AMERICAN
CASSANDRA

BOOKS BY PETER KURTH

Anastasia
The Riddle of Anna Anderson

American Cassandra
The Life of Dorothy Thompson

AMERICAN CASSANDRA

The Life of
Dorothy Thompson

PETER KURTH

Little, Brown and Company

BOSTON   TORONTO   LONDON

FIRST EDITION

Excerpts from this book appeared in *Vanity Fair*.

Rebecca West's correspondence is reprinted by permission of the Peters,
Fraser, Dunlop Group Ltd.

Excerpts from "The Lesson of Dachau" by Dorothy Thompson, copyright
1945 Meredith Corporation, are reprinted from *Ladies' Home Journal*
magazine with permission of the Estate of Dorothy Thompson. All rights reserved.

Excerpts from John Chamberlain's review of *Listen, Hans* by Dorothy Thompson,
copyright 1942 by the New York Times Corporation, are reprinted by permission.

Unless otherwise noted, all photographs are from the Dorothy Thompson Archives
at the George Arents Research Library at Syracuse University.

Library of Congress Cataloging-in-Publication Data
Kurth, Peter.
    American Cassandra: the life of Dorothy Thompson/by
Peter Kurth. — 1st ed.
    p. cm.
    ISBN 0-316-50723-7
    1. Thompson, Dorothy, 1893–1961. 2. Journalists —
United States — Biography. I. Title.
PN4874.T43K87 1990
070.92 — dc20
    [B]   89-14000
                                                       CIP

10 9 8 7 6 5 4 3 2 1

MV-PA

Designed by Barbara Werden

Published simultaneously in Canada
by Little, Brown & Company (Canada) Limited

PRINTED IN THE UNITED STATES OF AMERICA

FOR DINAH

in grateful memory

"In the dust of my firmament you are an
abiding star"

I know now that there are things for which I am
prepared to die. I am willing to die for political
freedom; for the right to give my loyalty to ideals
above a nation and above a class; for the right to
teach my child what I think to be the truth; for
the right to explore such knowledge as my brains
can penetrate; for the right to love where my
mind and heart admire, without reference to
some dictator's code to tell me what the national
canons on the matter are; for the right to work
with others of like mind; for a society that seems
to me becoming to the dignity of the human
race.

DOROTHY THOMPSON,

1937

What then should we *be?* That each will answer
for himself. But for myself and to myself I say:
Though stripped of every armor, be a warrior —
a warrior of the spirit, for what the spirit knows.

1955

Contents

Illustrations appear following
pages 176 and 400

Preface and Acknowledgments

THIS book began as the result of a wild-goose chase — an ill-conceived and rather suddenly abandoned novel about the Spanish civil war. In the spring of 1985 I was poring over the memoirs of American newspaper correspondents who had gone to Spain to report on the fight against Franco. Among them was Vincent Sheean, whose *Not Peace But a Sword* led me, out of sheer enthusiasm for Sheean's life and character, to a whole shelf of his books: *Personal History, First and Last Love, Between the Thunder and the Sun.* Around the same time, I was reading *The Nightmare Years,* the second volume of William L. Shirer's *Twentieth-Century Journey,* and there I took note of Shirer's incidental references to Dorothy Thompson. He spoke of his arrival in Berlin as a foreign correspondent, in the summer of 1934: "An old friend, H. R. Knickerbocker, a veteran correspondent, whose ten-year love affair with the Germans had begun to turn sour, told us that the Gestapo probably suspected I was an accomplice of Dorothy Thompson, who under police escort had departed the railroad station an hour or two before we arrived. She had been given twenty-four hours to get out after an enraged Hitler had learned what she wrote of him in her book, *I Saw Hitler.*"

I cannot recall how it was, or when, that I first discovered the name of Dorothy Thompson, but I already knew before I read Shirer's book that she was a prominent American journalist and that she had gone into battle almost single-handedly against the Nazis. In college I had read Brendan Gill's *Here at the New Yorker,* and I vividly remembered the scene in which Gill, as a young graduate of Yale, witnessed a nasty, drunken battle between Dorothy and her second husband, Sinclair Lewis. I was aware that Dorothy sometimes turned up on seventies-era lists of people who were "really homosexual" (though I did not realize, and am glad she never lived to find out, how much more lasting this barely substantiated reputation would be than her brilliant record as a journalist and commentator on world affairs). In 1985 I had not seen Mark Schorer's biography of Sinclair Lewis; or my hero Sheean's *Dorothy and Red;* or Marion K. Sanders's *Dorothy Thompson: A Legend in Her Time,* which was commissioned by Dorothy's literary trustees in the belief that Sheean's quirky memoir was not up to snuff. I did not know why Dorothy Thompson was sufficiently important in the mind of Hitler to warrant her expulsion from Berlin. But I knew after a single week of reading — and especially when I consulted her enormous archive at Syracuse University — that she had not yet found her biographer.

I was lucky, when I started work on this book, that so many people who had known Dorothy Thompson at the height of her fame were still alive and willing to talk to me about her. I was privileged to consult at least one person from every phase of Dorothy's life (including Marguerite Jarvis, her spirited friend and playmate from grade school, and George Abbott, who remembered the wedding of Dorothy's *father* in 1903). If I acknowledge these people in alphabetical order, along with others, living and dead, who helped me to flesh out the narrative of Dorothy's life, it is a mark only of my gratitude to all of them:

George Abbott, Anthony Adams, Nat Andriani, Tania Alexander, Joseph Alsop, Christa Armstrong, Marion Ascoli, Julian Bach, Eileen Agar Bard, Tish Belanger, Diana Beliard, Erich W. Bethmann, Marina and Otis S. Blodgett, Nigel Bottome, Marguerite Jarvis Bourne, Mary Branham, Paul Brooks, Michael John Burlingham, Mrs. Howell Chickering, Patricia Cockburn, Chris Coffin, Malcolm Cowley, Dr. and Mrs. Richard C. Cullen, Ernest Cuneo, Marcia Davenport, Hans Deichmann, David De Porte, J. W. Drawbell, Peter F. Drucker, Herschel Elliott, Mary S. von Euler, Eve S. Faber, Clifton Fadiman, Denis Fodor, Nigel Forbes-Dennis, Roger Forseth, Diana Forbes-Robertson (Mrs. Vincent Sheean), Dorothea Seelye and Peter Franck.

Sally M. Gall, Renate von Gebhardt, Brendan Gill, Lillian Gish, Victoria Glendinning, Ellen Goodman, Mrs. Robert Gottlieb (Maria Tucci), Stephen R. Graubard, Mr. and Mrs. Richard E. Green (Madeline Shaw), Jane Gunther, Maria Winnetou Guttenbrunner, Leota L. Hall, Kay Halle, Pamela Harriman, Richard Edes Harrison, Kitty Carlisle Hart, Eric L. Hedstrom, Erna Heininger, John Hersey,

Celeste Holm, William V. Holtz, C. Alexander Hoyt, Jack Huber, Dr. Hans R. Huessy, Gillian Hughes, Mrs. Harry Hull, Don and Polly Irwin, Marianne Kortner-Brün, Eve Curie Labouisse, Andrew Lambirth, Ruth Levine, Bernadette Lewis, Flora Lewis, Dr. Alfred M. Lilienthal, Helen Linton, James Blair Lovell, Clare Boothe Luce, Roger Lea MacBride, Elisabeth Marton, Maggie Maurice, Mary McCarthy, Mary McGrory, Patricia Mooney Melvin, Yehudi Menuhin, Nancy Milford, Freya von Moltke, Sonia Moore, Lilian T. Mowrer.

Steve Neal, Evelyn Stefansson and John U. Nef, Steve Nichols, Marithé and William I. Nichols, Louis Nizer, Ted Pasca, Whitelaw Reid, Christa Reinig, Rebecca Brock Richardson, Elizabeth Sherburne Ross, Charlotte Cramer Sachs, Rinna Samuel, Bob Sarnoff, Lili-Charlotte Sarnoff, Ruth Schorer, Alan Schwartz, George Seldes, Lisa Sergio, Rudolf Serkin, Eric Sevareid, Virginia Shaw, Ellen Sheean, Linda Sheean, William L. Shirer, Louis Smythe, Max Anton Stolper, Leland Stowe, Roger Straus, Richard L. Strout, John Temple Swing, Alice Marie Tarnowski, Roger W. Tubby, Laura Tucci, Niccolò Tucci, Laila and Thurston Twigg-Smith, Alex Ullmann, Katrina Valenstein, Faith Waterman, Brenda Wineapple, Rhoda J. Wolfe, Helen Wolff, Jennifer Wood, Mrs. Edward J. Wynkoop.

For their assistance in research, I want to thank above all others Carolyn A. Davis, Reader Services Librarian, and the staff at the George Arents Research Library at Syracuse University, especially Kathleen Manwaring, Manuscripts Processor, and Amy Doherty, Diane Cooter, Lillian Davis, Karin E. D'Agostino, Mary O'Brien, and Mark Weimer. I can honestly say that this book would not have been written without the benefit of their cheerful expertise. I have never felt so welcome in a library that was so well organized and so sure of itself, and I am quite certain that this "user-friendly" atmosphere is what Dorothy would have wished for her papers (though how she would despise the term!).

I am further indebted to Kenneth A. Lohf, Curator of Rare Books and Manuscripts, and Ronald Grele, Director of the Oral History Project at the Butler Library, Columbia University; to Dr. William R. Emerson, Director of the Franklin D. Roosevelt Library in Hyde Park, New York; to Patricia Willis at the Beinecke Rare Book and Manuscript Library and Katharine Morton at Sterling Memorial Library, Yale; to Cathy Henderson at the Harry Ransom Humanities Research Center, University of Texas, Austin; Rodney Dennis, Curator of Manuscripts at the Houghton Library, Harvard University;

Dr. Frank Mecklenburg and Dr. Diane Spielman at the Leo Baeck Institute in New York City; Sidney F. Huttner, Curator at the McFarlin Library, University of Tulsa; Philip N. Cronenwett, Curator of Manuscripts, Kenneth C. Cramer, and Barbara Krieger at the Baker Library, Dartmouth College; Mary-Ellen Jones at the Bancroft Library, University of California, Berkeley; Eva Moseley and Anne Engelhart at the Schlesinger Library, Radcliffe College; Charles Kelly, Jeffrey Flannery, and Fred Bauman at the Library of Congress; Jean F. Preston, Curator of Manuscripts, and Jane Moreton at Princeton University Library; Saundra Taylor, Curator of Manuscripts at the Lilly Library, Indiana University; and Dr. Lola L. Szladits, Curator of the Berg Collection at the New York Public Library.

Thanks go also to Ulrike Bauer at Frauenoffensive in Munich; Mary R. McGee of the *Christian Science Monitor;* David Klaassen at the University Libraries, University of Minnesota; Donald E. Loker of the Niagara Falls Public Library; Kathleen Jackson of Cornell University Library; Dwight M. Miller and Jennifer Pedersen of the Herbert Hoover Library, West Branch, Iowa; Maida Goodwin at the Sophia Smith Collection, Smith College, Northampton; Elena S. Danielson at the Hoover Institution on War, Revolution and Peace in Stanford, California; Joseph Streamer and Iola Kimmel at the Hamburg Historical Society, and Joyce Van Note at the United Methodist Church in Hamburg, New York; Jonathan Walters at the University of Chicago Library; A. Demole, Procureur de la République in Chalon-sur-Saône, France; Nancy Johnson at the American Academy and Institute of Arts and Letters in New York City; Michele Anisch and Muriel Robbins at the Library of the American Jewish Committee; Joy Chute, Christine Friedlander and John Morrone at PEN American Center in New York; Mary Ann Bamberger at the University of Illinois, Chicago; Jimmy Rush at the National Archives (Diplomatic Branch) in Washington; and Cynthia Sundberg Wall at the Newberry Library, Chicago.

I am grateful once again to Mary Tondorf-Dick, my editor at Little, Brown, whose sense of what works and what does not is a priceless gift, and whose enthusiasm for Dorothy Thompson could not have been greater from the beginning; also to Cynthia Nickerson, Senior Editorial Assistant, and to Dorothy Straight, my fearless copyeditor; to my agent, Rafe Sagalyn, and to Lisa DiMona at the Sagalyn Agency; to my family (as always), and to friends who helped, and bore with me, through all the ups and downs of Life with Dorothy:

Alan Altshuld, Suzie and Georges Balaes, Fran Bradfield, Liz Calder, Andrew Chapin, Kaye Danforth, Margie Danley, Charles Debuire, June-Rose Futcher, Brooke Gladstone, Sue Small Grider, Maggi Hayes, Dr. and Mrs. Ross Hill, Fred Kaplan, Colin Kelly, Carol Kitzmiller, Marie Biche, J. Michael Estep, Mirella Fera, Brendalyn Fougeras-Lavergnolle, Jan Hokenson, Geoff Oates, and all the gang at the Villa Rondinella (with special thanks to Messr. Strauss), Kathy Layton, Genevieve Lyons, Linda Macfadyen, Frances Manacher, Walter Miller, Professor David Neiweem, Edith O'Brien, Eddie Pattillo, Debi Pike, Brad Rabinowitz, Gillian Randall, Tony Regan, Veronica Richel, Jill Robinson-Shaw, Laurie Rosenberg, Johanna V. Thomas, Jan and Nick Timbers, Pamela Towne, James Velvet, Jacquot Wagner, Jane Westervelt, Carol Good Whitman, K. K. Wilder, and Erla Youmans.

To Susan Mack, who listened with sympathy, patience, and humor while Dorothy took shape; to Karen Waters, without whom I am nothing; to Betty Berman, greatly cherished, still divine; and to Michael Ferrell, whose contribution is more than he knows — my love and thanks. I would close with the hope that *American Cassandra* might stand as a tribute to Dorothy Thompson in the eyes of her family: Pamela and Bob Reeves, John Paul, Gregory, and Lesley Dorothy Lewis, whose helpfulness and generosity during the preparation of this book were exceeded only by the joy it has given me to write it.

Burlington, Vermont
Lewes, Delaware
DECEMBER 1989

AMERICAN CASSANDRA

Prologue

THE Reverend Peter Thompson's elder daughter, according to family legend, ran away from home for the first time at the age of three, taking with her some docile, dimly remembered childhood playmate and her father's buggy umbrella and heading straight down the line of the Erie Railroad into the open world.

Her name was Dorothy, the year was 1896, and on this occasion she got no farther than a neighbor's gooseberry patch, where she promptly fell asleep. But the urge to flight was permanently fixed.[1] "I believed in dreams," said Dorothy later. "I believed in waking dreams."[2] Sometimes she found herself crouched over one or another of the bridges that spanned the tracks of the Erie line, watching the boxcars slide off to Batavia, Rochester, Geneseo, Albany, and New York, one day tossing her round straw hat directly onto the passengers' coach beneath her and laughing with pleasure as it glided away — "far away, far away"— its bright blue ribbon streaming back at her in the wind. "All my childhood in it," she wrote of that moment and the unbounded longing of her growing up, "all my youth";[3] "I wanted to run away, not *from* something, but *to* something."

She wanted to run away at first to England, and specifically to County Durham, "a wild country of storm-swept moors" where her father had been born and where, so he told her, there stood "a big house built of blocks of gray stone . . . formidable as a fortress," fronted by an iron gate and concealing within its high outer walls a garden of fantastic loveliness. This was "Mountsett," the ancestral home of some wealthy relations, like nothing Dorothy had ever seen among the flat, stripped fields of western New York State.

3

"There was a faded photograph of it in my father's study," Dorothy remembered. "I imagined myself walking in the garden all alone, wearing a droopy garlanded hat, carrying a basket on my arm. . . . I thought of myself in the third person, and spoke of myself to myself as of another person. 'Dorothy' came down the stairs. . . . 'Dorothy' was not a little girl but a young lady, invariably dressed in white or in pale, pale blue. People stood transfixed at her appearance. . . . No one praised her cleverness."

The mirror above her dresser revealed a solid, sturdy, handsome-featured, and wholly approachable child, with a freckled nose and short brown braids. But "in daydreams that began early and lasted late" Dorothy Thompson was always beautiful, "tall and slender, with raven black hair, large, thickly-fringed violet-blue eyes, and . . . skin like a rose in the snow." This fantasy she kept to herself, as she kept a great deal to herself. "What went on in the realm between reality and imagination could not be communicated to ever-so-loving adults or even to other children," Dorothy said. Children were not to be trusted. One could play with them, and laugh with them, and even seek their counsel,

> but never must one tell them what one could see if one screwed one's eyes very tightly shut, or, wide open in the dark, fixed them on a single point: strange faces, as clear and real as any one saw in church or in the streets; sometimes beautiful, sometimes ugly and menacing. Landscapes, too, that one had never seen in real life, streams falling down high, high mountains, trees with strange, twisted shapes that turned, as one looked, into human figures or those of beasts. . . . Other children would think me crazy, or that I was telling whopping lies. So I held my peace about the pictures. By and by, when I was older, and I do not remember just when, they ceased. . . .
> But I was still seeing them in Tonawanda, alone at night.

There was a rightness about the privacy of these moments, Dorothy thought; there was something personal about adventure, something intimate. When her mother sent her to school in the early dark of winter mornings, wrapped in six or seven layers of clothing and a welter of leggings and "Arctics," she felt herself "infinitely diminutive on a vast empty waste" and was prepared to be devoured by wolves. She knew it could happen. The world was a place of perpetual hazard: "We climbed and fell out of trees; . . . cut our toes with axes; skated on thin ice." [4] In the summer of 1900, just before her seventh birthday, Dorothy stood in her parents' house in Tonawanda and watched the approach of a killer cyclone. [5] Her mother had grabbed the younger children and hurried them down to the cellar, where they sat huddled together, the children wailing, between the furnace and the wall. Her father was at the bottom of the cellar stairs, shouting through the noise of the storm, "Jump, Dorothy!" But Dorothy stood mesmerized in the doorway, leaping to safety, finally, only at the very moment the twister hit the house. She landed square at her father's chest and was "suddenly glad, grateful for his arms around me. So we stood as [the storm] broke, with a terrible noise, the whole house shaking as if dynamited, stones tumbling out of the wall into the cellar, and sticks and stalks, rags and chunks of wood whirling in upon us through the gap."

"Are we going to die?" Dorothy cried, and her father answered what he always answered, words she had come to expect: "We are in the hands of God."

"What I later became aware of," said Dorothy, "was the therapy against shock. When there's nothing one can do, one is in the hands of God."

She helped to clean up when the twister had gone, staring in amazement at the collapsed shelves and broken windows, the kitchen larder strewn of its contents, and the hole driven straight through the top of the house by a flying railroad spike. An old woman ran by outside, laughing and shrieking, "I saw a pig flying! I saw a pig flying!" Meanwhile Dorothy watched the parlor fill with shaken and wounded neighbors and imagined that she was a nurse in the recent war with Spain.

"Someone named Admiral Dewey had sunk a foreign fleet," she recollected. "It wasn't English but *really* foreign, and enslaved peoples were going to be freed." She was proud to be an American, glad to be of service. It was not necessary on this occasion to be the center of attention: "I was a big girl now, going on for seven and the second grade in school, . . . already experienced in a catastrophe of nature, aware, if vaguely, of war, acquainted with death, half-consciously aware of evil, and of something in myself that Father said was wilfulness."

In the evening, before bed, she would climb in his lap and lean her head against his face. It was always cool, she remembered, and smooth, with "a nice clean masculine smell. . . . It would have been lovely to have been his youngest child, his only daughter, very slim and prim with little hands and tiny sandaled feet and carefully brushed-back hair."

"My impatient child," her father said. ". . . Listen, Thea, Dorothea. It means 'the Gift of God.' "[6]

PART ONE
Yearning

My Father is rich in houses and lands,
He holdeth the wealth of the world in His hands,
Of rubies and diamonds, of silver and gold,
His coffers are full; He has riches untold.
I'm the child of a King,
The child of a King,
With Jesus my Savior
I'm the child of a King.

≡

Hattie E. Buell
(Methodist Hymn)

1
CHAPTER

W HEN I was a very little girl," said Dorothy Thompson, "I fell in love with God because I was in love with my father. I was sure that Jesus came into the room with my father. He radiated light and kindness — love it was, for every living thing." [1]

Her first memory, so she always said, was the image of her father sitting before the kitchen fire, holding in his arms a baby wrapped tight in a gray woolen shawl. The child was Dorothy's infant brother, sick with whooping cough, and the cloth that wrapped him seemed to Dorothy to come *out* of her father, to be a part of him somehow. It was a part of them all, she reflected later; it bound them all together: "The shawl was to become cobweb thin; to spin out into a mere thread invisibly encircling my wrist. . . . But however far I wandered, whether in space, time, or my own mind, there was always 'Pahpie,' invisible in the background, pursuing me like the Hound of Heaven to bring me home and wrap me in the gray shawl of his love and solicitude."

In the country parishes of western New York, among people who may never have read the works of J. M. Barrie, the Reverend Peter Thompson was called "the Little Minister," not merely on account of his small stature and soft pink face, but because of his meekness, his gentility, and the apparently unworked-at generosity of his spirit. Dorothy Thompson herself characterized her father as "utterly (and sometimes distractingly) unworldly, sublimely innocent, happy and serene. This is not only my memory," she insisted, "but the testimony of all who knew and continued to remember him." In later life Dorothy would admit that her father had been "an awful preacher," and that out of the thousands of his sermons she had heard as a girl she

9

could recall only two with any distinction.[2] Somehow this had not mattered. Peter Thompson was a *minister*. He was "a shepherd," and in his daughter's estimation "a born poet. . . . He could pray a bird off a tree." It was in the attitude of prayer that she remembered him most vividly.

"He never stood to pray," she said. "He always knelt, and when he got down on his knees, poetry poured out of him. I had never heard anything like it as a child. . . . I can still say I have never met anyone who had such magic on his lips."[3]

An Englishman from the North Country, the son of a shiftless and drunken father who ultimately had abandoned his family, Peter Thompson had spent his youth more or less as a poor relation, passed from house to house and from uncle to uncle until, at the age of eighteen, he "heard the call" of Methodism and converted from the Anglican church. He began his ministry as a circuit rider among the miners of Wales and in 1890 traveled to America to visit an elder brother who had emigrated. It was never his intention to stay permanently in the United States. But in Pittsburgh he met and fell in love with Margaret Grierson, the eighteen-year-old daughter of working-class immigrants from Scotland. Despite opposition from both families — the Thompsons were "gentle," the Griersons were not[4] — Margaret and Peter were married, and would have returned together to England but for a protracted honeymoon in Niagara Falls. While passing through the industrial suburbs of Buffalo, the Reverend was persuaded to take over the charge of a homesick fellow preacher in the town of Lancaster, and thus it was that his first child, on July 9, 1893, was born a citizen of the United States.[5]

She was christened Dorothy Celène with water from the Jordan River, a decanter of which stood throughout her childhood on a battered table in her parents' parlor. The unusual middle name was taken from a French great-grandmother and abandoned early. "Translated into American," Dorothy explained, "with the accent dropped, the lovely moon word became 'Saleen.' It sounded to me like some kind of sleazy yard goods." She was proud, all the same, of her relatively exotic heritage, knowing "from the time I knew anything beyond sensory impressions that I was not really wholly American." Her parents did not speak quite as the neighbors spoke. They did not wear quite the same clothes, or eat quite the same food. Dorothy knew no self-consciousness on this account, because while her father was an immigrant, he was "a Cunard-line immigrant. . . .

We weren't looked down on as 'foreigners,' but rather looked up to because my parents were 'educated' and English."[6]

The family grew quickly, almost automatically, each child born two years apart: first Dorothy, then her brother, Peter Willard, and finally the baby, Margaret May, known ever after as Peggy. The Thompsons moved from Lancaster to Clarence and from Clarence to Tonawanda and from there to Hamburg, Gowanda, and Spencerport — all of them suburbs of Buffalo, all of them, at the turn of the century, discrete communities, sufficient to themselves, linked to the city only by horse and buggy and some distinctly rickety local rails. In the Methodist tradition, Peter Thompson was an itinerant preacher, which meant that he could expect periodically to be posted from one "charge" to another and, within each, to minister to the faithful for miles around. The saying among the Thompson children was that they had been "born and brought up under the faith that moves parsons." Every September their father left for the Genesee Conference of the Methodist Episcopal Church while his family waited at home "in breathless suspense over whether we would stay or be moved, what the next salary would be, and whether the next parsonage would have a bathroom."[7] Until Dorothy was twelve, as it happened, none of them did. She had lived in five different houses by that time, but she remembered only two in any detail, and in her mind, always, those two were fused together into one: the parsonage on Union Street in Hamburg.[8]

Hamburg Village lies fifteen miles due south of Buffalo, in open farmland that has only gradually (and, ironically, only with the decline of local industry) succumbed to "progress" and homogenized commerce. It was and still is a typical, very nearly mail-order version of the American small town,[9] the site of the annual Erie County Fair, with a Main Street and a Pleasant Avenue and an old hotel that seems to have been frozen permanently in time and the national consciousness. It was 1900 when Dorothy first knew it, "the era of mutton sleeves, long skirts, piled-up hair and golden brooches,"[10] "when wood fretted gables, towers and porte-cocheres made a 'mansion,' when verandas were thrown out in all directions, and the *ne plus ultra* was a window of quite hideously gaudy red-blue-and-green glass on the stairs: the age of golden oak, black walnut, Brussels carpets, lace curtains, whatnots, center tables, and bead curtains. . . . And always the lawns, with never a high hedge or fence against a neighbor."[11] A cousin who visited the Thompsons from England was surprised to discover that the flower beds in Hamburg were "open to the street" — "just like public property," she sniffed in disapproval. But Dorothy's father "grew the prettiest flowers in town — he was famous for it,"[12] and an open garden was in tune with every other aspect of the Thompsons' life at that time. "Here is the hospitality which forever indicates heroes," Dorothy remarked later[13]: she was quoting Whitman.

The Methodist parsonage itself was a white, green-edged wooden building of two stories, identical in appearance if not in exact construction to dozens of others in the neighborhood, set in the middle of the village, directly opposite the schoolhouse and across a wide lawn from the church where Dorothy's father preached on Sundays. "In the backyard there were old Baldwin and Greening apple trees," Dorothy remembered, "and a wonderful, wonderful barn." Two parlors indoors served as centers of activity. One was formal and cold, "where portraits of John Wesley and Frances Willard hung on the walls" and glared down at children, visiting dignitaries, and couples who came to be married. The other was comfortable, shabby, and always inviting, furnished piecemeal by the parsonage committee and reserved for "folks" and for living in. "It had an ingrain carpet on the floor," said Dorothy, "with patterns in maple leaves, and white muslin curtains at the windows. . . . There was a round iron stove, a very jolly stove, a cozy stove that winked at you with its red isinglass eyes."[14] This was where Dorothy and her family gathered at different times to read, pray, stitch, darn, rest, play games, converse, or simply wait for the Reverend to come back from the rounds of his ministry.

Life in the parsonage revolved around that ministry, just as the activities of the Thompson family, as a matter of course, revolved around the person of the minister. It was taken for granted that "Father's" needs were paramount: it was never resented. All his life Peter Thompson had been physically frail; he suffered from pleurisy and later on from heart trouble, and "it was for this reason," Dorothy observed, quite apart from the agreed-upon value of his work, "that Father was so tenderly treated."[15] She had no recollection of her mother's occupying any kind of secondary or degraded position in the home, however. On the contrary, the wife of a minister worked as long and as hard as her husband to set the example and the tone of right living in Christian society. Margaret Thompson was by all accounts the perfect minister's wife: dedicated to her husband's mission while committed to her own projects; subservient to the needs of the parish but prepared to take on as much authority as she had responsibility. She was dark-haired, slim, pretty, and immensely hardworking, "one of the sweetest, heavenliest souls," her husband said, "that ever tabernacled in the flesh." [16]

"I 'always knew' that my father and mother loved each other," Dorothy wrote later, allowing for the confusions of memory, "and very early that they loved each other more than most children's parents do." She could recall only one occasion when her parents had quarreled — and "if the sun had fallen out of the sky," she remarked, "no greater terror could have seized me. . . . [My] father never returned home after an absence of merely an hour or two but my mother, hearing his footstep, would rush to the door and they would embrace each other. My mother never returned from an errand — on which one or more of the children would usually accompany her — but that my father, from his study, would cry, 'Is that you, Maggie?' and rush to take her coat and kiss her."

There was nothing secretive about the physical basis of the Thompsons' marriage, nothing covert, for all the strict observance in Hamburg of Victorian propriety. Her mother, Dorothy remembered, "was prettiest in a batiste nightgown threaded with ribbons and with her hair loose," but she "did not see her many times in that garb, because going around practically undressed was immodest." [17] When Dorothy was a little older, her father wanted her to know that the physical consummation of love was the nearest thing — the next best thing — one could achieve on earth to the love of God. It was not the *same* thing, the Reverend warned, neither so great nor so necessary, but it was close, it was related, and Dorothy was not to be ashamed of it.[18] "None of his children . . . ever doubted that it was good to be born," she wrote in tribute, "or ever suffered any panicky fear of life, for my father believed that life was the most glorious gift of God. He really believed that God would take care of the human race and that no mistakes that we might make, as we certainly would, were irrevocable, and his own example was a living proof that as pleasure may lie without us, happiness certainly comes from inside." [19]

There was "too much solid piety" among Christians, in the Reverend's estimation, too much gloom and pessimism. The only one of his sermons to survive in print contains the charming remark that "it is our privilege to be winsome for Christ," along with the advice, cribbed from some philosopher, that if you have money enough for two loaves of bread, you ought to buy just one and spend the rest on daffodils.[20] More than once Dorothy's attention was drawn to the epitaph on the headstone of an eighteen-year-old girl who lay buried in the Hamburg Village cemetery: "She was so pleasant." Her father's ministry and his whole personality were infused with a kind of sunny wonder, with laughter and merriment and the telling of tales. He was known far and wide for his beautiful tenor voice "and would always liefer sing than preach." He loved especially "the old English songs," said Dorothy — "The Last Rose of Summer" and "Drink to Me Only with Thine Eyes." But he moved without effort from popular ballads to the standard hymns of the Protestant church, exhorting his children to remember that "the early Christians were a singing people."

"My father thought that the greatest hymn written in English was Isaac Watts' 'When I Survey the Wondrous Cross,' " Dorothy remembered, "and for sheer adoration it is surely without peer. I can remember the strange, holy sense of wonder, mystery and beauty it evoked in me as a child, and that I could not sing it without bursting into inexplicable tears":

> See from His head, His hands, His feet,
> Sorrow and love flow mingled down!
> Did e'er such love and sorrow meet,
> Or thorns compose so rich a crown?

"Today I need but close my eyes," said Dorothy later, "to hear the vesper hymn — 'Day Is Dying in the West' — . . . and smell the fruity scent of syringa swaying outside the opened June windows." At her father's knee she learned that the human personality was sacred and inviolable; that each man and woman was worthy in the sight of God; that each, regardless of circumstance, motive, or native wickedness, could be redeemed; and that the grace of God was free to all, at any time and for the asking. This was an explicitly Methodist view, an extension and refinement of John Wesley's dictum that a Methodist is "one who lives according to the method laid down in the Bible" — who is guided, that is, in all matters, by the common principles of Christianity. Beyond that, Dorothy suspected, there was probably a lot of room to move.

From an early age she traveled with her father on visits to parishioners, comfort calls, deathbed vigils, and other church business, journeys that often took up whole days and carried them miles from home. "His parishes were usually wide," Dorothy observed, "[and included] many farm folk. . . . In fine weather these visits were performed by bicycle; he thought nothing of pedaling twenty or thirty miles a day."[21] Her own memories were mainly of jolting buggies and "horsey blankets,"[22] of mufflers and frozen noses and warm fires at the end of the road.

"I do not remember that these parishional visits had a particularly religious tone," said Dorothy. "Father, who had the mind and soul of a country man, talked about crops, new fertilizers he had read about, the weather, [and] other church members, not being above a little unmalicious gossip."[23] It was different if someone was sick. Then the pleasantries stopped, and the Reverend Mr. Thompson would take the patient's hand and ask, "Would you like me to say a prayer for you?" And if Dorothy asked him later, "Is Mrs. Powers *very* sick, Papa?" he would tell her the truth: "She is dying."[24] The reality of death was easier for Dorothy to accept because nobody ever tried to hide it, and because guides to salvation came at her so directly, without analysis or the slightest ambiguity. Even her reading lessons were "composed entirely of homilies: Pray to God, Love God, Fear God, Serve God, Do Not Swear, Do Not Steal, Do Not Cheat," and so on; these abbreviations of the Ten Commandments were then broadened almost imperceptibly into a whole line of secular admonitions: Count Your Blessings; Eat What's Set Before You; Don't Whine About Your Condition.[25] "In all this there was immense emotional *security*," Dorothy explained. "One knew where one was. One could count on things."[26]

One thing the Thompson children could always count on was the fact that their father had no money, and very likely never would have. Her family was "poor," said Dorothy flatly: "We were so poor you wouldn't believe it."[27] During the whole of his thirty years in America Peter Thompson never earned more than a thousand dollars a year. Part of this money was tithed, and frequently, when his parishioners themselves fell on hard times, his salary came to him only in the form of foodstuffs and other goods and services. "Let them pay in what they can!" he declared with a laugh. "We are all in the same boat together."[28] For one memorable period of about six months, during a strike of the barge workers on the Erie Canal, the Thompsons subsisted almost entirely on rice and apples, seeing out the hardship by reflecting on the Reverend's breezy remark that "more than two-thirds of the population of the world lives on rice" and that "the heathen, . . . admirable people in some respects, were able to teach us many things." Later Dorothy affirmed that with the notable annual exceptions of Thanksgiving and Christmas, she never once rose from the table at home without wishing she had had more to eat. But there were hidden advantages to this kind of poverty. "We had a freedom characteristic of royalty," said Dorothy:

> freedom from talk about money. I never heard money discussed in my father's house or used as a standard of measurement of ourselves or others. When, as children, we asked for things the household could not afford, we were told so; and although the telling no doubt brought on pangs, they were not bitter. For relative wealth or poverty was not linked with relative superiority or inferiority. . . . There is a kind of complete humility that, in a sense difficult to define, equals complete pride; especially if pride, as I think it does, equates with total indifference to the impression one makes on others. My father was trying to keep up with a standard much higher than the Joneses'.[29]

It was a good deal easier to be poor in Hamburg than it might have been anywhere else, because practically everybody was poor in Hamburg, and those who were not had very little to distinguish them from those who were. People lived much the same way, in Dorothy's recollection, no matter what their status — "in separate houses with lawns around them and flowers in summer." Such differences as existed were mainly of degree. "Wealthier people had more of *the same* things," said Dorothy: "their children had more nickels to spend on licorice whips, horehound drops and milk chocolate, and had shinier bicycles, and their small daughters . . . had several best dresses instead of one. But we all wore the same kind of clothes, every kid's spending money was in nickels — I never saw one flash a dollar bill — and our mothers did all or most of their own housework."[30] Life was simple, always "reckonable," but never dull and not without variety. Trim and pretty, resolutely Anglo-Saxon in tone, Hamburg Village nevertheless contained a perfect hodgepodge of races, creeds, and colors, if the Indians from the nearby Gowanda reservation were counted among the German and other European immigrant populations. Germans, in fact, were the first settlers of Hamburg, and in Dorothy's day a host of Ueblackers, Niefergolds, Eckerhardts, Federspiels, and Schunks were among the elite of the town.

"Somewhere," said Dorothy (and she hastened to point out that it was not through her father), "I was exposed to the notion that English were best, Germans next best, and Irish, Poles and Eyetalians not good at all." There were reasons for this in the small-town mind:

"The Irish were dirty. Poles and Eyetalians worked in mills, and all of them were Roman Catholics and Papists, which was a terrible thing to be." The Pope, indeed, "had horns and a tail"[31] so far as Dorothy was concerned, and might well have been responsible for the "real" poverty she sometimes saw in the world around her. Once or twice she had ridden up to Buffalo on the "Sunshine Trolley" (so named because it ran only when the sun shone) and caught a glimpse of another America, the flip side of her own rosy comfort.

"I had seen houses with children playing outside," she remembered. "The houses were all crowded together, one beside the other, black-colored, and without yards, not a leaf nor a tree. The air was dark and smokey, too, and women sat on stoops and did not look nice at all." Later Dorothy learned that these were the families of workers in the Lackawanna mills, and that they were "poor" in a way she could not imagine. This confounded her. "I knew *we* were poor," she protested; "Grandma Grierson had always said so."

Grandma Grierson was Dorothy's mother's mother, a handsome, big-boned woman with jet-black hair and hazel eyes, who periodically descended on Hamburg and "always knew everything better than anyone else." She had been deserted years before by Dorothy's grandfather, "a black Scot" and radical union organizer[32] who had left her with a colossal chip on her shoulder and some fierce opinions about the working class. Her visits filled Dorothy with dread: "She would begin by clutching each of us to her bosom, which was capacious but not soft, and following these too hearty ministrations by criticizing everything in the house, would promptly set about to put it right. . . . My mother was working too hard, the children's manners needed improving, the food was impossible, all the furniture needed polishing, father's income wouldn't support a churchmouse and nothing in America was as good as in England. . . . She had an inexhaustible energy and no sensitivity whatever." There was something askew about her racial theories, too, Dorothy could tell, because while Grandma Grierson herself was half Irish, "she wasn't dirty: she was so clean that it hurt."

Such were the sour notes in a childhood untouched by neurosis, played out, Dorothy knew, in a world of authentic innocence. She was accused in later years of having a hopeless sentimentality in regard to her upbringing, but she dismissed the charge with a wave of the hand and was not alone in doing so. Her memories of Hamburg, her memories of that America, were no different from the majority of her neighbors'. She remembered a world of church suppers and sleigh-ride parties, of ice cream socials and benevolent orders, of swimming and skating and canning and quilting, choir-singing and berry-picking, candy-making and chestnut-roasting. She recalled an existence that had turned on community, on "neighborliness," on mutual and voluntary cooperation, in which the sick were nursed by the well and no one, not even a stranger, was ever left to suffer a holiday by himself.

"I was certainly thankful for being alive," Dorothy remarked, "with that intense, exuberant, receptive aliveness of every healthy, observant child. . . . I knew that I was born in debt, not to the secular state but to life itself."[33] To be an American, she wrote,

> meant to have been born free, and to be so recognized — and therefore not to talk about it much. It meant to *live* democratically. . . .
> It had nothing to do with superior material comforts — but rather the opposite. [Ours] was a social democracy that had nothing to do with "ideology." [It] was a life of confidence — in the country, in one's fellow Americans, and in oneself. One was not confident that there would be no reverses in life — no "hard times." One was not confident that one would "succeed" or ever enjoy luxury. One was confident merely that there would always be *some* kind of opening for willing and competent hands and heads; confident that one was surrounded by good will; and confident that life, with all its ups and downs, setbacks and frustrations, was going to be a rewarding adventure and experience.[34]

In this atmosphere of hope and credence, Dorothy Thompson could kneel at night and thank her Maker for the world as it was, "God-blessing Papa, Mama, Willard, Baby, . . . the kitten, the dog, the neighbor's dog, . . . and whatever or whomever [else] I could think of, including Grandma Grierson."

In this atmosphere, too, shortly before her eighth birthday, when her family had been in Hamburg for less than a year, Dorothy's mother suddenly died.

WORD got around Hamburg — or rather, the story got absorbed into local legend — that Margaret Thompson had died "in childbirth," of complications that were common enough to be expected by any pregnant woman at the turn of the century. In fact, she had died at the hands of her own mother, Grandma Grierson, who believed that

Mrs. Thompson should not be burdened with another child and had therefore, "against her daughter's knowledge," brought on a miscarriage by administering "such herbs and potions as old wives knew about and used for such purposes." Mrs. Thompson began to hemorrhage, Grandma Grierson was afraid to confess, a doctor "plugged the flow, sealing in the poisons," and Dorothy's mother died of septicemia within forty-eight hours.[35]

It was Easter, and while her mother lay sick in the parsonage, Dorothy stayed outdoors, listening to the music that came across the lawn from inside the Methodist church — "a rehearsal for an Easter cantata." The younger children, Willard and Peggy, had been sent across the street to stay with neighbors. At length Peter Thompson joined Dorothy in the garden: "He took my hand, and we walked up and down . . . and I said that the night which was falling was dark without a star in the sky and Father said in a voice like a groan that it was the darkest night he had ever known. That was all he said except, after a little while, that my mother wanted to see me.

"I was afraid," Dorothy remembered, "though how could I be afraid of Mama?" She knew how when she found her mother lying in bed, "her lovely eyes sunk in pools the color of bruises, smoke-dark hair like a mourning wreath spread on the white pillow, her head moving restlessly, white hands on the white coverlet restless, plucking and plucking at its threads."

"Hello, Mama," said Dorothy, and she tried to smile, to pretend that the wasted creature in front of her was just one of the neighbors, some parishioner she and her father were visiting, somebody else's mother: "I touched her hand and recoiled, because it was icy cold, but she held mine and spoke rapidly as though she had no time."

"You are the oldest," Mrs. Thompson said. "Promise me you will always care for your little sister and your father."

"Oh, Mama," Dorothy replied. It was all she could think of: "Oh, Mama."

She did not cry when her mother died, though ordinarily she cried easily and without shame. She recalled an atmosphere of "unreality," a breakfast of "mush and milk," her father's solemn words — "Your mother is with the angels" — and the whining questions of her brother and sister: "When will she be home?"

"Whenever you think of her," said the Reverend, "and remember."

"But even now," said Dorothy, "I could not remember her. Only the face on the pillow and the hands on the coverlet, that were not

Mama's." She refused to kiss the corpse's face when the body was laid out in the "good" front parlor, "Grandma Grierson sniffling" on the sidelines, various friends and neighbors huddling together and muttering condolences.

"I ran out of the room with screaming silent in my throat," Dorothy recalled. "Father followed me. . . . He was not mad at me. He held me very tight."

"Your mother has a new life," her father said, "a beautiful new life." But he was crying, and because he was, Dorothy did too — "a little."

Her tears came out in a flood at the cemetery — "the burying ground," as it was called in Hamburg — where the Thompson family and, it seemed, the entire village had ridden in buggies, and where Dorothy's mother was laid to rest under a hemlock tree.

"Mama had colored Easter eggs," Dorothy explained, "and we would have rolled and cracked them against each other, and gobbled them up afterward with bread and butter and tea and cake, and now we would not, and I began to cry now, thinking of that. . . ." A woman murmured, "Poor little motherless child," and Dorothy wept harder than ever, because she had been thinking about the eggs and not her mother. As she left the cemetery somebody pressed into her hand a copy of *The Wide, Wide World,* by Susan B. Warner; she guessed what kind of book it was without even looking inside — something along the lines of the Elsie Dinsmore stories for girls, one in that series of hugely popular, "sadistic, masochistic, even necrophilic" books that "Father said were 'morbid,' because in them some mother was always dying." When she opened to the flyleaf she saw "a drawing of a little girl in the arms of a lady with wings, who was her guardian angel, and sure enough it was the tale of Ellen Montgomery, whose mother had died. . . .

"That was what I was now," Dorothy lamented, "someone set apart, the only little girl in Hamburg without a mother." Not long after the funeral, her father sailed for England — an event that "deepened my dismay," said Dorothy, "but registered in my mind again the realization that Father's ties were not all in America, and that in trouble one went 'abroad.' " Meanwhile, the Thompson children were sent to spend the remainder of the spring and summer, until their father came home, as guests on a neighbor's farm.

This last, at least, said Dorothy, was "cheerful news."[36]

* * *

SHE hardly ever spoke of her mother in later years, except to say, as if offhandedly, that "she died when I was young," or to illustrate that children will adapt to anything if they have to. Margaret Thompson's death had "put out a light" in her daughter's life, "never to be rekindled,"[37] but once she recovered from the shock and the strangeness of her loss, Dorothy — and indeed all of the Thompson children — appeared to adopt her father's tranquil view of things. For several years they all went out weekly to Prospect Lawn cemetery in Hamburg, carrying flowers and a picnic lunch and listening intently to the Reverend's stories of their mother's life.[38] Sometimes Dorothy found herself lying on the ground beneath the apple trees, staring at the sky and scanning the clouds for a glimpse of her mother's face.[39] She was already thinking about the larger questions.

"You must understand that discussing the will of God had been as common a topic in my parsonage home as discussing the weather," she explained. "I had cut my eye teeth on theology. . . . That death . . . was only a transition from one form of life to another I believed with simple faith. So, though my mother's death had been a crushing blow to Father and to us all, it had not, I thought, been hard on Mother. Mother had been gathering flowers in the garden one day, and then in two days she was gone, to gather flowers perhaps among the asphodels."[40]

She was taking seriously — very seriously, at the age of eight — the promise she had made to her mother that she would look after her father and her sister. (Her brother, Willard, everyone assumed, would fend for himself in time.) It was Dorothy who now met the Reverend Peter Thompson at the door when he came home from his rounds, Dorothy who took his coat and muffler, fetched his slippers, stoked the fire, and made the tea. She was granted a certain amount of leeway by the Reverend's sister, Elizabeth Hill, who in 1901 arrived from Chicago to take charge of the house. A widow with ten grown children of her own, Aunt Lizzie was the kind of sober, middle-class American matron, "crackling with starch and reeking of cleanliness," for whom the term no-nonsense was invented.

"She seemed to have a permanent age," Peggy Thompson remembered, and knew "no troubles, physical or mental, that could not be cured by a dose of castor oil, a good cup of tea, and faith. . . . She had never read a book on child psychology and had never heard of inhibitions. If she had, she would have been for them."[41] Her regime lasted for two years and was, in Dorothy's memory, a time of sturdy discipline and unquestioned love. Balance was restored, life went on, and Dorothy entered the third grade.

Her classmates in Hamburg, long after she became famous, remembered Dorothy as a "remarkable" child, "extraordinary," quick of tongue and pen and frankly "highty-tighty" — a girl who "flipped around the room in such a sassy manner" that mothers drew their daughters aside to say, "I hope you'll not become friends with *that* pert little thing."[42] Wooden sidewalks led directly from the parsonage on Union Street to the redbrick schoolhouse, where, for fifty years, Miss Lavina Robbins took charge of the younger children. All of the teachers in Hamburg were women; indeed, they were all maiden ladies: "Any mischief was rewarded by a smack on the palm of the hand with a heavy 24-inch ruler. If a student was really bad, he was sent to the principal, who administered a sound beating with a piece of rubber hose on the rear end."[43] The activities of boys and girls were strictly segregated on school grounds. "We all loved to skate," Dorothy protested, but rules were rules: "Boys built log cabins. . . . We made paper dolls."[44] If she resented the sexual restrictions of the era, she did not let them hinder her spirits. The redheaded, bespectacled Marguerite Jarvis, her best friend and sidekick in Hamburg, remembered that "Dorothy, even as a little child, stood out among the rest of us. She was very bright, very independent, extremely devoted to her family and also, I'd say, very sensitive, although she covered it with bravado."[45] For her part, Dorothy "just loved Marguerite. . . . Her father and mother were both English — I mean American, but they had come from England. That, I thought marvelling, makes us practically twins."[46]

Eighty-five years later Marguerite Jarvis still had the air of someone "telling tales" when she talked about her childhood friendship with Dorothy Thompson; about their practical jokes and their moonlight raids on cupboards and melon patches; about the time they locked the janitor in the basement of the church; and about their famous cat cemetery, which they had consecrated under a quince bush in order to provide a Christian burial and hope of resurrection to uncounted numbers of martyred kittens, drowned at Aunt Lizzie's command. The girls were widely known as "a couple of cards," and when, from time to time, Hamburg wanted for entertainment, Dorothy and Marguerite were pressed into service, "to sing a song or speak a piece."[47] Nobody forgot Dorothy's spirited performances in church once a month on Temperance Sunday, when she bellowed out doggerel at the top of her lungs:

Oh sell no more drink to my father,
   It makes him so strange and so wild!
Heed the prayer of a heartbroken mother,
   And pity a poor drunkard's child![48]

Her imagination, vivid and febrile in the calmest of times, sprang to new life in the year her mother died. As Dorothy explained it, "I discovered books."[49] She could not recall having learned how to read. It was something that had gone on for as long as she could remember, that was all: one read, and one read aloud, beginning at the breakfast table. After washing and scrubbing in icy water from a bedroom basin — "What polishing of cheeks, what brushing of hair!"[50] — Dorothy piled into as many as ten or eleven layers of clothing on winter days and joined her family in the kitchen to listen to stories from the Bible and offer up her morning prayers. "This was part of the routine of every day," she recalled, "and only in sickness could we ever escape it." At one of these lessons, as her porridge grew cold, she experienced what amounted to an awakening, something that "partook of the intense excitement of falling in love."[51] She was accustomed already to take refuge in fantasy and had recently become "addicted" to the puzzles, conundrums, and popular tales of travel and adventure published for children in *St. Nicholas* magazine. With her father she read *Five Little Peppers and How They Grew, Mrs. Wiggs of the Cabbage Patch, Tom Sawyer, The Water Babies, Hiawatha,* and *Evangeline* ("the reading of which occupied several evenings and taught me that Protestants could persecute Catholics, which was news").[52] But this was something else.

"I suddenly discovered," said Dorothy, "that the words I was obediently and absently attending were beautiful. I *heard* them for the first time. My father, I remember, was reading the Book of Job, and I found myself saying, 'Go on, go on.' "[53] She "heard words that rose and fell like a powerful melody, like the greatest, strongest hymn I had ever heard. . . . The words sang, and out of the singing a story came, not like the stories in my little books, but another kind of story, a terrible story about a man who believed in God when God let the most awful things happen to him. . . . I felt terrible about Job, but exhilarated. . . . The end was beautiful. The story was terrible and beautiful. I had not known before that a story could be terrible and beautiful at the same time."[54]

From this moment, at a time when books were expensive and prized beyond cost, Dorothy read without cease — "voraciously," "compulsively," anything to hand, of any length and density, whether she understood it or not: "Dickens, Thackeray, Scott, George Eliot, Hawthorne, Emerson, Mark Twain, Shakespeare, Palgrave's Golden Treasury, the Bible (compulsory), Hugo and a good deal of American and European history, as well as . . . what my father called 'cheap' novels, taken from the village library or left in the house by my low-brow Uncle Willie." [55] There was very little of world literature that the Reverend Peter Thompson forbade his daughter, as it happened. "If I read passionate love poems and songs," said Dorothy, "as I certainly did, . . . my father evidently had no apprehension that they would make me sexually precocious" (though George Abbott, who grew up in Hamburg before going on to become one of the great theatrical producers of Broadway history, distinctly recalled having to smuggle *Quo Vadis* out of the public library so that Dorothy could read it). [56]

"Reading became such a compulsion," Dorothy went on, "that in lieu of anything else I would read sermons or theological and philosophical theses." Punishment was meted out to her in the form of poems to be memorized and lessons to be learned. Once when she had slapped her sister, Peggy, her father locked her in a closet and would not let her out until she could recite Shelley's "Adonais" from beginning to end. [57] By the time she was grown, Dorothy could deliver without pause whole chapters of the Bible, the sonnets of Shakespeare, great chunks of *Leaves of Grass,* Chesterton's "Lepanto," dozens of the Psalms, and the entire Constitution of the United States. In a diary she kept many years later during a lecture tour, she recalled these days under her father's tutelage:

> He loved [Peggy] most, because she was like mother. "A clever child, Doro-thea, but not much comfort." . . . Why wasn't I a comfort? I loved him so. Lying on the floor in his study, . . . I could see his feet. In their nicely polished shoes. "I do hate untidy shoes." . . . He had nice feet and was vain of them, and nice hands, small and neat, and a little feminine.
>
> "Listen, Thea, Doro-thea . . . Listen." He had all the poetry of the English language in his shelves. That clear tenor voice. "Some time when your heart has ached a lot, you will love these people most of all." "Don't neglect Byron. A bad fellow they will tell you. A proud and aristocratic soul. Worth two of that shrill fellow, Shelley. But you are young. You will prefer Shelley." . . .
>
> He let me read Walt Whitman. "From pent-up aching rivers . . .

I celebrate myself, and sing myself . . ." "Rubbish, let the child read. There's magic in words. All the magic in this house is in these covers. Let her read what she likes. Won't hurt her."

"And seeing the multitude he went up into a high mountain, and he opened his mouth and taught them, saying . . ."

"That's pure poetry . . . Listen: Thea, Doro-thea. . . . Don't think it's enough just to be bright. Sit down there and learn the 13th chapter of First Corinthians. See if you can tell it to me in an hour. And then remember it. Especially the first verse." . . .

Oh, my dear father! I was never a comfort to you and you live in me like the truth of a thought. I wanted to grow up, amount to something, do something for you, make you proud of me.[58]

Her relations with her father changed abruptly, and permanently, in the summer of 1903. It was known far and wide in Hamburg that Peter Thompson was "hopeless" on his own. "He would talk to everybody," Dorothy explained. "He always had time for people. Anybody who came to our door was made welcome; he would invite the strangest people in to lunch. . . . We had the greatest difficulty once in preventing him from giving away our cooking stove."[59] The story got around of the day the Reverend met a beggar on the road and sent him off with the key to the parsonage, inviting him to help himself to food, clothing, and a bath. When the children arrived home from school, they found an empty cupboard and a note: "Thank you very much for the food. It was delicious. I took the liberty of cleaning the place up a bit. It needed it."[60]

Now, on Sundays, Dorothy sat with her family very primly in church, "second pew at the left," measuring the length of the service by the stages of her father's delivery, waiting for "those sweet words of release, 'And may the peace of God which passeth all understanding be with you now and forevermore,' "[61] and not failing to notice how ingeniously certain ladies of the parish managed to elbow their way to the Reverend's side on their way out the door. First among them was Eliza Maria Abbott, the church pianist, daughter of one of Hamburg's wealthiest citizens, and, in the words of her nephew George Abbott, "one of the homeliest women ever invented." Eliza was already forty in 1903, "over-sweet and weak," a sheltered spinster who lived with her parents and "seemed long ago to have withered on the vine."[62] Marguerite Jarvis remembered her as "a pain in the neck," the last of a breed, "the grandmother of all old maids,"[63] and undoubtedly the shock felt by the Thompson children when they realized that their father was going to marry her had something to do with the contrast she presented to their beautiful, physical, sexual mother.

"I know what she wants," said Dorothy to her sister when she first saw Miss Abbott leaving church on the Reverend's arm. "She wants Father, that's what. . . . I've heard the big girls talking. . . . You wait and see."[64] She was proved right on August 5, 1903, when Peter Thompson and Eliza Abbott were married at the home of the bride's parents, with Dorothy herself acting as a reluctant flower girl. George Abbott ventured that the most likely explanation for the wedding was the simplest: his aunt Eliza was "an ardent church worker, and since she would, by small-town standards, eventually come into quite an inheritance, Mr. Thompson put on the blinders, so to speak, and married her for her money and to give his children a mother."[65]

As things turned out, Peter Thompson's children did not want a mother, nor did Eliza Abbott ever betray the faintest aptitude for the job. "You children must understand," she announced on moving into the parsonage, "that I am mistress of this house and I shall run it, not you." This was a point that had not come up before, so far as the children were concerned: "It had just been home, ours, every-one's." But Aunt Lizzie was sent away as soon as was decently possible, and the new Mrs. Thompson set about to obliterate every vestige of her sensible presence. "You must conquer children with love," she proclaimed, reminding her charges with unconvincing regularity that she cared for them "as if they were my own"[66] and swooping down to kiss them with her "unattractive, wet lips,"[67] her eyes magnified so grotesquely by her thick spectacles that they looked as if they belonged to some hilarious garden bug. This poor creature came equipped with a whole series of hypothetical dicta about happy homes and healthy minds, and when her opinions failed to win her either obedience or respect, she took to a wheelchair and a bottle of patent medicine, a mixture called Viava that was meant to "strengthen her blood" but actually made her drunk.[68] "Whatever her other virtues," said Dorothy, who hated her, Eliza Abbott "was a self-pitying hypochondriac bravely but futilely struggling against an allergy to children."[69]

From the beginning Eliza and Dorothy were at odds, and their antipathy went far beyond the normal aggravations of stepfamilies. "She's a problem," said Eliza, "she really is."[70] With some difficulty Dorothy was persuaded to call Eliza "Mother," but she could not muster any kind of affection for her and deeply resented what she regarded as Eliza's meddlesome "religiosity." Her stepmother was "a scolder," Dorothy remembered, who "kept prying into your soul and your motives and getting between you and your own conscience."[71] Eliza, for her part, fairly persecuted Dorothy, teasing her and taunting her and publicly calling attention to her faults, her insecurities, and her adolescent want of grace, until Dorothy was reduced to helpless tears and Eliza could remark with maddening satisfaction, "What a cry-baby you are. Mercy on me, you're ready to cry if anyone looks at you." Once on Christmas — always an important and happy holiday in Dorothy's life — Eliza handed her a small, daintily wrapped package, which, when opened, was found to contain a baby's bottle and a card: "Merry Christmas to a cry-baby."

Dorothy was so taken aback that she could only exclaim "Oh!" before dropping the bottle on the floor and running to her room.

"Eliza, how *could* you?" Peter Thompson demanded. But he did nothing to halt or even mitigate the hostility that existed between his wife and his daughter. Indeed, he seems, in some extraordinary way, simply to have dropped from the picture, content to be henpecked, to defer to his ailing wife, to listen in silence to her mounting complaints about his lack of ambition and the "shabbiness" of all of their lives. Later on, only Peggy Thompson was willing to concede that Eliza Abbott had probably done the best she could in a difficult situation. "For forty years she had led the life of a protected daughter," said Peggy, "a little proud of the fact that she was 'delicate' and must not tax her strength too far. She had never engaged in any more strenuous pursuits than playing the church organ and giving piano lessons to a selected few of Hamburg's young." It was Peggy's guess that Eliza had probably dreamed of leaving her small-town life behind her when she married Peter Thompson, perhaps imagining that she would become "the charming hostess in the parsonage of one of Buffalo's more elegant churches. . . . The story of her life with us must have been one of such bitter disappointment that I can only skim its edges, a life of such frustration as to end in her dying request that Father . . . be buried beside her in the Abbott lot in the Hamburg cemetery, instead of beside our mother whose grave we used to visit. He promised, and since he had never been known to break a promise in life, it was done, a pitiful testimony to Eliza's final success."

In 1905, when Dorothy was twelve, the Reverend Peter Thompson was transferred to a larger parish, at Gowanda (a town that differed from Hamburg mainly in size), and there the conflict between Dorothy and Eliza came to a head. The rebellious child was developing into a troubled teenager — "putting on airs," in her stepmother's opinion, choosing her friends from among the "worldly and pleasure-seeking" of Gowanda's rather more upscale society,[72] one day coming home suspended from school for having satirized a pompous male teacher in an underground poem.[73] When Eliza decided that Dorothy, as a punishment for some misdemeanor, should pray aloud for forgiveness in front of the whole family, Peter Thompson put a stop to it, but it was rather late in the day for this kind of defiance. Dorothy was finally pushed out of the house altogether when the family moved to Spencerport and Eliza declared that "she just couldn't cope" if her stepdaughter came along. Arrangements were made for Dorothy to live with two of her father's sisters in Chicago, there to finish high school and, as Eliza explained to inquisitive Methodists, receive "advantages" she could not hope for in the outskirts of Buffalo. Willard Thompson remembered that her parting from the family was "cheerful,"[74] but her sister, Peggy, had a quite different recollection.

She "went about in a sort of daze," said Peggy. "She felt that Father had deserted her at last." It would have been unusual indeed if she had not. But she was not by nature given to holding grudges, and in future years — certainly after Eliza's death, in 1916 — Dorothy was content to remember her stepmother good-naturedly, as a sort of joke and a family distraction.

"That's a bright girl the preacher has," people said when, over the next several years, Dorothy returned occasionally to Spencerport or Gowanda, or to Hamburg to visit Marguerite Jarvis.

"She's having advantages," her stepmother would reply,[75] and anybody who looked at her could see that she was. Her father's greatest legacy to Dorothy might have lain in her being forced to strike out on her own sooner than anyone expected — down the line of the Erie Railroad, in pursuit of "waking dreams."

2
CHAPTER

DOROTHY spent five years in Chicago with her father's sisters Margaret and Hetty, the one a widow, the other a spinster, distinguished in conversation as "Aunt" and "Auntie." It was a happy time for her, notable mainly for the opportunity it gave her to finish out her girlhood in an atmosphere of toleration and respect. There were indeed "advantages" to living in one of America's premier cities, and Dorothy welcomed them all: theater, ballet, music, art. She was held in some awe by her friends in New York State, who remembered her during this time as having her "head in the clouds," talking "high-brow" and "sort of romantic" on her visits home.[1] Her aunts encouraged her to develop her "feminine" qualities, and along with them "some expensive tastes."[2] They "rearranged my hair," Dorothy recalled, "and [dressed] me for the first time in my life very becomingly. Also they kept telling me I was pretty. I can't tell you what a difference it made in my young life, and in my relations with everybody."[3]

In 1908 she was enrolled as a student at the Lewis Institute in Chicago, which, before it merged with the Illinois Institute of Technology, functioned as a junior college and prep school for "the poor but proud."[4] Here, paying a tuition of eighty dollars a year, Dorothy traveled every morning on roller skates to sit through upper-level classes on serious subjects, a far cry from the dusty schoolhouse curricula of Hamburg and Gowanda. She was the only female on the debating society (where, said the yearbook, "all of the debaters, including Miss Thompson, acquitted themselves like men").[5] She played on the girls' basketball team and continued her romance with English literature under the instruction of Professor Edwin Herbert

Lewis. Looking like the ghost of William Shakespeare, and seeming to believe, as Dorothy recalled, "that the preservation of the English language . . . had been entrusted exclusively to his care," Professor Lewis left on his students the kind of deep-felt impression that only a showman can. Like all great teachers he was a man of terrific prejudices and something of a prima donna.

"It is impossible to kill the mystery of things," Lewis thundered to a room full of middy-bloused, taffeta-bowed girls, who evidently had missed the point of some Elizabethan poet or other. "Here I try to introduce you to sheer magic, but all you will ever be good for is to rustle pots and pans!"

"No," answered Dorothy, "I won't." She was actually known to rise out of her seat in discussion with her teachers, striding up the aisles and waving her hands in the air as she argued her meaning.[6] Lewis took her on as a personal favorite and stayed in touch with her for many years after her graduation, cherishing the memory of "you with your wit. You with your charm. You, going out all innocent to see the world, but concealing more dynamite of venturesomeness than any academic fossil could guess."[7]

It was Professor Lewis who sought to console Dorothy when, in the spring of 1912, she came to him with the news that her family could not afford to send her to Vassar, Smith, Bryn Mawr, or any of the other outstanding women's colleges she had hoped to attend, and that instead she would have to take advantage of a scholarship at Syracuse University, for the children of the Methodist clergy.[8]

"You could do much worse," said Lewis, reminding Dorothy that Syracuse, while not in the Ivy League, offered a perfectly admirable course of study, a fine faculty, and, perhaps most important, a long tradition of providing opportunity for women: at the turn of the century nearly half the student population at Syracuse was female, and one of its most famous graduates was Elizabeth Blackwell, M.D., still remembered as "the first woman doctor" in America. But Dorothy Thompson, at nineteen, was "restless, dissatisfied, and extremely unsure" of herself, her "hunger for the aesthetic" balanced by "a desire for the sophisticated and urbane." It was pouring rain when she first laid eyes on the Syracuse campus; the massive, ashen limestone buildings seemed to radiate dismay as she approached. Syracuse was a scattered city, "more Victorian than Gothic," split in half by the New York Central Railroad and the Erie Canal. "The one touch of romance was 'The Castle,' " said Dorothy, "a duplicate of an English

Tudor mansion built by the Russell Sage family and donated to the college."

Thanks to her schooling in Chicago, she entered Syracuse as a junior and was able to complete the requirements for a bachelor's degree in a scant two years. She pointed out later with distinct satisfaction that she had "never studied specifically for anything, and left college without knowing what I wanted to 'be ' " — that is, what she wanted to do for a living. American university students were not concerned in those days with job training or even very much with "careers." Education was a privilege and a priceless commodity, and it would not have occurred to Dorothy or anyone else to think otherwise. She knew that if she wished to be educated, she would have to extend herself, to venture into areas of study for which she might have no gift and that she might not ever "use." "Above arithmetic," for example, she "was about medium-moron," [9] but all the same she slogged through algebra, plane geometry, trigonometry, and a variety of natural sciences, enduring the difficult and the incomprehensible with the same high spirits that propelled her through languages and history, literature and philosophy — for their own sake. Dorothy was abetted in this approach by a system that knew no sentimentality when it came to laziness; by a faculty that demanded results; and by a host of other young women — an earnest collection of Florences and Ethels, Graces, Doras, Louises, Ruths, Ionas, and Paulines [10] — who felt, as Dorothy did, that they were in the vanguard generation, privileged by birth and upbringing to realize and broaden the American dream.

Dorothy was among the first company of women in America who, if they could not take their higher education for granted, still knew that it was available to them and nowhere beyond their capabilities. "The knowledge that we were a selected and limited group had a sobering influence," she wrote. "We owed something, something above and beyond what others owed. . . . The social obligation may have been particularly emphasized at Syracuse, for the Methodist persuasion strongly emphasized the social gospel," and Syracuse was a Methodist school. But there was more to it than that. Dorothy came of age at a time when the whole United States seemed about to burst with promise and good intentions; when science offered the hope of general salvation; when "security" was thought to be a tangible commodity; and when *progress* was the word on everyone's lips — "unremitting and unending human progress. . . . The turn of the century was seeing a spurt of invention without parallel in the history of mankind," said Dorothy, "and we were aware of this." In later years she had to force herself to remember that until she was fourteen years old she never lived in a house with electric lights or rode in an automobile, that airplanes did not fly any distance until she was well into her teens, and that they were actually expected, when they first appeared, to put an end to war "by making wars too dangerous." [11] The books she read, the people she met, the sermons she heard, and the lessons she learned all encouraged Dorothy to believe that society was capable of perfecting itself, and that mankind, collectively, was swimming straight into the millennium:

> As a young woman I saw the future stretching straight ahead of me to a shining goal, and I had a quite clear chart to follow it with. My generation had begun seriously to question the existence of God, but we had another religion in its place, to which we were as fanatically devoted, and that was the religion of progress. We were unquestioning in our loyalty to democracy. We were very much under the influence of Darwin. We believed that man had evolved from the anthropoidal ape and would inevitably, along with society, go on evolving onward and upward forever. Universal education, a further extension of democracy — votes for women — and above all, science and technique [i.e., technology] would solve all our problems eventually. All a person had to do was study hard, keep the rules, be thrifty and hard-working, and he would get along.

Of course, there was still the problem of poverty, as Dorothy discovered. There was the problem of injustice. There was the question of evil. As bright as the future may have looked to a middle-class girl at Syracuse, a great deal of what she actually saw around her was mired in squalor, and the twin companion of "progress" in those days was "reform." The last generation in America had witnessed the rise of the muckrakers and the birth in the cities of the settlement-house movement. The settlement houses, highly politicized, "had gradually grown far beyond their original purpose," said Dorothy; they "were championing trade unions, fighting commercialized vice, and . . . appealing for social and political action through the churches." For a while Dorothy volunteered her services at a group home in Syracuse, and there, for the first time, she saw "a really seamy side of life." She was supposed to teach cooking to impoverished and "fallen" women, and was forced "to face the fact, however vicariously, that the world of my childhood and early youth was representative of only a segment of American society.

"I experienced a wave of revulsion and indignation," she remembered. ". . . I wondered to what extent the protection I had had and still did have was paid for by the unprotected. . . . I wondered about my father's faith in the innate goodness in every human being; I wondered whether any amount of law and policing could remove evils as long as there were evil people. . . . It was as though, from a serene heaven of birds and books and music and flowers and 'suffer little children' and 'How firm a foundation' and 'Jerusalem the Golden,' the cover had been ripped off the bottomless pit." [12]

She discussed these matters quite seriously with her father on her visits home, telling him that she would rather place her faith in science and in the social vision of women such as Lillian Wald and Jane Addams than in the Bible and the churches. She was "by no means convinced," she said, "at that point in my life, that 'the soul' existed apart from the body," and she was beginning to think that "man had invented God and not the other way around." Her father replied that if she was right, "it was the greatest expression of man's genius," because "nobody invents what he does not feel the need of!" [13] Inevitably the Reverend warned Dorothy that spiritual problems would need spiritual solutions, and that "progress" would mean nothing at the moment of death.

"He saw the world as a continual struggle between good and evil," said Dorothy, "virtue and sin. To his mind, . . . progress was furthered only through creative individuals, whose example and achievement leavened and lifted the mass. The business of each person on earth was to perfect himself, with the help of God, in the image of the ideal of Christ." [14] For the time being Dorothy was content to think of her father as "a somewhat charming old fossil." Before she left Syracuse she led a vespers service on campus in which she addressed the subject of "Outgrowing Things"; one of the things she had clearly outgrown was the Methodist creed, at least in its formal state. Henceforth her relations with the Almighty were going to be "purely personal."

The truth of the matter was that Dorothy, by her own admission, "was not really breaking my rather pretty head over any problems other than my own. I was imbibing what I would later digest." On her arrival at Syracuse she had been accepted as a member in Alpha Chi Omega, whose chapter house sat in a great turreted pile at 709 University Avenue, just down the hill from the central campus.

Dorothy was "irritated" by the lack of privacy in the house, finding it difficult to concentrate "in a room full of fudge-making, confidence-sharing girls," but she fitted in well with her companions and gave no lasting impression of condescension. Her friends remembered her as a "hearty" associate, "one with us all" and extremely practical ("I could whip up an evening dress for a gal with a special 'date' quicker than any dressmaker," said Dorothy) but given to sudden moods, spontaneous bursts of affection and tears, "intense" conversations, and the incessant recitation of poetry. "Her head was full of remembered rhymes," said her roommate, Ruth Hoople, who was herself the daughter of a Methodist minister. When she first met Ruth, in fact, Dorothy responded impulsively, with a stream of poetic quotation, and Ruth thought, "She's worth knowing."[15]

It was an opinion shared by an astonishing number of people, and the kind of remark that would follow Dorothy all of her life. Fresh with health and strapping good looks, her skin as pure and pink "as a six-month-old baby's,"[16] she was "the laughingest girl one could meet,"[17] "hectic, lovely, exciting,"[18] possessed of an extraordinary personal magnetism that was somehow, and by all accounts, far greater than the sum of its parts. She "fitted like an easy glove over the mind of any stranger,"[19] one of her companions wittily observed. She was a compellingly, overwhelmingly *social* personality — so much so that a classmate at Syracuse retained memories exclusively of "Dorothy and other people, never of Dorothy alone, as though it were the presence of others which [heightened] her own not inconsiderable color."[20] Studious though she was, she worked hard not to be "a greasy grind";[21] she joined the groups her girlfriends joined, entered their contests, played their games, and — because, as the daughter of a Methodist preacher, she was forbidden to dance — she sat contentedly on the sidelines at their showers and parties.

She was acquainted with "the facts of life" by the time she got to college; she had "read anatomy" and once discovered a girlfriend "petting" with a boy under some bushes in Gowanda,[22] but she had "not the slightest interest in marriage," and sexually, she said, "even for those times, I was retarded rather than precocious." Dorothy remembered "a great deal of flirting" at Syracuse, in spite of strict discipline among the sorority girls and repeated warnings about the fate awaiting any woman who relaxed her moral standards. One sister at Alpha Chi Omega who got drunk on a date was expelled from school without so much as a hearing; cigarette smoking was seriously (if circuitously) alleged to lead to insanity and death; and two of the top-selling books of Dorothy's college days were Jane Addams's *A New Conscience and an Ancient Evil*, which dealt with the horrors of prostitution and the white slave trade, and Eugène Brieux's *Damaged Goods*, an overwrought dramatization of the effects of syphilis on the French.

"I liked boys well enough," Dorothy admitted, "and they did not dislike me, but they often bored me with their damp hands and callow shy advances and I frightened them off with my rather highfalutin speech." There was a legend at Syracuse for many years that a date with Dorothy Thompson had meant a walk in the moonlight and a talk about Hegel. "She knew too much," said one turtlenecked boy of the day. "A fellow felt inferior."[23] Dorothy hardly cared: she was proud of her accomplishments, engrossed in her studies, and warmly contented with the devotion of her friends. This was the era of the "passionate attachment," when half-altered mores and a glimpse of the world only strengthened women's dependence on each other, and when one girl could say to another, without self-consciousness, without anxiety, "I love you . . . I adore you."

Men, of course, were bothered. Gordon Hoople, the older brother of Dorothy's roommate, Ruth, worried about Dorothy's influence on his sister and stepped in uninvited as her suitor and escort while loudly complaining that "Dot" was "unfeminine."[24] She was not unaware herself, at least in retrospect, of the "faintly erotic"[25] nature of her relations with women, but her greatest crime appears to have been that she did not take men seriously enough for their liking. Men were "incapable of quite completely understanding a modern young woman," said Dorothy later, with a note of both truth and smugness.[26] She would rather sit and laugh with Ruth, or talk politics and economics with J. Winifred Hughes, the captain of the women's basketball team, or read poetry into the small hours with Jean Marie Richards, the beautifully tailored, Boston-born Dean of Women, the "epitome of all worldliness, elegance, culture and refinement" in Dorothy's eyes.[27]

"I adored her," Dorothy recalled. "She had an exquisite speaking voice and beautiful diction. She was altogether an exquisite woman. Her clothes, I remember, had a caché [*sic*] rather rare in western New York. She spoke beautiful French, had travelled much in that country, and she had a real passion for literature. Some students, who thought her English too English for western New York, called her a snob. . . . We became real friends." The attachment was ardent and mutual, having begun to develop during Dorothy's first semester at

Syracuse, when she submitted a theme paper to Miss Richards in which she quoted Plautus at some length.

"She kept me after class," Dorothy remembered, "and remarked ironically that it would be better for me to write of what I knew than to drag in some second-hand quotation." Afterward, over long afternoons and uncounted pots of tea, Dorothy found in the beautiful, bookish Miss Richards much more than academic guidance.

"The fact that she paid some attention to me somewhat assuaged the uncertainty, even fear, that I felt about my capacity to meet life," Dorothy explained. "It has always astonished me that so few people then or later were ever aware of this inner uncertainty. I was not then, nor have I been ever, pleased with myself." The question of her professional future bothered her more and more as graduation approached. Her father, who had recently taken charge of an urban parish in Buffalo, had made enormous sacrifices in order to give her an education, and Dorothy knew that this was a debt she would have to repay. It was agreed that she would find a job immediately on leaving Syracuse and that she would, in turn, contribute to the cost of educating her younger brother and sister.

"I will have to get anything I can to earn some money," she told Miss Richards sadly. "I won't really be free for some years." Such ambition as she had was still amorphous, too — inexplicit, adolescent. "I want to see the world," Dorothy said, "all phases of it, in more than one country, and write about it. But I don't think I have any creative talent as a writer."

If she was waiting for Miss Richards to contradict her, she was bound for disappointment. "She gave me no fulsome encouragement," Dorothy remembered. "She told me that many people earned a good living from writing who would be forgotten when their pens ceased functioning. And she told me that if I wanted to write 'about the world' every experience I had of the world would help me."

The point was not too simple for Dorothy to grasp. Her father had told her much the same thing when she went to him in a moment of panic and high drama, facing graduation and the suddenly looming fear that she would never amount to anything, that her dream of being "a writer" would never materialize, that she would probably perish at some meaningless, grinding work before she found her way. Peter Thompson looked at her quizzically, half amused, and answered firmly, "My dear, you don't know how hard it's going to be for you to starve."[28]

*　　*　　*

THE main thing, said the Reverend, was to find work you were willing to do for no pay at all and then contrive to be paid for it. "You must never do anything *just* for money," he warned.[29] So far Dorothy's acquaintance with the world of work had been distinctly unpoetic. She had toiled one summer as a waitress in a restaurant on Lake George; had sold ice cream cones on the boardwalk at the Methodist resort of Ocean Grove, New Jersey; and had peddled encyclopedias door-to-door with her friend Ruth Billard, a brilliant, "maverick" mathematician who died suddenly of appendicitis soon after Dorothy's graduation. But this was not the kind of life that Dorothy had in mind for herself.

Wanting to be a writer, she had submitted a number of dreamy, exalted short stories to different monthly magazines in New York City, and when these were rejected — "The editors were cock-eyed," said Dorothy later; "the stories weren't bad at all"[30] — she abandoned fiction and turned her efforts to more directly "social" concerns. She turned a deaf ear on her father's suggestion that she do some kind of church work, nor did she care to follow Ruth Hoople as a missionary to China. She remained determined to combine work with a cause she could believe in. She found it in September 1914, when she was offered a job stuffing envelopes, for eight dollars a week, at the Buffalo headquarters of the New York State Woman Suffrage Party.

There were six years still to go, in 1914, before the ratification of the Nineteenth Amendment granted women in the United States the right to vote at the national level. The drive to enfranchisement had actually begun very close to Dorothy's own upstate territory, in 1848, when Elizabeth Cady Stanton had called for the first suffrage convention at Seneca Falls. Since then New York, with its great size and predominantly rural population, had proved to be one of the most hostile and recalcitrant of all the states debating the suffrage question; when Dorothy came aboard, it was thought to be the last state in the nation in which passage of the amendment really mattered. Without New York there was no hope for woman suffrage in America, and in New York, from 1914 to 1917, were concentrated the major efforts of all the women's parties. Here Carrie Chapman Catt, the stern and stately leader of the movement, heiress to the legacy of Mrs. Stanton, Susan B. Anthony, Lucrecia Mott, and thousands of their unheralded supporters, organized something like two million women nationally in the final push for enfranchisement. Here Dorothy Thompson, who had become "an ardent suffragist as soon as [she] heard of the movement,"[31] put theory into practice to gain "an extraordinary experience and education — in politics, publicity, public speaking, organization, and insight into every variety of the human condition."[32]

She graduated quickly through the suffrage ranks, moving from her dreary work at the desk in Buffalo out onto the road to stump for suffrage in "every town and hamlet in western New York." The state had been organized into nine campaign districts, and Dorothy worked the eighth, itself broken down into assembly areas that comprised Buffalo proper and half a dozen upstate counties — some 6,600 square miles of "difficult and discouraging territory."[33] Within a year Dorothy was earning seventy-five dollars a month and bore the title of "Organizer," which meant that she performed every kind of public-relations and propaganda work that the situation demanded at the grass-roots level — "everything that fire, imagination and high purpose could evolve."[34] She made countless speeches and wrote hundreds of press releases; she arranged parties and parades, dances and flower shows, cross-country runs, baseball games, and boxing matches, all in the cause of suffrage. In addition, Dorothy acted as a liaison between the women's parties and the voters, and after the fight was won she claimed without apparent exaggeration that there was not a single village in the district "where I do not know the leading citizens, and where they do not know me, and for the most part very happily."[35] "I do not think that any movement from those days to this," she later wrote, "has been carried on with so much energy and imagination."[36]

She rose frequently at five in the morning, "gritty with sleep," to catch the milk train from Buffalo and "make the turn around the county," sometimes stopping overnight at ramshackle inns or the houses of sympathizers, sleeping in "damp beds," as she remembered, and living on fried steak.[37] At any particular town, depending on the degree of local awareness, she might plead with the mayor or other officials to grant her a permit to hold a meeting in the town offices or grange hall, or might be obliged to deliver her speeches from the tailboard of a farm wagon. It was her primary responsibility, after "haranguing the populace," to form a suffrage committee in every town or village where none existed, and to see to it that the local women received practical instruction in furthering the cause.

"Make people love you," read the advice from headquarters. "Be careful not to antagonize anyone. Don't allow yourself to be entangled with other issues. Remember your *only* business in that community is suffrage. . . . Don't be ashamed or afraid to ask for money. . . . Don't forget collections at every suffrage meeting of any kind." It was much the same in regard to the press. There were more than eleven hundred weekly publications in New York State, as well as two hundred dailies and six hundred monthlies; over time Dorothy staged literally hundreds of stunts and suffrage "events" and learned to write publicity swiftly and to order, again on headquarters' advice: "Take up a newspaper and note how much of the news of the day is about men. There's your path blazed for you — relate suffrage to the things men are interested in. Men are tremendously interested in themselves." [38] For years the story followed Dorothy of the time she tried to make a speech from a soapbox in Friendship,[39] a resolutely antisuffrage village where she had been invited to speak during Old Home Week ("probably in order to provide some extra fun for the holiday"). A street carnival was in progress, and Dorothy stood gravely next to the mayor on a platform in the center of town.

"There's a young lady here from Buffalo," the mayor began, with no apparent enthusiasm, but his words were lost in the noise of a marching band that happened just at that moment to strike up a patriotic tune. Shrugging his shoulders in Dorothy's direction, the mayor climbed down from the stage and left her to shout her message over the din. But the harder she tried to be heard, the louder the band performed, until finally she caught sight of a child's blackboard on display in the window of a furniture store. She jumped to the ground, ran across the street, bought the blackboard for a dollar, and, returning to her position, commenced to write out her speech in chalk.

"Noise is not an answer to truth!" she began, then erased the message and added in a snappier vein, "Is this the treatment a lone gal gets?" Opinion was unanimous later that she had won the audience, if not their votes.

Dorothy's own favorite memory of the campaign concerned a dainty conservative lady who disapproved of the idea of votes for women but contributed a lot of money to the cause anyway. Asked why, she replied, "Because it's such a good show."

"It *was* a good show," said Dorothy, looking back. "It was the last romantic political movement this country ever had." [40] She hated the actual work of organizing, however,[41] and had uneasy feelings even then about single-issue politics. She remembered an occasion when she debated Lucy Price, a famous antisuffrage speaker, before a crowd of "ten thousand farmers" in Jamestown. The audience was "packed" with suffragists, said Dorothy, "in the fashion which we 'pure' women, who were going to reform politics, always used so blithely." Mrs. Price was quoting Longfellow:

> Stay, stay at home, my heart and rest,
> Home-keeping hearts are happiest. . . .

While Dorothy could not endorse the sentiment as used, there were other aspects of Mrs. Price's argument that did, on reflection, make some sense to her ("One being that politics was not only no sphere for women but no sphere for anybody").[42] Still and all, she could not but take sides against an opposition that called in doctors to affirm that the average suffragist, "measured by the fair rules of intelligence testing," had "about the mental age of 11," and that put forward its arguments against the Vote and the "extradomicilliary life" with such vaudevillian bad taste: "A suffragette is a sting of beauty and a jawer forever. . . . Not satisfied with the last word, she also wants the first. . . . She is a woman who would rather break windows than clean them . . . who spares no 'panes' to get what she wants . . . whose troubles are certainly not 'little ones' . . . who spends more time airing her views than viewing her heirs."[43]

It was the suggestion that they were somehow unfeminine, "unnatural," "sex-antagonized," or worse that most rankled Dorothy and her cohorts. The "Antis" were advised to be on the lookout for short-haired women and pretty-faced men, but if there had ever been any basis for these stereotypes in the suffrage campaign, it had long since disappeared. What had begun as an alien, forbidding movement among a handful of righteous middle-class women had developed, by the first decades of the twentieth century, into a cause for the mass of Americans — a manifestly nonradical demand for equal participation in a system whose basic structure almost everybody was ready to accept as it was. In her suffrage work Dorothy did encounter for the first time large groups of working and immigrant women — socialists, anarchists, and progressives of different stripes, who hoped to see the cause of suffrage flower into a larger movement for social reform. She became acquainted with factory workers, union organizers, political theorists, and (a turning point in her "limited, neat, placid" existence)[44] a host of Jewish intellectuals. But suffrage drew its main strength from the college campuses, where faculty and students alike joined forces to fill the ranks, and from "Society," where "smart young matrons and aging dowagers, with large fortunes at their command, were swinging into line."[45]

The roster of Dorothy Thompson's friends in the New York suffrage campaign reads like a page straight from the Social Register: Mrs. J. Borden Harriman, Mrs. O. H. P. Belmont, Miss Anne Morgan, the ravishing Mrs. Norman DeR. Whitehouse, Mrs. Frank Vanderlip, Mrs. James Lees Laidlaw, Mrs. Ogden Reid. Forward-thinking, mainly liberal-Republican wives and mothers, they set the tone for a whole generation of civic-minded women in the United States. There was Mrs. Charles L. Tiffany, the president of the College Equal Suffrage League, who warmly approved of Dorothy's efforts in the cause and introduced her to her sisters, the Misses Henrietta and Gertrude Sumner Ely, Philadelphia suffragists, philanthropists, and Democratic party stalwarts who became her lifelong friends. There was Mrs. Tiffany's sister-in-law, Dorothy Tiffany Burlingham, daughter of the designer of the Tiffany lamp, one of the first women in America to be psychoanalyzed and, later on, the disciple and companion of Sigmund Freud and his daughter, Anna. There was little Mary Gawthorpe, the vivacious, Lancashire-born speaker and organizer who came to Buffalo directly from her work with the Pankhursts in England and "made the papers blossom with columns of suffrage news."[46] Finally there was Gertrude Franchot Tone, mother of the future movie star, daughter of a New York State senator, wife of the president of the American Electrochemical Society and the Carborundum Company of Niagara Falls, and mentor to the young Dorothy Thompson — "your sister," as she signed herself, "mother, guide, philosopher and friend."[47]

It was the greatest disappointment of Gertrude Tone's life — a life that ultimately degenerated into alcoholism and pathetic, blowsy comedy on the streets of New York — that she had been born a woman and, she believed, at precisely the wrong moment, just before women had begun to take their place on the wider stage of American affairs. The wife of one of her brothers remembered that Gertrude "had a horrible inferiority complex because she lacked a college education. . . . She was *just* a female and God! how she resented it." A beautiful woman "with *piercing* dark eyes and almost beetling brows," Gertrude had shocked her neighbors in Niagara Falls by dabbling in Eastern religion and a variety of spiritual and social correctives that brought her "as far left politically as she could get without being a card-carrying Communist."[48] For a time she was director of the Women's Peace Union of the Western Hemisphere, which held as its stated goal the passage of "a constitutional amendment declaring war for any purpose illegal and prohibiting altogether the maintenance of armed forces."[49] When Dorothy met her, Gertrude was active (and heartily appreciated) as chairwoman of suffrage's eighth campaign district, but she described herself in letters as "that tragic member of the bourgeoisie," "this voice from the void," trapped, she explained, in endless "dog days . . . , with a bowl of cherries by my side."[50]

"God," said Gertrude, "if only I were something besides a question-mark. . . . I don't really belong anywhere!"[51] She certainly did not belong in Niagara Falls, where Dorothy spent many weeks as her guest and apostle, sitting at her knee to absorb her mournful wisdom, getting to know her children, theoretically despising her hidebound Republican husband, Frank, and not knowing for sure whether she was in love with Gertrude or with Gertrude's dashing younger brother, Ned Franchot. It was not something she examined very keenly at the time. "I wanted to be close to her," Dorothy remembered, "to be like her." More than once she contrived to turn up "accidentally" on the lake at Gerryowen, the Tones' summer camp in Canada — "just to be near her," just to be able to say, as if in surprise, "Why it's you — so near!"[52] When the New York suffrage campaign was brought to its successful conclusion in November 1917 — the suffragists had won by a margin of 94,000 votes — Dorothy traveled to Manhattan, East Sixteenth Street, to be exact, on the fringe of Greenwich Village, where Gertrude had taken an apartment. There she set about to rearrange the furniture, hang art on the walls, and provide new chintz curtains for the drawing room before moving in herself.[53]

The woman suffrage movement had triumphed, in the end, largely as a consequence of World War I. When America entered the European conflict in the spring of 1917, the women's parties never hesitated to exploit the flag-waving spirit to their own advantage: the suffragists' organizing skills and the issue of women's enfranchisement were entwined directly with the battle for democracy and the War to End Wars. Even Dorothy, whose basic instincts told her that the war in Europe involved "no fundamental ideological concepts" and was, in fact, only "a power-political struggle" and "a form of mutual European suicide," found herself rooting wholeheartedly against the Hun.

"My brother had gone to war," she explained, "and soon we heard he had gotten a bad infection in the trenches. . . . We were perpetually worried about our personal friends. Within one week my nicest English cousin and a dear school friend were killed."[54] She wanted to go to Europe herself to help with the war effort, to join her friend Gertrude Ely, who was shortly to be awarded the French Croix de Guerre for her work in the field. She was told, however, that she had no qualifications for paid war work, and she was beginning to wonder just what she was made of. For about six months she toiled in an advertising agency in Manhattan, earning more money "than [she] had ever seen in her life," but she disdained to pass her existence "writing phony blurbs for soap and mouthwash" and "got out of it," as she said, "because I could not see that I was contributing anything either to my own development or to the society in which I lived. On the contrary."[55]

She was joined in New York by her best friend from the suffrage campaign, Barbara De Porte, the daughter of Russian-Jewish immigrants, a graduate of Cornell, whose thick accent and brainy opinions had made her something of a sensation among suffrage women. Barbara and Dorothy had met in the last summer before the vote was won and had quickly become inseparable, bound together not just by temperamental sympathies but by ideals that seemed to reach higher to the skies with every passing day. The first generation of fully emancipated women in America was operating without a map, hoping to face life squarely and to be liberated, as Dorothy later put it, "from any *artificial* repressions, conventions or traditions." Dorothy was a virgin at twenty-five — all of her unmarried girlfriends were — but she was "awakened and conscious of her sex," attractive to men, and very much aware of "the tragedy of the modern young woman," whose opportunities for love and marriage seemed to dwindle in precipitous ratio to her desire for independence. In quest of experience, "in love with the world," Dorothy liked to think that she was guided by benevolent, autonomous forces — "some magic beauty, some grand sense." She laughed in delight when Gertrude Tone wrote a poem in her honor and told her that she was "a daughter of the gods."

"I believed it," said Dorothy. "I used to feel, *really* feel, that the gods loved me."[56] In September 1918 she wrote to Pauline ("Paul") Newman, the radical union organizer whom she had met at Gertrude Tone's apartment in New York:

I'm still "in quest of the one beauty" and the one purpose. I am afraid that I am temperamentally doomed to be forever a reed shaken in the wind. All this allegory in answer to your exhortation to get into the labor movement. If the movement could use me, I should be there, my dear. But labor is so scornful of us, whose whole background is middle class. We have to struggle so hard to live it down! No matter how fiery our hearts and indignant our tongues, how warm our sympathies — labor looks at us with skeptical eyes and demands that we show the mark of the nails in our hands — our hands that have never worked. And so we go to "Social Units" which are very good things I maintain, and make their own contribution to the democracy and right thinking of the world.[57]

The "Social Unit"[58] Dorothy referred to was the brainchild of Wilbur C. Phillips, the veteran community organizer whose crusade against infant mortality, earlier in the decade, had revolutionized welfare systems in New York and around the country. With his wife, Elsie, the passionate, thirty-eight-year-old Phillips had recently combined experience and philosophy to form the National Social Unit Organization, an experimental assembly of philanthropists and social workers who came together "for the purpose of finding some way to increase health, happiness, and the other good things of the earth" among the impoverished and disenfranchised of America's larger cities.

For purposes of demonstration, the Social Unit had focused its attention on issues of family hygiene and nutrition in the Mohawk-Brighton district of Cincinnati, Ohio — a thirty-one block area of "a typical American city."[59] It was there that Dorothy went in the summer of 1918 as publicity director for the experiment and the "personal representative" of her friend from suffrage, Mrs. Tiffany, who sat on the Social Unit's board of directors and helped to finance the project.[60]

"The questions which this community is trying to answer are: 'Can the advantages of village life be restored to the city, supplemented by the opportunities the city affords?' " Dorothy wrote in an article for the *New York Times Magazine*.[61] " 'Can neighbors get to know neighbors and organize for mutual benefit? Can the problems of health, recreation and living conditions be met and solved by the people themselves, pooling their social skill and experience? Can complete democracy be brought in by friendly counsel and cooperation?' " It was a bold experiment for 1918. With America at war, everyone Dorothy knew was making sacrifices of one kind or another — "knitting socks and mufflers, going without butter and sugar, buying war bonds, working for the Red Cross."[62] Meanwhile, when she was not lecturing for the Social Unit, writing press releases, or preparing a weekly bulletin for Unit participants, Dorothy edited and typed a newspaper of her own, the half-satirical, half-informative *Home Fire News,*[63] which she copied and dispatched to her brother, Willard, in France:

> Great rejoicing has been manifested in these parts due to the announcement received here to-day that Private Pete [i.e., her brother, Peter Willard Thompson] had arrived safely in France and "liked the life." This afternoon's papers also announced that the Germans had made a new peace offer. We knew they would.
>
> Miss D. Thompson and Miss Regina Kronacher [a colleague of Dorothy's at the Social Unit] ate chicken and watermelon at the Zoo last night for the Fatherless Children of France. Great patriotism. . . . The celery and onions of the Allies came out victorious this week in the first engagement against the Hun weeds. . . .
>
> Miss D. Thompson, known the world round as a record breaker for speed in talking, will address members of the Americanization institute Friday evening, on "Home and Community Aspects of Americanization." Miss Thompson says that her lecture might [as] well be called "How to Talk on What You Do Not Know."
>
> A rising young authoress of this city whose name is withheld because it is already too much in evidence and we do not believe in publishers being their own press agents has had a saddening experience. She recently wrote an article and, modestly underrating her ability, sent it to three magazines, all of which have accepted it. She is thinking of enlisting to escape the consequences.

She wanted the Social Unit to succeed; she wanted to think that it represented something beyond fine words and feelings, but she hated with a passion what she later called "organized uplift"[64] and above all "the social workers' jargon, the way they discuss people in case loads."[65] Her work in Cincinnati, none too exciting in the first place, included writing articles for such recondite journals as the *Shipbuilders News and Navy Yard Employee.* On one occasion, for a parade in honor of "Children's Year," Dorothy arranged to borrow some pelicans from the zoo and sent them down the streets of Cincinnati beneath a banner that read, "Eat Fish and Win the War. We Do!"[66] The only real excitement came after the Armistice, when the mayor and a group of Ohio businessmen concluded that Wilbur and Elsie Phillips were "Bolsheviks" advocating "violence, pacifism, free-love and other obnoxious ideas" among the poor.[67] Dorothy secured permission to address a meeting of the local government and, according to one report, "peeled his honor's hide off in a memorable philippic."[68] But the Red Scare was in full swing, the damage was done, and the Cincinnati experiment was disbanded for good.

Dorothy might have stayed longer in social work if she had not gone back to New York at the end of 1919 as the Social Unit's national publicity director, and if, by the time she got there, she had not been head over heels in love with Wilbur Phillips. It was her first "affair," if that word may be used to describe a relationship that remained entirely platonic — "sincere," said Dorothy, "conscious, frank, . . . with an overwhelming sense of things mental and spiritual involved,"[69] but never moving past vague intentions and heated declarations of feeling. These declarations were mutual, as Dorothy did not hesitate to point out, and evidently she had reason to believe that Phillips might divorce his wife in order to marry her. There were "things," she said later, "circumstances — which made it hard and me unhappy. We could not be real lovers and I thought I couldn't live without him."[70] For a time she endeavored to function as a sort of dewy younger sister to both of the Phillipses, whose relations, at least at the emotional level, were open and "modern." But ultimately the exercise left her furious and bored. "Distraught, disappointed, and terribly hurt," she resigned from the Social Unit at the beginning of 1920 and resolved "to set her feet upon entirely new paths; to jerk her life up by the roots, as it were."[71]

It was a long and miserable spring, Dorothy's last in New York for many years. She liked to tell the story of a prostitute who had found her weeping on a bench one evening in Washington Square and remarked (with a quick glance at Dorothy's "shabby pumps"): "Cheer up, dearie, it's only your shoes."[72] In fact "the sensation of falling *out* of love," when it finally came, was "wonderful" to Dorothy. She was with Phillips one day, "calling on a friend, and there was a conversation, peculiarly revealing, and as they sat there talking and I sat listening, suddenly, like a flash, I noticed things about him — absurd things — a certain smugness, and conceit — it doesn't matter what. Only then, just like that, I knew I *could* live without him. Quite well. And when we went out in the street I could have sung for joy and waltzed in the street because I knew I was I and I was free again. Of course there was a relapse — still it was a great moment."[73] In a letter to Beatrice Sorchan, her onetime assistant at Social Unit headquarters, she remarked that "men are brutes" and that "*nothing* will make you happy except what you can find in yourself. I tell you, Beatrice, nothing else matters *much* except keeping your own self respect and having satisfactory work."[74]

Her sister, Peggy, had left college in 1919, and for the first time in six years Dorothy was free from financial obligations to her family, ready to do the work she liked, "and for a crust and a garret if need be."[75] With Barbara De Porte, her beloved, Russian-born "Varya," she seized on the idea of going abroad — running away, with no clearer idea than that the two of them would become "journalists" together. Thanks to Dorothy's work in suffrage and with the Social Unit, a number of her pieces had already been published in New York, in the *Times,* the *Sun,* the *Tribune.* Now she turned to editors all over the state looking for assignments in Europe. She hoped to write a series of travel articles for readers around Buffalo, where she was well known and could count on a large audience. Or she might write on the ramifications of the peace, a subject that stirred her deepest passions. Woodrow Wilson's Fourteen Points had "burst upon our world like a great sunrise," Dorothy remembered, "after a darkness filled with nightmares. That, we thought, was the Voice of America! That was a real peace! No revenge, no reprisals! No annexations and no indemnities! Democracy in Germany and then, forgiveness." She had wept aloud in 1919 when she read the terms of the Treaty of Versailles, seeing in them nothing but broken promises and the wholesale betrayal not just of Wilson's idealism but of everything her own generation held dear: Freedom, Justice, Toleration. One thing only, said Dorothy, "still kindled our hopes and aspirations. . . . That was Russia, symbol formerly of the blackest reaction in our minds. . . . The Russian Revolution . . . seemed the only bright light on the horizon. Here, it seemed to us, something was unfolding which had the grandeur of the doings of days and nights, the elemental force of nature itself, sweeping away the old and outworn, and creating in blood a whole, great new order of things."[76]

So Dorothy and Barbara would go to Russia. The idea was to sail for England and move on through Europe to Moscow, where "the sun was rising" on the Socialist experiment and where Barbara's native connections might give them a head start in the field of foreign correspondence. With this in mind Dorothy approached a number of banks for a loan to finance the trip.

"Miss Thompson has ascertained that she can make herself self-supporting . . . through correspondence for American newspapers," she wrote in a cover letter, "provided she can borrow sufficient money to secure her expenses, pending delivery of her articles."[77] But no assignment was forthcoming, no encouragement from editors, and no money from the bank. Ultimately Dorothy and Barbara pooled their own resources (about five hundred dollars between them), booked passage to London on the SS *Finland,* and left town on the nineteenth of June, 1920, waving good-bye at the pier to Gertrude Tone and the Reverend Peter Thompson, Dorothy's father, who had traveled down from Buffalo to give her his blessings and advice: she was to call on her relations as soon as she got to England; she was not to create any extra work for them when she did so; she was to write home every week, and would doubtless have "abundant material for a long letter" before she even left the ship.[78]

"Since you are obliged to earn your own living," the Reverend remarked in closing, "it will not always be possible for you to remain a lady. But I pray you, Dorothy — please promise me, that you will always remain a gentleman."[79]

He must have been joking, and Dorothy laughed uproariously in future years when she repeated her father's words. Her acquaintances had thought she was "mad" to leave home and harbor and "a country full of friends" for a life overseas and a completely uncertain career. But it was never a question of sense or practicality. Dorothy Thompson was twenty-seven, and she thought she could see her youth sliding by — "the time of life that fears nothing, believes everything, suffers everything, bears everything, is happy in everything, is ignorant of everything." She sailed for London "happy and lighthearted, . . . on the knees of the gods, . . . and never, for an instant, sorry." That was because she was listening to her own counsel; "that was because I was doing what I did with my whole heart."[80]

3

CHAPTER

WHEN Dorothy looked back on her first days in journalism — days of wonder, exhilaration, and storybook triumph — she insisted that her success had been due "nine-tenths" to a run of luck. "Inexperience alone," she maintained, "could have accounted for the serendipitous adventures of that first year abroad.[1] The SS *Finland* took twelve days to cross the ocean, and during the voyage Dorothy was virtually thrust into the story that began her career.

It was a "heavenly" crossing, with "blue, blue weather" and quiet seas. "I have put on at least five pounds of flesh," Dorothy told a friend in New York, "and have gotten cheeks like apples, and a return of a measure, at least, of calm and equipoise." Settling in for the trip, she looked around her and discovered that she was surrounded by Zionists: rabbis, writers, lawyers, and propagandists on their way to London for a conference on the future of Palestine.

"To an anti-Semite the trip would be a torture probably," said Dorothy with some candor, "but to me, to whom an alien temperament is always stimulating, it has been altogether amusing." She spent most of her time for the duration of the trip talking with these "extraordinary people" and boning up on the history of the Diaspora. "If I keep on," she remarked, "I think I shall perhaps become the leading Gentile authority on Judaism."[2] What sort of headway she might have made without the help of her Jewish friend Barbara De Porte is open to question, but before the trip was over Dorothy had astonished even Barbara with her transcendent curiosity and her ability to ingratiate herself with the Zionist leaders.

"She won their interest and their hearts," Barbara recalled. "She listened to them debating and discussing. She questioned them far into the night."[3] She flirted with them, too, by her own account, "outrageously," and "to the scandal of the ship's Jewry."[4] By the time she got to London she had an article in her head and the beginnings of a legend on her hands — the legend of a fresh-faced girl from the American heartland, "an amiable, blue-eyed tornado"[5] who roared through Europe stirring up trouble and making news happen wherever she went. "She was a Richard Harding Davis in evening gown," said one reporter, with just respect. "Nothing prosaic ever happened to her."[6]

The story quickly got around of two hard-bitten newspapermen moping in a bar. "Have you heard?" said one. "Dorothy Thompson got into town at noon."

"Good God," said the other. "What happened at one o'clock?"[7]

On their arrival in London she had gone with Barbara straight to the offices of the International News Service, which at that time, when American news syndicates had just begun to build up their foreign coverage, relied heavily on free-lance contributions. It was not difficult for Barbara to convince Earl Reeves, the London chief of I.N.S., to let her cover the upcoming conference on Zionism: she had been a Zionist practically from birth, and not long before had met and fallen in love with Meir Grossman, a Russian-Jewish compatriot whose dedication to the establishment of the Zionist state was the central fact of his life. Dorothy's credentials, on the other hand, were rather less conspicuous. On what authority did the daughter of a Methodist minister from Buffalo seek to write about Palestine, Earl Reeves wanted to know.

"I know more about Zionism than anyone else," Dorothy answered.[8] It was all the authority she needed. Her earliest dispatches were filed under a joint byline with Barbara, but the articles she produced on her own about the Zionist conference[9] were so thorough and so convincing that later in the year she was offered a position as a reporter for the Jewish Correspondence Bureau. "I'd have the opportunity to become a *real authority* on the Near East," she exclaimed. "They offered me the job because, through a series of circumstances, I've come to know more about the Jewish problem than most Jews, and I've just written an article on the Palestinian emigration that is being translated into Yiddish! Imagine. However, I'm still considering."[10]

She was "considering" all that summer, while she lived with Barbara in a microscopic rented room in Brunswick Square and cooked her meals on a metered stove ("deposit a shilling").[11] Between visits to her father's relatives, she began to hobnob with "the Fleet Street crowd" and to learn the ins and outs of string correspondence. "The truth is I'm writing for anything and everything that will buy from me," she reported later on in 1920. "I've had some stuff in the N.Y. Eve Post, loads in the Xian [i.e., the Christian] Science Monitor, a long article in the Outlook . . . , and I've sold quantities of stuff to the pestiferous Hearsts." With careful planning and some nimble, picturesque vignettes of London life — "a certain kind of rather flippant little sketch that I do," she said[12] — she managed, with Barbara, to keep the funds they had brought with them to Europe more or less constantly replenished. Barbara herself was a talented writer, but she admitted that Dorothy's capacity for "sheer hard work" had far outstripped her own: her passion for detail and her willingness to go to any lengths for a story and to invest any amount of time and effort in writing it were the very things that separated Dorothy from the general run of hopeful young women in journalism.[13]

"Do you know anything about rats?" she asked a friend one day. "Do you know where they come from?" She was getting ready to do a story about a latter-day "Pied Piper" in Budapest:

> They come from the Ural Mountains [said Dorothy], from the same place the Hungarians come from. Do you know that there were no rats in Europe 200 years ago? I've been looking up rats in the encyclopedias. All that's known about their origin is that, about two centuries ago, they started to migrate out of the East. No one knows why. They came down in great numbers to the Caucasus, and there they met and fought and conquered the tribes of rats living there, and intermixed with them, and produced the European rat. They spent about forty years in the Caucasus, and then they continued their migration across Europe. They reached Paris at the time of the French Revolution. The French thought it was part of the catastrophes at the end of the world. . . . And after that, the rats took to ships, and made their way to America, and multiplied there, and went on across the American continent. That is the history of rats. . . . Don't laugh.[14]

She got her first "scoop" completely by accident, when she sailed off to Ireland to hunt down relatives and wound up interviewing the leaders of the Sinn Fein rebellion — among them Terence Mac-Swiney, Lord Mayor of Cork, who was thrown into prison for sedition barely an hour after Dorothy left his office. (No reporter ever saw him again: MacSwiney embarked on a hunger strike immediately after his arrest and died two months later.) According to witnesses — and she was not ashamed to tell this story on herself — Dorothy had no idea of the value of her notes until, some time later, she carried them back to England, stuffed casually in the pocket of her coat.

"What have you got?" Earl Reeves asked her when she turned up again.

"Oh, I saw everybody, and everybody told me something. I learned a lot of things."

"Whom did you see, for instance?"

"MacSwiney for one."

"MacSwiney?" Reeves couldn't believe his ears. "You saw MacSwiney?"

"Yes."

"Sit down at a typewriter, girl, and write out those notes!"[15] Her articles on Ireland, published on the front pages of newspapers across the United States, were sufficient to convince the New York office of I.N.S. that she ought to be given credentials.

"Chief likes your Irish series," Reeves cabled Dorothy, who on September 1 had crossed the English Channel on her way to Paris. "Asks me advise net cost your making month's survey Austria. What shall I tell him?"

Tell him *yes*, Dorothy answered. She and Barbara De Porte were still intent on exploring Russia. They hoped eventually to enter the Soviet Union from the south, interviewing peasants and workers as they made their way to Moscow; Austria would be a good place to start.

"The sense of adventure was strong in us again," Dorothy wrote in her diary on her arrival in France. "Did we not have still the charmed $500? Had not the Cheval glass in our more or less sumptuous abode shown us pink cheeks and shiny eyes? Did we not have roses in our belts from admirers in England? . . . We pinched each other's arms in pure glee." There were "absurd quarrels" to contend with,[16] little jealousies and shifting humors brought on by proximity ("Varya and I led a communal life for so long," Dorothy wrote the following year, "that she once remarked to me, 'We have a headache this morning ' ").[17] But the main mood of Dorothy's diary was beatific:

The waiter lighted our cigarettes and tutored us in French. When he looked at us his eyes were full of laughter. . . . Varya smoked with gleaming eyes. She looked so lovely . . . so young. . . . We talked of how wonderful everything was . . . how expansive life: How good it had been to us. We had started with so little, but the little somehow miraculously remained. . . . In the spring we would go to Russia. We *would* write . . . a novel perhaps. . . . Women *could* be friends, couldn't they? Didn't we prove it? Here we were, racially different; brought up under the most opposite conditions and environment. She eastern, I western . . . now casting our lots together under the most trying circumstances — so intimate, so difficult, yet loving and appreciating each other more and more each day. . . .

How beautiful and good everything was . . . how romantic! . . . how heavenly to be alive . . . how much ahead and beyond!

Thus our first night in France.[18]

In Paris they took a room at the Hotel Cayré on the Boulevard Raspail and went to work, along with hundreds of other would-be expatriates and the "jetsam of the war,"[19] writing publicity at a penny a line for the American Red Cross. It was tedious labor, "odious" to Dorothy, but it left her time to polish her French (which was execrable) and to hunt down new material for her articles. She hoped to write fiction eventually, like everyone else in Paris, and, indeed, over the next several years, she tossed off many hundreds of pages of mawkish, self-conscious prose ("It was awful," she admitted, "and I knew it").[20] As far as journalism was concerned, Dorothy's interests at this time were centered almost exclusively on left-wing politics and labor relations; before long she had had the pleasure of hearing herself addressed by a French syndicalist as "Mademoiselle Comrade from Amérique."[21] In Paris she and Barbara hooked up with Joseph Schlossberg, an organizer for the Amalgamated Clothing Workers of America and a friend of Barbara's from New York, who hurried them off to Rome before long with assurances that "trouble" was brewing there. At issue were the rights of metalworkers, recently unionized and determined that their wages should be increased to reflect the cost of living.

"Under normal circumstances," Dorothy wrote to a friend, "the workers would have struck, but the Italian labor movement has been dominated for some time by a new idea in labor tactics, which is this: Why strike, suffer, and make the public suffer? Why not *lock out the employers?* And that, my dear, is exactly what they did."[22] This radical notion had spread all over Italy and nearly brought down the country; by the time Dorothy and Barbara, wide-eyed, entered the Fiat factory in Rome, the workers had won the fight and were in a mood to entertain. They invited their American visitors to join them for music and minestrone, and gave Dorothy her first close-up look at European socialism. She had already been flabbergasted to see the words "Viva Lenin!" shrieking in red paint across the columns of the Temple of Augustus; now the factory workers wanted to know if she thought Eugene Debs would win the presidential election that year in the United States.

No, Dorothy answered, she feared it would be Warren G. Harding.[23] But she did not laugh at the naïveté of the Italian working class. She listened, she took notes, and she came to understand, if she had not understood it before, that she had arrived in Europe at a moment of permanent crisis, when "everything, apparently, had been cut loose from its moorings. Democracy, socialism, nationalism, were all assuming new, strange forms. All traditions were disintegrating." Dorothy was an avid student of the politics of chaos, eager to learn and tireless in her effort to find the story *behind* the story. And the cool serenity of her published work — the detachment and imperturbability that were already evident in her best reporting — stood in eccentric contrast to the artless, gushing confessions of her letters and diary.

"I *hate* sightseeing," Dorothy grumbled following a tour of the remains of an Etruscan village outside Florence. She agreed with Barbara that "it had swell ruins," but ventured that Florence itself, when viewed from a distance, looked very much like Cincinnati.

"I still maintain that the resemblance is really quite strong," Dorothy remarked in response to hoots of laughter, before marching off on her own for an evening of "contented loneliness" in the Boboli gardens.[24] "I am a hideously uncultivated person," she feared, "and I never realized it so poignantly and humiliatingly as when I was in Italy."[25] She was also lovesick, still smarting from the fiasco with Wilbur Phillips and urgently in need of affection, but she could find no appropriate object for her desire. As they advanced across Europe, at each stop Barbara found letters waiting for her from Meir Grossman, her suitor on board the SS *Finland*. Dorothy had no use for Grossman — she would have had no use for anyone in love with Barbara — but now he was begging Barbara to marry him, and the prospect of losing her companion to matrimony cast a long shadow over Dorothy's life. She tried, in response, to be gay, to be wise, to be sophisticated and "smart." She wrote reams that autumn about the different men who had approached her in stations, "mashed" her in taxis, accosted her on trains, and left her wondering how much longer she could remain a virgin on the continent: "To be twenty-seven and loverless in Italy is a crime against God and man."[26] Her diary was suddenly passionate, even erotic in tone. In October she went by herself to Genoa to interview Giuseppe Giulietti, the leader of the seamen's union, and nearly fainted with pent-up longing:

> He had his back to the door as I entered, and I got a very pleasant impression of tallness. (Most Italians are so short!) Then he turned around suddenly — and I fell in love with him! I mean it literally. . . . I have never been so stimulated and magnetized by any man in my life. As we talked we constantly broke into laughter and his eyes watched me with the most expressive, the most inviting, the most *speaking* expression. . . . We were obviously delighted and charmed with each other. . . . I was tremendously aware of him physically every moment I was with him and felt that he wanted me to be. I noticed every detail of his person. The way his hair grows, like a small boy's, all over his head in great hyacinth locks, curling from the center. His soft, round impulsive chin — the jaw, which is very muscular and manly, redeems it; even his lower lip, very full and red and half pouting, and the lines that deepen engagingly in his cheeks when he laughs. He wears a short, close-clipped moustache — dark, of course. His mouth is really beautiful. . . .
>
> "Addio, *Cara*," he said finally, looking right into my eyes with that delicious smile.

She saw Giulietti again the next afternoon at a socialist rally and carried the flirtation as far as time and her nerves would allow; she was supposed to leave Genoa that night for Milan, where Barbara De Porte was waiting:

> His hair was down over his eyes and he was clawing the air and rolling out great sonorous sentences in a gorgeous baritone voice. The crowd was distinctly as radical as the speaker. There were many interruptions of "When do we have a revolution!" "Don't be reformist!" etc.
>
> I went closer to the ladder on which he was speaking. I suppose my unconscious was urging me on. Anyway in descending he saw me. The same delighted smile flashed across his face. He came to me and led me to a room behind the ladder — a vacant store, I think. . . . Anyway it was dark and there were only a few people there. But I

could see his teeth flashing and I could *feel* him. I was actually trembling a little. . . . When I gestured with one hand he caught it — just for the briefest second, but it was an indescribable caress.

"When you go?" he whispered. (We were talking sotto voce not to disturb the meeting at the door.)

"Tonight," I replied. "I go to Milan."

His face fell so frankly that I laughed. . . .

"But I do not want you to go. I want to be with you. Is it possible?" he asked. "Is it possible?" he repeated very softly.

"I'm afraid not," I said. I was trying to be matter of fact, but I was simply flaming.

"Will you not stay with me — two-three days?" (he was whispering again). "I do not want you should go —" He wasn't touching me but I might have been in his arms! "Do you not desire also?" — he went on whispering and I could see his tantalizing head and even the little dents on each side of his mouth. I simply didn't dare to trust myself to speak and fortunately someone came up at that moment and dragged him away. "I desire greatly to stay with you. Surely you desire also to stay with me." Those were his last words. And there was a little more in this strain. . . . I had just time to catch my train. We said another *addio* in the street and kissed each other with our eyes.

"This may be disgusting," Dorothy wrote in her diary that night, "bumping along in a third-class carriage" to Milan, "but it is a true chronicle." She was not, on reflection, happy to have withstood Giulietti's advances: "I know that I should not have resisted him. Himself, my mood, and Genoa — that wonderful shore — those dim romantic streets — I'm not even glad to be saved. . . . And I still have an accelerated pulse . . . huzzy that I am." She arrived in Milan shortly before dawn, frustrated, cross, and with a burgeoning case of the flu, and when she found out that her hotel had canceled her reservations, she burst forth in a torrent of desperate, ungrammatical French.

"*Je suis une femme!*" Dorothy cried. "*Jeune! Je suis seule! Je ne savez pas la ville!*" ("I am a woman! Young! I am alone! I don't know the town!") She spent what remained of the night on a table in the dining room, crying herself to sleep. Later that day her pocket was picked while she waited for Barbara at the train station.[27]

"I must acknowledge occasionally a bit of homesickness," Dorothy admitted several days later. "But always accompanied by a loathing of coming home."[28] Things seemed to go from bad to worse. Dorothy had already fallen thirty lire behind in her budget when Earl Reeves telegraphed from London to say that I.N.S. had decided not to send her on assignment to Austria after all. Now Barbara dropped another bomb: she was going to marry Meir Grossman, and she was going to do it just as soon as she could get to London. But first the two women set off for Como, Trieste, and Venice in the company of Joseph Schlossberg (who "was in the most boresome mood," said Dorothy — "*would* talk about the purity of his relations with women").[29] There was still some discussion between Dorothy and Barbara about their mutual plans, about the books they would write and the trips they would take together: Barbara suggested that they might go to Russia in the spring, once she and Grossman had had a chance to settle down. But Dorothy knew the friendship was dead, at least in the form it had taken up till now. At the wedding in November she stood next to Barbara "like the dear friend she was," upsetting the rabbi when he discovered that she wasn't Jewish[30] and admitting later to "a bad taste in my mouth — somehow there was something insincere about it all." There is no doubt that she was bitter.

She went back to Paris, to the Hotel Cayré, and plunged into work and self-pity. She was laboring hard, exploiting her contacts and publishing general news reports through American syndicates, but she was obliged to go back to the Red Cross to supplement her income, "manufacturing publicity" at ten francs per hundred lines. She despised the work, and despised her compatriots in Paris.

"The whole place is cluttered up with almost successful people," she complained. "Scenario writers, magazine writers, photographers. They know their job well. Do it. Make a 'good living.' But oh, their shallowness. Appalling! . . . I hate them! Hate them! . . . Every night I come back to my little room on the top floor of this absurd hotel, where never an American stayed before. I write, but what I write is so thin. And I feel so much. I feel so much that I could burst the room open." She had begun to fear that she was gifted for nothing but hackwork. "Oh," she cried, "I wish that I were either more talented or less intelligent. . . . I could weep because I cannot express how I feel and make it count. . . . Oh, why, why haven't I talent?"[31]

Of course she did have talent: it was only a question of recognizing where it lay. In January 1921 she embarked on a three-day walking tour of the Loire Valley with Rose Wilder Lane, the independent, individualistic, incomparable daughter of Laura Ingalls Wilder, the author of the *Little House* books. Born in Dakota Territory in 1886,[32] Rose Lane had been raised first on the prairie that her mother made famous and later on a farm in the Ozarks; when she broke away to hunt down her own identity, she worked variously as a telegraph operator, a real-estate agent, a biographer of Henry Ford, and a San Francisco newspaperwoman. She arrived in Europe after a failed marriage, as a sort of floating correspondent for the Red Cross — their "chiefest writer," Dorothy remarked in her gloom, "with her sob stuff."[33] But Dorothy did Rose a disservice. Noted for her weary, even Zenlike view of the world — "The worst thing about life," said Rose, "is the necessity of trying to do something with it"[34] — Rose Lane was nevertheless in love with living, her fatalism tempered by an unquenchable curiosity and an enthusiasm that fully equalled Dorothy's own. She had a great deal to say about the realization of talent, and the passionate friendship she forged with Dorothy in the winter of 1921 would last, with interruptions, to the end of their lives.

"There has never been anyone like you," said Rose to Dorothy, "for clearing away this muddle in which I struggle to live, for somehow giving me fresh air, and light, and the freedom to be."[35] No one could doubt that Rose was "in love." Over and again she likened Dorothy to light, to air, to all the elements of science and myth. "I [want] you to be forevermore the Dorothy of 1920," she wrote in later years, "a song, a poem, a flame in the sunlight." Dorothy, less ardent, was no less devoted to Rose — "Roses," she called her, "Rose of Roses." That first weekend walk on the banks of the Loire, which they undertook in the pouring rain with Kate Horton, another struggling writer in Paris, stayed with Dorothy as "an illumined moment, which I shall remember and be grateful for, forever." They stopped overnight at country farmhouses, dining on "strange, sweet soup" and stews that might have been made of "hare or rabbit or squirrel" (or cat, Rose suggested) and talking every night till dawn about life, love, art. "How cool it was," said Dorothy, "how spontaneous, . . . transitory, but caught at the moment, and therefore eternal."[36] She went back to Paris invigorated and ready to get on with her work.

Through a chance acquaintance with the daughter of a banker from Kiev, one of a hundred thousand Russian refugees in Paris at that time, Dorothy had obtained an interview with Baroness Wrangel, the wife of one of the leaders of the anti-Bolshevik forces in the

Russian civil war. Her piece on the politics of the Russian emigration was sold for twenty dollars to the *Philadelphia Public Ledger* and soon came to the attention of Paul Scott Mowrer, the chief of the Paris bureau of the *Chicago Daily News*. Shortly thereafter, Mowrer invited Dorothy to join him for dinner and a talk about her future. She was "more attractive," he remembered, "quicker-witted and stronger-willed than the normal run."[37] But did she have any idea how many men and women were in Paris at that moment trying to be writers? Wouldn't it make more sense for a beginner in journalism to choose some *other* city to report from, go there, and corner the market?

Dorothy knew that this was the right advice, and she also knew, without any doubt, which city she would go to and make her own. On her way out of Italy she had paused for ten days in Vienna to interview the leaders of the socialist municipal government, which at that time was struggling to rescue the city from famine and financial collapse. The situation in Austria was "heartbreaking,"[38] and Dorothy felt with perfect certainty that Vienna was calling her now. She went one morning to the office of Wythe Williams, the head of the *Public Ledger*'s European news bureau.

"You haven't got a correspondent in Vienna," she began.

Williams answered that the *Ledger*'s correspondent in Berlin normally covered the entire Central European territory, and that Vienna, in any case, was a "second-string" city, a dying beat.

"You ought to send me there," said Dorothy,[39] arguing her own bona fides so forcefully that Williams finally offered her terms: she could use the *Public Ledger*'s credentials in Vienna and introduce herself as its special correspondent, but she would be paid only for work the *Ledger* actually published (in other words, there would be no salary), and she was not to imagine that the agreement contained any promise of advancement.

That would be fine, said Dorothy. She had already made arrangements to write publicity for the Red Cross relief administration in Budapest (near enough to Vienna, under the circumstances), and as a matter of principle she did not believe in worrying about money. "People will always give you a job," she advised, "if there is no risk involved."[40]

"I wish I could tell you without sounding like an evangelist that I believe being happy doesn't count," she wrote to a friend before leaving Paris. "Happiness doesn't matter. Getting somewhere does. . . . My dear, only fools and cows are happy. No intelligent human being is happy. There are moments of release, moments of bliss, Thank God for them, but don't hope to keep them, because it is in the eternal nature of things that you shouldn't. . . . If you suffer — well, what is that? Everyone suffers except horrible people who have no capacity. But one doesn't whine, and certainly one is never sorry for what has happened. *Never.* . . . Courage and self-sufficiency are *beautiful* virtues." [41]

With that, and alone, she left for Vienna, boarding a train at the Gare de l'Est and composing sonnets in her head, like the heroine of a novel she wanted to write: "The beat of the train was conducive. She felt herself a part of it; it was a great iron body, like an armor which she had put on, and she was in it, striding away, . . . rattling away across the lush Danubian meadows, and the turreted castles with their round towers, alongside the flowering trees to the mountains." [42]

VIENNA in 1921 was a dark and rotting place, [43] once the center of a magnificent empire, now the capital of a picturesque rump state brought into existence more or less arbitrarily by the Treaty of Versailles. Until 1918, properly speaking, there had been no such thing as "Austria." The Austro-Hungarian empire had actually comprised nine major nations and some fifty million people.

"Insofar as a man thought *nationally* in the old Empire," Dorothy wrote later, "he thought of himself as a Hungarian, a Pole, a Czech, an Italian, a Croat, or a German. When he thought of himself as an Austrian, he thought of something quite different: allegiance to a monarch; a certain form of life; a curious culture, compounded of many clashing and complementing elements." [44] Under the dual monarchy of Austria-Hungary, the different populations and regions of the empire had enjoyed a limited but functional autonomy; economically, they constituted one of the best-balanced and most self-sufficient organisms in Europe, with a free flow of peoples, free trade, and a common defense. But under the terms of Versailles, in the spirit of "self-determination," the Austro-Hungarian complex had been split into fragments, rival countries purporting to follow historical lines and each adhering to its own set of laws, finance systems, customs barriers, and mode of government. Borderlands in the north were returned to Poland, and in the south to Italy and Yugoslavia. Czech, Slovak, and Sudeten German territories had been welded together to form modern Czechoslovakia, while large portions of Hungary were handed over to Rumania, and the Balkan states, never known for their stability, were left to feud and war among themselves.

The result was an immense complication of European affairs and, ultimately, a total failure. Austria proper, finding itself penniless, with a worthless currency and few natural resources, had hoped and agitated for union with Germany. This was expressly forbidden by the Allied powers, however, and specifically by France, which had formed a bullying alliance with the so-called Little Entente of Czechoslovakia, Yugoslavia, and Rumania, and had effectively caught Austria in an economic and geographic stranglehold. Whereas Vienna, in the days when it was the capital of Middle Europe, had been the clearinghouse of the empire, the center of all things administrative, cultural, and financial, it was now isolated, choked off, unable to provide for its own nearly two million citizens or for the four million others who occupied the western rural sections of the country. Vienna was never designed, under any circumstances, to be the hub of a tiny, reactionary Tyrolean hinterland, the "scenic little slum"[45] that was Austria between the wars.

When Dorothy had thought about Vienna in earlier days she had thought, like everyone else, of "Strauss waltzes, Spanish Baroque, damask interiors, . . . a sumptuous court." What she found in reality was "a city of dread," on the edge of famine, teeming with refugees, soldiers, welfare commissioners, freebooters, profiteers, displaced peasants and an assortment of "gentlefolk, starving gracefully in Biedermeier salons."[46] She wanted "to get out among the people" and was given a choice by the *Wohnungsamt* (the dreaded, all-powerful Viennese housing authority): she could have an apartment with a kitchen or an apartment with a bath, but not both. She chose the bath ("the only hot bath in all Austria," she told Rose Lane),[47] and took a room at Rainergasse 5, "a proletarian house" in the Margareten district.

"A little lower down on the same street were gray and yellow palaces in weedy gardens," Dorothy recalled. "At our end of the street . . . the houses were very modest — [with] tiny groceries or sausage shops in their ground floors, or butcher shops advertising horse meat. The stone stairs were worn and uncarpeted; the stenciled walls had not been painted for a long time; the paint was peeling from them and sometimes the plaster." In exchange for English lessons, Dorothy was granted kitchen privileges next door by the Murbachers, the working-class family who became her first "authentic" Viennese friends and who introduced her to the native delights and customs of the city. With the Murbachers she went by tram on Sundays to "lie under the trees" in the Vienna Woods, "or walk in the Prater," or stroll in the gardens of the green-domed Belvedere Palace, which had recently been opened to the public by the socialist government.[48] An eerie atmosphere of grandeur and high culture still hovered everywhere in the starving city. The air was filled perpetually with the mingled smells of "kraut and lilac," and it seemed to Dorothy that she never left the house without hearing musical instruments being practiced in the background.[49]

Her first articles in the *Public Ledger* were of the Sunday-supplement, local-color variety — lengthy, flavorful pieces about traditional Vienna life: "the good strong coffee" and "the bad sour wine"; the combination in the city of "Germanic cleanliness and Latin ease"; the "soft slurring" of the natives' speech; that "mixture of easygoingness, carelessness, laziness and easy tolerance" which in Vienna calls itself *Schlamperei;* and the peculiar, morbid hangover the city was suffering from the loss of the empire. With wonder and astonishment Dorothy observed that "the Viennese' favorite entertainment . . . was to take part in a nice funeral." People actually advertised these events in the newspapers, hiring mourners and parading to the cemetery in ornate carriages drawn by horses crowned with flaring black plumes, even as the infant mortality rate rose to staggering heights and foreign travelers were warned not to drive their cars too fast in the streets because the local citizens, faint from hunger, could not move out of their way quickly enough. Simultaneously, in that summer of 1921, the first festival of modern music was held at Salzburg, where Max Reinhardt had also revived the Grosse Welttheater. There was "an extreme blooming of culture" in Austria, against a background of complete disorder, poverty, anarchy, "plot and counter-plot."

"Half the songs in Vienna are sung to lovely ladies," Dorothy wrote one day, "and the other half are sung to the city itself, and the mood is not much different. . . . The Viennese know what sort of hairpins, stockings, and system of financing is well received in Krakowitz and Belgrade, and of this knowledge the political constellation cannot completely rob them."[50] It was no small matter buying hairpins or anything else in the Vienna of those days; Dorothy was shortly introduced to the workings of the black market, which, like almost everything else in the city, was centered in the coffee houses: the Café Louvre, the Landmann, the Museum, the Herrenhof.

"Coffee in Vienna is more than a national drink," Dorothy explained. "It is a national cult. Palaces have been built for it: palaces where there are satin-brocaded walls, deep divans, onyx-topped tables, great windows curtained in gold-colored silk. These palaces are the center of Vienna's social, intellectual and spiritual life, and coffee-making remains one of Vienna's most perfected cultures." Every café in town was an institution in itself, "sometimes a club, sometimes an office, sometimes just a restaurant, but always full of life, atmosphere, and — smoke."[51] For the equivalent of ten cents Dorothy could order one of a hundred different brews and spend the rest of the day and night, if she liked, at her table, reading newspapers, conducting interviews, or writing her articles. There were cafés to cater to every taste and social group: workers, artists, musicians, politicians, journalists, actors, whores, and *Schieber* — those shadowy, more than usually unscrupulous profiteers who overran Austria after 1918, "lolling in lilac velvet and plate-glass limousines. There were plenty of that sort in Vienna then," said Dorothy. "They swarmed from Poland, or wriggled up from the debris left in Austria by the war, and through their special abilities managed to keep on top of the slime."[52]

In Vienna, the black marketers congregated mainly at the fabled Café Atlantis, on the Ring, directly opposite the Imperial Hotel.[53] "It [was] a great, gaudy, showy place," Dorothy remembered, "the last place you would look for anything illegal. Yet here, for a flick of the eyelid toward the waiter, you could be put in touch with someone — at a neighboring table — who would sell you anything you liked, or buy from you anything you had to sell, from old clothes to Gobelins."[54] Everyone at the Atlantis had his apportioned and never-deviating position: currency speculators in the heavy, red-leather armchairs; *Schieber* at the center tables; main-line prostitutes to the right of the door, homosexuals to the left; and in the corners, night and day, "every revolutionary in the Balkans." Dorothy got in the habit of buying "wonderful cigarettes" — she was already a chain-smoker — from a group of what she had taken to be "Macedonian bandits, . . . magnificently dressed in pale-blue frocks, deep blue breeches, silver jackets with broad striped sashes, jammed full of pistols and knives." She had approached them at first with some trepidation, "hoping to hear strange details of [their] wild mountain life," and was not a little surprised when one of them grinned and bellowed out, "We speak English, lady. We're all California boys."[55]

A good deal of Dorothy's early work, perhaps to balance the grave condition of Central Europe as she found it, was written in a merry and even impertinent vein. She filed comic dispatches on the awful perils of the Gellert baths in Budapest ("I estimate that in America alone there are ninety-nine million people who never took a Turkish bath. . . . Better a thousand times, I say, that they should go bathless than that they should attain cleanliness at such a cost");[56] on food, cuisine, as the only reliable international currency, or "The Tie That Binds the World Around";[57] and on her own mind-numbing encounters with the Austrian bureaucracy. Until the end of the war, no one in the Austro-Hungarian empire had needed to carry a passport or any other official identification. Now a whole new breed of functionary had sprung up: the customs official, the housing officer, the visa-dispenser.

"You cannot buy a railroad ticket or post a letter or register at a hotel in Vienna," Dorothy wrote, "without being reduced to tears or profanity as your temperament leads you."[58] There was "no depth of perjury or embezzlement to which you can fall," she said, "that will not only be justified by your fellow travellers but applauded and probably copied by them." During her first two years in Vienna Dorothy was forced to move no less than four times, driven out of her apartment on each occasion by the *Wohnungsamt* on the grounds of suspected "irregularities." Before long she had developed a bold and, she affirmed, surefire method for dealing with anybody in an office or a uniform. When one of them spoke to her in German, she answered in English — *American* English — enunciating each word slowly and at the top of her voice: "I don't *know* what you say. I don't *care* what you say. *Please go away.*"

"That worked," said Dorothy. "It always does."[59] In fact, her German was excellent. She had studied the language at Syracuse and was now taking lessons three times a week, revealing a greater affinity for the sense of German than for the grammar. The playwright Carl Zuckmayer, who got to know her later, in Berlin, remembered that Dorothy evidenced a certain beguiling contempt for the formalities of the German language, speaking to an important government minister, for example, with the familiar mode of address, *Du,* and then turning immediately to his dog, whom she patted carelessly on the head and addressed with the stiff and formal *Sie.*[60] She looked "like a lady who would forget her pajamas," according to a hotel porter in Warsaw,[61] but in fact she was "sharp as a tack."[62] Hunting down one of her first stories, she went to interview the leader of a nationalist youth movement and brought along a German interpreter. She swiftly grew impatient with the stilted, too-literal translations the fellow was giving her.

"That isn't what he means," Dorothy complained. "*Look* at him while he's talking."[63] A journalist had to watch faces, she said, and the set of the shoulders, and had to consider a person's tone of voice in order to know what was really going on. For all of that, Dorothy was not reluctant to submit her stories from time to time in direct, question-and-answer form, without commentary and with no embellishment, if she felt it would better make a point. She trusted her hunches, in other words, and later claimed to have absorbed only one set of rules when she started out: "Get the news accurately. If possible, get it first. Don't let your likes or dislikes obscure the facts, and remember the laws of libel and slander."[64] Over the next several years she would interview more than her share of world leaders — Gustav Stresemann, Aristide Briand, Chicherin, Trotsky, Atatürk — and the Great Men of science and culture — Freud, Strauss, Romain Rolland. But she was always more interested in ideas than in personalities, and she "saw stories," according to one of her colleagues, "that were not stories to more experienced correspondents."[65]

Women fared especially well at her hands. When Dorothy went to Bulgaria to cover a nationalist uprising in 1923, she spent more time with Nadeja Staneioff, the top aide and presumed mistress of Prime Minister Stamboliysky, than she did with any of the revolutionaries.[66] She interviewed the brilliant Soviet emissary Alexandra Kollontay[67] and a whole delegation of "peace women" led by Jane Addams, who descended on Vienna to press for international disarmament.[68] Always, inevitably, there was a royalty story. In 1923 King Zog of Albania let it be known that he was looking for a queen, and Dorothy reported his quest as "undoubtedly the finest opportunity to enter the ranks of royalty since before the war." "Job Offers Annual Revolution," her headline read, "Big-Game Shooting, Private Mountain Climbing and Blood Feuds As Well As Crown — Monarch Must Finance State."[69]

She was shuttling back and forth all of this time between her apartment in Vienna and the Ritz Hotel in Budapest, four hours away by train, where she was working as a publicity agent for Captain James Pedlow, the white-haired, Irish-born American Red Cross

Commissioner in Hungary. After the war, the Red Cross had taken the lead role in the rehabilitation of the devastated nations of Central Europe, and Pedlow was currently "a name to conjure with in Budapest." He was "the uncrowned King of Hungary," "the ipse dixit of the Hungarian people."[70] Dorothy's job was to promote Pedlow's work for the benefit of disgruntled citizens in the United States, who were alarmed by the spread of Bolshevism and always suspicious of foreign entanglements. As the months went by, she developed a fine rapport with "Pedlow Kapitan," who gave her the nickname "Angel Face" and greatly admired the disarming way she had "of blurting out questions that an ordinarily cautious correspondent would have led up to crabwise."[71] This same guilelessness and frank demeanor (not to mention "the beauty of her tender skin")[72] was what most appealed to the man who now stepped in as Dorothy's friend and mentor to guide her through the tangled maze of Central European politics: Marcel W. Fodor, the correspondent in Vienna and Budapest for the *Manchester Guardian*.

Dorothy met Fodor in Captain Pedlow's office in Budapest at the beginning of March 1921. A Hungarian by birth, member of a prominent banking family, Fodor had been educated as a metallurgical engineer and then later moved to England, where, at the outbreak of World War I, he was interned with other enemy aliens "very comfortably" on the estate of the Duke of Norfolk.[73] After the Armistice, with no particular experience in journalism, he went back to Hungary as the *Guardian*'s special correspondent and quickly distinguished himself as the most knowledgeable man in the field. Short, balding, in his own eyes "roly-poly,"[74] Fodor was "a round, rosy-faced man, with little gray eyes twinkling behind his spectacles,"[75] an intellectual and a political liberal who never wavered under the reactionary onslaught of postwar Europe. Nobody called Fodor by his first name, Marcel, which he despised. It was "Mike," or more often just "Fodor." There was not a reporter in Europe between the wars who did not know his work and benefit from his expertise. "I have never known a man," said his friend and colleague William L. Shirer, "and especially a journalist, who gave so much of himself and his knowledge to others."[76]

Dorothy never hesitated to give Fodor the credit for her own ultimately supreme erudition in the politics and culture of Central Europe. She went so far as to say that Fodor had launched her career, but if that was so, he had *merely* launched it — she was riding her own rocket through the journalistic skies. "She was an activist," said a friend who knew her in Vienna, "a positivist. She believed in free will. She believed that she could exert command, that she could control events."[77] Not long after their meeting, Dorothy was obliged, firmly but with genuine gratitude for his attentions, to decline Fodor's proposal of marriage. He "got over it wonderfully," she reported, "and relaxed into the friendliest and most humorous acceptance of his lot. . . . Fodor and I might be priest and nun as far as the utter sexlessness of our relation is concerned (although I am not sure the illustration is apt)."[78] Relieved, on further acquaintance, not to have become "the slave of a human dynamo,"[79] Fodor entered into a devoted and sympathetic professional collaboration with Dorothy, introducing her to, among other things, the mysteries of the Balkans, those "wildly improbable countries"[80] whose secret societies and murderous politics were his specialty; and to the exotic, "scented," hothouse world of Budapest, "the most hedonistic city in Europe."[81] Here the Danube flowed more majestically than anywhere in Vienna, and here, Dorothy wrote, "the manifold issues which perplex all the nations of Central Europe . . . are concentrated and magnified. Every issue is stretched to the breaking point."[82]

If Austria, after the war, lacked any clear sense of national identity, Hungary did not. "The Magyars are a strange, mystic people," Dorothy ventured,[83] a people in 1921 seething with resentment and, to judge from Dorothy's dispatches, engaged more or less to a man in political intrigue: "Nowhere are capital and labor farther apart; nowhere is the Jewish question more strained. Here is the center of the monarchist fight. Here is the most vigorous irredentism. Here is a nation whose social structure has been more violently assailed than that of any European country except Russia." Following the abdication of the Habsburg emperor Karl I — who under the dual monarchy had also been King of Hungary — the country had endured five months of Bolshevik rule under the fearsome Communist Béla Kun, and then a period of benighted reaction under the anti-Semitic, right-wing government of Admiral Miklós Horthy. Although the king was in exile, Hungary was still technically a monarchy, and the great political questions when Dorothy came on the scene were these: would there be any serious redistribution of land to the peasants? and who, in the future, would wear the Crown of St. Stephen? Not a day passed without rumors of a monarchist coup d'état. In fact Emperor Karl made the first of his abortive attempts to regain the Hungarian throne immediately after Dorothy arrived in Budapest:

This is a country in which every man is his own party [she wrote]. But if one goes out to Kobanya, where several thousand people are living in old hospital barracks eight or ten in a room, or to the villages on the outskirts of Budapest, one cannot find many people who are worrying about St. Stephen's crown. What is possessing these people is not the question of Republicanism vs. Monarchy, but the problem of how they shall get enough to eat and wear. Above all, they are obsessed with a desire for peace — for freedom from the atmosphere of fear and terror in which they have been living ever since the first revolution. If the return of [Emperor] Karl promises them these things, then they are for Karl. They would be for anyone who could promise the same.[84]

Dorothy was not to know for several months more how closely entwined her life and career would be with the fortunes of Hungarians. For the time being, she was fascinated by the whole spectacle of a nation in bedlam, noting with something like pleasure a sudden spectacular revival of dueling in the capital.

"One would think with all this slashing and shooting going on that the casualties would be great," she wrote, "but as a matter of fact no one is ever killed, and it is very seldom that anyone is even seriously wounded."[85] In the spring of 1921 she embarked with Fodor on a journeyman's swing through Prague, where she obtained her first penetrating interviews with Edvard Beneš and Tomáš Masaryk, the founders of modern Czechoslovakia. She talked with Masaryk for five hours straight and was loath to cut a word of their conversation later, when her articles appeared in the *Public Ledger*. On a quick trip to England she interviewed Ramsay MacDonald and looked in on Barbara De Porte, who was expecting a baby and living (said Dorothy meanly) "a drab little life with a cook general."[86] Then she sped back to Vienna and a series of feature articles that seemed to have been sent to her directly by "the gods" she relied on. She hunted down a collateral descendant of George Washington in a crumbling Tyrolean castle; an aged porter in a hotel in Budapest, who, as a onetime soldier in the Union Army, had helped to capture John Wilkes Booth after the assassination of Abraham Lincoln; and the extravagant Queen Marie of Rumania,[87] who had traveled to Belgrade to help one of her daughters start life as the new queen of Yugoslavia and who unburdened herself to Dorothy about the troubles in Greece, where another daughter sat on another, shakier throne.

"Dreadful, isn't it," sighed Queen Marie, and Dorothy agreed that it was, "miserably wondering," at the same time, "whether [she] could manage a swoop to two queens at once" when the time came to leave the room. Marie relieved her of the obligation, as it happened, by rising herself, pinching her nervous daughter on the cheek, and warning Dorothy, "You must remember that she is a very young queen. But she is going to be a very good one, one of these days."

"With which motherly patronage," said Dorothy, "she withdrew, looking very much like herself, if I may judge from pictures and reports, as though she might be gracefully wearing a train, which she wasn't." Left alone with the little queen of Yugoslavia, Dorothy found that talking to royalty — and doing so, as custom required, entirely in the third person — was an arduous business. What did Her Majesty feel about — well, about being a queen?

Oh, said Her Majesty, who was "perfectly sweet and thoroughly incompetent," she liked it. She really enjoyed it — though "kings and queens are more put to it than they used to be."

This was not a point that Dorothy would have argued. In October 1921 she was the only journalist privileged to witness, "under unforgettably romantic and tragic circumstances," the final act in the drama of the last imperial family of Austria.[88] She had had "a hunch" that Emperor Karl was going to make another grab for the Hungarian throne; she was not alone in thinking so, but she was more prepared than most. Fodor turned up at her door in Vienna one morning with the news that Karl and his empress, Zita, had left their exile in Switzerland and might arrive in Hungary at any moment to try to reclaim the crown.

"You go," said Fodor. "You are a woman. You may get farther than the men. . . . Cover for both of us. I'll be here."

Dorothy was on the next train to Budapest, along with nearly every other reporter in Central Europe. The attempted coup came at a particularly troubled moment, when Hungary, furious over the loss of its lands, resources, and prestige after the war, had reoccupied certain western territories, in clear defiance of the Versailles treaty. "The country was seething with troops," wrote Dorothy, "with diplomats, with military missions, with ultimatums . . .": the allied powers and the Little Entente regarded the proposed reestablishment of the Hungarian monarchy as an act of war, a step toward the restoration of all the old dynasties and systems. Faced with the prospect of a military invasion, the emperor himself backed down, and the adventure was over almost before it began.

"He should have been given the title 'Karl the Rash,' " Dorothy suggested. "His specialty in putsches is arriving too soon." Pending disposition of their fate, the emperor and empress were secluded in the Esterhazy castle at Tata, not far from Budapest. Strict censorship was imposed throughout the country, and the members of the foreign press corps, in Dorothy's words, "were the maddest bunch you can imagine."

"You know what it's like," she told Rose Lane later, "full of a story that you can't get out. . . . I was the only woman correspondent, and you know how men — well, [they] don't take you any too seriously on a job. If I could scoop them all I felt I'd die happy." It was her position as Captain Pedlow's assistant that came to her rescue. Empress Zita was pregnant with her eighth child, and that gave Dorothy an idea.

"All right," she said to Pedlow, "the Empress needs medical attention, and I need an interview with Karl. *You* are going to visit the castle and take me along as your medical assistant."

Pedlow was shocked, or at any rate he professed to be. "What do you think I am?" he said.

"A romantic Irishman with a sense of adventure," Dorothy answered.[89] She left the Ritz Hotel dressed as a Red Cross nurse, and two hours later, to the consternation of her competitors, rode across the moat into the castle at Tata.

"Never shall I forget our entrance into the courtyard," said Dorothy, "nor the palpitating moments on the drawbridge at the outer gate before we reached there." Inside she found a situation "full of dangers" — on her first night at Tata there was an attempt on the life of the emperor — and a cast of characters that seemed to come straight out of a comic opera by Lehár: the remote and dignified imperial couple; the swarm of bemused courtiers; the puffy-eyed, red-faced ringleaders of the thwarted coup; and the delightful Countess Lulu Esterhazy, "young, irresponsible, and head over heels in love" with one of the plotters, a country girl who had never attended the Habsburg court and had to be warned not to click her heels when she greeted the empress. While Pedlow talked with the emperor, Dorothy stood hidden behind some heavy velvet curtains and took frantic notes on the conversation. Later the empress gave her a short letter and begged her to transmit it to her son Crown Prince Otto.

"It was not a matter of state," said Dorothy. "It assured the child that they were safe. It admonished him on no account to worry. It sent him the tenderest greetings, and was signed: 'Mamma.' " Dorothy was still in the castle when the emperor and empress were removed to a monastery on the shores of the Balaton Lake, where, for all anyone knew, they might have met their deaths. As it happened, they were exiled instead, to the island of Madeira, and not six months later Karl died of pneumonia. It was the end not just of the Habsburg adventure, but of any notion that Europe might yet turn back the clock.

"It scooped the world, of course, that story," said Dorothy later on. "The only interview with Karl. The other correspondents were — well, you can imagine." After the emperor's death she attended a memorial service in Budapest and mingled again with the remnants of the Hungarian aristocracy: "The women, famously beautiful, wore crepe of the heaviest silk, skillfully cut, and long veils framed their lovely faces, ever so slightly rouged, the lips ever so palely red." Dorothy was not impressed by titles, nor did she argue at any point for the restoration of monarchy ("What fails fails," she said), but she felt a certain affinity now with the last of the Habsburgs, and she followed their fortunes closely to the end of her life. She had made her mark in Ireland, in Paris, in Rome, and in Vienna, but it was the episode at Tata that sealed her reputation and brought her the beginnings of a personal fame: from this point on, no one in the world of journalism ever asked her to prove herself again.

FODOR and Rose Lane had both been with Dorothy in Paris in May 1921 when she ran out of the offices of the *Public Ledger* crying, "I got it! I got it!"[90] "It" was a position as the *Ledger*'s salaried correspondent in Vienna. Dorothy had filed so many stories already on space rates that her editors decided they could save themselves some money by offering her a regular job. She was now to be their representative for all of Central Europe, with an office of her own, a salary of fifty dollars a week, and a tiny expense account. Her territory, besides Austria and Hungary, would include Yugoslavia, Czechoslovakia, Rumania, Bulgaria, Albania, Turkey, and Greece.

"I hold the cup of happiness tremblingly in my hands," Dorothy wrote Gertrude Tone not long after, "and fear that at any moment it may spill."[91] On the very day she was given the *Ledger* correspondency, she also received a telegram from her sister in New York, which told her that her father had died on May 4. She fainted when she read it: "I remember that. The bedroom had a pink striped paper and a red carpet and I could see the wash-bowl waving up and down when I opened my eyes. . . .

"There was no other word," Dorothy wrote that night, "excepting a letter from Father himself, dated April 15, in answer to a very racy one which I had written him from Budapest. His letter is cheerful, even gay. He exhorts me not to be a coquette, comments on the Budapest Royal Palace, and ends by saying he is feeling a bit depressed. . . ." The Reverend Peter Thompson had suffered from angina for a long time, but had gone about his business normally until he found that he could no longer stand up.

"It looks very bad, darling," he remarked to Peggy Thompson, "but it is not as bad as it looks." Then he died.

"That, then," said Dorothy, "is the last word from my father." [92] It would have meant a lot to her to know that he had heard of her success: "So I remember moments when I was quite a child, walking up to the top of the highest hill surrounding Gowanda, so I could see the wide, wide world, and thinking of the glorious things I should do, and the wonderful places I should see, when I grew up." [93] She was proud, later, to tell whoever asked, "My father follows me everywhere." [94]

4

CHAPTER

DOROTHY was having drinks with Fodor and other friends in Vienna on the afternoon of December 1, 1921, when word reached her that rioting had broken out in the city. That morning the League of Nations had turned down the Austrian government's request for a loan to help restore the economy and give some value — even an artificial one — to the nation's currency; now a mob of unusual ferocity, "most un-Viennese," had marched from the Parliament building to the Opernring and started looting the more elegant shops and hotels. Clothes, furs, jewels, and accessories were ripped from the mannequins in store windows; furniture was smashed in the sidewalks; food was torn from grocery shelves and stuffed into sacks and coats to be taken home and hoarded.

"Seeing a Vienna population like that," said Dorothy, "was like seeing some mild-mannered, polite gentleman whom you had known for years go suddenly, ravingly, hideously mad."[1] Within minutes she had left her table and was "down in the midst of it, . . . in a state of wild excitement,"[2] noting with affection and approval that the Viennese had not completely forgotten themselves even in the heat of the hour. When the first bricks went crashing through the windows of the Hotel Sacher, interrupting any number of wealthy travelers munching on tea cakes and *Gugelhupf,* passersby in the street outside were warned considerately to step out of the way. Before the day was over Dorothy herself, dressed in a heavy wildcat fur and looking exceedingly prosperous, was drawn aside by one of the more obliging rioters.

"Miss," he began, "I think maybe you should take that coat off. We don't want to hurt you, and it might excite somebody."

From this experience Dorothy drew an important lesson: "Never wear a fur coat when you go to a revolution."[3] She would go to a number of them in the next several years, and would "observe daily," as she wrote to Rose Lane in Paris, "the complete failure of the political remedy" in Europe.

"I should say more accurately the failure of politics as a remedy," Dorothy corrected herself. "These countries are going to rack and ruin."[4] Things began to change in 1922, when the League of Nations finally relented and granted Austria a huge recovery loan in exchange for guarantees of neutrality. Within weeks (or so it appeared on the surface) prosperity returned to "Red Vienna." The unemployment rate fell, and "a new heaven-on-earth" — vast, clean, sturdy housing developments, subsidized by the government — sprang up around the city, to the amazement of the populace and the admiration of all Europe. Other circumstances also conspired to aid the public welfare. In Germany, the French were about to occupy the Ruhr valley on the pretext that the Weimar government had defaulted on the payment of its staggering war debt — the 132 billion marks fixed by the Allied Reparation Commission as Germany's penalty for its role in World War I. The result of the French action was a crippling of German industry and trade and the beginning of an inflation that made Austria's look trivial by comparison; more important for Austria, Germany's troubles meant that large orders for steel and iron were diverted from the north and more money — real money — was pumped into the country.

"No one who was not in Vienna during the months that followed could imagine the change which occurred," Dorothy remembered. "[The] international talk about Austria began, almost imperceptibly, to take on a different tone. Word went out, 'No more sob stuff.' " Foreigners were streaming into the capital — some to attend the opera and art galleries; some to take advantage of skiing in the outlying mountains of the Semmering; others to enjoy "the cafe life, the easy-goingness, the direct charm and gaiety of the town."[5]

"Now, more than ever," Dorothy wrote, "Vienna [was] crowded with music lovers, music critics, and students."[6] It had always been a musicians' city, but in the early 1920s musical history was again being made in Austria. At the Opera Dorothy heard Maria Jeritza in the premiere performance of *Die Tote Stadt;* Lotte Lehmann in *Die Frau Ohne Schatten;* Elisabeth Schumann or Maria Olczewska in *Der Rosenkavalier.* Elsewhere she listened to Beethoven, Mozart, Haydn, Lehár, or, with a will, to Schönberg, von Webern, and Alban

Berg, whose works were "born and cradled" in Vienna during the sweep to modernism.[7] Literature and drama were no less conspicuously in flower, led by Robert Musil, Arthur Schnitzler, Stefan Zweig, and Ferenc Molnár. In addition, Vienna had seen an unprecedented influx of American artists and writers after the war. Waldo Frank was there, and the poet Louis Untermeyer with his wife, Jean Starr, and Edna St. Vincent Millay, who blew into Dorothy's life at the end of 1921 and went with her to Budapest, that "city of laziness, music and lust," as Dorothy called it,[8] — aptly, in the circumstances.

"Miss Millay was not a correspondent," a reporter for *The New Yorker* remarked some years later, in a profile of Dorothy, "but, as an acquaintance of hers once observed, she is a poet who likes to get around."[9] Dorothy knew and loved Edna's work and was not surprised to discover that Edna herself was as bright and sensual and "modern" as her verses. "A little bitch, really," said Dorothy with no diminishment of affection, "a gamin, a genius." Many years later, when an American woman who adored her sonnets ventured in conversation that Edna Millay seemed "very frail," Dorothy wanted to reply, "As a matter of fact, she has the strength of a racehorse. Any normal woman would be dead." But she held her tongue about Edna and confided what she knew only to her diary:

> In Budapest she had two lovers. . . . Both from the embassy; keeping them apart was a *Kunst* [an art — i.e., no minor feat]. The missions had filled all the hotels. Everything [was] crowded. She sat before the glass and combed her lovely hair, over and over. Narcissine. She really never loved anyone except herself. Very beautiful, with her little white body and her green-gold eyes. "Dotty, do you think I'm a nymphomaniac?" she had asked. Then she comes in a Grecian robe and reads aloud to the Ladies' Clubs, "What lips my lips have kissed. . . ." And what a sonnet that one! I had to go back to Vienna, and left her the toast of half the town; being painted by [Eugene] Feiks, dined at all the embassies, the adoration of Bohemia. . . . Handed her all I had . . . because . . . she was an angel. A bright angel. . . . We went swimming in the Danube, stark naked, late at night. . . . And drank champagne, afterward. And drove out to the castle, and danced, and in the morning we ate an immense breakfast.[10]

It was a long way from Syracuse; Edna Millay was not the only one who had come to Hungary for the sake of a lover. In the spring of 1921 Dorothy met Joseph Bard in the lobby of the Ritz Hotel in Budapest, where she sat having tea with Fodor. "[She] looked up and saw Joseph standing in the doorway," one of her friends reported. "It was the thunderbolt, the *coup de foudre,* love not only at first sight but at a glance. . . . There was no turning back thereafter."[11]

Fodor introduced them. At that time Joseph Bard was working in Hungary as an occasional correspondent for Reuters and the Associated Press, but as Dorothy discovered, his true interests lay elsewhere: in literature, history, philosophy. That very evening Dorothy spent with Joseph at the home of his friend and mentor, Professor Rusztem Vambéry, Hungary's leading criminologist and most liberal scholar of the law, who was also a counselor at the British Legation in Budapest. It was the first of many doors that Joseph would open for Dorothy, not all of them professional in nature. She made no secret of her utter infatuation, as she made no secret, later that spring, of the much-desired surrender of her virginity. Joseph was the man she had been waiting for, she said, the love of her life, "the flame Aladdin struck from out his lamp."[12]

Joseph Bard had been born in Budapest in 1892, the son of a Jewish father and a Croatian mother whom he described as "domineering," "a cold woman, a frigid person."[13] Madame Bard was a Protestant — "a ferocious Protestant"[14] — in a land where few apostates cared to live. She sent her son to progressive but nevertheless Catholic schools, a situation that allowed her, in some fundamental way, always to know best: until her death in 1927 she never ceased to advise Joseph that he was a special case, "some kind of Svengali," she liked to say.[15]

"I am Slav and Magyar," Joseph told Dorothy, "and perhaps a little Turk, but mostly Jewish."[16] Trained as a lawyer, able to speak faultless English, he had studied at the Sorbonne and served as a conscript in the Hungarian army during the war. Now, in peacetime, Joseph was very much preoccupied with his future. When Dorothy met him he was already at work on the book that was supposed to be his magnum opus, a huge, ponderous treatise on society and culture that he was writing in three languages simultaneously and called "The Mind of Europe."[17]

"He looked like an Egyptian prince," Dorothy remembered, "his hair lay on his head like burnished wings and his body was smooth, his limbs slender. . . . Something emanated from him. . . . Not desire, exactly, not so . . . centered. Tenderness . . . beauty . . . one felt always shy before it. A little blinded."[18] It was a typical passage among many hundreds of self-absorbed ruminations, naive and overinterpreted, that Dorothy spun out to document her first authentic love affair. "Your charm for me is essentially an erotic one . . . ," she confessed to Joseph later. "The gulf between us of race, culture, above all of early training, was bridged for you by the will to rise into what you believed to be a better, cleaner and more secure world; for me the only bridge was eros . . . sex lifted into something more. Something imaginative, kindling, kind, strong, passionate, clean-cutting, well-holding. Creative companionship: inner loyalty." [19] There was nothing imaginary about the depth of Dorothy's feeling, to be sure. And when it came to Joseph Bard, she was not the only one with the sun in her eyes.

"Joseph was, as every woman recognized at once, an accomplished flirt," wrote his friend Louis Untermeyer, "and a devastating charmer." He was "suave, slender, black-haired, black-eyed and strikingly handsome — a description that makes him sound fictionally slick and even sinister. There was, however, nothing the least malevolent or mean about him. On the contrary, he was a delightful companion, a stimulating conversationalist, and a brilliantly spontaneous raconteur." [20] The British novelist and Adlerian Phyllis Bottome, one of Dorothy's closest friends in Vienna, remembered Joseph as "considerate, unselfish and most entertaining . . . a kindly and pleasant friend, full of humor and good fellowship." [21] It is a tribute to Dorothy's discrimination, possibly, that all of her friends liked and admired Joseph, something she had never expected ("not because he isn't the most likable person on earth," she explained, "but because one's friends never do like the men one loves"). [22] An exception was Rebecca West, whom Dorothy got to know in Berlin and who remarked of Joseph that he was "not an unkindly soul, but the equivalent of a hairdresser, with a naive passion for fancy vests." [23] But Rebecca was known to exaggerate.

In view of subsequent developments, there is a small irony in the fact that it was Joseph, not Dorothy, who was the suitor and pursuer in the first months of their courtship. "He is a gentle and remote soul," Dorothy proposed, "interested in abstract philosophy. He does *not* crush my personality. He approaches with courtly bow and humorous eyes." [24] Anxious for reassurance, desperate to get out of Budapest ("this hot and smelly town," he called it, loathing it with all his heart), [25] he begged Dorothy to marry him almost from the start. "She appeared to Joseph in the light of Joan of Arc to the beaten Charles," said Phyllis Bottome, but "he simply had not got the moral stamina to make a way for himself that was compatible with the kind of life Dorothy had to lead — in order to *be* Dorothy."[26] She had given herself to Joseph "with equanimity" — "What shoals ahead I dimly guess, but '*Vivimus, vivamus*' was my class motto at prep school — let us live while we live."[27] All the same, Dorothy was not prepared to surrender the life she had begun to make for herself in Vienna, and she was not at all sure about Joseph's protestations of love in view of his persistent and evidently quite casual sexual infidelity. He had told her that this was a "Hungarian" trait, that "it was a national pastime in Hungary for men to pinch each other's girlfriends."[28] Dorothy was not convinced. She had been given a taste of what life with Joseph would be like when Edna Millay returned to Vienna twisting "a little green ring on her finger."

"Joseph gave it to me," said Edna to Dorothy ("absolutely brutally," in Dorothy's opinion). "But he really cares for you."

"It's all right, Edna," said Dorothy, "I know he does." She was "full of furious tears" and determined to guard against erotic lunacy.[29] Joseph accused her of having "inhibitions," a going word in the days when Sigmund Freud was still seeing patients in his office on the Berggasse. But it was Joseph who was "horrified" when one of Dorothy's American friends, an alumna of the suffrage campaign, endeavored to give her contraceptive advice and exhibited what Joseph called "a purseful of sexual objects." He was "offended," apparently, "by this breezy practical approach to the mysteries of love."[30]

"I don't *like* eroticism," Dorothy sighed in a letter to Rose Lane. "I don't *like* wallowy, mucky love. I don't *like* to be squashed by my emotions or anyone else's."[31] It was a very real concern for a woman who had constructed her whole life around the central fact of her independence.

"Sometimes I want love," Dorothy went on, "and protection — yes, *protection,* not of the practical kind, but the protection of love itself . . . the surrounding kindliness and sympathy of someone who loves you more than he loves anything or anybody in the world. And I desperately need to love someone who needs me. I feel this in my heart." She wanted "a home," too, she thought, "some course to my life . . . some stability in the compass. But then, at other times, my heart sits in me and bleeds like a thing in chains. I am half-inclined to throw my things into a suitcase, lock the door of my flat, take the only one hundred dollars I have in the world, and start away for another city, and a new environment. . . . I want so to be free.

I know if I marry I'll never take risks again in the same way. I'll never start off across the world with nothing in my pocket and be able to say, 'Well, it's my *own* life, isn't it? And if I *do* starve?' "[32] As she pointed out to Rose, "I have been a 'wild cat walking by my wild lone self' most of my life since 16 — but — but — ."[33]

Must there *always* be a man? Dorothy wondered. Must a woman bow perpetually to the whims of a masculine world? She had had any number of suitors in Vienna, and was credited in newspaper circles with one of the greatest brush-offs of all time. "Yes, dear," she is supposed to have said to an Austrian beau who was begging her for a kiss, "but right this minute I've simply *got* to get to the bottom of this Bulgarian business."[34] Tongues in Vienna were wagging now, not so much on account of Dorothy's "illicit" affair with Joseph Bard — after all, "sex in Vienna was strictly free enterprise"[35] — but because, though she was known to be "betrothed" to Joseph, she was still seen around town with Fodor.

"Dirt dogs!" she cried. "They simply won't believe that a man and a woman can be intimate friends, can collaborate together on work, can be seen rather often in one another's company, and not be lovers."[36] She was having a hard time reconciling one thing with another. Phyllis Bottome, the Adlerian, who saw Dorothy through all the stages of her love affair with Joseph, felt that a certain barely suppressed "rivalry with men" had come into play. Dorothy "fought" with men, said Phyllis, though she bore them "not the slightest ill will *as* a sex. On the contrary, she liked to attract men; and as a woman she *did* attract them." She was at the height of her rather vigorous appeal, "always attractive to look at," in Phyllis's view, "and sometimes radiantly pretty. I remember in particular a soft green leather costume trimmed with brown fur, in which she looked like the incarnation of an early spring day."[37] Dorothy's colleague John Gunther, who met her within a year of her arrival in Vienna, remarked that she might have been mistaken for "a gym teacher in a girls' college" were it not for "the marked femininity that colored her responses. She was all woman."[38] And Carl Zuckmayer, the playwright, went into raptures when he recalled her brightness and her charm:

> In her late twenties she seemed nineteen. She was marvelously healthy; her face always looked as if she had just been running in a stiff sea or mountain breeze; and her bright, clear eyes flashed and glowed with eagerness and enthusiasm, whether she was arguing or

agreeing with you. Even when her fine, well-proportioned figure was becoming a little plump, she loved to wear very light, rather girlish dresses which were wonderfully becoming to her. There was nothing about Dorothy that reminded you of the typical career woman who is intellectually overstrained or riddled by the craving for success, who never has time for herself and therefore becomes an irritant to everyone. Dorothy had time; despite all her professional work she took time to live, to be a woman and a human being. She could laugh, she loved gaiety and enjoyed simple pleasures. She cooked well; she could hold most drinks and any in quantity. The one thing that betrayed her hidden nervousness and did her no good was her incessant, hasty, uncontrollable cigarette smoking. In her greedy inhaling, her careless crushing out of a half-smoked cigarette and immediately lighting another, I saw a sign of inner restlessness which she otherwise locked within herself, as she did all the difficulties, the complications, and the tragic aspects of her life.[39]

"Gertrude," Dorothy wrote from Vienna to her friend Gertrude Tone, in one of those clipped and sweeping generalized statements that would become her stock-in-trade, "the relations between men and women will take years to resolve." Of one thing Dorothy was certain: "Sexual love is possessive. Sexual love is a bar to freedom."[40] She did not suppose that sex — "the life of the worm and the fly" — in itself was "odious." "But," she maintained, "in the atmosphere of this day and generation — subjective, over-emphasized, perfumed, refined, saturated — much of it is very odious indeed."[41] In a long letter to Gertrude, Dorothy outlined her position:

The closer I come to understand my lover, the more I love him, the less I want to marry him. But he, alas, does not feel that way. He wishes passionately to marry me . . . and a cloud crosses my mind, as I write, because I believe that if I do not marry him, after awhile he will go away. Don't ask me to explain this. I can't. Only . . . he will. Very well . . . then I must stand it. For oh, Gertrude, will any loving man ever realize that to be lonely, to be insecure, but to be free; to make one's friendships where and as one will, without artificial restraint; to violate never the integrity of one's own spirit; to give oneself because one wishes to give and never because of habit or custom — to give oneself generously, but never to be owned — will *any* loving man believe that any loving woman can count these things greater even than love? I wonder sometimes if I am not supremely selfish . . . if my love of freedom isn't a neurosis. . . . If I were to tell the truth I would say, 'I matter more to myself than anyone in the world matters to me.' I could say that to you, and you would understand it. I think. But not to my Joseph. . . .

Ah, well, let us not foresee the unforeseeable. I am very happy. Joseph and I drift a little. . . . Alone, in Vienna, I work. When he comes [from Budapest], which is every fortnight or so, we run away to the mountains, to ski and walk, and talk about his new philosophy of law, in the evening, by the fire. Or he comes to Vienna, and we joy in the theatre, and in work together. . . . This for that. As you know I have always had the banana peel philosophy. (Why worry about the future, when you may slip on a banana peel tomorrow?) [42]

She did not crack under Joseph's pressure until April 1923, more than two years after they first met. In the summer of 1922 she went to Berlin in order to fill in for Beach Conger, the *Public Ledger*'s regular correspondent, who was on leave in America. Berlin was a beat of world importance, and Dorothy aimed to do it justice: she stayed in the city for five months and had little time for a lovesick swain. After paying her a short visit, Joseph compared the experience to an airplane ride.

"Everything went at such a bewildering speed," he wrote Dorothy. "Somehow that speed has a very bad effect on my mental power, it gets troubled like water in wind, whereas your mind, dear girl, becomes white hot in motion." Joseph's letters were now filled with longing:

Sweetheart, I am young and I want you — desire you with an aching heart, desire you like scorched sand the rain or scorched lips a soft kiss.

with complaining:

When I think of how little conscious you were of my presence [in Berlin] I feel I have some reason to be dissatisfied.

with reproaches:

You told me once that you would be satisfied with a very simple life, a little house, garden, friends, books, work you like. But as a matter of fact you want much more from life, you are drunken with life, you would grab everything, live in a wild flush, and besides — write thoughtful books.

with blackmail:

> I have humbled myself before you; I have eaten dust. . . . I have had very little love in my life. . . . Once you told me to tell you sincerely whether I love you or not — and not be a "wretched coward." I ask you now Dorothy, tell me how much love you really feel for me, and how sincere and strong your love is?[43]

And so she married him, against her first and surest instinct but, when the time came for it, in wholehearted commitment. "I have in me the capacity to be deeply faithful to one man whom I love and who loves me," she told Joseph later on; "what I want is to . . . build a life with him which shall have breadth, depth, creative quality, dignity, beauty, and inner loyalty."[44] When it came to men, this theme of "creativity" was a constant in Dorothy's thinking. She described her union with Joseph as "an adventure into life: an attempt with all the powers I possessed, of health, and will, and joy to life, to make a creative marriage, to make out of two people who were not much — a boy from a bad environment in Budapest and a girl from an American village — a life which should be productive, warm, hospitable, comradely, creative."[45] Joseph had told her that she was "a bearer — a life-giver," and Dorothy, entering into what can only be called the first of her earth-mother phases, was not unhappy with the thought.

"For so I believe I am," she wrote; "it is my one consciousness of worth — the feeling that there is in me a source of strength renewed from some deep inner spring, some rich abundance of nature, which others who have talent to give it form can draw upon."[46]

Following their wedding in the town hall in Budapest,[47] the Bards set up house in a spacious, high-windowed apartment on the Prinz Eugenstrasse in Vienna, overlooking the Belvedere, where Dorothy "[ground] ahead at journalism"[48] and Joseph, freed from financial worry and other distractions, set to work in earnest on "The Mind of Europe." Only occasionally, during the next two years of "perfect bliss," did Dorothy have cause to remember her initial reservations: "Delirious with love, I was, delirious with youth and love together, and yet in the midst of it that blackness over my heart, that certainty of apprehension: This man will let me down; I shall break my heart over this."[49] She actually said that once to Joseph, "on the slope of

a hill" outside the city, but he answered her coldly: "Don't be boring."[50]

DURING her earliest years as a reporter in Europe, Dorothy operated
very much like other correspondents of the time: on her own, from
an office she had set up in her apartment, with "a multitude of problems" and nothing to guide her but her energy and her wits.[51] "I had
nine countries to cover," she remembered, "over an enormous territory, each one of them with a different history and problems. I had
no assistance, not even a secretary." There were "no fancy umbilical
links with the home office," no "apparatus of journalism" to fall
back on. Dorothy's success depended entirely on her own quick
thinking, her swift feet, and a variety of floating stringers and tips-
ters — "good local men with plenty of 'ins' " — who hovered on the
edge of events in Europe and were paid according to the value of
their contacts.[52]

"Those were the days before governments and their agencies, and
especially our own, had even attempted to take us into camp," Dorothy observed, "flatter us, consult us, make partners of us, transport
us around the world, set up press clubs for us — and offer us government jobs." Nothing like the prestige and high seriousness of a
later age had as yet adhered to the profession of foreign correspondence. Nor was there any reliable tradition, when Dorothy came on
the scene, of the reporter-as-celebrity, a phenomenon that may be
traced for all intents and purposes to the Hearst and Pulitzer correspondents of the Spanish-American War and, in Dorothy's own
time, to Floyd Gibbons, the roving correspondent for the *Chicago
Tribune,* who set the pace of foreign reporting in the 1920s when he
sauntered into the Sahara trying to find an Arabian sheikh to rival
Valentino for the folks at home.

"Floyd's notion of journalism was confined to being wherever
anything was likely to happen," said Dorothy (who admired him
greatly and had pretty much the same notion),

> and to dramatize the occurrence to the hilt. The first predilection had
> cost him an eye as a war correspondent in World War I; the ever-
> immaculate white patch over its empty socket was worn as debonairly
> as a monocle and served only to emphasize the blazing blueness of
> the other. He travelled, even to report a revolution, with a ward-
> robe trunk, was a superb raconteur with a seemingly inexhaustible

repertory, and had the reputation, carefully cultivated by himself, of being irresistible to women of all nationalities. Nobody was more engaging, and as a racy describer of what his eye could see, unencumbered by philosophical introversions of any kind, he was a first-rate reporter.

Gibbons was only the most flamboyant character among a colorful and varied crew of "high-flying young falcons" — the American newspapermen who came to Europe after 1918 and changed the face of modern reporting.[53] Up through the end of World War I, the emphasis in foreign correspondence had been placed almost entirely on the ups and downs of international diplomacy. The advent of the airplane, the cosmic implications of the theory of relativity, the discovery of the tomb of King Tutankhamen — each was credited at one time or another with launching the race to "features," flashes, stunts, and scoops among newspapermen. In New York the *Times*, under Adolph Ochs, had taken the lead in the sharper, brighter reporting of the 1920s, but for sheer ebullience nothing could equal the *Chicago Tribune*, "the world's greatest newspaper," as Colonel Robert Rutherford McCormick, its owner, always called it. The Colonel was one of those exasperating, illiterate businessmen with power, "a twenty-million-dollar ignoramus" who knew "nothing" about journalism and one day asked, after a session of the Versailles Conference in which the fate of the Ukraine was discussed, why the delegates had spent "so much time talking about a musical instrument."[54] But the Colonel's men were widely held to be the best in the business. The word went out to all reporters: "Compete."

From the central offices of the *Philadelphia Public Ledger*, Dorothy Thompson received the same instruction. For generations the *Ledger* had been among "the staidest of Philadelphia's institutions," unimaginative, sanctimonious, and dull, "the perfect embodiment of the conservatism and propriety of Rittenhouse Square." In 1919, however, the paper was bought by Cyrus H. K. Curtis, the publisher of the *Saturday Evening Post*, who announced that he would not be outdone by Chicago and New York and that "unlimited sums" would be spent to turn the *Ledger* into a national newspaper;[55] as a result, Dorothy enjoyed a larger expense account than most of her colleagues and had the added advantage of a wide syndication. In 1924 the *Ledger*'s foreign service merged with the *New York Evening Post*'s, giving her an even broader audience in America. She was the undisputed queen of the overseas press corps, the first woman to head a foreign news bureau of any importance, but her fame was still largely impersonal, within the trade.

"This isn't enough for me," she confessed to Phyllis Bottome. "It's not what I really want. I'm nothing in my own country. I want to be something there — something no other woman has been yet."[56] It is probably the most significant aspect of this whole period of American journalism that a correspondent such as Dorothy was given so much room to move. She was completely independent, freed of any ideological, corporate, or associative restraints.

"This was before journalism became institutionalized," said John Gunther, the blond, "rangy" Adonis[57] from Chicago who, like Dorothy, had arrived in Europe on his own initiative, with the goal only of reporting what he saw. "We were scavengers, buzzards, out to get the news, no matter whose wings got clipped. . . . Most of us travelled steadily, met constantly, exchanged information, caroused, took in each other's washing, and, even when most fiercely competitive, were devoted friends."[58] They had to be friends, said Dorothy, because they were the only ones who knew how to help each other in a pinch. She relied on her fellow correspondents not just for news and ideas but for secretaries, typewriters, lodgings, cash, and a great deal of moral support.

"In the nature of things we all knew each other," Dorothy reported, "for the number of foreign correspondents was never large. But we were engaged in a highly competitive profession, and in background, viewpoint, temperament, and personality we differed from one another almost as much as is humanly possible." There was the "gentle, gravel-voiced" Raymond Gram Swing,[59] the *Public Ledger*'s correspondent in London, "soberly meticulous" and devoted in private life to the composition of music. There was Clarence Streit, who defied the subsequently sacred notion that a journalist was "impartial" and infused his reporting with "a messianic urge to improve the world."[60] There were A. R. Decker, Junius Wood, Bill Stoneman, Negley Farson, Frazier Hunt, Larry Rue, and H. R. Knickerbocker, who came to Europe as a student of philosophy and stayed to become an expert analyst of German-Russian relations; Jay Allen, "an extraordinarily gifted man"[61] who distinguished himself later as a courageous and humane correspondent in the Spanish civil war; William L. Shirer, remembered by his colleagues as "utterly real"[62] and "totally nice";[63] and Edgar Ansel Mowrer, the "persistently engaging," wonderfully educated, "passionate, gloomy, explosive"[64] brother of Dorothy's onetime mentor in Paris, Paul Scott Mowrer.

Finally, there was the man whom Dorothy embraced, along with John Gunther, not just as a colleague and a friend but as a soulmate, a companion of the heart: Vincent Sheean — "Jimmy" — who went on to command an enormous, well-nigh idolatrous following in America after the 1934 publication of *Personal History,* his ground-breaking memoir of the correspondent's life.

James Vincent Sheean had come to Europe, in 1922, like so many others of this group, directly from the American Midwest — from Pana, Illinois, to be exact, where he grew up in an Irish-Catholic household and passed the better part of his adolescence trying to find a quiet place to read books and escape the attentions of his baseball-playing neighbors.[65] "He talks," said John Gunther, "in practically all languages, with the utmost fluency, clarity, grace and humor. All told his erudition matches, I think, that of any American I know; once . . . I heard him quote the Talmud, Spinoza, Tagore, Dante (for years he never traveled without the *Divine Comedy* in his pocket), Plutarch and Tolstoy in the same evening of casual talk."[66] Jimmy met Dorothy for the first time in 1926, in the bar of the Hotel Adlon in Berlin, and recognized at once that he had found a woman who understood him. Over the years their affinity developed into a sort of kinship, the kind of spiritual and emotional bond that might exist among happy siblings. Indeed, for many years Jimmy called Dorothy "my Protestant sister,"[67] and never forgot the way she wrapped up their first conversation.

"Well," she had said, "from the point of view of God, I suppose all human differences are insignificant."[68] Then she laughed in purest satisfaction, and Jimmy felt himself flush with admiration for this "fresh, smiling, pink-and-white, bright-eyed" American girl.[69] In the exclusive club of foreign correspondence, Dorothy remained to the end of her life a much beloved, even revered figure — "our Doro-thy," as the cable men in New York referred to her[70] — a reassuring female presence in a group that sometimes tried too hard to be tough. Raymond Swing once remarked, obnoxiously or not, that Dorothy was the only woman he had ever met in journalism "who was not a hellish nuisance to work with,"[71] while George Seldes, Colonel McCormick's man in Berlin, called her "the only woman news-paperman" and meant it as a compliment. "She never used sex-attraction to get her story," said Seldes. His implication was, of course, that other women did,[72] but in any case this view of Dorothy was echoed by all of her colleagues. A story made the rounds about a long night over coffee and Schnapps in a Vienna café, where the correspondents had gathered to determine "whose brains, among all those assembled there, would, if removed and pickled, make the best paperweight." It was generally agreed, and never begrudged, that Dorothy's brains "ranked first."[73]

"So far as I have observed," Dorothy wrote in 1926, "no single one of the many difficulties which have beset my path as an inexperienced adventurer in a new profession in strange lands arose from the fact of my sex." What she had mainly had to contend with, she explained, was "the difficulty of my own ignorance, of the fact that I had failed to absorb from my university training a vivid and accurate historical sense, a clear idea of economics, or fluency in any foreign language. I had been brought up on the easy-going theory that knowledge was 'knowing where you can find a thing,' and I had to learn that there is only one place where one can quickly get information in an emergency, and that is from one's self."[74] The idea that women were somehow unfit for the rough-and-tumble life of correspondence was too absurd for Dorothy even to refute. She was shot at for the first time in 1923, on a balcony in Sofia during a Bulgarian uprising, and fainted when it was over; on the other hand, she was never drunk on the job, and she liked to point out that this put her way ahead of most of her colleagues: "I think we can call it quits."[75] Dorothy was not, however, above exploiting the *fact* of her womanhood in the interest of a story. Once in Czechoslovakia she was stranded during a storm with no money and tried to wire her article to Vienna collect. When the clerk at the telegraph office demanded payment in advance, she quickly wrote out a message in German. It was addressed to Edvard Beneš, the Czech foreign minister.

"Beloved," Dorothy began, "will you bring pressure to bear to have the officials in this post office fired?" She signed it "Sweetie" and got results: her story was wired on the spot.[76] None of the correspondents ever balked at a little cheerful bribery to get a story through, and none hesitated to use a disguise or forge a passport if necessary, "trusting a reputation for American 'craziness,'" said Dorothy, "to save us from the worst if caught." She was well known for her resourcefulness. Due to a certain confusion in the American Expatriation Act of 1907, her American citizenship was suspended when she married Joseph Bard,[77] and for several years she blithely used the red seal from a can of coffee to make her travel papers look official.[78] One night in 1926 she was at the Opera in Vienna when news came that revolution had broken out in Poland. It was late, the banks were closed, and the only thing Dorothy could think to do was call on Sigmund Freud, who ordinarily kept the fees he had collected from his American clients in cash in his office. Dorothy had interviewed Freud for the *Public Ledger* and felt no compunction about asking him for a loan, and she set off that night on the train to Warsaw still dressed in her evening gown and slippers. Before the adventure was over she had traveled by train, bus, and peasant cart and then on foot; she straggled into Warsaw at dawn two days later, just in time to discover that Floyd Gibbons, having heard about the ambush of a car full of reporters on the outskirts of the city, had wired her obituary to Berlin.[79]

In these circumstances, and having had such adventures, Dorothy was not particularly interested in a discussion of "femininity" as it related to the effective conduct of journalism. She had no use for "the specious feminism of the women's magazines, which persist in finding cause for jubilation every time a woman becomes, for the first time, an iceman, a road surveyor, or a senator. . . . This playing up of women is a disservice and an anachronism. . . . The see-what-the-little-darling-has-done-now attitude ought to be outlawed."[80] Historically, Dorothy argued, women had made notoriously good spies; why should they not also be good foreign correspondents? "Their chief trouble is that they suffer from an inferiority complex and that they sell their services too cheap." She had some advice for women who hoped to enter the field: "Don't accept for an instant the theory that it's a man's job, and don't be flattered by the phrase, 'You write like a man.' That's only a man's badge of approval, and it doesn't mean anything."[81]

It was easier for a woman to be a correspondent in Europe, Dorothy felt, than it was in America, because in Europe "women are accepted as indigenous," and European men "are accustomed to talk about art, literature, and affairs of state with women. Had it not been so, the salon could not have existed nor played the role which it has."[82] Dorothy herself had become a leading figure in the most exciting salon Vienna knew between the wars, held in the home of Dr. Eugenia Schwarzwald, the last and most tellingly influential of all her female mentors.[83]

Dorothy was at a loss adequately to characterize Genia Schwarzwald. Everybody was. "Only that nearly obsolete word 'humanist' describes her," said Dorothy. A short, plump, round-faced, round-eyed, steely-haired Jew from "the far end of Austrian Poland," Genia was one of the first women in Europe to earn a Ph.D.; to the hundreds of young girls who attended her famous "Gymnasium" in Vienna she was known only, always, as "Frau Doktor." The Schwarzwald School had been the first fully accredited preparatory school for women under the old empire, and Genia was not just its founder but also its master and its guiding spirit. The future world economist Peter Drucker, whose parents were friends of Genia's and who grew up more or less in the Schwarzwald orbit, confessed that he had never met a more compelling teacher.

"Of all those I have seen over many years," said Drucker, "only Martha Graham, teaching a class of beginners in modern dance, radiated similar power and held the students in the same iron grip. . . . Genia taught every subject and on every level. . . . She had the gift of holding twenty third-graders spellbound while drilling them in multiplication tables, without jokes, without telling a story, but by making demands and more demands on them." Genia had no theory of education beyond the advice that it should be achieved "by mutual agreement,"[84] and no goals for her students except that they receive a solid foundation in the liberal arts. A "Schwarzwald girl" was an educated girl, and a confident girl in the normal run of things, because Genia's other talent, her particular genius, lay in the opening of doors. This advice she passed on to her students, and to Dorothy: "Never ask a person what to do; always tell him or her. If it's the wrong thing to do, or if there is a better way, they'll come back and tell you. But if you don't tell them what to do, they won't do anything but make a study."

During the war, in the knowledge that her school was well established and could function without her continual supervision, Genia Schwarzwald had turned to work in the social services as an "unpaid and unofficial but highly effective 'ombudsman,' battling red tape and bureaucratic callousness on behalf of individuals." She had no particular affiliation and represented no particular group of people. Her view of life, her self-definition, practically, was summed up in the question "What needs to be done next?" When Dorothy met her she had already established her fantastically successful "open kitchens" in Vienna, where she fed more than fifteen thousand persons daily in a cooperative venture that put the Socialists (and everyone else) to shame. She ran summer camps for the urban poor, a nursing home for impoverished Austrian aristocrats, a dormitory for young artisans and apprentices, and a bed-and-breakfast for selected friends at her summer house on the Grundlsee, near Salzburg. In addition, Genia's home in Vienna, an unexpectedly elegant, eighteenth-century stone villa tucked away in a courtyard on the Josefstädterstrasse, was transformed almost nightly into a kind of living theater, "unrehearsed, spontaneous, free-form, flexible and fast," where the leaders of Vienna's literary, intellectual, and cultural life gathered for the most strenuous and dazzling conversation in town.

At Genia's Dorothy got to know Arnold Schönberg, Adolf Loos, Bertholt Brecht; the Danish writer Karin Michaelis; the young Prussian *Junker* Helmuth von Moltke, who later lost his life as a leader of the anti-Nazi Christian resistance in Germany;[85] and Oskar Kokoschka, whom Dorothy knew as "Koko" and who had formerly taught art at Genia's school. (Kokoschka was dismissed on the order of the educational authorities in Vienna, who pointed out that he had no teaching degree; when Genia protested that he was a genius, the bureaucracy replied, "There is no provision for geniuses in the curriculum.")[86] Genia's husband was Dr. Hermann Schwarzwald, "Austria's financial czar," a high-level, low-profile wizard-behind-the-scenes at the Ministry of Finance. Bald, lame, and devotedly unpleasant, as sharp-edged and angular as his wife was doughy and round, "Hemme" Schwarzwald normally held court in the library, "breathing on the dry bones of national economics," in Dorothy's phrase, while Genia's mighty personality "blew like a purifying and not always too tender west wind" through the rest of the house.[87] According to Peter Drucker, the Schwarzwald salon flourished "precisely because Genia knew that a salon is not private but public. It flourished because Genia knew that a salon is performing art. . . . She also knew, I am convinced, that the salon is the only performing art of the bourgeois age that does not serve the male ego and male vanity and does not manipulate women for the sake of male gratification." Genia's rather terrifying invitation to nervous guests, who might be attending her salon for the first time, stayed with Drucker for the rest of his life.

"I'm having a little trouble hearing you," Genia would say cozily. "Why don't you sit next to me and tell us what you think." Until he first saw a television talk show many years later, Drucker found Genia's approach "puzzling. . . . Of course there was no TV camera in Genia's living room. But if Genia asked one of her guests to come and sit next to her in the corner on the settee, the guest knew that he or she was 'on camera.' Genia was the mistress of ceremonies, and the best I have ever seen. She never humiliated a guest, always brought out the best he or she had to offer, always was kind and considerate. But she also knew how to get rid of a guest who did not shine."

Dorothy shone. She had precisely the qualities that Genia was looking for in her "stars" — "intellectual incandescence, independence of mind, and radiant beauty," "a physical radiance," in Peter Drucker's memory, "that [went] beyond being physical." And she learned well from Genia's example what it meant to be a hostess. It was not long before the personalities of the Schwarzwald salon spilled over into Dorothy's own parties and dinners, first in Vienna, and then in Berlin, where, in the summer of 1925, she was officially transferred as the *Public Ledger*'s permanent correspondent. She had earned the new appointment, and she knew it. But along with the Berlin office came a legitimacy and a prestige that she hitherto had survived without; she was going to miss the struggle to establish herself.

"We had a wonderful, risky, unforgettable time," she wrote more than thirty years later, looking back on Vienna and "the bubbling, blazing days" [88] of American foreign correspondence. "Often I think that were there more of the old individualism, the press [in America] might help create a climate more favorable to peace. But neither side now welcomes the detached mind and judgment, with its unpleasant connotation of neutralism. . . . We may be forgiven if among ourselves even those of us who have attained a renown we never sought or anticipated tell each other without wistfulness or nostalgia, 'Those were wonderful days. Those were the best times of our lives.' " [89]

THE apartment that Dorothy found for herself and Joseph Bard in Berlin, after months of searching, was tucked away in a far corner of the Haendelstrasse, a curving, tree-lined street on the edge of the Tiergarten. Actually, she had hunted down a thirteen-room house, and through some majestic sleight of hand had managed to obtain a housing permit, "the precious *weisser Schein*," which allowed her, as a foreigner, to rent the place for more than three months at a stretch. Her friends Edgar and Lilian Mowrer, who had been trying for two years without success to get hold of the same kind of permit, were invited to occupy the ground floor of the building, while Dorothy took the six rooms upstairs. "Look," she said, "I can put in a kitchen," instantly knocking down a wall and beginning her renovations. [90] When she was finished she declared the apartment "enchanting and paid for. I have never lived in such a charming place. The plays of light are amazing; and the quiet a boon." It was Dorothy's intention to establish not just an attractive setting where she could work and entertain, but a "real home" for herself and her husband in "this birdnest . . . among the trees."[91]

She had arrived in Germany at the very time — it seemed to her neighbor Lilian Mowrer to have been almost on the very day — that the unimaginable postwar inflation finally ended and the German nation entered a period of spectacular economic recovery.

"There was a brief period which seemed full of promise," Dorothy remembered. "That was between 1924 and 1929, following the stabilization of the mark. In that brief five years truly remarkable progress was made in Germany. The inflation had wiped out the internal debt; everything began to be rebuilt, entirely on borrowed money — borrowed from America — but nevertheless rebuilt."[92] But the nightmare of the inflation — when the price of a sausage or a pack of cigarettes had been known to rise by a million or even a billion marks in a single day — was not easily forgotten. It had been just the cap on six years of government crises, putsches, ultimatums, invasions, plebiscites, murders, "incidents and results," and it was Dorothy's hunch, borne out by later developments, that the intense uncertainty and paranoia of the time had somehow fundamentally unhinged the German people.

She was not the only one who thought so. She was living in the city of *Caligari* and *Cabaret*,[93] where Expressionism, neo-Paganism, Oriental mysticism, and "a new theory of universal brotherhood," Nazism, were combining with jazz, sex, alcohol, and drugs to form a "startlingly new," totally nihilistic culture. Art, said Dorothy, had "assumed the most outré forms. To depict anything in a representational manner was to be branded immediately a Philistine. Harmony, whether in color or music, was considered outlived, and the paintings and music which got the greatest critical applause were marked by brutality, jaggedness, and chaos. . . . Characteristic also was the falling-away from any repulsion for the obscene. Every horror was played up luridly in the penny press. . . . Every sensationalism was indulged in."[94] A series of grisly murders in the countryside had recently stunned and riveted the city, and Dorothy went along with thousands of others to a bizarre police exhibition of the pathology and technique of crime. It was something to make the Chamber of Horrors at Madame Tussaud's in London look like "a show for infants," she said.

"It is amazing," wrote Dorothy, "how much perversity of a peculiarly repellent nature will go down with the German public." Here, if one was interested, one could "make a study into the methods of strangling babies."[95] Here was "a charming exhibition of bombs — tiny, pretty little bombs for individual service, designed to blow up one grown-up or perhaps two children," or larger bombs for terrorist outrages, "guaranteed to bring down an embassy." Here was recreated the squalid bedroom of a mass murderer in Hannover — "nice, cold, respectable Hannover" — who, stalking the toilets in the train station, had lured twenty-six young men to their deaths.

"If one wants a glimpse of the miserable den in which this monster killed his victims," said Dorothy, "if one longs to see the cot where he strangled them, the table where he carved them, the buckets in which he stored them, one must stand in line for half an hour."[96]

That night, as she did most nights, Dorothy escaped to the theater. She had not before paid any great attention to the stage, but it was not unusual now to find her at a play four or five evenings a week. Here, and in the world of literature and publishing, she felt herself part of a tradition that was not lurid, a culture that was not deliberately sinister and out of whack. "These were the brilliant, feverish years when Berlin was, in a cultural sense, the capital of the world," said Dorothy. "These were the days when the German mind was open to every stream of thought from every part of the earth. Every current beat upon Berlin." In the winter of 1925 she went to the premiere of Carl Zuckmayer's *Fröhliche Weinberg* ("The Merry Vineyard") and saw in it the perfect antidote to the conceit and cynicism she found elsewhere in the town. *Der Fröhliche Weinberg* was "more than a play," she wrote:

> It was an orgy. It was an orgy of sunshine, harvest, love, lewdness, tenderness, satire and gargantuan mirth. The mirth was not intellectual and not wisecracking. It was a mirth that arises from a robust affirmation of life. I missed a quarter of the lines because the actors spoke dialect. It did not matter. I laughed, everybody laughed, the world laughed. For the first but not the last time in my life I felt as if an outburst of German laughter might sweep the world clean. The play was coarse — coarse and clean — all the coarseness scrubbed with the soap of imagination and honesty. I was crazily happy. So was everybody else.[97]

She invited Zuckmayer into the center of her ever-widening social circle — Zuckmayer was married to Alice Herdan, one of Genia's "Schwarzwald girls" — and kept him there, with the likes of Ernst Toller, the novelist Jakob Wassermann, Klaus and Erika Mann, Franz Werfel and Alma Mahler, Kurt Weill, Lotte Lenya, Brecht, Piscator, Max Reinhardt. Now more than ever her work revolved around entertaining, and not just when it came to the luminaries of culture. She was beginning to move in even more rarefied strata, counting among her friends and acquaintances Albert Einstein, the very brilliant Barbara Morgan, wife of an assistant to the American reparations commissioner, the economists Gustav and Toni Stolper, and a number of visitors from abroad, who were drawn to Berlin's atmosphere of intellectual freedom and social ambiguity: Rebecca West with Lord Beaverbrook, her lover of the time; Lady Diana Manners; Maxim Gorki and H. G. Wells and their reciprocal paramour, the fabulous Moura Budberg; Harold Nicolson and Vita Sackville-West; the American writer Margaret Goldsmith (who took a job as Dorothy's assistant and fell in love with Vita); and Frederick Voigt (who reported from Berlin for the *Manchester Guardian* and fell in love with Margaret).

"Berlin sometimes reminded me of a huge railway station," said the English-born Lilian Mowrer, who was herself writing for British newspapers and, like Dorothy, spending a great deal of time at parties. "It was the stopping-off place between eastern and western Europe; everyone travelling from Paris to Moscow, sooner or later, came there." The embassy parties were the most interesting, Lilian remembered, and the parties at the Soviet embassy on Unter den Linden were the best of all, "for the Russians did not halt at conventional social boundaries, and collected around them artists, writers, intellectuals."[98] From there it was only a short walk to the Hotel Adlon, just inside the Brandenburg Gate, where all the correspondents gathered when they were in town and where, at the bar, a poker game for Americans was kept running day and night. The Adlon was not only Berlin's most magnificent hotel but "probably the greatest newspaper haunt in history," according to George Seldes, the correspondent for the *Chicago Tribune*.

"The theory that we were all in this together isn't quite right," said Seldes. "We were friends, yes, but we were rivals, we were all competing. And at the Adlon we could keep our eyes on each other."[99] If Dorothy's colleagues were not drinking at the Adlon bar, they could often be found having dinner with her in the Haendelstrasse, and if not with her, then with Sigrid Schultz, her only significant female rival in the world of foreign correspondence.

Sigrid Schultz, though born in America, had lived in Germany since before World War I. In January 1926 — that is to say, about six months after Dorothy obtained her bureau post in Berlin — Sigrid inherited the *Chicago Tribune* correspondency from George Seldes and thus achieved a kind of parity with Dorothy. She was never so successful as the latter, a fact that she resented, but she was a shrewd and talented reporter and was able to help Dorothy a great deal.

"She lives in a studio apartment with her mother," Dorothy wrote, "an old lady beloved by the 'boys' from one end of Europe to the other, . . . and by way of setting an excellent table and being able to create a jolly atmosphere, [she] has become intimately acquainted with a great many people in key positions."[100] It was Sigrid's belief that the only way you could find out about a person was to "invite 'em to the house," and this she did: painters and writers and opera singers "and a little group of members of our Embassy, who were just a little bit snooty about correspondents." Then there were the Nazis. When the first seats in the Reichstag began to fall to the National Socialists, Sigrid dispatched one of her assistants to the Parliament building with this instruction: "Look those guys over, and find out which of them has the kind of table manners that I can invite 'em."[101] The future Field Marshall Hermann Goering, as it happened, had that kind of manners, and through Sigrid Dorothy began to meet some "very important fellows, . . . long before the Nazis came into power and when nobody thought that they ever would."[102]

That was Berlin — a series of dinners, parties, and press conferences, nightclubs and gay bars and "those tiring journalistic evenings" that Claud Cockburn, the correspondent for the *Times* of London, remembered "used to start about 6 in the afternoon and rarely ended until 6 or 7 in the morning."[103] All of Dorothy's stories were now filed through the combined syndicate of the *Public Ledger* and the *New York Evening Post;* the *Post* was an afternoon paper, which meant that she often did not begin writing until night had fallen in Berlin. She got in the habit of staying up late, sometimes whipping off feature pieces as the sun was rising over the Tiergarten and Diana Jane Mowrer, the daughter of Edgar and Lilian, was getting ready for school downstairs.[104] It was easier for Dorothy to lead this kind of life because she was sleeping, for the most part, alone.

For some time now, at least from the moment of her move to Berlin, Dorothy and Joseph Bard had been living apart. There was no formal separation, and none desired, at least not by Dorothy. Nothing about her work had ever lent itself to an easy Monday-through-Friday existence; she and Joseph had grown used to each other's absences. Nonetheless, Dorothy was redecorating the flat in Berlin with Joseph in mind. She talked about him incessantly, and she explained his absence to her newspaper friends, who sometimes wondered if he really existed, by saying that he hated Berlin, or that his work was keeping him in Vienna, or that his mother needed him in Budapest. Dorothy did everything but admit to herself that the marriage was in trouble, though "in my unconscious mind," as she wrote to Phyllis Bottome in January 1927, "I've known for over a year that he didn't love me anymore. . . . I thought perhaps it would change." [105]

Joseph did hate Berlin — Dorothy was not wrong about that. He told people later that he had been very happy with Dorothy in Vienna and that if she had not been quite so busy "scampering around the world," things might have worked out differently between them. [106] Joseph was a committed, even a fanatic, Anglophile, and much of the time after Dorothy moved to Berlin he spent in London, ostensibly for purposes of research and to hunt down a publisher for "The Mind of Europe." A telling, if minor, aspect of their relationship was that Joseph always used the English spelling of his name, while Dorothy, dreamy with some notion of the Hungarian soul, persisted in addressing her letters to a Magyar, "Josef." Lilian Mowrer met Joseph Bard during one of his infrequent visits to Dorothy in the Haendelstrasse and concluded that Dorothy's conception of her husband was quite simply askew.

"He *was* rather attractive," said Lilian, "if you could stand that sort of obvious thing." She remembered that Joseph was "hard at work on some great, serious, unfinishable tome," but in Lilian's opinion he was no match for Dorothy, and "he just didn't seem to be a part of the picture." While she refrained from any open judgment of Joseph's motives, Lilian still knew what all of Dorothy's friends did: he was dependent on Dorothy for money, and he was not sexually faithful to her as a husband. [107] It was no secret that he had been to bed with a number of her closest friends — "I gather that every cat and dog in Berlin, Vienna and Budapest was well aware of it," said Jimmy Sheean [108] — and, according to Dorothy, he had even seduced another woman on their honeymoon.

"Have you ever met a man who has slept with 126 women?" she asked John Gunther.

"Perhaps," said Gunther. "I don't think so."

"Excluding cocottes," said Dorothy grimly.[109] Up till now none of Joseph's "affairs" had led to anything deeper, but the situation was rapidly becoming more than even she could endure.

"What if I do support him?" she snapped to their friend Louis Untermeyer. "He is my best investment. Besides, should I divorce him because his glands happen to be more active than mine?"[110] Dorothy believed in Joseph's talent as a writer. Many people did. She was working hard to justify their ever more distant connubial existence by casting Joseph in the role of "Genius" and herself in that of "Maecene"[111] — by which she meant that she was a combination patron and muse, a spark for her husband's brilliance, undoubtedly, but an aesthetic second-in-command. All at once Dorothy began to talk about how much she hated daily journalism — "It tears at my nerves, it kills the best things in me"[112] — claiming that she only continued in it for Joseph's sake, for the sake of the home she was trying to create and the life she was trying to make for *him*. "I could expend my energy on journalism as long as Josef was there to complete the circle of my life," she remarked, "with what I believed would be a beautiful, inner, and permanent work. His work was indeed the justification of mine."[113]

Somewhere along the line she had made a complete about-face. She had capitulated. "Oh, Rose," she wrote to Rose Lane when she realized that her marriage was over, "because I could never do anything except with all of me I loved Joseph with all of me, and was so proud, so proud . . . friends didn't matter anymore, nor that I should make beautiful things . . . he would make beautiful things for me, and I would make a beautiful life for him. He writes, 'You have such a splendid life . . . go on with it. . . .' But I haven't any life, because he has gone. Rose, I am afraid. . . . I am afraid of being hurt, and I have never been afraid of anything in the world before."[114] She remembered an afternoon in a hotel room in Munich, when she had still been in possession of herself and in love with her life. Joseph had asked her calmly, "If I have a friend with whom I can work, and talk, and who suits my peculiar temperament — would you mind? You always said you didn't care so long as you don't know about it."

Dorothy had taken a moment to think before she answered. "I see the scene vividly," she wrote to Joseph later, "with myself throwing things into a suitcase and you lying on the couch with that *verlogen* look which sometimes used to freeze my heart. . . . And I replied, with absolute clearness — 'Josef, I don't particularly mind little affairs, if they are discreet, spontaneous, and don't influence your feeling toward me, but if you find the woman you describe, then go to her, because she is the wife/woman/friend that you want.' And I said, 'I have the courage to break if you have not.' "[115] But she didn't. When Joseph actually fell in love with another woman, Dorothy was nearly undone.

The woman was Eileen Agar, a beautiful, wealthy, sublimely confident English student of painting, six years younger than Dorothy and already wiser for having had a failed marriage of her own. Like Dorothy, Eileen Agar was a rebel, determined to follow her lights and not too concerned with public opinion ("Why don't you *buy* pictures if you're so keen on painting?" her anxious, upper-class English parents had asked Eileen when they heard that she wanted to become an artist.)[116] "I was no husband stealer," Eileen remarked,[117] not in defense of her own conduct but in a pure statement of fact. Joseph Bard wanted out of his marriage, had wanted out of it for a long time, and it was a matter of sheer good fortune for him that he met Eileen when he did. George Seldes saw Joseph and Eileen in Paris around this time and reported that Joseph was in a state.

"He told me how unhappy he had been with Dorothy," Seldes reported. "He told me I couldn't imagine what his life with her had been like, how domineering she was, how she told him every minute what he should do, what he should eat, when he should sleep, when to get up, when to go out, when to stay home. It was too much for him."[118] A particularly nasty remark he made about Dorothy can be traced to this period of marital distress. "Like all intellectual women," said Joseph, "she thinks you can starch your prick at the nearest man's laundry."[119] Even so, at the beginning, Joseph was not prepared to ask her for a divorce. For a while after she found out about his affair with Eileen, Dorothy was content to go along with an obscure plan she had worked out with Joseph, which stipulated "that we should each go his own way, and yet stay together"; that she would not "oppress" him any longer and would even consent to regard him as a "sometime husband"; that Joseph would live with Eileen while he worked on a novel, a roman à clef; and that all of them, in the meantime, would be friends.[120] Joseph's failure to make a clean break of it might have been called despicable if Dorothy had not been so ready herself to overestimate her powers and indulge in the most absurd ideas about the human heart. In December 1926 she wrote to Eileen,* though the two women had not yet met:

> I am sending this boy of mine back to you. I mean, I am letting him go. He wants to, so much! You can do a great deal for him now, and, believe me, dear Eileen, he is worth doing something for. Beauty is in him, and goodness. I know you, through him, to be a woman of sensibility and goodness and simplicity and that is why I feel that I can write to you so. I believe if we knew each other, we should be friends. Perhaps you will come and see me one day in Berlin. . . .
>
> Dear Eileen, be wise and free. Only so can you help yourself and anyone else. Including this boy, who happens by a curious and not altogether fortunate circumstance to be my husband, but who is, more importantly, my most beloved friend.[121]

It wasn't long before Dorothy lost her attitude of benevolent tolerance. "If she had been older and more experienced in the hazards of the affections," said Phyllis Bottome, who was always ready, whether invited or not, to step in as a counselor for Dorothy, "I think she could perhaps have afforded Joseph more room to live. I think too that Joseph might have easily been convinced of her necessary claims upon him had she given him more room to swing his cats in."[122] As it happened, Dorothy suffered a perfectly normal reaction and one night found herself drunk in a bar, "love-hungry, sex-hungry," lonely, and weeping. As she explained it herself, she "suddenly flung herself into the arms of the first wayfarer who, not having a prostitute handy, happened to want her — into the arms of someone she didn't in the least love, and whom she hopes and prays she'll never see again." It was Floyd Gibbons, comically enough, whom she was bound to see again. This did nothing to lessen Dorothy's mortification when she sobered up, or Joseph's, either.

"You might have given me syphilis!" Joseph exploded when he heard about the episode with Floyd[124] — because of course Dorothy

---

*During the period of their separation and divorce, from 1926 to 1927, Dorothy wrote literally hundreds of letters to Joseph Bard. Many of these are now in her files at Syracuse, either because she never sent them or because Joseph returned them to her at some later date. Dozens more are in London with Eileen Agar, who remembers that Joseph also tore up a number of Dorothy's letters when they arrived. Sometimes she wrote him two or even three times a day. I have found no evidence to explain why she kept some of the letters and not others, and I have here and there combined passages from both sets of letters in the interest of space and clarity.

told him. This was a couple with a larger-than-average number of Freudian and Adlerian friends. One of Joseph's attempted conquests, in fact, was Dorothy's friend from suffrage days, Dorothy Burlingham, who had come to Vienna for analysis and was soon to become a permanent fixture in Dr. Freud's household. Everybody's conversation, and all of Dorothy's correspondence, was filled with talk about "ego strivings" and "transferences" and "compensations." Only after several months was Dorothy angry enough to identify Joseph as "a pathological Don Juan"[125] and to repudiate his rather impudent suggestions about her own sexuality. There are references in her correspondence that point plainly, if unspecifically, to homosexual experimentation on Dorothy's part; Joseph, at least, never hesitated to affirm that a number of her friends were lesbians. She did not save his letters from this period, but from the dozens that she sent to him, and the dozens more that she wrote and never mailed, it is clear that she and Joseph were both playing what a later age would call mind games.[126]

"It is impossible," Dorothy wrote, "to leave a healthy, spirited, and sexually attractive woman for months on end, and expect her to be *sexually* true, unless you can deceive her into making a sacrifice for what she thinks is some higher good, or convince her that you are faithful, or hold her by genuine passion of one variety or another."[127] For a short time at the beginning of 1927 Dorothy was disturbed enough to enter into treatment with Theodore Reik, a student of Freud's.[128]

"I have been driven into a state of hysteria," she reported. "I have aged in this last year shockingly: my hair turned gray and came out. I lost my figure, and I even became much more stupid (a lot of this has changed)." Her letters to Joseph soon took on a new boldness:

> I must repeat, Josef, that our lives were never one, and that insofar as they approached fusion it was through my efforts, not yours. . . . I cannot let you get by with this stuff about "life and freedom" without reminding you that you tried repeatedly and always to hamper *my* freedom. Your whole effort was to concentrate upon yourself and upon yourself *alone, all* my love: all my friendship, all my intellectual interests; all my erotic being. You were jealous and suspicious; if you have forgotten, I have your letters to prove it. . . . My instinct, which is pretty sound, knew you better than my mind did. . . .
>
> I have also my complexes, of course. They are quite clear to me.

But three talks with Dr. Reik showed me that they aren't nearly so serious as you tried to persuade me to believe. . . . If you're going to be a novelist, why not analyze what happened to a girl who became all woman in your arms and then was thrown back into a semi-homosexual state of adolescence by Budapest eroticism? . . . Why do you think I had those awful rages? . . . Why did you teach me all those tricks, throwing me back into an infantile narcissism, into an adolescent homosexuality which would have been completely overcome? Which *was* overcome? . . . You said things to me in those mad days which would simply have *finished* me if I had not known that I am, actually, rather exceptionally attractive to men. On this issue you can go to the devil, my dear, dear.[129]

She was lucky to have recovered her balance: the night she spent with Floyd Gibbons appears to have been the excuse that Joseph needed to forge ahead with his new life. ("The double standards, you know," Eileen Agar commented. "What a man did in those days didn't matter. But for a woman of Dorothy's high moral standards — shocking!"[130] At the beginning of 1927 Joseph advised Dorothy in his best lawyer's language that "under no conditions and in no form" did he "wish to resume matrimonial relations" with her.[131] This news, she remembered, "disintegrated [her] whole personality."[132] Genia Schwarzwald was the first to give her the only advice that would suit in the circumstances: "Make an end of it."[133] But Dorothy was not ready to concede to Eileen. She was not ready to lose Joseph, and it was Genia's belief that she came near to killing herself that spring.

"I tell you I won't get over it," Dorothy cried in a letter to Phyllis Bottome, "not ever — I know. . . . Endurance was bred into me, but I'm afraid I'm going to break. . . . I'm done for, Phyllis."[134] She had told Phyllis before that "Joseph always lets me down in the little things," but "if it ever came to a great crisis, he would be at my side." Now, she wrote to Joseph, "I know that if you and I were shipwrecked and there was just one spar, you would seize all of it, and say to yourself, 'She is strong and can swim — and I must follow my destiny.' "[135] She allowed herself the luxury of heaping some abuse on her husband:

> You have done me every wrong a man may do a woman and every wrong one human being may do another. You seduced me without love. . . . You won my adoration on false pretenses. . . . You

married me knowing you could never be faithful to me. . . . And when I had eaten myself fat as a compensation for love denied; and worked myself gray for the illusion of your ambition, . . . and turned away all the men who might have cared for me, then you left me, cast me off. . . . I tell you you have been as base as ever a man can be — Base, base, base — And I tell you that you are no less base this moment than you were last week. And I tell you . . .[136]

And on she went, for several months, until she got tired of it, filling reams of paper with pleading and diatribes, character analysis, affirmations of love, and the resolute promise that she would never again submit to this kind of thrall. "I am resolved to make myself free," she proclaimed later in the year. "Innerly free. There is no medium I will not take to accomplish it. It has become the deepest necessity of my whole being."[137] From Albania, where she had set up house in the capital city of Tirana and was living in pashalike contentment with her companion, Helen Boylston, Rose Lane invited Dorothy to drop everything and come join her.

"It really does look like a nice little war here, perhaps, along in June," said Rose. "Though of course it may end in nothing but another bitter diplomatic explosion. . . . Golly, how I *love* the Balkans!"[138] By grace of some amazing natural sobriety, Rose was the only one of Dorothy's friends who counseled her not to work too hard at figuring things out: "Go on, for a while, on your brain, my dear. . . . You needn't do anything about the days, you know. They will keep on going by . . . if you'll just not try to 'see' anything — or do anything, or think anything. It isn't necessary. Everything goes by, dear Dorothy, *everything*. You needn't do anything at all about it, you needn't even just let it go. . . . Oh, my dear, there's something in you, too deep down for even you to know it's there, that knows what you need, and gives it to you."[139]

This was the advice that Dorothy, at length, was prepared to take. She knew instinctively that no amount of arguing or thinking could resolve a crisis such as this, and she was getting ready, so she told Joseph, to "leave it to God, or to nature, or to what you call 'destiny.'" "The world will comfort me," she said: "the beauty which I worshipped in happier days, when I belonged to myself and was free in my heart . . . the feeling I begin at last to have again, of power: power to make the world open for me because I love it and understand it."[140] Matters were helped along considerably in May 1927, when Dorothy traveled to Geneva to cover the world economic conference of the League of Nations and finally met Eileen Agar, who had come to Switzerland without Joseph just for that purpose. The two women liked each other immediately — Eileen remarked later that if it hadn't been for Joseph they might have been good friends — and following one more harrowing plunge into insomnia and grief, Dorothy felt her ambition and high spirits come surging to the fore. She wrote to Joseph:

> I have got, in one way or another, to reevaluate and change my life. I don't know what I shall do, but I know that I have got to go another way than I am going now, find another way of life in which I can live. Because this person who receives people, makes interviews, is so efficient, is not me. It is the curious mask I have made for myself. Underneath it is something . . . I don't know exactly what . . . but something passionate, which is best under risks, and which has perhaps something to express. . . . I have been awfully muddled, Josef, awfully tied up, but I have got somehow to get back to the person who is me, who has been somehow lost in you.[141]

She had filed for divorce in January 1927, but at least twice before the decree was final she asked Joseph if he would not reconsider. "Are you sure you don't want to try again to make a life with me?" she pleaded. "I think it would go better with us in some ways. . . . I have learned a great deal."[142] In the meantime she was "carrying on trying not to throw the inkwell at the dear friends who tell me how brave I am. . . .

"Good old work!" she exclaimed. "I hated it so, and nagged at it, and felt it kept me from higher things. . . . In fact I was thoroughly treacherous to my work — but it stood by me and doesn't let me down. Good old routine, good old head that functions automatically at the sight of a newspaper."[143] She could take comfort in the fact that when all was said and done she managed to remain friends with Joseph Bard — excellent friends, as a matter of fact. It was as though they had gone back to the beginning, or even further, without "this erotic wrongness" to contend with, "this sex thing which is so cruel."[144]

"I cannot hate Josef," said Dorothy; "I cannot get over my queer feeling of responsibility for him," though "a little less poetry and more facts would have made everything easier for both of us. . . . At least I got him out of Budapest."[145] After a while Joseph and Eileen moved to England, where Eileen developed a significant career as a painter and Joseph, ultimately, became president of the Royal

Society of Literature. Although he did finish his novel, which contained a thinly disguised portrait of Dorothy and her circle, and later published two or three quite beautiful short stories, he never completed "The Mind of Europe."[146] "What's the use of mending a chair on a ship that's sinking?" he asked.

"He loved *talking,* you see," said Eileen, who understood Joseph in a way that Dorothy never had. "He was such a philosopher." Eileen refused to marry Joseph until 1940, during World War II, when her mother was dying and she felt she could afford to grant someone else's wishes in the matter.[147] Even so, Joseph and Eileen spent much of their married life in separate apartments, she upstairs, he down, and Joseph could be seen from time to time walking up Piccadilly in his plus-fours, more English than the English by the time he died, and wearing around his neck, according to witnesses, a locket with a picture of Dorothy in it.[148]

For her part, Dorothy was left with the knowledge of failure and the reassuring feeling that when it came to her memories of her first love,

> Josef has nothing to do with it, whatsoever. . . . I have been living in a world of illusion, and it has gone. Now, after all my passionate attempts to re-seize it, I bend myself quietly to receive this knowledge. . . . In so bending, so releasing, and so receiving the pain which is mine, I begin to find myself, and in myself alone find strength. . . . I go to a mirror and say, "And you, Dorothy?" And then I like myself. My body, that is sturdy and strong, my head which is high again and free, and my eyes that have the sea in them. And then I say: ". . . You will be well again, and ill or well you are you, Dorothy, all of one piece, and I like you."
>
> So sometimes I lean a cheek against that reflected cheek in the cold glass, and somehow it comforts me.[149]

NINETEEN twenty-seven was the year of the airplane, the year that Charles Lindbergh made his solo flight from New York to Paris and the *Spirit of St. Louis* became the spirit of the decade. In June Dorothy rushed to Kottbus to greet the arrival from New York of Chamberlin and Levine, the first twosome to cross the Atlantic, who in doing so actually bested Lindbergh's distance record. For fourteen days she followed the new heroes in their procession around

Germany, persuading them to grant her exclusive pictures and interviews in exchange for her services as an impresario.[150] It wasn't
the first time she hijacked a story. She practically "owned" Sigmund
Freud, for example: George Seldes remembered that "no American
journalist had even *seen* Dr. Freud without Dorothy's permission."[151] She grew accustomed to being shown a certain deference
and to doors' being opened at the mention of her name. In the year
of her divorce, she did not hesitate to throw her weight around.

On the eighth of July she went as usual to the weekly afternoon
tea given by Gustav Stresemann, the German foreign minister, for
the benefit of the press in Berlin. Dorothy was a well-known figure
at the foreign ministry, and it was only natural that one of her colleagues, the redheaded, warm-hearted H. R. Knickerbocker, should
have introduced her that day to Sinclair Lewis, the American author
of *Main Street, Babbitt, Arrowsmith,* and *Elmer Gantry;* Dorothy
knew that Lewis was in the city and had already cabled the news to
her papers. It was just as natural for her to invite him to dinner the
following evening, July 9, which was her thirty-fourth birthday and
the day that her divorce from Joseph Bard became final.

"I will never, never forget how you looked," she wrote to Lewis
many years later, "or how I felt, that first night."[152] He had amused
her mightily at their first meeting, pinning a Rotary Club button to
his jacket and introducing himself to foreign ministry officials as the
correspondent in Berlin for the *Volta Review*. Dorothy did not need
to dig around in her Freudian lexicon to detect in Lewis's humor a
compensation for his undeniable and, at first glance, startling ugliness. "Rufous," "gawky," bony, spindly, with "glaring bloodshot
popeyes"[153] and skin that looked "like canned tomatoes with the
seed in it,"[154] Lewis was known to his friends as Red; no one who
met him for the first time could say for sure whether this nickname
was given to him on account of his wispy orange hair or, cruelly,
because of his "hickeys" — the scarlet, precancerous lesions left by
acne on his cheeks. One of Ernest Hemingway's wives ventured that
he looked as if he had been hit in the face "with #7 shot at twenty
yards,"[155] while Dorothy was left with the unearthly impression that
he had "survived a battle with flame-throwers."

> I saw a narrow, ravaged face [she remembered], roughened, red,
> and scarred by repeated radium and electric needle burnings, less of
> the face below the hawkish nose than above it, where it broadened

into a massive frontal skull, crossed by horizontal lines; reddish but almost colorless eyebrows above round, cavernously set, remarkably brilliant eyes, transparent as aquamarines and in them a strange, shy, imploring look; red-blond hair, already retreating, very fine and silky; a small and narrow mouth, almost lipless, drawn away from the long teeth by repeated burnings, and which in the course of a few minutes could smile a dozen ways. . . . I felt that if one but touched him with the softest finger tip, he would recoil. My instantaneous reaction was, God, what a lonely, unhappy, helpless man! Somebody *must* love and take care of him! And, of course, I was fascinated.[156]

She entertained Lewis at her birthday dinner — and divorce party — along with H. R. Knickerbocker, Helmuth von Moltke, and the former Hungarian Prime Minister Count Károlyi. One of the other guests was Lilian Mowrer, whom Dorothy dragged upstairs for the occasion even though her husband, Edgar, was sick with flu and she did not want to go out.

The Mowrers had known Sinclair Lewis already in Italy, where they had been posted for some time with the *Chicago Daily News* and where Lewis, following the first huge success of his books, had traveled extensively with Grace Hegger, the wife he was now divorcing. Perhaps because Lilian's was a familiar face among strangers, Lewis spent the entire evening at Dorothy's talking to her — or rather, as Lilian remembered, *not* talking to her. Where he had been funny at Stresemann's tea, witty and gregarious and as personally charming as he was physically frightful, he was now in a somber mood, "vile, solemn, and *miserable*." He sat at Lilian's side in stubborn silence, uninterested in her, his hostess, and all of the other guests. Lilian kept running downstairs to check on Edgar, and finally, bored equally with the party and with Lewis's churlishness, she made her excuses to Dorothy.

The next morning at around eleven the telephone rang. The Mowrers were used to Dorothy's calling when she woke up, to say hello or check on the weather or pick up stray bits of news. But there was something different about her voice today. It sounded happy. It was a voice Lilian Mowrer had not heard for a long time, and the words were flying over the phone in a rush: "After you left last night . . . that appalling evening . . . as soon as you had gone . . . recovered his manners . . . charming . . . perfectly wonderful man . . . and when everybody else had left he wouldn't go home . . . and he went *on* and *on* . . . and he *stayed* and *stayed* . . . and at three o'clock in the morning he asked me to marry him."

There was no more than a second's pause before Dorothy added, "Shall I?"[157]

5

CHAPTER

T HE first thing Lilian Mowrer told Dorothy about Red Lewis
was that "Red was a drunk" — not "a heavy drinker," not "an
artist" with an artist's need for speedy release, but a full-blown alcoholic, whose benders, brainstorms, and table-smashing sprees were
known to literary society across the United States and Europe, in
New York, in London, in Paris, in Rome, and now, by the looks of
it, in Berlin. There was nothing rancorous about Lilian's characterization, even at a time when alcoholism was little understood. She
was telling Dorothy the truth, and if Dorothy doubted it, she had
only to stay put: she would see for herself soon enough what drink
had done to America's best-selling novelist of the 1920s.[1]

"Mr. Lewis!" Dorothy had exclaimed, laughing, at the end of that
long summer evening in Berlin when Red first proposed to her. "I
don't even know you!"

And what did that matter? Red replied. Dorothy was the only
woman in the world for him. No one else could make him happy.
It was fate. Kismet. They would marry and return to the United
States. They would buy a farm in the country, in New England. They
would write books and milk cows. "I have been looking for you all
of my life," said Red.

Somewhere in the back of Dorothy's mind the same words were
playing: "I have been looking for you, too."[2] But instead of saying
so she burst out laughing and told Red that he really ought to go
home.

All right, said Red, he would go. But he would be back. And he
would propose to her henceforth every time they met, in public and
in private, for years, if necessary, until she accepted him.[3]

"No doubt this was all embellished with a rare foliage of nonsense," wrote Jimmy Sheean, who over the years heard the story many times from both parties, "since Red's conversational style was like that, and yet Dorothy was left with an uneasy sense (half terror and half delight) that this madman was deeply in earnest and meant precisely what he said."[4] On July 11, 1927, she wrote to her exhusband, Joseph Bard:

> The divorce came on my birthday: a strange gift — and on the same day a man came into my life, who seems, and quite inevitably, about to be the chief factor in my destiny for a while to come. For how long I do not know. He is a very curious and demonic person, hard-drinking, blasphemous, possessed, I often think, of a devil. Stimulating to weariness: a countryman of mine, of my own blood, and in many ways of my own nature, and although he is rather famous, I think him far greater than anything he has yet done. I do not know whether this new and strange friendship, which seemed just to happen, will last long or not — he is getting a divorce and wants to marry me, but I am very doubtful. But it is opening new vistas in my life, and giving it new significance. It may change all my plans. I wanted to tell you about it — I feel, somehow, that you should know. . . .
>
> The man is Sinclair Lewis. You will, of course, say nothing to anyone about it.[5]

She saw Red again that very evening, at a dinner given in his honor by his German publisher, Ernst Rowohlt. Midway through the party Rowohlt asked Red if he would like to address a few words to the assembly, and Red rose to his feet.

"Dorothy," he declared, "will you marry me?" Then he sat down. He had nothing more to say. Over the next several days he proposed to her in nightclubs, in taxis, in the park, at the theater, at the Adlon, at the palace of Sans Souci, in the offices of the *Public Ledger,* and finally in midair, as, unexpectedly, the two of them flew to Vienna. Word had come from Fodor on July 17 that revolution was brewing in Austria. The Palace of Justice had been torched by a leftist mob, in revenge for the acquittal of three right-wing assassins who had murdered an old man and a child during a socialist rally. Now a press blackout had descended on the city, and Dorothy sped to the scene.

"Dorothy," Red cried, "marry me, will you?" It was dawn on the morning of July 18, and Red had followed her in a taxi to the airfield at Tempelhof. She laughed as usual when she heard the question, but answered that she might consider it if Red would get in the plane with her and agree to write a couple of articles for her newspapers. Red had never flown before, but he clambered aboard and shouted above the noise of the propellers: "Dorothy, will you marry me?"[6] Sitting between them was John Gunther's "leprechaun" wife, Frances,[7] who, according to modest contemporary accounts, "was pressed into service as a chaperon."[8] Red was happy to observe that the interior of the plane "was exactly like a large, comfortable limousine, with gray whipcord lining, big leather seats, windows to open and close . . . and nice little paper bags to be sick into."[9] Dorothy, for her part, wondered if this was not the exact moment, somewhere around five thousand feet up, when she first knew for sure that she would accept Red's proposal. It was certainly when they got to Vienna that they became lovers.

"Altogether there is a wind in this love," said Dorothy later, "which pleases me, a ripple of mocking laughter, a thumbing of the nose at the world."[10]

Harry Sinclair Lewis — "Red" to the public, "Hal" to his family and both of his wives — was born in 1885, in Sauk Center, Minnesota, population 2,807, the town he made famous as "Gopher Prairie" in *Main Street,* his classic put-down of American provincial life. Red was the third son of the local doctor, one of Sauk Center's leading citizens, a "cold, rigid," habit-ridden gentleman[11] who was invariably described as "austere" and who was unimpressed at any stage by his son's prodigious talent. Red's mother died of a "quick consumption"[12] when he was six; two brothers and a stepmother whom he adored evidently were unable to fill the hole left in his emotions (if indeed there can ever be any accounting for these things) by his physical unattractiveness and his irreparable loss. His face was ravaged by acne by the time he was fifteen. He grew up lonely, awkward, nearsighted, a show-off, athletically inept and with a harrowing trigger temper. But he was "gentle," too, people said, "kindly, boyish and vividly entertaining."[13] He was "restless, driven, ranting, panting, febrile — and electric."[14] Like the woman he later married, he was "afflicted with Wanderlust"[15] and wanted more than anything else, when he was growing up, to run away from home.

He was educated at Oberlin and Yale, and before becoming a novelist worked in advertising; in public relations; as a janitor at Helicon Hall, Upton Sinclair's socialist commune in New Jersey; and as a journalist, editor, and free-lance writer. He had written poems, short stories, and a "potboiler for boys." He had lived in New York, California, Iowa, Panama, Canada, Mexico, and Provincetown, Massachusetts, where the Greenwich Village literati were inclined to search for "Vagabondia"[16] in the years before World War I. The atmosphere in Provincetown was self-consciously Bohemian, even "proletarian," and the influence on Red was likewise left-radical: though fundamentally he was nonpolitical, his work was informed from beginning to end by the spirit of social activism. He was the sworn enemy of "conventionality, conformism, hypocrisy, commercialism, cant."[17] He regarded himself in the first line as a critic, and his novels satirized an assortment of "boosters," preachers, businessmen, and all-American hucksters whose perfect names had no equal outside Dickens: Myron Weagle; Roscoe Geake; Berzilius Windrip; Fatty Pfaff; and George F. Babbitt, the real-estate salesman from "Zenith," the mythical midwestern town, modeled on Cincinnati, where Red set his most violent attacks on American sleaziness and mediocrity.

It was *Main Street,* his hugely successful sixth novel, that first propelled Sinclair Lewis to the forefront of American letters. There had never been anything like it: *Main Street* changed the way America thought about itself. Exquisitely drawn, irreverent, funny, and merciless in its condemnation of small-town values, the book caused an uproar when it was published in 1920 and set Red squarely on the path of iconoclastic satire that most distinguishes his work. Questions were common even then about his consequence as a writer — was he a novelist of stature, the critics wondered, or merely a caricaturist, a sharp-witted social philosopher? — but it never mattered one way or the other to his vast, indignant readership, who gobbled up each of his novels in succession as if they had sprung from some cantankerous national oracle. *Babbitt* followed *Main Street,* and *Arrowsmith* followed *Babbitt,* and Red was the man Americans loved to hate. By the end of the decade his position was secure as the upstart heir to the mantle of Theodore Dreiser, the only novelist in America whose books rivaled Red's own in their social impact. Dreiser was thought to represent the "naturalist" school, while Red — along with Sherwood Anderson, whose *Winesburg, Ohio* had appeared a year before *Main Street,* in 1919 — was credited with launching a "new realism" in American letters. All three men were united by a common outrage, a contempt for the ugliness, vulgarity, superficiality, and basic inhumanity of the Main Street state of mind.

"Don't you understand," said Red to the journalist Frazier Hunt, "don't you understand that it's my mission in life to be the despised critic, the eternal faultfinder? I must carp and scold until everyone despises me. That's what I was put here for."[18] He was never a stylist in the "literary" sense. He was no threat to Hemingway, F. Scott Fitzgerald, or anyone else of the "Lost Generation," and would not have been welcome at the feet of Gertrude Stein. Red was an observer, a chronicler of events. He was a naïf and an incurable sentimentalist. His work has been described variously as a search for the balance between "illusion and reality" in American life and a throwback to an earlier idealism, a longing for the nation that might have existed in the early nineteenth century, before the swell of commerce and the technological age turned it into a car salesman's paradise. Few would argue with the judgment of Mark Schorer, his biographer, that the works of Sinclair Lewis, "whatever their aesthetic limitations, . . . played a major part, probably *the* major literary part, in the transformation" of American society between 1918 and the Great Depression.[19] "Not one" of his contemporaries "kept so close to the main channel of American life," according to Carl Van Doren. Red was "America telling stories."[20] His books were translated into dozens of languages, and when he met Dorothy Thompson, in 1927, *Elmer Gantry,* his biting attack on Christian fundamentalist chicanery, had just enjoyed the largest first printing of any book in history up to that time — a hundred and forty thousand copies.[21]

"His suits were made from Savile Row," said Dorothy, and his shirts, too, were all custom-made in London. He was a man of compulsive neatness and terrifying perfectionism, with "a fetish about cleanliness"[22] and an almost prudish decorum that vanished completely when he drank. And he drank nearly all of the time — beer and wine, whiskey and gin, cognac and schnapps and anything else that might hurl him from one moment to the next. His friends were hard put to describe the crashing muddle, "the nervous brightness, easy laughter and incessant clatter"[23] of his life. He was like "a helpless missile, rocketed along by some furious inner propulsion."[24] The poet Ramon Guthrie, who spent several weeks with him just before his trip to Berlin, paraphrased a line of Red's own and declared that "he was one of those people who are born knowing that they will never sleep again."[25] The air of demonic energy that surrounded him was only heightened by his grotesque appearance, stranger even than his scarred and pitted face would indicate.

"The first impression . . . was of a man put together with connections unlike those of most human beings," said John Hersey, who worked one summer as Red's secretary. "All his joints seemed to be universal. His long, slender hands seemed to turn all the way around on his wrists. Wolcott Gibbs had once described him emerging from a car — 'a tall man, getting up in sections.' . . . I would have sworn that he was hideously ugly until he started to talk, when his face suddenly turned on, like a delicate, brilliant lamp."[26] Jimmy Sheean maintained that Red's "famous 'ugliness' was hardly more than the most transitory impression to most people. . . . I have known women who did not even think him ugly — who were, in fact, attracted by the sheer oddity of his peaked face and staring eyes, the eyes of a small child or a frightened animal looking through a woodpile."[27]

It was something his friends and acquaintances needed to learn, if it was not immediately apparent to any sensitive mind: the drinking and the clowning and the sometimes heartless chatter were all masks, in Red, for the same "awful, involuntary humility."[28] "He had another gift," said Brendan Gill, a much younger Yale graduate who knew Red at the height of his fame, "and that was for turning a simple, friendly gesture on his part into an occasion for making lifelong enemies of everyone within reach of his scalding, vituperative tongue."[29] Red's conversation was peppered with oaths and scatological outbursts that never got into print, and he was the kind of drunk who turned up at parties with his pants held up by a towel, or sat on the floor at formal dinners and held conversations with imaginary cats, discussing the other guests as if they weren't in the room and urging his unseen friends to join him later at his hotel so they could *really* talk. As a personality (not to mention as a houseguest) he would have been merely horrifying were it not for his sense of humor, his generosity, and his unmatched talent as an entertainer and raconteur.

"In company he organized games," said John Hersey. "Once with John Marquand and others he passed around pads and pencils and made everyone see how many names of rivers beginning with M they could write down. He would assign guests outrageous names from telephone books and tell them to converse in character with the names. He would hand out a set of end rhymes and get people writing sonnets with them against the clock."[30] Red's own record for a complete sonnet was three minutes and fifty seconds.[31] He was a brilliant mimic, a master of accents and dialects who reeled off extemporary monologues of quite staggering complexity and boasted that he could parody any poet of the modern age, "on any current news topic," perfectly and without a moment's preparation. When challenged, he would prove it, to the astonishment of everyone within earshot. Milton, Wordsworth, Tennyson, Blake, Matthew Arnold, Vachel Lindsay, Edward Lear — it didn't matter: Red knew all of their styles and all of their rhythms and could imitate them down to the last caesura. Rebecca West, no idler herself when it came to words, described his conversation as "wonderful," and added: "After five solid hours of it, I ceased to look upon him as a human being. I could think of him only as a great natural force, like the aurora borealis."[32]

In 1914, before his first success, Red had married Grace Hegger, a former staff writer for *Vogue* magazine and a consultant at Elizabeth Arden in New York. Gracie was a "pretty, clever, ambitious" woman,[33] "who floated and emoted rather"[34] and fueled her husband's barely hidden snobbery with her own brand of innocent social climbing. "Titles went to her head like strong drink," said Lilian Mowrer, who remembered the day Gracie learned that an Italian office boy working for Edgar Mowrer was "a *real count!*" ("She had no way of knowing," said Lilian, "that half the men in Italy are counts.")[35] In 1917 she had given birth to a son, Wells Lewis, a beautiful child who was named for his father's hero, H. G. Wells. Gracie left Red only when she reached the end of her tether, after twelve brave years. In 1926 she met and fell in love with Telesforo Casanova, a young Spaniard "of distinguished lineage"[36] and no visible means of support, whom Red liked "genormously"[37] and whom he was happy to see become his successor.

"I shall never get used to him," said Grace Lewis in a novel she later wrote about Red, "as long as I live. Not a husband, not a father, not even a jealous lover. Just an author."[38] What Dorothy did not know when they met — what she had no way of knowing — was that Red himself was at the end of his tether. He had come to London in February 1927, just ahead of the outraged scandal that greeted the publication of *Elmer Gantry* ("slime," said his churchgoing critics in the United States, "pure slime," "sordid and cowardly," "venomous," "unprincipled," "an insult," "filthy").[39] The book sold more than a hundred and seventy-five thousand copies in the first six weeks of its existence, and simultaneously Red embarked on a crazy, drunken journey through Europe, part car ride, part walking tour, that took him to Yugoslavia, Greece, Corfu, Vienna, Munich,

Strasbourg and the Black Forest. He was forty-two, and since leaving Yale had never lived in the same place for more than six months. ("Is the wanderer like me homeless," he wondered, "or does he just have more homes than most people?")[40] In Vienna Red was actually desperate enough to consult a doctor, who told him that unless he stopped drinking he probably would not live out the year. He was "in a bad way," according to Ramon Guthrie, who warned Dorothy that Red had only "one chance in ten" of surviving. "You are that chance," said Ramon. Dorothy believed it.[41]

"It has been a curious spring and summer," she wrote to Joseph Bard with considerable understatement, "spent mostly in the air. I have flown — on air assignments — some ten thousand kilometers and discovered amongst planes and pilots a whole new world. I grew to love the sudden starts at early dawn, the silvery planes, rising into a rosy sky, the long flights over massive cloud, which stretched grayly under us, like a vast Arctic sea, like a world of snow and ice and sunlessness." Dorothy did not care to say much to Joseph about her new love affair. She was still writing to him frequently, and she had a long way to go toward emotional detachment.

"I shall never, ever, care for anyone as I loved you," she told Joseph. "There is no reason why I should not say this. There is no possibility of happiness for me so great as the possibility I thought I had three years ago." In the meantime she would try to enjoy herself. "Lewis" was wonderful, she remarked, the most marvelous companion.[42] Some time later she wrote to Rose Lane:

> It isn't quite the same. I approach life with more humor. This is a gain and a loss. I cannot ever again reach that transcendental state of feeling myself one, flesh of flesh and eyes of eyes of another individual. I am not nearly so much "in love" — whatever that may mean. I cannot stretch my imagination to believe that S.L. is the most beautiful person in the world. I know him to be compounded of bad habits, weaknesses, irritabilities, irritancies. But he pleases me. He is a superb comrade. He amuses me: the first requirement of a husband. He heightens my sense of life. He opens a future for me, so that for the first time in years, I dream of tomorrow, as well as enjoy today. Thus, he gives me back the gift of my youth. I like him, enormously, amusedly. I admire him, immensely and impersonally. I am absurdly happy in a quite head-on-my-shoulders kind of way.[43]

She had returned to Berlin from Vienna with Red after several comical and amorous days at the Hotel Sacher and a revolution that, yet again, failed to materialize. Red had penned three articles for the *Ledger-Post* syndicate and pronounced modern journalism to be "as unromantic as a Ford carburetor."[44] Dorothy, in turn, dismissed Red's work as "not much good — all about me."[45] They made no secret of their new relationship, but the terms of Red's divorce had yet to be finalized, and since ultimately a great deal of money would be involved, it was best, for the time being, to keep a low profile. Dorothy was tired — "I don't look ill," she said, "but I am afraid I am really not very well — I've taken to passing out now and then"[46] — and in August she left with Red for a hiking tour in England. Red was a serious walker, covering ten or even twenty miles in a day and never happier than when "chastising the vegetation"[47] with a stick.

"We are going sans baggage," Dorothy told Joseph in London. There was no room for a change of clothes on a proper hike: if you were worried about hygiene, said Red, you could bathe in your underwear; in the meantime, you needed room to carry your books.

"Oh, the weight of those rucksacks," Dorothy moaned after two weeks on the road in Shropshire and Cornwall,

> oh, this exaggerated love of literature. . . . At no time have we had less than twelve or fifteen books disposed about our persons. . . . En route we lay plans; each plans a mighty work of fiction. . . . The day always begins, "Have I told you of my plan?" . . . You see I have found me a companion who will *always* tell me a story! Only Hal's stories never begin, "Once upon a time there was," but always, "Now, I've often thought I would . . ." or "When we grow up, let's. . . ." Slowly again I find myself at home in the world, which I do truly love and always have. It is fitting that I should marry a tramp."[48]

She always called him Hal, the nickname of his boyhood, and not Red, which smacked to her of whiskey and cronies. He was "off drink," Dorothy reported — which meant that he was drinking only beer and wine — and he informed his own friends in New York that because of her he was "a new man," "a reformed character." She was giving him "a care and an understanding which was bringing [him] back to life after something dangerously like passing out."[49] In a letter to H. L. Mencken, one of his best friends in America, Red joked that "I positively never get drunk oftener than once a fortnight, and I have become so phlegmatic that sometimes I let other people talk for a minute at a time."[50] From the outset Dorothy's relations with Red were more playful than romantic, "amusing rather than ardent." [51]

"You," said Red to Dorothy one day, "you are . . . a . . . a pudding . . . a bread pudding . . . made of the divine host." He paused and added, "That's a compliment no one ever made anyone before." [52] They called each other Waffle and Mrs. Waffle, Mr. Minnikin and Mrs. Minnikin. They joked about the child they would have together, a serious little girl called Lesbia. They knew for certain that they would buy a farm when they got back to the United States, "somewhere where there are frosty autumns," as Dorothy said, "and round hills and great trees and mellow old houses." [53] They were happy on their holiday.

It is, of course, one of the saddest as well the most certain aspects of any alcoholic's life that these periods of good intentions and natural high spirits do not last. "A cloud" had already begun to descend on Dorothy by the time she got back to Berlin. She had left Red at Koblenz, drunk, in the company of Ramon Guthrie, and realized with some dismay that her lover had begun to obsess her. She was "excessively nervous, restless, almost ill. Consumed with fears, which are indistinct, nameless. It is curious I do not believe, emotionally, that I am going to be happy," she said. "(Or is this feeling only a defense against disappointment?)" [54] She was reading Red's books that autumn and stewing a great deal about her own professional future. Her letters and diaries make it plain that she felt inferior to Red on the professional level, and she struck up the same theme she had played earlier with Joseph Bard: Red was "a genius," while she was . . . she didn't know what.

"I am so deeply, painfully, still, aware of futility," said Dorothy. "It is curious that a new love and a new life cannot cure old wounds. But it is true — for me, at least. I do but wall them up: segregate them: stop them spreading. But in cold weather they ache." [55] At different times before the end of 1927 Dorothy announced plans to write three different books: one on Germany and its recovery from the war; one on "American Protestantism"; and finally a compendium of interviews — she was going to travel around the world and ask prominent people to reveal their inmost thoughts about God. [56] Or maybe she would write a book about men and women, about what men *did* to women:

> The reason why modern women are so unhappy [wrote Dorothy] and why they unconsciously hate men, is because they have gotten

better and men have gotten worse. They will not let men swallow them up, because the swallowers aren't good enough. . . . Women *know* that making money to buy motors and country houses, shoving around lumps of money to the most profitable places, or selling more and better tooth paste, isn't admirable, isn't worth the expenditure of whatever flame of life is in them. . . . I've never known a woman who thought adding up a column of figures was important.

She was given to think about her own situation, about her hopes for the future and her fear of failing again:

[Joseph] never took me wholly . . . he knew he couldn't digest me. . . . It is true that I was never married to him. It was an enchantment of the senses and a rare intellectual companionship; no inner fusion. We learned a great deal from each other, but we never, for an instant, became each other.

Yet I am not sure that this, that I have written, is not the rationalizing of a blind urge. . . . I am not sure it is true. Perhaps what we need is not to find the man who completes ourselves — perhaps, indeed, that is impossible — and what we need is to create a man *in* ourselves (or a woman if we be male). Der Mensch is neither male nor female, but like a tree, carrying all the elements of life within himself.[57]

She might have developed this theme further if it had not depressed her so, if she had not been so aware of the stresses and pulls of her own life. "I am afraid to work," she confessed; "I am afraid of my own 'striving, energetic, ascending' mind. I feel the conflict between myself as a mentality and a personality and myself as a woman and a lover. I am divided. Broken."[58] She was helped not at all by the alcoholic nightmare she had entered. Red returned to Berlin in September, a week or two after Dorothy, and took a lease on an apartment about a mile from her flat, in the Herkules-Haus. He was no longer "off drink." Soon enough "insane quarrels" broke out among the high and funny times. There were sudden violent fits of screaming in the street, "permanent" ruptures in the backs of taxis, and tearful reconciliations on the stoop.

"God, I'm lit again, darling," Red groaned on these occasions, the picture of contrition, while Dorothy "cried like a small child" and asked herself what on earth was the matter with him. Or with her. "I still feel poisoned from the sound of the hatred in his voice," she wrote after one particularly awful scene at a party in Berlin. "And

this time I was part of his hatred. He hated me, too. . . . What lies
in his soul, when the inhibition is lifted? What contempt, what rage
with himself? . . . This darkness in him which comes up like a tidal
wave, drowning his spirit, when drink beats down the dikes —
should I resent what causes him such agony? . . . I do not feel re-
sentful, only weary, and afraid. I want to be alone. I want terribly
to be alone."[59] Her diary of that autumn could stand as a testament
to the suffering and bewilderment of anyone who has ever loved an
alcoholic:

Sept. 21.

A dreadful night. We were to go to Mrs. Israel's for a dance; I was
invited and wangled an invitation for Hal. Hal said, "We will have a
fine party . . . dinner somewhere grand, dress clothes . . ." I wore
the little Lanvin taffeta and spent the afternoon having my hair done,
and nails. . . . H. was to come at 7:45: at 8:00 I was watching for
him from the window. I knew that he wouldn't come. At 8:30 he
'phoned. His voice was thick. "I'm shot . . . come here, darling." I
didn't intend to go. I intended to go directly to Mrs. Israel's. Yet,
when I got into the taxi I gave his address to the chauffeur. At the
Apartment House the porter leered at me when I asked for Mr. Lewis'
room. I was wearing the Lanvin frock and my most scrumptious evening cloak. All the lights were on in H's apartment and he was on
the bed in his underclothes and dressing gown. Dead to the world. I
was beside myself. I washed his face but he only came to enough to
smile at me with fishy, dead eyes. . . . I cried terribly. Something in
me collapsed. I shook him. I was enraged that he could lie there escaped from it all. I thought, "I will get drunk, too," but when I went
into his sitting room there was only one cognac bottle and it was
empty. He is on cognac now. He said, "Take off your dress. . . .
You will spoil your dress —" I was lying on his bed — he thinks of
the queerest things. I said, "No, I am going home." I knew I had to
go home. I couldn't, I thought, stay all night in a man's apartment
. . . a drunken man's apartment. When I said that, he held my wrists
tightly and recovered enough to say, "No, no. . . . Stay here. . . .
I shall die if you go." I took off my dress, and my pretty silver shoes
and the shiny rosy stockings. Suddenly he sat up, winked the sleep
out of his eyes, and said, "I will get you some pajamas." He laughed
when I put them on — white silk ones. I was sobbing all the time. He
lifted me into his bed, clasped his arms around me, and went fast
to sleep again on my breast. All the time I was sobbing. I saw how

everything is going: our house in the frosty New England country, the gay wanderings about the world, the baby I want from Hal; I who never wanted [Joseph's] child. I saw that everything has been a dream . . . like the dream of a child who says, "When I grow up. . . ." I saw that this thing will always dash the reality away — I saw all this, and thought, "I will get up and go. Somehow I will reconstruct my life. There is still work. . . ." And I knew that there was not even that. I saw that being a woman has got me, at last, too. I saw that if Hal goes now, I am finished. I cannot live by myself, for myself. All my heart cried out: this is my man, the one man, and he has come too late! Nothing left for me but to become brittle or to rot. All the time Hal was making love to me. Feebly, but tenderly. I kissed his breast, and he yearned toward me. I wished I could lift him up and carry him to a high hill, where wind would be blowing.

Things got worse as the night went on. At two o'clock in the morning Red decided that he needed something to eat and staggered out of the house trailing his pajamas.

"I shall bring you a nice little sausage," he mumbled to Dorothy, and left her sitting in his bed, shivering:

I was terrified after he was gone . . . in that state . . . he might be run over . . . he might fight with a policeman. They would bring him home and find me there. How unspeakably sordid it all was! My eyes burned like fires, and my heart was palpitating. He was gone over an hour. He brought back potato salad, sausages and a bottle of cognac. He had had a drink, too. He smelled dreadfully of brandy. His body like rank weeds. He tried to pull out the cork. It stuck because he had not properly cut away the tinfoil. I watched it, fascinated. It seemed as though my whole life hung on the tinfoil, on the tinfoil's holding. "It won't come out," he said, looking up at me, and smiling like a foiled but good-tempered child. "It won't come out," he said incredulously.

Dorothy was weeping still, and suddenly Red was filled with remorse. "I cannot ruin your life," he whimpered. "You are wholly good . . . wholly good. Get up — you mustn't stay here — I will take you home. . . . Tomorrow I will go away. . . . You will never see me again. I am finished." But he was too drunk to take her anywhere, and after a while they both collapsed, exhausted:

In the morning, sitting up, the hand holding the eternal cigarette up before his face as though to ward something off, his thin, pale, fine hair all on end, his whole body quivering, he said — "Sweet, sweet . . . I know it's giving up spirits or giving up you. And I can't give up spirits. A man takes a drink, the drink takes another, and then the drink takes the man. And it's got me. I don't know how it began. It was my father and Gracie. They both hated me. And you will hate me, too. I am a rotter. . . . But I won't go like Verlaine — like Oscar Wilde. . . . I'll take care not to get that far. When I get that far . . ."

All my heart dissolved in me. I hid my face on his knee. "Hal," I said, "I know it is true — If you don't give up spirits, of course I can't marry you. Of course we must separate. But that's no solution for me either. You're my man. I'm thirty-three years old, and I've been married once, and I've had lovers, but it was all a search for you. I won't get over this." He held me so closely. So dearly. I said, "Oh, Hal, you'll get over this! It *will* be all right."

At breakfast he was quite himself. "I won't take another drink for two weeks," he said, "or just beer. Tell me, can I drink beer?"

I said I thought so. "Damn it, I want a whisky now," he said. "And I don't need it at all." His hands were shaking. All the time he talked of the future. Of our house in New England. "I will learn to lay bricks and we will build our own wall," he said. "If I work with my hands, that will help me."

After breakfast he said, "Now you must go . . . I must work."

But I had the feeling he wanted me to go because then he could take another drink.[60]

"Why did she marry him?" asked Mark Schorer, Red's biographer, never pausing before he answered his own question: "For the obvious reason that most women marry the men they choose to marry: she loved him."[61] It may be so. But there were many in Berlin who remembered how doubtful Dorothy was about the whole undertaking. Lilian Mowrer (who thought she was "crazy") recalled the many hours Dorothy sat with her, analyzing the situation, hashing it out — but always refusing her advice.[63] Others referred to Dorothy's "acute sense of journalistic timing" and "certain opportunistic elements in her decision."[63] The truth was that after seven years in Europe she had suffered a failure of nerve: "I cannot live by myself, for myself . . . being a woman has got me, at last, too." Even in November 1927, when the *New York Evening Post* sent her to Russia to cover the tenth anniversary of the Bolshevik Revolution — it was "the most interesting assignment of my life," said Dorothy[64]

— she could not get Red out of her mind. She had left him in Berlin, where he had begun work on the novel that would become *Dodsworth*.

"I arrived in a blizzard," she wrote from Moscow.

> It's terribly cold and bleak, but my room at the Savoy is warm, and I have the titillating expectation of new experience. All along the road today the unkempt fields, the wooden houses with their little verandas, the groves of silver birches, the woods which must have been cut away, leaving fields of stumps, the immense horizons — all so different from the infinitely civilized landscape of Europe — reminded me of home, as did the sharp cold, and the rutted roads through the thin snow. Suddenly I wanted intensely to go home, and to live in America again, with you.[65]

But it was going to be a long assignment. Dorothy's editors had ordered a major series on the New Russia, twenty articles at the minimum, and for the next two months she had nothing to do but listen and look. "I have a most uncomfortable feeling of having left behind me something essential," she wrote to Red, "I can't think just what, but I'm lost without it. Could it be you?"[66]

She worked hard — very hard — on the Russian project. "Such days!" she wrote.[67] "I am painfully aware of my inability, here, to scratch more than the surface; painfully, because I have never been in a place which is so challenging, or where I more genuinely desired to know what was going on."[68] Besides, she said, "Every day I change my mind about everything I've made it up about the day before."[69] She had been welcomed to Moscow with open arms, not just by the Soviet officials, who were trying out a friendly approach to the West, but by the host of American writers and journalists who were covering the Soviet anniversary and still clinging passionately to the idea that Russia was the modern utopia. Theodore Dreiser was there, Red's rival, flirting with every woman in the Kremlin and spreading rumors that he was sleeping with Dorothy in Red's absence. Scott Nearing took her around town and lectured her on the evils of capitalism. The dedicated Anna Louise Strong gave her socialist pamphlets and leaflets and a pair of galoshes when her trunks failed to arrive from Berlin ("Now you see how it is," Nearing remarked in triumph, "to lead a worker's life without any clothes").[70] And Jimmy Sheean turned up at the last minute from China, chasing the woman he was in love with and hoped to marry: Rayna Prohme, a fiery, left-leaning beauty from Chicago, "who had balled up her life inextricably," in Dorothy's opinion,[71] and was now, over Jimmy's protests, about to join the Communist party.

"The atmosphere of this place reminds me of suffrage campaigns," Dorothy wrote to Red in Berlin. "Discomfort and enthusiasm." Moscow itself, said Dorothy, looked "entirely different than I thought. Rather straggly and shabby like a small town, rather like Zagreb, or any Slavic-Austrian provincial city, with sudden wonders of towers, and spires, and domes." At bottom the city was "as puritan and pure as Sauk Center. There's an unquenchable social settlement house smell about it — carries me back to my glowing youth."[72] Dorothy was not at all perturbed to relate that nearly everyone she had met in Moscow, Soviets and visitors alike, had asked her about Red. But she had refused to discuss their relationship, smiling and answering only that "Mr. Lewis" was in Berlin, writing. She walked through the streets with her interpreters, pausing to interview "housemaids, droshky drivers, artists and intellectuals," asking them serious questions that they couldn't answer — "What is a communist?" "What do you mean by *bourgeois?*"[73] — and thinking, all the time, about Red: "You say, 'I can't believe you can go on liking me among surroundings so stirring.' I say: Perhaps I am a little glad to have come away like this, to know, without any touch of your hands, or sound or sight of you, how you live in me, and *are* me. This comfort and this quietness."[74]

"I can see you," Red wrote to Dorothy on November 7, the day of the Moscow anniversary celebrations, "beige-suited and defiantly spectacled, swinging about from office to office, learning seventy things a second."[75] He was writing well, and drinking little. "You would have given me at least a D.S.O.," he reported, "if you could have seen me refusing cocktails at Frau Valentin's tea. . . . I suppose I'll break out in gum-chewing or an admiration for André Gide or something."[76] These were the notes of promise, the warm, adoring thoughts that helped ease Dorothy's mind about the future. This was "Hal when he's himself."[77]

"I can never tell you," Red wrote to Dorothy in his letter of November 27, "— indeed, I doubt if ever, in the moments of the utmost gloomy frankness, I could [even] tell myself — quite how I have missed you. After having been brought very near to the black gates of madness and death, and to what is kin to madness, a sense of complete futility, I found you, and I began to live again — no, not *again,* but for the first time in my life!"[78] He told her he would join her in Moscow as soon as he had reached some natural break in his book. In the meantime, there were rumors of a revolution in Rumania, and he issued orders: "You're to let it revolute by itself. . . . Let Fodor go."[79] And on November 28 he sent a cable: "Fifty thousand words done and cannot endure longer without you. Leaving for Moscow tomorrow."[80] Red arrived in Russia to a hero's welcome. His works were popular in the Soviet Union, and he was greeted at the station by a brass band and a delegation of writers. There was an address by the chairman of the Soviet Society for Cultural Relations, and the inevitable invitation to make a speech. Why had Mr. Lewis come to Moscow?

"To see Dorothy," he replied.

But what was the purpose of his trip? What had he come to see? "Dorothy," was the answer. "Just Dorothy."[81]

"Why else should I have married him," Dorothy asked many years later, "considering my own position when we met, except because of that pull of his genius and my faith in his almost agonized protestations, at times, that he *needed* me?"[82] Red joined her in Moscow at a time when she needed *him,* in truth. On November 21 Rayna Prohme, Jimmy Sheean's leftist fiancée, had died suddenly of a cerebral hemorrhage. Dorothy had nursed her in her final hours and "risen out of the chaos" to comfort Jimmy.

"I did not know her until then except in the most superficial way," Jimmy wrote. "I had no notion of her indomitable courage, no concept of the grain or texture of her character, no remote idea of the heights to which she could rise."[83] Privately, she was desolate. She was frightened. "It is dreadful, Hal," she wrote to Red, "to die alone in a beastly hotel room. . . . And I've wanted all day to run home to you, because it scared me."[84] She had followed Rayna Prohme's "absurd little coffin . . . all the way out to the crematorium," walking "five weary, icy miles, on cobblestones."[85] It was snowing, and she had only a thin blue cape to wrap around her shoulders as the bells of a nearby monastery rang in mourning for a girl she hardly knew.

"I want to come home," Dorothy repeated. "I am home-sick. I am Hal-sick."[86] It didn't matter about her career. She would find her way. She would quit her job when she got back to Berlin. She and Red would go south, to France or Italy, while Red finished *Dodsworth* — to "some village," Red had suggested, "where we could be outdoors when we weren't writing, and where there was color, outdoor cafes, 'native costumes.' "[87] Perhaps Dorothy would write a book herself. She would turn her Russian articles into a book. "But

I'd really rather grow peaches," she confided, "and raise Lesbia to regard the world with gustoish laughter. (How do you make an adjective of *gusto*? Gustic? Gusty?)" [88]

"Let me believe that one can grow in wisdom!" Dorothy cried to Joseph Bard.

> Let me believe that experience can bring an irony of mind to protect me from too great hurts again. . . . I will still make a life for myself that has sense, and content, and beauty. I say, though, I *will*. I pray with my heart and mind that I will be for Hal what he needs. Because he is a good person, as I know goodness. He is the most incredibly good person I have ever known. I am not good enough for him. He shames me, by his love for me. And I am certain, with a deep certainty, that he has saved my life. . . . So don't be afraid that I am not going to give him all I can, all I have; *all* there is. . . . And tear up this letter, which is very sincere, however unwise. [89]

To Hal she pledged her love and the promise of her loyalty: "You, beloved, furnish the passion. I shall try to understand." She would marry him "so gladly," she said,

> with the old marriage service, for better or worse in sickness in health and forsaking all others — until death do us part. . . .
>
> Because in swearing this to you I swear it to something else. To a life-ideal. To the belief in loyalty, to the belief in comradeship, to the conviction that nothing comes of any human relationship except through the sacrifice of the unimportant. . . . In the end, Hal, it is as my friend that I think of you clearest, love you best. My comrade. Not that I belong to you or you to me but that we two together belong to something bigger than either of us. . . .
>
> Ah, my friend! I see you with your torn-open eyes, your face scarred as though with flames, your long-legged body leaning against the wind, the pain in you, the sweetness in you, the mad anger in you. . . . Hal, I do not want to touch you. Hal, I do not want to speak. . . . I only want to see you . . . to feel you are there . . . to know you are in the world, somehow breathing into me power without divesting yourself of it, somehow receiving from me strength and thereby increasing mine. Hal! Hal! [90]

IN the spring of 1928 they went to Italy. Having completed her Russian series, Dorothy surrendered her post at the *Public Ledger* (it was "more of a wrench than I supposed," she said),[91] closed the flat in Berlin, and set off to find a house in the sun where she and Red could write in peace.

"I'm going to have months and months of doing *nothing* except getting younger and healthier," she wrote to Joseph Bard. "And then we are going to tackle the U.S.A. together again. I confess to some apprehension at the prospect, but thank heavens, we won't be marooned there — we can always come away when it gets too bad."[92] Red's divorce would not be final until April, and in the meantime he continued to deny publicly that he was engaged to marry anyone. Privately he and Dorothy were planning a May wedding in London, followed by a long honeymoon spent traveling around the British Isles in a caravan. They had bought the trailer already, for two thousand dollars; it was waiting for them in England.

"My sense of propriety is entirely met by the idea that our first house together should be one on wheels!"[93] Dorothy wrote to Rose Lane, while she joked to Red that she was "going to turn domestic. . . . And occasionally go to Tibet."[94]

In Italy, after days of looking through "deserted casas" — "and how deserted!" said Dorothy. "And how deserted! I, too, would desert them"[94] — they took a lease on a small house in the gardens of the Villa Galotti at Cape Posillipo, near Naples. It was really "nothing but a crenelated tower," Dorothy told her sister, Peggy, "which rises sheer above the Mediterranean. . . . Down below is a sort of pediment wider than the tower itself, in which gardeners or somebody live; we never see them, although occasionally we hear the gurgles of their innumerable babies." They were attended by "a fat chef in a high wide hat" and a diminutive Austrian maid named Elsa, who was "terribly scornful of the Italians" and ran about the house in a state of perpetual indignation ("These Italians, they steal like crows. Would you believe it, that gardener's wife has stolen a cake of kitchen soap! Would you believe it!").[96] For six weeks Red continued his work on *Dodsworth*, while Dorothy expanded her Russian articles into a book-length manuscript. Thanks largely to Red's connections, she had secured "a corking good contract" with Henry Holt in New York,[97] and in her spare time labored over a translation of Lion Feuchtwanger's satirical verses, *PEP,* which Ben Huebsch had commissioned for the Viking Press.

"Some of the rhymes are astonishing," Dorothy reported. "In fact an adequate preface to the entire volume would be the couplet":

This book as art
Ain't worth a ----[98]

"In the afternoon the sun shines on this promontory," she went on, "and it is all gold and rose-colored. . . . Outside . . . is a big terrace on which one can pace up and down and regard the sea and Naples — a sort of roof garden, with palms in pots, and wicker chairs." She felt "magnificent."[99] There were only two or three drunken scenes during the whole time Red was with her (one of them, unfortunately, played out in the company of Joseph Bard and Eileen Agar, who were visiting Italy at the same time).[100] Later Red dedicated *Dodsworth* to Dorothy, and she appeared in it as the pacific, life-saving Edith Cortright, "a woman of 'spaciousness' "[101] whom Sam Dodsworth encounters at the close of the story. Words she had spoken to Red at Posillipo turned up in the manuscript and haunted Dorothy to the end of her life: "Have I remembered to tell you today that I adore you?"

On March 15 the *New York American* announced in its morning edition that Sinclair Lewis would marry Dorothy Thompson as soon as his divorce was final. On March 17 Red denied the rumors to the Associated Press.[102] One month later Grace Lewis was granted her divorce in Reno, and on April 23 Red left the Villa Galotti to prepare for the wedding in London. He was arranging everything himself, somewhat to Dorothy's confusion.

"As both of us are divorced," Red reported, "we can't be married in a pukka church, so the actual tying is [to be] done at the registrar's office."[103] A religious ceremony would follow at the Savoy Chapel. "I've talked to the verger and one of the clergy," he informed Dorothy, ". . . and Monday I'll see 'em again and try to fix [the] hour for marriage, then begin to invite any kings and queens who are in town."[104] Dorothy herself had submitted only a modest guest list: she wanted some newspaper friends to be there, as well as a colleague or two from suffrage days and a pair of "female cousins . . . sweet and English and unimportant." She was impatient to have it done.

"I want to come to you," she wrote to Red from the villa, "and I think I ought to help a little on this wedding."[105] She peered out over the bay toward Naples and reflected on the dreamlike quality of her life:

It's odd that I find suddenly that marrying you is frightfully important. I have felt so married to you for months. And yet — now, suddenly, it seems as though this nine months were only one long day: a holiday which began when you kissed me at Rowohlt's in Potsdam; as though we walked home then, by a long way 'round; a path that went over tall cliffs beside a wild ocean, and through gracious lanes with fat, sappy trees; as though we stopped in a clear room for tea, walked on a little farther through funny streets of people gibbering an unknown tongue, where golden cupolas peeked over crenelated walls, and then — when we were sweetly tired — slept in a little room with a stone floor, in a tower above a swishing sea. And now it's morning and another day: with Vesuvius's smoke blowing in quite the right direction.

But I'm greedy and want yesterday back, to live all over again.[106]

She spent the last days before her marriage trying to lose weight. She had grown "round-faced" and "hefty," and by her own description was "ever so faintly — please agree faintly — sear." At one point she "went three days with nothing to eat except oranges and boiled grass. But today at suppertime," she reported to Red, "I had such a roaring headache and felt so sick that I had a tiny piece of veal and some asparagus."[107] Meanwhile, news of her engagement had been confirmed in the newspapers, and according to her sister, Peggy, caused "a furor" in the United States.[108] At a time when a fundamentalist minister in Virginia, made livid by the success of *Elmer Gantry,* had invited Sinclair Lewis to "come down and be lynched," it was thought to be significant that Dorothy Thompson was the divorced daughter of a Methodist preacher.[109] The story even got into the *New York Times* that the appearance of *Elmer Gantry* had "wrecked Miss Thompson's fondest ambition." She had "yearned . . . to write a novel unveiling religious shams," the *Times* affirmed, but after reading *Elmer Gantry* she concluded that her future husband had said it all.[110] In Hamburg, New York, Marguerite Jarvis, Dorothy's favorite playmate from childhood, heard the news of her engagement over the radio.

"To say I was surprised and excited was putting it mildly," wrote Marguerite, who knew the works of Sinclair Lewis and had this advice for Dorothy: "Swat your future husband for me, and tell him there are a few back doors on 'Main Street' that he didn't peek in. I suppose you have heard that until you get sick of it."[111] It seems not to have occurred to Dorothy until she arrived in London that she was going to be famous — or, rather, that being famous was going to be unlike anything she had ever experienced. On the fourteenth of May, 1928, she stepped out of St. Martin's Registry Office in Henrietta Street and faced a row of cameras for the first time from the celebrity's side. She was wearing a blue silk suit from Chanel, "a charmeuse coat," and a wide-brimmed hat,[112] and "every flashbulb," so Jimmy Sheean thought, "must have been in some respect like a notification of things to come."[113]

The civil ceremony had been performed in the presence of Red's English publisher, Jonathan Cape, and the church service that followed was remembered by all of the guests as a curious, only distantly religious affair, performed by the Reverend Hugh D. Chapman and consisting mainly of an exhortation to Red to write more books.

"It was a rigmarole," said Anita Loos, who attended the wedding with her husband, John Emerson, "a lot of hocus-pocus, all done in deadly earnest, with the preacher shouting at the top of his lungs to drown out the starlings who were making an ungodly racket on the Thames embankment."[114] Luncheon followed at a restaurant in the Savoy, where Red "addressed the assembly as if they were jute merchants and he were reviewing the situation in the jute trade throughout the British Empire."[115] Dorothy, meanwhile, was getting ready for her caravan honeymoon, and a bright, smart, up-for-anything tone had entered all of her writing and conversation:

> What can you carry in a caravan? Bacon and butter, beer and wine, oranges and bread, cakes and beans, olives and jam, honey and eggs, jugs and plates, cups and forks, books and paper and pencils and ink. . . . In short, everything which a civilized human being wants, if his wife knows how to cook, to make a bed, and to wash dishes without afterward smelling of them. And is that possible?
>
> But of course! Out of that little oaken chest of drawers, she takes a white pot of cold cream with a French mark. She rubs it thick on her hands and pulls on rubber gloves over them. That is all. And back goes the pot and shut goes the drawer. Everything is possible if you only keep ship-shape.[116]

This was unbelievably chirpy stuff coming from a woman who had just interviewed the leaders of the Soviet Union. Louis Untermeyer, an old friend of Dorothy's from Vienna, saw her after her wedding and reported that she was "radiant," mesmerized by her husband's "violent loquacity" and paying "the same rapt attention to his least considered disposals as she would have given to a world-shaking oracle." Untermeyer detected "concealed tensions."

"Isn't it good," said Dorothy, "to see two people who suffered so in their previous marriages now so happy with each other?" There was no pause before she went on: "You don't have to answer. The real answer is that we needed each other. Of course, now he needs me more than I need him; don't you, Hal?"

"Indubitably, my dear," answered Sinclair Lewis in his best mock-British voice. "And I'm going to go on needing you until you can't stand me."[117]

With that they bumped off into the countryside. "I need a collaborator," Dorothy wrote to Rose Lane. "I really think that's why I go around marrying. I am sure I saw in Josef Bard a creative talent to express my own creative instinct and will, and with quite glorious zeal devoted myself to making for him the atmosphere and mood to write my books for me. . . . Now, for a change, I have married me a demon, who writes as never I could write, but . . . from an angle ever so foreign: all his values topsy-turvy from mine." They would be on the road until August, she announced. Then they would come back to New York. They would find an apartment in Manhattan and a house in the country with great lawns around it.

"And *my* work," said Dorothy. "What? How? Where? . . . I feel as though I should never write anything again, neither reports on Russia nor sonnets to record the soul's travail, the soul's ironic victories. I cook, my dear, in the caravan. But I cook well. 'What's worth doing at all —' my father used to say."[118]

"Where does the light of the candle go when it is blown out?" Rose asked mournfully when she read Dorothy's honeymoon letters. That spring Rose had left Albania to look after her aging parents on their farm in the Ozarks, and she wondered now why Dorothy, who had no such daughterly obligations to fulfill, should voluntarily have surrendered her freedom — her career, her future, her whole identity, as Rose saw it: "I knew you when you were young and proud and gay, and true to yourself as easily and instinctively as the compass is true to the north. . . . My God, Dorothy. . . . You have all the gifts, and are you going to be wrecked and ruined by a humility which in your blindness you sincerely feel — a humility absolutely false, a damnable lie? A thousand times I have said in my soul that if I could kill Joseph Bard I would do it."[119] But she put this answer aside and instead sent Dorothy a note of congratulation.

"I may as well refrain from thrusting upon you a counsel not asked for," said Rose. "Who am I — whose memories of experiencing it are so dim that I hardly remember I have them — to send opinions about [marriage] to you? . . . Be happy, my dear. I, too, am a good cook. Be happy, and come home to a country which may not quite be God's own (since we have abolished God) but is most certainly the greatest country on His footstool. Come home to your house in green lawns. And perhaps we shall talk there — if I am not too shy." [120]

Shy? said Dorothy, surprised: "What do you mean *shy?* Neither of us will be more shy with each other than such nice people as we are normally are." [121] She had "fallen forever out of that love which grows into the flesh of another." The world was "wide and beautiful, on Broadway and in Albania." [122]

"Did I say that one reason I'm glad I'm going home," she concluded, ". . . is that then — as I dream — you'll come and stay with me a *long time,* and we'll talk . . . and talk . . . and talk." [123]

PART TWO
Fusion

Hammer and tongs, hammer and tongs.
When a suffragette marries she'll right no more wrongs;
She'll sit by the fireside, where she belongs,
And instead of parading she'll sing cradle songs.
For the married career she secretly longs,
And if given the chance will drop hammer and tongs.

≡

Antisuffrage doggerel

In other wars they used to sing
Of the girl he left behind.
She fanned herself with a turkey wing
And wept her poor eyes blind.

The girl today nor fans nor weeps,
She has no time for pining.
She crops her hair and dons the pants
And undertakes the mining.

O 'ware you well, ye Kaiser Bill,
And 'ware ye Hunnish horde.
For the hand that used to wield a fan
Today can wield a sword.

≡

Dorothy Thompson,
1918

6

CHAPTER

THEY found not one house but two, on opposite sides of a wooded valley in the hills of central Vermont. There were old stone fences, as Dorothy wanted, sweeping lawns, "birches, tamaracks, maples and spruce," "run-down orchards," "delicious air," and, from the front of the larger of the two buildings, a "grand long" view of Mount Ascutney.[1] About two miles to the west was the village of Barnard, and south of that was Woodstock, the quintessential Vermont town, whose steepled churches, white clapboard houses, and famous covered bridge had not yet been washed and prettified by a flood of Rockefeller money. For three hundred acres and two authentic farmhouses, each more than a hundred years old, Sinclair Lewis paid precisely ten thousand dollars. It was the first home he had ever owned, and it was called Twin Farms.[2]

The hunt for the place in the country was given top priority when Dorothy and Red arrived in New York, on August 27, 1928. They stayed in the city for only a few days, while Red looked after various business matters and Dorothy made her first appearances as a Literary Wife. Yes, she told reporters at the pier, they had had a wonderful honeymoon. Yes, she had cooked for her husband every day. Yes, she was going to call herself Mrs. Lewis. "After all," she said, "a woman takes her name from her father. I can see no reason for annoyance at taking her name also from her husband."[3] In the meantime, she had never lived under Prohibition and was scared to death of "bathtub gin." What did the boys advise?[4]

The parties started immediately, first in Manhattan and later in Riverside, Connecticut, where Dorothy and Red traveled shortly to stay with Red's American publisher, Alfred Harcourt. Here

Dorothy — "little Dorothy," as Red kept calling her[5] — met some of the smartest figures of New York's literary elite: Bernard De Voto, Harrison Smith, Edna Ferber, Dorothy Parker, and those two cynical, woman-hating confederates, George Jean Nathan and H. L. Mencken. Mencken hoped to write off Dorothy as an aberration, "a hearty gal with red cheeks,"[6] "bosky" and "of considerable bulk," "like a Kansas milkmaid." But privately she got under his skin.

"How do you like her?" he asked Charles Angoff, one of his sidekicks and his future biographer.

"I think she's nice," Angoff replied.

"That's no way to describe a grown woman. No grown women are nice."

"I like her," said Angoff.

"I don't know her too well myself," said Mencken. "But I've heard about her. She frightens me. . . . She looks like Hindenburg as a young man."

"I still like her."

"You're stubborn."[7]

In September Dorothy sent Mencken a jocular postcard from Plymouth, Vermont, the birthplace of Calvin Coolidge, as she drove with Red and her sister, Peggy, in search of the perfect house: "Stopping in this idyllic spot today we bared our heads and in your behalf as well as our own, sent up a prayer for the welfare of our Pres. and the success of the Party."[8] Before leaving New York, she and Red had rented an apartment for the winter, a duplex at 37 West Tenth Street; it would not be available before November, however, and in the meantime they wanted to call on their landlord, Lyndow H. Connett, who had a place in Vermont where he spent his summers. When they saw Connett's two houses and the land that surrounded them, they knew that they had found what they were looking for. The papers for Twin Farms were signed on the spot, and within twenty-four hours, to everyone's amazement, Mr. Connett had left for a comfortable retirement in Florida. The whole transaction was so quick and so unbelievably simple as to seem foreordained.[9]

The older of the two houses at Twin Farms, the one on the west side of the valley, had been built in 1796 and was fully furnished when Dorothy and Red moved into it. "It had everything the city dweller wants on his precarious adventures in the country," said Jimmy Sheean, whom Dorothy invited to join them while they set up house, "bells and baths and furnaces and all, but at the same time it did not *look* like something run up for the summer folk, the *villeggiatura*. It really did look like a Vermont farmhouse, which was, historically and architecturally and I dare say spiritually, just what it was. . . . It had not been improved, embellished or amended in any particular." [10] Across the ravine, at the crest of the valley and visible through the trees in winter, was the second, larger building, called the Chase House in 1928 and derelict when Dorothy and Red first saw it. At one time this had been the showpiece of the property, and immediately Dorothy set about to restore it to its rightful condition.

She commenced remodeling at once — "without an architect," as she liked to point out, "and without a contractor, carpenters working from pencilled drawings that I made." [11] At first it was a question mainly of painting and papering, strengthening roofs and floors and walls, replacing windows, and renovating an old barn that stood at right angles to the building. Red wanted there to be "one great room" in which "various persons might do various things without interfering with one another. That is, at one end there might be a poker game and at the other end a seminar, without a clash of interest, without even an annoyance." So the barn was gutted and connected to the main house by means of an elegant, "obscurely wrong" loggia of Dorothy's devising. [12] The "Big Room" became the focus of living and entertainment at Twin Farms, while its reconstruction and other renovations cost Red nearly twice as much as he had spent originally on the purchase of both houses. [13]

From the windows of the Chase House — already people were calling it Dorothy's House — one looked out over ledges, slopes, and an ambling, gracious lawn toward the southern end of the Green Mountains. Here, at the bottom of the terrace, Dorothy tended to her flowers. She planted more than three thousand bulbs at Twin Farms that first year [14] and laid the design for what was to become one of Vermont's most beautiful and most expertly maintained formal gardens, a dazzling arrangement of roses and dahlias and delphinium and sweet peas, spread out along graceful pathways and framed by a splendid perennial border. It was in conference over the garden, in fact, that Dorothy first came in contact with "authentic" Vermont life. The entire state at that time had no more than three hundred and fifty thousand residents ("which makes it only slightly greater in population," Red observed, "than that not very distinguished community, Jersey City"), [15] and the inhabitants were a stable, famously cryptic folk, not known for their lowliness. When

Dorothy started giving orders to the handymen she had inherited from Mr. Connett, she was swiftly put in her place.

"Woman," said one of the hired men ("more man than hired," Dorothy remembered), "you think you can go through me just like you went through Russia."[16] She had arranged to employ a cook and housekeepers from the village, but the women who "did" for her in Vermont "were not in the very least 'servants.' " They drove their own cars; they called her by her first name; they sent their sisters or their daughters or their nieces to work for them if they were too busy to come themselves; and somehow they managed to remain as inscrutable as they were congenially familiar and polite. Dorothy "had been accustomed to that 'gracious lady' treatment of Vienna, Budapest and Berlin," Jimmy Sheean pointed out,[17] and it was months, even years, before she got used to the tone of Vermont. Trying to make conversation with Mr. Quimby, her chief gardener, she asked him one day what he thought of President Coolidge, and he answered simply, "There's a hell of a lot of Coolidges ain't in the White House."[18] She had no idea what he meant, but it was the kind of remark she came to adore.

She was putting the last touches on the galley proofs of *The New Russia* that fall, while Red finished *Dodsworth* and Jimmy Sheean, starry-eyed, hung around the house writing something — he could never remember in later years what it was. "I saw between Dorothy and Red a genuine affection," said Jimmy, "which, in a more tepid manner, spilled over upon me and made me glad to be there. . . . They had asked me to stay more or less forever, and I almost did." It was an election year; Herbert Hoover was running for President against Al Smith, "promising not only a chicken in every pot . . . but silk stockings on every leg." At night, Jimmy recalled, "we sat by the fire and roared with uncontrollable laughter" as the candidates delivered their campaign speeches over the radio: "They spoke every night, and they were unbelievably funny. I do not think anybody since then has touched their ineffable silliness."[19]

Life was cheerful that autumn, life was fun, and the world, to Dorothy, was still "entrancing."[20] To prove it she only needed to open her windows and look out at the hills of Vermont, "impossibly beautiful" in the October sunlight, "wildly, insanely, cock-eyed lovely," in Ramon Guthrie's words, "like a couple of million drunken rainbows in a brawl." As neophytes to a Vermont autumn, the inhabitants of Twin Farms were given to shouting and whooping and leaping out of chairs, telephoning their friends to urge them to drop what they were doing and come look at the view. When Guthrie moved to nearby Hanover, New Hampshire, to take a job as a professor of French literature at Dartmouth, a kind of rivalry developed between the two households.

"Come over here and look at this, quick!" Red would cry over the phone.

"You come over here!" Guthrie would reply. "My country is even better than yours!" Then both would holler in unison, "Liar! It can't be!" and hang up.[21]

"I really love it," Dorothy wrote H. R. Knickerbocker, her successor at the *Public Ledger* in Berlin, "and it's the only spot in this country that I *do* love. . . . It's the only place that reconciles me to being in America."[22]

She was finding it even more difficult than she had feared to read-just to life in the United States. It was "a sterile country," she complained, "crass" compared to Europe and "fundamentally hostile to women."[23] There is no doubt that Dorothy's attitude was at least partly affected, born of insecurity and a cynicism that was all but mandatory among her husband's friends. She wanted to keep working if she could, and Red wanted it, too. At least he said he did. When they got back to New York in November, he arranged for Dorothy to have lunch with a number of important editors,[24] and in the meantime she took free-lance assignments from the *Ledger-Post* syndicate. But she had no reputation as a reporter on American affairs, and she was very much aware that she would have to build one from scratch.

"The paper wants me to do special stories and columns or something . . . ," she remarked to Knickerbocker. "But I have only queer introverted ideas in my head that come out in the form of unsalable fiction. I've started on a history of the woman's movement (Mauve Decade sort of stuff) 1910–1920, but find myself so fundamentally out of sympathy with it that I wonder whether I can do the book." She went on for a while about her plans and her houses and her neighbors — "George Seldes is living across the street from our N.Y. flat," she observed — then asked outright, "Do they still remember me in Berlin? Damn it all, Knick, I'm not yet quite adjusted to not having a regular job. I miss you all like the devil." She had discovered, however, that it was an easy matter for "Mrs. Sinclair Lewis" to arrange public appearances, and recently ("God forgive me") she had embarked on a lecture tour of the Midwest, talking to women's clubs about Russia, Germany, art, theater, and European politics in general.

"I thought it would be a good way to see the country," Dorothy protested, "[but I] find the country's all alike, and one sees chiefly Pullman sleepers." The work itself, she maintained, was "easy, remunerative, boring and demoralizing."[25] But she was good at it — very good at it — and she was going to see an awful lot of Pullman sleepers over the next several years. The following autumn, just after the New York stock market crash, she stopped overnight at Terre Haute, Indiana, and notified her husband, "You may tell the world that Zenith and Main Street haven't changed any unless possibly for the worse." Dorothy was impressed most strongly and most unfavorably by "the cheapness of all standards, the shoddiness of all values" in a land full of Woolworths and Piggly Wigglys:

> But more than that [she wrote Red] — there is as far as I can see not a single public place in town where you can meet anyone for a quiet talk. . . . The houses are atrocious. The town still burns lots of soft coal, evidently, and most of the houses are painted a dingy gray turned alm black with smoke. . . . There is no standardization of architecture whatever. The streets are a hodgepodge of ugly frame houses, also flimsily built and cheap. In fact cheapness is the main thing.
>
> And yet everyone seems contented. After my lecture yesterday a lot of women came up to speak to me and almost all of them said, "Well, aren't we lucky to be living in America." . . .
>
> Darling — I am so lonely. This is a lonely country. It is so Goddamned empty. I am turning mystic. Surely there is something different in the very air of a city where civilized people have lived, worked, dreamed, loved, and enjoyed civilized pleasures for hundreds of years. Living must produce some sort of radio-activity which lingers in the atmosphere. I begin to believe in ghosts. Gentle ghosts which keep one company in ancient towns. Here there are none.[26]

She might not have been so depressed by "America" — indeed she might not have gone lecturing at all — if her life in New York had turned out to be more stimulating or at least more scintillating than it did. The duplex on West Tenth Street, in the heart of Greenwich Village, had been furnished with Dorothy's own belongings, "the accumulated loot of her eight years in Europe,"[27] and she had even transported Hedwig, her German maid, from Berlin to New York in anticipation of an elegant and civilized existence.

"Dorothy expected something far more brilliant, more of-the-

great-world, than she got," said the ubiquitous Jimmy Sheean, who
was now living around the corner, on Fourth Street. "She certainly
must have expected . . . that life with the most famous of American
writers, in the largest of American cities, on an income which even
for the United States was really large, would have had some elements
of variety, glitter, change and excitement. Not at all."[28] Red had
started drinking again as soon as they returned from the country,
and when he was not holed up in some hotel or other — he needed
solitude and "quiet" for his work, he said — he filled the house with
card-playing drunks and total strangers, whom Dorothy might find
at any hour of the day or night raiding the cupboard or sprawled
unconscious on the floor. It was the era of "wonderful nonsense,"
in Westbrook Pegler's famous phrase, the last blast of the Jazz Age,
and the abuse of alcohol was as much a part of the literary scene in
New York as smart-aleck novels and caustic reviews. At the Algon-
quin Hotel, almost daily, Robert Benchley, Dorothy Parker, Alexander Woollcott, and a dozen other wits and quipsters drank their
lunches and honed their jokes. Scott Fitzgerald passed out in taxis;
Ernest Hemingway gripped "queers" by the throat. At the end of
1928 Dorothy characterized the whole New York experience as
"hell," and the memory of her earlier happiness at Twin Farms
seemed bitter indeed. A Christmas holiday at Hot Springs in Virginia — a time of "inexpressible boredom," said Dorothy, "sustained only by my love for Hal" — left her "aching for a society in
which I feel at home." Red had decided that they would go to Florida
for a while in February 1929:

> [We] are off day after tomorrow [wrote Dorothy], because Hal is
> "tired." I agree, because he has been drinking terribly again and only
> some such trip will make him stop it, but my heart is heavy and re-
> bellious. My God — Florida mud flats, and all next summer in Ver-
> mont! Not one enjoyable dinner party the whole winter; not one
> evening at the opera; not one concert, not a single human relation-
> ship — Can't bear it. I *won't* bear it. I had rather go and work in
> someone's kitchen than lead this sort of life, chased, pursued, ha-
> rassed by fear's fear. . . . Oh, my God, I really don't know whether
> I love or hate him — but tonight I was *bored* with him.
>
> I say to myself, "You are totally unimportant and you are married
> to a man of genius — if you give up your life to making him happy
> it is worth it."

But it isn't! It isn't! I can really do nothing for him. He is like a vampire — he absorbs all my vitality, all my energy, all my beauty — I get incredibly dull. If ever I begin to talk well he interrupts the conversation. . . . He is completely without consideration of me, yet he protests with the greatest tenderness that he loves me, and it is true: he does. He insults people in the house which is mine as well as his — the house where I am hostess. He invites strangers to dinner and goes away and leaves them. All social finesse, all delicacy and gaiety of intercourse, all subtlety of contact — all the things I prize in the world, all beautiful civilized manners and forms, he violates. If I cross him in anything; if even I irritate him by weeping, out of sheer nerves and exhaustion, he yells at me that I am driving him crazy, that I have designs to make him feel like a scoundrel, and he never fails to tell me that I am just like Gracie. He thinks then that when he says he is sorry our relationship is the same. But it is not . . . too much has been piled upon too much; I am inexpressibly weary and sore. I want to get away, somewhere, forever.[29]

It was going to be the story of her marriage, an endless repetition of the on-again, off-again, up-and-down shivaree they had sung to each other in Berlin. It had nothing to do, at least to Dorothy's mind, with the love she felt for Red. It was his "demon" she had to fear, his "illness, . . . rooted in psychic complications too deeply bedded ever to be eradicated."[30] There was no treatment for alcoholism, then or later, that could be effective without the alcoholic's wholehearted willingness to be helped. Alcoholics Anonymous would not be founded for another six years, and in any case Dorothy was still pinned to the notion of her husband's "genius": she would never have consented to think of Sinclair Lewis as just another drunk. Along with everybody else in the sloppy, suicidal world of late 1920s literary society, she accepted as normal a certain amount of pandemonium and appalling behavior, and for a time she even tried to beat Red at his own game, drinking like a sailor and adopting a hearty, entirely artificial air of bonhomie among his blistered friends. For all her doubts and the agony brought on by drink, and despite their "crazy fights"[31] and lengthy separations, Dorothy and Red were very much a couple in those days. Something always came along, as it usually does in an alcoholic marriage, to draw them together when the panic got too real.

The first thing that rescued them was a case of plagiarism. In October 1928 Dorothy's *New Russia* was published to excellent reviews (not a single one of the critics failed to mention that the author was also "Mrs. Sinclair Lewis"), and one month later Theodore Dreiser issued a book of his own about the Soviet Union. He called it *Dreiser Looks at Russia*, but Dorothy thought it would have been better titled *Dreiser Looks at the Evening Post*,[32] because it contained whole passages (she counted three thousand words in all) that had been copied directly from her book and reproduced without citation.[33] His biographers all agree that Dorothy was not mistaken in her conclusions: *Dreiser Looks at Russia* was "pieced together"[34] from different sources by secretaries and editors, and evidently Dreiser did not even read it carefully before publication.

"The old beast simply lifted paragraph after paragraph from my articles," Dorothy complained in a letter to Rose Lane. "I'm not speaking of material — we all got that where we could — but of purely literary expressions. And, of course, ideas."[35] When confronted with these charges, Dreiser first denied them and then "asserted that [Dorothy], in the course of talks with him in Russia, had obtained from him material later incorporated in her articles and book."[36] He began "a whispering campaign" to the effect that he and Dorothy had been lovers in Moscow, and that she, taking advantage of the intimate situation, had "purloined his *notes!!*" She was aghast: "*That* swine!"[37]

"As I recall it we only met two or three times," she told reporters in a carefully worded statement, "and then had merely casual conversations about what we'd seen and been doing. . . . Here are two books in which actual verbal passages of purely descriptive matter, literary passages, let us say, are identical. I protest against this, and have asked for an explanation, because I feel, even if Mr. Dreiser doesn't, that it puts one of us in a bad light."[38] She declined to sue him because, as she told Rose Lane, "I know too much about literary suits. It would simply be furnishing wisecrackers with something to wisecrack about, and it is clear that Dreiser will stoop to anything."[39] But if Dorothy wanted the incident forgotten, she hadn't counted on the reaction of her husband, who was "enraged beyond measure," stewing and storming and threatening action.

"To Red it seemed deliberate plagiarism," said Jimmy Sheean, "an insult to Dorothy and therefore an insult to himself, etc., etc. . . . Dorothy, who had a far more accurate view of the probabilities, never did think Dreiser had deliberately stolen her descriptive sentences. She merely thought, as we all did, that he ought to have been more careful — and that he ought to have read his book, at least, before signing his name to it."[40] Ultimately, there was enough of a scandal to entertain the press.

"The world will never know whether or not Dreiser lifted 3,000 words from a book written by Mrs. Lewis," said the *Minneapolis Tribune,* in a fairly typical comment, "and we suspect its indifference will be fully equal to its ignorance. . . . If guilty, there is at least one thing to be said in favor of Mr. Dreiser. When he is on the literary prowl, he shows at least a burglarious sense of values in that he steals his stuff from Mrs. and not from Mr. Lewis."[41] The dynamic of Dorothy's marriage actually went public in 1929, when she and Red took opposite sides of a published debate in the *Pictorial Review.* "Is America a Paradise for Women?" the magazine asked, and Red answered that it was, while Dorothy insisted that it wasn't. Her head was brimful of ideas about the country's imperfections; she was beginning to realize, too, that she could make herself heard over the din at West Tenth Street. At one dinner party, while Red sat under the table bellowing about the food and reciting from memory whole chapters of his books, Dorothy held forth calmly about the situation in Europe.[42] They were both talking at once, and it may have been as early as this that Red was first heard to explode: "The situation? The situation? God *damn* the situation!"[43]

"What *will* happen to them, Henry?" asked Sara Haardt, the teacher from Alabama who was soon to marry H. L. Mencken.

"No telling," said Mencken. "Red will drink and Dorothy will talk until they both go *meshuggah.* But you never know."[44]

After *Dodsworth* was published in the winter of 1929, the Lewises left New York and motored around Florida for nearly six weeks, starting out in Homosassa and moving on through Tampa, Winter Haven, Miami, and Palm Beach before Dorothy headed north for a lecture date and a visit with her sister in Pittsburgh. "I am trying to write fiction," she told Rose Lane, "and failing utterly. If only I really believed that it was important to express myself. But I am so sick, sick, SICK of people expressing themselves."[45] April found her in Quebec City, at the Château de Frontenac, hard at work on a series of articles about the effects of Prohibition in Canada. Then in May it was back to Vermont, where life went on very much as it had the previous year, with one exception: Red was planning a new book, a multigenerational novel about the American labor movement that he spoke about as his masterwork. Twin Farms was filled to bursting that summer with union officials and other experts on labor relations, as well as communists, socialists, politicians, and businessmen: Red never wrote anything without researching it to the core. The purpose of good documentation, he always said, was "to know how much you can leave out,"[46] but with the labor novel he never got past his obsession with detail.

"Everybody except Red himself was desperately buckled down to the job of getting the novel written," said Ramon Guthrie, who came over frequently from Hanover and suspected that Red was in well over his head. Dorothy thought so, too, though for the moment she did not say so. She agreed with Guthrie that her husband had only one sustained political conviction — "politicos are scoundrels"[47] — and for a woman who lived and breathed social movements and the workings of statecraft, this was disconcerting. But she delighted in the company that Red's research gave her, and she made a strongly favorable impression on a number of his friends, among them Clarence Darrow, Carl Van Doren, the "labor journalist" Ben Stolberg, and Frances Perkins, who later became secretary of labor in the Roosevelt administration. Miss Perkins judged that Dorothy was "more interesting" than Red at this time.[48] She was right. Dorothy was in the front line of journalists and writers who sensed that the frantic tone of the 1920s was about to give way to a more thoughtful and social-minded literature. Letters were going political. For a while Dorothy and Ben Stolberg talked about starting a monthly magazine, a "journal of ideas" that would be, in Dorothy's words, "socio-critical" and "definitely high-brow."[49] While she pondered this idea, Red kept on drinking and one day turned up at a party in New York, where he asked a doctor of his acquaintance "how much danger was involved to a woman in her thirties having her first baby." The doctor replied that while it might be risky, it wasn't actually perilous, and Red declared, "Well, it looks like I'll have to get on my bicycle and pedal."[50]

Dorothy was pregnant by the time they left Twin Farms in the autumn. That was the second thing that rescued them.

DOROTHY'S pregnancy was trouble-free, and the birth of her son, when the time came, almost painless.[51] Until then, however, since she had never had a baby "or anything" (as she put it to Jimmy Sheean),[52] she was anxious enough about it not to want to stray too far from New York, where she enjoyed the services of a doctor who gave her "confidence and peace of mind."[53] After a final swing through the Midwest on an autumn lecture tour, she settled down on West Tenth Street to await her confinement.

"Whether it's a girl or a boy," she warned Red, "I *won't* have him or her brought up in this country. I *won't*. . . . She said with a flash of the old spirit."[54]

"I'm sure there's no need to worry, my dear," Rose Lane assured Dorothy from her hideout in the Ozarks. "Thousands of women have thousands of babies at thirty-six, and if one is thinking of danger, what else do all of us live in every moment of our lives? Nevertheless I do worry, because you are so precious to me — and even forgetting me, so precious, so valuable, as a person, as an end-in-itself. You have always trusted fate, and the nettles have been soft to your grasp; and I truly believe they always will be."[55] At the end of 1929, looking for magazine assignments and relief from boredom, Rose arrived in New York and took the opportunity to get drunk with Red. She was meeting him for the first time, and she enjoyed herself so immensely that she was able to tell Dorothy, "Darling, you are going to affront all the literature of the ages by triumphantly combining great beauty with the happy ending. . . . My objections to this marriage are hereby withdrawn *in toto;* I'm *for* it!"[56] Rose had caught the Lewises on an upswing, buoyed by the prospect of parenthood and, for the moment, infused with tenderness for each other.

"Do you know how dearly, how sweetly, how, sometimes, even terribly I love you?" Dorothy had written to Red not long before.[57] It was difficult for her to remember, in the good times, how bad the bad times were. It was hard enough in any case to resist a man who sent her such charming love notes. "I'm so lonely for you that I could howl," Red wrote one day. "Owwwwwwww!"[58] And telegrams: "WOULD SAY I ADORE YOU BUT WORD ADORE TOO BANAL."[59] And letters: "Now you look here young woman, I'll tolerate almost anything except your ever busting up with me. As a matter of fact I would like to make this entire letter simply this: Darling, darling, darling, darling, darling, darling, darling, darling, darling, darling, darling, darling, and so forth and so forth."[60] When she was on the road, especially, living in hotel rooms during the lecture season and reflecting on her marriage from a comfortable distance, Dorothy fell in love with Red all over again.

"When you spoke to me [on the telephone] this morning," she

wrote from Quebec City, "when I heard your voice, my heart sang. It sang: Hallo Hal, darling Hal, funny Hal, wonderful Hal, belovedest Hal, *my* Hal. It sang, 'How I'd like to kiss you, hold your dear face in my hands, love you —.' " She did not often get the chance to kiss him, she complained, she could not often hold his face in her hands — "because you move it away so quickly. Loving you is a bit like loving mercury."[61]

The truth of that statement was proved again at the beginning of 1930, when Red suddenly announced that they would spend the rest of the winter in California. There were "some questions about alimony to settle" with his ex-wife, in Reno,[62] and with that excuse he dragged Dorothy, five months pregnant, across the Continental Divide. The only consolation for Dorothy was the promise of a trip to San Francisco, a city she had always longed to see. But no sooner had she begun to enjoy herself there than Red whisked her away again, south to Monterey, where they rented a rose-covered cottage among "the rich, fashionable and dull Pebble Beach crowd."[63] Here Dorothy mingled with a maddening assortment of writers and golfers and *wives* who regarded her only as an appendage to Red, "the little woman" he had brought back with him from Europe.

"This place is filled with cypresses, polo ponies and morons," wrote Dorothy from Monterey.[64] If the landscape was "dramatic," and if the garden was "full of roses, mimosa, blossoming quinces, narcissi, etc.," the company she was forced to keep still bored her to distraction. She was "vegetating," she said, she was "loafing shamefully" along with everyone else: "Looking down on myself the other day I decided I should be snow-capped if this kept up — so I've gone on a diet of 1500 calories a day to keep myself from becoming too like the High Sierras."[65] While she worried about her weight and the course of her life she was reading *A Farewell to Arms* and confessed to being "astounded" by the experience. The book was "almost pure poetry," she declared: "whole passages sing in my brain."[66] She was not afraid to contend that if America ever produced a really great novelist, it would be in Hemingway's generation. In the meantime, she doubted that there were many great novelists anywhere.

"Thomas Mann is perhaps a great novelist," she had earlier written to Rose Lane. "I think Ford Madox Ford almost is — the most underrated writer living. Hal — my Hal — has the talent and the spirit to be, only he does not know enough."[67]

Her opinions were wasted, however, in Pebble Beach, where the chief entertainment under Prohibition was the cocktail party, and where Colonel Charles Lindbergh, by way of a practical joke, was busy spiking the Burgundy with bottles of Listerine.[68] Later Dorothy remarked that her main recollection of that winter was of "scooting around hairpin curves at three in the morning" while Red drove them home, "praying that [if] my own neck was broken the chee-ild would somehow survive."[69] By the time she and Red arrived in Los Angeles for a visit with Red's friends Bill and Helen Woodward, Dorothy had had enough. She told Red that she could not cope with another minute of this "vacation," and that she wanted to go back to New York.

"Yes," said Red, "you go. I'll follow." Dorothy left California in March, by herself, not knowing when she would see her husband again, and, in the circumstances, not caring much. Many years later she told Red's biographer, Mark Schorer, that "this was the point at which she knew that her marriage was not going to be a marriage after all, that she must protect herself in preparation for its collapse";[70] when Red joined her in New York later that spring, she did only what she could "to keep [him] from drinking himself to death."[71] Even when Michael Lewis[72] was born, on the morning of June 20, 1930, Red could not see his way to staying sober. There had been a party at West Tenth Street the night before — Dorothy's labor pains started over the punch bowl — and when Red took her uptown to the Woman's Hospital, the revelry kept on in their absence. Jimmy Sheean called on Dorothy the following day and found her "blooming — all pink and white and relieved," as much interested in the process of motherhood as she was in the baby himself. Red was nowhere in sight.

"Here we are," said Dorothy, "in the year 1930, with every possible advancement of science upon us in every conceivable field, and yet nothing whatsoever has been done to mitigate or diminish the boredom of childbirth. . . . What has been the practical use of all this progress through the centuries when a woman is faced with her fundamental and indeed quintessential function in the life of her species, which is to reproduce it? One might as well be a Bulgarian peasant inured to parturition in a furrow. I protest."

"When she ended up with 'I protest,' " Jimmy remembered, "we both laughed and she rang a bell. A nurse came in. Dorothy lifted an imperious and well-arched eyebrow. She really felt well that day. " 'Bring in the child,' she said."[73]

*　　*　　*

THE news of Michael Lewis's birth, according to Dorothy's friend H. R. Knickerbocker, spread around the world "like the war bulletins of drum-thumping Africans, and in less than no time it was impossible to get a rise out of anybody with the question, 'Did you hear the latest? Dorothy has —' 'Oh yes,' they all break in, 'it weighs eight pounds eleven ounces.' " But did Michael Lewis have his father's red hair, Knickerbocker asked — "Does he look like another great author?"[74]

She had received notes and telegrams from the great and near-great among writers on two continents: Edith Wharton, H. G. Wells, James Branch Cabell, Rebecca West. "He comes into a lonely world," said H. L. Mencken from his seat in Baltimore, "and must be taught to remember that he was born during the Hoover administration."[75] Dorothy laughed at the thought.

"The Michael whom you hail is red-headed," she answered Mencken when her son was a few weeks old, "has a mighty nose, a quivering nostril, a prodigious frown, a tremendous yell, and a charming grin. There is no question of his legitimacy."[76] To others she was not afraid to acknowledge that she felt a certain sense of unreality about Michael's very existence.

"It's been a strange, an incredibly strange year," she wrote from Twin Farms in October. "Looking back on it, it seems less an authentic experience than something read: a fantastic novel: but here I am at the end of it, with restored and all too blooming health and my boy who is too appallingly dear to me."[77] She was never less than effusive in her expressions of adoration for Michael: "They say the angel is 'like unto God.' . . . He is the most lovely thing that ever happened to me . . . the deepest joy I have ever had."[78] But she raised him from the start in a manner that owed more to money and perceived ideas than it did to tenderness, and that did not bear even the very faintest resemblance to her own warmly remembered childhood in Hamburg, New York.

"I want my boy to grow up at home in the great world," Dorothy wrote to Tish Irwin (who, with her husband, the writer Wallace Irwin, was appointed as guardian for Michael in the event of his parents' death), "not over-impressed by famous names or grand houses or family traditions, but not sneering at them, either, merely out of a sense of inferiority." She had exact hopes for Michael:

I don't want him to adore money, and neither do I want him brought up, as I was, to think that money is something disgraceful.

. . . I want him to be modern, that is to say, at home in his own age, and not frightened or paralyzed by it. . . . And teach him, Tish, if he ever comes into your hands, that no social, economic, or political system is eternal or worthy of profound reverence; that reverence should be preserved for life itself and for those human spirits who have made life more intense and luminous. . . . Tell my boy, if you have the opportunity, that this is a grand world, and that his mother never for an instant apologized for putting him into it.[79]

She went with the baby to Twin Farms as soon as she was well enough to travel; when they got there, she sent him to live in the old farmhouse with a team of nurses and attendants, while she and Red moved into the remodeled Chase House and filled it with summer guests. In fairness to Dorothy, it was Red who insisted on keeping Michael at a distance. He was busier than ever with the research (but not the writing) of his labor novel, and he "found the nursery atmosphere and the child's noise uncongenial."[80] As a father, Red "was inclined to pay a child a visit once every other day, . . . waggle a long finger at the baby's nose, and go away again."[81] He had already spent thirteen years ignoring one son, the lonely, golden-haired Wells Lewis, who stayed at Twin Farms that summer and got on his father's nerves terribly. Wells was "a beautiful and neurotic child,"[82] Dorothy reported, "[whom] I am intensely sorry for and don't much like,"[83] but if she was aware of Red's contribution to the boy's unhappiness, she did not say so at this stage. Such warmth and affection as her own son received, nevertheless, came entirely from her and from the various people she employed to look after him.

The first of these were the Haemmerli sisters, two expensive Swiss nurses to whom Dorothy gave full authority over the needs of the baby. In doing so, she behaved no differently from any other wealthy woman of the time, and despite the peculiar living arrangements at Twin Farms, she saw her child as often as most mothers in her position. A woman who came down from Burlington to see her found Michael happily settled in his playpen while Dorothy moved from room to room, chatting with her guests and stopping every now and then to make note of a thought at one of a dozen typewriters scattered around the house. But she always returned to check on the baby, and was demonstratively affectionate toward him.[84] From the beginning, too, she tried to fill the house with children who could serve as companions for Michael; by the mid-1930s Twin Farms had begun to resemble a kindergarten, as the sons and daughters of maids and gardeners and cooks romped through the grounds and drove Red to the edge of distraction.[85] He was peeved enough already during the first summer of Michael's life, when the only children on the place were Wells, Wallace and Tish Irwin's son Donny, "the housekeeper's lusty and husky girl, aged ten," and little Pamela Wilson, the daughter of Dorothy's sister, Peggy, and Peggy's husband, Howard. Dorothy loved this "beautiful, quaint little girl, black-eyed, coppery haired, tiny, and with an Alice-in-Wonderland wiseness." Many times, with "Pammy" in mind, she said that she wished she had a daughter of her own.

"Our place is spacious and simple," she wrote to Joseph Bard in that summer of 1930. "People come and go; Hal works quietly; we swim, play tennis, dig in the garden. I write some fiction, some articles, and sell them all, for varying prices, in proportion as they are good or bad (when good, little money, when bad, much)."[86] There were dogs and cats and hens and pigeons and a herd of cows on the hillside that Red liked to say had been "hired for the effect." Mencken came to visit, on the assurance that he would not be "compelled to play tennis, take walks, meet the neighborhood or admire the baby."[87] Old friends dropped by, including Captain James Pedlow, Dorothy's onetime superior at the Red Cross in Budapest, and Gertrude Tone, who was waging her own battle with alcoholism and taking thyroid for a mysterious swelling of her legs.

"I'd like to take it for my hips," Dorothy reflected. "My brain has gone *phut* but that's due to domesticity (which is unavoidable. Show me a woman married to an artist who can succeed in her marriage without making a full-time profession out of it. Oh, Jesus, God!!)."[88] She was at peace with Red for the time being. Michael had helped to settle them — the *idea* of Michael had — and her mind, in any case, was on other things. In the fall the Lewises left Vermont for Westport, Connecticut, where they had arranged to rent the house of their friends Frank and Esther Adams. (Franklin P. Adams was "F.P.A.," the witty, poetical columnist for the *Herald Tribune* and the *New York World,* and Esther was his beautiful wife, "very possessive of Dorothy," as acquaintances remembered, and "mad" about the psychology of Carl Jung.)[89] Westport was ideal for Dorothy's purposes — it gave her the illusion of living in the country but was close enough to New York to enable her to stay in the city several days a week "and still be in touch with the baby." She was already determined that her life, with or without Red, was going to take a different course.

"As for my own problems," she wrote, "a couple of months by myself seems necessary and desirable — [though] a couple of months away from my very little boy — ten or twelve days' journey away — seems brutal." But she was willing to risk it in her own interest. She would go abroad that winter, "to Germany and Russia on a fast trip — perhaps two months. . . ."[90] She would go alone, if necessary, back to the work she had done so well before.

She was in New York for a conference with her editors on November 5, 1930, when Red reached her by telephone. The phone was a wicked instrument in Red's hands, and Dorothy was used to jokes and tricks when it rang. Once, when a German professor had called to talk with her about some translation or other, Dorothy had thought it was Red using one of his accents, and had shot back, "Come off it, you son of a bitch. I know you. You can't fool me again."[91] This time, however, Red was serious and very upset.

"Dorothy," he gasped over the wire. "Oh, Dorothy!"

She was frightened for a moment, and she answered quickly, "What's the matter? What is it?"

"Dorothy," said Red, "I've got the Nobel Prize."

It was the third thing that drew them together in those years, but it took a few minutes for the news to sink in.

"Oh, have you!" said Dorothy. "How nice for you! Well, I have the Order of the Garter!"[92]

7

CHAPTER

THE only ones more surprised than Red and Dorothy by the announcement of the 1930 Nobel Prize in literature were Red's enemies and rivals in the world of letters. For a long time now the more broody literati had been writing Red off as a scribbler, "a commercial hack" whose reputation grew in direct proportion to the vulgarity and lack of discrimination of the reading public. The young Ernest Hemingway, whose pretensions normally ran in another direction, dismissed the awarding of the prize to Red that year as "a filthy business," and remarked that the only positive thing about it was the fact that it had not gone to Theodore Dreiser.[1] Four years earlier Red had showily declined the Pulitzer Prize, for *Arrowsmith*, on the grounds that "all prizes, like all titles, are dangerous";[2] the excuses he offered now for his altered sentiments were as lame as they were forgivable. It was no secret to anyone that Red had coveted the Nobel with all his heart and regarded his selection as a kind of apotheosis. But if he was proud of his good fortune, defiant and even cocky in public, in private he was terrified.

"This is the end of me," he remarked to his friend Lillian Gish. "This is fatal. I cannot live up to it."[3]

It was left to Dorothy to deal with the "immense commotion"[4] at the house in Westport while Red answered questions, went to parties in his honor, worked on his acceptance speech, and saw a doctor in New York to get rid of his "hickeys" — the pustular lesions, formed by acne, that were forever erupting on his face. There was never any doubt that Red would go to Stockholm to accept the Nobel award, or that Dorothy would go with him. The only thing that needed settling was the question of the baby: it did not occur to either of the Lewises to take Michael along.

Rose Lane was in New York, fortunately, at the end of that year, more desperate than ever for a change of scene. Before long Dorothy had pressed her into service as a sort of governess. She ensconced Rose in Westport with the usual assortment of nurses and domestics and then rushed back to New York for emergency oral surgery. On November 26 she had ten of her teeth extracted, and traveled the next day to Philadelphia for a conference with the editors of the *Saturday Evening Post,* who had agreed to publish any reports from her European journey, if she could turn it to professional account.

"I never saw a person so busy," said Rose in a letter to her mother, "in bed at her hotel with a nurse on one side changing dressings on her gums, and a telephone at her ear and messengers coming and going and packages being delivered and telegrams arriving. She is going from Sweden on into Russia, and then out to Germany where she will join Hal again. He's going to England while she goes to Russia."[5] The Lewises both arrived in Stockholm exhausted, on December 9, after a rough and stormy Atlantic crossing. They took possession of a suite at the Grand Royal Hotel and embarked on a solid week of banquets, receptions, speeches, and parties.

"Stockholm was dark," wrote Dorothy later. "Eight o'clock in the morning is black as midnight now; but where else in the world would the door open to admit a beautiful apparition, dressed in white, with hair of pure gold flowing over her breast and shoulders, on her head a crown of evergreens and flaming candles, in her hands a tray of cakes and steaming coffee?"[6] It was the season of the festival of Santa Lucia, when young girls in Sweden are dressed to promise the return of the sun, "and it is said in Stockholm still," Mark Schorer noted later, "that on the first night that [Red] was in his hotel, such a creature appeared in his room and, with her mythological appearance, terrified him into screaming."[7]

Dorothy's head was swimming already, even without the imposition of folklore. "I wonder whether I have sufficient evening dresses," she asked herself. "My husband groans in anticipation of successive struggles with shirt studs."[8] The following day they arrived at the Concert House for Red's presentation to Gustav V, King of Sweden and of the Goths and Wends. The court was in mourning for the queen, who had died in April, and Dorothy was afraid that Red might trip or otherwise embarrass himself as he moved down the long red carpet to greet the royal family. In fact, his performance that whole week was flawless. He never once got drunk and never insulted anyone, endearing himself to the Swedes but greatly disappointing his cronies at home, "who had expected him to rush about bussing the little princesses."[9] Even his denunciation of the American literary establishment and his accusation of "crudeness" on the part of the American people were delivered without rancor, with supreme self-confidence, and to thunderous applause. "Our American professors," said Red, "like their literature clear and cold and pure and very dead."[10] An article in the *Chicago Tribune,* reflecting the reaction at home, dismissed the acceptance speech as being "in singularly poor taste,"[11] but the Swedes were given no reason to think that Red was *not* the author who best represented his country. When the ceremonies were over, "dancing began, liquor flowed," and Red and Dorothy set out to attend a series of Nobel balls.[12]

Dorothy had sat by quietly through the festivities in Stockholm, turning aside questions with an airy hand and letting Red do most of the talking. ("Please be thrilled," a secretary at the American embassy had urged her as she left her hotel for the banquet to honor the Nobel laureates. "Please don't say you don't get any particular kick out of it!")[13] At dinner she was placed beside the king's brother Prince Eugen, and later told reporters that he was "swell — we have a date for Sunday." But she had not felt well from the start of the trip, and she could not have been happy to see herself described in *Time* magazine as "buxom, brunette Mrs. Lewis."[14]

"I've always wanted to be blond," she sighed one day to Ramon Guthrie, in what Ramon took to be a moment of fatigue, "— blond and kittenish."[15] By the time she and Red left Stockholm for Berlin, on December 21, Dorothy was ready for a reunion with old friends: the Gunthers, the Mowrers, the Knickerbockers, and others. There was a great celebration on Christmas Day, with "many speeches and uproarious fun,"[16] and at around midnight Red decided that it might be entertaining if the whole party nipped down to Vienna on the train. But reason prevailed, and it was a good thing it did, because at three o'clock in the morning Dorothy was suddenly stricken with a ruptured appendix, and she wound up, seriously ill, as a patient in the Mommsen Clinic.

She stayed in the hospital for about ten days and followed that with an extended recuperation in the Thuringian Forest. "Your son has gazed upon snow,"[17] Rose Lane informed her in a cheerful Christmas letter, before sending a telegram that purported to come from Michael himself: "LETTER RECEIVED AM HAPPY AND GAY

GAINED FOUR OUNCES WEIGHT STUDYING SWEDISH CALISTHEN-
ICS AND ORATORY LOVE MICHAEL."[18] In the meantime Dorothy
had canceled her trip to Russia, partly on account of her illness and
partly because Germany itself offered so much material for any reporter in search of a story. When Red went to London as planned
after New Year's, Dorothy stayed on alone in Berlin, at the Adlon.
Her friends had warned her that the Germany of 1931 was not the
Germany she had left three years before; all the same, it was a shock
and a bewilderment for Dorothy to discover just how great the transformation had been.

In February she went along to the *Sportpalast* in Berlin, where,
for the first time, in a hall hung with swastikas, standards, and oversize portraits of Adolf Hitler, she heard Joseph Goebbels declaim the
Nazi creed — that "peculiar mixture," Dorothy called it, "of Nordic
myth, anti-Semitism, militaristic tradition, desperado nationalism
and moronized socialism." In the elections of September 1930 the
Nazis had garnered more than six million votes and won a hundred
and seven seats in the Reichstag, which gave them an influence in
parliament second only to that of the majority Social Democrats.
They had succeeded so far largely on the basis of one theme, decrying
"Germany's spiritual and financial enslavement to the war victors;
Germany's ruin through reparations," and the betrayal of the Fatherland, which had been "stabbed in the back," they maintained,
by both internal and external foes.[19] There were not a great many
analysts of the situation, in Europe or in America, who failed to see
that something in Germany was about to give way.

"National Socialism began as a protest against a lost war," Dorothy observed. "It has been throughout the entire course of its development a protest against the lost war. Not only against the peace
treaties, not only against the dictates of Versailles — against the fact
that Germany lost the war at all."[20] The situation was exacerbated
and indeed ignited by fiscal disorder and the world economic crisis.
German recovery after 1918 had been based almost entirely on foreign loans, but now, with the onset of the Great Depression, there
was no more credit to be had and no money anywhere with which
to meet debts. By the end of 1930, six million German workers were
unemployed. Banks were failing; industries collapsed; the Weimar
government, under Chancellor Heinrich Brüning, was operating at a
huge deficit and had recently invoked emergency powers to rule by
decree. "If it were only the Nazis who talk[ed] of Germany's ruin,"
said Dorothy, "one could write it down to irresponsible chauvin-

ism."[21] But everywhere she went that winter she met a people obsessed with "injustice" — the injustice of reparations, the injustice of the ban on rearmament, the injustice of the seizure of German territories and borderlands, the plots of finance capitalists, the leverage of Communists, the conspiracies of Jews.

"It seems to me," said Dorothy, "that every conversation I had in Germany with anyone under the age of thirty ended with this phrase: *'Es kann nicht weiter. Es muss etwas geschehen.'* 'It can't go on. Something must happen.' Nearly everyone of the generation coming of age believes this." Meanwhile, all over Germany, hundreds of thousands of persons were meeting in "monster demonstrations." Two hundred thousand young men — "usually called S.A. men," Dorothy noted crisply, "not with reference to their sex appeal"[22] — had already been organized into Adolf Hitler's private militia, the *Sturmabteilung,* and were battling it out with Communist and leftist factions for control of the streets in Germany's largest cities. Arson, torture, kidnapping, murder — all manner of anarchy and violence had come to be expected, a matter of course, in a country whose citizens normally placed such a high value on public order that during the revolution of 1918 they had fled the rioting along clearly marked pathways because the signs in the parks told them to "Keep Off the Grass."

"It is a curious experience to go out from the vast hall," said Dorothy, "where 15,000 people have been listening to a word picture of their ruin, into the streets of Berlin; to drive through the wide and brilliant thoroughfares of the west side, with its cafes and theatres, its superpalaces for motion pictures, its Lucullan restaurants; to travel, perhaps, in the newest underground, that paragon of subways, finished since I was last in Berlin three years ago — lofty and light as day, with mural decorations on its station walls." Dorothy was looking around her for some exterior sign of the Germans' ruination, that act of "international treason" which figured so centrally in the Nazi mythology. She wanted to know if the German people were really worse off than anyone else in the Depression:

> How could a ruined people [she wrote] have developed the greatest aviation system in Europe and built the most successful dirigible? How has this ruined people built the world's fastest and most luxurious ships? Out of what financial ruin has it erected the finest and most modern hospitals, the most grandiose radio and exposition emporiums, the most numerous popular swimming pools and sports

palaces? How can a ruined state subsidize Europe's most lavish theatres? What financial catastrophe is represented by the magnificent
industrial plants stretching from Silesia to the Ruhr, from Hamburg
to the Alps?

Only twelve years ago I entered, for the first time after the war, a
shabby, decadent and demoralized Germany. Today, coming into this
country from east or west, from north or south, the visible manifes-
tation of a great reconstruction meets the eye. Here, one thinks, is a
nation of workmen, a nation of builders. Here stands a mighty state,
its equipment new, efficient, rational. By all odds the best equipped,
the best built, the most luxuriously administered nation in Europe,
and in some ways in the world. But when I voice this impression
timidly to a German companion, he says glumly, "Yes, we are the
best outfitted poorhouse on earth!"[23]

She went back to New York with Red at the beginning of March
1931, and in May published "Poverty De Luxe," the first of her mas-
terful pieces on the fall of the Weimar Republic. She was building a
reputation in America, largely through her lecture appearances and
articles in national magazines, that carried her far beyond her position as a reporter and correspondent. She was becoming famous.

"Oswald [Garrison] Villard wants you to consider being man-
aging editor of the *Nation* beginning next fall," Red wrote to Dorothy around this time. "He is also considering Raymond Swing.
. . . Villard is crazy about you, and wanted to see you in Berlin.
. . . I take it from what he says he'll pay $7,500 a year, top-notch.
Might be worth considering; certainly it would link you to America
if later you wanted to do articles there and give you grand American
political dope while, perforce, keeping you in touch with European
politics. . . . Mick and me could live on Long Island."[24] But it
wasn't enough for Dorothy.

"How *can* I take the *Nation*?" she answered Red. "What about
Vermont? Europe? I *see* you staying home and minding the baby.
Du!"[25] She worked on a profile of Al Smith (which was never published) and was consulted by President Herbert Hoover on the matter
of European disarmament.[26] But her heart was in Germany, in "the
situation," and there it would remain for a good long while. In the
rise of the Nazis she had found the platform she was looking for.

" 'Two souls, alas, dwell in this bosom,' " she wrote, quoting
Goethe. "Certainly two souls dwell in the National Socialist bosom,
however few clear ideas dwell in the heads of its leaders."[27] From

now until the summer of 1934, when Hitler, having secured the office of chancellor in Berlin, suspended civil liberties and purged the Nazi party of "radicals" and "leftists" to become Führer and master of the Reich, Dorothy produced more than a dozen pieces on the new Germany for the *Saturday Evening Post*. "Why Call It Postwar?," "Back to Blood and Iron," "All the King's Horses," "Gangway for Mars"[28] — her articles took weeks and sometimes months to prepare; they were "longer than God," she declared, running to eight and ten thousand words apiece and fulfilling her own cherished definition of superb foreign reporting: "the type of despatch that would give the complete social, diplomatic and economic history of a country if assembled over a period of years."[29] These were the days when the readers of a popular magazine in America were assumed to be capable of following an argument and of paying attention to a certain amount of detail, and these were the articles that secured Dorothy's reputation as, in John Gunther's words, "the best journalist this generation has produced in any country, and that is not saying anywhere near enough."[30]

Dorothy had tried to see Hitler for the first time in 1923, immediately after the Munich "Beer Hall Putsch," when, on the run from the police, he had taken refuge with acquaintances of hers in the mountains of Bavaria. But she had not been quick enough, and later, after serving a short prison sentence for his role in the attempted coup, Hitler had remained "lofty and remote from all foreigners."

"Germany for the Germans!" Dorothy explained. "Scorn for Americans, the dollar-chasers, the money-grubbers, the profiteers."[31] She read *Mein Kampf*, in the meantime, and recognized it for what it was: nonsense, "one long speech" filled with lunatic diatribes about nations and races, "eight hundred pages of Gothic script, pathetic gestures, inaccurate German, and unlimited self-satisfaction."[32] The people were to awaken — if Dorothy did not completely misunderstand the text — "and Hitler's movement was going to *vote* dictatorship in! In itself a fascinating idea. Imagine a would-be dictator setting out *to persuade a sovereign people to vote away their rights*."[33] But by 1931 it looked as if the dictator might just succeed, and anyway, as Dorothy observed, "reason never yet swept a world off its feet."[34]

She was back in Europe that November, having established Red and the baby in a swank new apartment on East Ninetieth Street. "I wonder sometimes whether you don't resent all the activities that take me away so much," Dorothy wrote to her husband from the road. "But don't dearest. The great thing isn't being with someone every minute but knowing that someone is always there." [35] At the moment she was in England, where her hotel room was "strewn with pamphlets, reviews, newspapers and articles" and she was trying to make some sense out of the European chaos.

"I have read books and books all about gold standards," she wrote to Red, "and deflation vs. devaluation and this and that, and the more I read the less I know, but I am banking on my theory that the England of indecision is the England that will stand for a long time yet." [36] Noel Coward's *Cavalcade* was playing to packed houses in the West End; it was "an emotional orgy of nationalism," Dorothy remarked, "three hours of showing how well the British behave under stress. . . . I found that to mumble in one's throat about this show and to say that, after all, it didn't present the world with many new ideas, was nothing short of lèse majesté." It was no different anywhere else in Europe — not in Hungary, where, in the twin cities of Buda and Pest, lying on opposite sides of the Danube, Dorothy encountered "the final idiocy" in a sign that read, "Buda Citizens Buy Buda Products"; nor in France, where Aristide Briand, the foreign minister, "managed to make the most moving and pathetic speeches for disarmament while his country maintained the largest standing army in the world." The French had a bit less "backtracking" to do, Dorothy conceded, inasmuch as "no French statesman ever for a moment questioned the advisability of France first." But the attitude in Paris was symptomatic of an illness that had infected the entire continent.

"The Greeks had a name for it," said Dorothy bluntly: "xenophobia. . . . The gilt is off the international gingerbread. . . . The whole world is retreating from the international position and is taking its dolls and going home." [37] By the time she got to Berlin again she was "horrified" at the extent of the nationalist retrogression and the simultaneous "tooting of horns." "Unless things change radically," she announced, "there will be war in Europe within the decade — before the 1930s are out. And I've been where it will start." [38] She had met the man who would start it, too: Adolf Hitler, "the awkward Austrian," "the perverter of Nietzsche," "the champion of the blond beast." [39]

Her interview with Hitler [40] was arranged by his press attaché, Ernst ("Putzi") Hanfstaengel, "an immense, high-strung, incoherent clown" [41] who regarded the meeting between Dorothy and the Nazi leader as a great feather in his own cap. On the eve of their victory the Nazis were suddenly interested in making a good impression abroad. Hitler, said Dorothy, was "going very high hat and frock coat. He associates with industrialists. He goes to tea with princesses. . . . [He] is in control of propaganda and organization funds estimated at $8000 per day."[42] And his interview with Mrs. Sinclair Lewis was thought to be a matter of some importance to them both.

"There was a lot of fussiness connected with the preparations," Dorothy remembered. "Not, somehow, what one would expect from a man to whom The Deed is everything."[43] Already she suspected that the ranks of the National Socialist party were filled with men of a particularly dubious virility, "a lot of wavy-haired bugger-boys," she called them later, "pink-cheeked mediocrities" making a fetish of brotherhood and "talking about woman's function in bearing SONS for the state." Dorothy never hesitated to use the word *perversion* when she wrote about the Nazis, or to attribute to Hitler's closest associates a homoerotic exaltation.[44] When, in December 1931, she finally saw Hitler "shoot" through the lobby of the Kaiserhof Hotel "on the way to his rooms, accompanied by a body-guard who looked rather like Al Capone," she could well believe that he was "a man who owns an army. A man who terrorizes the streets." She was "a little nervous," she confessed: "I considered taking smelling salts." But her general impression of "sickness" and "inversion" was not dispelled when, at length, she received her summons to appear:

> When finally I walked into Adolf Hitler's salon in the Kaiserhof Hotel, I was convinced that I was meeting the future dictator of Germany. In something less than fifty seconds I was quite sure I was not.
>
> It took just about that time to measure the startling insignificance of this man who has set the world agog.
>
> He is formless, almost faceless, a man whose countenance is a caricature, a man whose framework seems cartilaginous, without bones. He is inconsequent and voluble, ill-poised, insecure. He is the very prototype of the Little Man. . . .
>
> The eyes alone are notable. Dark gray and hyperthyroid — they have the peculiar shine which often distinguishes geniuses, alcoholics, and hysterics.
>
> There is something irritatingly refined about him. I bet he crooks his little finger when he drinks his tea.
>
> His is an actor's face. Capable of being pushed out or in, expanded or contracted at will, in order to register facile emotions.

As I saw him, I thought of other German faces.

The President, [Paul] von Hindenburg: A face cut out of rock. No imagination in it; no light; no humor. Not exactly an appealing face. But one revealing a character so defined as to determine its owner's destiny.

Chancellor [Heinrich] Bruening: The head of an eighteenth century cardinal-statesman. A high-bridged, sensitive nose. A finely cut mouth. The convex profile of obstinacy. Quizzical, wise, humorous. . . .

I thought of this man before me, seated, as an equal, between Hindenburg and Bruening, and involuntarily I smiled. Oh, Adolf! Adolf! You will be out of luck! . . .

Looking at Hitler, I saw a whole panorama of German faces; men whom this man thinks he will rule. And I thought: Mr. Hitler, you may get, in the next elections, the fifteen million votes which you expect.

But fifteen million Germans CAN be wrong.

The interview itself proceeded without a great deal of interest. It was "difficult," said Dorothy, "because one cannot carry on a conversation with Adolf Hitler. He speaks always as though he were addressing a mass meeting. In personal intercourse he is shy, almost embarrassed. In every question he seeks a theme that will set him off. Then his eyes focus in some far corner of the room; a hysterical note creeps into his voice which rises sometimes to a scream. He gives the impression of a man in a trance. He bangs the table." Every now and then Dorothy managed to interrupt the "stream of eloquence" by bluntly repeating one of her questions, but all Hitler really had to say was this: "I will get into power legally. I will abolish this parliament and the Weimar constitution afterward. I will found an authority-state, from the lowest cell to the highest instance; everywhere there will be responsibility and authority above, discipline and obedience below."

"So that's that for the Republic," said Dorothy.[45] It was a great annoyance to her in later years to hear about the "blunder" she had made when she claimed that Hitler would never come to power in Germany. John Gunther called it "her comico-terrible gaffe."[46] William L. Shirer remarked, somewhat more kindly, that it "was a rather surprising judgment for so veteran and astute a Berlin correspondent."[47] But these were the verdicts of hindsight and essentially unfair, because in the article she published based on the Hitler interview, and in the small book, *"I Saw Hitler!,"* that she developed from the article, Dorothy had made some swift and sound predictions. She stated quite accurately, for example, that the Nazis would begin to suffer a decline in the popular vote and that they would enter the government in Berlin, if at all, only by being invited as part of a coalition. By the time this actually happened, in 1933, Dorothy had long abandoned any notions she may have had about Hitler's ineffectiveness. She never changed her mind, however, about his *person*. Like Hannah Arendt many years later, she recognized "banality" as the outstanding feature of the Nazi movement — "Nazism is the apotheosis of collective mediocrity," she declared, "in all its political and sociological aspects"[48] — and she was not the first or the last to meet the Nazi leader and wonder what all the fuss was about. As late as 1934, when Hitler had consolidated his power and there was no longer any question of a "gaffe," Bill Shirer saw the Führer riding through the streets of Nuremberg, "and for the life of me," said Shirer, "I could not quite comprehend what hidden springs he undoubtedly unloosed in the hysterical mob which was greeting him so wildly."[49]

Everyone underestimated the Nazis: it was no sign of shoddy journalism to have faced the onslaught with disbelief. "Whatever else the Hitler revolution may or may not be," wrote Dorothy, "it is an enormous mass flight from reality." If she made a mistake, it was not in minimizing Hitler, but rather in thinking that civilized people would have to realize, as she did now, that the Nazi menace was a world menace, that this "revolution of the *déclassé*"[50] had let loose forces stronger than even Hitler knew. From the moment of Hitler's rise to power until his death in a bunker twelve years later, there was no one in journalism, anywhere in the world, who spoke louder than Dorothy in the fight against nazism:

> [Nazism] is a repudiation of the whole past of western man. It is . . . a complete break with Reason, with Humanism, and with the Christian ethics that are at the basis of liberalism and democracy. . . . In its joyful destruction of all previous standards; in its wild affirmation of the "Drive of the Will"; in its Oriental acceptance of death as the fecundator of life and of the will to death as the true heroism, it is darkly nihilistic. Placing will above reason; the ideal over reality; appealing, unremittingly, to totem and taboo; elevating tribal fetishes; subjugating and destroying the common sense that grows out of human experience; of an oceanic boundlessness,

Nazism — that has been my consistent conviction — is the enemy of whatever is sunny, reasonable, pragmatic, common-sense, freedom-loving, life-affirming, form-seeking and conscious of tradition.[51]

She stood at the balcony of her room at the Hotel Adlon more than a year later, in March 1933, and saw the first legalized Storm Troopers tramping down Unter den Linden, saluting and shouting: "*Jude Verrecke!* . . . Perish the Jews! . . . *Heil Hitler* . . . *Sieg Heil.*" She had been reading Bertrand Russell's *Scientific Outlook* and Aldous Huxley's *Brave New World,* and as she watched Hitler's victory parade she heard a voice inside her head saying, "Your world has slipped."[52] "With unbelieving eyes"[53] she had witnessed the seduction of a nation, the triumph of "hatred, envy, greed, vanity and cheap heroics,"[54] and that day she suddenly had an intense longing for America. She wanted to run into the street, she remembered, and shout the Gettysburg Address in the faces of the soldiers.

"I saw them," said Dorothy, "in my mind's eye, marching on and on, over frontiers, north, east, west and south. . . . I saw, in my mind's eye, the machine guns that would soon be in their hands, the planes that would fly over their heads, the tanks that would rumble and roll with their tread." And she knew — and said, when very few others would say it — that "post-war Europe was finished, and pre-war Europe had begun. . . . The boiling kettle had exploded."[55]

"YOUR little son today entered your room," Dorothy wrote to her husband in February 1932, when Michael Lewis was just eighteen months old, "opened the drawer of your night table, took out a passport picture of you, kissed it, brought it over to me and said, very wisely, and quite clearly, 'Papa!' He then took it back, closed it into the drawer, and said again, but sadly, 'Papa!'

"Before you completely melt into tears," Dorothy went on, "let me hasten to add that he then turned sharply around, re-opened the drawer, extracted the picture with an air of great firmness, and threw it into the wastepaper basket without saying anything at all."[56]

Dorothy was alone with Michael for several weeks that winter while he recovered from a bout with scarlet fever and she placed herself "in quarantine" at the new apartment on Ninetieth Street. She had come back from Germany and the Hitler interview just in time for Christmas, and had then promptly embarked on a lecture tour when the holidays were over. ("It's work," she maintained, "and it keeps one somewhat in touch with reality. With people. With, for instance, Brooklyn school teachers.")[57] On her return, Red had left on a research trip, and they were back to functioning as they functioned best: apart.[58]

"Whenever I separate from Hal," Dorothy confessed, "it is as though I come out of a delirium into sanity, out of a maelstrom into a quiet place. And yet my heart goes rushing after him as he careens his way outward."[59] There had been no diminishment of craziness on the home front, no change in Red's drinking, no variation of either of the Lewises' now-you-see-me, now-you-don't approach to love and marriage. Their new apartment had two sitting rooms, one for her and the other for him, and when, rarely enough, they found themselves in the same city at the same time, it was obvious, at least to their friends, that they had little to say to each other.

"Much of the conversation at Dorothy's gatherings was in German," Bill Shirer recalled, "in which she was extremely fluent but which Red scarcely understood. He felt shut out of the talk, and his inevitable reaction, which was mercurial, was to stomp out and leave not only the party and the dwelling but the city. He was always taking off in a huff for other parts."[60] Dorothy had actually known her husband to rise in the middle of dinner and announce that he was on his way to Kansas.

"He would decide to go abroad in twenty-four hours," she said, "or a week. . . . He would rouse up the chauffeur or his man secretary, or hire a car from a garage, and start — for the Adirondacks, the sea, the mountains. . . ." Red was abetted in these escapades by his driver and amanuensis, Lou Florey, a crack stenographer and amateur nurse whom his family remembered as "charming and literate"[61] but whom Dorothy hoped to blame for her husband's waywardness if ever she could. ("I think I am unjust to Lou," she once admitted. "Can't be helped . . . unhappy memories . . . a complex.")[62] If she was critical of Red's style of living, however, and of his choice of companions, her complaints were as nothing compared to Red's sporadic attacks on her. It was a question of alcohol, as always. It was never anything else.

"You with your important little lectures," Red snarled at Dorothy. "You with your brilliant people. *You* want to talk about foreign politics which *I* am too ignorant to understand."[63] She had just begun to find the kind of company she wanted to keep in New York — groups of artists and writers and thinkers who were concerned, as she was, with ideas and the flow of events. She was playing hostess also to a variety of gifted socialites: Clare Boothe Brokaw; Alexander Woollcott; Noel Coward; the publisher John Farrar; the oversized, "catalytic" Ernestine Evans, a children's writer and editor at Putnam's; and Efrem Zimbalist and his wife, the diva Alma Gluck. Alma's daughter, Marcia Davenport, the biographer of Mozart, also was a regular guest. At none of Dorothy's gatherings was "chit-chat" tolerated for long.

"Mildred Wertheimer came to dinner last night," she noted in her diary, "and we discussed Arthur Salter's book [probably *Framework of an Ordered Society*] which I, for one, do not find very good. You have to accept in it the fundamental thesis that such far-reaching changes as the abandonment of national sovereignty can be accomplished without revolution."[64] While Red sat and brooded in corners or fled the house to his makeshift offices, Dorothy went right on talking — arguing, lecturing, disputing, correcting, and demanding a reasoned response from her friends.

There were comical moments in the decline of this marriage — plenty of them. Once at Twin Farms, while Dorothy held forth at one end of the "Big Room," Red sat casually in an armchair and every now and then remarked, not quite under his breath, "Blip!" The talk that night was about Hitler and the Nazis, and whenever Dorothy or one of her guests reached a particularly dramatic point in the discussion, Red would say it again — "Blip!" — until finally somebody asked him what he was up to.

"I'm just trying to get a word in edgewise," he replied.[65] At times he was known to split the party into two groups — those who wanted to talk about "It" with Dorothy, and those who wanted to talk about "something useless," something else, with him.

"Is she talking about *It?*" Red would ask, sotto voce, if he stumbled late into one of Dorothy's soirees; if she was, he would often stumble out again. "He had betrayed a dislike for political argument," said Jimmy Sheean, "abstract discussion, journalistic excitement and table-pounding from the earliest days; now this dislike was not only betrayed but asseverated, enforced as a rule. Many is the time I have heard him say, 'No more *situations* or I will go to bed.' Ultimatum. Generally he pronounced it *sityashuns* in order to make it seem more contemptible. *Sityashuns* referred to events on the continent of Europe, in general, and in particular to events in Central or Eastern Europe or to anything connected with Adolf Hitler." It was not difficult to guess that Red was deeply threatened by his wife's erudition and her involvement in world affairs; as the decade wore on, he was heard to say more and more frequently, "If I ever divorce Dorothy, I'll name Adolf Hitler as co-respondent."[66]

It is plain from Dorothy's diaries and letters* that her relationship with her husband, except on the rarest days, had ceased to be physical. It had never been sexually intense. "I exist mostly above the neck," Red told Dorothy once, "half-whimsically, half-apologetically."[67] Many times, according to Mark Schorer, he tried to persuade her "that the erotic relation between people did not really matter at all."[68] She claimed not to be bothered by it.

"There is a love of the body and of the body alone," she wrote, "and the Church, which knows a thing or two, calls it Lust. And I'm not so set against lust as the Church is, but lust never yet caused me to lose my head."[69] She was just as happy to forget about lust altogether on those infrequent occasions when Red, "drunk and demanding," staggered into her room smelling strangely, vilely, of "rotting weeds."[70]

"He was a perfectly potent heterosexual man," Dorothy pointed out calmly, more than twenty years later, "but he could never hold a woman sexually. . . . He could be tender, playful, delightful with women *except* in the sexual relationship. . . . He performed the act without tenderness, and the moment it was over [he] left for his own bed and room without a parting caress." His awkwardness, to be sure, was preferable to his hostility. "On occasions," said Dorothy, "he would follow up lovemaking by starting a violent quarrel, invariably over nothing at all, or over something in the past that had been smoldering for a long time. . . . His rages could be formidable — terrifying — he would all but foam at the mouth, eyes starting from their sockets, lips twisted over his teeth." Dorothy never tried

---

* A word on Dorothy's letters, here and throughout: she wrote to Sinclair Lewis in the same way she had written to Joseph Bard — that is to say, constantly, sometimes several times a day, and without an eye for repetitiveness. It was her habit all her life to write the *same* thing many times. Hundreds of her letters to Red have been lost or discarded; others she saved for her files (either the originals or in carbon). Still others were never sent. As was the case with the letters to Joseph, I have found no *internal* evidence to distinguish sent from unsent letters; we may assume that the letters Red received from Dorothy were no different in style and tone from the ones she kept for herself.

There are several particularly lengthy letters at Syracuse ("sermons," Red called them) that date from 1937, 1939, and 1941, after Dorothy and Red had permanently separated. Although they are slightly out of context chronologically, I have included them in this chapter because they comment *generally* on Dorothy's marriage and its demise.

to argue with Red in these moments (she was afraid of him, she admitted) but instead worked to impose "a frigidity" in their relations and "got the hell out of it." Her friend Rebecca West reflected later that "Dorothy probably got a good many mean blows that we don't know about. . . . It was a sign of her insulation from reality that she ever fell in love with Red, . . . but I think she probably locked herself in with a triple turn of the key because she was scared by Red's cruelty."[71] She was bound to Red by their common misery, certainly, as many people who love each other are:

> A hundred times you have begged me, and made me promise, not to leave you [she wrote to him at the end of their marriage]. Always I gave my promise. I stuck when sometimes it seemed impossible, in the days when you were terribly drunk and absolutely unreckonable. . . . I blame myself that sometimes I fled from what had become pure torture. But I stuck because I happen to care for you more than for anyone else alive. I cannot explain the nature of that caring. Perhaps one merely cares for one's own sufferings and joys. I'm sure I do not know.[72]

It was difficult for anyone who knew the situation to imagine what held her to him. "I love him with my soul," Dorothy protested. "There must be a soul, because otherwise, what on earth *do* I love him with? I feel as though we had been born in the same nursery and quarrelled through all our childhood, and studied together, and argued, and talked each other down in school, and fought and made up. . . . He's the only man I have ever known in my life that I really understand. Even why he drinks so. Only it hurts my feelings that he does . . . makes me feel inferior . . . one ought to have more charm than a whisky and soda, one thinks."[73] People marveled at Dorothy's ability to keep her head during the most embarrassing and degrading scenes. A popular cigarette of the 1930s promised tranquillity and "nonchalance" to the initiate, and Dorothy was heard to remark at a party, gazing at her husband's passed-out form, "I have to smoke so many Murads."[74] Her resolution to accept Red exactly as he was involved a certain radical change in her feelings — a very real emotional withdrawal, something that reminded her of "an amputation." She wrote to him in 1934:

> I too must shoulder my burden . . . must walk off . . . must free you. I picture my home dissolved . . . our home. . . . I speculate what to do with Micky. . . . I work myself into a state of anxiety

approaching hysteria. I lose all touch with reality . . . what is real
and what is imagined. . . . I have no security with you . . . no inner
security. What can a woman do under conditions like these except
try with all her will to make herself *innerly* independent, innerly free?
Tell me, if you know the answer. Do you think that being innerly free
means that you don't love another person? On the contrary. It is only
then that you know what love really is. . . . Oh, Hal — you and I
were made for each other — I feel that, and I think you feel it. . . .
God damn soul mates. And then suddenly this feeling which seemed
so solid is blown into atoms. And I sit in the dark.[75]

In the end she was obliged to operate exactly as Red did: alone,
and with her own needs foremost in mind. Her own needs and those
of her son, that is, about whose welfare in a drunken household she
was already seriously concerned. It was with "Micky" as a shield
that Dorothy wrote to Red, in one of a dozen extended appeals:

I hear from home that you have been ill again and had to have
Jerry [Ziegler, his doctor] out and the news depresses me. Darling
when if ever, will you do something about your health and something
about your pathological drinking? I do not blame you for it any more
than I would blame you for having nephritis or diabetes, but I suffer
intensely from it as everyone about you does, because when you are
drunk you act exactly like an insane person. You are cut off from so
much. . . . I don't blame you, as I have said, but what I do blame
you for and often very bitterly, is that you refuse to face it and take
no steps whatever to deal with it. And no one is permitted to mention
it . . . we all must treat you when you are ill as one treats a most
exacting patient . . . you yourself insist then that you shall be treated
as a victim of an illness which he cannot help — but when you are
clear-headed and could take measures then you (and I) are expected
to act as though everything were all right. . . .

It is not going to do you the least bit of good to force your will
on the matter and to go on the wagon and all that; what you have
to get over is the obsession with it. And of course if you don't, I
shudder to think not only of your future but of mine and above all
Micky's. As far as I am concerned, I feel able to deal with the situations that your illness creates, although it has taken me several years
to learn to do so, and often now . . . I feel quite incapable, and as
though your drinking had become my phobia, a mania under which
I will eventually crack. But the future of the child worries me to distraction. I don't need to go into this because you have sufficient imag-

ination yourself. Often often often I think that I ought to take him away now, now while he is still very young.[76]

As time went by, she got better and better at speaking her mind. "In this story," she wrote, "as it involves [Red's] personal life and relations, *there are no heroes or heroines.* [Dorothy's emphasis.] I was inadequate to a relationship I undertook in fairly alert awareness. It required a far more sacrificial soul than mine. Intellectually, and rationally, I *think* that that would not have worked, either. But nobody *knows* this. All I do know is that I have too strong a sense of self-preservation (perhaps, even, of self-worth) to have immolated myself on the altar of his genius."[77] And so she threw herself into her work. It was the one thing she could count on, she maintained, as being both "impersonal" and "so demanding."[78] The odd thing was that the further apart Dorothy and Red grew in reality, the closer they became in another sense — in that largely imaginary, "creative" realm she always sought to inhabit in her relations with men. The game suited them both equally: their correspondence in the early thirties was far more ardent than their marriage had been at any time. They wrote to each other nearly every day when they were apart.

"I have at this moment a great need to be lovely to you," said Dorothy to Red. "I wish to say the tenderest things, tender as the faintest, softest, littlest kiss that you can imagine. . . . Oh dearie me. . . . Oh dearie me."[79] And again: "I beseech you to be kind to my darling, who is yourself . . . tell my darling, who is yourself, that this is a fascinating and lovely world full of many strange things and thus and thus."[80] Red, for his part, whenever Dorothy was gone, sent her thrilling words of reassurance, mixed in with New York gossip, news from the farm, and nonsense: Carrie Chapman Catt had written asking Dorothy to serve on some committee or other ("Don't you do it!" warned Red); Gertrude Tone could be seen all over town at speakeasies, "terribly soused"; the Empire State Building was having an affair with the Holland Tunnel.[81] And in Vermont, "after three dreary days," it was "heavenly" again. The sun was soft, the breeze was gay, the clouds were rolling by: "And hot or cold or shy or bold, whatever I may be, in North or South I kiss your mouth, announcing I love Thee."[82]

"I hope you have not been captured by Fascists . . . ," said Red incidentally. "Oh my dolly my dolly my dolly. . . . Talking to you on the phone yesterday . . . lovely . . . it made me believe in mod-

ern inventions. . . . I was homesick for you. I've never loved you
so much!"[83] He agreed with Dorothy that her work should take
priority, and when she wasn't in town he spoke to everyone proudly
of her success — so proudly, in Brendan Gill's recollection, and so
effusively, that it was "something of an embarrassment to their
friends."[84] If Red was scornful, in private, about Dorothy and "It,"
in public he leapt to her defense at the slightest provocation, and got
his face slapped by Theodore Dreiser for his pains.[85]

The occasion was a dinner at the Metropolitan Club in honor of
Boris Pilnyak, a Russian novelist who was visiting New York at the
beginning of 1931. A number of other writers and critics, miffed at
the awarding of the Nobel Prize to Red, had been making snide remarks about Red's talent, and Red himself, of course, was drinking — "eating little sausages, drinking, drinking, and drinking."
When Dreiser walked by his table to offer brusque congratulations,
Red "replied by puckering up his face and emitting a Bronx cheer."
Later in the evening he rose to make a speech.

"I'm very happy to see Mr. Pilnyak," he said. "But I do not care
to speak in the presence of one man who has plagiarized 3,000 words
from my wife's book on Russia." At the end of the meal, Dreiser
came up to Red's table.

"You made a statement about my taking stuff from your wife's
book," said Dreiser. "I know you're an ignoramus, but you're [also]
crazy. You don't know what you're talking about." Red refused to
apologize, and Dreiser "smacked" him. "And I asked him if he
wanted to say it again," Dreiser recalled. "He said it again. So I
smacked him again. And I said, 'Do you want to say it again?' "

"Theodore," said Red, "I repeat that you are a liar and a thief."

"Do you want me to hit you again?" said Dreiser.

"If you do," said Red, "I'll turn the other cheek."

"Aw, Lewis, you shit!" Before long the literary giants were forcibly separated. "I'll meet you any time anywhere," Dreiser shouted,
while Red was heard to mumble soddenly to one of his rescuers,
"Why didn't you let him hit me again?"

It was "the year's greatest literary sensation" — "hilarious news
for the countryside," the *Literary Digest* felt sure. Red, at least, was
not above milking the incident for publicity. "I don't like scraps,"
he told reporters, "or rather scrapes. I'm just a country 'hick' living
on a farm, and every time I leave it I get into trouble." Baby pictures
of Michael Lewis were soon appearing in the newspapers over the
caption, "Say 'Dreiser' to this young man and he'll punch you on

the nose," while Red was observed to stop in front of his son's perambulator and command in a knowing voice, "Don't you be a writer. Writing is an escape from something. You be a scientist."[86]

At the end of 1931, after nearly three years of work, Red gave up on his labor novel. "In the first planning," he wrote to Dorothy, "it was all great fun — this picture of the great sweep of a novel covering practically all of American History." But as work progressed, he found that the subject bored him. "The labor leaders seem to me mostly a dreary and futile lot," he remarked. "Yet on the other hand I haven't the pleasure of disliking them enough so that I would get any pleasure out of satirizing them. . . . So quite suddenly I ups and chucks it, and I have been delighted ever since." He was especially happy because a new idea had already begun to take shape in his mind. He was going to write a novel about a Great Woman, a woman who had the audacity to try to succeed at her career and simultaneously at her life. It was the book that became *Ann Vickers*.

"I am going to do something that is important," Red wrote to Dorothy, "and that, so far as I can remember, has scarcely been touched upon in all fiction, and has never been adequately done except perhaps in the case of Mr. Shakespeare's Portia. In doing it I am thinking of Genia Schwarzwald — of Frances Perkins — of Susan B. Anthony — of Alice Paul — of such lovelier and more feminine, yet equally individual women as Sarah Bernhardt — of Jane Addams with all her faults — of Nancy Astor — of Catherine the Great — and if you don't mind being put in with such a gallery, a good deal of yourself."[87] The resulting combination of nimble social history and Sinclair Lewis make-believe (*Ann Vickers* was another huge best-seller) involved a wicked parody of the fight for women's rights, a look at the role of women in business, and some titillating excursions into "free love" and lesbianism.[88] It bore only a minor resemblance to Dorothy's experience, and none whatever to anything by Mr. Shakespeare. But there is no doubt that Dorothy served as the model for Ann[89] — so plainly, in fact, that Red was worried about stealing her thunder: she had often talked of writing her own novel about suffrage days.

"I should be infinitely proud if anything I might ever have said, or thought, or been, or felt, should excite your imagination,"[90] she wrote when she heard about Red's plans for the book. She was aware on some half-acknowledged level that in writing *Ann Vickers* he was attempting to come to terms with the reality of their marriage. Red was aware of it, too. He told Dorothy that Ann's "great tragedy . . . is that she has never found any man big enough not to be scared of her,"[91] and Dorothy was uncomfortable enough at that to apologize to him.

"Often I think the greatest service I could do you as an artist would be to leave you," she wrote, "— to make you free . . . or that it were better were I less demanding of life, myself, more truly the servant of my master. I can so well understand why artists marry their cooks. And I wish in my heart very often that I could abandon the world for you. But — it's no good — I can't. The world was my first love, and I have a faithful heart."

She was writing from a hotel room in Brussels, a dingy, dreary bedchamber "better suited for a lone suicide. In just such a room," Dorothy observed, "the heroine of a cheap novel, deserted by her lover, betrayed by her husband, takes the fatal draught. . . . It is quite incredible to me that I should be in this room . . . in this town."[92] She was waiting for an interview with the exiled Empress Zita of Austria. It was to be a follow-up to her famous report on the 1921 Habsburg putsch at Tata, and when the article was finished she called it "Water under Bridges."[93] The whole of her most recent trip to Europe had been like an extended journey into the past. In London she had called on Joseph Bard "and wondered how in the world I had ever found anything to talk with him about, and why in hell I had ever thought him good-looking."[94] In Berlin she had been able to think of nothing but Red "and our lovely early days together."[95] Then she had gone down to Vienna by train, "all day long through the country that next to Vermont I love most of any. . . . And to-night Genia's house, where I feel so extraordinarily, so peculiarly at home. Nothing ever changes in it, or in the warmth of the welcome. And good old Fodor on the station, fatter but otherwise the same . . . loquacious . . . full of tales." She had made up her mind, while sitting among the lilacs in the Belvedere gardens, to move to Vienna again.

"They say it's dead," Dorothy remarked, "but for me better the corpse of Vienna than any other place."[96] With Genia Schwarzwald as her agent, she took a lease on an apartment in the Wohllebengasse and rented a villa in the mountains of the Semmering, where she meant to spend the whole of the next winter, 1932–1933, whether Red came with her or not. There had been another "awful scene" between them not long before. The *Saturday Evening Post* had sent Dorothy to Paris to report on the upcoming reparations conference, and she had cabled Fodor to ask him to meet her there and afterward accompany her on a tour of the East — Prussia, Poland, Czechoslovakia, and Hungary. Red, drunk, trailed her to Europe and begged her to cancel her plans.[97] When she refused — "You know me, Fodor," said Dorothy: "We are going on"[98] — he became abusive, wildly angry, and flew to England swearing divorce and custody battles and other kinds of revenge. The week-long bender that ensued was evidently so serious that Red himself, without any prompting from Dorothy, abruptly swore off liquor.

"Yes," he wrote to her, "— no spirits. None."[99] This time he really meant it: he was going to stay sober "maybe for seventy-seven years and maybe only for life."[100] There followed the usual reconciliation through the mails.

"Can it be that I *miss* you?" Dorothy wrote to him when she heard how well he was doing. "Can it be that I want Micky? But that would be *absurd* in a Saturday Evening Post reporter.

"Can it be that I don't think it's very *important* to be a Satevepost reporter?

"I'm afraid I think it isn't."[101] She returned to America in May of 1932 and announced that she would begin work on a book, an extended essay on modern politics that she called "The End of Bourgeois Morality." "For me, the closely reasoned argument has become the nearest thing to art which I can achieve," she wrote to Rose Lane from Twin Farms. "I have definitely forsaken the divine urge for the more seasoned thought." She would need "to read and read and read" before she could even get started,[102] but there would be plenty of time for that when she got back to Austria.

In the meantime, summer in Vermont was more beautiful than anyone had remembered. There had been a sudden flood of money into the Lewis household. *Arrowsmith* and *Dodsworth* had both been purchased for the movies, while Dorothy's *Post* articles were earning her two and sometimes three thousand dollars apiece. When she sailed for Europe again on August 24, this time with Red at her side, it was in the midst of "the best six months we have had since we met."[103] The baby was walking and talking — "Hal swears he is going to be a brat with his front teeth out," said Dorothy, "and his hair all mussy"[104] — and Red's pledge, so far, had held: he had not touched a drop of liquor all summer. Disembarking at Cherbourg, the Sinclair Lewises were the very picture of the happy, healthy, wealthy American family — "so terribly lifelike," said Dorothy to Red, "that you almost convince me that's me, until suddenly my heart is crying outside a locked gate, with the other 'me' inside."

She would be left there alone again before long, she suspected, "looking in on the false me, with you." [105]

THERE is nothing in Dorothy's letters or diaries to indicate the precise moment when she began to take lovers. That she did take them she acknowledged herself, with considerable serenity, in a long essay she prepared for Mark Schorer about her marriage to Red. A diary she kept at the end of 1932 refers several times to "E." as a guest at the Villa Sauerbrunn, the house on the Semmering where Dorothy and Red spent their weekends.[106] Dorothy went so far as to declare that she was "in love with E., and happily married, too," and yet looking still for "tenderness" — "that curious tenderness, that pervading, warm tenderness" that she never seemed to find:

> I went for a walk with E. and in the woods he turned suddenly and put both hands on my cheeks and we clung together. His mouth tasted deliciously of love, like the smell of semen, and I could have lain down with him right there in the woods then and there as I could have done for five years, except that we agreed that we wouldn't . . . the old leap of the heart and womb was there, and we walked along, greatly shaken.

She got in the habit of writing about her romantic encounters, not out of prurience, but because she was a reporter, and because she hoped that in writing she might hit on some useful truth about herself. "There's a critic in me these days," she said, ". . . who takes me firmly by the hand, pushes aside the curtain and insists upon my looking forward, down the road. . . . I must at last try to understand myself, because if at forty one has no wisdom . . . in two years I'll be forty . . . then what has one?" Dorothy did not describe her sexual adventures in detail, and she did not name names. ("You ought to have a locked book like the Queen of Rumania," she told herself, "and wear the key on a bangle: only I would lose the bangle.")[107] But the little books and wads of paper that she carried with her everywhere were filled with ruminations on the nature of love, what it was and was not, what it meant and did not, what the differences might be between lust and passion and "resonance . . . physical resonance, mental resonance, and resonance of feeling."[108]

These thoughts could sometimes be found squeezed in between reports of Dorothy's conversations with the Nazi Gauleiter of Bavaria and the grim statistics of the Polish national debt.

"The sexual tyranny which people who pretend to love each other exercise over each other has nothing to do with love," said Dorothy. "It is plain and sometimes vicious possessiveness, unbridled, undisciplined and unbeautiful, and eventually it kills even sexual passion." She "never could understand . . . the idea of the exclusiveness of love. People get caught in dilemmas," she thought, ". . . only because they are not innerly free and innerly courageous."[109] In January 1933, in the back of one of her research notebooks,[110] she left fragments of a sonnet in pencil:

> I have broken myself often on the rock
> Of man's hard love. Oh where is tenderness? . . .
> If in your arms I for a moment feel
> Utterly safe, . . . with what words will you steal
> This right from me? . . .
> Like man, I turn to woman in great need,
> Back to the source from which no one is freed.

There had been a party on the Semmering over Christmas — one of the great parties of the 1930s, a fabulous, week-long bash that went on through New Year's — arranged by Dorothy and Red for some of their closest friends. The entire autumn and early winter had been passed in a flurry of concerts, receptions, and openings of different kinds. The Lewises had gone off for a while on a walking tour of Italy and then returned to Vienna for what was really the last of prewar Austria's brilliant social seasons. Very little work got done by either of them, and the Christmas party at the Villa Sauerbrunn — a house "as thick with comfort as a coffee cake is with sugar"[111] — was meant to cap the holidays before laziness took over permanently as a way of life.

The Gunthers came, and the Mowrers and the Fodors (in 1922 Fodor had married the beautiful Martha Roob, a fellow Hungarian), along with newer acquaintances from Vienna and around Europe: the poet Robert Nichols and his wife; Edgar Wallace's daughter Patricia, and Patricia's fiancé, the publisher A. S. Frere; Marcia and Russell Davenport; Phil and Lily Goodman; the "tall, willowy, beautiful, sensitive, vivacious" Virgilia Peterson,[112] an American writer who was soon to become Poland's Princess Paul Sapieha; and Nicholas Roosevelt, who at that time was the American ambassador

Margaret Grierson
Thompson, photographed
in Buffalo in the 1890s.
The baby is probably
Dorothy.

The parsonage on
Union Street in Hamburg:
"It was a tall wooden
house with a narrow
veranda . . . , and it
looked across a lawn
at the church where
Father preached on
Sundays."

The Thompson family,
motherless, 1901. *Left to
right:* Willard, the Reverend Peter Thompson,
Peggy, Dorothy.

*Courtesy of the United Methodist Church,
Hamburg, New York*

The wedding of Peter Thompson and Eliza Abbott (*center*), August 25, 1903. The photograph was numbered for newspaper publication. Dorothy (no. 3) holds a basket of flowers; third from right (no. 16) is George Abbott, future director, playwright, and producer extraordinaire.

Dorothy in fourth grade.

Dorothy in Chicago with two of her father's sisters, "Aunt" and "Auntie," around 1911. "They rearranged my hair," she said, "and dressed me for the first time very becomingly."

The Women's Basketball Team at Syracuse, 1914. "Dot" Thompson is at the center of the top row.

Dorothy (*right*) with an unidentified companion during the campaign for woman suffrage. She was " 'in quest of the one beauty' and the one purpose."

Dorothy at the start of her career.

Top to bottom:
John Gunther, Rose
Wilder Lane, and
M. W. Fodor — three
of Dorothy's closest associates during her early
years in Europe. The
friendships she forged in
the 1920s would last to
the end of her life.

Joseph Bard during an outing on the Semmering, September 1923.

Dorothy at the Haendel-strasse in Berlin, around 1926. She was the first American woman to head a foreign news bureau.

Dorothy and Joseph in their apartment in Vienna: "Delirious with love I was, delirious with youth and love together. . . ."

Dorothy in Moscow, November 1927.

Sinclair Lewis in 1928. Within two years he had won the Nobel Prize in literature.

"Miss Dorothy Thompson." This photograph was sent to American news agencies with the announcement of Dorothy's engagement to Lewis. She was described in the papers as "the divorced daughter of a Methodist minister."

London, May 14, 1928: "I will marry you so gladly, with the old marriage service, for better or worse in sickness in health and forsaking all others, till death do us part." A month later Dorothy wrote in her diary, "It was a nice day. Hal didn't lose his temper with me once."

Starting off on the cara-
van honeymoon. The
Lewises' movements were
chronicled by newspapers
all over England.

On the road: Dorothy
shows Red how to wash
a teacup.

Dorothy with Michael Lewis. He "has a mighty nose," she reported, "a quivering nostril, a prodigious frown, a tremendous yell, and a charming grin. There is no question of his legitimacy."

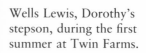

Wells Lewis, Dorothy's stepson, during the first summer at Twin Farms.

Opposite: In Barnard, Vermont: The "Big House" (*top*) — or "Dorothy's House" — and the smaller "Old House" at Twin Farms. Dorothy and Red paid ten thousand dollars for the two houses, on three hundred acres.

Fun times in Italy: Dorothy and Red on a rare relaxed holiday, late summer 1932.

Christa Winsloe.

The party on the Sem-
mering, Christmas 1932.
On the sled are (*left to
right*) Peggy Wilson,
Lilian Mowrer, Dorothy,
and Mrs. Robert Nichols.
Christa Winsloe (with
head bowed) stands next
to Peggy. Red and other
guests look on.

Red, Michael, and Dorothy Lewis — "so terribly lifelike," said Dorothy bitterly, "that you almost convince me that's me."

Dorothy and Red at the Brandenburg Gate, January 1931.

At the Nobel Prize ceremonies in Stockholm: Red (*at right*) prepares to deliver his speech — an attack on the American literary establishment.

to Budapest. Also on hand were Dorothy's sister, Peggy Wilson, who had had "a God-awful two years" in the United States and was staying indefinitely with Dorothy and Red in Vienna, and five children: Michael Lewis and his cousin, Pamela; Denis Fodor; Johnny Gunther ("Punch"), to whom his father later paid tribute in *Death Be Not Proud;* and Diana Jane Mowrer, the daughter of Edgar and Lilian. The idea, as Dorothy kept telling people, was to have *fun.*

"We've arranged for extra rooms and breakfasts in the house next door," she wrote to Knickerbocker in Berlin; "with any luck there will be ski-ing and tobogganing; there will be tea-dances at the hotels, and dinners and lunches by us, and if you don't come you will be making a mistake and we shall be most disappointed. It's our party from start to finish so all you need (but you are probably rolling in money) is carfare." [113] Unfortunately for everyone, at least in view of Dorothy's plans, there was hardly any snow on the Semmering that Christmas — "*not one flake,*" Lilian Mowrer remembered [114] — and so there was no skiing and very little tobogganing and not much to do except eat, sleep, and drink. There was, to be sure, a great deal of all three. Dorothy had rented a *dépendance* next door to the villa, a larger building that had once housed Empress Elisabeth, and it was here, every night, that the party repaired to dance and talk and booze until dawn. [115]

To everyone's amazement, Red Lewis was the only one at the Semmering party who abstained from alcohol. He went to bed at eleven o'clock each night and left his guests to get drunk by themselves. So unfamiliar was the spectacle of Sinclair Lewis sober that it had the opposite effect of what was intended: it actually made for tension in the house, because everybody present, knowing his record, had to wonder just when he would fall off the wagon. They were expecting Red to take a drink at any moment, and what with the lack of snow, the diversion of entertainment from the slopes to the bars, and a couple of fierce Prussian servants who kept ordering the guests from one room to another, the atmosphere in the villa was decidedly electric. Midway through the week, John Gunther took to his bed with a bad attack of asthma; his wife, Frances ("who was a B-I-T-C-H," in Lilian Mowrer's view), was constantly late "and holding *everybody* up"; [116] the children were starting to hit each other with shovels and snowshoes; and Dorothy, three days after Christmas, realized that she had fallen in love with one of her guests — a woman, a German writer and sculptor named Christa Winsloe:

Dec. 28.

So it has happened to me again, after all these years. It has only, really, happened to me once before: with G. [Gertrude Tone]. (Then I was twenty, and G. was 37, and I see her still quite vividly. She wore a black broadcloth tailored suit with white frills and a *jabot* and a big hat. She was very handsome, full-figured and womanly, and I wanted to be close to her, to be like her. . . . I fell in love with W. [Wilbur Phillips] before it wore off, or went away, and all the time my feeling for G. was in the background. Sometimes I think I loved her better than anyone, and there's a queer tenderness between us still.)

I don't count F. ["F." is unidentified, but obviously she was a friend of Dorothy's in Berlin in the twenties.] Then, so many other elements entered. (Are there similar elements counting now?) But one was curiosity, and that plays no rôle now. I behaved awfully badly with F. In the end I hated (and feared) her. Just the same I still remember when she pulled my cheek down to hers that afternoon in Berlin (Schiffbauerdamm 28 [where the *Philadelphia Public Ledger* had its offices]) and her soft scented mouth —

Only I should like to have left it there. I should have left it there. The rest seemed such a perversion, a perversion of a love for a man. One loves men differently, and the culmination of love for a man, with me, is very simple. Those forms of sapphic love were like making love to . . . being made love to by . . . an impotent man. One sickens.

There's something weak in it and, even, ridiculous. To love a woman is somehow ridiculous. *Mir auch passt es nicht. Ich bin doch heterosexuel.* ["Anyway it doesn't suit me. I *am* heterosexual."] Even according to the very simple Freudian definition which determines the matter by the location of the orgiastic sensation. Like Marguerite in Faust, the *womb* throbs — not something else, more surface. All this petting is nothing without the deep thrust to the heart of one.

Well, then, how account for this which has happened again. The soft, quick, natural kiss on my throat, the quite unconscious (seemingly) even open kiss on my breast, as she stood below me on the stairs. . . . What was the sudden indescribable charm in that too-soft face, and the heavy-lidded eyes. (The upper lid is very arched, the lower straight.) Anyhow immediately I felt the strange, soft feeling . . . curious . . . of being at home, and at rest; an enveloping warmth and sweetness, like a drowsy bath. Only to be near her; to touch her when I went by. She has a quite simple, unconscious way of kissing the inside of one's arm — I say "she has a way" and she only did it once. "Don't go away." I wanted to say, "Don't go."[117]

Christa Winsloe was the divorced wife of the Hungarian Baron Ladislas ("Laci") Hatvany, an old friend of Dorothy's and Joseph Bard's from Budapest and one of the leading figures of Hungarian belles lettres. Christa was born in Darmstadt in 1888, the daughter of a Hessian cavalry captain, and raised in Berlin, where, for several years, she was a student at the *Kaiserin-Augusta-Stift*. This was the "strange, stiff and solemn" Prussian girls' school that Christa later recreated in *The Child Manuela*,[118] the story that became the basis for the notorious "lesbian" film *Mädchen in Uniform*. When Dorothy first knew her, in the early twenties, Christa was still married to Hatvany, but she lived most of the time by herself — both in Munich, where she kept an atelier for her work as a sculptor (and an accomplished one, at that), and in Berlin, where the "Manuela" story, in Christa's stage adaptation, enjoyed its first scandalous success. It was not, in fact, a scandalous piece; it is a classic of feminist literature, the drama of a young girl in love with one of her teachers, but its openly lesbian sensibility and its violent ending ensured that it would be remembered mainly for its shock value.

There had been no hint of a romance between Dorothy and Christa during the first years of their acquaintance. There had been no hint even of any particular friendship. "This never happened to me, then," said Dorothy. She had appeared in Budapest as Laci Hatvany's friend, not Christa's, "and surely in those days I bored her," she thought; "I belonged to the political side of the dinner table." But 1932 was the year of Christa's greatest success, the year that *Mädchen in Uniform* was made into a film, and Dorothy had invited her to the Semmering in the knowledge that she could hold her own with any celebrity there:

> Her name suddenly had a magic quality. C[hrista]. I wanted to say it. To use it. I talked about her to others, to hear her name. Like holding an amulet in your hand, that was what saying her name was like. I love this woman. There it stands, and makes the word love applied to any other woman in the world ridiculous.

Dorothy left the Villa Sauerbrunn on New Year's Day — without Red, and without Michael — and went east with the remnants of her Christmas party, through Vienna, past Budapest, and all the way to Hatvan, the Hungarian country estate of Christa's former husband,

Laci Hatvany. ("For two divorced people they are the most married couple I have ever seen," said Dorothy later. "They write to each other about five times a week.")[119] Christa, who had gone to Hungary herself a few days before, met the party at the train station in "a black fur coat — lamb, with a high collar of sable and a brown tilted hat"; she "looked exquisite," in Dorothy's view, "beautiful and worldly, as I remember her":

> The curious thing is how vividly I remember things about her after all these years. Once at Lainz, in summer, there was a tea party, which dragged on. She was going somewhere to dinner later and wore a white dress — some thin stuff, embroidered all over with small white beads. Consciously, I only thought: she looks beautiful. But years afterward I bought a dress like that, because she had worn one. Another day we walked through the villa [at Lainz] — it was an ugly house, with big bare rooms full of bad furniture and the usual imperial taste. When we went through her bedroom, the bed had been opened for the night, and the bidet pulled out. I was somehow shocked at the insouciant and quite unveiled presence. . . . I wondered what sort of life she led. She had the animals which she loved and modelled in the garden. I could see her in tweeds, always walking alone. She seemed to me always lonely, repressed and volcanic. Even then I wondered at her relation with Laci. I don't usually speculate about people — what they do in bed. I have inhibitions — and I hate that people should speculate about me — still many thoughts crossed my mind about Laci. . . . I think he never understood her at all, but was fascinated by her . . . and still is.

Christa was a beautiful woman by anyone's reckoning, dark and sophisticated, soft, languid, and intensely feminine, despite her tweeds and her "mannish" haircut. Helen Wolff, who knew her through her husband, the publisher Kurt Wolff, remembered glancing into Christa's closet at a hotel in Paris and seeing row upon row of identical tailored suits, ties, blouses, and tweed skirts, which Christa wore as a sort of uniform. She was not, for all of that, merely "a woman's woman." She was "appealing to men," "beautiful, . . . in her speech warm, spontaneous, straightforward."[120] The other word always used to describe her was *sensitive*. She was "almost too sensitive," said Jimmy Sheean, and "could pass without transition from tears to laughter and back again. If anything moved her to pity or terror she would say, '*Ach, Gott!*' under her breath, and it was a prayer."[121] In *The Child Manuela* Christa had given vent to the most

elemental and genuine girlhood feelings, and it was this same simplicity, this authenticity of emotion, that was echoed now in Dorothy's diary: she was acting like "a baby" over Christa, she feared,
like "a love-struck adolescent."

"Believe me," said Dorothy, "I laugh at myself. I am perfectly
conscious that I am absurd." An unexpected contretemps between
Christa and her ex-husband at Hatvan that New Year's — a dispute
over money — left Christa in tears and Dorothy with a heart "like
lead. I could hardly speak during dinner. . . . [But] immediately
afterward she was kind and warm, and she put her arms around me,
and the rest of the day was heavenly."

> I put the incident down here as a record of my own sensibility to
> this woman [continued Dorothy]. What in God's name does one call
> this sensibility if it be not love? This extraordinary heightening of all
> one's impressions; this intensification of sensitiveness; this complete
> identification of feeling? It was so when I read her book and suddenly
> felt that I *must* translate it, because in its essence I might have written
> it myself. *I* was Manuela, as she is Manuela, and everything that has
> happened to her has, in essence, and other circumstances, happened
> to me. This incredible feeling of sisterhood. . . .
>
> We came back after visiting the wide-horned white oxen in the
> stalls, and watching the sheep moving about the barnyard like un-
> dulant brown waves, and spending half an hour sampling wines in
> the wine cellar. . . . We talked, C. and I . . . and talked of this and
> that and I was happy.
>
> At the house again gypsies played while we had tea and talked,
> and the little maid and the coachman sang. C. lay on a deep divan
> and I beside her, and she held her cheek on her hand, and looked
> quite young. . . .
>
> So then we had supper and left and went home.
>
> We kissed each other and she called me "liebling" and said: "I will
> write to you and telephone, and you will not get rid of me." And I
> felt full of beatitude.
>
> I put all this down to look at it: The result: There is not the *slight-
> est* indication that the extraordinarily intense erotic feeling I have for
> this woman is in any way reciprocated. I *feel*, of course, that it is —
> but the wish is so easily father to the thought. And if it isn't, I stand
> to make a damned bore of myself to a woman from whom, in the
> last analysis, I want only a warm friendship, and the opportunity to
> go on loving her no more articulately than heretofore.

Dorothy went back to Vienna on the night train and "dropped into bed" in the flat she had taken for the winter in the Wohlleben-gasse, then rose again at midday and made the two-hour drive to the Villa Sauerbrunn. "Above Glognitz the sun was brilliant," she reported. "Suddenly I was glad, glad, glad to be home with the party over." She went directly to find Red and saw that he, too, was happy to have seen the last of their guests:

> I could see that he was awfully glad. I stood a long time in his arms, loving his familiar feel and smell, rubbing my face on his face. What are you going to do? he said, and I said: First of all, take a bath. So he said: Stop in on your way down. I stopped in in a dressing gown and nothing else and he said: Come to my bed. So I did and it was awfully good. Especially good, with me just too tired to expect it to be and suddenly it was there and very wonderful. . . .
>
> I write all this out to be clear. Obviously there are two quite different feelings. I don't love Hal any less. Rather more.

They lay together for a long time, much longer than they were used to doing. Finally — "quite a while afterward" — Red turned to his wife.

"Darling," he said, "I didn't do anything. Did you?"

"And I hadn't," Dorothy realized. "And I didn't. It would be nice to have a new child as the end-of-the-party. So I slept all afternoon." Around six o'clock Michael came in and woke her up, climbing onto the bed and dropping a book in her lap: "Mammy wead."

"I kissed the back of his neck," said Dorothy, "and he smelled delicious, like a kitten. 'Mammy's pet,' he said and grinned delightfully. I think he will be a terribly attractive male."

"I have been very, very happy," she concluded. "And all the time, every moment, I have thought of Christa."

FOR just a little while after the Semmering party, while she and Red stayed on in Vienna in their rented flat, Dorothy tried to believe that her life had entered a new phase of contentment. She was pregnant, as she had hoped she would be, and the days with Red passed "happily," in "a gentle languor."

"I am not sure that having a child," Dorothy wrote, "actually bearing a child, isn't, for a woman, the only entirely satisfactory sexual experience. . . . I should like to have that long-legged red-headed girl that I imagined Michael would be. But — But —

But —" She had made no progress on "The End of Bourgeois Morality," and was working instead on a novel, a memoir of her marriage to Joseph Bard that was also destined never to be completed. Most of the time she spent reading and snoozing. "I thought I had married a serious publicist," Red told her one day, "a traveller, a conversationalist of parts, an economist, a reader of belles lettres. And what does she turn out to be? A cake-eater! A sleeper in chairs!"

"He only jeers at me when he is liking me a lot," Dorothy pointed out. They were both happy. In January, hoping to ward off another serious weight gain in her second pregnancy (and also, she suspected, because the heroine of *The Child Manuela* had loved to skate), Dorothy took up ice-skating, wobbling along to her lessons in Vienna three times a week. "My skating is atrocious," she admitted: "my left ankle is so weak that I cannot take a long glide upon it. . . . But I shall keep it up." It was worth the cost of the lessons, and much more besides, just to watch the children at the rinks. One couple in particular, a young brother and sister of world-class ability, seemed to Dorothy to express everything that the winter in Vienna meant to her:

> Suddenly the boy lifted the girl high [she wrote], his hands at her little waist, and then they were off, dancing together, she spinning at the end of his arm: now they skated with feet spread and calves turned out, their bodies flattened against the wind: now entwined together, with only two legs between them — he holding her foot, she his — now drawing away behind them: now pirouetting: now low on the ice their little feet dashing from under their crouched bodies. . . . And I noticed that whenever . . . she floated away, he was after her, swiftly, and whenever he glided away, she followed him, her long, pale, childish legs seeming to trail after her narrow, eager body.

She got home from skating one day and found that Red had wrecked the apartment — he was drunk, and in an alcoholic frenzy he had smashed the dishes, the pictures, and the rented furniture. When she screamed at him, he hit her, something he had never done before, and very soon she realized, "I must save myself; I must really, now, save myself." [122]

8

CHAPTER

"D ARTHY is leaving Wredde," Philip Goodman wrote to H. L. Mencken from Vienna, using the wise-guy nicknames the two of them had devised for the battling Lewises. "Yesterday was the pay-off when they came to blows that were actual and not rhetorical." For as long as it lasted, Dorothy made no secret of her resolve to have done with the marriage:

> Her charges will be simply that he's a dirty son-of-a-bitch [Goodman explained]. She wishes no alimony, but only to be rid of him. Say what you will, the woman is all decency and dignity. Her stories are long, it is true, and that she is a lady journalist (worse, a lady foreign correspondent who is always privy to wars that are being secretly made between countries whose names she is unfortunately not at liberty to divulge) is also true. But she's not without steel in her character, and her inner self stands erect and rather proudly. As against Wredde, I'm all for her. . . . She has her own ego, and it goes marching down the street behind a brass band at times, and she is an energetic money-maker; but she is honest and not cheap, and she hates all of Wredde's vermin friends. More: she tells him so. Her plan is to earn enough to support herself and her baby, and to give Wredde the rest of the earth in which to get drunk and make a public damn fool of himself. At least, all this was the earful Lily and I got last night. For all I know, as I write this they may be in one another's arms.[1]

In fact, they were not even in the same country. In February 1933 Red took off for London while Dorothy stayed in Vienna to close up the apartment and the Semmering villa. She did not write to him at all for the better part of a month and may well have relished the uneasy tone of his letters to her as he sought to contain the damage.

"Darling," wrote Red on February 12, "did you note that on the 7th inst. I became 48 (forty-eight) years of age? I'm so sorry. I tried every way to keep from it. I skipped rope; I skied down appalling mountains; I read P. G. Wodehouse; but still I came to 4–8."[2]

A week later Red was more deeply in earnest, if not altogether clear about the nature of their trouble: "You seem to me in my mad life my one refuge and security. You see, I don't care a damn — not any more at least — for fame and all those amiable experiences, but only (and this is a not-too-easy contradiction) for you and Mickey on the one hand, and Freedom (whatever that empty thing may be) on the other."[3] And then, by the beginning of March, he was seriously alarmed. Red and Dorothy had talked about spending the spring together at Twin Farms, and he held the vision out to her now almost as a last hope:

> My lamb! Be happy! Vermont! . . . I long to be there with you. It is true, isn't it, that there will be apple trees, and flaming lilies, and the moon over the low mountains and you and me, after dinner, sitting smoking on the terrace, and inside, when it becomes chilly, the fireplace and lamplight and lots of books? Love me, so we can go home.[4]

She forgave him, of course; she forgave him in the end with the same rush of longing and forgetfulness that she always marshaled from a distance: "Oh, Hal, oh my darling my dear, it's a long time, and why did we ever quarrel, and why did you go back to spirits, and will we ever be happy and quiet again, and do you love me, and . . . and . . ."[5] But something had changed between them, something had snapped, and when Dorothy came back to the United States in the middle of May, she did not come alone. She brought with her the two great passions of her middle years: the struggle against Hitler, in which she was about to play a leading part, and Christa Winsloe, who by that time — if only for a short while — was her inseparable companion.

They were somehow curiously entwined in Dorothy's life, at least at the beginning, the twin issues of a sapphic romance and the mounting peril of the Nazis. Dorothy had suffered a miscarriage just before leaving Vienna — she had nothing to say about it except that it made her "depressed"[6] — and it was to Christa that she turned for relief. They had not seen each other since the New Year's party at Hatvan, but now they made plans to meet in Portofino, on the Italian Riviera. Dorothy had already packed her trunks and dispatched them to Italy with Michael and his nurse, the younger of the Haemmerli sisters, when suddenly, almost on a hunch, she boarded a train for Berlin.

"I know that you will forgive me," she wrote to Christa in Portofino, explaining the delay in her arrival, "because I know you will understand how I feel about the German situation."[7] Adolf Hitler had just become chancellor in Germany, and an election campaign was now under way in which the Nazis were hoping to secure a majority of the seats in parliament.

"There never were such elections in a modern western state," Dorothy reported later. "The entire opposition press was muzzled, and for much of the time suppressed. The chancellor's private army, the S.A. troops, and their picked division, the black-breeched S.S. men, broke up opposition meetings, terrorized the streets, staged rows, beat up Social Democratic deputies, and even assaulted leading Catholics."[8] Already the Nazis had turned their special attention to the persecution of the Jews, but at this stage of things, within weeks of their coming to power, anyone who opposed them was fair game. Dorothy was in Berlin on the night the Reichstag burned, and she stayed for ten days more to record the outbreak of "sadistic and pathological hatred" that attended the Nazi victory.

"It is really as bad as the most sensational papers report," she wrote to Red in New York. "Italian fascism was a kindergarten next to it."[9] She had intended to whip off an article for the *Saturday Evening Post* on her return to Vienna, but the atmosphere in Austria, too, "had gotten so poisonous that it even drifted in through closed doors, into one's writing room, like a poison gas, a disease germ, or a bad smell. It looks as though Austria [will] also go Nazi. And it looks as though the result of the Hitler putsch [will] be hell-to-pay."[10] Before leaving Vienna, Dorothy sent an agitated report of the Nazi takeover to an acquaintance in London, the pianist Harriet Cohen. Harriet was friendly with Ramsay MacDonald, the British prime minister, "and I can only think," she reflected later, "that [Dorothy's] unspoken reason for sending me this letter was that she knew I would take it, or send it, to him — which I did." There was no shortage of sound reporting on the violence that attended the Nazi takeover; it was front-page news around the world. But Dorothy and her fellow correspondents would learn soon enough how thick the walls of diplomacy were, and how difficult it was to rouse anyone outside Germany to the menace of Hitler:

> Harriet [wrote Dorothy], you must believe it, because I saw victims with my own eyes, and read many, many affidavits. . . . These S.A. men have gone perfectly mad. . . . They have a pretty habit of breaking into the houses of people whom they do not like — and they don't like anyone who is a pacifist, an internationalist, a Jew, a socialist, a Catholic, or a radical . . . dragging their victims out to so-called "*Braune Etagen*," which are big flats, usually used as dwelling quarters by numerous S.A.'s, and there simply torturing the victims. . . . They beat them with steel rods, knock their teeth out with revolver butts, break their arms — a favorite trick — give them a liter of castor oil; bring them out of unconsciousness by throwing water in their faces, or mustard in their eyes, urinate on them, make them kneel and kiss the *Hakenkreuz* [the swastika]. . . .
>
> Not a single newspaper dares to bring [out] anything of true events. The *Berliner Tageblatt* is unrecognizable. Three days ago the leading article was devoted to an account of conditions in Chile. Every single writer of any distinction has left the country: Thomas and Heinrich Mann, Erich Remarque, Arnold Zweig . . . Lion Feuchtwanger . . . Bert Brecht, [Ludwig] Renn. You must have read in the papers that Bruno Walter and Fritz Busch were prevented from giving concerts! . . .
>
> I keep thinking what *could* be done. I am so afraid that something bad will be done — that the liberal world will turn with hatred against Germany. I feel myself starting to hate Germany. And already the world is rotten with hatred.
>
> If only someone would speak: someone in a high important place who has the ears of the world.[11]

She was still hammering away at this theme when she got to Portofino in the middle of March. To Dorothy, the most amazing thing about the Nazi revolution was that nobody had protested against it — no one in authority, that is. "Most discouraging of all is not only the defenselessness of the liberals but their incredible (to me) docility," she said. "There are no martyrs for the cause of democracy."[12] From New York, where he had returned at the beginning of the month, Red was sending her news of the economic crisis in America, the bank failures that had shut down the country, the inauguration of Franklin Delano Roosevelt, and the onset of the New

Deal. It was a time of panic and confusion around the world, when people everywhere were clamoring for "leadership" and even such a sage and sober figure as Walter Lippmann, the political columnist for the *New York Herald Tribune,* could advise President Roosevelt that "the situation was critical" and that Roosevelt might "have no alternative but to assume dictatorial powers." [13]

"Apparently Roosevelt really is going to do something," said Red eagerly.[14] But Dorothy had heard it before: the Nazis, too, had been elected to "do something." She was working to develop the voice that would carry her, soon, to the top of her profession and beyond, not just as a spokesman for the forces against Hitler, but as an advocate of the strict defense of America's democratic institutions. "I am homesick and patriotic . . . ," Dorothy remarked. "I hope we behave well." [15]

> My own political credo has been reduced to an extremely simple formula [she wrote]: I believe the best kind of world is the kind of world that I and people like me can exist in most happily. It may sound terrifically egotistic, but I don't think it is. . . . If the world of thought, if individual human character bows to this mob rule of cynicism, unreason, confusion, and rage, we are going to be done for. . . .
>
> I shall write what I can. But it's not a time for exposition but for eloquence. . . . I wish Roosevelt could put into words for the American people what I feel: that I don't care, at this moment, whether the banks ever open or whether I ever have again a quarter or a tenth of what wealth I had five months ago; I don't care if I have to go and live in one room and do manual work for a living; I don't care *what* happens to me, if I can believe that decent human feelings between men and men, between races and races, between peoples and peoples can be preserved in this world. I hope this doesn't sound . . . like a melodramatic tirade.[16]

She set up house in Portofino with Christa and Michael, Nurse Haemmerli, and an effeminate Italian butler named Giovanni. "He does everything but [our] hair," she told Red; "he arranges our clothes, and keeps the house supplied with the loveliest arrangements of flowers. . . . Portofino is below us, and looks like a cheapish stage set for *Cavalleria Rusticana* — all front and no back. . . . I like it here. . . . If I can't live with you in Vermont I had rather live with Christa here than anything I can at once imagine." Every morning Dorothy and Christa worked in their separate rooms, Dorothy on "Back to Blood and Iron," her article for the *Saturday Evening Post,* and Christa on a "spiritualist" play she was writing. "Then we walk until one," said Dorothy, "lunch very lightly — the kind of lunch women living alone have — sleep for a little while — work again until tea; sometimes visit a neighbor then; have our baths, dine at eight; work an hour, or read, or talk, and go to bed at ten." The house was charming, though it had "very little sun."

"I wrote 'sin' instead of sun," said Dorothy, "— page Mr. Freud — and that, alas, is also true!" But Christa was "an angel," and Dorothy had decided "that what every worker needs is a wife."

She was trying to be funny: at no point in her correspondence, with Red or with anyone else, was there any frank admission of a love affair with Christa, and the unavoidable questions about their friendship — whether or not it was physical, whether it was *consciously* homosexual, or merely intimate, special, "tender" — were not going to be answered to anyone's satisfaction. Christa Winsloe was just "the most sympathetic woman I've met in years and years," said Dorothy. She was careful to advise her husband that it was "terribly funny sharing a house with another woman" — it reminded her of Syracuse and college days. And she added, "As for your last admonition to me — do you remember it? — have no fears, I ain't thata way."[17]

It would appear that she really believed what she said. She had written already that lesbian love was "ridiculous," "a perversion of a love for a man," and her notebooks now were crawling with protests about the nature of her attraction to Christa. As often before, Dorothy's thoughts came out in the controlled, self-conscious framework of a poem:

> What can I do, then, with this so great love,
> I being woman? There is no release
> In intermingled flesh; I cannot prove
> With lips and hands my love. There is no peace
> For you in me, no shudder bringing rest.
> These bones like yours, these too receptive thighs,
> This yielding flesh, these arms, this too soft breast,
> Offer you nothing, for they say who lies
> With her own flesh lies with futility.
> Shall I then sue for pity, beg of you
> Pardon for loving, in humility?
> Rather I swear, I know this to be true:

This love will find its form nor be less fair
Because it is incarnal as the air.[18]

It may have been this sonnet, among the several she wrote that
year, that Dorothy gave to Christa Winsloe at Portofino, and that
Christa carried with her one whole afternoon while she paced the
terrace outside the house. She experienced "a frightful longing"
when she read it and recited the words to herself "over and over"
that day. There is (and was) no doubt about Christa's feelings, nor
any question that she was far more comfortable than Dorothy with
the fact of their affair.

"Dotto," wrote Christa, "hold close to me, please . . . or I'll collapse. You are dearer to me than you know. . . . *Liebes Dotto Du.*
Whenever I think of you I see your dear gray . . . no, they're blue
. . . your dear blue eyes, filling with tears. . . . *Liebste Herzens-
gans,* don't cry. . . . I kiss you, darling, and stroke your hair, my
Grauli Mauli, Du."[19]

They would both look back on their six weeks at Portofino, when
they were working well, and eating well, and drinking a lot of wine,
as the happiest time they ever knew together. "My God," said
Christa later that year, after she had followed Dorothy to Vermont
and New York and been caught up in the whirl of American life,
"where is Portofino? . . . just to sit with you again in the scented
pine forests, to sweat with you in the sun . . . to look at the sea
. . . with you . . . again." Most of Dorothy's letters to her were
lost in World War II, but Christa's own ardent pages — typed, usually, in a "burry, furry" mixture of English and German[20] — were
kept in Dorothy's files to the end of her life. No attempt was made
either to censor or to explain them.

"Good night, darling," wrote Christa one day. "I love you, and
I rejoice to know how your care and your love surround me. I have
slept in your eiderdown, I have drunk your wine, I am using your
face-cream and wearing your slacks. . . . It's as though I exist only
as the creation of my Dotto. . . . *Such* a Dotto as no one else has,
so kind, so dear, so good, and *ach* . . . sometimes *so-o-o* sweet."
Christa was no less discreet than Dorothy when it came to explanations — none was needed between them — but no one reading her
letters could miss the references to the lesbian culture of the time, or
doubt the deeper meaning of her words. Did Dorothy know that the
hummingbird was called, in Hungarian, the *Sappho madár,* asked
Christa — "Sappho's bird"? Had she watched the cats at Twin

Farms? Pansy, the latest addition to the clowder, had fallen for Silver King, the big white tom — "so completely that we were sure she was a girl. And then right in front of my eyes Pansy started using Silver King as if *he* were the girl. . . . Oha," said Christa, ". . . ain't it *awful!*" She signed herself "Christian" in her letters to Dorothy, or sometimes just "Chris," and often employed the German masculine pronoun for them both.

> And if *you* have reason to be sad [wrote Christa], still you have to say to yourself: the thing with Christian, *that* I did well. . . . Darling, I lay my arms around your neck and whisper in your ear: Your cares are mine. . . . I am with you. . . . I *am* you . . . because with you I am myself. I am with you, and I love you, and I don't need to give myself up.
>
> . . . Many, many little kisses, and a last one, finally, on your sweet Baby mouth.

"Red knew all about it," said Jimmy Sheean, who was the first to see the correspondence between Dorothy and Christa after Dorothy's death.[21] That opinion was second-hand, however, and Jimmy did not believe that Dorothy's affair with Christa had "amounted to much. Naturally it aroused her keen curiosity, her desire for self-analysis, etc., etc." Dorothy's sister, Peggy, who knew her better in a certain way than anyone else, also confessed that she was "surprised to hear about [Dorothy's] love for Christa Winslow [*sic*]." But Peggy knew how jealous Red had been of the women in Dorothy's life — "Red thought that Genia [Schwarzwald] was in love with Dorothy," Peggy remarked, "and that's why he hated her so"[22] — and she also knew that Christa, during the summer of 1933, had been asked to live with the Lewises at Twin Farms, then sent away again, and then abruptly asked back, in what looked like the workings of an overwrought triangle.

Dorothy never asked for her husband's permission to bring Christa Winsloe to Vermont. She merely asked him to send her a note of welcome. She took the position that the author of *Mädchen in Uniform* could not go back to Germany under the Nazis (though Christa did go back, many times, over the next several years), and so she said to Red, "Please write a note to Christa and tell her you are glad she's coming. She's a little nervous about you, and afraid."[23] Red and Christa got along well enough temperamentally, and in other circumstances they might have been good friends, because Christa liked men, even if she did not take them seriously. She called

Red "*der Rote,*" and acknowledged to Dorothy that "he really does care for you a great deal. . . . He's jealous." But if there was some effort at Twin Farms that summer to hold feelings in check, there was not, strictly speaking, any concealment of the facts. Dorothy's sexual ambivalence may have been the object of a certain amount of speculation during her years as a foreign correspondent; it had never, until now, been the object of gossip.

"They were a couple," said John Farrar about Dorothy and Christa. "If you asked Dorothy to dinner, you asked Christa, too."[24] In 1933 Farrar published *The Child Manuela,* and that year he and his wife, Margaret (the champion and popularizer of the crossword puzzle), saw a great deal of Dorothy and Christa both. It became a matter of interest to see them *apart,* so that Christa could report to Dorothy after a party at Carl Van Doren's, "Clare Brokaw [later Luce] graced the company in diadem and lilies and black velvet and was pleased to ignore me. . . . She asked about you. . . . Whenever I go out alone with people they peer around and say: 'How is Dorothy? Where is Dorothy?' . . . I like it when they think of us together. I like it, that people think of Dotto when they look at Christa." The same evening, with great ease and satisfaction, Christa fell into conversation with "a painted fairy" of Clare's acquaintance, a little man "who wanted to talk about Nijinsky and planted himself at my feet, thinking that I would understand him, and he was right, I did. I thought he was lovely." Lilian Mowrer remembered the night when Christa and Dorothy, "tight" and laughing over some private joke, "staggered" into Dorothy's apartment on Ninetieth Street and "fell into bed together." She remembered it because Dorothy had apparently forgotten that she had invited Lilian to stay, and because Lilian, up to that point, had never thought of Dorothy as "an active lesbian."[25]

"Almost never in my life have I been able to bring this mess which is the original me," Dorothy wrote to Christa, "plus the cultivated me (cultivated in the agricultural sense of the word) into harmony." She was making another mighty effort at self-analysis, as she always did when having a love affair, and she had developed a theory of herself almost as a split personality: "Sometimes the original me has fallen in love, and that has been grand love, and I have tired of it from one day to another; sometimes the other me has fallen in love, and when that has happened the love has died of malnutrition, and settled into an amiable friendship, but if ever the two parts of my nature have found any outlet in a single person, at once, then it has been a fatal business, and so far that has only happened to me once, before this . . . before this." She would not give up on the old idea that her own talents were somehow inferior:

> At the very center of me and part and parcel of all of me [she wrote to Christa] is a belief in life and in creation and a terrific discouragement with myself that I put nothing new, nothing unique into the universe. Hence this passion, this urge to do something, to serve more creative natures, this admiration for some better self, which lies at the root of my attachment to Hal, and also at the root of my attachment to you. I think, you see, that you are very much better than I am. I think, perhaps, that I have something which this very-much-better-than-I-am person can use.[26]

She was careful to link her friendship with Christa — privately, in her own mind, as well as in public — to the menace of Hitler and the danger posed to the world by fascism. When they first came back from Portofino, Dorothy and Christa actually met the press together on the pier in New York, and Dorothy (after first denying that she and Red were headed for divorce) introduced "the Baroness Hatvany" as one of the leaders of the anti-Nazi crusade. They were just about the only anti-Nazis in New York at that time, though Dorothy was already being asked to explain the "mistake" she had made in her Hitler interview: had she not dismissed Hitler as "a little man" only a year before?

"I still believe he is a little man," she replied at once. "It is the apotheosis of the little man." The Jews of Germany, in the meantime, just to mention one example, were "truly in a helpless state."[27] Before long Christa and Dorothy, as experts on the situation, both embarked on lecture tours, and Christa got Dorothy "all excited" about a "tragic revue" she wanted to see produced on Broadway, "a kind of cavalcade of war which is obsessing her at the moment."[28]

"You know well," wrote Christa, "that the world, our world, is passing away. . . . I want so badly to write something, something that will shock people awake, a terrible warning about what is coming. *Vor Krieg, Dummheit und Wannsinn* ["Before war, stupidity and madness"]. But I am so talentless, Dotto. I have only rage inside me, and no power . . . why, Dotto, why am I not a MAN?"

She was writing to Dorothy from the Princess Pat, a hotel in Virginia Beach, where she was staying, in one of the civilized gestures that typified the time, as the guest of Sinclair Lewis's ex-wife, Grace Casanova. Red had ordered Christa out of the house at the end of "a wild summer of coming and going,"[29] which had included, for Dorothy and Christa, a quick trip back to Austria, and, for Christa alone, a brief fling with a married man, the playwright Sidney Howard. Howard had been commissioned to draft a script for the stage version of *Dodsworth* and spent many days at Twin Farms that summer in boozy consultation with Red.[30] Like Dorothy, Christa had a penchant for "creative" men, and like Dorothy, she was given to the editorial view of sexual relations.

"I know I'm an idiot . . . ," she wrote to explain her liaison with Howard. "Perhaps I love the affair itself, and not *him*. I'm no different from other women. I love to love, and I want to be loved. And when somebody makes a gesture — somebody like that — I stand there in flames." There was no cause for Dorothy to be jealous, Christa hastened to add. It was advice she needed to repeat: "Essentially nothing on earth can come between us . . . not a man . . . not on my part, anyway. . . . What we have together lies on another plane. . . . Men for 'us' are only good for a time, but not *à la longue*." And if Red Lewis could not tolerate her presence in the house any longer — well, Christa could understand that, too. She had done what she could to be friendly to Red — to be "*menschlich*," unthreatening — and had even written to him lightheartedly when she and Dorothy were in Austria:

> Dotty is doing a lot of shops. I . . . did not always join her because it was too much for me. Dotty has the strength and perseverance of six men, and I mean I have not. One day I promised to join her later. I found the young man who had taken her around, under a heap of curtains, he had fainted. The lady who had taken his place screamed with hysteria and just got carried off by the firebrigade. The boss of the shop was on his knees before her, imploring her.[31]

But it was all too much for Red, and the only thing Dorothy could think to do while Christa licked her wounds in Virginia was to step up her own lecture engagements. She went to Bermuda for a while with Red and the child whom Christa was calling "Micky, the Wrath of God"; then Red started talking about moving to England. Dorothy let him talk: "I get so goddamned tired that I feel like crawling into a mousehole and dying there."[32] In fact, her health was giving cause for alarm. In 1933 she was diagnosed as having diabetes and embarked on the first of many dozens of strict diets, regimens that were meant to stabilize her condition and help her lose weight but that she always found reason to abandon eventually.[33] When Red abruptly (and only temporarily) removed himself to Chicago, Dorothy called Christa back, and the two of them managed to spend the rest of the autumn together. They were defiant. "Who is Red going to throw out of the house next time," said Christa wickedly, "if he's all by himself?"

They were living in Bronxville, north of New York City, in a sprawling, mock-Tudor mansion at 17 Wood End Lane. Red had bought the house for Dorothy on her most recent return from Europe, and over her vigorous protest: she had wanted to keep the apartment in New York. Ideas were never easily gotten out of Red's head, however, and presently she found herself cast in the role of suburban matron — "a Kansan," as she described herself to Charles Angoff, Mencken's friend.

"I looked into the mirror this morning," said Dorothy, "the bathroom mirror, and I do look like a Kansan, and I say this without any disrespect to Kansans. Really, I mean it. A Kansan in Westchester!"[34] There is evidence to confirm that she was deeply unhappy at this time. She was in a foul mood when it came to "It," at any rate — "the well-known 'situation.'"[35] Angoff heard her muttering about "bad women's magazines" and the menace they posed to culture. Democracy was "too successful," said Dorothy, "and since there are more silly women than silly men, it's going to be terrible."[36] In 1933 she was introduced to Dale Warren, who represented her friend Phyllis Bottome at Houghton Mifflin, and who became, over time, one of Dorothy's own most cherished companions. Dale knew her from the start as a vibrant and incurably "sanguine" personality, and he was surprised, one day, meeting her at the house in Bronxville, to find her practically immobilized with gloom.

"I am glad to see you," said Dorothy without conviction, "but I don't feel well and am very depressed." And with that she withdrew to her room, even though Dale had been invited to dinner.

"I don't see why I am so depressed," Dorothy continued when she emerged again. "Spring is here, and I have been to the matinee."[37] It transpired that she had gone to see *The Children's Hour,* and Dale thought to himself that this was sufficient explanation for her despondency, because one of the heroines of Lillian Hellman's drama hangs herself at the end of the story rather than confront her attraction to another woman. Of course Red was drinking, and that would have had its own bearing on Dorothy's frame of mind. Jimmy Sheean recalled the Lewises' "half-controlled hostility" on the "very few occasions" when he actually saw them together during these years;[38] others spoke of a "deadly rivalry" and actual violence — as when the young Brendan Gill, fresh out of Yale and calling on Red to patronize some alumni project, visited the Bronxville house and watched as Dorothy and Red fell into a shouting match. The dispute concerned a housemaid whom Red had fired without Dorothy's permission.

"Lewis started cursing her," Gill remembered, "she returned his curses, and for the first time I heard on the lips of a woman an expletive that I had supposed was reserved for the use of men. Bitterly mocking his reiterated use of the term, she said to him, 'Ah, balls, balls!' I sat aghast with wonder . . . so this was what marriage between superior people came to." Gill had already looked on in horror as Red, drunk, struck little Michael "hard across the mouth" and then collapsed in "paroxysms of drunken remorse, crooning and gibbering, of course to no avail."[39] The household at large had perfected a kind of mass vanishing act that was performed every time Red came home drunk. Dorothy could be found on these occasions sitting tensely with the servants in their quarters, knowing that Red, while he might behave abominably to his family and friends, was "very much the grand signor" when it came to his "inferiors," and would never dream of entering their rooms uninvited.[40]

"I suspect Red of liking to receive deep bows from servants," his friend Philip Goodman opined,[41] but these days, more and more, he was just hungry for company — anyone's company. Night after night he sat up late with Emily Walker, the hardheaded Scotswoman who had stepped in as Michael's nurse and became a virtual factotum in the Lewis house, "the top domestic employee" among a small army of workers. ("She's little," said Red, "but she keeps that brat of mine quiet.")[42] At Bronxville, till all hours, Red sat reading books, or listening to music, or just staring into space while Emily discreetly watered the Scotch.

"He worshipped the ground you walked on," Emily told Dorothy many years later, reminiscing about Red. "When he heard you were coming home from a trip, he would send for the barber to shave him, insist that all his clothes should be in apple-pie order, dress as though he were going to court. And then, often you'd hardly be in the house, when he'd start a quarrel, and then, as likely as not, he'd call the car and leave next morning. You don't know how often I'd go to my room and cry. I never understood why he acted so."[43] In a last effort to manage the situation, Dorothy and Red agreed on a system of rationing his drinks, but it was an absurd proposition and it failed at once. The servants all remembered the day when Red arrived home unexpectedly in a taxi. Dorothy and Christa had been drinking martinis, and at the sound of the cab Christa grabbed the bottles and glasses and stirrers and olives and dashed for the pantry, only to trip over the stairs and land at the butler's feet, where Red found her, gin pouring all over the floor.[44] On this occasion he laughed aloud, but he might well not have, and there was no better moment to dramatize how deeply he had been frozen out of Dorothy's life.

Christa went back to Europe just after New Year's 1934. "I think you'll be coming after me soon," she wrote to Dorothy confidently. "You've got to separate from Red somehow, that's for sure — otherwise you're *kaput* with me." But Dorothy was touring America, facing "shoals and shoals of women"[45] on her lecture dates, writing "a great many book reviews and some dramatic criticism,"[46] and fighting off depression while she wondered what to do. She was in a veritable temper by the time she got to Twin Farms in the spring, and she took on a tone with the Vermont staff that hitherto she had not dared to assume. Bill Lucia, the carpenter, Mrs. Currie, the cook, Mrs. Waller, her secretary, and "Stub," her nemesis in the garden, all came under Dorothy's supersensitive scrutiny that year.

"A vegetable garden is a garden," Dorothy advised the farm brigade in a cranky memorandum. "The only reason we have a vegetable garden is for beauty and pleasure. It costs about five times as much to grow vegetables with the wages we pay as it does to buy them." In the meantime, the grounds were a mess: "You dig out weeds and leave piles of them overnight or for several days. They look like hell. No gentleman's place ought to look like that. . . . If you don't want to do it my way, then find someone else to work for. . . . I am very serious about what I am saying."[47] She was still fuming over the presence at Twin Farms of Lou Florey, Red's secretary and companion, whom she accused of feeding Red's mania for alcohol and indulging his worst instincts for pranks and shenanigans. Although Red did take an interest in the running of the estate, more and more he was calling it "Dorothy's creation" (which more and more it was), and one night at dinner, after she had prepared "an epicurean salad" from her herb garden, he called the guests to order.

"I'll tell you the best way to eat herbs that ever was," he announced. "You go out to the garden and pick every damn herb in sight and take them into the kitchen, tell the cook to throw them all into the garbage pail, and use salt and pepper instead."[48] The relations between the Lewises had become so icy by this time, and "so goddamned polite,"[49] as to make their outright battles seem preferable. Frequently Red deserted Barnard for Woodstock and holed up there with George Seldes, who had been one of Dorothy's colleagues in Berlin and well remembered Red's complaints as the marriage neared its end.

"George," asked Red one day, "you don't know anyone around here who is looking for a job as a mistress — at least a part-time mistress — do you?" Another time he demanded to know "why in hell he had had to marry a Roman senator." After Dorothy went back to Europe in June of 1934, the phone at the Seldes house sometimes rang in the middle of the night; on the other end was the German housemaid at Twin Farms. "Mr. Seyldes!" she cried. "Komm kvick! Mr. Lay-vis vill have D.T.'s!"[50] There was no one left to care for him except the servants and, for the time she was there, Peggy Wilson, with whom Red had developed a very real rapport, something approaching intimacy.

"Red used to say, when he was very drunk, 'I made a mistake and married the wrong Thompson girl,' " Peggy recalled. The thought had occurred to Dorothy as well. "He should have married you," she told her sister, and she seemed to be serious about it. But while Peggy agreed that Red was "wonderful" when he was sober, "kind and generous and without vanity,"[51] she also knew that he was in love with Dorothy, and it touched her profoundly to see his distress that summer when news came from Germany of the "Night of Long Knives" — the Nazi purge that eliminated, in one bloody wave of murders and executions, Kurt von Schleicher, Ernst Röhm, Gregor Strasser, and other "radicals" among Hitler's entourage. Dorothy was still on her way to Berlin when the assassinations took place, but Red was "hysterical" for her safety all the same, and "it required the whole evening to calm him."[52] Forthwith, as if to counter this unexpected emotion, he embarked on "some vague midwestern motoring"[53] and abandoned Twin Farms to Micky, the servants, the secretary, the gardeners, and "a hell of heat."[54]

Six weeks later, without warning, Dorothy Thompson was expelled from the Third Reich on the personal order of Adolf Hitler. It was the first time any such action had been taken against an American foreign correspondent, and it was the event that set the seal on Dorothy's rise to fame.

"Well, what do you expect me to do about it?" Red snapped to reporters when they came to him for a statement. "She's no poor, weak little woman who needs my help." But his voice cracked when he said it, and his hands were shaking more violently than usual.[55]

THE expulsion order was brought to Dorothy by an agent of the Gestapo while she finished breakfast in her room at the Hotel Adlon, on the morning of August 25, 1934. She had been in Berlin already for ten days, having come from Austria, where she had gone to gather information about the unsuccessful Nazi coup in Vienna and about the murder of the Austrian chancellor, Engelbert Dollfuss, and where she visited Genia Schwarzwald at her summer house on the Grundlsee.

"Of course Austria is very sad," Dorothy wrote. "Vienna put me in a suicidal frame of mind. . . . It is terrible to see the collapse of a world where once one has lived so safely and happily. It concerns me, I find, more than I would have dreamed."[56] Entering Bavaria later, alone and by car, she was surprised to discover how easy it was to move from one country to the next in a time of upheaval.

"I never knew just when I passed the border into Germany," she recalled, "because no frontier official stopped me. I thought it odd that there should [have been] border warfare so recently and all sorts of secret police, and yet no customs officials in sight, but it was so." She realized that she had entered Hitler's kingdom, finally, only when she saw the flags:

> They hung from all the houses. They were bright red with a black swastika in a white circle in the middle, and sometimes they hung from the second storey to the ground. They gave the streets an odd Chinese look. There were often several on one house — one for every family who lived there. They made the streets look very gay, as though there were a festival. If there is a flag for every family, there must be more than ten million flags in Germany, I thought, and all manufactured during the last year and a half. Ten million new flags because the old ones were different. Any flag that will stand the weather costs fifty cents, and the big ones five dollars or more. Someone must be making money in Germany, I thought.[57]

She took her time driving to Berlin from Freilassing, passing through Garmisch-Partenkirchen, Munich, Nuremberg, Coburg, and the southern reaches of Saxony and Prussia. Her arrival coincided with the death of President Paul von Hindenburg and the merging of the offices of president and chancellor into the person of the

Führer; a plebiscite had been called for August 19 to ratify, pro forma, Hitler's new position as head of state. Everywhere Dorothy saw evidence of the Nazi *Gleichschaltung* — that national "co-ordination," that "bringing into line" that accompanied the tightening of Hitler's grip. Whipping came back in the schools; dueling was restored in the universities; the loose federation of autonomous states that had constituted the German nation "was abolished overnight by *force majeure*," and an absolutely rigid, absolutely fascist form of government took its place.

"There are to be no minorities of opinion in the new Germany," said Dorothy, "and no division of loyalties. . . . Most men will wear uniforms, the badge of their membership in that secret, mystic community of blood-brothers, the German state. Women will, by preference, wear kitchen aprons and will stay at home and take care of the children, which they will gladly bear in large numbers for Germany. They will not hold political opinions — but then, neither will anyone else."[58] As she drove north, Dorothy passed row upon row of campaign posters, produced and delivered by Joseph Goebbels's brand-new office of Public Enlightenment and Propaganda.

"The election banners and posters did not explain any program," she observed. "They did not explain why it was good that Hitler should be the whole show, the head of the army and the navy and the civil service, and even head of the supreme court when he wanted to be, more powerful and supreme than any other person in the whole world. And of course there weren't any posters on the other side. You couldn't put up a poster: 'Hitler is a big stiff. Vote No!' It wouldn't even have been fun to try." At Murnau, Dorothy stumbled onto a summer camp of the Hitler Youth, "six thousand boys between the ages of ten and sixteen," brought together on the Führer's business. Still unmolested, bewildered by the eerie tranquillity of the scene, she took the opportunity to look around:

> They were beautiful children. I did not think they would ever grow up to be thick-set beer drinkers with rubber-tire necks. They sang together, and no people sing in unison as the Germans do, thousands of them, in the open air, young voices, still soprano, and the hills echoing! It made one feel sentimental.
>
> An enormous banner stretched across the hillside [and] dominated the camp. It was so huge that you could see it from the farthest point. It was so prominent that every child could see it many times a day. It was white, and there was a swastika painted on it, and besides that

only seven words, seven immense black words: YOU WERE BORN TO DIE FOR GERMANY!

There's lots of time to think when one drives a car. From Murnau to Munich thoughts kept racing through my head. "Little child, why were you born?" My father, who was a minister, would have said, "To serve God and your fellow man." My teachers would have said, "To become the most you can. To develop the best that is in you." Times change.

When I looked at my speedometer I was driving sixty-five miles an hour. I wanted to get away from there.

She arrived in Berlin and went straight to the Adlon, where the smiling, slick-haired bartender welcomed her with a martini and asked her for news of her trip. "It was good to be there," said Dorothy, "like home. . . . There was the big porter who can always get you anything you want — reservations when the airplane is sold out and money when the banks are closed. There was the manager who always remembers how many people there are in your family and what room you had last time. Oh, I was glad to be back! The French doors were open into the garden and the fountain was sparkling and the little lawn was as smooth as the finest broadloom, and a man in an apron was actually sweeping it with a broom. It was all the courtesy, all the cleanliness, all the exquisite order which is Germany." While she munched on plum cake and caught up with friends, Dorothy reflected that courtesy and cleanliness and order, in the years to come, would probably make their own contribution to the Nazi horror:

> I kept thinking of Doctor Klausener's ashes. He was a Catholic leader, and while they were killing the others [during the June purges], they shot him too. I couldn't find out just why. They cremated him and sent the ashes to his wife, parcel post, registered. At least I read this in an English paper. I kept thinking how it must have been when the postman rang the bell. I could imagine the postman — a nice, jolly sort of man. "Good morning," he would say. "I have a package for you this morning." Probably she would put it under her arm while she signed. Then the postman would tip his hat. They are awfully polite in Germany.[59]

In later years, after she became identified around the world as a leading opponent of the Hitler regime, Dorothy never exaggerated or misrepresented the circumstances of her expulsion from Berlin. In fact she played down the event as "a not-very-important incident in a dramatic revolutionary development,"[60] and emphasized that she had "not encountered the slightest discourtesy" when Hitler's agents came to call.[61] She knew that she was being punished for her mocking depiction of the Führer in 1932, in *"I Saw Hitler!"* What she did not know — what no one then could quite comprehend — was why Hitler had chosen this particular moment, so soon after the brutal purge of the S.A., to outrage foreign sensibility even more than he already had. For Dorothy's expulsion was not, as she liked to say, a minor incident. It was unheard-of in Western Europe at that time; it was a sensational, unprecedented development in international affairs, and it caused "a great deal of excitement and anxiety" in a world that was just getting used to dictators.[62] The journalist Bella Fromm, a social columnist for the *Vossische Zeitung* and one of the best-informed women in Berlin, learned that the Nazis had been contemplating action against Dorothy for some time.

"The Fuehrer is going to have to let off steam against someone," an officer of the S.A. told Miss Fromm after the summer purges. "Perhaps it will be against Dorothy Thompson. They've established a Dorothy Thompson Emergency Squad that rushes translations of every word she writes. It won't be long now. They're just waiting for an excuse to kick her out of the country."[63] So far Dorothy had been no more condemnatory in her reporting of the Nazi dictatorship than many of her American colleagues (particularly Edgar Mowrer, who had left Berlin for Paris in 1933). But she was a lot more famous than most, and she had ridiculed Hitler in a way no gentleman would: "I bet he crooks his little finger when he drinks his tea." She found out later that Hitler had been especially bothered by some articles she wrote in opposition to his racial policies for the *Jewish Daily Bulletin* in New York. "They were articles of fact," she maintained, "not opinion. They were reports."[64] But the letter she received from the Gestapo in August 1934 made reference only to her "numerous anti-German publications," and advised her in the most diplomatic tones that "the German authorities, for reasons of national self-respect," were unable to offer her "a further right of hospitality."[65] She was asked to leave the domain of the Reich "in anticipation of formal expulsion," and given twenty-four hours in which to do so.

"The general feeling in the foreign colony here over the incident," the *New York Times* reported in its front-page story, "is that Nazism has once more demonstrated its utter inability to understand any mentality but its own, but in this instance it has outdone its previous efforts. Mrs. Lewis is the first correspondent actually requested to leave Germany. . . . However, there is more to the matter than that. There is good reason to believe — and the belief extends to the highest diplomatic circles — that the case of Mrs. Lewis is merely the first step."[66] Dorothy had wanted to test the waters and find out if the Gestapo meant business — that is, to see whether she would be removed from the country forcibly if she did not go by herself[67] — but the American ambassador, William E. Dodd, advised her against it, and in the end she decided not even to take advantage of the one-day extension Dodd had managed to gain for her through some careful diplomatic pleading. On the morning of August 26 Dorothy left Berlin for Paris on the *Etoile du Nord,* her arms filled with bunches of American Beauty roses, which her fellow journalists had given her as a token of their esteem and solidarity.[68]

"Nearly the entire corps of American and British correspondents went to the railway station to see her off and wish her good luck," the *Times* continued. As the train pulled away, Dorothy was seen to be weeping — not with regret, she insisted later, but in gratitude for the immense show of support she had received that day.

"I wish to protest warmly against the charge that anything I have written emanated from hostility to Germany," said Dorothy in a hastily prepared statement. "Were that so I should be a most ungrateful person, for I have spent some of the happiest years of my life here and enjoyed the hospitality of this country. I have immense respect for the great gifts of this people." She refused to equate the aims of the National Socialists with the greater good of the nation, however, "or to believe that what we see here now is the final state of Germany." She would not bow to threats and intimidation. The function of journalism, she said, was "to deal with ideas as well as with action. It is, of course, the right of any government to answer with an order of expulsion."[69]

As far as I can see [Dorothy explained], I really was put out of Germany for the crime of blasphemy. . . . My offense was to think that Hitler is just an ordinary man, after all. That is a crime against the reigning cult in Germany, which says Mr. Hitler is a Messiah sent by God to save the German people — an old Jewish idea. To question this mystic mission is so heinous that, if you are a German, you can be sent to jail. I, fortunately, am an American, so I was merely sent to Paris. Worse things can happen to one.[70]

She returned to New York on the *Leviathan* in the middle of September,[71] and when she did, for the first time, the reporters waiting for her at the pier were more interested in her tales of the Nazis than they were in the state of her marriage.[72] Her expulsion from Berlin had turned her overnight into a kind of heroine — a celebrity of note, the dramatic embodiment of the nascent war against fascism. Red came down to meet the ship and stood quietly on the sidelines, as she had done so many times for him, while she told the press what they could expect in the future: "tyranny," "murder," "blackmail," and war. "For the aim of the Hitler regime appears to be single," said Dorothy, and there would be no turning back from the course, not for Hitler, and not for her.[73]

"Germany has gone to war already," Dorothy said, "and the rest of the world does not believe it."[74]

SHE was in New York for only a short time before she disappeared "into the Stix,"[75] setting out on a thirty-city lecture tour, the first of three that would take her, over the next eighteen months, into every corner of the United States. Her lecture agent, William B. Feakins ("Management of Distinguished Personalities"), had announced that she was available to speak at universities and to women's clubs on a variety of topics, but it was Hitler that her audiences wanted to hear about, Hitler and the Nazis, and in fact all of Dorothy's lectures in this period revolved around a single theme. It was a theme that had begun to obsess her and that gave the twist to one of her husband's most successful books, *It Can't Happen Here*. Red's novel of a fascist takeover in America would never have been written, according to Mark Schorer, if he "had not been married to Dorothy Thompson, if he had not absorbed a good deal more than he often pretended from those excited discussions, in which she was the center, of the situation in Europe."[76] It *could* happen here, Dorothy warned, and it *would* happen if Americans were not careful.

"The German people have not had Mr. Hitler thrust upon them," she had written in the *Saturday Evening Post*. "He recommended himself and they bought him. . . . They bought the pig of autocracy in a poke, because they did not know or even ask exactly what form it was going to take." That the Nazi victory had come as a shock to so many people was due almost entirely to "sentiment," said Dorothy, and to "a couple of illusions fondly and incurably cherished" by the Anglo-Saxon mind: "One is the illusion that all peoples love liberty, and that political liberty and some form of representative government are indivisible. The other is that peoples are less aggressive than their rulers."[77] But they were not. It had nothing to do with being German; the vast majority of ordinary mortals, in Dorothy's experience, were impatient in troubled times, and Hitler had come to power in Germany "largely because so-called civilized people did not believe that he could."

> But civilized people were wrong [wrote Dorothy]. They thought that the complex of prejudices, standards and ideas accumulated at the cost of great sacrifice over a period of some hundreds of years was really greatly cherished by all men. Civilized people did not see that this culture is, actually, to the vast masses no treasure at all, but a burden, which can be borne only under exceptionally favorable circumstances. Beyond that point — if, for instance, by reason of economic malfunctioning masses of people are, for years, hungry and idle — the will grows to look upon civilization as a restraining, impeding force, and to identify revolt against it with freedom.[78]

She saw this principle everywhere in action, she believed, as the "Nightmare Decade" wore on. At the end of 1934 George Horace Lorimer, the right-leaning editor of the *Saturday Evening Post,* invited Dorothy to broaden her base, to abandon her preoccupation with European politics for the moment and turn instead to domestic affairs. Lorimer wanted three articles about the first New Deal (which, like all good Republicans, he abhorred), and Dorothy spent the opening weeks of 1935 buried in Washington, toiling "from nine in the morning till two in the morning, literally,"[79] in exploration of the mysteries of the federal government. The Roosevelt administration, beginning in 1933, had pushed through Congress a whole body of legislation that was aimed at curbing the miseries of the Depression and revitalizing the American economy from the top down. The "Hundred Days" that followed Roosevelt's inauguration had seen the introduction of banking acts, relief acts, conservation acts, and unemployment acts — all of them controversial, none of them tested, many of them headed for the political dumpster as the economy, very slowly, began to right itself. More significant than any purely economic effect of the New Deal, however, was the transformation it brought about in the federal bureaucracy and in the mind of the electorate. It is no exaggeration to say that American political opinion was split down the middle by Roosevelt's interventionist approach to the crisis. In an era of "conservative" editors and journalists, meanwhile, the press, when not overtly hostile, was mainly dubious.

"I have had one of the most interesting weeks of my life," Dorothy confessed at the start of her investigation in Washington. "I've spent days in the relief administration going through reports, looking at pictures, talking with people. . . . Here you can get a real picture of the line-up of forces, the whole struggle of American life is visible here. But it is *gruelling* work to get it, requiring terrific patience, because the picture is smothered in paper." She had nothing but admiration for the good intentions of the New Dealers: Interior Secretary Harold Ickes, Cordell Hull at the State Department, Henry A. Wallace, who at that time was secretary of agriculture, Homer Cummings, Rexford Tugwell, Jerry Frank, and above all Harry Hopkins, the enterprising head of the Federal Emergency Relief Administration. She suspected, however, that these "bright boys" knew "a lot more about things and economics than [they did] about people," and she came away from Washington convinced that the New Deal itself was "on the rocks."[80] For Dorothy it was the beginning of an ongoing quarrel with the policies of the Roosevelt administration — a very public quarrel, as it turned out, vociferous and even bitter at times, that would last through the end of the 1930s.

"I am the voter who in 1933 welcomed the New Deal," Dorothy affirmed several years later, in a speech before the Union League Club in New York. "We welcomed it because of its quality of awareness. Because it ceased the mumbo-jumbo about this being the best of all possible worlds, and set out to do something about it. We believed that something ought to be done about it. We knew that mistakes would be made, inevitably, but we believed that the effort itself might remain pure."[81] Now, in the fifth year of the Depression, Dorothy was looking for results. What had been the long-term benefit of throwing billions of dollars in welfare relief at a full 20 percent of the American population? What would be the ultimate effect of "State charity" on individual initiative? on national productivity? on human dignity? Why had there been no systematic, nationwide attempt to break down the unemployment rolls for careful analysis, "to find out how many people on them have ever worked, how many are genuine victims of economic maladjustment, how many are bums?"[82] Dorothy was deeply suspicious of the administration's emphasis on works projects — that is, the official policy of creating jobs to match the talents of the unemployed — and she feared the end result of a program that was ready to try out "not just anything, but everything at once" in the interest of economic recovery:

> This administration has been truly encyclopedic in its sympathies [she wrote]. It has tried, in the midst of depression, to raise wages and preserve profits. It has encouraged monopolies and sought to protect labor. It has advocated high prices and the protection of the consumer. . . . It is probably the most literate administration that this country has ever had since the early days when politics was believed to be a gentleman's profession, and it is certainly the most talkative. It is also probably one of the most truly representative of administrations, for it shares practically all the illusions of the typical American intellectual. It believes that any action is better than none; that the scientific attitude is synonymous with being willing to try anything once; that economic reform can be interpreted in terms of social uplift; and that the lion and the lamb can be brought to lie down together by persuasion.
>
> This is pre-eminently the administration of good will — on all sides. But the good, says the proverb, die young.

For Franklin Roosevelt himself, the man who had "gathered the whole kit and caboodle of the destitute to [his] bosom," Dorothy had normally respectful, but decidedly skeptical, words.[83] She did not labor under the assumption, common to a later era, that the President of the United States ought to be protected from criticism by virtue of his high office, or that he should somehow not be held accountable for the actions of his subordinates.

"Probably Roosevelt will be reelected," Dorothy remarked in a letter to Red, "but if things move in the present tempo I think we may easily have a Republican-fascist dictatorship by 1940."[84] She was not joking, and she did not imagine that there would be any difference between Republicans and Democrats when American fascism came.

"I do not like the constant reiteration that something — anything — must be done," she complained, "now, at this moment, in this instant, otherwise the whole country is going to bust. . . . In country after country, under one slogan or another, the people are retreating from freedom, and voluntarily relinquishing liberty to force and authority, with instructions to bring order into men's affairs. . . . Everywhere there is a demand for more efficient instruments of political power. And accompanying these demands is a growing tendency toward personal leadership and personal government."[85] It was easy enough to laugh at the crank element in the Depression, at the Dr. Townsends and the Father Coughlins and the Reverend G. L. K. Smiths, that seemingly endless parade of scripture-quoting charlatans who monopolized the papers and the airwaves. It was even possible not to take seriously a homegrown fascist such as Huey Long (though Dorothy did take him seriously, and made no secret of it). What could not be ignored was the rapid centralization of the American government under the office of the Chief Executive, and "the move away from an *informed* public to a *persuaded* public" — an electorate looking to be relieved of the burden of thinking for itself, so far as Dorothy was concerned, looking to be confirmed in its prejudices, looking to be told what to do by some dynamic and charismatic leader.

"This is the essence of the quarrel that many of us have with the New Deal," Dorothy wrote some time later,[86] when she had had time to formulate her opinions more clearly and when the actions of the Roosevelt administration had convinced her "that the President is intent on substituting himself and his own ideas, his own policies and his own hunches, for the checked and balanced government of this country."[87] The lion's share of New Deal legislation had been simply railroaded through Congress, a body so craven in the face of the public clamor for "action" as to be almost completely superfluous, in Dorothy's opinion. It was not because she thought Roosevelt had any particular aspirations to dictatorship that she insisted so stoutly on the primacy of means over ends, of form over content, of law over government itself: "What we are interested in is neither the dictatorial talents nor the dictatorial predilections of the President. We aren't concerned with whether he *wants* too much power, but with whether he can *get* too much power."[88] There would be no swastikas in the next American revolution, Dorothy supposed; there would be no need for them:

> No people ever recognize their dictator in advance. He never stands for election on the platform of dictatorship. He always represents himself as the instrument for expressing the Incorporated National Will. When Americans think of dictators they always think of some foreign model. If anyone turned up here in a fur hat, boots and a grim look he would be recognized and shunned. Likewise anyone resembling six Roman Emperors, or someone you must greet with a stiff arm and a Heil. But when our dictator turns up you can depend

on it that he will be one of the boys, and he will stand for everything traditionally American. Since the great American tradition is Freedom and Democracy you can bet that our dictator, God help us! will be a great democrat, through whose leadership alone democracy can be realized. And nobody will ever say "Heil" to him, or "Ave Caesar," nor will they call him "Fuehrer" or "Duce." But they will greet him with one great big, universal, democratic, sheeplike bleat of "O.K., Chief! Fix it like you wanna, Chief! Oh Kaaaay!" [89]

She was packing in two and three thousand people a night on her lecture tours, and had begun to move beyond her accustomed circle of "women and gardenias" and into the larger realms of public debate.[90] In New York she addressed the Foreign Policy Association and the American Society of Newspaper Editors and was one of the lead speakers at the Herald Tribune Forum, the prestigious nonpartisan conference on current affairs that was held every year at the Waldorf Astoria and broadcast simultaneously throughout the country. During her first appearance at the Forum, Dorothy shared the billing with President Roosevelt (whose speech was broadcast from Washington) and Carrie Chapman Catt, who gave her opinion that the feminist movement was "going forward" while Dorothy insisted it was "dead" — "as dead as last week's newsreel." [91] CBS had approached her with the offer of a position as a free-lance radio commentator, but she held out for better terms, and got them — from NBC.[92] From then until the end of World War II she was never far from a microphone, the instrument that did more than anything else to speed her rise as "an American oracle, one of those very few people who have the corporate, general permission to tell people what to think." [93] Always an effective speaker, she was also an entertainer, and she began to appear in news stories and press releases as "Miss Dorothy Thompson." Her voice was "well-pitched," said a critic for Scribner's magazine, "and needs but a little grooming, a little more experience, to qualify her for political campaigning. She could easily become the Lady Astor of America." [94]

At home, meanwhile, with Red, Dorothy's life continued in the same pattern it had always followed. Christa Winsloe had returned from Europe and gone to Hollywood to write film scripts "for better or worse," [95] while in Vermont it was "the end of summer, and not yet winter, and not yet even fall." The apples were "red and heavy"; the dahlias and gladiolus were "nothing but colored-stained rags." And "all the time" Dorothy was thinking "about what is important and what isn't, and that Micky was right when he said . . . 'Life is to be lived.' And that living was mostly loving when you were most alive, and that nothing else mattered so much."[96] Now and then it looked as though Red was serious about staying sober: "candy and music" were his chief companions in 1935 and 1936[97] — though he was drunk again the night he addressed a gathering of the League of American Writers and fired away at their socialist affectations. It was the heyday of the American Communist party, the era of the Comintern and the Popular Front, and *It Can't Happen Here* had been praised to the skies by every left-wing critic in New York. Dorothy sat silently (and "sourly," in the memory of at least one person there)[98] on the dais next to Red when he rose to make his speech.

"Boys," he began, "I love you all, and a writer loves to have his work praised. But let me tell you, it isn't a very good book — I've done better books — and furthermore, I don't believe any of you have *read* the book; if you had, you would have seen that I was telling you all to go to hell."[99] As Dorothy remembered it, Red was forever being asked to take sides against fascism by endorsing something dreadful in its place — some different ism, popular at the time, that invariably he knew nothing about.[100] "Now, boys," he concluded, "join arms: let's all of us stand up and sing, 'Stand Up, Stand Up for Jesus.' "[101] The young Granville Hicks, who was present that evening, suspected that Red might have been won over to the Communist line if it had not been for Dorothy's influence.

"I felt that she was afraid Lewis's high spirits and his desire to be liked might betray him into a kind of commitment to the Popular Front that she didn't want him to make," said Hicks,[102] and certainly Red was heard to answer more than once, when pressed for an opinion on current events, "Ask Miss Thompson. Miss Thompson is the political expert. I am not."[103] The reporters who came out to Bronxville now were coming to meet *her*; it was Dorothy's picture that graced the magazine stands, and she who was beginning to be quoted across America as "a sounding-board for world affairs." In January 1935 a lengthy and loving profile by her friend John Gunther appeared in the *New York Herald Tribune* under the title "A Blue-Eyed Tornado." There were stories in the *Literary Digest,* the *Pictorial Review, Time, News Week,* and the United Press, which reported somewhat mysteriously that "Dorothy Thompson — more recently Mrs. Sinclair Lewis — is going to drop lecturing, cease to be a world traveler and go home to be a mother to little Michael Lewis. The woman who interviewed Hitler and was brave enough to say she thought him neurotic, also is brave enough to rearrange her career in favor of her 4-year-old-son." [104] It was the kind of misinformation that Dorothy sometimes let drop in her weaker moments, but nothing could have been further from the truth.

"I want to live for four hundred years!" she shouted one morning, whooping for joy. "Well, three hundred, anyway. The world is so interesting, and I am so alive!" She was sitting in front of her bedroom mirror at Twin Farms, doing her hair and chatting with Marjorie Shuler, a friend from suffrage days who was on assignment to profile Dorothy for the *Christian Science Monitor*.

"It was to be a quiet day in the country," Miss Shuler supposed, until Dorothy informed her that "H. G. Wells was practically on my heels"; that Alma Mahler and Franz Werfel were coming to lunch, and Alice Roosevelt Longworth, and G. B. Stern. There were to be thirty guests that afternoon, said Dorothy, "or maybe 50." Michael Lewis was discovered on the terrace arguing with his violin teacher, stamping his foot and eloquently insisting, "You will never make me a musician. I shall be better with words. I don't like to study . . . I must live my own life," while his father mimicked radio personalities in the "Big Room" and Dorothy swept down the stairs in midspeech, swearing that the two-month lecture tour on which she was about to embark "would be her last, positively her last."

"Why go around in trains," she asked Miss Shuler, "when you can talk over the air to two million people, without leaving your husband and child for more than an hour or so? [105] It was a sensitive issue even for her — or perhaps especially for her, who was used to blazing her own trail — and her views on Marriage and the Family seemed to interest her audiences almost as much as did the threat of fascism. "Is woman happier in the home?" Dorothy was asked in 1935, during her lively and much-quoted radio debate with Sir Gerald Campbell. She answered that she would have thought the question had been settled already:

> I notice you say WOMAN, as though there were any such thing as an abstract WOMAN. I'm sure I don't know whether women as a whole are happier or aren't. You might as well ask, "Don't you think the Negroes were happier under slavery?" Or "Don't you think that mankind was happier in the feudal era than in the industrial?"

Or "Aren't people happier on farms than in the city?" But you couldn't restore slavery, or feudalism, or put every human being on a farm even if the answer were yes.

She was vividly entertaining on this subject, and refused to be side-tracked by the typical male objections to women's liberation:

Now look here. This business of whether women ought or ought not to have jobs comes up every time there is a depression with serious unemployment and men begin to say that women are taking away their work. . . . The fact of the matter is that men have been horning in on women's jobs ever since the Industrial Revolution began. Men have been taking away women's traditional work for the last hundred years. They began taking it away when factories were established to make clothes, and to can and package food, when hospitals were founded to care for the sick, and schools to teach and train the young, and hotels and restaurants established to feed people. Whenever women's work could be taken out of the home and operated for profit, men took it out. . . . The only work that is still absolutely reserved for women is bearing and nursing children, and I really believe that if having children could be made painless and profitable, men would try to do that, too.[106]

But Dorothy was not a "radical feminist," at least not in the trivialized sense that would later be attached to the term. She not only accepted the inherent differences between women and men, she cherished them — she *relied* on them, in fact, for the preservation of the race and as the only hope of world peace. When she declared that feminism was "dead as a doornail," she meant only that feminists had failed to keep up with their historic mission: "to make a new world," to produce "stronger, freer, more co-operative" human beings.[107] It wasn't enough to have won the vote.

"If the world is going to be regarded as a continual hunting, fishing and fighting expedition," said Dorothy, "— if it is to be regarded in terms of the primitive male activities — then it will go on as it has gone on, with booms, depressions, and wars. . . . It's going to be Caesars and World Wars throughout a long future, or it's going to be just the opposite."[108] Only when it came to the rearing of children were Dorothy's opinions and the facts of her own life noticeably at odds.

"No normal woman wants to leave her children when they are small," she maintained, and "no man will ever realize the agony that women go through, trying to give their attention to a job and [being] worried [also] about their children." On the other hand, Dorothy was confident that children would "understand it" if their mothers were absent from the home for long periods of time because they were engaged in some "useful and necessary" work.[109] With this reasoning, and with her arms full of toys, she hoped to deal with her own son, who had begun to articulate his unhappiness rather chillingly. She often worried about the effects of her traveling on Michael, but she was even more dismayed when she heard him say one day about Sinclair Lewis, "I think when I grow up I am going to kill my daddy."[110] Normally the child had "a funny babyish tact" when it came to Red, but it was becoming increasingly difficult for him to understand why his father, especially when he was drunk, ignored him so completely.

"Why does Daddy go away?" Michael asked "with a pained and hostile gaze," and Dorothy lied, as she had been lying to him already for some time, "He is tired."

> [Michael] sat up [she wrote], in his little plaid dressing gown, and put his little hands on each side of my face, pushing my hair back from my ears. "Moosey," he said, "I'll make a Moosey out of you." He has said that since he was a year and a half old. There is some special tenderness in it. He leaned his head on my breast. "Boonies," he said. Meaning bosom. He held my hands, then, lover-like. . . . Miss Nelson said that after I had gone next day he threw himself on my bed and wept bitterly. Now and then he asks suddenly for me, and is sad. He is terribly bound to me. . . . But independent and intractable. Very imaginative, [with] an extraordinary sense of words. "It's shocking that you go away," he said. "Simply shocking."[111]

But there was nothing Dorothy could do about it — or nothing she wanted to do. She was lecturing in more than forty cities during the winter of 1935–1936, moving from Pittsburgh to Akron and Chicago and St. Louis and down to the Mississippi delta, where she found "the highest rate of illiteracy in the country" and "the greatest amount of physical degeneracy and disease. . . . I never knew that we had such an economy in our borders as the cotton economy is, and I realize for the first time that we are an empire, not a nation, and have our own India and white man's burden."[112] She was exhausted by the trip and by "the difficult three-ring circus of my life,"[113] but she pressed on nevertheless to Cedar Falls, Iowa, and Wheeling, West Virginia, and Topeka, Kansas, past "miles of cornfields" and "wide, wide prairies," "grimy main streets" and "straggling, casual villages."[114] She insisted in later years that she had learned more about the United States on her lecture tours than she ever had in her official capacity as a journalist; that the time she had spent in strange towns and hotels, brushing coal cinders out of her hair and sponging down her black cocktail dress, with its reversible collars and its "so many buttons," had put her more deeply in touch with the shifting moods of the nation than all the interviews she had ever conducted. One morning she found herself in Tulsa:

> B'nai B'rith here and the Jews [she wrote]. . . . It is very early and my skin has that tight drawn feeling, dry and gritty that a night in a sleeper always gives it. We go to a hotel and the coffee room. Breakfast and more of the delegation. Eager, kind, interested. I am smothered in eagerness and kindness. But they have rooms ready for me, and flowers, and a pint of rye whiskey — Okla. is dry — cigarettes; thoughtfulness, hospitality, everything except leaving me alone "in my own temper." They want to talk about Hitler — the Jews — the Protestant revolt in Germany. I talk. I feel like a phonograph record. Coffee, orange juice, indigestion. Nerves getting jagged. Jumpy. Would I like to be alone? I would rather be alone than anything on earth. In my room undressing. A bath, Bed. Sleep. Clean clothes. . . . Clean stockings. A tiny lunch, all by myself, I think. But this doesn't come off. Lots and lots of people for lunch. All eager. All wanting to talk about Hitler and the Jews and the Protestant revolt and the Olympics.[115]

She got in the habit, never broken, of chatting with her neighbors on the train as she moved from town to town. Many times she sat up well into the night listening to their troubles, offering advice and sometimes practical assistance. One man worried that his wife was "smarter than he was, and what was this world coming to, and didn't [Dorothy] think that this country was really run by women, etc., etc."[116] A woman who worked in a beauty shop told bloodcurdling stories about the horrible things that could happen to you in a hair salon — "blindness and burns and poisoning and even death" — and insisted that "none of this ever got into the papers. . . . Not a word."[117] A mousy girl from Massachusetts was having romantic difficulties: her boyfriend had got another girl pregnant, a girl he didn't love but felt bound to marry anyway. Dorothy answered that the trio should "consider all sides" and that if they *really* wanted to do something, it would only cost them two hundred and fifty dollars:

She said she had that much. So I told her the name of a friend in Boston and said if she wrote me I would find a first rate physician, etc. And there I was all embroiled in the life of a total stranger and about to break the law of the land.

But I couldn't help it. I *hate* the hypocrisy and the class discrimination whereby a helpless girl like this can ruin her life and a woman like myself can do pretty much as she damn pleases.[118]

Sidney Howard's adaptation of *Dodsworth* was playing in Chicago when Dorothy got there at the end of 1935, and it made her think about the days when she and Red had first been in love and were living together at the Villa Galotti on Cape Posillipo. It gave her "that curious feeling of exposure, of revealed intimacies," to hear the characters speaking lines that had once come from her own mouth: "Have I remembered to tell you today that I adore you?"[119] She was calling her husband Red in her diaries, and not Hal, as if she wanted to distance herself from him even further than she already had. All the same, she "felt horrible" when he called her up at her hotel and gave her an ultimatum: "You will have to choose. I can't stand this. You live and move in another world than mine. I haven't a wife."[120] Dorothy had taken at least one and possibly, to judge from her diaries, two different lovers on this most recent tour of the Midwest; far from being happy with her choices, though, she was filled with contempt for the "adolescence of American males."

"High school boys," she called them, "every one of them . . . hopeless as lovers, all scared of their wives, undeveloped, childish, arrested. . . . This whole damned country is full of impotent men." It was a problem of "emotion," Dorothy figured. American men were afraid of it: "Afraid of emotion. But emotion is the life-source of everything; the eternally renewing spring. . . . The source of *growth*." Her suitors could learn something from their own sports heroes, Dorothy concluded; they could learn from Olympic skiers, for example, "that one leaps the precipice only when one is relaxed and *légère*. Free. Innerly free."[121]

"Oh dear God," said Dorothy as she hurtled across America, "I love to be the age I am, I wouldn't do away with a year or a day of the experiences of these years, but I *shall* grow old, and I don't want to."[122] She was riding through upstate New York on the Erie Railroad, thinking about the past, remembering:

It has not changed . . . autumnal fields, the broken fences, the stripped earth and winter coming. So familiar this upstate landscape.

216 = AMERICAN CASSANDRA

. . . A hundred memories, riding from Rochester to Geneseo, on the Erie. . . . Where did I used to go in the suffrage campaign . . . somewhere near here . . . Batavia. That was it. Batavia. One made the turn around the county. . . . And then, finally, one came to Batavia. . . . One lay in bed at night with a little light, and the room a cavern of shadow, and shadowy shapes coming out of it, and read poetry. "Oh wild west wind thou breath of autumn's being. . . ."

She stopped for the night with three women she had known in the suffrage campaign, women who had never left the territory and who were frozen now in "spinsterhood," relics of the good fight, "elderly . . . all passion spent. Was there ever a passion there?" asked Dorothy. "Two of them have lived together for nineteen years. Were they ever in love? With a man? With each other? Such things happen, they say." [123]

Her friendship with Christa Winsloe, her "affair," had petered out and then effectively ended when Christa fell in love with someone else. Dorothy and Christa had been together in Austria in July of 1934, just before Dorothy's expulsion from Berlin, when Christa developed a wild crush, an unaccountable passion, for the Italian basso Ezio Pinza, who was singing at Salzburg that year.

"Of course there are thousands of Italian soldiers and fishermen . . . who look as good as he does, and better," Christa admitted after she had chased Pinza, literally, from Salzburg to San Francisco, "and who can sing nearly as well, with less training. And none of them ever meant anything to me." It was Christa's way of assuring Dorothy that the shine she had taken to Pinza would dull completely in time. But Dorothy was not mistaken in sensing an underlying restlessness in her friend, an impatience, a cessation of "tenderness."

"I feel that something between us has broken," she wrote Christa in California,

and like all that love I wonder now if it was ever there. Oh, yes, it was there, but didn't all the threads run from me to you, and none really run back? You will not answer me, nor help me, perhaps only because you do not want to hurt me. I write with my eyes full of tears, and my heart full of tears, and I wish they flowed because of someone else, because then perhaps you would comfort me. Or would you? Why is it that one's *own* love can sustain one for so long without any reciprocity, and then, suddenly, it can't anymore?

I had a strange dream last night. I dreamed I was putting out into a very rough sea in a frail ship, and the crew were all women. I was afraid, and woke up, sweating. . . . Christa![124]

But if it was over, it was over. Dorothy had "never been a clutcher." She had "always let 'em go the moment they veered away. And always always except with J [Joseph Bard] — fallen out of love first."[125] Before long Christa was able to admit that her feelings for Dorothy had been "elevated to a higher plane," and she acknowledged, too, when she arrived in Los Angeles to try her hand at screenwriting, that she was "ready for a new intimacy," a new friendship.

"I can't be alone," Christa told Dorothy. "*You're* responsible for that, you made me dependent, you got me used to it." In the meantime, she was "happy to be back on [her] own thematic turf," writing a script about a young boy's struggle with homosexuality. Her adventures in Hollywood were comical indeed: so-and-so was a lesbian, she reported, though she was married to a studio boss; somebody else could be found every night at "a homo bar," though currently he was the romantic idol of the nation. But Christa was not suited to this kind of hypocrisy, and no one in Hollywood had the nerve or the wit to produce her scripts. She went back to Europe for the last time in 1935.

"You have Mike," she reminded Dorothy before she left the country. "Mike . . . Work . . . Success. Be satisfied." It sounded to Dorothy like nothing so much as the parting words of Joseph Bard, eight years before, in Berlin. This time she did not struggle; she did not plead; she did not even protest. "I do not know how to change my feelings," she advised Christa. "It is inadept of me . . . unworldly. Do you suppose I'll ever learn? Do you?

"Whether or not," Dorothy finished, "for everything, for *everything,* thank you."[126] There is no evidence that she ever loved another woman in the same way again; indeed, there is no evidence that she ever loved *anyone* in the same way again. She was joined now — "fused" — with something larger than a lover or a husband, something "vast, casual, radioactive," something she thought she could detect in the American landscape as she shot by it in her train: "A world unfinished, taken up and dropped, begun and interrupted. The frontier is not yet conquered." There was "room to breathe in" still, room "to risk things in, to adventure in. I love it," said Dorothy, "love it . . . love it . . . love it."[127]

9

CHAPTER

NINETEEN thirty-six was the year of Dorothy's exaltation, the year she broke away from the main current of American journalism and shot to "astronomic heights" as a free-flying pundit — "a molder of opinion, a power in the land." There was not a reporter in the United States who would not already, in all likelihood, have pointed to Dorothy Thompson as the foremost woman journalist of her time. But she was about to make the transition (to borrow one of Jimmy Sheean's constructions) from journalism into history.[1] She was about to embark on her soul's adventure as a political columnist for the *New York Herald Tribune* and the leading American voice in the war against fascism.

The column was the brainchild of Helen Rogers Reid, the wife of the publisher of the *Herald Tribune* and herself a vice president of the newspaper's board.[2] Dorothy and Mrs. Reid had known each other since 1915, when Helen was treasurer of the New York State Woman Suffrage Party. In the intervening years, as her husband, Ogden Reid, made a slow descent into alcoholism, Helen had taken an ever more determined hand in the shaping of the *Herald Tribune*'s business and editorial policies. For years the *Tribune* was the most prominent and most respectable right-wing newspaper in America, "a blindly conservative foe of social change"[3] and the tool, generally speaking, of the eastern Republican establishment. It was Helen Reid's personal triumph that she managed to open the paper's doors to the twentieth century and let some oxygen whistle through the halls. She did this not only by encouraging her husband's selection of more liberal reporters and editors, but also by flooding the *Tribune* with women staffers. The southern-born, open-minded Irita

218

Van Doren edited the book review; the diminutive Marie Mattingly Meloney — "Missy" to her friends — was producer of *This Week,* the *Tribune's* justly famous Sunday magazine; and Helen Reid herself served as the personal liaison between the *Tribune* and its dimly enlightened patrons on Wall Street. When Dorothy's column was added to the list of Helen's acquisitions, Sinclair Lewis joked that he was planning "a new sort of girls' book" for the edification of the people: *Helen, Missy, Irita and Dotty, Or: The Herald Tribune Girls in Harlem.*[4]

"I think I said I would do it because there are so many things that I care a great deal about," said Dorothy, reflecting on the origins of "On the Record," the column she began in March 1936 and continued to produce without interruption, three times a week, for the next twenty-two years. "I couldn't bring myself to turn the opportunity down."[5] The *Tribune* had wanted "a column about politics, wars, and domestic and international problems written so that women could easily understand it and would not always have to be seeking information from their husbands."[6] Such, at least, was the explanation of the husbands, after "On the Record" became a national success. In correspondence with the Reids, Dorothy asked for an office, a secretary, two months' annual vacation, and "a guarantee of freedom to write as I please, provided that I remain within the canons of good taste and within the libel laws." She had never written a column before and had no way of knowing whether she would do it badly or well. But she saw no reason to sell herself short, and she asked that "On the Record" be positioned, on alternating days, in the space directly opposite Walter Lippmann's "Today and Tomorrow," the momentous commentary that graced the front page of the *Tribune's* second section. That, at any rate, said Dorothy, would "keep me very much on my toes."[7]

"I like enormously having you as a neighbor," Lippmann wrote to Dorothy in a friendly note of welcome, ". . . but have you any idea of what a term of hard labor you have committed yourself to? When I see people sign up to write columns I can understand why young men, in spite of all the horrors of war, still enlist when the drums beat."[8] In fact Dorothy was about to join an elite and very powerful corps of "personal journalists" in America, what H. L. Mencken (who abhorred the trend) was calling "the self-exploiting, individualized star system" of news commentary.[9] The phenomenon was unique to America and particular to the twenties and thirties. Through conglomerations, expansions, the quest for higher revenues, and the perceived demand for an "objective" viewpoint, American newspapers had already begun the slide into that facile and predictable uniformity which, even before the triumph of television, obliterated all but a few of the major dailies from the national scene. In 1936 the editorial pages of the world's largest democracy were reflective mainly of a desire to please — or, more accurately, a desire to minimize offense, and not to take responsibility when offense was given.

"The gloomy truth," wrote Charles Fisher in *The Columnists*, his 1944 exposé of America's leading pundits, "is that the newspaperman as a newspaper *publisher* has almost vanished from the earth he once troubled so sorely. The owner who stomped in to write his own editorial under the sting of some boiling rage has given way to a board of directors worrying over the Little Dewdrop Drain Cleaner account. When inequity is mentioned, or an unpopular cause, the bookkeeper is called in first. The emasculation of the country's editorial pages was inevitable under this arrangement."[10] And the syndicated columnist — the man or woman whose judgment could be said to mirror "independent" thinking but who was picked or dropped solely in accordance with advertising revenues and readers' polls — was a magic answer for an industry made cowardly by the quest for profits. Generally speaking, the columnists started out as surrogates for a strong editorial position. They were front men, scapegoats, lightning rods for public opinion. They represented every shade of political conviction (though most were conservative) and every style of newspaper writing. They quickly became celebrities.

"Strange," said Frederick Lewis Allen, who made a career out of chronicling the changes in American popular culture in the first half of the century, "that the old tradition of personal journalism, so nearly killed by the transformation of the American newspaper into a standardized corporate entity, should thus reassert itself on the grand scale!"[11] Americans were used by now to the potent views of former sportswriters such as Heywood Broun; nasty gossips such as Walter Winchell; blustering reactionaries such as Mark Sullivan and Westbrook Pegler; and the lofty male highbrows, generally reformed left-liberals, such as Walter Lippmann. But something in her sales figures would indicate that the nation was also ready for Dorothy Thompson, whose particular blend of solid reporting and naked emotion had never before been seen in a syndicated column. "She gave herself her own assignment," the *New York Times* reported later, "which was no less than the whole human situation."[12] Her call to conscience, her emergence on the American scene as an almost mythic heroine, "half mother and half firebrand," gave Dorothy a place in the history of journalism that was entirely her own:

> One of the seven and a half million readers of Dorothy Thompson's column [a *New Yorker* writer reported in 1940], which is syndicated in some hundred and fifty newspapers in America, had a dream about her the other night. She appeared in this dream as a trained nurse, starched, crisp, and tender, hovering beside a bed in which a sick world lay. The sick world was depicted by the familiar cartoonist's symbol of a frail figure with a bandaged globe for a head, and Miss Thompson was ministering to it by taking its temperature with one hand while she deftly gave it the hotfoot with the other. The chart that hung at the foot of the patient's bed was labelled simply, "On the Record." [13]

She delayed the start of the column for several months while she rented an apartment in Washington and continued her study of the politics and personalities of the Roosevelt administration. She had been hired by the *Herald Tribune* in the first place largely on account of her opposition to the New Deal, and word got around Washington now that she was preparing to run for the Senate. "There was even gossip to the effect that her friends were proposing her as a presidential candidate," Mark Schorer noted; Sinclair Lewis, when he heard this news, is supposed to have remarked, "Fine. Then I can write 'My Day.'"[14] He was referring to the syndicated column recently begun by Eleanor Roosevelt, but in fact he showed no disposition to settle down happily into the role of consort: on March 1, only two weeks before "On the Record" made its debut, Red departed suddenly for Bermuda, leaving Dorothy with nothing but an "abusive" letter to explain his absence. She was either too used to his antics or too preoccupied with her work to issue more than a perfunctory reprimand:

> If I ever pulled anything on you like that I would never hear the last of it. You've heard the last of it with this note. I shan't bring the matter up again, but that's only a smug demonstration of my really superior nature.[15]

She was billed in the *Herald Tribune* as the spokeswoman for a new brand of "liberal conservatism" — the first of many expressions of general confusion as to her political sympathies — and the advertisements for her column[16] were accompanied by a photograph "of such haughty beauty" that her friends had trouble recognizing her.[17] Only once in the *Tribune*'s promotion was Dorothy described as the wife of Sinclair Lewis; thereafter, and for the rest of her life, she needed no such introduction. She opened on March 18, 1936, with a discussion of the Corporations Tax Bill, signifying in one unvarnished stroke that she had no intention of writing "for women":

> Some time ago I decided that it was the duty of any student of public affairs to learn something about the money economy under which we live, and in pursuit of knowledge I waded with damp and corrugated brow through volumes by experts Austrian, German, Swedish, English and American. I found that a great many serious and gifted men have devoted their entire lives to the subject, and come to definite conclusions, but I also learned that these conclusions by no means agree. . . . Obviously it is not for a layman like myself to decide between distinguished gentlemen. I know now that there is one field of human knowledge that is forever closed to me. I, like 120,000,000 other Americans, will probably never grasp the truth about the money system. Professor Einstein also admits that he doesn't understand it, so I am not as humiliated as I otherwise might be.[18]

And with that she was off, transforming the "cozy, woman-to-woman chat" the *Herald Tribune* had wanted into a "sensationally informative," wondrously unself-conscious tour de force, "an endless procession of passionate certainties" that propelled her, by the end of 1936, to the front line of syndicated opinion.[19] Most of the columns in "On the Record" ran to a thousand words apiece, and Dorothy proved to be as comfortable discussing the major issues of world economics and the New Deal as she was addressing the United States' foreign policy, military affairs, the ups and downs of capital and labor, the genius of Toscanini, or the butterfly collection of the emperor of Japan.

"The universe was centered in her sights from the start," Charles Fisher observed. "She took virtually every phase of human life under her supervision, untroubled by any inner doubts and adopting from the first an air of authority that her clients found irresistible."[20] On March 20, in her second column, Dorothy ran her readers through an abbreviated political dictionary, explaining how the word *honor*, for example, had been debased in the modern world to mean "prestige"; how *defense* now signified a preparation for war; how *unity* meant "uniformity" and *truth* had become a code word, "quite frankly, [for] whatever may serve as an instrument of national policy."[21] The third column dealt with the mechanics of statecraft,[22] and the fourth with party politics and the baser nature of man, "the only paranoiac amongst the animals."[23] On April 2 Dorothy called for the establishment in Washington of a permanent, professional civil service on the British model; two days later she switched themes and attacked whatever ghoulishness was inherent in American life that would account for her having been invited to witness the execution of Bruno Richard Hauptmann, the convicted killer of the Lindbergh baby.

"Perhaps I am just a little bit squeamish," she conceded, "but I am willing to take the word of a prison doctor, the executioner, the spiritual adviser, and the other necessary officials as to how and when [the] prisoner died. . . . I do not presume to speak for the American people. . . . But as I live I believe that I speak for more of them than can be imagined."[24] Then, on April 9, when she heard that President Roosevelt had left Washington for a fishing trip, she suddenly emerged in her column as a seriously funny woman:

> As long as the President is fishing, dark omens of impending dictatorship will fade. Whoever heard of a dictator who was a fisherman? Mussolini plays the violin and rides horseback, but so did Nero. Hitler loves dogs, but so did Napoleon. These hobbies are not incompatible with tyranny. . . . [But] ours is the Anglo-Saxon tradition. Has no one observed that whenever a cabinet crisis occurs in Great Britain the Prime Minister rushes to Scotland and catches a salmon? Then the fears of the public are allayed. All is quiet; the outlook is serene; conditions may be serious but not hopeless. . . .
> And yet where is the completely convincing, non-circumstantial evidence that the Chief Executive has ever really caught a fish?[25]

She wasted no time running after the Chief Executive, Roosevelt, whom she more and more suspected of leading the country down the road of benevolent despotism. (In this she was entirely in accord with the editorial position of the *Herald Tribune*.) This was another election year, and "reluctantly" Dorothy threw her support behind Alfred M. Landon, the valiant Republican governor of Kansas who had mounted a hopeless campaign to unseat the incumbent. Many people besides Dorothy, including Walter Lippmann, were backing Landon on the tepid theory that if he won, it would not be "catastrophic" for the nation.[26] But it would have required a far more exciting candidate than Landon to drive "That Man" from the White House.

"From this serene and quiet distance," Dorothy wrote to Red from Twin Farms, "I read Brother Landon's speeches, and observe that the Star of Destiny is not shining on the gentleman's brow. I should like to be for him, but I am neither old enough nor discouraged enough. Nor have I any passion for a lost cause. Only for thee, only for thee!"[27] She told Oswald Garrison Villard, the publisher of *The Nation,* that she found it "difficult" to write about the presidential election for a Republican paper: she was worried about losing her perspective.

"I cannot tell you why," she reported, "but I have an increasing distrust of Roosevelt and the people around him. It is a kind of smell. . . . I have to keep reminding myself that it may be the *Herald Tribune* atmosphere."[28] Dorothy was always careful to absolve the President of any malevolent *intention* as he moved ahead with his plans for the second New Deal. But Roosevelt was still, to Dorothy's way of thinking, a frighteningly "charismatic" leader, and he had "worked himself up to the point where he believes that a mystical compact exists between him personally and the American people."[29] It was the sine qua non, Dorothy feared, of the modern fascist state.

"The idea of this compact between the masses and a man is the very soul of Fascism," Dorothy maintained, "and it is from this that it derives whatever psychological power it has. . . . The concept is that the leader . . . acts exclusively in the interest of the general welfare, as contrasted with the selfish motives of special groups."[30] In the summer of 1936 she attended the national political conventions as a radio commentator for NBC and watched in fascination as something that she called the Roar Machine ("a contraption conspicuously mounted on a tier of boxes in the middle of the auditorium") measured the intensity of the delegates' responses to campaign rhetoric.[31] She was already concerned about the effect of radio advertising on the American mind, about the adoption of slogans and catchwords in place of "principles" and honest thought, and she was not at all surprised to discover that when the words "Almighty God," "the Constitution," "Liberty," and "Free Men" were spoken at the conventions that summer, the Roar Machine practically sputtered through the roof. As it was, she spent a great deal of time in her column worrying about the wisdom of the common man ("The Common Man is important," she said, "because there are so many of him")[32] and speaking "In Defense of Adults," of whom she saw very few around her. To Dorothy there was "nothing more fearful and wonderful than a society congealed in the pattern of an adolescent mind,"[33] and when Roosevelt, accepting the nomination for a second term, declared that "this generation of Americans has a rendezvous with destiny," she replied that "this generation had better not make any blind dates."

It was pure Thompson, the kind of verbal KO that became Dorothy's trademark and made her, for a while, the most quotable of all the national pundits. "Now let's get this clear," she began one morning, preparing to take on the Wagner Labor Relations Act. "This column believes in trade unions."[34] She did not hesitate to quote the Bible, Shakespeare, Homer, Whitman, Jefferson, Hamilton, Madison, Lincoln, or the Reverend Peter Thompson as it suited her purpose. She was capable of the most undaunted egotism when it came to world affairs ("I have expected for years," she declared, "that the blindness and folly of nations and men would bring about apocalyptic upheaval in my lifetime")[35] and could close a discussion of the fascist threat with a line straight from Scripture: "He that hath ears to hear, let him hear."[36] But she switched without strain from the pontifical manner to the snappy style, remarking of Roosevelt, for example, when he tried to push through some legislation that she found obnoxious, "Before we sit upon the ground to tell sad stories of the death of kings, it is better to sit in our chairs and review how we got into this jam."[37] For a number of years, every February, Dorothy published a column called "To My Valentines," in which she awarded popular books to public figures: *How to Win Friends and Influence People* to Adolf Hitler; *My Life in Art* to Shirley Temple; *Death Comes for the Archbishop* to Mrs. Wallis Simpson; *If I Have Four Apples* to the Dionne quintuplets.[38] She also developed a number of fictional alter egos who allowed her to comment in a whimsical manner when her weightier pronouncements got the better of her. One of her more diverting creations was "Mrs. William J. Rattler, President of the Cornucopia Club," who periodically made an appearance in "On the Record" to speak to the women of America.

"We had intended to take up the nineteenth century this afternoon," Mrs. Rattler told her audience of attentive Republican wives, "but so many of the ladies have asked me to take up the program for the next session of Congress that we will put off the nineteenth century until next week. I hope that each and every one of you agree with me that it can wait. . . . We are all, I am sure, interested in agriculture, and nobody more than the members of our agricultural committee, whose zinnia campaign last summer was one of the brightest chapters in the history of this club."[39] Dorothy was a gardener herself, and when the criticism of her column got too heated, she was quick to point it out.

"I have never known a gardener, now that I think of it, who was a stuffed shirt or a reactionary," she wrote, responding to charges that any Republican must of necessity be an arch-conservative. One of her good friends in Vermont was the Republican Governor (later Senator) George Aiken, an expert on gardening and horticulture who in 1936 published a learned book about fruit trees. "And if you spend your life producing hybrid delphiniums, acclimatizing Alpine plants, and naturalizing wild flowers," Dorothy observed, "I don't see how you can be very deeply committed to the theory of laissez-faire. Gardening is a continual struggle *not* to let nature take its course."[40] Readers of her column got to know a good many things about Dorothy's life in Vermont, about the "polite, courteous, gentle-spoken people" who lived there[41] and the natural conservatism of anyone who kept his nose to the ground. It was the first rule of gardening, said Dorothy, that "if a thing is growing all right where it is, don't move it . . . for heaven's sake, leave well enough alone!" She was firm on this point: "Good gardeners know their limitations. One can't, for instance, change the North into the South, or vice versa. Don't hope to grow hybrid tea roses on a Vermont mountain top. Don't yearn for magnolias."[42]

But she was not sentimental about "the land," or about farming as anything but an arduous way of life. When it came to the crisis of modern civilization, Dorothy somehow knew instinctively that "the landscape will not furnish the solution for the problem."[43] She was appalled to discover how little most Americans knew about the structure of their own democracy, and appalled, too, at the enduring influence in America of "cracker-box radicals" and "so-called Christians" — those "anti-socialist, anti-liberal, anti-alien" white male supremacists who had gone such a long way already toward cornering the market on "patriotism." Dorothy was not afraid to devote whole columns to the exposure of bigots, racists, and the more colorful tassels on the lunatic fringe,[44] and she was one of the first in the nation to make an appeal for gun control. ("The criminality of the United States is not debatable," she wrote. "We are simply the most criminal country in the so-called civilized world.")[45] She rapidly developed a reputation as a debunker, an iconoclast, and a scold, who could be counted on to criticize not just the sloppy thinking of politicians and intellectuals but the passing fads of all Americans: dance marathons and "boogie-woogie" and the outrageous shapes of women's hats.

"I read a poem once about a tree that could in summer wear a nest of robins in its hair," said Dorothy. "I am not that tree. Are you?"[46] She acknowledged that she was "something of a carper about moving pictures,"[47] and she totally rejected the idea of "film" as "art." In 1940 she emerged from a screening of Disney's *Fantasia* "in a condition bordering on nervous breakdown":

> I felt as though I had been subjected to an *attentat,* to an assault. . . . All I could think to say of the "experience" as I staggered out was that it was "Nazi." This word did not arise out of an obsession of mine. . . . The illustrations of the Beethoven *Pastorale* are sufficient to raise an army if there is enough blood left in culture to defend itself. . . . If [Beethoven] had lived to see the inside of a concentration camp his torturers might have driven him mad by [this] performance.[48]

But the most famous of Dorothy's creations, and the character who frequently got the best lines in "On the Record," was "the Grouse," the cantankerous, oracular breakfast companion who made his debut in October 1936 and was widely understood to be Sinclair Lewis in disguise. Dorothy did not deny that Red had been her inspiration, but she took full responsibility for the Grouse's opinions[49] and only discontinued him in the 1940s, when she thought he had become "lame." The inaugural column was one of the best:

> "Good morning. Have you got the papers? What's in them? How is the campaign going?"
>
> "The Giants are three up."
>
> "Don't be silly. I mean the political campaign, of course."
>
> "The political campaign? I am decreasingly aware of a political campaign. . . . Furthermore, I do not wish to discuss situations or conditions. I hope that you have noticed that it is an exceptionally beautiful day. Your dahlias froze last night, but the asters did not. Can you explain that? Why do dahlias blossom last and freeze first?"
>
> "I want to talk about the campaign. You act as though there were no issue."
>
> "There are many issues. But the chief one is whether there are more nuts in this country or stand-patters, whether there are more

lookers-back upon a lovely yesterday or gazers-forward into a betin-seled future. If the nuts have the more influence the present incumbent will remain. If nostalgia is tops the contestant will succeed."

"So you think the present government is nutty?"

"As nutty as this glorious autumn. It is thoroughly nutty."[50]

In February 1937 Dorothy used the Grouse to launch her boldest attack to date on the Roosevelt administration:

"There is one certain remedy for a headache," said the Grouse crankily. "It is cheap, instantaneous, and guaranteed. That remedy is decapitation."

"I fail, as usual, to follow you."

"I refer to the President's way with that bothersome old lady, the Supreme Court. He says the Supreme Court has, and is, a headache. He proposes to cure it. But he is a busy man. It's a long way upstairs to get the aspirin, and the doctors disagree, anyhow, as to just what's wrong with Auntie. So he has jumped into the kitchen for a cleaver, and the sure and lasting cure. Nice fellow, the President. Can't bear the sight of long drawn-out pain."[51]

The fight revolved around Franklin Roosevelt's proposed reorganization of the federal judiciary, which, had his legislation passed Congress, would have allowed him to appoint as many as six additional justices to the bench of the Supreme Court. Among the arguments put forward in favor of the Judiciary Bill was the evidence that the nation's dockets were overcrowded and that aged federal judges were badly equipped to handle the mounting volume of cases; in reality, however, since 1933, the New Deal had suffered a series of crushing defeats at the hands of the Supreme Court, and the Roosevelt administration hoped to "pack" the bench with judges who would be more sympathetic to the President's agenda. Since he had just won reelection with the largest electoral margin ever witnessed in America (523 to 8), and since Congress was both overwhelmingly Democratic and timid in the face of this mandate, it looked as if the President might be unstoppable. But the outcry against him was swift and acrimonious, and one of the loudest voices in the fray was Dorothy's. Between February and July of 1937 she devoted no less than eight columns to this one subject, speaking in tones of such rich indignation that Interior Secretary Harold Ickes gave her the nickname Cassandra.[52] She was accused of "hysteria," "emotionalism," wild exaggeration, and rampant paranoia, but she was not disturbed to be mocked in the cause.

"Say what you will about Cassandra," Dorothy remarked, "the chief thing about her, and the unfortunate thing about her, is that she was always right."[53] Dorothy's first column on the Court-packing plan set the righteous tone for hundreds of others, on hundreds of subjects, in the years to come:

> If the American people accept this last audacity of the President without letting out a yell to high heaven, they have ceased to be jealous of their liberties and are ripe for ruin. . . .
>
> This is the beginning of pure personal government. Do you want it? Do you like it? Look around the world — there are plenty of examples — and make up your mind.[54]

She was so violently opposed to the Judiciary Bill that she took to the podium herself, delivering a series of lectures at Town Hall in New York, entitled "Essentials of Democracy."[55] She had been reading and rereading the basic texts of American government, and one day in her column published a string of excerpts from *The Federalist,* hoping to demonstrate once and for all that the President of the United States had got things backward.[56]

"The method of legitimate Constitutional government," Dorothy wrote, "is to say: 'If you don't like the law, change it. If you don't like the powers of the Supreme Court, limit them. If the meaning of the law is doubtful, clarify it.' That is exactly the opposite of saying, 'The law means what I and the current majority in Congress say it does, and we shall fix it so that the judges and we see eye to eye.' . . . This is no proposal to change the Constitution. This is no proposal to limit the powers of the Supreme Court. This is a proposal to *capture* the Supreme Court."[57] When the Senate Judiciary Committee prepared to debate the Court proposals, Dorothy was called to Washington to testify as an expert witness; later, when the President had been introduced before a speech as "the Head of the Nation," she responded with icy precision that "under the American system there is no such thing as the 'Head of the Nation.' The President of the United States is not the 'Head of the Nation.' The Constitution does not provide for presidium government."[58] In her Senate testimony Dorothy conceded that she was "not an expert on constitutional law" and that her only qualification for speaking was her experience as a foreign correspondent. She had been "an observer at the collapse of constitutional democracies," "a researcher into the

mortality of republics." She knew how quickly "reform" could turn
to despotism in the modern world:

> Political freedom is the condition of all freedom [she declared], as
> the people of Russia have learned, as the people of Italy have learned,
> and as the people of Germany have learned. They gave up political
> freedom to get something else which they thought at the moment was
> very much more important, and then they found out that there is not
> anything more important. . . . I have never suggested that President
> Roosevelt is trying to establish a dictatorship. I would not be so fool-
> ish. But I have said that if any President wanted to establish a dic-
> tatorship and do so with all the appearance of legality, this is the way
> he would take. The modern *coup d'état,* by which so many demo-
> cratic systems have fallen, does not destroy the legal apparatus of the
> State.[59]

The matter was settled in the end through that mixture of fizzle
and compromise which attends most legislation in Washington, and
which in this case only proved Dorothy's point about the separation
of powers. A series of rulings favorable to the New Deal left the
President less urgently in need of allies on the Supreme Court, while
some of the lesser provisions of the judiciary package were allowed
to pass through Congress when the established system for appointing
judges was no longer threatened. Dorothy neither gloated over the
victory for the "conservatives" nor apologized for her own "hysterical" approach to the crisis.

"Well," said a woman of her acquaintance, "she's wonderful
when she's hysterical."[60] Another lady, riding to New York from the
suburbs on the train, was observed to poke her finger at a copy of
the *Herald Tribune* and demand of her startled husband, "Do you
know who most of the people *are* who are reading Dorothy Thompson's column? *Men!*"[61] Within a year of the debut of "On the Record," Dorothy had made a contribution to American public opinion
that was as difficult to pin down as it was to ignore. Not long after,
a radio station in St. Louis, during the broadcast of one of her
speeches, cut her off the air in midsentence with the argument that
she was "against *everybody.*"[62] This was not, in fact, an accurate
assessment of the "Thompson Philosophy." Nearer the mark was
Dorothy's own revisionist reply to the suggestion that she hated
Franklin Roosevelt and all he stood for.

Not so, she said: "When he is right, I am for him; when he's wrong, I'm against him."[63] Dorothy had actually spent the night of Roosevelt's reelection in 1936 in the friendly company of Harry Hopkins, the head of the Relief Administration and one of the President's most trusted advisers, whom she had often had occasion to criticize in her column. Dorothy and Hopkins had had dinner together at the Iridium Room at the Hotel St. Regis while the election returns were tallied and the hotel's wealthy, almost entirely Republican clientele danced through the night to the strains of a balalaika orchestra.

"Every soul in the room was obviously for Landon," Dorothy remembered, but when Landon conceded defeat, at around midnight, nobody paid the slightest attention. It was as if the announcement had not been made, as if the election had never taken place. Hopkins laughed out loud.

"My God," he exclaimed, "they don't know what's going to hit them."

"I didn't awfully like this," Dorothy recalled, "but I did think the behavior of the crowd was preposterous," and so she said to Hopkins, "Get up and propose a toast to the President of the United States."

"Here?" Hopkins replied. "Are you crazy? We'd probably be lynched. Why don't you do it yourself?"

"If you won't drink a toast to your own candidate," said Dorothy, "why should I?"

"Because you're the stickler for proprieties."

"All right," said Dorothy, "if you think I'm afraid, I will." And she rose to her feet and declared, in the loudest voice she could muster, "Ladies and Gentlemen, I should like to propose a toast to the President of the United States, Franklin D. Roosevelt." Still the crowd paid no attention; apart from the balalaikas, there was nothing but "a painful silence" in the Iridium Room. As Dorothy and Hopkins drank their toasts, Hopkins choked with laughter "and spurted champagne," said Dorothy, "just past my nose.

"I think that was the first time I was ever really for Roosevelt," she reflected later, "and, as ever after, it was not so much he as his opponents who made me so. I thought I had never seen such rotten sportsmanship. After all, the decision was made, the people in the room would have to accept it, so why not with better grace?"[64] Such was the attitude of hearty realism behind "On the Record." This womanly common sense, in a nutshell, *was* the "Thompson Philosophy":

No longer are we puzzled
By events across the sea,
No longer do we have to think
"To be or not to be." . . .

Is Der Fuehrer really hated?
Is Il Duce pixilated? . . .
Mrs. Babbitt's syndicated
Up and down the whole countr-ee.[65]

DURING the first twelve months of its existence, "On the Record" was licensed through the *New York Herald Tribune* to seventy different newspapers in America.[66] By 1938 it had been sold to a hundred more, and at the height of Dorothy's fame, in the years just prior to World War II, the column was read by an estimated eight to ten million people a day. A 1940 *Fortune* magazine poll ranked Dorothy Thompson second only to Walter Winchell, the "Broadway" columnist, in the breadth of her popularity, while *Time* magazine, in a cover story, remarked that next to Eleanor Roosevelt, she was "undoubtedly the most influential" woman in the United States.[67]

"She became sufficiently important for writers and cartoonists to satirize her," said Charles Angoff in "Kansan in Westchester," his essay about Dorothy. "She was portrayed as giving advice to the Pope, to the President of the United States, to the King of Sweden, to the Emperor of Ethiopia, to the President of the New York Stock Exchange, to the President of Harvard University. She became the Woman of the Year. She became the Woman of the Decade. She became the Woman of the Twentieth Century."[68] During just one week in 1937 Dorothy was obliged to turn down seven hundred different requests to speak at rallies, conventions, clubs, forums, dinners, commencements, and business roasts.[69] That year she received honorary degrees from six major colleges and universities (among them Dartmouth, Columbia, Tufts, and Syracuse, her alma mater) and became the first woman ever to address the Harvard Club and the Union League Club of New York. She was profiled in *The Nation, The New Yorker, Collier's, Scribner's,* and *McCall's,* while every wit, pundit, and political stuntman in America was busy constructing epigrams at her expense.

"Dorothy Thompson is perhaps the only person in the United States who makes a career out of stewing publicly about the state of the world," said Jack Alexander in "The Girl from Syracuse," his two-part portrait of Dorothy in the *Saturday Evening Post*. "She ingests the cosmos and personalizes its pains." Sir Wilmott Lewis, the Washington correspondent for the *Times* of London, quipped that Dorothy had "discovered the secret of perpetual emotion,"[70] while Alice Roosevelt Longworth, in a line that has been famous ever since, declared that she was "the only woman in history who has had her menopause in public and made it pay."

"Alice is so funny," said Dorothy when she heard this crack;[71] she was used by that time to jibes and put-downs. She was a "breast-beating Boadicea," a "wet nurse to destiny," "our self-appointed anti-fascist Joan of Arc," combining "the seeing-eye of Cassandra and the appearance of Brünnhilde with the gusto of General Patton and the holy fire of a crusading apostle."[72] There was no other columnist on the national scene — and no other woman at Dorothy's level — whose writings and personality so lent themselves to exaggeration. Reference was made repeatedly to her "emotionalism," her "stridency," her "flexible logic," and "her curiously split personality."[73] She was dismissed as "a woman," in other words, when she could not be dismissed any other way — "although," said Charles Fisher in his hilarious analysis of Dorothy's work, "the fact is that in her approach to momentous concerns she displays the conventional attitude of omniscience which is beyond sex or, for that matter, beyond most earthly things. Only one small sign of frailty is evident in her Writings: she is more inclined than the gentlemen practitioners to shake her subject, take it by the two shoulders and rattle its frame while she says shrilly, 'Now . . . you . . . pay . . . attention . . . to . . . me!' "[74]

"The best of Dorothy Thompson is her militant generosity," wrote John Chamberlain in the *New Republic*. "The worst is a failure of clarity, a punditical 'either-or' method of analysis that results in an oversimplification and even a complete falsification of issues."[75] Chamberlain was not the first to draw attention to Dorothy's "philosophical haziness" or her tendency to be "always choosing, with a great dramatic gesture, between good and evil in the name of freedom."[76] She was "the Delilah of the Ink-Pot," in Chamberlain's scenario, "a dangerous woman" who ought to be avoided "simply because she has the gift of unsettling your mind with an appeal to your emotions."[77] In 1937, following the Supreme Court fracas, the liberal columnist Jay Franklin dismissed Dorothy's work as "an avalanche of tosh,"[78] while Heywood Broun, in an article entitled "The Right People," declared that she was the "victim of galloping nascence," "greater than Eliza," said Broun, "because not only does she cross the ice, [she] breaks it as she goes. Moreover, she is her own bloodhound. . . . If all the speeches she has made in the last twelve months were laid end to end, they would constitute a bridge of platitudes sufficient to reach from the *Herald Tribune*'s editorial offices to the cold caverns of the moon." Broun was hardly alone in being suspicious — or indeed, in resenting — Dorothy's unparalleled rise to the top:

> Possibly I speak out of a certain prejudice [he wrote]. Some months ago I had an engagement to talk at the New School for Social Research and was unable to attend on account of illness. I ran into a man who went and asked him who took my place. "Who do you think?" he said. "Dorothy Thompson." And so of late I always sit tense and worried in that interval at Episcopalian weddings where the minister pauses and asks if anybody has anything to say, and I look around furtively to see if by any chance Miss Thompson is among the congregation.[79]

She came in for her most severe criticism in the arena of domestic political affairs, where, according to her detractors, "she never struggled much past a state of mental disorder."[80] Margaret Marshall's 1938 profile of Dorothy in *The Nation* was perhaps the most perspicacious of all the critiques of "On the Record," understanding as it did that there was "a perpetual dualism" in Dorothy's writing, and that her basic conservatism was tempered by "a sense of conflict" and a rich humanity that went a long way toward accounting for her alleged inconsistencies in print. She was "the most interesting and dramatic personality among the columnists," Miss Marshall avowed, and if she were to be judged exclusively "on the basis of her comments on foreign affairs, she would be set down as a liberal of good will who sees the totalitarian flood advancing over Europe and wishes to stop its course."[81] Rather, it was her persistence in spying "fascism" behind the New Deal that most annoyed Dorothy's leftist critics — that and the "incredible arrogance and irresponsibility" with which she attacked, among other Democratic monuments, the Social Security bill. Dorothy's initial objections to Social Security were the usual ones: the program was being pushed through too quickly, she feared, "without study," without deliberation, without due consideration of the experience of other nations. Later on, when the bill had been more clearly framed and was actually approaching passage, she dismissed it as being, in her own case at least, completely superfluous.

"I wish to stand on what I consider my constitutional right to be insecure," said Dorothy, in what many of her friends considered to be a shocking attempt at humor. "It seems to me that all this solicitude for human rights ought to include the voluntary right to live dangerously, just for those who happen to like it that way. The government doesn't know what kind of an old lady I am going to be, and neither do I, but I think I can guess better than the government. And so I want to provide for that particular old age that I, particularly, anticipate." If the government *really* wanted to do her a favor, Dorothy went on, the IRS might allow her to take a depreciation on her brain power when she filed her income tax:

> If I earned my income from a lead mine [she wrote], I could demonstrate its gradual exhaustion, but apparently my head and my nerves are inexhaustible. . . . If the government would just be logical and apply the security tax philosophy to the income tax, they wouldn't have to worry about my old age at all. They could take me right off their minds.[82]

She was no less irritating, if somewhat more qualified to lecture, when it came to such things as the Fine Arts bill, which provided for the continuation of the Federal Writers' Project of the WPA:

> The framers of the bill ought to make up their minds whether they are providing for the relief of the indigent or whether they are contributing to the cultural standards of the country. There is no connection between the two aims. The WPA artistic projects are full of people who have no better claim to be actors, writers, designers, painters or sculptors than I have to being a locomotive engineer. . . .
>
> The writer needs paper, pencils, a roof over his head and an adequate amount of food. If he is really a writer, and has these primary needs supplied, then nothing on earth can keep him from writing. For writing is, to the writer, a terrible whip and a form of somewhat excruciating self-indulgence. If indigent he needs relief, but he doesn't need a "project," and if he really has anything to say, he will shun a project as he would the plague.[83]

It was on the evidence of statements such as these — and particularly in view of her stubborn hostility toward organized labor — that Dorothy was accused of having deserted her own liberal principles in the interest of winning fame and the approbation of the rich. "Don't quote Dorothy to me," President Roosevelt warned Jimmy Sheean. "She's the oracle of Wall Street."[84] In 1938 her old friend George Seldes, in his book *Lords of the Press,* lumped Dorothy together with Walter Lippmann as a notorious journalistic turncoat and added that "by denying she was ever among the Leftists [she] thereby claims immunity from criticism."[85] Dorothy was outraged at Seldes's charges and demanded (and obtained) changes in the second edition of his book.[86] She had *not* backtracked from the liberal position, she proclaimed; she had never been a "liberal" in the sense that Seldes meant,[87] and if people mistook her for a reactionary now, it was only because she was fighting for something they did not comprehend — "the liberalism of the Founding Fathers," as she rather grandly understood it, the "aristo-democratic" tradition of the eighteenth century. Part of the problem, said Dorothy, was that no two people meant the same thing when they tossed the words *liberal* and *conservative* around.

"We do not even have a vocabulary of words which convey semi-precise meanings," Dorothy complained.[88] "To be a liberal means to believe in human freedom. It means to believe in human beings. It means to champion that form of social and political order which releases the greatest amount of human energy; permits [the] greatest liberty for individuals and groups, in planning and living their lives; cherishes freedom of speech, freedom of conscience and freedom of action, limited by only one thing: the protection of the freedom of others."[89] By that definition, Dorothy Thompson was a liberal of impeccable credentials. She did not believe, for all of that, that the American Revolution had been fought to guarantee the ascendancy of stevedores and riveters; she did not believe in "the divine right of the underprivileged to rule the state." The class struggle according to Marx she dismissed as an idle syllogism. ("We tell our children," she said, "that all history is the story of a conflict between social forces. But nobody ever saw a social force in his life. There's no romance in a social force. Nobody ever died for a social force.")[90] She reserved her greatest scorn for the kind of leftist demagoguery "which exploits the sufferings of the poor, and breeds in them the very vices which have been denounced in the successfully predatory. . . . There is nothing inherently more noble in a worker thinking exclusively of wages and hours than there is in a capitalist thinking exclusively of profits."[91]

But even that was not really the problem, said Dorothy. The problem was that modern society was a materialist society, and a profoundly ethical conception, "the idea of self-realization, of self-development," had given way in America to "a totally amoral one: the idea of self-interest." Thus "the ideal of a society trying to *be* something" had degenerated "into the ideal of all individuals trying to *get* something."[92] It was not a question of right or left. It was not even a question of economics. The modern crisis was *spiritual* — and in saying so, Dorothy departed significantly from every one of her colleagues in punditry. If she was contemptuous of leftist ideology, she was no less so when it came to "roughshod capitalism." She had no use for rightist patter about "the sacredness of property, the infallibility of the democratic way of life, the efficiency of the capitalist system, . . . the goodness of God, the equality of man, and the Christian ethical code.

"I am unable," she said, "whether I trust my instinct or my intellect or that combination of them both which is intelligence, to lump these things all together in this fashion. Capitalism and Christianity do not . . . have equal value in my mind; the sacredness of property and the democratic way of life are not of equal value. . . . I find a difference between the property accumulated by a change of hands in a stock market speculation, for instance, and the property which a farmer builds up by his toil; and I think that one conceivably has rights that do not belong to the other."[93] She was apparently sincere when she said that she was "not prepared to lift a finger to save the capitalist system or the cross of gold," and she made no secret of her belief that socialism — some kind of socialized democracy, at least — was inevitable even in the United States.[94] "I can accept this with equanimity," she declared, "because the capitalist system is not one of the things that I am prepared to live or die for."

> As for democracy [Dorothy went on] — if a preposterous tangle of pressure groups and their agents, plus professional politicians who live by serving them, is political democracy, then I am not willing to live or die for that, either. If social democracy means the subservience of culture to money or the dictatorship of mass taste . . . ; if it means the jungle of ruthless competition and shady deals that block our economic life; . . . if it means a maze of legalisms in which law is mocked and crime flourishes; if it means an impotent plutocracy plus a self-satisfied, smug, bridge-playing, golf-playing, automobile-riding middle class . . . ; if this is the whole sum of it, then what person in his right mind would not herald its inevitable decline and fall?[95]

She was not afraid to take this theme on the road and to develop it further in lecture halls and on college campuses, where she had become one of the most sought-after commencement speakers of the 1930s. The intellectuals who read her column and dismissed her as "the Florence Nightingale of the wounded Tory intellect," "the Clara Barton of the plutocrat in pain,"[96] must not have been listening when she told the students at Syracuse, Russell Sage, St. Lawrence University, and a dozen other places that their main problem was "to find a substitute for self-interest as a driving force in economic life,"[97] or when she implored them to bear in mind that "Man has devised a system of economics to serve the perfection of Man. If it is not serving that purpose, kick it into the ashcan and make another. Man has created political systems to serve the perfection of Man. If they fail in that purpose, do away with them."[98] In a hundred speeches, Dorothy warned against "the damnable idea of work as a commodity, . . . detached, as it were, from the worker himself,"[99] and urged the youth of America not to sell itself short. "Why do you sell yourselves at all?" she asked. "But you are trained to 'sell yourselves.' . . . Why would you rather write an ad for shaving cream than plant an acre of trees? . . . I tell you you hold yourselves cheap. I tell you that you do not dream of the possibilities you contain. You are a man, or a woman, and priceless."[100]

She was no less forceful an advocate of individualism when it came to the demands of citizenship, arguing that she had "no conception of 'nation' in terms of geography and consanguinity" and "no patriotism in the sense of continuous allegiance under all circumstances to whatever [forces] may choose to steal the words. . . .

"I love my own country," Dorothy affirmed, "insofar as its myth and the expression of that myth are a unique part of the universal civilization which is 'Western.' [But] if America, for instance, should disavow Lincoln and Jefferson and Walt Whitman, or pervert them into nonsense, . . . or rewrite or reinterpret *The Federalist* into (let's say) an apologetic for Marxism, then 'America' for me would be either a nostalgia or a battleground. Since the conception of America is not disassociable in my mind from the conception of freedom, a free Englishman, Frenchman, German or Hottentot would seem more akin to me than an enslaved resident of the United States, and I'd either join them, or stay home and fight the usurpers, or get me to a nunnery. . . . The [actual] territory . . . would get no allegiance from me whatever."[101] Only fanatics were patriotic in that blind sense, Dorothy observed; nationalism was the natural province of the fascist:

> And the enemy of Fascism is not the masses but the people — those "private persons," individually or in aggregate, who insist on calling their souls their own. The enemy of Fascism is reason. Its enemy, also, is religion, which evokes loyalty to concepts above the state, above race, empire and class. Its enemy is humanism, which insists that personality is sacred, and that man is a being capable of constant development. Its enemies are all those manifestations of the human spirit which derive from profound personal experience — art, for instance, and thought.[102]

Her critics were not mistaken when they said that a "radical" element had entered all of Dorothy's work. In the spring of 1937 she added to her other chores the production of a monthly column for the *Ladies' Home Journal*,[103] and it was here, in a more overtly female environment, that she wrote some of her strongest and most beautiful pieces — lengthy, thoughtful essays on love and liberty and marriage and children and the need for women to reclaim their role as the architects of society and the guardians of the peace. It was fashionable to say that Dorothy Thompson had abandoned feminism along with liberalism when she rose to prominence, but this was a trite and inaccurate judgment of her work. She had merely identified the struggle for women's rights with something other than access to the boardroom and equal opportunity to lead a sterile and meaningless existence.

"Society is deranged," Dorothy advised the three million readers of the *Ladies' Home Journal*. "It is very sick indeed." It was dominated "by intellectual giants who are moral and emotional morons,"[104] and it could not be left indefinitely to the care of men. Dorothy wanted women to *be* women, and to pursue their own activities with confidence and pride. She wanted them to recognize their function "as a *conservative* influence, cherishing, nurturing and developing the best that we have in our individual and social experience." She invited women to cooperate "with all the forces that make for greater unity in society [and] with all the forces which try to overcome class and sex prejudice," and she called for "sabotage and opposition, organized and individual, against all attempts to force society into a rigid pattern under an omnipotent state.

"Sabotage and opposition," Dorothy repeated, "against militarism in all its forms." [105] As time went by and she grew more and more fixed in the mode of a certain kind of homey wisdom, she wrote some appalling nonsense about a woman's place by the hearth ("I should hate to see most women so exteriorize their lives as I have done. I have an ever-increasing respect for those women who stick to their knitting"), and she devoted a great deal of space in her *Journal* column to discourses about flowers ("It is never futile to grow sweet peas, or arrange roses in a bowl").[106] But she was strong in her depiction of women as the only consistently life-affirming, life-protecting force in human history, and she was without peer in her warning that it was not women's business "to produce for death."

"We want to live in a world," wrote Dorothy, "in which we have such things as contentment, freedom, personal pride, opportunity for self-development, love, affection, and spiritual purpose. We want to live in a warm world, a kind world, a human world. We want to be on good terms with ourselves and with one another. And whatever new program or governmental system fails to assist these very simple human desires is a ghastly failure, even if it produces more goods, greater wealth, more economic stability and more national power than has ever been produced or concentrated before." [107]

This was the message, finally — this broad appeal to the conscience of civilization and the extended family of man — that rested at the heart of Dorothy's work and secured her position as one of the leading voices of humanity and legitimacy in American life. This was the basis of all of her power, the foundation of her authority, the one unassailable force in the battle she was waging against "the world's dark hocus-pocus." [108] It was pointless to tag Dorothy as a liberal or a conservative in the face of the stand she took. It was pointless to talk about Republicans and Democrats, capitalists and socialists, right and left. In 1937, after she denounced General Francisco Franco and his army of "Catholic rebels" in the Spanish civil war, Dorothy had the pleasure of hearing herself called a "Red" by Father Charles E. Coughlin, the anti-Semitic "radio priest" whose broadcasts from the Shrine of the Little Flower in Detroit had struck the most sensitive and paranoid nerve in the American people. In Jersey City, New Jersey, Dorothy was actually banned from public speaking by the Catholic mayor at the very moment when the American Communist party, irked by her refusal to endorse the Soviet-backed government of the Popular Front, was attacking her most vehemently for her "right-wing" views on Spain. But barbarism was barbarism, said Dorothy — there was no political remedy; there was no middle ground.

"There is only one effective revolution," she told the graduating class at Syracuse in June 1937, "and that is the revolution represented by the evangelical idea of conversion: that men see where they have been wrong; that a light dawns upon them; and that they change their ways. For it is the spirit that quickeneth, and the spirit that forms."[109] Dorothy realized that "the spirit" was not the favored medium of any government that had tasted power, but she could see no other answer to the challenge of the times. More than once she was heard by her staff to be sobbing while she wrote her column,[110] and following the Austrian *Anschluss* of 1938, when Hitler's troops marched into Vienna and set off a wave of pogroms and persecutions unparalleled in Europe up to that time, she went so far as to say that she would have given her life to save Austria from the Nazis.[111] There was not one among her friends who doubted that she meant it.

> Write it down [she cried in her column]. On Saturday, February 12, 1938, Germany dictated . . . a peace treaty to make the Treaty of Versailles look like one of the great humane documents of the ages.
>
> Write it down. On Saturday, February 12, 1938, military bolshevism, paganism and despotism started on the march across all of Europe east of the Rhine.
>
> Write it down that the world revolution began in earnest — and the world war.

She looked around her in that year of "horror walking"[112] and remarked that in Austria, at least, "every gallant soul I have ever known — from the highest aristocracy to the last intelligent trade-union leader — is dead, murdered or a suicide, or is in prison, in concentration camp, or in exile."[113] Treaty after treaty had been broken by the Nazis; the "terrible barbarities" of the Hitler regime were being dismissed as "an internal affair" of the German nation; "the civilized world has had its face slapped and turned the other cheek so often that it's become rotary"; and the West was now confronted, by virtue of its complacency, with "the necessity of a titanic resistance, . . . the necessity of either taking a last stand against heavy odds, or going under for generations."[114]

That was the choice, said Dorothy. "Truth" was the weapon of survival — "integrity," "legality," "a new and great idea. . . . We have got to face the reality that liberal democracy is the most demanding of all political faiths, and, in the world today, the most aristocratic. It is a political philosophy which makes painful demands. That is its price. That is also its glory." [115] And if Dorothy could contribute in any way to a renaissance of democratic values — if "Cassandra" should be heeded at last — then all of the wisecracks would have been worth it: "For, believe it or not, there are such things in the world as morality, as law, as conscience, as a noble concept of humanity, which, once awake, are stronger than all ideologies." [116]

RED left her, more or less permanently, when "On the Record" was about a year old, at the end of April 1937. There was no immediately defensible provocation for the break, and no better explanation from Red than that Dorothy's work — and her stupendous success — had "ruined their marriage" and "robbed him of his creative powers." He stood in the front hall of the house in Bronxville, "quite cold and quite possessed," and told Dorothy with a straight face that she was to blame for his diminished productivity, and that he wanted a separation in order to rescue his career from oblivion. [117] "I want to go away," Red announced, "and be by myself for a couple of years." [118]

"Who in hell does he think he is?" Dorothy demanded to know, quoting her inmost thoughts in one of those lengthy, deliberative letters that always accompanied the ruptures in her life. "He has written a whole shelf of books and four of them, certainly, and probably more, are classics of American literature already. Or five, or six. One would be enough for a normal genius. . . . Some time, he will have to resign himself to sit under the vine and ruminate on the past." Between 1935 and 1937, in fact, Red had completed one novel, a number of essays and short stories, some criticism, a bad play — the ill-fated *Jayhawker* — and a good one, the stage adaptation of *It Can't Happen Here,* which in 1936 was produced simultaneously in eighteen cities across the United States under the aegis of the Federal Theatre Project of the WPA. The truth is that Red had been unceasingly "creative" ever since the publication of *Ann Vickers,* and the excuses he gave Dorothy for wanting a formal separation were only that — excuses.

"This business that you have built up now in your mind about me and you," she chided him from Bronxville, "about being the husband of Dorothy Thompson, a tail to an ascending comet and what not, is only because you are, for the moment, stymied, and you have

been that many times before. . . . I know all about you, my darling.
I know what is eating you and [what] always, periodically, has eaten
you."[119] So far as Dorothy could tell, Red had been more amazed
than disturbed by her mounting celebrity. Frequently he had helped
her to edit the columns in "On the Record"; he almost always had
something constructive to say about them, and occasionally had to
be stopped from reading them aloud, over and over, to his friends
and dinner companions.

"He was fascinated by the power of the telephone company,"
Brendan Gill remembered. He assured everyone in earshot "that he
had only to say to the operator, 'Get me Dorothy Thompson,' and
they would promptly 'get' her, although she might be hundreds of
miles away."[120] Red's jokes about Dorothy's prominence were becoming famous throughout America. He told all sorts of people
about an improbable Sunday morning when he had answered the
telephone in bed and, hearing the White House secretary at the other
end of the line, handed the receiver to Dorothy. For half an hour,
Red insisted, he had lain there with the telephone cord stretched tight
across his neck while Dorothy and the President talked about foreign
policy.[121]

"Let us not discuss it," Red pleaded whenever he got home and
found guests in the house. "I mean, let us not discuss It. O.K.?"[122]
Everyone knew what "It" was by this time, but evidently Red's humor was only a mask for his genuine discomfort. "He had a horror
of being known as 'Mr. Dorothy Thompson,' " Jimmy Sheean explained, "and in one way or another this phobia was made known
to all of his friends." Dorothy herself told the story of a hairdresser
in Los Angeles who was reluctant to extend credit to "Mrs. Sinclair
Lewis" but not to Dorothy Thompson.

"Are *you* Dorothy Thompson?" the young woman asked.

"That's my name," said Dorothy.

"Well, why didn't you say so? Of course you can charge it."[123] It
was just the kind of thing — ridiculous, but more and more common
as time went by — to nourish Red's towering paranoia.

"I couldn't help being on Lewis's side," said John Hersey, who
worked as Red's secretary during the summer of 1937. "I must have
been too young to recognize the bitterness of an exhausted gift, and
of course I was ignorant of the drinking history. Dorothy Thompson
seemed to me an overpowering figure in a Wagnerian opera, a Valkyrie, deciding with careless pointing of her spear who should die
on the battlefield. Some things about my boss's home life, if it could

be called that, did make me uneasy."[124] Jimmy Sheean's young English wife, the talented and beautiful Diana Forbes-Robertson, met Red around the same time as Hersey and remembered that he was "almost sheepish" in his attempts to put himself forward.

"I wrote a book once," Red remarked with a sigh, then shouted amiably in Dorothy's direction, "Dotty! Don't lecture!"[125] Mrs. Sheean — "Dinah" to her friends — was the daughter of the great Shakespearean actor Sir Johnston Forbes-Robertson and the niece of Maxine Elliott, one of America's most celebrated leading ladies in the early part of the century. Red himself was about to embark on a long and, in Dorothy's opinion, obnoxious love affair with the stage. "Everyone should have a new interest at some time or another," she remarked coldly,[126] but in Red's case it became an obsession and ultimately led him to a series of much-publicized acting jobs in summer-stock companies and regional theaters. The shared bond of the theater undoubtedly did a great deal to draw Red and Dinah Sheean together as special friends — that and the fact that they both were regularly overwhelmed by the highfalutin talk at Dorothy's parties.

"Red was charming to me," said Dinah later. She did not recall ever seeing him drunk, and retained only the warmest and happiest memories of his company: "He made me feel important, which I wasn't. With Dorothy, I was more or less invisible, just 'Jimmy's wife.' "[127] This proven ability on Dorothy's part to ignore the feelings of other people — her reluctance to acknowledge, sometimes, that they were even in the room — infuriated Red more than anything else.

"God damn it," he cried when the jokes wore thin, when Dorothy had commenced for the sixth or seventh time to expound on the fate of the West, "if I hear anything more about 'conditions' and 'situations' I'll shoot myself." He made a rather memorably embarrassing scene one morning when Dorothy, watching an American Legion parade from an apartment window in New York, began to pontificate about the fascist impulses of the American male.

"Oh, Dorothy," Red groaned, "let those men have a little fun! Some of them haven't had a chance to get away from their wives for years. Let 'em have their fun, for God's sake!"[128] By this time, according to Jimmy Sheean, Dorothy was unable "to speak for ten consecutive minutes without bringing in the subjects that governed her mind,"[129] and Red had begun to mimic her in a way that was not quite gentlemanly and not quite nice. "Now I am Dorothy Thompson," he would announce to a company of friends (or even total strangers): "Ask me anything." [130] Six years later, when they were divorced, Red painted a wicked portrait of Dorothy in "Winifred Homeward," a character in his novel *Gideon Planish:*

> But Winifred, Winifred Marduc Homeward, that was something else; that was a woman, *the* woman, the American woman careerist, and it is a reasonable bet that in 1955 she will be dictator of the United States and China.
>
> Winifred Homeward the Talking Woman.
>
> She was an automatic, self-starting talker. Any throng of more than two persons constituted a lecture audience for her, and at the sight of them she mounted an imaginary platform, pushed aside an imaginary glass of water, and started a fervent address full of imaginary information about Conditions and Situations that lasted till the audience had sneaked out — or a little longer.
>
> She was something new in the history of women, and whether she stemmed from Queen Catherine, Florence Nightingale, Lucrezia Borgia, Frances Willard, Victoria Woodhull, Nancy Astor, Carrie Nation or Aimee Semple McPherson, the holy woman of Los Angeles, has not been determined.
>
> Winifred was as handsome as a horse, a portly young presence with a voice that smothered you under a blanket of molasses and brimstone . . . she had the wisdom of Astarte and the punch of Joe Louis, and her eyelids were a little weary. . . .
>
> In all her dissertations occurred the face-saving phrases: "Oh, just a second. There's one other thing I wanted to bring up. I do hope I'm not talking too much tonight. Just let me speak of this, then I'll shut up."
>
> She wouldn't, though. Winifred Homeward the Talking Woman. [131]

There was gossip at the time of Dorothy and Red's separation in 1937 that Red had caught her in flagrante delicto — or at any rate, in deep conversation — with David Cohn, the suave Mississippi-born writer and man about town who was one of her great friends and most favored escorts at the time. When "On the Record" first appeared, Dorothy rented a studio apartment on West Sixty-seventh Street, which she used as a combination office and drawing room, a place to rest between interviews and lecture engagements and a convenient setting for any kind of impromptu congress. The story goes that Red arrived there one evening unannounced and found her with

Cohn. Certainly the servants at Bronxville all remembered the night he raged about the house in a fury shouting out the details of his wife's supposed infidelity,[132] but there is no reference to Cohn or to any other third party in the great pile of letters that Dorothy began to send, now, to her unsteady husband — "my man," as she persisted in calling him throughout their long separation. "I know this sounds like Frankie and Johnnie and a Mae West film," she wrote Red truthfully, "but kitsch, as you have often remarked, is often true."

She had experienced "a sort of delayed shock" when she realized that Red was serious this time about leaving her — that he no longer wished to live with her and wanted no part of her "sentimentality" about their marriage.

"When you stood there yesterday with the collar of your polo coat turned up against the back of the head," Dorothy wrote to him later, "you looked so [much] like the photograph that Yvonne took of you in London at the time we were married that my heart contracted. There were so many things that I wanted to say to you, but I could not. Seeing you standing there made me go back, to find out why you should be standing there now, and saying goodbye to me."[133] Almost immediately after walking out the door, Red had canceled Dorothy's power of attorney and begun to talk matter-of-factly about financial arrangements, property settlements, the sorting out of books, and the establishment of a trust fund for Michael. He did not want a divorce, he maintained. He only wanted to quit an intolerable situation. When Dorothy protested that she loved him — that she had always loved him, and always would — he answered that she was mistaken, that she had confused "love" with some idea she could not let go of, some theory she had about women and men, some philosophy of character.

"You have continued to declare that you veritably love me," Red sniped at Dorothy some time later, "that no one else so greatly cherishes me, even while by a thousand omissions you demonstrate that your attitude toward me is not love nor even any very lively affection, but rather a mixture of nostalgia, amusement at such humor as I may have, admiration of me as a workman, and, above all, hurt pride."[134] It was a not inaccurate reading of Dorothy's feelings, but then again, it would be a not inaccurate reading of the feelings of anyone who had given years of her life to an appallingly difficult marriage. There was some justification in Dorothy's complaint that she had been done a dirty trick, that all her commitment had been for nothing.

"When I married you," she reminded Red, "I didn't do it because I thought I would be happy. All my intelligence — that cold part of my mind — warned me. I knew that I wouldn't be happy in any ordinary sense. . . . I knew that you would make me a great deal of pain. But always, when I was with you, I felt that I was alive. You were, and are, a constant, living experience." [135] It was the "experience" that she would miss most of all. She made no secret of it: "I know how damned difficult and often horribly unhappy our marriage has been, and that has been true for me, too. But I honestly thought, with the deepest part of me, that we belonged together 'forever and ever.' " [136] Then, too, said Dorothy, "You used to sing to me about a lady fair and kind was never face so pleased my mind . . . I did but see her passing by . . . and now I love her till I die. . . . I thought you meant it. I always believed everything you said." [137] She continued:

> I am trying to tell you about myself as truthfully as I can, because of the need to be understood, because of the faint hope I still have that we might understand each other, because of the wanting that our marriage shouldn't go and the thought that maybe now, in this last hour, we can be truthful enough with each other to save it. I don't really think it can be saved because I don't really think you want to save it. Also I am held back by the embarrassment that you may think I am running after you and trying to "clutch" and "devour you." One great trouble with our marriage has been its false attempt of each to spare the feelings of the other.

To these words Dorothy added a line in pencil: "except when you were tight." Then she went on:

> Well, maybe you are proud of the mess we have made of this attempt to make a life. Maybe you think that that's what life is, and maybe you are right, or right for you. But I don't think it's what life is. . . . I think it is so wasteful, undignified, unloving and unhuman that I hate myself. It becomes neither of us. It is beastly to the child. At some point I shall have to tell this child: Your father left you because he did not love your mother anymore, and that will hurt this child irreparably, as it hurt your other son. I suppose everyone gets hurt irreparably some time, but I don't like to be the instrument. [138]

She was obliged to take sleeping pills at night for more than a month after Red left Bronxville: the demands of her column and her determination to avoid "utter shipwreck in emotion" both called for a certain amount of rest. She was not, however, by her own admission, completely undone by events. "I have been desperately, agonizingly unhappy," she acknowledged in a letter to the twenty-year-old Wells Lewis, Red's son from his first marriage, "but as I told you once, I have no really great talent for it. Once in my life, I really broke my heart. That kind of heartbreak doesn't happen twice. . . . I find that I continue, remorselessly, to be vastly interested in the spectacle of the world, and profoundly moved by it. And deeply curious as to how it is all going to turn out. Does that shock you?" It was easier for Dorothy to maintain her balance, probably, because nobody in the Lewis family was able to take Red quite seriously any longer, and because the story, with Red, was never over; the game was never played out.

"So many many times," Dorothy observed brightly, "the best thing one can do . . . is just to wait and see what life turns up." [139] In this case, only a few weeks after his dramatic farewell, life turned up a drunken, broken Red, fallen to the floor of a rented room at an inn in Old Lyme, Connecticut. He had taken off on one of his "country jaunts," and when Dorothy, alerted to his disappearance from New York, rushed to his side, she found him in the throes of delirium tremens, suffering from three cracked ribs and gibbering for his wife. On the advice of doctors, she took him immediately to the Austen Riggs Center in Stockbridge, Massachusetts.

"It was an incredible, tragic drive," she recalled, because Red, in his hallucination, imagined that he and Dorothy were "together" again, that the clock had been put back ten years and they were making plans to return to Europe, to hop in the car and "go places." The Riggs sanatorium did not specialize in alcoholic patients, but the doctors in Stockbridge were not about to turn away a Nobel Prize–winner in distress.

"They strapped him up," said Dorothy; "I stayed for several days, but when he was sober again he did not want me around and I returned to New York." [140] She saw her husband several times more over the course of that summer, but it was beginning to dawn on her that her company made him unhappy, and by the end of 1937 she had resigned herself to the fact that the two of them would have to live apart — "amicably," as all of the papers and gossip columnists were quick to assure the world.

"So funny," said Dorothy in a letter to Red that she kept in her files and headlined only "On our parting." "You go away and you say you will go forever and suddenly I don't see how I can even write my column. If you won't read it, if you won't like it, or dislike it, or criticize its punctuation . . . then why should I write it at all? For money, because I like work . . . but the little pleasure, the proud pleasure of being praised by you . . . that was always the fun in it." [141] Red had not entirely disappeared from her life, to be sure; in an odd way, nothing between them had changed. After spending the summer in Stockbridge, he took a penthouse apartment at the Hotel Wyndham in New York, and there, "at once disaffected and still dependent," he clung to the tails of Dorothy's existence, "hovering in her neighborhood," as Mark Schorer put it. [142] The guests who turned up at Dorothy's parties never knew whether they would find Red smiling at the door, all ease and hospitality, or just hanging around, aimless and drunk, waiting to be introduced.

"This is my husband," Dorothy would say, "Sinclair Lewis." [143] By 1937, when she was at the height of her fame, her hair had gone almost completely white and she had abandoned her "lady-journalist" tailored suits in favor of "sweeping, gorgeous chiffon creations" [144] from Saks Fifth Avenue and Bergdorf Goodman. The contrast she presented to the awkward, pockmarked creature at her side could not have been more pronounced. Red's friends were relieved when, in the summer of 1938, he took up acting and left New York for New Jersey, New Orleans, Los Angeles, Ogunquit, Maine, and Cohasset, Massachusetts. He was having "a ball," he told Dorothy; he had "never been happier nor learned more" [145] and was able, at least in his letters and telephone conversations, to be a friendly and supportive presence in her life. He could tell her that she was "a great gal" and that he liked her a lot. [146]

Thus it was that Dorothy clung to the idea, through some combination of romantic fantasy and stiff-necked pride, that she and Red might one day come together again as husband and wife. She asked him to promise her only one thing: "Don't do anything rash or hasty about Vermont." Red had given her full ownership of the house at Bronxville, and now she ventured that Vermont — Twin Farms — was "the best expression in life of both of us — beautiful, comfortable, hospitable and unpretentious." It could not be abandoned without psychic consequences.

"You have loved it very much," Dorothy warned, "and you have been very happy there and very productive. (Also unhappy, I know, but happy, too.) There is something about places where one has loved and been loved. Michael was conceived there, and there I came with him. I don't want to read my emotions into you, but I love that place. It is the place you promised me the day we met, and it is my home. . . . I could walk out of [Bronxville] tomorrow and shed no tears. . . . But I would sacrifice a good many things to keep Vermont, and even as I write about it, I feel how much I love you . . . God knows how . . . but how close I am grown with you. . . . Go away for six months, or three months, or six years, or three years. I shall sit at home, *our* home, and be there when you come back to it. . . . I am, therefore, in a not very classic way, the very picture of Penelope."[147]

She was undoubtedly sincere in what she said, but she must also have realized at some fundamental level that "conditions and situations" suited her perfectly.

10

CHAPTER

T HE first thing Dorothy did when it became clear that "On the Record" was going to be not just a success, but a smash hit, was to ask her employers for a raise. Her contract with the *Herald Tribune* guaranteed her ten thousand dollars annually and 50 percent of any syndication proceeds in excess of that amount. In January 1937 she estimated her income from the column at only twelve thousand dollars a year and determined without difficulty that she was worth a great deal more than that.

"I can earn $1000 a week net on the lecture platform any time I want to do it," she wrote to Helen Reid in a shrewdly worded letter of complaint. "Lord knows why, and Lord knows I don't like the travel and the dinners and the eventual utter boredom of hearing my own voice, but as work it is incomparably easier than writing three articles a week. . . . I need some assistance in research. I can't read and digest the amount of stuff I have to go through if I am to do this column as well as I can." In 1936 Dorothy had spent more than three thousand dollars out of her own pocket just to produce the column:

> And I have had lots and lots of long distance telephone calls, which I haven't put on the office account because they were made from home. Furthermore, the work is so demanding that unless I am utterly to neglect my family, and work myself to death, I cannot do anything else. I have turned down thousands and thousands of dollars' worth of speaking dates, book contracts, article contracts — the sum of those already *offered*, unsought, is far more than $12,000 a year. And the copy I have produced, at the rate which I have been able to

command for a long time, would bring me certainly $32,000 a year in the magazine field — and be easier to do, because it is a lot easier to write one six-thousand-word article than six one-thousand-word articles.[1]

A year later, with "On the Record" in wide syndication and her revenues already significantly increased, Dorothy was still dissatisfied with the terms of her employment — "really distressed," in fact, "at the prices at which my column is being sold."[2] The story went around New York that she had gotten wind of certain money-making clauses in Walter Lippmann's contract with the *Herald Tribune* and been moved, one afternoon, to "unleash an oral column" on Helen Reid.[3] She was taking a stab in the dark, however, because no reliable standard existed by which to measure her value on the open market. In his book *The Columnists,* Charles Fisher maintained that there was no basis even for guessing when it came to the income of any of the national pundits.

"Figures in such cases are secrets shared only by the writer, the syndicate and the Income Tax Bureau," Fisher insisted. "It isn't even possible to make an appraisal from the number of subscribing newspapers." Columns were sold at different prices around the country, depending on the circulation and readership of the papers buying them; the exact number of people who read any one columnist was to be found "only through sorcery and incantation."[4] (By way of comparison, however, Walter Lippmann's biographer puts his salary at sixty thousand dollars a year.)[5] Many times, until she got what she wanted from the *Herald Tribune,* Dorothy threatened to abandon the column entirely and go back to magazine writing.

"I am perfectly aware that under my contract I cannot take my column to another newspaper," she snapped to John Moses, her main literary agent, "but I believe that nobody can be held to compulsory labor, and that I can discontinue it altogether. . . . I don't know what other columnists in this field make, but I know they make a great deal more than this, and I am not the least bit impressed by the argument that they have been writing for years. I shall not write a better column five years from now. . . . These are the most productive years of my life; these are the years I must make whatever money I am going to make."[6] It is safe to say that in the end, all of Dorothy's demands were met, because by 1939, when *Time* magazine published its cover profile, her annual income was estimated at

$103,000 "from all sources." This figure was widely quoted and never denied.*

"The more profitable I am to the Herald Trib," said Dorothy frankly, "the freer I feel to write as I please. I find it awfully hard to bite the hand that gives me my evening clothes."[7]

She sublet the house in Bronxville in September 1937, having found herself bored with it, depressed by its associations, and wanting to be in New York again, in the thick of things. That fall she signed a lease on an L-shaped, "Baron Haussmann–style"[8] apartment at 88 Central Park West, on the corner of Sixty-ninth Street. The living room and Dorothy's bedroom both looked out over the park, and at the back of the house was "a large and delightful nursery" for Michael, who had turned seven in June. There were, in addition, a room set aside for Sinclair Lewis (should he ever decide to spend the night), an ample kitchen, a pantry, a dining room, and what Dorothy called "the usual offices."[9] These began to fill up rapidly, not just with file cabinets, typewriters, and boxes of clippings and research notes, but with personnel — the myriad secretaries, housemaids, companions, and assistants whose job it was to keep the Dorothy Thompson industry going.

First among the servants was Emily Walker (later Carter, later Haberman), the congenial Scotswoman whom Red Lewis had liked so much and who, over the years, must have served Dorothy in every capacity that a hired woman could. ("What *was* her precise function?" Dinah Sheean wondered, noting that Emily had started out as a nurse, stayed on as a governess, left to get married, returned as "head housekeeper," married again, left again, and finally wound up as a maid-of-all-work.)[10] Next came Mimi Stadler — "Fräulein" — Michael Lewis's "good, solid, meat-and-dumplings" Austrian nanny, who, like most of Dorothy's subordinates, transcended the bounds of her office and was regarded, for as long as her employment lasted, almost as part of the family.[11] There were Josef and Greta Schmidt, a husband-and-wife maid-and-butler team whom Dorothy had inherited from Genia Schwarzwald and whom she sometimes lent to Red when he needed help with the "tidying-up" in his hotel rooms and makeshift apartments. Finally there was Marie, the cook, "one

---

* To get some idea of what $103,000 might amount to in current terms, the figure would need to be multiplied at least by ten. Dorothy's financial records for 1939 are not among her papers, but on her 1937 federal income-tax return, a copy of which is at Syracuse, she listed personal income of $31,207 and a tax liability of $3,551.17.

of the really *great* cooks" and reportedly the last woman in New York — apart from Dorothy herself — who knew how to make a perfect consommé.

"The pair also share, in Miss Thompson's estimation, pre-eminence in the art of buttering bread for tea," said Jack Alexander in the *Saturday Evening Post*. "(You butter the end of the loaf first, then cut off a thin slice, butter again and slice, and so on.)" If Dorothy had "any pet hates which rival her aversion to Hitler," Alexander went on, "they are bungled broth and clumsily buttered tea bread," and for that reason alone Marie was deemed to be irre-placeable.[12] She was short, stout, nearsighted, and French, and she came with a strapping, handsome grandson, Henry Studley, whom Dorothy eventually helped to put through college and whom she treated with the kind of friendly condescension that drove Red Lewis into fits.

"Her charities," said Dale Warren, who was to become Dorothy's editor at Houghton Mifflin,[13] "[were] private rather than public, . . . widespread and wholly spontaneous. It gave her a deeper plea-sure to send a deserving child to school or summer camp, or an ailing friend off on a European holiday, than to contribute to one [charity] or another merely by reaching for her checkbook."[14] In 1938, ac-cording to *Time*, Dorothy gave away a full 20 percent of her earnings after taxes, asking of the beneficiaries of her largesse only that they not "disappoint" her. There were some who suspected that she avoided organized charities mainly because she liked to control any cause she was involved in; that she suffered from a certain "Lady Bountiful" complex; that here, as in many areas, she had lost contact with the basic reality of other people.

"I have a terrible impulse when I'm with Dorothy," said a woman of her acquaintance, "to suddenly stretch my mouth with my thumbs, push my eyebrows up with my fingers, and shriek, 'The cat is on the mat!' I'm positive Dorothy wouldn't notice anything out of the ordinary."[15] It was not unheard-of for Dorothy to greet her guests at the door, when she had invited them for dinner or a late-night party, with a bright smile and the words, "How *are* you? You look wonderful. You simply *must* hear my column. It's terrific — the best I've ever done. Listen!"[16] And she would launch into a reading, unabashed even when encouraged only by the most perfunctory nods and sighs of admiration. She frequently laughed aloud at her own humor, and common wisdom held that if nobody were present to laugh with her, she would laugh by herself.

"Often," said Dale Warren, "very often, she appears to regard those within earshot as constituting a lecture audience, and proceeds at length to deliver (in private or semi-private surroundings) what is regarded as a public lecture. What she is really doing is using present company as a sounding-board in an effort to clarify her own ideas."[17] In Dorothy's defense, it should be stated that it was never the sound of her own voice alone that held her in thrall. She invariably had "a literary passion" going, and anyone who came to dinner at Central Park West could count on a fireside recitation from *Leaves of Grass,* or some book of philosophy Dorothy was reading, or an article in *Foreign Affairs,* or a novel she admired. She was extremely generous with information and ideas; "she had no negatives of ambition,"[18] and was sincerely interested in advancing the reputation of anyone whose work she thought was important. "She can do more for a cause than any private citizen in the United States," said *Time* magazine,[19] and if she talked too much, it was best put down to a kind of amnesia, or the natural and somehow forgivable abstraction of an especially busy mind.

"No chit-chat about Noel Coward tonight," one New York hostess warned her friends. "Dorothy's coming. You know what *that* means": there would not be "a subtle sentence" all evening.[20] Her old friend Phyllis Bottome felt that global success had only intensified Dorothy's basic messianic qualities:

> She was always one-ideaed; and difficult either to work or play with, unless the idea she had was shared by her playfellow. She was a most uncertain hostess. I can remember many parties of Dorothy's that were successes, but none which could be *counted* on . . . to be successes. You might even (as happened to my husband and myself on more than one occasion) be invited to dine — and get no dinner at all; or you might be transferred from the party you had been invited to, to another one, not really to your taste; or again Dorothy might give the party and be so absorbed in writing an article, or getting material for one from one of her guests, that all of her other guests felt themselves superfluous. . . . Whether you enjoyed these social occasions or not simply depended upon whether you understood what Dorothy was up to. . . . Her aim was always wider than any private occasion. . . . Some of her secretaries complained bitterly of her as an employer; but I remember a little hunchbacked German man . . . who told me with shining eyes that to work with and for Dorothy was the inspiration of his life. If the secretaries shared Dorothy's

absorption in the job, . . . they did not mind working like demons, with all the explosive force and unexpected diversities that Dorothy introduced. She never spared them; but then, she never spared herself.[21]

"Now listen here," Dorothy advised a secretary she was breaking in. "If I speak sharply to you, you're not allowed to cry."[22] It wasn't personal, said Dorothy; it was just that the times were perilous. Her manner in conversation was normally "calm," unless, as *The New Yorker* reported, "people turn out to be as stupid as she expects them to be," in which case she was apt to shout out "Pah!" and "Pooh!" and "Don't be ridiculous!" without imagining that anyone she was talking to might be offended.[23]

In fact, many people were. Women in particular often found themselves, much to their annoyance, treated as "ciphers" in Dorothy's company; the wives of her colleagues and unofficial advisers sat out many an evening at Central Park West "in a cold fury" while their husbands formed a ring, literally, at Dorothy's feet.[24] "To hold a conversation," said Louis Nizer, her attorney, "you must let go once in a while. She rarely did. She lectured and we learned and enjoyed it." She was the mistress of a private "brain trust," a varied network of political theorists, economists, journalists, editors, cabinet ministers, agrarians, playwrights, publishers, and Broadway producers, who gave her their advice free of charge and were generally thought to be the hidden power behind "On the Record."[25] As time went by, Dorothy became eager to counter the impression, prevalent mainly in leftist circles, that she was "a kept journalist," "the white-headed girl" of business interests.[26] It was no secret, however, that she preferred the company of men to that of women, and when Henry Luce put her on the cover of *Time*, the caption under her picture read, "Dorothy Thompson: She rides in the smoking car." Even the furnishings at Central Park West seemed designed to put men at their ease.

"No self-conscious period pieces remind the guest of the occupant's taste in antiques," said Jack Alexander. "The chairs are deep and comfortable and of no more specific design than those in a men's club. The ash trays are capacious." The Scotch flowed freely, and bowls of loose cigarettes lay scattered around the tables.[27] "I wonder we ever *saw* one another," said a friend of Dorothy's, thinking back on the clouds of smoke that always hung in the air in her company.[28]

Alexander Sachs, the bespectacled, Lithuanian-born vice president

of Lehman Brothers, was Dorothy's chief financial consultant for
"On the Record," along with Frank Altshul of Lazard Frères and
Gustav Stolper, whom she had known in Vienna and who with his
wife, Toni, formed an independent, two-party think tank on economic affairs. All of these people were political liberals and fiscal
conservatives — "dissident Democrats" in the New Deal years —
and they gave Dorothy a sound training in the obliquities and ca-
prices of international capitalism and high finance. It was not unusual for Dorothy to receive a twenty-page memo, even a direct
outline for a series of columns, from one or the other of her banking
friends. When she needed a legal opinion, she went to the "witty,
tweedy, bow-tied" Morris Ernst, the liberal activist and future board
member of the American Civil Liberties Union, who in 1933 had
undertaken the successful defense of James Joyce's *Ulysses* against
obscenity charges and thereafter enjoyed, in perpetuity, a lucrative
royalty from the Joyce estate. Ernst was "a man of lively, jumping
mind, curious about everything, skeptical about many things, liberal
in all his general assumptions, maybe too free in passing judgments
in a few fields in which he [was] not professionally versed."[29] He
was, that is to say, much like Dorothy. William I. Nichols, who went
on to edit *This Week* in New York, remembered a party at which
Dorothy and Ernst had sat together on a sofa in the middle of the
room and "talked *at* each other, simultaneously, uninterruptedly,"
for more than twenty minutes.[30] The membership of Dorothy's
"brain trust" was, in fact, fluid and constantly changing, because any
authority she met in any field was likely to be pumped for information within the first hour of their acquaintance.

"Oh, that's good!" she sometimes exclaimed in the middle of conversation. "Can I have that?"[31] She was criticized for "brain picking," but she answered the charge by asserting that no one person
could possibly be expected to know everything, and only a man
would try. "To the best picker" belonged the brains, said Dorothy;
it was just too bad that there weren't more of them.[32] She had access
to the Roosevelt administration through Frances Perkins, Robert
Sherwood, Harry Hopkins, and Jerome Frank; a line to Hollywood
through Arthur Lyons; an expert on education in Dean Christian
Gauss of Princeton University. Wendell Willkie advised her on utilities; David Sarnoff on communications and entertainment; Harold
Nicolson, Herbert Agar, and Hamilton Fish Armstrong on foreign
affairs. In addition, Dorothy was never far from her familiar circle
of crack reporters and foreign correspondents — Jimmy Sheean and

John Gunther, especially, who were both enjoying fantastic success on the home front, the equivalent of superstardom, John with the first of his *Inside* books and Jimmy with *Personal History*. If Dorothy could not always be counted on to cite her sources in her column, she never quoted anyone directly without permission, and the regularity with which she did use quotes gave the lie most dramatically to the accusation that she never stopped talking herself. Being summoned by Dorothy Thompson, the saying went, was like being asked to lecture before the French Academy: you had the best audience in town, and your words were bound to turn up in print sooner or later.

"I was delighted to find a phrase or an idea of mine — mostly on fascism — in one of her columns," said Max Ascoli, the Italian journalist and refugee from Mussolini who later on became editor of *The Reporter* in New York. "I was just writing for the *Yale Review* and other small-circulation magazines in those days, and I was glad to have a wider platform. . . . Sometimes Dorothy and I would go around the corner to an Italian restaurant — it had been a speakeasy — for dinner. Then we'd go back to her place and sit up, sometimes till four in the morning, talking, with Dorothy writing away furiously on her golden pad."[33]

She was seen more and more often in the company of men such as Ascoli; Raoul de Roussy de Sales, the brilliant liberal aristocrat who was correspondent in New York for *Paris-Soir* and other French newspapers; and the ruddy, blue-eyed Peter Grimm, the real-estate developer who gathered together the properties in midtown Manhattan that formed the site for Rockefeller Center. With all three of these men Dorothy was reputed to have had affairs, and with all three of them, possibly, she did.[34] She was seen in their company dining at "21," "whisking up and down the aisles" at the Philharmonic, speaking at testimonial dinners, and applauding at Broadway premieres.[35] She had become, by the late 1930s, almost preternaturally beautiful — "radiant," as the wife of her agent, John Moses, remembered, "statuesque" and "gorgeous" in her Bergdorf and Neiman-Marcus gowns.[36]

"She *became* beautiful," said a woman who met Dorothy in 1939. "Literally, she shone with success and power."[37] She had never been interested in fashion, but she got used to being complimented on her appearance, and every six months or so she would sally forth in a taxi and come home with half a dozen expensive new evening dresses, two or three conservative red hats ("I couldn't wear red when I was young," said Dorothy, "with my red cheeks and dark hair I looked like a tomato"),[38] dozens of pairs of high-heeled shoes, and, when everything was tallied up, "an uncommonly varied collection of fur coats."[39] These she proceeded to wear casually, almost sloppily — "as if she were impatient with the necessity for bothering about clothes," said Jack Alexander. "A watchful observer gets the feeling that she puts them on hastily and then forgets about them, and that the tilt of her shoulder straps may be imperiled by her next gesture."[40] In a letter to Alexander Woollcott, whose summer place at Lake Bomoseen in Vermont was not far from Twin Farms, Dorothy complained that she was never depicted "as a woman" in the newspaper and magazine profiles. She was tired of being told that she had "the brains of a man."

"What man?" she wondered. "My strength is altogether female. . . . I wish somebody would say that I am a hell of a good housekeeper, that the food by me is swell, that I am almost a perfect wife, and that I am still susceptible to the boys. That's all heresy which the feminists wouldn't like, but it's a fact. . . . Work with me has always been a by-product and a secondary interest. I'd throw the state of the nation into the ashcan for anyone I loved."[41] No one who knew her could take these protests seriously (they were always fleeting, in any case), but neither did the men in Dorothy's entourage deny that she was "a magnificent animal," an intensely female presence, "a woman you felt it would be fun to go to bed with."[42]

"Suggestions that her incessant intellectual gymnastics obscure her feminine qualities irritate her a great deal," Charles Fisher observed. "Miss Thompson's feeling appears to be that despite the excessive numbers of her gray cells and the responsibilities she has shouldered, she is all frail womanhood, by God, and anybody who doubts it can look for a clout in the ear."[43] She was "the worst-photographed woman in America," said John Gunther;[44] in her own estimation, she always came out looking like Sophie Tucker. Only the people who knew her personally could have had any idea of how lovely she was — how her flawless "roses-and-cream" complexion combined with her blue eyes and her prematurely white hair to make her look like a woman out of Nordic legend, "like a snow goddess."[45] Dinah Sheean's first memory of Dorothy was of watching her at a party at the Hotel Lombardy, laughing, "tossing her leonine head in that way she had" and "seeming to look down on everybody from a great height."

"She wasn't *haughty*," Dinah pointed out, "just *high*."[46] According to Klaus Mann, the German writer and son of Thomas Mann,

Dorothy had begun "to assume the appearance of a Roman Empress, whose imperious charm we can still admire — not without respectful trepidation — in certain busts of the decadent period." Everything about her was "*mächtig,*" said Mann — "powerful": "Every time I see her I am spellbound anew by that electrifying force she emanates." These comments were recorded in a private diary and were not hyperbolic.[47] Dorothy was "incapable of doing the simplest acts without infusing drama into them in some way," Jack Alexander remarked. "Her friends say that she snips her nails with indignation."[48] Poets and movie stars were no less enthralled with her than were journalists, writers, and professors of economics. The radio personality Ilka Chase watched in amazement one evening as the great Arturo Toscanini ran up to Dorothy at a party in his honor and "greeted her with a warm kiss."

"[Dorothy] observed complacently that he always did that," Miss Chase remembered, "because she was the one person who didn't fuss over him."[49] In 1939, in a column for "On the Record,"[50] she drew up a list of the twenty people she would invite to "the perfect party" if she had the chance. They included Helen Hayes and Katharine Hepburn ("on account of such modest earnestness in the midst of so much good looks"); the comedienne Beatrice Lillie (who was "the funniest woman alive"); Helen Reid of the *Herald Tribune;* Alice Roosevelt Longworth; the beautiful and enigmatic Eve Curie, daughter of Marie Curie, "a woman who [had] everything," in Dorothy's eyes, and who enjoyed a famous romance with the French boulevardier Henri Bernstein; the pianist Ania Dorfman; the artist Neysa McMein; Noel Coward; Charlie Chaplin; Clare Boothe Luce (who already went to every party in New York and could "discuss politics, letters [and] fashion with equal vivacity"); and Dorothy's "personal favorites," Sir Wilmott Lewis of the London *Times* and Stringfellow Barr — "Winkie" to his friends — the president of St. John's College, in Annapolis.

"Sinclair Lewis can come to any of my parties," Dorothy added in a wry exercise in public relations, "and not because it is his right. Nobody living talks better if he likes the party; nobody can kill a party sooner if he doesn't. But he'd like this party. . . .

"And as for Dorothy Thompson," she concluded, "she is terrible. She always talks politics and has a horrible habit of holding forth. Given the slightest opportunity she makes a speech, and nothing that she says to herself in the cab on the way home seems to cure her." Dorothy's reputation for "logorrhea" — "tongue-wagging for tongue-wagging's sake" — was so secure that it became the butt of jokes even overseas.[51] Closer to home, Waverley Root, who at that time was a member of the Association of Radio News Analysts in New York, remembered the dismayed reaction whenever it was suggested that the association should open its doors to women: " 'We think we're liberal and up-to-date,' somebody would say. 'We ought to think about admitting women.' The response was always the same. 'Of course we should. But the first woman we would have to admit would be Dorothy Thompson.' Silence would fall, and after a moment someone would introduce a different subject of conversation."[52] There were always two or three guests at Dorothy's parties, meanwhile, who hung nervously in the background, dreading the moment when she might ask one of them a question and expect an answer.

"Did you ever meet a nicer young man," she might mutter abstractedly when a newcomer had left the room, "— or a duller one?" She was "lightning quick" when it came to recognizing a serious conversationalist, and her sincerest compliment, especially in characterizing another woman, was to say that she was "witty." "In men she looked for other qualities," said Dale Warren, "but regardless of the sex her preferences were for people who were 'gifted,' and responsive as well."[53] Klaus Mann recalled the night when Dorothy sat up until dawn arguing with Henri Bernstein in Bernstein's apartment — "flashing, polemicizing, joking, explaining, vying for points." At about four in the morning Bernstein began to get tired, finally winding up prostrate on the sofa, "finished," muttering in stupefaction about his beloved Eve Curie.

"Eve est incomparable!" moaned Bernstein from the couch. *"Ah, comme elle est belle! Quelle femme! Elle est incomparable . . .* incom-pa . . . *rable . . ."* Dorothy, on the other hand, was growing "fresher by the minute," and only when the sun came up over the East River did she finally look at her watch, "put an end to her astonishing monologue," and depart with the words, "My secretary is waiting for me. I have to dictate a couple of articles before lunch."[54]

BY 1939 she had three secretaries, all of them, funnily enough, called "Madeline." The spellings were different, but the pronunciation was the same, and if nothing else, this allowed Dorothy to confine herself to a single brisk shout when she needed assistance. Madeleine Clark was a Frenchwoman and Dorothy's "right arm" from 1937 to 1941, when she retired for reasons of health; Madelon Schiff was a quiet and dedicated worker who died during World War II; and Madeline Shaw, who came to Dorothy fresh from the Katherine Gibbs School and lasted in her employ, with interruptions, for twelve years, was a bright, good-natured, auburn-haired girl who "put up with a lot of guff and kept on laughing."[55] Because she was single and just starting out in her career, Madeline Shaw was willing to accompany Dorothy on her annual migrations to Vermont and to live there full-time in the summer. Thus she became "a real part of things" and was expected not just to take dictation, answer mail, arrange appointments, and shoo away guests, but also to baby-sit Michael, pass around drinks, do the shopping in Woodstock, and keep her eyes open for the kind of silk stockings that Dorothy liked.[56]

On an ordinary working day in New York, two of Dorothy's secretaries could be found at her office in the *Herald Tribune* building, a place that she rarely visited herself — "because the phone never stops ringing"[57] — but had decorated tastefully, with globes and maps and a framed copy of the expulsion order that the Gestapo had issued for her in Berlin in 1934. Next to this hung a cartoon that James Thurber had drawn for *The New Yorker*. It showed two women staring, half tolerantly, half incredulously, at the husband of one of them, who was seated at a typewriter and visibly fuming. "He's giving Dorothy Thompson a piece of his mind," the caption read.

Certainly it was Dorothy's enormous correspondence that kept her secretaries most exactingly on their toes. Mountains of letters arrived at the office every day — sometimes, particularly after Dorothy made a radio speech, they had to be delivered in special sacks — and all of them, except for the most obvious crank pieces, were answered sooner or later. It was the secretaries' job to decide which letters Dorothy should see personally and which not, and for that they had to be completely informed about her work and her interests. They checked her facts, they kept accounts, they scanned a wide variety of domestic and foreign publications for news and comment, and they knew how to take care of a paragraph such as the following, which struggled down from Central Park West one day and needed to be edited before it was published in "On the Record":

In 1929–30 Finland spent blank per cent of her total national budget on education and public health, blank per cent on defence. Sweden spent blank per cent of her budget on education and social welfare, blank per cent for defence. . . . In the great states the expenditures are reversed. Great Britain spent blank per cent for defence and only blank per cent for education and public welfare — proportionately less than blank as much for the latter as Denmark, exclamation point.[58]

Ordinarily Dorothy wrote out "On the Record" by hand, in bed, where she lay most mornings until well after noon, reading newspapers, telephoning friends, answering mail, drinking black coffee, and chain-smoking Camel cigarettes. One of the secretaries was always in attendance to take down her dictation, but unless she had other writing to do — a speech or an article or one of her regular radio broadcasts — she preferred to work on the column by herself, and only when she was happy with the way it sounded would she rise and read it aloud to anyone who might be in the room. When a column was finished, it was hastily typed up and sent by messenger to the *Herald Tribune* office, where it was checked for libel and grammatical errors (but rarely edited otherwise) and then dispatched by airmail or telegraph to subscribing papers around the country. Dorothy was then free to rise, get dressed, and pace the apartment for the rest of the day, a yellow legal pad clutched tightly in her hand so she could easily jot down ideas as they came to her. Quantities of foolscap, as well as Parker pens and L. C. Smith typewriters, were scattered the length and breadth of the house because Dorothy never knew when she might "get curious" and need to write about something. She would keep on writing, annotating, telephoning, and talking things out until the cocktail hour, when her friends would begin to drop by for drinks.

Strict rules of privacy and quiet, in the meantime, applied in the household on "column mornings," three times a week. "Lady callers," wrote Charles Fisher, "permitted the intimacy of dropping in while Miss Thompson breakfasts in bed, have reported her spirit romping about in indignation long before the body was ready to follow it. . . . Luncheon and tea have found her dunking her crumpets, so to speak, in the world situation."[59] In the *Saturday Evening Post* Jack Alexander drew a portrait of Dorothy at work that entered the national imagination as no other could. Having agreed to be interviewed by a lady reporter,

> she was sitting up, in negligee, in a bed that was strewn with newspapers, books, cablegrams and letters, and she was dictating her column for the next day. A secretary, seated at a typewriter, pecked out

the dictation. Miss Thompson, talking as if addressing a mass meeting, was trying out phrases and sentences in various combinations until she was satisfied with their ring. She talked at a giddy clip, simultaneously brushing her hair in jerky sweeps. She used gestures for emphasis, waving the hairbrush in the air or bringing it down smartly on her free hand.

Fascinated by the spectacle, the visitor sat down near the door. When the column was finished, the secretary left the room and a maid came in with a breakfast tray of prunes, toast and coffee, and set it down across Miss Thompson's knees. The interviewer opened with a casual remark about a move which Germany had made the day before. The effect was as if she had touched off the fuse to a string of firecrackers. Miss Thompson, who thinks and has freely stated that Hitler is a maniac, launched into a rousing diatribe against *Der Fuehrer* and all other dictators. She delivered herself so forcefully that at times the tray rattled and the prunes jumped about in their saucer.

The caller was so taken by the sight of the volcanic columnist in eruption that she forgot to bring up a list of questions which she had prepared in advance. She came away convinced that she had seen one of the natural wonders of America at close range.[60]

"I am living on quantities of adrenalin[e]," Dorothy confirmed, "self-distilled, from the fury I feel at every waking moment. The fury I feel for appeasers, for the listless, apathetic and stupid people who still exist in this sad world!"[61] She was living, also, on speed — Dexedrine pills and a variety of "uppers" that her doctors gave her in the belief that she could not function under such high pressure without assistance. In 1938 Dorothy wrote 132 columns for "On the Record" (a thousand words each); twelve lengthy pieces for the *Ladies' Home Journal;* more than fifty speeches and miscellaneous articles; uncounted radio broadcasts; and a book, *Refugees: Anarchy or Organization?,* which she developed from an article in *Foreign Affairs* and which dealt with anti-Semitism and the crisis of modern statelessness. Two collections of her columns were also published at around this time,[62] one of them under the "friendly, want-to-be-helpful" title *Dorothy Thompson's Political Guide,* and the other as *Let the Record Speak,* which became a best-seller in New York and which the *New York Times* thought would have been better called *Let the Record Shout.*

"This is not because Miss Thompson's prose style sometimes produces with extraordinary fidelity the effect of having someone bellow in your ear," the *Times* reviewer remarked. "It is because her book shows how often she has been prophetically right." When it came to discussing her opinions, meanwhile, there was only one rule to follow: "When you agree with them, you say so. When you do not, you don't actually say so; you say, instead, that she is too emotional."[63] Dorothy's "emotion" was still her greatest asset, according to Lewis Gannett, who, on rereading the columns in *Let the Record Speak*, went so far as to compare her to Winston Churchill.

"Churchill writes pungently," Gannett observed; "Dorothy Thompson writes fierily. Sometimes she seems to write almost hysterically. . . . She gets mad. She pleads; she denounces. And the result is that where the intellectualized columns of her colleagues fade when pressed between the leaves of a book, these columns still ring."[64] The effect of the columns was only enhanced by the air of immediacy they carried. They were written "in a white heat" and left that way; rarely did Dorothy find time for revision. She was not even sure where she found time to read books, but read she did, with a voraciousness made more acute by the pressing of time. Jimmy Sheean liked to say that any book Dorothy owned was actually two books: the one that had originally been written and the one she wrote in the margins while she read it. A reporter who interviewed her for the *Christian Science Monitor* looked over her shoulder while they talked and was staggered to see some of the titles on her shelves: *Dynamics of Population; Government Publications and Their Use; Political Handbook of the World; Meritism — The Middle Road —* she needed every bit of assistance her secretaries could give her.[65]

"Darling," wrote Dorothy to Alexander Woollcott at the end of 1937, "for no fee and not even for love would I make any more speeches than I have contracted to do this year. . . . I speak so much as it is that I am emptying my not very competent brain much, much faster than I can refill it."[66] That summer she had been given her own radio program. Sponsored variously by Pall Mall cigarettes, General Electric, Savarin Coffee, and Clipper Craft Clothes, Dorothy was billed as an "all news commentator" for the NBC "Hour of Charm," and for thirteen minutes, every Monday night, she broadcast what amounted to "a topical swing session" on any subject she chose. Her program was "not recommended for those suffering either from complacency or cardiac disorder." She had a way of punching her words on the air that was nothing short of electrifying, and her voice had by this time taken on a kind of thirties fruitiness that led one critic to describe it as "an intriguing blend of Oxford and Main Street."[67] Anyone who read her column regularly would have known already about the breadth of her interests, but on her radio program, at least until war broke out in Europe, in 1939, she tried to limit herself to discussing "Personalities in the News."

She talked about the Duke and Duchess of Windsor, whose recent marriage in the south of France had capped "the romance of the century"; about Charles Lindbergh, whose open admiration of Adolf Hitler had begun to puzzle his compatriots; about Justice Hugo Black, whose appointment to the Supreme Court of the United States in 1937 was accompanied by the revelation that he had once belonged to the Ku Klux Klan. If the news that week was dull (it rarely was), Dorothy might turn her attention to the luminaries of history: Booker T. Washington, Clara Barton, Napoleon and Josephine. She talked about Ireland's Prime Minister Eamon De Valera and about Mexico's President Lázaro Cárdenas; about Hjalmar Schacht and Andrew Mellon and a veritable stampede of Balkan royalty: Magda Lupescu and King Carol of Rumania; King Zog and Queen Geraldine of Albania; Crown Prince Otto of Austria-Hungary and his mother, Dorothy's perennial favorite, the Empress Zita. On one occasion she had planned to discuss the career of Admiral H. E. Yarnell, Commander of the Pacific Fleet, but on the same day Adolf Hitler named himself minister of war in Berlin, and she thought it much more important to explain to her audience exactly how frightening that was.

"What has happened today is a defeat," she said, "of the forces in Germany who have been trying to stop [Hitler's] wild adventures. . . . The German foreign minister, Baron von Neurath, has been replaced by Joachim von Ribbentrop, ambassador to London. The ambassadors from Tokyo, Rome and Vienna have been recalled. At the same time, a new secret council has been formed. This is a war council, of course."[68] Over time, Dorothy's sponsors began to worry about her "belligerent tone." General Electric, at least, "caught between the glories of free speech and the perils of libel," felt the need to issue a statement affirming that Miss Thompson's opinions were her own; and an effort was made to "soften her diatribes" by introducing her on the air to the strains of Phil Spitalny's All-Girl Orchestra, which welcomed her with reassuring tunes such as "Love Sends a Little Gift of Roses" and signed her off with a soothing rendition of "Thank God for a Garden, Thank God for You."[69]

It was absurd, of course, but Dorothy would have gone to greater lengths than these to get her message across. She was so preoccupied with world events and the menace of Hitler that she even failed to notice, according to witnesses, the great hurricane of 1938, which swept through the northeastern United States in September of that year and caused particularly heavy damage in Vermont. Dorothy was in New York at the time of the storm, broadcasting editorials "night and day" in response to the Munich crisis and the Nazi dismemberment of Czechoslovakia; only after two days, while waiting her turn at the NBC microphone, did she chance to overhear a weather update, realizing in one awful moment that Twin Farms — along with her son, who happened to be there — might well have been blown to smithereens.

But she was always distracted in moments of crisis. One night in 1939, just after the outbreak of the war in Europe, she was invited to dinner by Jimmy and Dinah Sheean. The Sheeans had been living that summer in the smaller "Old House" at Twin Farms, and another of their guests that evening was the actor Otis Skinner, a Vermont neighbor and good friend of Dorothy's. Dorothy was expected at seven, but by eight she had not yet turned up, and eventually the Sheeans and Skinner sat down to eat without her. They were halfway through the soup when Dorothy suddenly appeared, framed dramatically in the doorway as the shadows of evening fell around her.

"Jimmy," she declared, without any preamble. "The Russians are in Poland!"

"The startled silence that met this announcement," said a woman who talked with Dinah Sheean later, "reminded her of her manners, and she moved at once, flowingly, to Otis Skinner's side. 'Oh, hello, Owen dear,' she said."[70]

VERMONT was the place where Dorothy went to relax, if "relaxation" can be understood to mean that she did not reduce her journalistic output by more than a hair. "Even in the midst of a weeding orgy, a bout of berry-picking, or the arrangements for a luncheon party," her editor Dale Warren reported, "there was often the refrain: 'Can you bear it? This is the day I have to write a column.' She was not essentially a do-it-yourself girl. She was, however, distinctly a how-to-get-it-done girl, and she was eternally mobilized to this end."[71] Her secretaries would sometimes find her on her knees in the kitchen, scrubbing the floors and insisting that "she *was* working" on the next day's copy: housework helped her to think, she said.[72] In 1938 she was appointed president of American PEN and elected to the American Academy and Institute of Arts and Letters; shortly thereafter, she began to decline invitations to make speeches and public appearances, except in the most urgent causes.

"I am convinced that I have lately received too many honors," she wrote to Pearl Buck, who wanted to present her with an award as the American Women's Association's Woman of the Year, "and have consequently been publicized much more than I really like to be."[73] This was not the only reason, however: she had had a hysterectomy, too, and she told Missy Meloney at the *Herald Tribune* that her doctors had actually ordered her not to take on any more engagements.

"You should know what happens to people who overwork," said Dorothy.[74] And so she took up farming. More than a hundred acres of her property in Vermont were devoted to agriculture after 1939, when Sinclair Lewis, getting ready to ask her for a divorce, deeded full ownership of Twin Farms to her. Dorothy was not, of course, in any position to get up at dawn and sit behind a plow, but neither was she merely playing "Marie Antoinette in the mountains."[75] She was serious about making Twin Farms productive. With a great deal of patience (and an awful lot of help from the succession of professional farmers whom she hired to manage the place), she built up a thriving eggs-and-poultry business, some fine herds of sheep and dairy cows, a working fruit orchard, and a vegetable garden that in summer could feed half the neighborhood. She knew the names of all of her cows (she called one of them "Madeleine" after her secretaries),[76] and could discuss fertilizers and soil conservation with anybody in the state.

"She was forever trying to bring some God-forsaken patch of rock and sorrow back into cultivation," said Jimmy Sheean, who was proud to report that during all the years of their acquaintance, Dorothy never prevailed upon him to pull a single weed. "For a great many years she was convinced that Twin Farms was productive, that it was useful to the United States and contributed to the food supply; she even thought for some years, thanks to clever bookkeepers and other legerdemain artists, that it made money; she thought her herd of Guernseys and Jerseys were paying for the artesian well and the furnace and the long distance telephones; she believed the henhouse sustained the Cadillac and paid at least half the liquor bill."[77] It was Dorothy's boast during World War II that Twin Farms could produce all of its own food and might even have turned an excellent profit were it not for gasoline rationing and other "absurd" regulations of the time. In 1944, some devilish confusion arose along these lines about Dorothy's chicken coop and the number of chickens she was allowed to keep in it.

"Shoot if you must this old gray head," she cried to the War Production Board, "but spare your country's hens, she said."[78] Indeed, nothing stirred her to outrage faster than bureaucratic interference in the running of her farm — unless it was the *lack* of interference that ordinarily greeted her advice and protestations to the state government in Montpelier.

"It gave her no pleasure to look out of the window at sunrise and watch deer and woodchucks, and whatever else could get over or under the 100-proof fence, at work on her *mange-tout* peas and six-foot delphiniums," said Dale Warren, who spent part of every summer with Dorothy at Twin Farms. "To Governor after Governor, to County Agent after County Agent, she used to point out the simple fact that if Vermont were to be an agricultural state, it could not likewise be a wild-life preserve. To her it seemed a truism that you could not have it both ways and both at the one time, as they still say in the country."[79] Dorothy was forever counseling the state authorities on rural matters — "occasionally privately," as she reported to a friend, "and more often publicly at the top of my lungs" — but after twenty-five years as a "flatlander" in Vermont, she was forced to admit that she had "an unblemished record: none of my advice has ever been taken."[80]

"You know," said Dorothy, "people seem to think that Vermont is a reactionary state. I live in Vermont and I know that's pure nonsense. Vermont is a *poor* state. Just about all we've got is landscape."[81] During the presidential election of 1936, Vermont had been one of only two states in the union to cast its vote for Alf Landon (Maine was the other, and Dorothy remarked in a celebrated crack that if Landon had made one more speech, he would have lost Canada, too). Much of what Dorothy admired about American democracy could be found in Barnard on its annual Town Meeting Day, when all three hundred of the village's adult citizens would gather to govern themselves and deal with any problems that might have arisen in the course of the year. Green Mountain conservatism was "live-and-let-live" conservatism, like Dorothy's own; it was based in a long tradition, in toleration, in common sense, in "the divine right of every citizen to be left in peace." Mrs. Patrick Campbell's famous dictum about the British — that they didn't mind what you did, really, so long as you didn't do it in the street and frighten the horses — applied very nicely in Vermont, and if its citizens were poor, they were poor in cash only, not "the way people in the slums of cities are poor," said Dorothy, "or in run-down mill towns, or on broken-down Southern plantations."[82] Barnard, Vermont, was very much like Hamburg, New York, at the turn of the century — "For that is the other thing about Vermont," Dorothy wrote: "it always reminds people . . . of home. Englishmen say it is like Cumberland; Germans like Thuringia; Austrians like Upper Austria; Frenchmen like parts of Savoie. Indeed, its verdured hills are very ancient; and in its contours, its clouds, its gusty rains, its winter stillness, its soft air, there is a sweet and nostalgic melancholy."[83]

She left New York every year around June 1, bundling up books and papers and secretaries and Michael and heading north, by car, up the Hudson to Vermont. Sometimes she would go through Connecticut and the Berkshires, but whichever route she took, she always drove herself, and since she was, by common agreement, "the worst driver in history,"[84] the annual "safari" was thoroughly dreaded by her staff. Madeline Shaw never forgot the sight of Emily Walker cowering on the floor of Dorothy's black Road Master as they roared off to Barnard, Dorothy at the wheel, laughing and chattering and appearing to look over her shoulder, or out the side window, more often than she ever did at the road. She "never understood the function of a clutch." She was "abstracted" at traffic lights, and it was rare indeed for her to go any distance in a car without hitting something.[85] All of her friends heard about the time Dorothy ran a red light in Bennington and was "chewed out" for it by a traffic cop. While she fished for her driver's license (which in any case she always had trouble finding), the policeman kept "yelling" at her, and finally, quietly, she looked at him and said, "I crossed the red light. I broke the law. You can give me a ticket, but you can't give me any lip. Hear me?"

The cop was "struck dumb," according to witnesses, but Dorothy wasn't.

"I am a citizen of the state of Vermont," she proclaimed. "I pay my taxes and they help pay your salary. So take me to the courthouse, but don't treat me to that abuse."[86] Dorothy was forever being brought into court on one traffic violation or another, and while she was plainly guilty of vehicular mayhem, she preferred to approach each complaint on a case-by-case basis, even going so far as to ask for a jury trial if she thought she had been unfairly charged. But each year, at the end of the summer, knowing that she had to get back to New York, she would usually turn over all of her unpaid tickets to Loren Pierce, her attorney in Woodstock, and instruct him just to take care of the fines.

It took about eight hours to drive from New York to Barnard in 1939, and on the way up the Taconic highways or on Route 7, Dorothy would make frequent detours — at restaurants and flower shows and a variety of junk and antique shops, which she plundered every summer with an eye to decorating Twin Farms. She was always on the lookout for brass doorknobs, for example, and collected glasswork, cider jugs, and candle molds; the houses in Barnard both wound up furnished in a weirdly appropriate mixture of Maria Theresia, Heppelwhite, Biedermeier, and Governor Winthrop styles. The smaller house, after Sinclair Lewis left, was given over to guests or even rented out for months at a time, but in the main house Dorothy continued to undertake renovations, "building things and changing things and adding things on to other things, so that the original shape of the house was really quite lost."[87] Eventually she appended a wing to the western end of the main building, featuring a combination "bedroom-boudoir" governed by the same rules of privacy as her workspace in New York. A sign hanging over the typewriter said:

GOD PROTECT US

FROM

TRAITORS AT HOME

AND

TYRANTS ABROAD

In the kitchen, meanwhile, where Dorothy took a much more active hand than she was used to doing in New York, bright-red canisters stood on neatly ordered shelves and were labeled, in German, *Pfeffer, Salz, Zucker, Kaffee, Brot, Gewürze, Tee*. She was accustomed to walking around the farm in pretty frocks and printed aprons, looking "like a very pleasant, well-dressed cook,"[88] her hair tied up in knots and sometimes swept back in a frilly bandanna.

Normally Dorothy would have only a week or two by herself in Vermont before her guests began to arrive. She went to Twin Farms every year with the intention of getting "some really serious work" done, by which she meant something above and beyond her regular journalism. She had the equivalent of a standing blank contract with Houghton Mifflin for any book she wanted to write, "big or small,"[89] and for many summers in Barnard she worked hard on a novel about her childhood, which was never published. She called it "As the Hart,"[90] taking the title from her favorite psalm, the Forty-second: "As the hart panteth after the water brook, so panteth my soul after Thee, O God." One year she announced that she was starting a book "about America,"[91] and two other manuscript drafts, "I Try to Think" and "The Moral Crisis of Our Times," were also begun and abandoned at Twin Farms.

"I am counting on the novel being the major part of your summer 'vacation,'" Dale Warren wrote to Dorothy in 1940. "Tell all three secretaries to put it down in all three engagement books."[92] Besides being her editor at Houghton Mifflin, Dale was Dorothy's closest male companion for many years, "a little gentleman," in her somewhat heartless view, "pink" and "proper" and "the best friend any woman ever had."[93] They shared the same birthday, July 9, and generally celebrated it together in a colorful, "feudal" gathering on Dorothy's lawn.

"It was really a meadow," said Denis Fodor, Marcel Fodor's son, "and it kept turning back into a meadow," despite all of Dorothy's efforts to tame it.[94] The Fodors had been rescued from Czechoslovakia by Jimmy and Dinah Sheean, literally in advance of the German armies, when the Nazis occupied Prague in the spring of 1939. Now they were living on and off as Dorothy's guests, while Fodor lectured at different universities[95] and his thirteen-year-old son provided some sorely needed companionship for Michael Lewis.

Sixty or seventy people might turn up at Twin Farms for Dorothy's annual birthday celebration; it was never unusual after that date, for as long as the summer lasted, to find a dozen overnight guests in her house. They came by train to Rutland or White River Junction, or by plane to Lebanon, New Hampshire, where they were collected by the staff and driven the twenty or so miles to Barnard. If they arrived at a civilized hour, they would be greeted with drinks on the terrace and, while they waited for Dorothy to appear, could look out at the mountains; or play with Kippy and Bongo, the dogs; or climb the immense, incongruous observation tower that Red Lewis had had erected on a hill behind the Big House and that everyone knew as Lewis's Folly. There was tennis for anyone who wanted it, and swimming a mile or two away, at Silver Lake, where Dorothy had acquired a number of boat docks and beach cottages and where she herself could sometimes be found in the late afternoon performing a majestic breaststroke. (She characterized herself as a "tugboat" swimmer — "very hard to sink, but with neither speed nor elegance.")[96]

At dinnertime a small gong would sound, the signal that "It" had begun — "something high and theatrical and yeasty and weighty," in Denis Fodor's memory.[97] "I did tell you, didn't I," Dinah Sheean wrote to a friend, "that Jimmy used to call Dorothy 'Stern Daughter of the Voice of God' from Wordsworth's 'Ode to Duty.' There was an immense amount of quoting and reciting at Twin Farms. . . . My stock went an inch higher because I knew a hunk of English poetry by heart, and even some German (Heine, Rilke) and some French (Villon, Charles d'Orléans, Ronsard). . . . I was much bolder on those sessions of roaring poetry than in other conversation."[98] It was difficult to keep up with Dorothy at the best of times, harder still on a stomach filled to bursting. She served enormous repasts in the country, "heavy Viennese meals" with lots of wine. Her digestion was "something to make both goats and ostriches run to cover,"[99] and not two hours after the company had finished eating, while her guests sat smoking on the terrace or, in cool weather, in front of the great stone fireplace in the Big Room, plates of sandwiches and bowls of fruit and ice cream would be brought in to tide them over.

"It is a noble thing to save mankind," Dorothy observed, "but it is also a contribution to humanity to be able to bake a good coconut cake or a first-rate apple pie."[100] Every now and then, concerned about her figure, she would pause in front of her mirror and say firmly, "This has simply got to stop"; but she was just as likely to rise from her chair at two in the morning and announce to her friends, "Come on, let's get tight."[101] The eating and the drinking and the talking went on in Vermont, as they did in New York, until they could not go on any longer, and even so, Dorothy's guests sometimes heard the clacking of her typewriter in the middle of the night, when they were trying, finally, to get some sleep.[102]

Mornings found her out in the garden, yanking weeds and sweating away the excesses of the previous evening while her friends slept till noon or just wandered about the estate, hung over, in a torpor. Many were the tales of transplanted New Yorkers who stumbled onto Dorothy arguing with "the natives" or conversing with delegates from one or another of the Woodstock women's clubs, who were forever pestering her to join a committee or pour a tea. Dale Warren told the story of the policeman in Middlebury who gave Dorothy directions to the high school auditorium one night when she was late for her own speech.

"Down there," he said helpfully. "But you can't get in. Place jam-packed. Dorothy Thompson speaking tonight."

She made a point of staying on good terms with her neighbors in Vermont, and especially with the "Barnardites," on whom she depended for more than comic relief. ("I would thank you not to suggest moving any more perennials this year," Dorothy's gardener told her once on her arrival from New York. "I have plenty to do as it is.")[103] She was most definitely a celebrity in the area, and not all Vermonters were so good-natured or so docile as to fail to take advantage of her fame. When she made improvements on her land or her houses, for example, the town selectmen would always drop by to ask her if she thought her taxes should be raised, and if so, by how much; and prices at the general store on Barnard Green were elevated "ever so little" in her case.

"This would be irritating," said Dorothy, "except for the counter fact that if 'tis known you're hard up, the grocer thoughtfully puts them back to what everybody else pays. There is a terribly old-fashioned and unregenerate idea up here that you shouldn't kill the goose that lays the golden egg, even if he is just summer folks."[104]

Not content with the six separate buildings — including garages, guesthouses, studios, and whatnot — that eventually sat on Twin Farms, Dorothy began to buy up land and houses in the village of Barnard itself. Before long she had also purchased an entire block of commercial property in Woodstock, a town that was already well on its way to becoming the chic and costly borough it remains today and that Dorothy did as much as anyone to rescue from mere prettiness. Half of Windsor County appeared to be populated with her friends and confederates. These were not just regulars such as the Sheeans, the Fodors, Dale Warren, and Raoul de Roussy de Sales, but political refugees as well, stateless immigrants on the run from Hitler who had come to the United States under Dorothy's sponsorship. Bill Nichols, who lived for many years in Vermont with his wife, Marithé, remembered that the streets of Woodstock on Saturday mornings looked much like those of a Bavarian village on market day, the groceries, restaurants, and sundries shops "filled with nothing but people in dirndls and lederhosen, speaking Deutsch."[105] In the meantime, Twin Farms and the whole area around Barnard and Woodstock were transformed into something that Sinclair Lewis was pleased to call "Mittel-Vermont," a haven and vacation spot for some of the more prominent exiles of the Nazi period. "Does anybody at Twin Farms speak English nowadays except Jimmy?" asked Red.[106]

Carl Zuckmayer, the novelist and playwright, who came to Vermont in 1938 and took up residence at Backwoods Farm in Barnard, was probably the most famous of "Dorothy's refugees,"[107] but there were many others in the area who owed their comfortable exile to her, and no German national for miles around lived outside the reach of her émigré network. The Austrian Princess Annie Schwarzenberg, daughter of one of the oldest noble houses in Europe, found a home in Bethel, seven miles north of Twin Farms, where she ultimately became the director of a commercial home knitting enterprise and won Dorothy's wholehearted admiration for her fortitude and hard work. The last democratic chancellor of Weimar Germany, Heinrich Brüning, wound up in Norwich, along with Eugen Rosenstock-Huessy, the legal historian, sociologist, theologian, philologist, and "educationalist," whom Dorothy knew through Genia Schwarzwald and with whom she maintained an extensive and well-nigh impenetrable correspondence on philosophical matters.[108] After the war two of her dearest friends in Vermont were Hilda von Auersperg, who served briefly as her secretary, and Hilda's husband, Baron Louis de Rothschild, a Jewish aristocrat from the Austrian branch of the Rothschild dynasty, whom the Nazis had imprisoned in Vienna after the *Anschluss* of 1938 and then "ransomed" successfully for a staggering twenty-one million dollars in cash.

But Dorothy was not particular when it came to the economic and professional status of Hitler's victims. "She was the address for every German-Jewish refugee whose name was suggested to her," said Meyer Weisgal, the Zionist spokesman and theatrical producer who was closely associated with Dorothy after 1938; "she found work for dozens of them, places to live, comfort, encouragement."[109] Ethel Moses, the wife of Dorothy's literary agent, recalled that she never saw her in these years without "an envelope full of immigration papers in her handbag. She was always collecting affidavits of support for someone."[110] It was the era of "the quota," a time of strict immigration laws and mounting xenophobia in American life.[111] The high unemployment rate and another serious recession in 1937 had left masses of people convinced that their jobs might be taken from them should the tide of Europe's refugees be directed to the United States. The death camps, of course, were a thing of the future; "the Holocaust" had not even been dreamed of, and Dorothy was one of the very few journalists in America — and the only one of her stature — who spoke out consistently in behalf of the European Jews. Even the leading Jewish organizations in New York, fearful of an outbreak of anti-Semitism to go along with America's economic paranoia, were largely silent on the refugee crisis, "eager to rescue fellow Jews from Hitler's reach," as one scholar put it, "but not at the expense of their own security." [112]

"I suppose we keep our sanity these days partly at the cost of our sensibilities," Dorothy observed in "On the Record," "and certainly we tend to subdue our imaginations rather than to use them. Otherwise the picture of what is happening to human beings in all parts of the world, as it is presented to us every morning [in the newspapers], would drive us into deep depression." In January 1938 the Jewish Council, the figurehead organization empowered by the Nazis to deal with Jewish interests in Berlin, had addressed "a heartbreaking appeal" to the Reich government, in which it acknowledged for the first time publicly that the Jewish population in Germany was in danger of extinction. Nobody was thinking about gas chambers. A series of promulgations and state-sanctioned boycotts had simply excluded the Jews from German national life; racial laws had restricted their freedom at every level; measures introduced to control the flow of money had enabled their property to be stolen and their means of livelihood smashed. Something like half a billion dollars in Jewish assets lay frozen in Nazi banks after 1938, "and for the Jewish youth inside the country," as Dorothy affirmed, "there is no future whatsoever. These are facts." [113]

The problem was not confined to Germany, or even to the domain of the Nazis. In Rumania, where anti-Semitism flourished with no help from Hitler, half a million Jews were threatened with deportation on the extraordinary and ridiculous charge that they had all arrived in the country "from the East" and that they were not really Rumanians to start with. "Loyalists" and "Rebels" in the Spanish civil war were each calling for the expulsion of foreigners from that country. There were Jewish deportations as far away from Berlin as Ecuador, and by 1938, in Dorothy's calculation, "at least four million people, a whole nation of people, [were] wandering around the world, homeless." They were the legacy of the Treaty of Versailles, "men and women who often have no passports, who, if they have money, cannot command it, who, if they have skills, are not allowed to use them. This migration," said Dorothy, "unprecedented in modern times," included "people of every race and every social class, every trade and every profession: Russian aristocrats and, more lately, Russian technicians; Italian liberal professors and Austrian Socialist workmen; . . . the flower of the prosperous Jewish bourgeoisie and the inhabitants of East European half-ghettos; nonconformists of every race and every social, religious and political viewpoint."

For Dorothy, the final straw in the refugee crisis was the proposed dismantlement of the Nansen Office of the League of Nations, the only body (apart from the Red Cross) that had even attempted to approach the problem of mass displacement from a standpoint of international cooperation. Brought to life at the end of World War I under the leadership of the Norwegian explorer Fridtjof Nansen, the Nansen commission had been empowered by the League of Nations to issue passports to stateless people and loosely to represent them before the governments of the "host countries." More than a million Russian refugees had been assisted by the commission in the wake of the Bolshevik revolution, and thousands of Greeks, Turks, Armenians, and Assyrians were resettled under its auspices. But Nansen's death in 1930 coincided with the onset of the Great Depression and a sudden slamming of doors throughout the world. The brief era of international toleration ended with the stock market crash.

"Almost all countries tried to bar new immigration," Dorothy reported. "It became a common experience for a refugee to find himself on a frontier, trapped between a country that had spat him out and a country that would not let him in. In that predicament he was practically forced to disobey the orders of one government or the other, by making an illicit entry and illicitly taking work. . . . The net effect was increased hostility to foreigners, and above all to refugees." The Nansen Office had been designed in the first place to deal only with what might be called "normal" refugees — the victims of war, revolution, and the alteration of borders, the sorts of political catastrophes that might befall anyone. Now, however, there was a new kind of exile on the international scene: the scapegoat; the racial pariah; the victim of organized bigotry and state-supported persecution. Thus, said Dorothy, "The attention of peoples is distracted from matters of the most urgent necessity to an issue that is a piece of bad fiction. . . . The refugee problem is economic, financial, social and political. It is not a Jewish problem at all, except as it is made so in men's minds." [114]

It would be several years, at least, before Dorothy or anyone else outside Germany realized that Hitler had devised his own "final solution" to the problem of the Jews, but she was never alone in her call for action to stem the tide of Nazi persecution. She counted as her allies almost all of her former colleagues in Vienna and Berlin —

Fodor, Gunther, Mowrer, Clarence Streit — and the editors of every major paper in New York, as well as Anne O'Hare McCormick, whose prestigious column on foreign affairs in the *New York Times* rivaled Dorothy's own in the breadth of its concern.* But there was a reticence even among journalists to admit that the Nazis meant business: it was impossible, before the war, to contemplate the willful and systematic destruction of an entire population. For a long time, perhaps naively, Dorothy labored under the assumption that Hitler might be ready to cooperate in a plan to remove the Jews from Germany altogether.

"Their number is not so overwhelming that they cannot be absorbed," she offered somewhat weakly.[115] She saw no reason why the Nazis should not want to see that happen: "For in the long run," she wrote, "— though they may find it gratifying to have the Jews 'liquidated' — it is uncomfortable to have in one's midst a body of desperate pariahs." With this in mind, in an article for *Foreign Affairs*,[116] Dorothy proposed a dramatic revitalization and expansion of the Nansen commission — the establishment of "an international corporation," really, "for trading in refugees."

Her plan was as bold as it was simple, as shrewdly considered as it was hopeless in the face of Nazi reality. She envisioned a world fund for the resettlement of all political exiles, a fund to be maintained by an "impartial, international commission" and financed by the "billions of dollars' worth of blocked German marks, blocked Hungarian pengös, blocked Rumanian leis, blocked Bulgarian levas — and heaven knows how many other blocked valutas" around the world.[117] Each refugee would be sponsored, so to speak, by the country that was throwing him out; money would be transferred from frozen accounts at some mutually beneficial rate of exchange and at guaranteed interest, so that a stateless refugee could arrive in Canada or America or Brazil with a cushion against un-

---

* Mrs. McCormick was the only woman columnist during the 1930s and '40s who could even approach Dorothy Thompson in terms of influence and prestige. In line with the policy of the *Times,* however, she was not syndicated, and so her readership was much smaller. "She is extraordinarily objective," said Dorothy, "and completely refutes the often-uttered criticism that women are always 'personal.' No American journalist is more impersonal than Mrs. McCormick. . . . I never miss a dispatch of hers, either from Europe or from Washington." In later years, Dorothy went on, she and Mrs. McCormick "often had a good laugh over friends who, in the hope of flattering us, had praised one of us to the disadvantage of the other. I thought she was tops and always said so. She honored me by her esteem."

employment, and the bandits who had confiscated his property in the first place could save face by skimming something off the top. In the case of refugees who had no money of their own, Dorothy suggested a kind of barter system: extending credit to the "sponsoring countries," say, or granting deferrals on the repayment of loans.

The idea was not without precedent: Jewish resettlement organizations in Palestine had already had some success in persuading the Nazi government to accept frozen Jewish funds as payment for exports. "By this method," *Time* reported, "some 82,000,000 marks in goods have been transferred to Palestine in the last five years, and 14,000 refugee families have been shipped there, who otherwise would not have been able to raise the needed capital." [118] Dorothy had the hope and expectation, based largely on the successful colonization of Palestine, that there might be some greater "organization of immigration" around the world — that refugees might emigrate in packages, that is, as pioneers in their own autonomous communities. It made more sense to Dorothy to "import" doctors and teachers and artisans in ready-made, self-sufficient groups than to sit by and watch them "sink or swim" on their own, and if this sounded a bit like the New Deal's philosophy of work relief, well, a great deal had happened on the international scene in the years since Roosevelt's rise to power.

"Obviously," said Dorothy, "this is not an ordinary business enterprise to be measured by daily experience and routine. Like all plans of great dimension, . . . its success does not depend upon commercial feasibility alone. . . . Jewish circles in America and elsewhere would not be enthusiastic about any plan which would seem to present the anti-Semitic governments with an easy opportunity to get rid of their Jews, or which would give other governments the notion that they too could follow suit. But the present emergency does not offer the possibility of choosing between one entirely satisfactory path and another entirely unsatisfactory one." [119] If Dorothy's plan was Utopian, if it presupposed a level of altruism and cooperation unheard-of in modern times, it was only a skirmish in the larger battle she was waging. Who would shoulder the burden of racial intolerance, she asked, if not the Western democracies? The world, she said, had turned into "a jungle, and the refugees are merely the people forced to run away from one part of the jungle to another. Their personal tragedy can only serve one great social purpose. They are and should be recognized as an advancing crowd shouting a great warning." [120]

"I hardly dare say what I am going to say now," Dorothy went on. "But I believe it completely. Nearly every man of vision believes it. Science believes it. Religion teaches it. Common sense must see it.

"Nationalism is dead. We are walking around with a corpse." [121] Her campaign on behalf of the Jews of Europe was widely recognized as being the spur that moved the American government to action, however pathetic that action may have been. In the summer of 1938 the State Department, on orders from President Roosevelt, convened an international Conference on Refugees at the French resort of Evian-les-Bains, a gathering that led to no concrete solution for the refugees themselves but did at least give the problem the stamp of official recognition.

"There need be no secret that the State Department's action was stimulated by an article by Dorothy Thompson which had just been published in the April 1938 issue of *Foreign Affairs*," said Hamilton Fish Armstrong, who edited *Foreign Affairs* and was the sponsor of the piece.[122] Hitherto the American government had adopted a program of strict "nonintervention" in regard to Hitler's persecutions, offering the excuse (backed up, in the main, by public opinion) that "direct intercession would only worsen matters" and that "traditional diplomacy" was the only hope for the Jews. In 1937 the State Department actually apologized to the German government when Fiorello La Guardia, the mayor of New York, characterized Adolf Hitler as "a brown-shirted fanatic who is threatening the peace of the world." [123] As the months went by and the United States showed no signs of deviating from its policy of "ostrichism" and appeasement, Dorothy's indignation turned to outrage, and finally to a kind of Homeric fury. It was estimated in *The New Yorker* that out of the quarter million words she wrote in "On the Record" between 1938 and 1940, about 150,000 of them — "or nearly three-fifths the total" — were devoted to attacking the Hitler regime and the "cowardice" that sustained it.[124]

"I have an impression from a fairly faithful reading of Dorothy Thompson in the *Herald Tribune* that she may sail at any minute in order to strangle Neville Chamberlain with her own hands," Alexander Woollcott remarked in a letter to Rebecca West. "Would this be a good thing?" [125] Chamberlain was then the British prime minister, and 1938 was the year of Munich, when the governments of Great Britain and France, desperate for peace, signed a pact with Hitler that allowed the Nazis to annex the Sudetenland from Czechoslovakia. Coming so soon after the Austrian *Anschluss,* the Munich

Agreements signaled to the world, effectively, that might made right — that "right is whatever serves us," as Dorothy put it, "our party, our group, our economic interests. . . . The spectacle of great, powerful, rich, democratic nations capitulating hour by hour to banditry, extortion, intimidation and violence is the most terrifying and discouraging sight in the world today. It is more discouraging than the aggression itself."[126]

"Let us not call this peace," cried Dorothy in the wake of the Munich accord.

"This peace has been established on lawlessness and can only maintain itself by further lawlessness.

"This peace has been established on dictatorship and can only maintain itself by further dictatorship.

"This peace has been established on betrayal and can only maintain itself by further betrayal."[127]

Less than six weeks after she wrote these words, the world found out just how bold the Nazis had become. In November 1938, in Paris, a seventeen-year-old Jewish boy named Herschel Grynszpan walked into the German embassy on Rue de Lille and assassinated Ernst vom Rath, a secretary to the Nazi ambassador. Grynszpan's family had recently been uprooted from an already penurious existence in the German city of Hannover and deported along with six thousand other people to Poland, where they were now living "under terrible conditions, in a no-man's land." Some time earlier Grynszpan himself had been sent to stay with relatives in France, but his visitor's visa had long ago expired, and the fate of his family had rendered him wild.

"He could not leave France," Dorothy reported, "for no country would take him in. He could not work because no country would give him a work permit. So he moved about, hoping he would not be picked up and deported, only to be deported again, and yet again. Sometimes he found a bed with another refugee. Sometimes he huddled away from the wind under the bridges of the Seine." And somehow he contrived to buy a pistol. He had "read the newspapers," said Dorothy,

and all that he could read filled him with dark anxiety and wild despair. He read how men, women and children, driven out of the Sudetenland by a conquering army — conquering with the consent of Great Britain and France — had been forced to cross the border into Czechoslovakia on their hands and knees. . . . He read that Jewish

children had been stood on platforms in front of classes of German
children and had had their features pointed to and described by the
teachers as the mark of a criminal race. He read that men and women
of his race . . . had been forced to wash the streets while the mob
laughed. . . .

He knew, no doubt, that the youths who murdered the Austrian
Chancellor Dollfuss [in 1934] are heroes in Nazi Germany. . . .
Maybe he remembered that only four years ago the Nazi Leader himself had caused scores of men to be assassinated without a trial, and
had justified it simply by saying that he was the law. And so Herschel
walked into the German embassy and shot Herr vom Rath. Herschel
made no attempt to escape. Escape was out of the question anyhow.

"Being a Jew is not a crime!" Herschel Grynszpan burst out when
the French police took him into custody. "I am not a dog! I have a
right to live and the Jewish people have a right to exist on this earth.
Wherever I have been I have been chased like an animal." He was
wrong on only one count, so far as Dorothy was concerned: "Animals are not chased . . . like this." [128] The immediate consequence
of the vom Rath assassination was the *Kristallnacht* — the "Night
of Broken Glass" — when "spontaneous demonstrations" throughout Germany resulted in a wholesale looting and burning of Jewish
houses, businesses, and synagogues, and scores of Jews were shot and
beaten to death as they fled their homes. Thousands were arrested
in the days that followed. Survivors who lined up outside American
and British consulates seeking visas to leave the country were attacked by passersby, clubbed with revolvers and knotted ropes, and
chased through the streets "while the police looked on, smiling." The
Nazi government had made it clear that every Jew in Germany would
be held responsible for the murder of Secretary vom Rath, and "that
if any Jew, anywhere in the world, protests at anything that is happening, further oppressive measures" would be taken. In the meantime, the Nazis had imposed a "fine" of four hundred million dollars
on the Jewish community.

In Paris it was announced that Herschel Grynszpan would stand
trial for murder. And on November 14, in "On the Record," Dorothy published an open appeal "To a Jewish Friend" (as the piece
was titled).[129] Her letter might have been dismissed as a mere pre-
sumption had it not been so conscious, and so demanding, of the
universality of the Jewish experience. It was certainly unique at the
time as an expression of solidarity:

My Dear Friend [wrote Dorothy]: I could find no words when we spoke on the telephone this morning. Should I merely add one more expression of revulsion, disgust, and grief? And would you listen to it, in any case, through all the bitterness that you feel? I hear in my ears your cry, "What will become of my child if this goes on?" . . .

It is perhaps hard for you to believe that the same cry that you uttered was in my heart, too. "What will become of my child!" You fear that this mob-madness will spread, and I share your fear. . . . But, if it does, what will become of my child, as well as yours?

Would you prefer your child to be brought up to be a persecutor than brought up to be persecuted? Would you like him to be taught to burn, and beat, and steal? Would you like him to preen himself on his fair hair as sufficient justification for his existence and his actions? Would you like him to be trained in prejudice and brutality and violence? You would not, and as you seek to protect your child, so I seek to protect mine, and we are, as we always were, on the same side, standing for the same things. . . .

You said, "I feel debased, degraded." But I cannot share that conception of honor. No one is debased by what is done to him. He is debased only by his own actions, and if we are to put this question on racial grounds then I, as what is called an "Aryan" in the idiotic parlance of the day, have more reason for furious protest than you against abasement.

And so I beg you to regard this horror as not more personal to you than it is to me, and to all the millions of others on this soil. . . . The crisis is not a Jewish crisis. It is a human crisis. . . . I would beg you not to isolate yourself in a fierce and bitter pride, but to have the courage to continue in the common front with which your life and your actions have allied you — the front of human decency.

She went on the air one week after the *Kristallnacht* with what amounted to an appeal to all nations that Herschel Grynszpan be given a fair trial in Paris. She endeavored to "enter his mind" and to explore the reasons for his "desperate act of protest," and while she would not publicly condone the assassination of Ernst vom Rath, in private she worked out an impressive theory of the role of political murder in history.

"There is a very great literature," she wrote, "poetry, philosophy and law, to support the thesis that if the individual cannot right his grievances by appeal to law because the law has been suspended by a tyrant, he has the right to destroy the tyrant, whether the tyrant is an individual or a regime. The political criminal has never been treated as an ordinary criminal." [130] Dorothy was compelling in her defense of Grynszpan's motives and in her claim that this one murder, at least, had been paid for many times over.

"Who is on trial in this case?" she cried. "I say we are all on trial. I say the Christian world is on trial. I say the men of Munich are on trial, who signed a pact without one word of protection for helpless minorities. . . . We who are not Jews must speak, speak our sorrow and indignation and disgust in so many voices that they *will* be heard." [131] Her own voice was heard over the radio by more than seven million people that night, and though she had asked for nothing but solidarity for Grynszpan in his ordeal, she received in the mail, over the next several weeks, nearly forty thousand dollars in spontaneous contributions. The response to Dorothy's broadcast was "so phenomenal," in fact, that she found herself directing the establishment of an international fund for the defense of Herschel Grynszpan. She was joined in this enterprise by some of the most prominent figures in journalism, including John Gunther, Leland Stowe, Hamilton Fish Armstrong, Heywood Broun, Edgar Mowrer, Raymond Swing, and William Allen White; the Journalists' Defense Fund set up offices on Fifth Avenue in New York, dedicated to Grynszpan's defense in particular and to the relief of Hitler's victims in general. Buttons and badges in support of Grynszpan were distributed at rallies across the country, while Dorothy urged that any future donations be sent by "non-Jews only."

"We want every cent of this money to come from Americans who are not Jewish," she declared. "The reason is a simple one. All the Jews in Germany are being held as hostages for whatever the members of their race do abroad, and we want to be able to say that not a [single] Jew has contributed to this defense fund. If you are Jewish and want to help, tell your non-Jewish friends, on our authority, . . . that thousands and thousands of Christians want to disassociate themselves from this terror and help secure justice for every human soul." [132] Dorothy herself had become the object of an anti-Semitic hate campaign in the wake of the Grynszpan case. The overwhelmingly positive response to her writing and broadcasts had left her convinced that there was sufficient sympathy in America for a relaxation, if not a complete abrogation, of the immigration laws. But at the same time, her mail began to fill with racist diatribes, death threats, and the kind of incoherent cursing that American bigots had developed practically into an art.

Why didn't the Jews go "back where they came from," one of Dorothy's antagonists asked — why didn't they go back "in leaky boats"? "You are Jewry's protegée," another one cried, swearing at the same time that Sinclair Lewis was really "the Jew Socialist Sidney Levy" and that Dorothy, therefore, was married to "a kike." "Alleged Gentiles" of Dorothy's stripe — anyone who spoke as loudly as she did in defense of "foul, Christ-killing Jews" — was probably a Christ-killer herself, a "refu-Jew," in racist slang. Dorothy did not answer this mail, but turned it over routinely to the FBI,[133] while from the podium and at testimonial dinners she talked about "little men — nasty little men — who run around pinning tags on people. This one is a 'Red'; this one is a 'Jew.' Since when has America become a race of snoopers?"[134] The story got around town of the night Dorothy was invited out to dinner and her host saw fit, in her presence, to make some "careless, semi-humorous remark" about the Jews.

"I will not remain in the same house with traitors to the United States," said Dorothy, and she left.[135] Just as she refused to regard Hitler's persecutions as a specifically "Jewish" problem, so she looked at the rise of anti-Semitism in America as an assault on the very foundation of American democracy:

> I am 44 years old and if I have been menaced by Jews I haven't noticed it yet. A Jewish physician saved my life once, and I assure you I wasn't interested in his grandmother at the time; I was only interested in what he knew about peritonitis. I speak of anti-Semitism in the United States, not because I stand here as a friend of the "Jews" — I say it is not American to speak of "the Jews" — there is no such thing as "the" Jews. The Jews include the gangster Arnold Rothstein and Chief Justice Brandeis, just as the Anglo-Saxons — the race to which, according to the best of my knowledge, I belong — include John Dillinger and Dr. Harvey Cushing. I am for trying the Jewish crook before a court of law, and I am for giving a Jewish genius like Albert Einstein a chair at Princeton University. And I am for allowing the courts of the United States to decide who is a good Jew and who is a bad Jew, and not a Detroit priest.[136]

She was talking about Father Charles Coughlin, "the Radio Priest," whose inflammatory broadcasts — unopposed, incredibly, by the Catholic Church in America — reached three and a half million people every week and had recently taken on a directly anti-Semitic tone. Father Coughlin once made the mistake of referring to

Dorothy as "Dotty" on the air, and was rewarded in her column ever after with the nickname "Chuck." In the late 1930s he founded something called the Christian Front, a hodgepodge of Protestant fundamentalists and disaffected Catholics, most of them from the lower middle class, who saw it as their task to rouse the world to the menace of "Christ-haters," "CIO racketeers," and "parasitical aliens." Coughlin's weekly tabloid, *Social Justice,* had even defended the atrocities of the *Kristallnacht* with the argument that they were "a defensive reaction by Germans against Jewish-inspired Communism."[137] It gave Dorothy a certain amount of pleasure to reply in "On the Record" that for committed fascists around the world, "the best thing that can possibly happen is the outbreak of Communism in any country where they have interests. . . . The Communist issue is essential," said Dorothy; "it is the rallying cry; it is the new shibboleth; it is the banner under which peoples are being prepared for war."[138] She had no use for communism as a political alternative, of course — and absolutely no regard for American intellectuals who belonged to the Communist party — but she knew a setup when she saw one, and she invited Father Coughlin and others like him to look to Germany to see where a truly Christian opposition lay: in "a few robust Protestant pastors" who were languishing in Nazi jails; in theologians such as Karl Barth, whose manifestos had cost him his professorship at Bonn; in priests and nuns who had openly defied Hitler and were paying for it now in concentration camps.[139]

If Father Coughlin and the Christian Front filled Dorothy with disgust, another organization filled her with dread. This was the German-American Bund, the protofascist "patriotic" association founded in 1936 under the leadership of Fritz Lieber Kuhn.[140] The Bund had started out, in Buffalo, as a more or less innocuous social club for Americans of German descent; over time, under Kuhn, it had moved to New York and developed a philosophy that was strictly fascist and a program that was strictly Nazi. Kuhn himself was a naturalized American citizen, and his "pro-America" Bund — complete with Storm Troopers, youth camps, swastika armbands, and the crudest kind of anti-Semitic and anti-Communist rhetoric — boasted nearly thirty thousand active members by the end of the decade. The American Nazi party itself had a membership of two hundred thousand by 1937, the same year that Hitler's government called on all Germans abroad — all foreigners, that is, of German origin — to swear allegiance to the Fatherland. Hitler had established what amounted to a "Nazi International," the fascist equivalent of Stalin's Comintern, and the German-American Bund, at least for a while, took its orders directly from Berlin.

"Now this is of the gravest concern to you and me," said Dorothy in one of her radio broadcasts. "All Germans, everywhere in the world, even when they are citizens of other nations, are to regard themselves, first of all, as Germans. It doesn't matter how many oaths of allegiance they may have taken to the American Constitution." The Nazi authorities were explicit on this point: "Whoever lives abroad is working *primarily* in the service of the Fatherland. . . . German Nazism is a world philosophy." [141] Although in 1938 the Nazis actually repudiated it as being "too radical" and not particularly helpful to German aspirations, the German-American Bund remained, in the public mind, the chief conduit of Nazi philosophy in the United States. More important, and more frightening to Dorothy, was the steady and undeniable conglomeration of American fascist groups — the Christian Fronters, the Silver Shirts, the Bundists, the Ku Klux Klan — under one "philosophical" banner: "Americanism."

"The tie-up between the Coughlinites and the German-American Bund is perfectly clear, Helen," said Dorothy in a letter to Helen Reid, "if you read their common literature. They are working both sides of the same street — although I know perfectly well that to mention it is dynamite." [142] Dorothy may have been somewhat loose in her characterization of Coughlin as a Nazi, but it made little difference to a Jew in New York, when he wound up in a hospital with broken bones, whether he had been beaten up by a Bundist or by one of Father Coughlin's acolytes. At the end of 1938 Dorothy called on the Federal Communications Commission to start investigative proceedings against Coughlin with a view to eliminating his speeches from the air; [143] and in February 1939, when she "dropped in" on a rally of the German-American Bund at Madison Square Garden, she saw Father Coughlin's *Social Justice* on sale in every corner of the hall. She saw, in fact, "the same scenes I witnessed in Berlin, seven years ago." [144]

The Bund rally was without question the most astonishing and "disgusting exhibition" [145] of organized bigotry that New York had ever seen. On the eve of George Washington's birthday, twenty-two thousand Nazi sympathizers, having first pledged allegiance to the flag of the United States, sat beneath gigantic swastikas and portraits of Adolf Hitler and roared their approval while the Bund's orators warned them about the "invisible government," "the Hidden Hand of International Jewry," and the socialist plots of President "Franklin D. Rosenfeld." Banners hung from the walls next to mounted basketball schedules and advertisements for beer: "Wake Up America — Smash Jewish Communists!" Outside, traffic was closed off for two blocks in order to keep an estimated one hundred thousand protesters from storming the Garden. Dorothy herself was admitted at the last minute only because she had a press pass.

She was on her way that night to deliver a speech to a meeting of the Phi Beta Kappa Society, and her decision to take a detour to the Bund rally was not so casual as it appeared. She had been worrying a lot recently about the limitations of the First Amendment. She wondered to what extent free speech might need to be curtailed in the interest of its own protection. She had no answer to the problem — indeed, she was to grapple with it for many years to come[146] — but she knew she would be on familiar territory in a sea of Nazi flags, and she arrived at Madison Square Garden with the express purpose of causing an uproar. She took her seat in the front row of the press gallery and commenced to interrupt the speakers with strident gales of raucous laughter, humiliating and infuriating the pride of American Nazism so deeply that after about ten minutes of this, while the Bundists shouted "Throw her out!," she was actually surrounded by a unit of Fritz Kuhn's "Storm Troopers" and muscled out the door.

"Bunk!" cried Dorothy as she left the auditorium. "Bunk, bunk, bunk! *Mein Kampf,* word for word!" She was followed out by her fellow columnist Heywood Broun, whose views on fascism often were at variance with her own but who persuaded her now to return to the hall. "Oh, boys, come *on!*" she exclaimed when a line of New York policemen stepped in to relieve the Troopers at her back and to envelop her in a kind of guard of honor. She laughed some more, and then went off to deliver her speech at the Hotel Astor.[147]

It may have been her finest moment — the indelible dramatization of her promise to Hitler that she would not be muzzled by thugs. She had "violated one of journalism's oldest traditions of courtesy," said *Newsweek*: she had laughed out loud.[148] According to *The New Yorker*, where the incident was written up in "The Talk of the Town," Dorothy's behavior "was more damaging to the composure of Herr Kuhn and his mob than all the angry clamor in the streets."[149]

"Perhaps it is a personal prejudice," she had written in "On the Record," "but I happen to dislike intensely 'liberal' fascists, reactionary fascists, labor fascists, industrial fascists, Jewish fascists,

Catholic fascists and personal fascists. When it comes to choosing the particular brand of fascism, I'm not taking any."[150] Generally speaking, coverage of the Bund rally zeroed in on all of the issues that Dorothy had hoped to raise. "It served formal notice," said *The Nation*, "that the gangsters are among us. . . . The richness of America makes it capable of buying more time than was granted, for instance, to the Weimar Republic. But the race is on."[151]

Within a year Fritz Kuhn had been indicted and sent to prison on charges of embezzlement, and the German-American Bund disappeared from view, its members condemned to a small-town racism or absorbed into more respectably xenophobic outfits such as America First. But the spectacle of Dorothy Thompson at Madison Square Garden — tall, fair, blue-eyed, and laughing in her evening gown at twenty-two thousand "little men" — was not a thing to be forgotten. Nor should it be forgotten, the *New Yorker* writer warned: "All these things called for laughter, and from various portents we read in the sky many more will before the spring comes in. We live in merry times, Dorothy. Take care of your larynx."[152]

She had begun to listen to her own publicity, and titled one of her columns "Cassandra Speaking."[153] "This business hasn't even started yet," she protested to a friend. "There will be massacres."[154] She celebrated the third anniversary of "On the Record" with a party at the St. Regis, then announced that she would take a vacation commencing in June. She had a private life to consider, she said.

11

CHAPTER

I N 1939 Michael Lewis was stricken with a bad case of pneumonia, and his mother (having proclaimed in "On the Record"
her immense relief that he did not have polio)[1] sent him away to
school — "to Arizona," she wrote to Red, "to a very small school
where he can live in a cottage with his nurse, and associate with other
children, and be out of doors." Michael was eight. He had already
spent time as a student both at Collegiate and at the Town and Country School in Riverdale, north of New York City, but he did not get
on well with the other boys and was, by common estimation, "a
problem."

"His teacher," said Dorothy, "who is a saint, and has taught children for twenty years, says that she has never known a child with
such intense feelings."[2] Others who knew Michael described him as
"a perfect little horror,"[3] a boy whose famous "sensitivity" posed a
real danger to himself and other people. He was both overdeveloped
and underdeveloped: "extraordinarily large and strong," as Dorothy
declared, but emotionally wild, given to furious tantrums and alarm-
ing bursts of violence. During one winter vacation, while playing
with the sons of Raymond and Betty Swing, Michael had grabbed
"a large open knife" and lunged at the other children with it — and
"Dorothy," said Betty, "these are symptoms which you CANNOT
overlook."[4] Frances Gunther, who would shortly be divorced from
Dorothy's friend John Gunther, left in her diary the record of a conversation she had with Mrs. Swing on this topic:

> Betty talked of D's boy Michael, their visit to Vermont, how she
> never left her boy John alone with Michael for fear he might hurt or

kill him — how he beat his nurse — how he was a monster — a sadist etc. — how D ought to take him to a psychiatrist — how terribly sorry she felt for D who had no time to be with her child. I said Why feel sorry? She could be with him if she wanted to. She'd rather be with her career. Much better if she stayed home and minded her husband and child instead of minding the nation.[5]

It was a typical statement, a typical belief, and a facile explanation for the problem Michael had become. Most of the women who knew Dorothy — and especially the wives of her colleagues in journalism — were inclined to look at her troubled family life in terms only of some "decision" they thought she had made, some conscious resolution on Dorothy's part "to put her profession ahead of her child." She was "a terrible mother" in this regard,[6] a "bad" mother, "not a mother at all, really," Dinah Sheean thought. Dinah remembered one Sunday evening when Michael wandered into a party at Central Park West to ask Dorothy if she would drive him back to school in Riverdale. He practically had to shake her to get her attention, and Dinah wanted to shake her, too, as Dorothy "came down out of that world she was in" — the world of international affairs, the world of "It" — and answered, "Oh, no, darling, I can't possibly go anywhere tonight. Fräulein can take you. Give me a kiss."[7] Marianne Kortner, the ten-year-old daughter of the German actor Fritz Kortner, who came with her family to New York in 1938 under Dorothy's sponsorship, enjoyed "a rather passionate childhood friendship" with Michael and believed that Dorothy was well aware, at some level, of her maternal failings:

> Dorothy was not a good mother to Michael. She tried desperately to make up for her lack of time and, probably, of motherly feelings for him by giving him everything else he wanted (and more). She even said she wanted to adopt me at one point (I never was sure how seriously she meant that) because she thought I was good for Michael. . . . She gave us ridiculous amounts of money, and if we wasted it all, she gave us more. I was very critical and serious at the time, and funnily enough she listened to me. She even tried to change her ways a little, but that never lasted long.[8]

"She loved Michael," said Denis Fodor, who spent weeks and months with the Lewises in New York and had a perspective that many others lacked. "She loved him very much." Some other child than Michael, a different little boy, might have taken Dorothy's peccadilloes in stride, because she was "terribly nice" to children in the normal run of things. "She was friendly," Denis thought. "She understood kids. She got down on their level." There were many who thought she would have done better with a daughter: she often said that she envied her sister, Peggy, whose only child, Pamela Wilson, was a source of real pleasure in Dorothy's eyes. But if her son was lonely — if he was neglected, like his father, in favor of "It" — his sufferings nevertheless were not Dickensian. Rather, they were in the mode of Little Lord Fauntleroy's sorrows.

"He was left alone with all kinds of people," Denis Fodor remarked in a fascinating sentence. "It wasn't as if he was kept in a cold dungeon." There were always friends around the house, dozens of people for Michael to talk to: secretaries, journalists, handymen, "Marie in the kitchen, baking cookies." In addition, said Denis, "he could have anyone over he wanted to play with, to spend the night, whatever. He wasn't a terribly lonely child. And she genuinely loved him."

"Mama," Michael would say when Dorothy was leaving on a trip, or just going out for the evening, "do you *have* to go? When will you be back?" Dorothy "always sounded sorry" when she answered: "Yes, I really do have to go." "And Michael understood," in Denis Fodor's memory.[9] At least he *said* he understood. At least Dorothy kept telling people that it could not be helped.

"I know my son much better than you think I do," she wrote to Betty Swing in 1938, endeavoring to answer Betty's charges about Michael. She was not prepared to worry about "tantrums"; she did not want to hear stories about knives: "I was a hellion myself, and I have kept out of an insane asylum until now." Dorothy became writerly on this subject, as on many others:

> I know [Michael] because I know myself, and I know his father. I know him because I enjoy a warm, affectionate, candid and, at the same time, fairly detached relationship with him. We love each other. I know what his reactions are, and why he reacts as he does. I know that in another year or two, he will react differently, and better. I like him very much, and I am not in the least worried about him. . . . If a child is physically strong and large beyond his years, if he is intelligent, and imaginative; if he is also combative and proud, and if, plus that, he is an only child, you are bound to have a "difficult" little boy! He is difficult. But that does not constitute a case for a psychi-

atrist. . . . And if you keep on regarding him as one, I shall be, eventually, annoyed.[10]

But Michael really was a case for a psychiatrist, and over time, very slowly, even Dorothy began to realize it. She found out from other people that Betty Swing was right — that Michael did, for example, "beat his nurse," the adoring Mimi Stadler, who was ready to do almost anything Michael asked, apparently, and took his blows without a word of complaint. As a very small child, Michael had sometimes been locked in a closet for hours at a time by his governesses, the Haemmerli sisters, whose ideas of punishment were old-world, to say the least.[11] Dorothy put a stop to this treatment (and fired the Haemmerlis) just as soon as she heard about it, but there was no telling what kind of damage might have been done before she did. All in all, there was no telling what combination of character and circumstance might account for Michael Lewis — and when it came to that, said Dorothy, "What about Red?"[12] Why was it always the *mother* who was blamed when the child went wrong?

"If Sinclair Lewis had any affection for either of his sons," Dorothy wrote, "it was not obvious." Children "bored" him. For two or three years after his separation from Dorothy, Red managed to send Michael "some small Christmas present" every December, but he never once remembered his birthday, and only in 1944, "for the sake of the boy's own attitude toward his father," did Dorothy insist that he send him a monthly allowance of fifty dollars.[13] On the few occasions when he actually wrote or telephoned to say hello, Red invariably came out sounding awkward, put out, or a bit funnier than was appropriate. In 1939 he presented Michael with a five-year diary for Christmas — his gifts were never more expensive than that — and explained:

> The theory is that you will write on the same page on February 17th, 1940, 1941, 1942, 1943, and 1944 — if that astonishing last date ever does come around. But I think that if I were you, I'd make it a two-year diary, and use up the first two spaces on each page in 1940, and the last three in 1941, when you will be a very profuse author and (I hope) writing both my novels and your mother's columns, so that we may devote ourselves to bridge and the crossbreeding of catnip plants.[14]

In her letters to Red, Dorothy made no secret of her belief that his neglect of their son would one day have tragic consequences. She spoke of Michael often as "the re-incarnation of his father,"[15] and no doubt the "fairly detached relationship" she enjoyed with him was prompted in part by the fear that her assessment might be right — that Michael *was* like his father, that he was disturbed like his father, "violent and frail, gifted, unbalanced and charming, born to unhappiness, to ill-adjustment, to crazy joy and continual disappointment. . . . A sick, lovely, nerve-wracking, expensive child," in Dorothy's description.

"He was conceived in a night that I remember," Dorothy wrote to Red, "but you do not, and born in a night that I remember and that you . . . or do you? . . . He is dearer to me than my life, and he makes life almost intolerable."[16] The opinion hardened into legend in the Lewis family that Michael "never forgave" his mother when she threw up her hands and sent him to school in Arizona.[17] He had had a difficult recovery from his pneumonia, and a number of physical complications were still baffling his doctors.

"This was in the days before there were antibiotics," said Dorothy. "[Michael] was given injections of horse serum, to which he was allergic. The fever, which was almost fatally high, came down, but he broke out in hives and was given adrenaline for that. This illness was followed by an infection of the heels of the feet which caused him to walk on his toes. . . . No doctor here could explain the cause. [But] the family physician in New York . . . discovered a heavy albumen content in his urine — nephritis — and kept him in bed for some weeks."[18]

The family physician was Dr. Cornelius Traeger, "Connie" to Dorothy and Red and the horde of celebrities who consulted him in New York, a specialist in rheumatoid arthritis, an amateur violinist, and "a quack," in Denis Fodor's opinion. "He was much concerned about the growth of Michael's private parts," Denis recalled,[19] but in fairness to Dr. Traeger it should be pointed out that he was not alone in this. Alarmed by her son's condition, Dorothy had called in "a *great* specialist, Professor Lichtwitz, formerly of Berlin," who attributed the trouble with Michael's feet to the horse serum and the trouble with his personality to an endocrine imbalance.

"He is sub-pituitary," Dorothy reported to Red. "His sexual development, as a result, is subnormal. His genitals are those of a child of four, not of eight, he is overweight and the distribution of his fat indicates this sub-masculinity. Lichtwitz believes that his whole behavior is due to this."[20] It is hard to blame Dorothy for being relieved. Michael needed "exercise," the doctors said, "sunlight," "warmth." And so she sent him to the Palo Verde Ranch School in Prescott, Arizona. He was "very happy" there, she reported, basing her claim on Michael's letters home, each and every one of which, over a period of nearly a year, began with the same seven words: "Dear Mother: How are you? I'm fine."[21]

Private schools and desert retreats had likewise been the fate of Red Lewis's elder son, Wells, who was twenty-two years old in 1939 and who had become, in a real sense, closer to Dorothy than any other member of the family. Her initial distaste for Wells's company had given way to a warm and mutual devotion. "I not only liked him," said Dorothy later, "I loved him immeasurably. He was all that I would have wished in a son."[22] She was apt to make these statements in her own son's presence, unfortunately, and when it was pointed out to her from time to time that Michael might suffer from the comparison, Dorothy responded hotly that this was nonsense, that Michael loved Wells as much as she did. And probably he did. Wells was "Joe College" when Michael was growing up, a glamorous, smart, golden-boy older brother in a camel-hair coat, who published his first book — They Still Say No, a well-received and enduringly funny novel of sexual frustration[23] — when he was just out of Harvard. But there was "something ghostly" about Wells for all of his charm, something lonesome and ethereal, delicate of touch.

"He seems to have walked somewhat lightly through life," said Dorothy's friend Max Ascoli, "as if he wanted to observe what we were doing and report somewhere else."[24] His mother, Grace Lewis Casanova, was a beautiful woman, and Wells, too, was lovely to look at. He was a gentleman, always, and a great rescuer of other people — first his own mother, who after her divorce from Red was always in financial difficulty and possessed of one forlorn plan or another to make money, and then Dorothy, who dated her own heartfelt attachment to Wells from the night at Twin Farms, sometime in the early thirties, when Red had "lashed out at [her] with words of such brutality and vulgarity" that Wells, standing by, had grabbed an antique sword from the wall "and brandished it at his father."

Red, "for once speechless with fury," Dorothy remembered, "left the room in almost visible smoke. I looked at my Knight, waving the sword above his head and glaring with the countenance of an avenging angel, and simply collapsed with helpless laughter. I asked him what he intended to do, decapitate his pop? run him through? or merely hack out his tongue. We then plotted together the most gory mayhem, and having, as it were, quartered Father and burned him in oil, we went for a swim to wipe off the bloodstains, and felt fine, agreeing that Father was just hard on kids and wives and there was nothing one could do about it . . . except symbolically."[25]

Everyone who knew them also knew that it was Dorothy who had helped Wells Lewis to reach some modus vivendi with his father; that she had "opened her house and her heart to this boy"[26] and given him, for the first time in his life, a sense of family and belonging. When he graduated from Harvard, in 1939, she used her influence and got him a job in Greenville, Mississippi, where he went to work for Hodding Carter on the *Delta Democrat-Times*. The following year he accompanied Dorothy to the Republican national convention in Philadelphia and was rewarded with space in "On the Record" to air his views on the Willkie campaign.[27] Dorothy was "tender" with Wells, and thoughtful, and respectful, in a way that she rarely was with Michael, and it took no genius to see that she functioned far better as a stepmother than as a parent. She knew it herself. Some years later she wrote to Grace Casanova that she wished *Michael* had had a stepmother to help him along:

> Actually I think that Michael has had it worse with his father than Wells did, simply because of the absence of an intermediary. There again one's capacity to "face reality" enters. I could face the reality of Red-Wells-Grace with some degree of common sense because I could be dispassionate. I could not bring the same coolness to bear on the triangle Red-Michael-Dorothy. I was inescapably *parti pris* — not being a saint. . . . Michael, like Wells, needs reconciling, somehow. . . . But his father is not present ever. He exercises over Michael a distant fascination, compounded partly of envy, admiration, hatred, fear, wounded feelings. Michael has never had the opportunity to develop Wells' ultimate humorous casualness: "An old bastard but I love him." He was separated from his father too young to be sure he is an old bastard from first-hand experience; he has been separated too long to feel love. . . . Nor can he realize, as Wells came to do, that Red's resentments, his dearest treasures, are also a fount for his talent.[28]

Red's talent had been expressed, over the past two years, almost exclusively in regional theater, where he had made something of a splash acting in stock productions of *It Can't Happen Here,* Thornton Wilder's *Our Town,* and an original production of his own, *Angela Is Twenty-two,* which he had worked out in collaboration with the actress Fay Wray and which concerned the roving eye of a fifty-year-old man. In June of 1939 he spent two weeks at Twin Farms, "gently and quietly," in the recollection of Dinah Sheean, who was happier than ever to have some relief from Dorothy's "Teutonic" pastimes and spent hours with Red going over his lines.[29] The Sheeans were always "a convenient buffer"[30] for Red in his dealings with Dorothy: she had done nothing whatever to encourage his passion for the stage.

"I do not admire your present incarnation," she wrote with withering honesty, "or respect your present attitude toward anything. I did not like *Angela Is Twenty-two* because I think it is beneath the level of the author of *Arrowsmith* and *It Can't Happen Here.* I think it is a cheap concession to a cheap institution — the American Broadway Theater."[31] Dorothy's disdain turned to an ever more fixed incredulity, however, as time went on, because besides learning his lines, Red was also chasing girls — young girls, as Dorothy discovered, "nymphets," summer-stock ingenues and *jeunes premières.* He turned up at parties now with starlets on his arm and told the youthful Kitty Carlisle, among others, that he was prepared to divorce his wife in order to marry her. Since Miss Carlisle (who everyone agreed was not a nymphet) knew Red Lewis's wife only from the radio and the *Herald Tribune,* she was understandably "frightened out of [her] wits."[32] She made her excuses and was replaced in Red's affections by a woman younger than she, younger even than the eponymous "Angela" — an eighteen-year-old apprentice at the Wharf Theatre in Provincetown, Massachusetts, with whom Red promptly (and permanently) fell in love.

Her name was Marcella Powers; she was "a young girl with a great deal to learn," who was "fascinated" by the doting attention of Sinclair Lewis.[33] Nothing like scandal ever attached itself to their relationship, in the first place because Red was accustomed to introduce Marcella around town as his "niece," and in the second place because they were known to be sincere in their devotion to one another: Marcella cared deeply about Red. The affair lasted for the better part of seven years and may be said to have ended only when Marcella grew up and realized that she no longer wished to play Galatea to Red's Pygmalion. By that time Red's life was bitter indeed, but at the beginning of the relationship Dorothy asked only that he not introduce Marcella to his sons as their "future Ma."[34] In any case, she was not going to give him a divorce: she was going to save him from himself whether he liked it or not.

Red had asked for a divorce for the first time in the spring of 1939, before he even met Marcella Powers, when he and Dorothy both found themselves in Los Angeles for several weeks. Red was becoming more and more attached to the world of actors and, through actors, of filmmakers, and he was in California that year to negotiate with studio executives for a scriptwriting deal that never came off. Dorothy, as it happened, was in the same position. She was taking two months' vacation from "On the Record"; after a visit to Michael Lewis at his school in Arizona, she moved on to Hollywood to meet with Louis B. Mayer. Recently she had put together a screenplay treatment about the life of Alexander Hamilton and the founding of the American Republic; though it was never produced, it was sold to MGM "for a handsome price" as "the kind of motion picture America *ought* to be seeing" (in Dorothy's words).[35] She was guided in this enterprise by her own loftiest sentiments and by her dramatic collaborator, Fritz Kortner, the man who had become her "research assistant" and, in recent months, her lover as well.[36]

Fritz Kortner had been one of Germany's leading classical actors in the years before Hitler came to power. (It was a position he would resume when the Third Reich collapsed.) He was known as probably the finest interpreter of Shakespeare outside London, and with his tall and stately "Amazon" wife, the actress Johanna Hofer, had formed part of the ensemble corps of the Berlin State Theatre. He was short, "blue-jowled," Jewish, and heatedly dramatic in temperament; completely devoted to his craft; politically committed, with a strong leftist bent; and even more fiercely provocative in company, if this was possible, than his friend and colleague Bertholt Brecht. Many people found Kortner intolerable. "He had all the charm of Karl Marx," said Denis Fodor; since he played tennis in a hair net and "looked like the owner of a candy store," he was the object of a certain amount of ridicule among Dorothy's friends.[37] But Dorothy's passion for "creative" men had not been diminished in any way by time or experience. After Kortner emigrated to the United States, she single-handedly arranged to obtain entry visas for the rest of his family — his wife, his two children, and even his mother — and for some time, on the promise of Kortner's talent and his proven reputation, the entire clan lived in New York and California at Dorothy's expense.

That Dorothy and Kortner were lovers, and not just collaborators, was a matter ultimately of minor importance, because the affair was brief and because neither of them, in 1939, was especially interested in "personal" satisfaction. When they came to work in the morning, Dorothy's secretaries would sometimes find rambling, unfinished essays sitting in her typewriter — passionate, even salacious accounts of her most recent liaison, which she had tossed off in the middle of the night and which the secretaries would promptly burn, in the interests of her reputation.[38] But Dorothy was always more devoted to Kortner intellectually than she was sexually or emotionally, and she was able to take a superior tone with Red precisely because *her* involvement with the theater was "useful" while Red's was "commercial." As one of the best-known and most influential friends of German refugees around the globe, and with Kortner as her anchor, she had resurrected in her salon the world of the Berliner Ensemble and was mingling again with the likes of Ernst Piscator, Salka Viertel, Oskar Homolka, Emil Jannings, and the whole of the German exile community in Hollywood.[39] According to Kortner, Dorothy also "put pressure on the State Department" to grant an entry visa to Bertholt Brecht in 1939, and she certainly gave Brecht money to live on when he came to America. She would not have been surprised, however, after the war, to discover that this notoriously unpleasant person had been left with "a bad impression" of her character.[40]

"It has been my fate during much of my life to be mixed up in one way or another with geniuses," Dorothy explained years later, in the *Ladies' Home Journal.* "I don't know what there is about me that attracts them. They see me coming. They spot me a mile off."[41] In 1939, with Kortner, she wrote and polished a full-length play about the plight of Hitler's refugees. It started out as *Spell Your Name* (the title taken from one of the more obvious degradations of exile) and ended up as *Another Sun,* a title taken from Virgil's *Georgics:* "For exile they change their homes and pleasant thresholds and seek a country lying beneath another sun." By the time it got to Broadway in February 1940, *Another Sun* was a wordy, well-intentioned, hopelessly static drama that only proved, in Dorothy's good-humored estimation, that "as a playwright I am a good journalist."[42] She was given an authentic comeuppance, as a matter of fact, in regard to the "cheap institution" of the Broadway stage.[43]

Dorothy put up something like thirty thousand dollars of her own money to see her play produced,[44] and it was the opinion of at least one member of the cast, the then nineteen-year-old Celeste Holm, that she had written it in the first place only in order to show Red Lewis how "Broadway" ought to be done. She would arrive at rehearsals laden with equipment, Miss Holm recalled — pads, pencils, clipboards, "and one of those metal, fold-down desk attachments for the chair in front of her, a little desk with a little shaded lamp on it." On this Dorothy would commence to draw pictures, evidently, "or maybe she got a lot of writing done," because she had nothing to say in rehearsals that anyone needed to hear. She was completely out of her league, and she was made to realize it all too keenly. One of the more demoralizing aspects of a nearly totally demoralizing experience was the spectacle of Fritz Kortner "humiliating" Dorothy along with everyone else in the cast. Kortner was directing as well as starring in *Another Sun,* and whenever Dorothy ventured timidly that one of the actors might want to try this or that or the other thing on stage, he would wheel around and holler at her "like a crazed gorilla, his face purple, his eyes bulging."

"Go up on the stage and take over the direction!" Kortner would command before stalking off the set. "Never" in his whole connection with the theater had he seen such arrogance! Three or four times a day he would declare that it was "impossible" to work with Americans, that he should have known better than to mix with *journalists,* "that he was through, through!" — until finally Cheryl Crawford, who as the producer of *Another Sun* was having a difficult enough time holding the company together, called his bluff and shouted back, "OK! OK! Let's quit! Let's forget it!"

"Since this was his first, and I think only, [directing] job in New York," Miss Crawford later wrote, "that was the last thing he wanted to do." He was persuaded to see the production through to the end, but he was remembered by almost everyone involved as a "pompous," "appalling" character —"a monster," in Celeste Holm's opinion. Kortner's wife, Johanna Hofer, was also a part of the cast, and when he began to yell at her, too, Miss Holm found herself crying out (much to her own surprise), "If you weren't a Jew you'd be a Nazi! You can't *yell* at actors, not in *this* country!" And with that she tore from the stage and threw up in her dressing room. "I don't think I'd ever spoken to anyone that way," she recalled. "Nor since." On the night before the opening, having quarreled with Dorothy, Kortner gathered the cast together and announced, "in great, self-pitying tones," "You no longer have a director. My friends have told me that I can't direct. I regret to say that you are a ship without a captain."

Altogether it was an unhappy production. After rehearsals, Dorothy and Cheryl Crawford would sometimes go to "a small, ugly bar" next to the Plymouth Theatre, where they would sit gloomily over drinks and commiserate about the difficulty of "being women in a man's world." The question came up inevitably, incessantly, in all of the interviews and profiles of Dorothy: what motivated her? what spurred her on? She was "the archetype of the American woman rampant," "articulate, emancipated and successful." She was supposed to have "limitless faith in herself," in her intuitions, in her judgments.[45] But she told Cheryl Crawford that she wanted a *man* — a "talented, strong and tender" man who might consent to let her be herself.

"Well," said Cheryl, "who doesn't, and where the hell are they?" Dorothy doubled over with laughter when Cheryl told her about the time she had "nervily" approached Edna Ferber with the question, "Miss Ferber, how does it feel to be an old maid?" and Miss Ferber had replied, "Well, Cheryl, it's rather like drowning — not bad once you stop struggling."[46] There was no other answer for a woman in Dorothy's position, no better explanation for her drive to success than her own romance with herself. "The numerous attempts to explain her by asking what she is up to all run completely off the track," Dale Warren insisted in the *Saturday Review*. "She is up to exactly what she is doing, writing or saying, and up to nothing else whatsoever."[47]

Another Sun opened on February 20, 1940, and closed a week later, after eleven performances and some of the cruelest reviews that Dorothy had ever seen. "Miss Thompson's and Mr. Kortner's sun has difficulty in rising," said Brooks Atkinson in the *New York Times*, "and no particular interest in setting before bed-time."[48] "So many things happened at once to so many people," another critic maintained, "that when one of the characters died in the middle of the stage the audience didn't notice it for ten minutes."[49] The consensus was that the Nazis would never be unseated by the Broadway stage, and about the only thing the critics could find to praise was the splendid accents of the cast. But since most of the cast was European to begin with, that was not saying a lot.[50] (Celeste Holm "truly felt" that *Another Sun* had failed because, "by employing so many refugee actors, it actually *disproved* the point it was trying to make" — that is, that the plight of the refugees was desperate.)

Dorothy took her defeat in stride, as might have been expected, and even drew from it some invigorating fire for "On the Record."

"I have no ambitions in the theatre," she pointed out. "I am the only person involved in this play to whom it is a matter of no great importance whether it stays on or goes off." She was, however, worried about the actors, and she was persuasive in her denunciation of the power of the critical establishment.

"I don't know what the intention of the critics was toward this play unless their intention was to destroy it," she wrote. "I have never written a column without a definite end in view, without thinking what the results might be. I have, for instance, attacked Father Coughlin with the definite intention, if I could, of destroying him. I take responsibility for that intention. If I could succeed I should be glad."[51] She gave a fifty-dollar bonus to every member of the company, but she never wrote another play,[52] and within a year she had fallen out with Kortner, too. The details of their rupture remain obscure — they were not known even to Kortner's family — but there was at least one "traumatic" scene in the presence of Wells Lewis, which came down discreetly in Dorothy's correspondence as "the Wells-Kortner episode" and which apparently involved another attempt on Wells's part to defend his stepmother against the verbal outpourings of an angry man.[53] Shortly afterward, Kortner and his family left for Hollywood, where they were a central part of the émigré community during the war and where Kortner, in the company of friends such as Brecht — "a redeeming blot on the beaming ebullience of this place" — felt more at home. He pledged his abiding loyalty to Dorothy, meanwhile, and said he would "remain a very attentive reader, and as good a friend as your mode of life permits you to accept."[54]

She was blamed by every man who ever left her for the breakup of their relations; it seemed to be her destiny never to find a man who would just admit that she scared him to death. "The strangest aspect of your great brilliance," Red Lewis wrote to her, "your power of analysis of masses and men outside yourself, is that you never — almost never — analyze your motives, or your feeling and relationship toward anybody near you."[55] As Dorothy's star rose higher and higher, stories abounded of her perceived heartlessness toward other people — not the refugees for whom she spoke so eloquently, but ordinary people, *real* people, such as her secretary Madeleine Clark, who in 1941 suffered a nervous breakdown and was not invited back into Dorothy's employ because, as Dorothy said, "I should constantly worry about you, and frankly I don't want to have to do so."[56] It was a fact, nevertheless, that Dorothy paid the bulk of Mrs. Clark's medical bills, and for anyone who knew her, this was "typical Dorothy."

"She would go to any lengths for you," one of her friends remembered, "if she knew what you needed, if she knew what the trouble was. If she didn't — if you didn't make it clear to her — she was just as likely never to ask you how you were." This unthinkingness was still — always — Dorothy's most obvious crime, as when she arrived in Chicago in 1939 and commenced to treat her sister, Peggy, as if she were some kind of supplicant.

"Peggy!" Red Lewis exclaimed in a chastising note to Dorothy, "your sister and probably your deepest admirer, the kind, tender, timid, lonely Peggy." Peggy was "bitterly hurt by your scarcely having written her in the past year or more," Red reported, "and by the fact that on your one day in Chicago, she could see you only in the presence of the noisy, chattering, parrot-preening Rosie."[57]

"Rosie" was Countess Rosie Waldeck, the notorious Jewish adventuress who was briefly Dorothy's research assistant and whom Red called the "Graefenberg-Ullstein-Waldeck Rosie lady" because she had had so many husbands and such a murky career.[58] Rosie had been born a Goldschmidt, the daughter of a banker in Berlin, and worked her way up the German social ranks through her marriages to a gynecologist, to the publishing magnate Franz Ullstein, and to an "invisible" count, whose title, more than anything else, allowed her to travel around Nazi Germany "with mystifying ease."[59] In the late 1930s Rosie published her memoirs and took New York by storm, acting as her own press agent and building her celebrity on what appeared to be sheer nerve. It was never proved that she was a foreign agent, as many believed, but it was soon discovered that she was an intriguer, and when Dorothy found out that she was also under investigation by the United States government, she was quickly shown the door.[60]

But Dorothy was more and more often the victim both of opportunists and of her own idées fixes. "Did you ever realize how much Dorothy is like the Statue of Liberty?" Walter Lippmann wrote to his wife. "Made of brass. Visible at all times to all the world. Holding the light aloft, but always the same light. . . . Capable of being admired, but difficult to love." In 1938 Lippmann had caused a scandal even in practiced journalistic circles by falling in love and effectively eloping with the wife of one of his best friends, the editor of *Foreign Affairs,* Hamilton Fish Armstrong; according to Ronald Steel, Lippmann's biographer, Dorothy "even discerned international significance in the divorce. A falling-out between two such ardent and influential internationalists [as] Lippmann and Armstrong, she feared, might weaken the willingness of Americans to confront the Nazi menace." Lippmann's own sympathies, meanwhile, were "with Sinclair Lewis": "You know," he said, "when I think of it, being moralized over by a woman who has made a mess of two marriages seems to me to be the height of impudence. Wouldn't it be fun not to have to be a gentleman all the time?"[61]

It was inevitable that anyone in Dorothy's position would make mistakes in judging character; inevitable, too, that she would be mobbed by people who were looking, so to speak, for a place at the foot of the throne. One of the reasons Fritz Kortner was so deeply resented by Dorothy's associates was that he had helped to persuade her, on the most dubious evidence, that the German nationals in her employ were "Nazi spies" — that they were reading her mail and her research notes and passing them on to Berlin. The FBI, which stepped in to investigate the situation at Dorothy's request, found no evidence whatsoever that her suspicions were true, but she fired the servants anyway, in a great dramatic purge: Josef and Greta, the maid and chauffeur; poor Mimi Stadler, Michael's governess; even the Duckers, a Vermonter couple who had been hired to farm Dorothy's land in Barnard.[62] She never acknowledged her mistake in this matter, and in fact she was generally beginning to react badly to the barrage of disapproval that attended her success.

"Ignorant bitch," H. L. Mencken was heard to remark as he posted a letter to Dorothy. "Shrieking hurricane. . . . Poor Red Lewis, stuck with that."[63] Red, too, had begun to step up his criticism of his wife's behavior. He declared that she was "wicked" not to give him a divorce; that she was keeping him in "exile"; that she had set herself up as "the Supreme Being" and would listen to no other counsel. She was as tired of Red's moralizing as he was of hers, however, and she shot off a reply that revealed the depth of her own indignation. "If you think it's wicked," she wrote, "— go ahead and get a divorce. I won't oppose it. I also won't get it. For God's sake, let's be honest. You left me, I didn't leave you. You want it. I don't. You get it. On any ground your lawyers can fake up. Say I 'deserted' you. Make a case for mental cruelty. You can make a case. Go and get it."

He had told her that her attitude was "incredible"; that if she honestly loved him, she would set him free; that months went by when she "never wrote," and that this in itself was proof of her insincerity:

> What is "incredible" [she asked] about my not writing? What is
> "incredible" is that I don't rush into the divorce court and soak *you*
> for desertion and "mental cruelty." I don't write because I don't know
> what to say to you. You have made it clear time on end that you
> dislike me, that you are bored with me, that you are bored with "sit-
> uations and conditions. And reactions." You don't like my friends.
> You don't know my friends. You resent my friends. Shall I write you
> that I think Hamilton Armstrong has done a brilliant piece of jour-
> nalism in his last book on the Munich conference? Or that Graham
> Hutton is in America and has a fascinating tale of Britain? Or that
> Peter Grimm has ideas on the Housing policy? . . . You are happy.
> Happier, you write, than you have been in years. I congratulate you.
> I am glad that you are happy. I happen not to be. I am not happy. I
> am not happy, because I have no home, because I have an ill and
> difficult child without a father. Because I have loved a man who didn't
> exist. Because I am widowed of an illusion. Because I am tremblingly
> aware of the tragedy of the world we live in.[64]

She lost the friendship even of Rose Wilder Lane by the end of
1939, having ignored a series of letters from Rose that were critical
of her style — not her literary style, certainly, but her style of living — and of the apparent recklessness with which she dismissed
other people as "fascists," "crooks," or ideological hacks. Rose was
hardening into a serious ideologist herself. She had lost everything
in the Depression and worked her way out of the disaster on a platform of self-sufficiency that made Dorothy's own natural conservatism look Bolshevist by comparison. After helping her mother to
produce the *Little House* books, Rose left the Ozarks once and for
all in 1937 and took up residence in Danbury, Connecticut, where
she spent the rest of her life as an apostle of the Libertarian philosophy and an opponent of "regimentation" in all its forms.[65] "Bad
luck, financial anxiety, rural isolation and political outrage run as
heavy dark lines through her diaries and letters," said Rose's biographer,[66] and an argument with Dorothy over the character of a mutual friend, the Russian-born journalist Isaac Don Levine, became
the occasion, for Rose, for an outburst of untrammeled resentment.

The dispute involved Levine's literary collaboration with a former
Stalinist agent, an exiled Soviet spy whose memoirs he ghosted for

the *Saturday Evening Post;* Dorothy, in a widely quoted speech, had criticized Levine and warned about the dangers of mixing ideology with journalism. A series of wayward letters and crossed telephone wires kept Dorothy and Rose from settling their differences, and after days of frustration Rose concluded that the friendship was dead. "You will hear nothing further from me," she vowed. "Once you were a fine person, sensitive, intelligent, witty, poetic, ardent for truth and justice. . . . Now you are coarse and stupid. . . . I could not believe what my reason told me. So I appealed to your honesty, your love of justice, and your patriotism; I told you that your charge against Don Levine is a mistake or a lie; I asked for a chance to prove that it is not true. You prefer to discard a genuine friendship."[67]

"I do not know how to answer your letter that I got the other day," Dorothy wrote to Rose in a weary reply. "If that is your opinion of me, there is no answer. You have a right to it." She was ready to apologize for her "careless and exaggerated" remarks about Don Levine, but she did not otherwise understand why Rose was so upset: "I know that I have neglected my friends. I have neglected many things that matter to me very much. I really live beyond my means in the work I am doing, but I wish you had told me personally how you feel about me."[68] The breach with Rose was eventually repaired, but the connection was never again so close, and the strain of this and other broken friendships, coupled with Dorothy's anxiety about the state of the world and the sheer volume of her work, left her, by the summer of 1940, "as near a nervous breakdown . . . as I have ever been in my life."[69]

"The awful thing is Mickey," she confessed in a note that she never sent to Red. "I don't dare to say it. But he seems utterly unreal to me. He doesn't seem like my child. And I don't seem like myself anymore, but like somebody else whom I don't know. Mickey was always you to me. Another you. But now I don't know you and I don't know him. Everything is dream-like — all the things people say to me and about me, and fame or notoriety or whatever it is. It all bounces back upon a vacuum which is me."[70] She was stretched so thin that her doctor, Connie Traeger, saw fit to remind her that the times demanded her continued well-being: "You must learn to conserve your resources," said Traeger, "because they will be needed for a long time. You have a responsibility not only to your friends but to the world, and we cannot let ill health or physical collapse interrupt your work."[71]

"Connie, of course," Dorothy reported, "tells me that my feelings are all due to my years and the operation last spring [her hysterectomy]. He takes down a book and reads me the symptoms. One of them is 'involuted melancholia,' and, of course, I may just be rationalizing a deficiency of hormones. Maybe that's all we are, anyhow, just electricity and hormones. I do observe that whenever Connie gives me a shot of whatever it is that he injects every week, I feel for a couple of days less inclined to end it all."[72] She was more "pepped up" than ever on drugs; "she seemed to be living on Dexedrine," and her agent, if not her doctors, "sometimes scolded her for guzzling pills."[73]

She canceled most of her lecture engagements for the 1940 season, saying that she would "rather live on fifty-three thousand dollars" a year "than die on a hundred and three,"[74] and in good time, after a rest at Twin Farms, she was restored to health and her accustomed equanimity. "My faults are, as a matter of fact, much greater than you dream," she had written to Red the year before; her letter might have served as a notice to all of her discomfited critics:

> There are things in my heart that you do not dream of, things that are compounded of passion and fury and love and hate and pride and disgust and tenderness and contrition, things that are wild and fierce . . . and you ask me to write you conventional letters because you are in "exile." From what? From whom?
>
> Give me Vermont. I want to watch the lilac hedge grow tall and the elm trees form, and the roses on the gray wall thicken, and the yellow apples hang on the young trees, and the sumac redden on the hills, and friends come, and your two children feel at home. Who knows? Maybe some time you might come home yourself. You might go a long way and do worse. As a matter of fact and prophecy — you will.[75]

AT the end of May 1939 the German writer Ernst Toller hanged himself in his apartment at the Mayflower Hotel in New York City, six years after his flight from Nazi Germany and just two weeks after he appeared with Dorothy at the PEN International Congress of writers and publishers at the New York World's Fair.[76] Dorothy was president of American PEN, and under her stewardship a conference had been organized with the aim of drawing attention to the spread of totalitarianism and the plight of the intellectual refugee — "the poet," as Dorothy urged all of her guests and speakers to regard themselves.

"I want to propose to you a conspiracy of poets," she proclaimed, "to offset the innumerable [other] conspiracies which have made this world a nightmare. . . . We need the intuitive imagination of the great poets, to comprehend in even a small way the nature of the forces that are moving the world." When Dorothy used the word *poet*, she did not limit her meaning to the craftsman of verse. She spoke of poets the way Walt Whitman had spoken about them in the preface to *Leaves of Grass*. She envisioned a "breed of men" as Whitman had envisioned a City of Friends: "full-sized, capable of universal sympathy, full of pride and affection and generosity."[77] She had the courage to assert that *she* was a poet, and that her colleagues in journalism all were poets, and that no writer in the twentieth century could afford to see himself as "some sort of ornament on the pillars of society. The days are Doric," said Dorothy. "There is no room for ornament. . . .

"Never, in the memory of anyone in this hall, have so many of our guild been men without a country," she remarked to the PEN congress. "Never, in the memory of anyone in this hall, have so many of our guild been in prison or in exile. For in much of the world today the word itself has been made captive. It walks in chains. Those who would free it do so at the risk of their own lives."[78] When Ernst Toller killed himself, Dorothy commented that the gesture was perfectly appropriate — that suicide, in Toller's case, was the only convincing response:

> They will say that Hitler killed him. That is true enough. But commend him not to hate who had in him no steely power to hate.
>
> His fate was to love the world and mankind, and most unhappily. . . . Being a poet, he was afflicted — with nerves and with imagination. . . . He looked upon the world with torn-open, incredulous eyes. They remained to the end incredulous eyes. They looked eagerly for beauty, serenity, dignity, justice, truth. What they saw appalled them. Toller was appalled to death.[79]

She had taken up her favored themes in "On the Record" and rolled them into a ball of outrage, which she commenced to hurl, over and over in the next two years, at the "cowards" and "appeasers," the isolationists, the America Firsters, and "the architects of cynicism" in American life. She had no other public concerns,

really, between 1939 and 1941. Her columns were not distinguish-
able from her radio broadcasts, nor her speeches from her open dis-
course. "Day by day," said Dorothy Canfield Fisher, her Vermont
neighbor and fellow writer, "with a clang like that of a powerfully
swung hammer, she beat upon [the] general confusion of mind till
the will to defend democracy was forged."[80] It was no American
virtue to put "America First," Dorothy argued: democracy would
"not save itself by repeating indefinitely that it is the most perfect
form of government" or by asserting with a shrug that Hitler, Stalin,
and Mussolini were mad. "If they are mad," she wrote, "there is
consistency and method in their madness, which is more than can
be said for the sanity of the rest of the world. In a contest between
twenty per cent of organized madmen and eighty per cent of disor-
ganized paralytics, the madmen will win."[81] She was tired of "the
'anti' attitudes." She was tired of people who were "anti-Hitler" but
"pro" nothing else; tired of a President who refused to take a political risk and declare outright that the Nazis were murderers; tired of
a Congress that had "become representative only of the articulately
negative elements in our society: the people who do not want to
starve, do not want to be taxed, do not want to lose their dividends,
do not want to go to war, . . . do not want to do anything dangerous."[82] Hitler himself had written in *Mein Kampf* that "you can
fight an idea only with another idea, and a better one," but better
ideas, in Dorothy's estimation, had gone begging:

> Integrity, honesty and every noble passion are held up to ridicule.
> The independent personality is the butt of every cheap joke. Let a
> man emerge amongst us of truly superior quality, and a thousand rats
> will begin gnawing at his legs to topple him down. If he is a poet, let
> him write one book inferior to himself and the jackals will howl with
> glee to proclaim him finished. Let him change his mind through the
> achievement of wisdom, and he will be called a renegade. A head that
> stands above the mass must expect to be removed.[83]

Still, she could stand on a lecture platform — on the ramparts, as
it were — and express her hope that America might revive, and that
the people might come to their senses before complacency and
mediocrity had totally swamped the heartland. She was moved to
rapture, sometimes, by the majesty of her vision: "Is this not a beautiful country, Ladies and Gentlemen? Is this not a miraculous country? Do you ever wake up in the morning and wonder by what stroke

of unearned good fortune you were privileged to be born in the United States of America?"[84]

She was heard on the air for fifteen consecutive days and nights at the end of the summer of 1939, the year Hitler invaded Poland and Europe went to war. It was one of her more attractive characteristics that she did not gloat when she was proved right. She was unable to resist a certain modest statement of fact, however, in this case: "Nothing is happening that has not been predicted." She had predicted the conquest of Czechoslovakia after the conquest of Austria, and the conquest of Poland — "or perhaps some other Eastern European power" — after the conquest of Prague. She had even foreseen the Hitler-Stalin pact, the "surprise" switch in Soviet foreign policy that freed Hitler to go to war:[85] Dorothy had long maintained that the Soviet Union *had* no foreign policy and that "something dreadful [was] being cooked up in Russia."

"So all the rats are together," she observed. "In a way, it's a rare opportunity. We will fight the first round of the World War, I hope, by getting rid of Communism and Fascism in our own country."[86] On September 3 Britain and France declared war on Germany, and thereafter, as Dorothy remarked three days later, in her final broadcast of the summer, "events . . . moved forward with kaleidoscopic swiftness to the point where we are tonight, when the Nazi troops stand at the gates of Warsaw, and the French troops at the Western wall of Germany. . . . More than a score of cities and towns have been bombed, the great capitals of Western civilization have been evacuated, millions of children have been put into gas masks. And men are conducting their affairs underground, away from the death that lurks in the air. . . .

"I think it is one of the most incredible stories in history," Dorothy sighed, "that a man could sit down and write in advance" — as Hitler had done in *Mein Kampf* — "exactly what he intended to do; and then, step by step, begin to put his plan into operation. And that the statesmen of the world should continue to say to themselves: 'He doesn't really mean it! It doesn't make sense!' "[87]

The question now, of course, was how long the United States could get by on simple incredulity. On September 5 President Roosevelt had issued two proclamations of American neutrality in the European war, while at the same time asserting (in what amounted to a confession of personal sentiment) that no American citizen could be expected to remain "neutral in thought." Two weeks later he asked Congress to lift the international arms embargo that had been attached to the neutrality laws of 1937. Although it was clearly understood that the repeal of the arms provisions was intended as a means to assist Great Britain and France in their struggle against Hitler, it was not until June 1940, and even then in open defiance of his military advisers, that Roosevelt broke with his own precedent and proclaimed himself on the side of the Allies. By that time a state of "limited national emergency" was in force; the Selective Service Act was passed the following September, but political feeling in the United States was still so overwhelmingly isolationist — in the strict sense that the American people wanted to keep out of the war — that Roosevelt, with France defeated and England enduring "her darkest hour" alone, was able to transfer military aid to Britain only in the guise of "Lend-Lease," and with the understated assertion that it was necessary for the defense of the hemisphere.

"This country is literally drunk with pacifism," said Dorothy's friend Raoul de Roussy de Sales in the autumn of 1939. "The war as an absolute evil in itself has become a mysticism. One no longer dares to pronounce the word nor to think of it except with pious horror. To spare our boys has taken on the value of a national mission." [88] While other columnists and national editors continued to call for the maintenance of neutrality, Dorothy, faced with "a spectacle of stupidity and hypocrisy rarely equalled" in American life, was heard to cry out about some Wall Street acquaintances, "God damn it, they've discovered that Hitler is a good Republican!" [89] She was positively reeling with indignation in her column, and it was not long before she began to get hate-mail addressed to "Dorothy Thompson, Warmonger." She had not, in fact, called for American entry into the war — at least, not yet. She had merely taken a carefully timed shot at Colonel Charles Augustus Lindbergh, who in September 1939 had broadcast a radio speech from Washington in which he dared to suggest that Hitler might not be the devil incarnate after all.

From the beginning there was something pathetic about Charles Lindbergh's defense of the Nazis [90] — something tragic and defeatist that was done for long before the calamity of Pearl Harbor finished it off. As America's most famous and probably most authentic national hero, stunned by the kidnapping and murder of his oldest son and by the media circus that followed, in 1935 he had left the United States for Europe, where he lived for nearly four years with his wife,

Anne Morrow, and where he developed "an aviator's admiration" (not to mention a conservative's sympathy) for the "efficiency" of the Nazi regime. Lindbergh never declared publicly that he thought America should ally itself with Hitler, but he did, as a prominent member of the America First Committee, make some unfortunate remarks about "the Jews" and the need for "new policies" and "new leadership" to counter Jewish influence. Privately, President Roosevelt himself never hesitated to affirm that "Lindbergh [was] a Nazi," and Interior Secretary Harold Ickes, who had many times been at odds with the opinions in "On the Record," had nothing but praise for Dorothy when she answered Lindbergh with "a smashing attack" in her column.[91]

"Colonel Lindbergh's whole argument deserves the most searching analysis," Dorothy wrote, in plain style. "For what Lindbergh clearly implied in his [radio] talk . . . was that unless this country is prepared to go to war with the full force of all its manpower and resources, the Nazis will win it; and, this being the case, it is better not to offend them in any way. Sentiment, pity, or personal sympathies ought not, he said, to influence our cold judgment of realities."[92] And with that in mind she went to work herself, using the sharpest blades at her disposal. She called Lindbergh a fascist; she called him "a cruel practical joker," a man "without human feeling"; she called him a Nazi before she was through, and she insisted — especially after his wife published The Wave of the Future, a befuddled exploration of fascism in action — that he was also intent on becoming an American dictator. He was "America's number one problem child," said Dorothy — a fallen hero who would not be satisfied until the United States bowed to Hitler.

"I cannot prove that what I say about Lindbergh is true," Dorothy admitted. "I have no 'inside dope.' . . . I know it because I recognize something familiar. I recognize the manner, the attitude, the behavior of the crowds. . . . This man has a notion to be the American Fuehrer."[93] She published three more columns against Lindbergh in 1939, six in 1940, and four in 1941. Her attacks on him did not cease until well after Pearl Harbor, when Lindbergh, with a dignity that no one could deny, issued a plea to all Americans that they rally behind the war effort; he then retired from public life. By that time opinion had swung unanimously to Dorothy's side. But when she first took on "this somber cretin" and his "noxious vision of the future," her desk was flooded with such angry letters from "Christians" and "patriots" that she confessed to Raoul de Roussy de Sales that she was afraid for her safety.[94] Apart from the usual anti-Semitic tracts and some crude certifications that Dorothy was "a homely-looking battleax" who had "missed out on love," there were a number of more deeply upsetting cables and menacing diatribes.

"Dorothy Thompson," one woman began: "I pray that the first bomb that is dropped on the U.S. will hit your Son." It was signed "A Mother." "Be a 100% U.S. Citizen," a second reader snarled, "not more British . . . than you are for the U.S. If you do not like what the great majority of citizens of the U.S. want why get out of the U.S. as we do not care to have your kind around. . . . If you was a male [I] would be after you to give you a good two-fisted beating the U.S. way. I get around the U.S. quite a lot and hope to meet you face to face."[95] When Dorothy turned up at a party one night with a bandaged finger, someone quipped, "Bitten by a Nazi, no doubt."[96] She was rarely given to joke about the subject herself. In 1940 a woman wrote to her with the prideful words, "I do not choose to have my son die fighting in Europe," and Dorothy, having read the letter aloud to a roomful of people, sat down at her typewriter and pounded out a response.

"Well, then," she asked, "just how *do* you choose to have your son die? From a cerebral hemorrhage? From cancer? In an automobile accident? Just how?"[97] In February 1941 a delegation of women protesting the Lend-Lease provisions attempted to hang Dorothy in effigy on the White House gate, because "she wants to give away," as their placards read, "a million boys' lives in blood and pain."[98] From time to time she tried to reason with her critics, as when a certain Clara Studer published "An Open Letter to Dorothy Thompson" in the *New York Journal and American* and asked what Dorothy would do if she had to fight the war herself, "knowing that it might cost you a pair of legs."[99] Dorothy invited Miss Studer to tea "to quarrel it out," but not before she drafted a bitter reply.

"What business have you to assume from anything I have ever written, spoken or said," she cried, "that I believe in war, want our country to go to war, or want to see a single human being killed in war? . . . If my life would end this war with a decent Europe I would die gladly, and die with torture, and I mean it."[100] She did not understand anyone who thought that "peace" was a matter simply of avoiding conflict at all costs. She told her friends repeatedly in these days that she was counting on "a tremendous renaissance of

Christianity" to defeat the Nazis,[101] and while she was never particularly clear about what she meant when she spoke of "Christians," she was specific indeed about certain brainstorms she had had. In August 1939, while the world waited to see what action the Allies would take in response to Hitler's aggression in Poland, Dorothy had sent an unusual ten-page telegram to Harold Nicolson in London, an astonishing plea for nonviolent resistance. At that time Nicolson was M.P. for West Leicester and a vocal critic of the British government's policy of appeasement:

HAROLD [Dorothy began] THERE IS A WAY TO WIN THE WAR OF NERVES AND AVOID THE HORRIBLE HOLOCAUST BUT IT REQUIRES A PRODIGIOUS ACT OF THE IMAGINATION. . . . THE BRITISH CABINET MUST . . . DELAY ITS ANSWER WHILE IT ENGAGES IN MEDITATION AND PRAYER TRUSTING IN GOD TO REVEAL TO ENGLAND'S LEADERS THE WAY TO A TRUE AND JUST PEACE FOR ALL PEOPLES EVERYWHERE POLES AND GERMANS AND ITALIANS AND FRENCHMEN AND ENGLISHMEN CALLING ON ALL CHRISTIANS THROUGHOUT THE WORLD TO HOLD FAST TO THE FAITH WHICH THEY PROFESS. . . . THE ENTIRE SHORT WAVE TO GERMANY SHOULD BE CONFINED TO THIS SIMPLE STATEMENT AND TO THE PLAYING OF THE GREAT RELIGIOUS MUSIC OF GERMANY THE PASSIONS OF MATTHEW AND JOHN THE GREAT GERMAN HYMNS AND THE GREAT HYMNS OF ALL RELIGIONS AND THE READING OF PASSAGES FROM THE BIBLE THE SERMON ON THE MOUNT THE TEN COMMANDMENTS THE THIRTEENTH CHAPTER OF FIRST CORINTHIANS THE GREAT PROPHETIC CHAPTERS OF ISAIAH ABOUT PEACE. . . . ENGLAND'S STRENGTH [is] NOT APPEASEMENT NOR WAR BUT A GLORIOUS CHRISTIAN RESISTANCE I MEAN THIS WITH ALL SERIOUSNESS I AM NOT AT ALL CRAZY LOVE FROM RED WHO THINKS I AM = DOROTHY.[102]

"Of course I do not think you crazy to take that point of view," said Nicolson in answer to Dorothy's telegram, "and I have often thought myself that we should be doing a wise thing to get away from all the ordinary diplomatic formulas and to state the issue in simple moral terms. . . . Dear Dorothy it is so welcome in this moment of terrible crisis to get messages from you and Red."[103]

She stayed away from the arena of war for as long as she could bear to, working on her columns and radio broadcasts, lighting Christmas trees at Rockefeller Center, gratefully acknowledging the compliment when somebody at the International Flower Show in

Manhattan named a sweet pea after her.[104] But in March 1940 she sailed for Europe, fresh from the disaster of *Another Sun* and hopeful that "a swing around the hot-spot circle"[105] might enhance her advocacy of Democracy's cause. It was the period of the "phony war," that extended, nerve-racking lull in hostilities — or rather, in actual military engagements — that followed the invasion of Poland. In April the Nazis overran Denmark and Norway, but it was still unclear how far they aimed to go. Dorothy herself was under no illusions: she had left New York with the unfamiliar impression that she was getting in over her head.

"I never remember feeling quite like that," she wrote in her diary: "suddenly not glad any longer; suddenly as though the whole journey were too frivolously undertaken."[106] She had planned a sweeping trip through her old territory — "I knew I had to go to every European country I could reach," she said[107] — and made stops at Gibraltar, Athens, Ankara, Budapest, Belgrade, Geneva, and Rome, where she donned a veil and visited the Pope. She had hailed the election in 1939 of Pius XII, who had previously been Papal Secretary of State, as a sign that the Catholic Church might be ready to adopt a more vigorous and more directly political role in world affairs. (She was wrong.) She praised Pope Pius's first encyclical as one of the great religious documents of the ages,[108] and whenever she passed through Rome in future years she never failed to arrange a private audience at St. Peter's. During a famous encounter at the end of the war, she made an appeal for papal assistance in the resettlement of refugee children and found herself pounding the table in front of her.

> The Pope smiled at me sadly [she remembered] and said, "I know, my child, I know."
> Here I was quite carried away and said, "Well, Your Holiness, if you do know, why don't you do something about it?"
> He lifted his hand gently. "Now I know that you are a Protestant."
> "How, Your Holiness?" I asked. "Is it because of my rudeness?"
> "No," he said. "It is because only a Protestant could so greatly overrate the powers of the Roman Catholic Church."[109]

Dorothy did not live to hear the worst of the accusations brought against the Vatican in the wake of the Nazi Holocaust (they came forward only gradually, with the opening of government and diplomatic files); in 1940, during her European tour, she was no more or less critical of the Church than of any other "legitimate body" in

Europe that had failed to counter the Nazi menace. Her friend Genia Schwarzwald was dying of cancer in Zurich, having been chased from Vienna by the Nazis; it was all Dorothy could do to control herself when Genia warned her from her deathbed, "You must not hate. . . . Everyone will hate, but there must be some who do not . . . though they fight like tigers."[110] Christa Winsloe was in the south of France, at Cagnes-sur-Mer, where she had taken up residence with a Swiss girlfriend named Simone Gentet. And Jimmy Sheean was in Paris with Dinah, and Edgar and Lilian Mowrer, and dozens of other journalists and diplomats who sensed, like Dorothy, that the "phony war" was in its final stage. On the morning of May 10, 1940, Dorothy awoke in her suite at the Hotel Meurice to find that the Nazis had invaded Holland and that all of France had been mobilized.

"Make room, make room!" the soldiers were crying later, "On a Paris Railway Station"[111] where thousands of young men were boarding trains for the front and where Dorothy composed one of the all-time classic dispatches of the war. No one was laughing, she observed, no one was singing as the trains pulled away:

> "What! No *Tipperary*? No *Madelon*?"
> The whistle blows. The officer holds his girl's cheek to his. The soldier kisses his girl on the mouth. Just one more!
> Nobody watches anyone else. No one pretends. No one is pretending anything.
> "Kill a Boche for me, darling." Didn't they say that in the last war?
> No one says a word about Boches or killing. Not a word. Not a flag. Not a salute . . . not an *au revoir*. They pull apart, and the men crowd into the cars. They wear good woolen uniforms and good thick boots.
> They look through the open windows — a thousand faces, a thousand different faces, not one like another, not one common expression, not one replaceable face.

She followed the army as far as Nancy and made a much-publicized tour of the front, where, from an underground fortification of the Maginot Line, in the vicinity of Wissembourg, she lobbed a series of artillery shots at the Nazi troops who had crossed the Rhone:

> The soldier managing each gun gave it a tap with the palm of his hand, no harder than a light slap. There was a noise that seemed to raise the top of my skull. The soldier facing me opened his mouth

and swallowed and indicated I should do the same, and I did. Another tap and again the terrific detonation. Ten times, in the roar, trying to keep my thoughts together, I began counting them: one for the Czechs and one for the Poles and one for the Norwegians and one for the Dutch, and then in the noise I lost track.[112]

When France collapsed she fled to Genoa, and was back in New York in time to respond to General Hugh S. Johnson's charge, inspired by her performance at the Maginot Line, that she was "a blood-thirsty, breast-beating Boadicea, urging us to flaming action" and bent on dragging the country to a foreign doom. The general was a popular syndicated columnist himself, a renegade New Dealer and one of the founders of the America First Committee; Dorothy only wished that he would "straighten out his classical references." She had just gotten used to being identified with Cassandra, and she did not imagine that she could make an easy transition to Boadicea, the warrior queen of ancient Britain. Besides, "there was a sort of lofty and elevated darkness" about Cassandra that she admired, something that put her in mind of her own childhood fantasies: "A pale, tall figure on the Trojan walls, foretelling doom in noble strophes. . . . I caught myself going around with a darkling air, and a brunette soul, cultivating an iambic pentameter style and wearing black dresses and a look of suffering."[113] But she reminded Julian Bach, then a young editor at *Life* magazine, more nearly of the Lion of Lucerne, the majestic symbol of liberty that stands watch over Switzerland, the oldest republic in Europe.

"Her hair was quite long at that time," said Bach. "It came down below her neck, and when she talked I kept thinking about the Lion, about liberty and freedom." Bach had dinner with Dorothy and several of her friends at the Starlight Roof of the Waldorf-Astoria just after the fall of France. "The times were unbelievably dark," he remembered. "I don't think there was a worse day than the day France fell. The one land army of Europe had been smashed; the nakedness of the democracies was revealed, so to speak; there was nothing to stand between the Nazis and the sea"; and Dorothy, back from the front, was rising to new heights of eloquence. She asked the party back to her apartment that night, and when they all got there she made a speech.

"She was standing in front of the fireplace with one arm on the mantel," said Bach, "and she spoke about the situation, democracy and the war. She spoke so magnificently that we all had our handkerchiefs out. We were crying. We were *weeping*."[114] Jane Perry Vandercook, who would later become the second wife of John Gunther, heard Dorothy talk at Carnegie Hall not long afterward and declared without reservation that "it was the best speech I have ever heard given by a woman. It was *absolutely thrilling*." Someone in the audience shouted at Dorothy, "Take off your hat!" and she started clowning for her fans.

"I haven't had time to have my hair washed!" she cried.[115] But she took her hat off anyway, to roars of approval, and nodded wisely when someone told her later that she had spoken "like an angel."

"And every word was true," she replied.[116] At an Aid-to-Britain rally in Springfield, Massachusetts, she attracted more than ten thousand people and delivered her speech in an alluring ashes-of-roses gown, her hair pulled back in a beaded snood and the bodice cut in such a way as to suggest that she was aware of the impression she was making. "What a woman!" said a man in the crowd. "Great speech!"[117] In Congress, some of the leading isolationist senators — including Burton K. Wheeler of Montana, Gerald P. Nye of North Dakota, and William E. Borah of Idaho — were talking about having Dorothy investigated as "a British agent"; she laughed at the idea, but welcomed the opportunity, when it came, to plead England's cause in a wider forum. A speech she made in Montreal in July 1940 was broadcast directly to London, where Jimmy Sheean, Edward R. Murrow, Eric Sevareid, and other friends of hers were reporting nightly on the Battle of Britain. She urged the British people to trust in God, in Churchill, in history, and in the "gallant company of ghosts" that hovered, in her view, around the map of England:

> Elizabeth is there, and sweetest Shakespeare . . . Drake . . . and Raleigh, and Wellington. Burke is there, and Walpole and Pitt. Byron is there, and Wordsworth and Shelley. Yes, and I think Washington is there, and Hamilton, two men of English blood. . . . And Jefferson is there, who died again, the other day, in France. All the makers of a world of freedom and of law are there, and among them is the Shropshire lad, to whom his ghostly author calls again: "Get ye the men your fathers got, and God will save the Queen."[118]

"If democracy perishes in Britain," Dorothy proclaimed, "it will not be because the British people did not fight Hitler with all they had; it will be because they were defeated in an unequal battle, and because the world's greatest democracy and brother free nation allowed them to perish without adequate aid."[119] So convinced was she that the fortunes of the United States and of England were tied together — and *ought* to be tied together — that in 1941, following the first of the wartime conferences between Roosevelt and Churchill and the adoption of the Atlantic Charter, she actually proposed "a union of the English-speaking world."[120] It was a specifically Thompsonian interpretation of Henry Luce's "American Century," and it was not the first such extravagant notion she had had. The previous spring, while still in Paris, contemplating the fall of France, she had concluded that America could not afford a change of leadership in that pivotal election year. Franklin Roosevelt had not yet declared his intention of seeking a third term, so Dorothy — to the astonishment of her friends and, above all, her employers at the *Herald Tribune* — declared it for him.

"The greatest thing, it seems to me, that the Republican party could do now," she wrote, ". . . would be to announce, and as quickly as possible, that if the President will accept a third term it will offer no candidate in opposition to him, but will offer, instead, only a Vice-Presidential candidate." Dorothy had in mind "a government of national concentration,"[121] and to that end she was even willing to overlook her own relentless criticism of the New Deal. She knew that when she came out for Roosevelt her critics would have a field day; she would be accused of "waffling," "flip-flopping," and every other journalistic insecurity her detractors could think of. Indeed, she *did* flip-flop quite a bit that summer as she sought to see her way clear. When her friends pointed out to her the sheer unmanageability of a two-party ticket, and when Helen Reid cabled her to request that she confine herself to writing "about nongovernmental people" for a while, Dorothy agreed to reconsider her position.[122]

"I think my column about a third term was a mistake," she admitted to Paul Block, the publisher of the *Pittsburgh Post-Gazette* and the *Toledo Blade,* who subscribed to "On the Record" and was horrified by the drift in Dorothy's thinking.[123] There was as yet no constitutional limit on the number of times an American President could seek reelection, but the very idea of a third term was anathema to most conservatives, and in earlier days, undoubtedly, any such proposition would have raised a cry of "fascism" from Dorothy herself. She tried to explain later that her views had been altered by events, that she was thinking realistically and had expedience in mind. After all, she wrote, "the year is 1940. We have behind us eight terrible years of a crisis we have shared with all countries. Here we are, and our basic institutions are still intact, our people relatively prosperous, . . . our society relatively affectionate. No rift has made an unbridgeable schism between us."[124] If the Republicans were determined to defeat the President, she said, they would need to propose "a new idea." They would need to propose another Roosevelt. And that being the case, Dorothy continued, "the only possible choice" for them was Wendell Willkie.

Dorothy had been singing Willkie's praises since April of that year, when she had declared in "On the Record" that "the job of being President . . . is not one to be jumped at with insouciant gaiety," and had picked off, one by one, the more traditional and predictable Republican candidates: Senator Robert A. Taft of Ohio, whose impeccable isolationist credentials disqualified him immediately in Dorothy's eyes; Thomas E. Dewey, who was "too young" and anyway "not wise enough"; and her good friend Arthur Vandenberg, who was simply "the wrong kind of man" for the job.[125] But Wendell Willkie was something else. Wendell Willkie was a thrilling candidate, and if Dorothy had not been so totally wrapped up in the war against fascism she might have stuck with him to the end.

Intellectually brilliant, physically attractive, filled with common sense and relaxed good humor, Wendell Willkie had left a thriving legal practice in the early thirties in order to take on the leadership of Commonwealth and Southern, the utility giant that stood in the vanguard of the fight against government regulation of industry during the Depression.[126] His strong identification with the bosses of capitalism, in 1930s America, ought to have turned him into political poison; instead it made him, as a business critic of the New Deal and in particular of the Tennessee Valley Authority, a kind of inverse populist hero — "a simple barefoot Wall Street lawyer," in Harold Ickes's stinging estimation, or "the earnest David of free enterprise," according to Richard Kluger, the historian of the *Herald Tribune,* "locked in combat with the Goliath of an oppressive government."[127]

Willkie was never a "politician." He joined the Republican party only two years before he ran for President, and it was this very independence of mind that Dorothy found most appealing about him. He was a patient, educated, liberal thinker after her own heart. He was also having an affair with Irita Van Doren, the book-review editor of the *Herald Tribune,* a fact that was known to all of New York society and to every journalist in the United States; no one thought it necessary in 1940, however, to expose a candidate's private life in the interests of democracy. Opinion was unanimous, in any case, that Willkie could not have achieved the Republican nomination had the world situation not been so dangerously unsettled and had not many, many Republicans been thinking exactly what Dorothy was think-ing — that the times demanded an independent, internationalist can-didate. At a Republican dinner earlier in the year, when Senator Robert Taft had continued to insist that the United States should remain neutral in the European conflict, pandemonium had broken out.

"Everybody began to scream at once," Martha Taft recalled, "with Dorothy Thompson screaming more at once than anybody else." [128] When Dorothy finally abandoned the Republican ticket in October 1940 — when she "jumped ship," in the bitter parlance of Wendell Willkie's supporters — she did so only because she had de-cided, in the middle of a tense and confused campaign, to trust her initial instincts.

She had declared earlier that she would support Willkie "to the hilt" if he won the nomination. [129] The New York Herald Tribune had done more than any other paper in America to create Wendell Willkie, and Dorothy confided (but only to her closest friends, and only when the Willkie campaign had been revealed in practice as a folly of compromise and mixed intentions) that she feared she had backed the wrong horse. Roosevelt had twice summoned her to the White House, once in June and again on October 1, 1940, and en-deavored, with an earnestness that impressed her, "to get this silly business of Wendell Willkie out of her head." [130] She wondered again if the essential difference between Roosevelt and Willkie was not, after all, the "vital question of experience." She wondered, never-theless, if Roosevelt could survive a third term — if he could actually "live through another four years of this kind of strain." [131] She was genuinely confused about what to do. But when Willkie, following some terrible campaign advice and trying to counter a slip in the polls, began to adhere to a strict anti-Roosevelt line — when he be-gan to make isolationist speeches and declared that "we shall not undertake to fight anyone else's war" — Dorothy concluded that the Republicans had undermined their own candidate, "that they were not real supporters of Willkie and intended to knife everything he stood for." [132] She made up her mind and she never looked back.

She took Willkie to lunch and told him that she could no longer support him. She saw Roosevelt again and pledged her devotion to him once and for all. Then she dropped the bomb at the *Herald Tribune,* in a column that ultimately got her fired.

"The President *knows* the world," Dorothy wrote.

> He knows it, in the most particular minutiae, better than any other living democratic head of state or ex–head of state. The range and precision of his knowledge . . . ; his understanding of conflicting social forces; his grasp of programs — all these impress every person whose life has been spent in foreign affairs. . . . I think I reached a quick decision before this campaign began, back in May, in France, when I saw two-thirds of the French Republic folding over the other third and knew that the great crisis was coming to a head. In that moment, I think, I knew that Roosevelt must stay in office and see this thing through.[133]

There was no greater scandal in that tense election year; certainly there was nothing more exciting among journalists than the spectacle of Dorothy Thompson bowing to Roosevelt, and of Ogden Reid, her boss at the *Herald Tribune,* being driven nearly to apoplexy when she did. The arch-conservative Mark Sullivan, who wrote for the *Tribune* and had frequently disagreed with Dorothy in his column, now accused her of being a traitor to conservatism; no attempt was made either to muzzle him or to soften his attacks. There were mutterings that Dorothy had "betrayed her class" (an idea that shocked her profoundly); that she had been "bought" by the Democrats; that she had "flipped her lid."[134] But she was not the only one of Ogden Reid's pundits to lose faith in Willkie. An estimated 90 percent of the nation's newspaper editors had backed Willkie at the start of the campaign, but nothing like that number stayed with him to the finish. Walter Lippmann, who, with Dorothy, was indisputably the most influential of Willkie's early supporters, fell completely silent before the campaign was over and refused to endorse anybody. If Dorothy had taken Lippmann's approach, she might have held to her position at the *Herald Tribune* awhile longer. But she was never known for her acquiescence under pressure.

"You think that my preoccupation with the foreign situation has blinded my view on the domestic situation," she wrote in an open letter to Mark Sullivan.

> You are quoting Miss Thompson against Miss Thompson. . . .
> [But] I do not see how any thinking person could have lived through the world experience of the last months without having to give hon-

est, careful reconsideration to everything he has hitherto thought and believed. As long as one's mind is alive, it changes. Do you remember the words that Goethe spoke to Merck in one of the "Conversations"? He said, "One must change one's skin seven times before one is master of one's own house. Let no one be ashamed to say 'yes' today if yesterday he said 'no,' or to say 'no' today if yesterday he said 'yes.' For that is Life. Only the shoemaker sticks to his last. Never to have changed — what a pitiable thing of which to boast!" [135]

She went to Buffalo on October 14 to make a speech, and from there she dictated a column that was meant to explain her position more clearly. She wanted it understood that she had no animosity toward Willkie personally, nor any doubts about his patriotism or his good intentions. She was "certain," nevertheless, that the Nazis were counting on a Roosevelt defeat, and that the people behind Willkie were playing straight into Hitler's hands. The Republican challenger had even been endorsed (with perfect incongruity) by John L. Lewis, the scowling president of the United Mine Workers and founder of the CIO, who was "miffed" at Roosevelt and, in Dorothy's opinion, had his own aspirations as a "Dictator-Boss." "If they don't take me," Willkie had said darkly to her, "they are going to get something worse." [136] Rightly or wrongly, Dorothy envisioned a giant, overriding conglomeration of discontented forces behind the Willkie campaign, a trend that seemed far more worrisome to her than anything about the New Deal:

Under [a] Republican administration [she wrote] we shall see the greatest concentration of political *and* economic power *and* military power that has ever occurred in our history. The industrialists of this country, engaged in making armaments, will not only be serving the state, they will *be,* to a great extent, the state. . . . The next President . . . will be Commander-in-Chief of the Navy and of the biggest peace-time Army in our history. He will have more power over industry and labor than any previous President. I do not want to see this vast power in the hands of inexperience, or in the hands of a man supported by Axis agents, whatever his personal attitude toward them may be. I do not want to see this power in the hands of a party which has never shown the slightest practical sympathy for the problems of the poor, the wage earner, the white collar worker, or the average man whose salary is under fifteen hundred dollars a year. . . . I take comfort in the belief that the average man and woman in the country has been smart enough to see what I see. [137]

But the *Herald Tribune* refused to publish Dorothy's rationale. A column scheduled for publication on October 14, in which Dorothy declared outright that "the Axis desires the defeat of President Roosevelt," was swiftly and simply suppressed.[138] Word came down from Ogden Reid that his columnists were employees, and that employees could not challenge editorial policy and expect to continue as before. The mail against Dorothy was running 19 to 1 (or so said Reid), and for two days, next to a formal disclaimer of Dorothy's position, the paper offered a sampling of its readers' ire. Miss Thompson was "an eyesore," one woman remarked; the space devoted to her column would be better given over to a crossword puzzle. It was "the candid opinion" of another subscriber (and "many of my friends") that Dorothy Thompson had "a Communistic tendency."[139] She was even the butt of some poetry in New York:

> Willkie's good
> And plenty hotty,
> To all the Reids . . .
> But not to Dotty.[140]

She was astonished at the *Tribune*'s "loss of temper" in this matter, and at the willingness of Ogden Reid to print "this abusive, illiterate, hysterical" drivel in place of her own explanations.

"Many [of the letters] were virulently anti-Semitic," she remarked in a diary entry. "More than ever does one see what forces gather behind W.W." An "acid" reprimand from Helen Reid left Dorothy feeling "lousy": "[I] don't like fights with old friends. [Mrs. Reid] attacked the column for being too long, said she had often complained the columns were too long, hinted the paper did not have space. I asked whether she meant that she would prefer not to publish the columns from now on. (My contract expires in March.) She said, apparently wounded, that she was not associating the two things in her mind."[141] But in fact she was. Dorothy never expected to convince the Reids that "Roosevelt represents the most conservative leadership — conservative in the deepest sense of the word — that we could have hoped for from 1940 to 1944," but if she was "positive of anything in this world, [she was] positive of that."[142] She took the opportunity to say so now as often as she could, and suddenly found herself in a nationwide "altercation" with Clare Boothe Luce, a Willkie supporter, who was persuaded to challenge Dorothy at a "Work for Willkie" rally in New York.[143]

"Eight years ago Miss Thompson had an interview with Adolf Hitler," Clare began, in what was to be her very first public speech, "and afterward she wrote that he would never come to power. Her judgment of the qualities it takes in a man to lead a nation, fight a war, or win a peace [is] surely open to question." Dorothy was "fighting mad" herself when she heard this, and Clare got back as good as she gave — better, really.

"Miss Boothe is the Body by Fisher in this campaign," said Dorothy, speaking of an especially elegant (but still mass-produced) automobile chassis and shrewdly calling her opponent by her maiden name; Clare had only recently married Henry Luce and begun to rise above her career as a socialite editor and "frothy" authoress. "She is the Brenda Frazier of the Great Crusade. She has torn herself loose from the Stork Club to serve her country in this serious hour." When Walter Winchell spotted Clare and Dorothy at the same nightclub one evening, he shouted out, "Ladies! Ladies! Remember there are gentlemen present!" It was a valuable lesson for Clare, a warning never again to criticize another woman in public.

"Differences of opinion between women are always treated by the press as inspired by personal dislike," Clare later explained, "and are used as evidence that every woman, at bottom, fears and hates every other woman for reasons of sexual jealousy. In our debate we were reported as having 'struck out with bared claws,' 'pulled hair,' 'hissed,' 'meowed,' 'scratched each other's eyes out.' The whole lexicon of a back-fence female cat fight was used to describe our speeches, although our arguments were supported by no less logic than is common among male campaign speakers."[144] In a letter to Henry Luce's mother, who had seen fit to praise her courage in the face of the Republican onslaught, Dorothy confessed that she, too, had been mightily upset by the quarrel over Willkie:

> I am a woman, Mrs. Luce, and not at all insensitive — something you may find it difficult to believe. The truth is I cry my eyes out a lot of the time. However, I dry them up again, too. . . . I think we shall have an awful time winning this election. All the organized forces are with Willkie: Big Business, Big Labor . . . Big press . . . all these plus the Nazi organization in this country and every little lunatic fringe fascist group, all organized, all given a "general line," and all singing the same song — well, you've got to have an awful lot of faith in the common man. . . . I am not optimistic. . . . I have been here before, I have seen exactly this mobilization of forces,

exactly this sort of election. I pray God on my knees every night that this time, here, at last, it will fail.[145]

The least disturbed of all was Wendell Willkie, who liked Dorothy and was never vindictive toward her. He suspected that she merely wanted "to ride with the winner"; weeks later he was "still chuckling" over her change of heart.[146] Although he lost the election that November by a wide margin — the forces behind him were not nearly so powerful as Dorothy had dreamed — he was well on his way to becoming one of America's most respected public figures, and he might have had an important future in politics had he not died so young (at fifty-two, in 1944). Dorothy remembered him afterward as "a prince" and "a part of America forever,"[147] but there was no use pretending that the events of his campaign had not rocked her to the core.

"It is being sweetly breathed into my ear," she wrote in a letter to President Roosevelt, "that in consideration of my overheated readers it would be well for me ('I am thinking of you, personally, my dear') to lay off writing about 'politics' and confine myself to 'those charming things you do so well' — little vignettes on rural life in Vermont, or 'How to Make Apple Butter,' I gather would be in order."[148] Shortly after the election, at a party, Dorothy saw Ogden Reid and challenged him to tell her where in her contract it was stated that she could not speak freely; when Reid responded that they had had a "tacit agreement" to hew to a common line, she declared that they had had no such thing.

"In the times in which we live, it is primarily as a citizen that I think of myself," she wrote to the Reids in January 1941.[149] She had "calculated the risk" in coming out for Roosevelt:

> I don't believe you know . . . how much I have risked and lost economically in the last years because of certain stands I have taken. The stand I took on Spain — which, as you know, I took wholly for larger political reasons, absolutely refusing to interpret the Spanish Civil War as a struggle between Christianity and Communism, insisting that it was a major move in power politics — cost me a year's radio contracts, because of organized boycotts and letter-writing campaigns. . . . [But] if I begin listening to the howls of the people who seem to think I have no rights as an individual citizen . . . why then I shall be simply paralyzed. I have never listened to them in the past, when the readers of the *Herald Tribune* were all agreeing with me, and I don't see why I should listen to them now — unless, of course,

their distress is actually having a serious financial result to the *Tribune*. I would consider that a justifiable reason for *your* listening to them, I mean.[150]

Her contract with the *Herald Tribune* was due to expire in March, and while nobody had said so, nobody needed to: Dorothy understood that it would not be renewed. The President of the United States had entered his third term "in a world where tyranny is young again, and Democracy old."[151] There would be many more quarrels, Dorothy feared, "as this war proceeds," many misunderstandings to stir up "all the sediment in the bed of what only a few months ago seemed a fairly placid stream."[152]

12
CHAPTER

T HERE was still a year to go before Pearl Harbor — almost exactly a year, in fact, during which time Dorothy renounced any semblance of "objectivity" and appeared to be welded, "fused," even, to the destiny of her country. It would scarcely be possible to exaggerate the extent to which she had become identified in the public mind with the struggle to preserve democracy. She was introduced on the radio one morning as "a cross between Harriet Beecher Stowe and Nurse Edith Cavell" by an announcer who went on to intone that "about her person are crystallized all the elements and forces which are arrayed against the barbarism threatening the civilization of our day."[1] Not long after, Dorothy appeared as the keynote speaker at a dinner given by the Committee for the Relief of German-Christian Refugees, and was praised literally to the skies by the clerics who were honoring her: "As we look over the European scene, alas, we cannot say, 'All is right with the world.' But 'God's in His heaven.' In His wisdom and mercy He has given us Dorothy Thompson to lead us in this great adventure."[2] Anyone who thought that her countrymen had simply been carried away by Dorothy's prolific energy and grande dame style could refer to a telegram from Winston Churchill, sent from London in May 1941 on the occasion of a tribute dinner, a celebration of Dorothy Thompson that attracted more than three thousand people to the Hotel Astor in New York.

"She has shown what one valiant woman can do with the power of a pen," said Churchill in his message, which was read out to the crowd by none other than Wendell Willkie. "Freedom and humanity are her grateful debtors."[3] That night Sara Delano Roosevelt, the mother of the President, unveiled a bust of Dorothy that had been executed by the sculptor Jo Davidson, and declared on behalf of her son that "no other individual so symbolizes the American qualities of courage, intelligence and a recognition of the dignity of man." There were words of praise from Governor Herbert Lehman of New York; from Fiorello La Guardia; from former President Herbert Hoover; from the prime minister of Canada; from Sigrid Undset, Eve Curie, Chaim Weizmann, and the ministers-in-exile of Norway, Denmark, Poland, Belgium, and Czechoslovakia. "Free Frenchmen" and "Free Italians" sat in clusters around the hall, and according to Raoul de Roussy de Sales, "the ceremony took on rather quickly the air of a revival meeting."[4]

"It will be a close race as to whether Dorothy or Willkie will be the next candidate for President," a good-humored friend of Roosevelt's reported to him the following morning. At least one man in the audience wondered that Dorothy's words had not been engraved on stone tablets and hurled down from the rafters,[5] because when she rose to make her own speech at the tribute dinner, after demanding that "America be placed at once on a total war footing," she commenced with a reading of the "Ten Articles of Faith" — her "political credo," in which she proposed "to re-state the meaning of democracy, freedom [and] internationalism in terms of twentieth-century needs."[6] She spoke about "the basic equality of all persons"; about the community of nations; about the "superior responsibilities" that go along with the "superior gifts" of freedom. She argued that "wealth [was] not the bookkeeping that is called Finance" and that "possession must be justified by use, with due regard to the conservation of resources." She insisted that "all creative functions in society are of equal human value" and that "the materialistic conception of history — Communism — and the biological interpretation — Nazism — are false. Man is Body, Mind and Spirit, with needs, desires and aspirations in all three elements of his nature."

At the end of her speech Dorothy took from her finger "a ring of curious symbolism" — a sort of modified Claddagh that she had designed herself and had fashioned for the occasion at Van Cleef and Arpels, consisting of three circles held together by clasped hands over a map of the Western Hemisphere. A copy of the ring, Dorothy announced, would be ordered for anyone who subscribed to her Articles of Faith and would endeavor to spread them further: "The condition of obtaining the ring [is] that every recipient must find two others to whom to present it. It must never be purchased by the recipient, but always come as a gift from one person to another."

Count de Sales, in the audience that night, ventured that the idea was "to create a kind of Freemasonry among the partisans of the new society,"[7] but in fact Dorothy's ambition was wider than that: she hoped to put a stop forever to "Lindberghism" and the evils of America First.[8] To that end, she proclaimed,

if I want to help my country in this hour, I must stop being afraid . . . stop being afraid. . . . We must realize that our American ideals are not passing currents of air but the rock on which the nation rests. We must stop grasping for extraneous solutions — solutions that can be promoted, advertised, sloganized and universally adopted. Anything that is universally adopted thoughtlessly by everybody is certain to be a quack panacea. . . . I am in favor, once and for all, of dismissing all doubts about the validity of democracy. Democracy is right. We are wrong. We are no democrats. Let us see what we can do to make ourselves right.

This was the beginning of the Ring of Freedom, the visionary, grass-roots "forum for democracy" that later in 1941 merged with the Fight for Freedom Committee and other liberal organizations to form Freedom House in New York. Within days Dorothy had set up an office on Forty-first Street to handle donations, correspondence, and the distribution of tens of thousands of "freedom rings" to subscribers around the country. Pamphlets were written, newsletters went out, and "aristocrats of the spirit" were encouraged to spread the word wherever they went — at home, in church, in the workplace, and ultimately at the voting box. The Ring of Freedom was more than a high-minded think tank. It was a club, a working fellowship that bore an unmistakable resemblance, at least in its method of organization, to the National Social Unit of Dorothy's youth. There were to be cells, blocks, whole neighborhoods of Ring affiliates; there was to be no discrimination based on class or sex. The goal of the Ring was to develop in its members a sense of their personal responsibility for democracy and for the social welfare, and to impress upon the American public the need for change, for activism in American political life.

"Let us tell each other the truth," said Dorothy: "we are being defeated. Our world is being defeated. There are two ways to face this reality. One is to retreat backward over the abyss; the other is to retreat forward. We had better retreat forward in a big way and along all fronts. . . . It is very, very late."[9]

She had left the *Herald Tribune* for the *New York Post,* where "On the Record" continued to appear three times a week. A deal was struck with the Bell Syndicate that actually increased Dorothy's readership around the country — by 1941 more than two hundred newspapers subscribed to her column — but there is no question that she felt the loss of the *Tribune* quite keenly.

"I want you to know that I do not suffer financially by the change," she wrote to Eleanor Roosevelt in a rather touchingly diffident note, "you are so kind, that I feared you might hear of it and that it would worry you, so I want you to know this." In those days the *New York Post* was a liberal paper, and of the second string, even under the vigorous editorship of Ted O. Thackrey, who was soon to be married to the *Post*'s powerful owner, Dorothy Schiff. Dorothy herself was aware that in the future, to a large extent, she would be preaching to the converted.

"I'm sorry," she went on to Mrs. Roosevelt, "because I think there ought to be a circulation of blood — I don't like to see all the Liberal writers in one place and all the Conservative in another, or all the pro-Administration people and all the anti-Administration lined up under separate roofs." In the meantime, she asked a favor: "Do you think that some time soon I could have a talk with the President? There are a few things that I am deeply anxious to discuss with him." [10]

It was part of the price Franklin Roosevelt had to pay for Dorothy Thompson's support in the 1940 election that for the rest of his life, and particularly throughout the course of World War II, he was obliged to listen to her advice. He was said to have greeted her banteringly, when they met for the first time after the election, "Dorothy, you lost your job, but I kept mine — ha ha!" [11] Now his desk was flooded with cables, notes, messages, and letters from her that urged him, basically, to "be bold," to "be *audacious,*" to "have courage" and "demand action." Roosevelt grew fond of Dorothy, and during his third term she was sometimes employed behind the scenes as an adviser on foreign affairs and a campaign consultant. During the war, along with her friend Robert Sherwood, she drafted quite a lot of material on Germany for the President, the State Department, and the OSS; Sherwood insisted that her advice in the last days of the 1940 campaign was among the best the President received, [12] and a new story (naturally apocryphal, under the circumstances) began to make the rounds. It concerned Red Lewis, after he listened to one of Roosevelt's "fireside chats."

"It was a great speech," Red was supposed to have said to Dorothy.

"I know," Dorothy replied. "I wrote it." [13] Having finally capitulated to Roosevelt's magnetic leadership, she remained somewhat gushy about him, always calling him "the President," for instance, and imbuing her pages and pages of earnest memoranda with a kind of maiden-aunt humility that must have kept him laughing.

"May I be permitted," Dorothy would begin; or, "Greatly as I dislike to ask a favor of your overburdened self"; and once, "May I beg you from a deeply troubled heart to go much further than you have gone thus far, and to risk your whole political life on it?" [14] She was regularly on the phone to the White House after 1940, and even smuggled notes to the Oval Office in the pockets of visiting dignitaries. [15] She told the President repeatedly that she had "no regrets."

"I remember that you once said to me, 'Don't take a stand unless you intend to stick,' " Dorothy wrote. "I hope that within the limit of my talents I have not too greatly disappointed you. . . . I would like only to be more useful." [16] She expected to be treated with a certain propriety, meanwhile, and she once amused John Gunther by departing a White House reception with impeccable solemnity and then reverting immediately, outside, to the snappy demeanor of her younger days. "Let's go out and get something to *eat!*" she said. [17]

She had begun to take on some of the more irritating characteristics of royalty — in her exaggerated devotion to "duty," in her appreciation of noblesse oblige, and in her personal mien, which had become "slightly breathless" and, in the estimation of Dinah Sheean, "a bit 'refained.' " Dinah and Jimmy and their two young daughters barely escaped incineration one night in February 1941, when Dorothy's house in Bronxville, which they had rented for the winter, burned to the ground. Dinah thought she was dreaming when she awoke to see the house in flames, and she could have sworn that Dorothy was wearing nothing but a fur coat and a bracelet when she arrived in the middle of the night to assess the damage. [18] Like royalty, she had also begun to go about without money, explaining that she was forever misplacing her pocketbook and that her secretaries normally gave her "a few dollars for the cab" whenever she left the house. By this time she was commanding up to twenty-five hundred dollars for a single speech, but if she thought it was for a worthy cause, to the despair of her agent, she was known to offer her services for nothing. She did not hesitate to ask anyone to help her, either, on any kind of project. She excused the demands she made on other people by pointing out that she herself was giving "half my time and a very large proportion of my income" to the things she had decided "*must* be done" — and if she could do it, anyone could do it. In keeping with her habit simply of "turning up" in support of a cause, in May of 1941 the following note found its way into the files of her lawyer friend Morris Ernst:

Dear Morris:

I will be glad to go to Washington to testify before the Naval Affairs Committee, since you say it makes no difference whether or not I know anything about the Navy. Sincerely,

Dorothy[19]

Meanwhile, through the agency of Dale Warren, Dorothy's publishers at Houghton Mifflin never ceased in their efforts to get her to write another book. "I think you are coming more and more to be bracketed in people's minds with Winston Churchill," wrote Ferris Greenslet, the company's editorial director, "as prophets of evil who were justified in the event." Greenslet was eager to publish "anything" that Dorothy had to offer, and went so far as to suggest that it was her "public duty. . . . You must have a wealth of notes," he insisted, "ideas, to say nothing of the material in some of the printed columns, to make the writing of such a book a comparatively simple matter." But Dorothy was too busy even to consider it.

"I wish I could find a ghost to write my columns and broadcasts!" she sighed one day to Dale. "I know you think books are more important and in a way they are. On the other hand, I think perhaps seeds, little seeds, repeating the same idea over and over again among the millions of column readers and radio listeners, may accomplish more in the long run, if you can't do both."[20] In-house memoranda at Houghton Mifflin described Dorothy's recent work as Plutarchian — "Plutarchian-cum-Thompson" — and the air she had taken on of infallibility and condescension naturally led, here and there, to a certain resentment. When she was asked one day to join the board of the Friends of Luxembourg, she answered that she would be delighted to but that at present she was "much more concerned about the United States," and added that if the United States did not manage to find out in short order "where it is going and how it is going there, there isn't going to be any Luxembourg."[21] She appeared one night on a highbrow radio talk show with Jay Franklin, Boake Carter, and a number of other male panelists, all of whom seemed determined to prove that "the First Lady of American Journalism" was filled with hot air. She was tired that night, "and even rattled," and as Franklin and the others pounded away at her arguments, she actually started to cry. Suddenly she burst out, "Well, I agree with the Pope!"

The Pope had not been quoted or even mentioned until that moment, and Dorothy's tormentors were at a loss as to how to respond; in the end, rather than admit that they had no idea of what she was talking about, they ceded her the evening.[22] She won many battles, many points, on the sheer force of her personality. Clifton Fadiman went to her apartment for dinner around this time and came away impressed forever by Dorothy's "supreme command of life's contingencies, small or large." It was winter, it was cold, and Dorothy had decided, in the middle of their conversation, to light the fire.

"Still talking vigorously," Fadiman remembered, "she casually struck a match and, just as casually, without a glance at the fireplace, she threw it on the logs. They burst into flame at once, as she continued talking. She had absolute confidence that the match would do her bidding."[23] And she had run out of patience for anyone who could not keep up. It was only to be expected, perhaps, that by the time the rest of the country began to awaken to the inevitability of war with Germany, Dorothy would already be thinking about the postwar period, and worrying that the coming conflict was going to be fought for all the wrong reasons.

"I don't need to explain to anybody that I want to stop Hitler," she observed in the summer of 1941, just before the breach of the Hitler-Stalin pact and the Nazi invasion of the Soviet Union, "but I want to know what we are going to have after Hitler. We are in about the middle of a world-wide revolution, involving the whole of humanity — a revolution of unprecedented scope — and [we] will only win it with another revolution, the revolution to end revolutions."[24] By the end of the year her rhetoric had grown bolder. "This war is futile," she maintained, "unless we fight it for a new world of cooperation. It is futile if by it we are trying to destroy the German and Japanese nations, or trying to enslave them. . . . If we are just to go on deciding which Great Power is to step on the face of the other for the next hundred years, or just defeat one Big Power and leave a vacuum of anarchy for a new gangster to occupy, the prospect is too bleak for effort."[25]

Already, again, she was somewhat out of step. She was ahead of herself, but she made no apology for that. There was no distinction any longer between her public and her private selves: she *was* the cause she was fighting for. "This is my story," she ventured to say, "this is my song, and this is the only thing in the world that I care about in this moment."[26]

IN July 1941 Dorothy flew to England, on a tour to "reconnoiter" that took on the air of a royal progress. She was already famous in the British Isles as a heroine of the war and a "friend of Britain"; in her transatlantic speeches, many of them broadcast at the height of the Blitz, she never hesitated to point out that she was of "English lineage" and regarded England as her second home.

"You have no idea how great your influence in England is," Phyllis Bottome had written to her that spring. "People in England imagine that they are not ruled by their hearts because they keep away from outward expressions of emotion, but the exact contrary is true, and where they have learned to love, as they now love you, the reward is amazing and will I know last forever."[27] In May the Germans had succeeded in bombing Westminster Abbey, the British Museum, the House of Commons, and Lambeth Palace, the South London residence of the Archbishop of Canterbury, all in one ghastly week; Dorothy equated the tragedy with the very demise of Western culture, and published a column in which she sought to live up to Phyllis's claims for her:

> This war is to stop the destroyers of civilization in their tracks. To defend the Abbey, the Museum and the Commons. To see to it that though they lie in rubble, and the very dead are exploded out of their tombs into the light of arson brighter than day, and the records of a thousand searching brains are mingled with the ashes of a surprised child's hair, and the representatives of the people must meet under the sky of a roofless hall — to see to it that nevertheless:
> The Abbey stands, the Museum lives, the Commons meet. Because the human will cannot be broken.[28]

She arrived in England after a stop for refueling in sunny, neutral Portugal, and was met at the plane by J. W. Drawbell, the editor of the *Sunday Chronicle* of London. The *Chronicle* had been publishing reprints of columns from "On the Record," and Jimmy Drawbell sensed in Dorothy's visit to England the opportunity for a sensational wartime propaganda campaign.[29] It was he who arranged for

Dorothy to occupy three suites at the Savoy Hotel for a solid month, where a bevy of secretaries and two or three bright young men from Fleet Street answered the phones, the mail, and the many hundreds of requests for Dorothy's attention. The entire Dorothy Thompson enterprise, in effect, had been transported across the Atlantic, the sole difference being that it was even more hectically pursued in London, if that were possible, than in New York. "I was an exhilarated wreck when she left," said Drawbell later. She had visited bomb shelters, war hospitals, munitions factories, schools, orphanages, the opera, the ballet, and the British fleet at Plymouth, where she lunched with England's naval commanders and shocked them into silence by demanding an explanation for some badly botched strategy in the Mediterranean.

"Gentlemen," said Dorothy to this gathering of "padlocked icebergs," "what I want to know is why you ever went to Crete at all if it was *not* important to get there; and if it *was* important, why didn't you *stay* there?"[30] She did not hesitate to give advice to the British wherever she went that month. She addressed the House of Commons and spent a quiet weekend with Winston Churchill. A series of "day and night receptions" was held in her honor. She lunched with Nancy Astor, dined with H. G. Wells, had drinks with J. B. Priestley, and went to the movies with Anthony Eden. She saw the leaders of "every government-in-exile currently in London" (including the boy-King Peter of Yugoslavia), and was presented with a Queen Victoria gold sovereign by an old-age pensioner in Birmingham, the first of several grateful Dickensian characters whose faces turned up next to Dorothy's in newspaper photographs. At the same time, nearly every day, Dorothy was broadcasting speeches over the BBC.

"Shall we ever forget what that voice, at that particular moment, did for us?" asked Jimmy Drawbell later on. "She brought the whole situation to the level of a personal struggle. And we saw it clearly for what it was, and knew as clearly what the outcome would be." Dorothy was so prominent a figure in wartime Britain that her movements were chronicled not just by the society columnists and news agencies but by Buckingham Palace itself, where she went to tea one afternoon at the invitation of Queen Elizabeth and where her departure for New York, at the end of August, was actually announced in the Court Circular.

"We sat for nearly three-quarters of an hour together," said Dorothy about her date with the Queen, "just the two of us, the Queen

and I. We talked of everything that two women would talk about —
I can't, of course, repeat it."[31] She was equally tight-lipped about
her conversations with Churchill, telling her friends only about the
prime minister's response when she asked him how, fighting alone,
he expected to win the war.

"That question has not yet crossed my mind," Churchill replied.
"I am presently concerned only with how not to lose it. And we shall
lose it, you know, unless you come in — and with all you have."[32]
Shortly after Dorothy's return to New York, Jimmy Drawbell published a book about her trip, *Dorothy Thompson's English Journey*,
which left British reviewers "gasping with admiration and vicarious
fatigue." Dorothy and Drawbell had discussed the possibility of
bringing out an American edition, too — it was "common ground"
between them — but when she got home, Dorothy was made to realize by her editors and "influential friends" that her reputation as
an independent journalist was at risk on account of her impassioned
support for Britain; Drawbell's adoring book (wherein Dorothy was
depicted as a figure of benevolent inspiration, very nearly the equal
of Florence Nightingale) might well have set the seal on the rumors
that she was an agent of the Crown.[33] As it was, she sent an angry
letter to J. Edgar Hoover asking for the assistance of the FBI in com-
bating "a program of abuse and vilification" that she said had been
launched against her by the isolationist Senator Burton K. Wheeler
and a number of other "ostriches" in Congress.[34] And to add to her
troubles, Sinclair Lewis had begun to pester her again with requests
for a divorce.

"We have not lived together for four and a half years," Red complained in July 1941, "and there is no chance that we shall ever live
together again. I know that it is impossible for me, and I imagine
that it is impossible for you, to compose any sort of normal and
decent life so long as we are held in this bondage. . . . You are now
the most prominent advocate in the whole country not only of Freedom but of generosity. . . . Are you going to deny your entire faith
by holding an unwilling ex-associate?"[35] His pleas for release were
answered only by the usual mountain of discursive mail, however,
and by a speech on the nature of "Freedom" that must have driven
him straight to the whiskey: "Freedom, Hal, is a concept that has
perplexed the philosophers for centuries, and the meaning of Freedom is the central question of the age we live in." No, in other
words — she would not grant him a divorce, nor ever deny that she
still loved him:

You see, one cannot undo one's life, unwrite one's marriage, go back, start over, or blot out a major experience as though it had not been. Hundreds of times, Hal, you made me promise that I would never leave you and never divorce you. I made the promise, because I meant it. . . . Why should I believe that you meant that and mean this, or that you did not know your own mind [then] and do know it now?

. . . I have been wretchedly unhappy, Hal. I have missed you desperately. I never come to Vermont but that I miss you again, with the sharpest missing anyone can feel. I never walk up the stairs to your room, without the feeling that I should be bringing you up a cup of coffee. . . . I think that you ought to come home, to a place that you once loved, and to a woman who holds you very dear — on any terms you please. . . . I think you should take an interest in your child. . . . If you cannot bear this idea, and I gather you cannot, then I think we should remain separated in a dignified and friendly manner. . . . But do not say that I try to hold you. I am held to you by my marriage and its fruits.[36]

She had joked with Red before she went to England that he probably would not need to worry about a divorce: London in the Blitz was a dangerous place, and they might be freed from bondage sooner than they thought, and "in a more thorough manner." But Red was past the point of jesting. His self-delusion in this matter was no less exasperating than Dorothy's own:

Come off it, Dorothy [he wrote]. Be the generous, realistic girl you usually are! . . . Be the girl for whom I did every damn thing it was in my power to do. If you get a divorce, life will be a hell of a lot saner for Micky, for me, for you.

I shan't write much. You're too excellent a dialectician for any novelist to argue with. But if you'll listen for it, you'll hear me saying this, earnestly, without rancor, wherever you are . . . whatever you may be writing. Dorothy! Be generous![37]

It was the appeal to the welfare of Micky that finally hit home with Dorothy and persuaded her, in November 1941, to give Red what he wanted. In a letter to Wells Lewis she affirmed that Red had in fact threatened never to see Michael again unless she capitulated. She understood from different sources that he was hoping to marry Marcella Powers, and simultaneously that Marcella was "desperately in love with someone else, and looking elsewhere for the comforts suitable to her age and temperament." Dorothy feared that her husband was "going to be let down this time, and made horribly miserable," but "love is blind," as she very well knew, and he would have to make his own mistakes. She wrote to Wells,

> I have felt that your Pop, who has not the sense he was born with, needed the protection of his marriage bonds, but that is obviously the attitude of a domineering woman. . . . I have been heartsick over this divorce business, for however quietly it is done, it is still a newspaper story, and oh, my God, how I long for a bit of private life. I think your father is the goddamndest fool of a great man anybody ever knew, and the Verlaine period is over, even if he were fitted for the Lothario role, which God knows he ain't. . . .
>
> But cheerio — I've always known that 1942 would be a bad year for the Allies.[38]

She filed for divorce as a Vermont resident, charging "willful desertion" and refusing to make any further statement. ("I will never," she declared later, "so help me God, ever write about him as a husband.")[39] There were many things to occupy her mind that fall. The insurance money that came to her from the fire at the house in Bronxville had been sunk into the purchase of a three-story brownstone at 237 East Forty-eighth Street, one of a number of quietly elegant, altogether exclusive townhouses that form a rectangle around Turtle Bay Gardens in Manhattan. It was a bad moment to buy a house, Dorothy realized, "just in time to have it bombed," but for her "237" was a dream fulfilled: as a young woman in New York, working as a publicist for the National Social Unit, she had sometimes stayed in Turtle Bay, at the home of her friend Beatrice Sorchan.[40]

"It's exactly as I remember it," she remarked wistfully, "and that is something that practically never happens." She spent more than twenty thousand dollars on renovations even so, and when the work was finished, at the end of 1941, she declared it "the most perfect small house I have ever seen . . . it fits me like a glove — two rooms on a floor — a fascinating kitchen that is half a small pine-panelled *Stube,* a dining room all wrought iron and glass, a really handsome salon and a small and lovely library" (which nevertheless had room for more than three thousand books).[41] The third floor of the building was given over entirely to Dorothy's workroom, and a reporter for *Look,* whom she invited to inspect the place, took note admiringly of the numerous gadgets and "labor-saving devices," the nine telephones, the intercom system, and the dozens of charts and strategic maps that hung on the walls upstairs: "It was a veritable command post."[42] Embedded in the door at the main entrance were eight painted glass panels that purported to show Dorothy, in vaguely medieval attire, pursuing her various tasks: writing her column, greeting her guests, reading aloud from her work. The motto she had chosen for the house was boldly emblazoned in Latin: *Gallus in sterquilinio suo plurimum potest* ("The rooster on his own dunghill is very much in charge").

"Five fireplaces," Dorothy continued, "— one in every major room. Clear bright colors. Elegant and unpretentious." In the drawing room, a huge, wine-colored satin sofa could hold five people at a time — five of "the most distinguished bottoms in New York," as Dorothy's friend Max Ascoli liked to say.[43] It was the kind of remark that no longer amused her, however. Very little, indeed, amused her in these last days before the war. In the winter of 1941–1942 Katharine Hepburn and Spencer Tracy teamed up for the first time in *Woman of the Year,* Michael Kanin's comedy about a chic and sexy, globe-trotting foreign correspondent and newspaper columnist, plainly modeled on Dorothy Thompson, who is cut down to size and banished to the kitchen by a sportswriter and "regular guy." Dorothy dismissed the film as "a sickening travesty and thoroughly unconvincing"[44] and even contemplated legal action until her lawyer, Louis Nizer, warned her that a lawsuit might only invite further comparison. Nizer had already had to obtain major rewrites in the script of a Broadway murder mystery, *Cue for Passion,*[45] whose central characters, at least as originally conceived, bore an unmistakable resemblance to Dorothy Thompson and Sinclair Lewis.

"It was as difficult to guess their identity as to answer the quiz: 'What countries were involved in the Spanish-American War?' " Nizer reported, though ordinarily he advised his client not to make a fuss about the unwanted offshoots of fame.[46] When the *Look* writer came to call, Dorothy was photographed at the piano, plunking out a tune, but she could "never find real rest anywhere," and Raoul de Roussy de Sales noted that she seemed "frankly defeatist."[47] On September 15, in "On the Record," she called for the first time for a declaration of war against Germany, hoping that America might still avoid the "craven, fat-headed, glazed-eyed" fate that isolationism promised. In a letter to Wendell Willkie she offered her opinion that "we are within ten minutes of losing this war" and that the international situation, compounded by Japanese aggression in the Pacific, was more dangerous than it had been at any time since the fall of France. "We must fight fast," said Dorothy, "and like hell-and-gone."[48] But mainly, these days, her columns were falling flat. She was "tired to death . . . , not physically but in my nerve ends,"[49] and when the war finally came — when Pearl Harbor put an end to any further discussion about the pros and cons of American neutrality — she did little to hide her discouragement.

"I know it is said that we went to war because we were attacked at Pearl Harbor," Dorothy later wrote. "That is childish. The attack at Pearl Harbor did not precede but followed the breakdown of peace negotiations opened by the Japanese in Washington. We could have had peace with Japan if we had been willing to recognize Japanese claims in China. I am no major prophet, nor minor prophet either, but I stated a full week before Pearl Harbor that we would be attacked by Japan, since the break-down of the Washington negotiations indicated war, and the predictable Axis tactic was undeclared attack."[50]

Michael Lewis and Denis Fodor found Dorothy in her bedroom at 237 on the night of December 8, 1941, when they came home from the movies. All the lights in the house were burning, the servants seemed to have vanished, and it was plain to see that Dorothy had been crying.

"It had obviously hit her like a hammer," Denis remembered, and when Michael, worried about his mother, asked her what had happened — "if someone was dead, or what" — she shook her head and just repeated, "No, darling, we've gone to war. We've gone to war."[51] It was a sorrow to Dorothy that the United States had only been brought into the fight against Hitler for "the usual nationalistic reasons." She took an exceptionally sharp tone with her readers in the *Ladies' Home Journal* and urged them to "see to it — *you* see to it — that this war degenerates into neither sheer aimless destruction nor a burdensome and antiquated imperialism. *You* see to it that this war ends, as it began for us and our allies, as a war of liberation."[52] Elsewhere she confessed to an "all but immeasurable apprehension" about "the next ten, twenty, or thirty years. There is not, I fear in my bones and brains, going to be any happy ending to this war. Not for a long time to come."[53]

Three weeks later she was in Vermont for her divorce hearing. She had ridden up to Woodstock on the overnight train, and in a small bound notebook she left the last of the entries about Sinclair Lewis:

> It was on July 8, 1927, and I had been granted a divorce in Hungary the day before, and I thought I had never seen anyone as unhappy as I except he, with a face like one who has gone through war and *"flammenwerfer,"* and a tongue so cynical and brilliant, and he said, "I have been looking for you for years. Will you marry me?" And I thought, "I have been looking for you, too." Then always those years of intense pleasure and blackest pain. Still the crazy conviction that he loved me and it would all add up to something. But it was so quickly over for him, or maybe never began. On that first day he said, "I will buy us a house in Vermont, this shape  and looking down a valley." And he did. And insofar as we were ever happy we were happy there. Now, to sit in the Woodstock Courthouse, charging desertion . . . and to feel nothing at all, literally nothing except some faint distaste. To have felt too much is to end in feeling nothing. Four years of loneliness and agony and work, all anodynes. The last terrible remembering in London. . . . But now it is the ratification of something that has been over and done with and not even Michael, anymore, reminds me of him. "Far and forgotten like a scene in cameo."[54]

The divorce was granted on January 2, 1942, on the condition that a trust fund be set up for Michael and that Red not remarry for a period of two years.[55] And with that the spell was broken, and broken permanently. The five entries that follow in Dorothy's diary are concerned almost exclusively with the conduct of the war. In the last of these, dated January 30, she told of telephoning CBS in search of a transcript of one of Hitler's speeches.

"They sent me 'highlights,' " Dorothy complained, "— I fear mistranslated and inadequate. [I] called again and asked for [the] full *German* text. Not available."

"Miss Thompson," said the secretary at CBS, "you are so *thorough*."

"Remember Pearl Harbor," said Dorothy, and she hung up.[56]

She was speaking as a professional, as a pundit, and naturally was unaware of the losses she herself would sustain in the days to come. Many of her German friends, for example, would be killed in battle, or in bombing raids, or in opposition to Hitler; her beloved Wells Lewis, who had enlisted in the army a full year before Pearl Harbor, would die in France, his head blown off by a sniper's bullet, in the last year of the war; and Christa Winsloe — "your Chris" — would be shot in 1944 by a gang of mercenaries in the disturbances that followed the liberation of Paris. Christa had settled on the Côte D'Azur, where she had hoped to live out the war unmolested by "politics." At the time of the Normandy invasion she headed north to Cluny with her companion, Simone Gentet, and then abruptly made up her mind to go back to Germany. It was Christa's fear that her record of weary pacifism would be misinterpreted by the Allies as collaboration with the Nazis, and indeed, when the news of her death first reached America, her executioners were described to Dorothy as leaders of the French Resistance. In fact, they were "ordinary criminal[s]," who set upon two middle-aged women — Christa being German, and the other being her lover — and murdered them in cold blood.

"Of course she was anti-Nazi," said Dorothy, who after the war demanded that the French authorities give her an accounting of Christa's death, "but of what consequence is that in these indiscriminate times? The life of that sensitive woman, made for beauty and for love, was a series of violences: the violence done to her by a Prussian school, the violence of the First World War, . . . the violence of Nazism that finally made her an exile. The drama, it seems to me, had to end, by the logic of destiny, just as it did."[57]

But those days were over when Dorothy Thompson could easily confide the depth of her emotion in a letter or a diary. She was aware herself of the dreamlike quality of all her past attachments. A young friend asked her, at the end of the war, what it had been like to be married to Sinclair Lewis, and she drew a total blank. She seemed not to understand the question. She took a sip from a large martini — it was the third one she had poured for herself that day — shrugged her shoulders, and advised her friend to go to a library.

"Read about him," she said.[58]

PART THREE
Getting Back

*Man is not at ease in the Frankenstein civilization his geniuses have created;
the civilization is diseased; but he thinks he must have 'progress' at all costs;
his civilization must be, he thinks, not only a machine but a perpetual
motion machine. The Swastika, the ever-turning wheel — symbol of the run-
away civilization — is it not the symbol of the whole of Western civilization?
Were not the Germans, always so protean, always so indicative of that
civilization, its most truly representative children, its 'master-race,' in the
sense, at least, of being the master example?
Such things pass my mind.*

≡

Dorothy Thompson, 1947
(used as the epigraph for
her unfinished memoirs)

*He is the happiest man who can join in close union the beginning with the
end of his life. . . . And how else should this be accomplished, except
through the endurance of affection, of trust, of friendship, and of love?*

≡

Johann Wolfgang von Goethe

13

CHAPTER

S HE would never have expected to fall in love again at the age of forty-nine, to find "in the midst of complete resignation," on the heels of "inner and outer storms" that left her "disgusted" with herself, "a serene happiness which seems like an undeserved gift of the Gods."[1] Dorothy had thought she was "beyond good and evil."[2] She was tired even of flirting with men and had said to herself many times ("with a slightly crooked smile"), "*Wie schön ist ein Leben ohne Liebe*" — "How lovely is a life without love."

"Not so untrue, my dear, either," she wrote to the man who proved her wrong, the "beautiful stranger" who "drifted in and took possession" in the summer of 1942.[3] He was Maxim Kopf, "a poor artist," "a penniless refugee," who came to Twin Farms to paint Dorothy's portrait and stayed to become her "*Prinz Gemahl*" — her consort and loving companion, "the man I should have married in the first place."[4]

She was presiding that summer over a gathering of the Volunteer Land Corps, probably the most inspired of all of her wartime projects, which brought together six or seven hundred "boys and girls" from Harvard, Dartmouth, and the Eastern Establishment cities and put them to work on farms in Vermont — milking, mowing, baling hay.[5] It was Dorothy's thesis that the average American, growing up, had "no earthly idea" of how the food on his table came to be there, not realizing, for instance, that milk "[did] not originate in a bottle" or that a slice of bacon represented an amount of work undreamed-of on city streets. Dorothy was already "desperately worried" about the future of the small family farmer, whose livelihood, she held, would be threatened inexorably by the wartime centralization of industry and the drainage of labor from the farms.

"We won't have any of them left," she complained in a letter to a Land Corps volunteer. "We will have nothing but factories on the farms. This perturbs me more than I can say, for as far as I can see nobody is taking the slightest interest in what is happening to the social structure of America as a result of the war. . . . We are going to proletarianize everybody in America before it is over — I mean proletarianize them at very high wages, but destroy all that is left of economic independence." It was a real concern for a woman who was still struggling to turn a profit from her own "chickens, potatoes, grain, vegetables, strawberries, dairy cows and flocks of sheep"; she would have gone a long way to preserve the way of life she had found in Vermont.

"I can see it," said Dorothy grimly, "in some not too distant future, becoming another Adirondacks."

> The houses will fall in and the villages which live from the farms will disappear, and all the comeliness that it is will be gone, and the future of other such communities seems to me a very high price to pay for a war of freedom; a grotesque price and a price that doesn't have to be paid if people would think and plan in another direction. I see the Land Corps as specific help for that kind of farm and that America, and that is why I am so passionately interested in it. . . .
> In this, of course, I am a "reactionary." And I am exactly that.[6]

"Dorothy Thompson has just summoned me to sing out for her Land Army," the Vermont poet Robert Frost wrote to a friend in August 1942.[7] She had opened Twin Farms as a kind of summer camp and recreation center for Land Corps volunteers, and she persuaded as many of her friends as she could find in the area — including Frost, Alexander Woollcott, and Dorothy Canfield Fisher — to join her in promoting the project. "[We] discovered at a certain stage of the game that we had more applicants than we had places," Dorothy wrote with pride,[8] and when she addressed the Land Corps from the lawn at Twin Farms, standing on a stone slab that commemorated the visit to Barnard, in 1828, of the Marquis de Lafayette, it was very much in the mode of a sponsoring angel: "I am trying to say this to you: Neither your personal life nor your social existence is a series of episodes. History is not a series of episodes. The creation of a personality and the creation of a nation depend upon the maintenance of continuity."[9]

Maxim Kopf, the artist and sculptor who was to become her third husband, stumbled onto this scene as the guest of Hermann Budzi-slawski, Dorothy's primary research assistant during World War II, a friend of Fritz Kortner's and a former editor of the *Weltbühne* in Berlin. "Budzi" was just one among a number of temporary residents and "accent hounds" [10] who, during the war, gave Dorothy's property the air of a refugee-processing center. He had the distinction of being, so far as anyone knows, the only person ever to dictate "On the Record" in her stead; [11] at this stage of the game, in the early 1940s, Dorothy trusted him absolutely. She did not want to sit for Maxim, however, when Budzi first proposed it. She was "too busy" to have her portrait painted, she said, and when she realized later how close she had come to missing the love of her life, she was "like to faint."

Maxim was a Czech, a German-Bohemian, born in Vienna in 1892 and raised in Prague, "in the oldest part of the medieval city, on the Hradcany Stairs." [12] His father was a petty civil servant of the old empire, a frustrated artist and "a slave," in Maxim's opinion, who "never did anything in his life that he really wanted to do" and drank himself to death before he was fifty. It was a powerful lesson for Maxim, who always insisted that his own gift was minimal.

"I believe that I got in the cradle a talent as an artist," Maxim remarked in a letter to Dorothy, "not a great one, a smaller gift, and that's harder than a successful one — but I believe I have to give an account for it one day. . . . I am a man who has been trying all his life to be an artist, the best artist God intended him to be. And my story is about how history interrupts and destroys and maybe makes and saves a man like me." Dorothy saw in Maxim's odyssey "the saga of the innocent bystander," [13] and when they briefly considered publishing a book of his memoirs, they called the narrative "Excuse Me for Living," the title taken from one of Maxim's favorite comments about himself: "By the law of averages, as the polls and the insurance companies reckon, I ought to be dead. If the world were what it seems to be, I should not be alive. . . . I have no excuse to be alive. That is why I say — Excuse me for living."

He was educated at the Academy of Fine Arts in Prague, having studied painting in Paris and Dresden. During World War I he was badly wounded at the front; a "nervous breakdown" that attended his convalescence was followed by a bout of tuberculosis that spared him any further experience of active warfare. Maxim traveled widely all of his life, through Europe and Africa and several times to the

South Sea Islands — "looking for color," as he explained, the "glorious, pulsating color" that many considered to be the chief distinction of his work. He had no special lineage as a painter; he was classified as a "neo-impressionist" and at the same time compared, often, to Oskar Kokoschka. He was "a more coherent and disciplined Kokoschka," said a *New York Times* critic in 1942, when Maxim's work was first exhibited at the Wakefield Gallery.[14] As an artist, Maxim seemed always to be "edging toward greatness"[15] without ever reaching it. In Prague he was a leader of the so-called Secession movement, "building a culture in an atmosphere of work and liberation," and after the invasion of Czechoslovakia, in a minor attempt to establish their legitimacy, the Nazis tried to claim him for their own. They claimed him, that is, as "a pure-blooded German." But Maxim refused to stay "in a country ruled by a maniac who thought he was an artist, surrounded by thugs who thought themselves Teutonic knights." He fled.

He returned to Paris, where he took up with a number of other Czech refugees, some of whom happened to be Communists. Maxim himself had no political affiliation, but in 1939, in the wake of the Hitler-Stalin pact, he was arrested anyway as an enemy alien and a suspected spy. He spent five months in solitary confinement in the Paris *Santé,* where he lost more than sixty pounds and half of his teeth through malnutrition. The Nazi occupation of France, ironically, set him free, but when he moved south to the Riviera and then on to Morocco he was promptly rearrested, this time by the Vichy police, as a "Free French" sympathizer. He was held in a concentration camp for more than a year and was released, finally, only through the intervention of Jan Masaryk, the exiled foreign minister of Czechoslovakia, who "pulled every diplomatic wire" at his disposal and arranged for Maxim, along with hundreds of other Czech refugees, to sail for New York.

"Concentration camp is a very intense experience of life," said Maxim later, in what was, for Maxim, a typical remark. He credited his survival to the fact that he had "never, never" allowed himself to be idle: "I took every chance to work. I got huge muscles." He was a large man to begin with, six foot one and strapping, a "stallion" and a "hunk," in the recollection of nearly everyone who knew him. In camp he served as a cook, and when he was not laboring to keep sane, he amused himself with pen and ink, manufacturing decks of playing cards and decorating them with pictures of women: "The more I drew, the more voluptuous they got. They weren't pornographic pictures — not that — but there was an awful lot of woman in them." Maxim told Dorothy later that he had made a bargain with the Virgin Mary during the worst days of his captivity.

"Mother of God," he had said, "if I get out of this, I will do something as long as I live to help people to remember your Son." Thereafter his canvases were filled with Crucifixions, Resurrections, Transfigurations, and a series of buxom women at the foot of the Cross. He "was one of a school of Mary Magdalene painters," said a friend with a wink,[16] and many of the people who met him at Dorothy's — where he seemed so "whole, healthy, happy, satisfied, lusty, funny, and kind"[17] — were shocked to be confronted with the obvious torment of his finest work.

But Maxim was not a painter who expected to be understood. He was "free of 'isms,' " and he knew very well the dilemma of the artist whose commercial success declines as his pictures get better. He was "a man all eyes and hands," said Dorothy; he was "inarticulate in four languages." He knew how to talk when it came to art, however, and he reserved his deepest scorn for "the howling mob" and the nihilistic "assassins" of the gallery scene.

"Art for Art's sake is a slogan," said Maxim with assurance. "It is meaningless. . . . Do you think that the artists of the High Middle Ages painted for 'Art's sake'? They painted for *Christ's* sake. Art is a very serious business." And life, said Maxim, was "a wonderful miracle. . . . Even at its lowest it is a miracle. I would not change my life for anyone's, and I think if everyone really digested his own life, he would not change his, either."

For Dorothy, it was the *coup de foudre* yet again: love at first sight, "crack-up," Destiny. Not since she first saw Joseph Bard in the doorway of the Ritz Hotel in Budapest had she been so smitten with a man.

"It is true that he reminds me of my first love," she wrote to her friend Gustav Stolper. "Perhaps there is some nostalgia in it . . . , but isn't one always looking again for that first love, with all its purity, isn't one always hoping for another chance for that first love?"[18] Dorothy knew that Maxim Kopf was married, and that his wife was waiting for him somewhere in Brooklyn; she knew that even though he enjoyed a rather loose connubial arrangement, there were bound to be difficulties. She didn't care. Maxim spent just one day working on her portrait at Twin Farms (she came out looking like George Washington, he complained), and that night, as a guest in the Big House, he crept up the stairs to her room, holding his shoes in his hand and offering no explanations. When he "kissed me on the mouth," said Dorothy, and climbed beneath the sheets, "I was idiotically happy."

> I have only been so once in my life [she wrote to Maxim later], when I was very young, for I have had bad luck in some ways. I mean if I liked a man's head and heart, even, then I didn't like the other, and if I liked the other I didn't like his head or his heart. But I like *your* head very much, the way you think, very clearly, and not *literarily*, which is a great relief to me. . . . And I think you are very good, and the rest was all wonderful, so I do not feel afraid of you at all. . . . I do not suffer. . . . I want to laugh — to laugh out of sheer appreciation and pleasure.

She told no one, at first, about her new affair, deluding herself that the household would not notice that she had dropped everything she was doing and was walking around the farm in a daze. Maxim had come to Vermont for only a week, and when he left again Dorothy found herself "living" for his letters, carrying them around in her pocket and trying to stay calm when the phone rang. ("You have to realize that everyone can listen in on the Twin Farms phone," she wrote to Maxim truthfully. "*Why* haven't I learned Czech!") One afternoon she piled into the Buick and "just drove around the valley" — to South Pomfret, Hanover, White River Junction — trying to remember what her lover looked like and quoting Edna Millay: "I looked in my heart while the wild swans went over,/ And what did I find I had not found before?"[19]

"You are my wild swans," Dorothy told Maxim, "and I want you to come over the town again, . . . and my complications and complexes interest me really less than nothing. That is why I love you — loved you 'at first sight' — because I don't have to explain myself to you, or you to me." She felt "quiet" in the thought of Maxim. She wanted him to "like" her. She wanted "to be taken care of," and "petted, and liked for what I never seem to get a chance to be." But she worried that he would drop her when he found out what her life was like. She feared she was not really his type. "Oh, hell," she concluded, "why all this analysis . . .":

> I think I am an awful woman in any man's life. It takes *so* much understanding. The world crowds in on me so terribly — I hate it; I suffer terribly from it. I would like you to believe that. I am not, by nature, made for what I do. I have nightmares sometimes of masses

of faces and hands; all staring and grabbing, and I wake up in a cold sweat and a terrible anxiety that I am going to be torn apart and eaten alive. . . . And yet, equally strong is the obsession that I must go on, that there is something I must help to create before I die: a more decent and intelligent society. It is not that I think I amount to much, except that the faith of those same consuming masses of faces gives me a power that I have to use. And my experience of intimate personal things has been very bitter. For it is hard for a man to be constantly shoved aside by the crowd.

But in Maxim she had found a man who was big enough to take it — large enough, generous enough. "I love your lively spirit," he wrote to her from New York. "I love your *gentillesse*. . . . I love your blue eyes, your little mouth . . . your wonderful body." When Dorothy wrote back to say that she was going on a diet, "to get a little thinner for you," Maxim told her not to bother.

"Don't be foolish," he remarked, "don't torture yourself. . . . I like you and love you so and so." He was "worried," true, "very upset and crazy with love," but he was proud to tell Dorothy, in his awkward English, "I do not hide it . . . you are the most charming woman I met in my life." He called her "my Great Woman," "Sweet Majesty," and swore that he would "never cause you trouble, never interfere" with the way she lived her life:

> It's a shame, Dorothy, to think all day long of you. To hope to see you again, to kiss you again, to touch you again, to say silly sweet things to you. . . . I will be very patient, it's only a week from now on, that I shall see you, kiss you, and answer all your good letters by word of mouth — and believe me, I have to tell you a lot. . . .
>
> You are wise, you are good. . . . You gave me so much happiness in a very wonderful way. . . . I kiss you. I kiss every spot on you.

The only problem was Maxim's wife, Lotte Stein. (She was, in fact, his third wife, the two others having been divorced in Czechoslovakia.) Lotte was an actress and a Jewish refugee, and Dorothy insisted that Maxim had married her in the first place only in order "to give her a passport." Certainly the Kopfs were united more by convenience than by sentiment. Even so, as things turned out, there was Lotte's pride to consider.

"The first days at home have not been nice," Maxim wrote to Dorothy, "— my wife saw at once how strong I liked you — but now I think everything is again all right, as long as she does not lose me entirely." For several months, then, with Lotte in mind, Dorothy and Maxim endeavored to conceal the depth of their feeling for each other. They met in secret and developed a series of elaborate signals for use in letters and on the telephone. While Dorothy, on the sly, was sending Maxim the most passionate love letters, she was also writing to Lotte in the guise of a helpful friend, hoping that Lotte would come to call, hoping that both of the Kopfs might "take a break" at Twin Farms. It was entirely disingenuous, and entirely unlike her. Only when she made up her mind to marry Maxim (she proposed to him herself, in the back of a taxi) did she put an end to this game and insist that Lotte give him a divorce.

Lotte refused. She refused most stubbornly, and it was rumored later that Dorothy paid something like thirty thousand dollars to "buy her off." Louis Nizer, who handled the matter for Dorothy and Maxim, confirmed that Dorothy sent Lotte a letter — a *long* letter — in which she confessed her determination to marry Maxim and "upbraided" Lotte for "holding on to a loveless relationship."

"She denounced [Lotte's] attitude as immoral," Nizer reported. "She advised her that Max and she were in love and that a thousand Mrs. Kopfs could not stand in the way of their happiness." Nizer was less concerned about Dorothy's happiness, however, than he was about her public reputation, in an era when "sexual freedom was still called licentiousness" and a well-timed charge of husband stealing could ruin a career. It seemed not to occur to Dorothy that she was being fantastically indiscreet. "Mrs. Kopf was not an admirer," explained Nizer. "She suddenly had in her hands not only written proof of her husband's infidelity, but a document which might destroy his mistress." The "satisfactory terms" that Nizer arranged for Lotte Stein were in practical fact a bribe: they bought a divorce for Maxim and the return of "the damaging letter" to Dorothy.[20] It was the one dark spot on a union that was — if any marriage ever is — happy from beginning to end.

The wedding took place at the Universalist Church on Barnard Green, on June 16, 1943. A remarkably varied crowd had gathered for the occasion, considering that it was wartime: Jimmy Sheean, fresh from a tour of the fighting in North Africa; Dorothy's sister, Peggy, with her husband, Howard Wilson, and her daughter, Pamela; and Emily Carter, Esther Adams, Helen Reid, Raymond and Betty Gram Swing. Michael was there, aged thirteen and already effusive in his devotion to Maxim. Red sent his congratulations by telegram. There were writers — Anita Daniel and Agatha Young ("the famous unknown author," as Jimmy Sheean liked to call her)[21] — and musicians — the pianist Ania Dorfmann and the diva Alma Clayburgh — and a number of Dorothy's former escorts in New York, including Peter Grimm, Alex Sachs, Gustav Stolper, and Connie Traeger. Finally there were a few friends whom Dorothy, already, was pleased to call "ours" — friends of her own and Maxim's, too: Hermann Budzislawski; Rudolf Rathaus, the Polish patriot who was Maxim's best man; Carl and Alice Zuckmayer, with their daughter, Winnetou (she was named for an Indian hero of the Karl May westerns); and the "wonderful, exasperating" Ernestine Evans, nicknamed "Teeny," whom Dorothy had known since her suffrage days and who was so colossally fat that she once got stuck in a doorway at Twin Farms.[22]

"It was the wedding to end all weddings," said the faithful Dale Warren, who arrived from Boston carrying a dozen live lobsters, an armful of wedding gifts, and "a blood certificate (or whatever you get married with), which I had been told to pick up in Woodstock." Toward evening, following a short ceremony at the church and an epicurean revel on the lawn of the Big House (there were "vast and delectable casseroles," "huge cakes," and "giant platters of cookies"),[23] Hermann Budzislawski led the guests in a Sufi dance, while Zuckmayer and Maxim ripped off their shirts and fell to the ground in a sweaty wrestling match. Previously Dorothy had professed herself "a little bashful at the thought of myself as a bride,"[24] but she was "flushed with pleasure" when the time came, and the witnesses at her wedding all agreed that they had never seen her look so happy, so excited, so expectant, so sexy, and, three weeks shy of her fiftieth birthday, so much like a young girl in love.

"Forgive this drooling," she wrote to Wells Lewis, who at that time, a year before his death, was serving with the American forces in North Africa, "but I've never before had any *fun* out of being married, and I had come to the conclusion that nobody ever did, and now I know that marriage is WONDERFUL. . . . I feel as though we ought to be celebrating our silver wedding or something. . . . I am so happy that I fear a sweet reasonableness is creeping into my style, and I shall end up clothed in fatuous grins. Only the follies of mankind keep me from slipping!" Neither Dorothy nor Maxim ever denied that their compatibility was based in a powerful sexuality — in *physicality,* rather, which came to them naturally, as the "simple souls," the "highly gifted peasants," they declared themselves to be.[25] They cooked, they ate, they gardened, they farmed, they sat at home and played gin rummy; there was not a whiff of introversion about this marriage, not a moment's self-absorption. Dorothy was completely frank about it — very frank indeed. "When I make love the house shakes," she told the publisher Cass Canfield during a rather tipsy Atlantic crossing in the late 1940s.[26] At a dinner party in New York, when Maxim used her as a model in a demonstration of how to create "a perfect goulash," she "blushed like a schoolgirl and squealed in delight."

"You cut from *this* part of the cow," said Maxim, smacking Dorothy squarely on the backside. "You cut from the rump" — *smack!* — "and from the loins" — *smack!* — "and you cut in *chunks*."[27] To say that a number of Dorothy's friends were amazed by Maxim's behavior is to understate the case: they were mystified, also, by the change in *her*. She had always been an absolute romantic when it came to sex — she "prepared for love by marshalling abstract nouns," said Rebecca West, who had known Dorothy up till now only in her relations with Joseph Bard and Sinclair Lewis.[28] But with Maxim Dorothy was "totally real," "rooted to the ground," and she minded not at all the most overtly sexual references in her presence. She realized that Maxim had "shocked the pants off some of my respectable friends." His own reply, however, "was that they'd had their pants off many times before they met him."[29] And it would have been a mistake, even without the convincing evidence of his painting, to conclude that Maxim was merely "a stallion." Rebecca West, who adored him, declared that he was "one of the best-read men" she knew in America, and that his knowledge of French and German literature, especially, was very wide.

"He was also always kind and considerate to Dorothy," said Rebecca sternly, "with a kindness and consideration I have never seen anybody else show to her."[30] Politics and world events did not interest Maxim in the abstract; he was no better equipped than Red Lewis had been for an endless discussion of "It." But he was miles ahead of Red when it came to inner poise, and he did not take Dorothy's monologues as a personal affront. "I'm just the janitor here," he liked to say;[31] when the talk got to be too much for him, he would simply disappear. Dorothy built him a studio on the hill above the Big House at Twin Farms, and this was where he felt most at home. "I have a silent profession," he said, "I have a profession that needs daylight — I go to bed [early] and have the happiness to see a beautiful morning — to see all the trees and plants how they prepare themselves to explode with life."[32] Maxim realized that many of

Dorothy's acquaintances regarded him as a gigolo and "an idiot," but no one who really knew them thought that, and anyway, the most he ever asked for was reassurance. His letters to Dorothy were always handwritten, unsophisticated, deeply loving:

> I need to be told that you love your husband, because that's the only real thing I want to have, the only possession I have, for which I fought and suffered, for which I put myself [now] in the background — to be the nice jolly fellow with the foreign accent. . . . Sometimes I wish I should have success, then maybe many of your friends would make an effort to be more interested in my work, or at least would try to include me in.
>
> But Darling, it is not against you — I don't complain — I love you so much. . . . I want to wrap you in gold and put you on a Christmas tree. . . . As long as I have a clean conscience I am all right.[33]

"I have a silly sort of feeling," said Dorothy, "that somehow, some way, I must have been a good girl after all; as though this were all a reward for something, not really deserved, and not to be taken for granted." She felt an "enormous *dependence*" on Maxim — "emotional dependence" — and told her friends that it was the greatest relief she had ever known.[34] Committed to the union, she went about her business, confident that Maxim would be waiting when she was through, cooking her dinner, mixing her drinks, and "lifting her up in his hulking arms,"[35] as he had done the day they were married. He swept her off her feet, literally, when their friends proposed a toast, and, to the astonishment of everyone in sight, tossed her in the air.

14

CHAPTER

I T was Dorothy's belief, as a journalist and as a human being, that "in all social and political matters nothing is less praiseworthy than consistency. It is a virtue only in the minds of fanatics — of those who, having made up their minds, are incapable thereafter of . . . changing them. All consistencies are foolish except those centered in character. A character centered in truth will prove to be inconsistent in relation to dogmas and ideas."[1] Having begun the war as America's undisputed primary agitator against the Nazis, Dorothy would end it, in 1945, as the strongest voice in America in defense of the German people — in pursuit of a "sane, rational, reasonable peace," that is, with the nation that Hitler had left in rubble. She realized that events had placed her in an odd position; she had been given "a thankless task in the middle of this war" and especially in view of "the uniquely hideous behavior" of the enemy.

"It might be difficult," said Dorothy, "for me to sustain in argument rational reasons for a dogged conviction that someday, somehow, Germany will lead herself and help Europe to a new humanism. . . . So let me make myself clear at the outset: I am neither pro- nor anti-Germany, as a nation and people, under all circumstances, past, present and future. And if I were, my personal antipathies, experiences and prejudices would not, I hope, influence what I have to say. I am pro-*human*. Pro-*reason*. And pro-*world cooperation* after this war, on as vast and inclusive a scale as possible."[2]

It had taken Dorothy some time to find her way in the months that followed Pearl Harbor; it was evident that the United States' declaration of war had robbed her of some of her heat. She wanted to assume an active role in the conflict, so once a week she went down to Washington to attend the "German Directive" meetings of the Office of War Information. She also sat on the Writers' War Board and was a member of the ad hoc committee that advised Colonel William J. Donovan, the director of the OSS, on matters relating to Germany. But she saw "no coherent policy" in Washington that was not strictly military in nature, and she was infuriated by what she regarded as the waste of the talents of America's journalists in wartime.

"At present all the government does is to call us occasionally and ask us to write an article on War Bonds," she complained in a letter to President Roosevelt, "or back the Scrap Drive; instead of being powerful instruments for the promotion of major policies, we are errand boys. We are sent masses of unconscionably dull and dead releases from all sorts of agencies — stuff that nobody has time to read, prepared by hacks, and usually telling us, who are interpreters, something that has appeared in the papers a week before." Dorothy was worried mainly "about the larger *political* aspects of the war"; she saw things "going off the track, both domestically and internationally."[3]

"Figuratively speaking I am on my knees," she went on in another memo to Roosevelt, begging for a propaganda assignment with the OWI. "Mr. President — eight million or ten million [dollars] for short-wave propaganda is worth a couple of battleships. We could, *with plenty of money,* organize the most brilliant war of nerves ever seen (or heard). Can't you get the means of setting up a thoroughly hard-boiled, really organized [propaganda] bureau, to drive Mr. Hitler into an insane asylum? It is the dream of my life."[4] She was doing what she could on her own turf, meanwhile. In the *Ladies' Home Journal* she called for the establishment of public-funded day-care centers to help women cope with being drafted into industry.[5] She exhorted women to turn their backs on the "short-sighted, lazy ideas" that drove American culture and to take their cue from the women of Great Britain, whose "stubborn lovingness" had saved England in the Blitz.[6]

"This is a terrible, terrible war," wrote Dorothy. "There is no good trying to make ourselves believe, because our cause is just, that it is not a terrible war." Nonetheless, as Dorothy never ceased to repeat, history would not support the thesis that "some nations are by nature peaceful and others by nature warlike. Nations change."[7]

If the war was to make any sense in the long run, it would need to be fought not for punishment, nor even for "victory," but for the reconciliation of the combatants:

> I think we ought to end this war the way it really began [she wrote] — with a book-burning. I think all the existing textbooks used in all the elementary and high schools of the so-called civilized world ought to be destroyed, and new ones made. . . . I believe that as a preface to a real and lasting peace we ought to create a universal world history, so that youngsters [would] learn approximately the same account of the life of mankind and the development of each of the national segments. . . . I am writing these words to women, because I think there is some hope in women. . . . This war ought to end in the determination to create a new spirit — the realization that God has no pets among nations.[8]

In the spring of 1942 Dorothy won her heart's desire and took the lead in an anti-Nazi propaganda campaign commissioned by William Paley at CBS and broadcast via shortwave directly into Germany. Paley had asked Dorothy to organize the radio project; she was to deliver the principal broadcasts herself, while also securing for CBS the services of four other anti-Nazis "who represented different backgrounds and could talk to different segments of the German population."[9] There was no central coordination of propaganda during that first year of America's involvement in the war; independent producers and the radio networks were encouraged to develop their own programs with the "advice and consent" of the Office of War Information. For the CBS series, proudly, Dorothy brought on board the theologian Paul Tillich; Professor Dietrich von Hildebrand of Fordham University; Max Werner, an expert on Russia and author of *The Great Offensive;* and Horst von Baerensprung, who had once been the chief of police in the German city of Magdeburg and whose anti-Nazi credentials were as powerful as she could have wished for.

"It's going to be a terrific winter," she wrote to her agent, John Moses, in July 1942, "and people with courage, realism and willingness to stick their necks out are going to be needed on the air. . . . I know that the President wants me on the air because he told me so."[10] Dorothy's speeches were conceived of as extended sermons on the evils of nazism and the inevitability of German defeat, and they were addressed, in German, to a fictional friend in Berlin, an enlightened Prussian *Junker* identified only as "Hans." It was thought that Hans was really Helmuth von Moltke, the leader of the so-called Kreisau Circle, "the foremost think tank" of the German resistance. Von Moltke was a Christian and a pacifist, a devoted friend of Genia Schwarzwald's, who two years later, in 1944, would lose his life in the mass executions that followed the plot to assassinate Hitler.[11] Many of Dorothy's "dearest friends," indeed, would be killed by the Nazis that year, evidence to her of "a tremendous resistance" inside Germany[12] — or a nascent resistance, anyhow — which the "Hans" broadcasts had been designed to encourage. She was being frank when she announced that her task as an Allied propagandist was "to foment revolution" in Hitler's Reich.

"I [have] asked you, German listeners," she proclaimed, "to spread it abroad that every Friday Dorothy is trying to reach Hans. For I knew if he got wind of such news, he would know who was meant, and would listen."[13] Her speeches were brimful of argument, history, analysis, polemic, and what her publishers called "a few Dorothyish shrieks."[14] But they carried with them an air of rippling enjoyment, of merriment, even, and there is no question that they hit their mark when they were transmitted into Germany. They were intended as a kind of concentrated tweaking of the enemy. In his own radio broadcasts Joseph Goebbels denounced Dorothy Thompson as "the scum of America,"[15] and he wondered in his diary, apparently sincerely, how it ever came to pass that "such dumb broads [so dumme Frauenzimmer], whose heads can be filled only with straw," were permitted to criticize "an historic figure of the greatness of the Führer."[16] Dorothy was especially rough on Hitler that week:

The guilt for this war is on his head; its blood is on his hands, and on the hands of those German leaders who, knowing better, did not have the strength of mind and character to oppose him. . . . I do not hold the masses of the German people responsible for this war. I believe they were as much the victims of this frivolous Narr as all the other people on this suffering globe. Their sin is not guilt for the war; their sin is that they did not take the responsibility for the fate of their own nation — that they followed blindly and obediently a leader whom millions in their hearts despised. . . .

Hans, Hans! Think and act before it is too late. Act for Germany and for Europe and for our common cause. . . . Not yet have thousands of American lives been lost in Europe. Not yet has the American hatred of Germany become the hatred of a nation with graves. But

the time to save Germany is running out. Your duty is urgent. It is
much later than you think.[17]

It was Dorothy's friend Ernestine Evans, "a catalytic presence" in
the calmest of times, who had the idea of gathering up Dorothy's
CBS broadcasts and publishing them "as a dollar-book" under the
witty title *Listen, Hans*.[18] Dorothy herself was "getting a great kick
out of this stuff," and in August 1942 ("working like a nigger," in
Dale Warren's unfortunate phrase)[19] she composed a hundred-and-
fifty-page essay to accompany the speeches. She called it "The Invasion of the German Mind" and poured into it her twenty years of
experience with, and knowledge of, the German nation. Malcolm
Cowley, writing in the *New Republic,* declared that the introduction
to *Listen, Hans* was "good enough to serve as a textbook for American propagandists,"[20] while Carl Zuckmayer, who had helped Dorothy as an adviser on the project, remarked that it was "one of the
best, if not the very best analysis ever written about the German people — written by a non-German, I mean."[21] The book received "sensationally good reviews," according to Dorothy's own report.[22] It
was "a brilliant textbook of timely propaganda,"[23] "one of the most
remarkable books to have come out of the war."[24] The critic for the
Christian Science Monitor, while noting unspecified "inaccuracies"
in Dorothy's account of German history, was prepared to overlook
them: "What matters is the future. And on that score every friend
of mankind must agree with the author."[25]
"Here we have the Dorothy Thompson whom I have always particularly admired and enjoyed," said John Chamberlain in the *New
York Times,* "— the Dorothy Thompson who does not confuse writing with oratory. This Dorothy Thompson does not attempt to be
both Socrates and literary Valkyrie. Writing carefully and exactly,
she seeks to isolate the quarreling elements that go to make up the
mind of the average German individual." Chamberlain was quick to
recognize the value of *Listen, Hans* at a time when American public
opinion had already begun to be divided on "the German question."
Basically, there were two schools of thought. One held that the German nation was utterly incorrigible and that it must be prevented,
at all costs, from ever menacing the peace of the world again. The
other took the view — which Dorothy subscribed to — that "sometime, somehow," the Allied nations would have "to discover — or
to create — some representative Germans with whom peace can be
made." In *Listen, Hans,* in "On the Record," in her radio broadcasts,

and in every other forum at her disposal — *Ladies' Home Journal, The American Mercury, Life, Look,* and *Foreign Affairs* — Dorothy devoted tens of thousands of words to her defense of the Germans as "a real people, in a real place," with a real history and real problems that might explain, if not excuse, the aberration of nazism.

"The Catos among us will denounce [her] for not wishing to see our modern Carthage obliterated and its fields strewn with salt," John Chamberlain continued. "But who among us has the inhumanity to recommend the destruction of 80,000,000 people? We cannot beat the Nazis by doing things which only a Nazi could do. The 'other Germany' must be found, even if it figuratively involves cutting Nazi tissue out of 80,000,000 brains by some as yet undiscovered super-surgery. Dorothy Thompson has some ideas about effective social surgery that are worth listening to here. And, happily, she has ceased to write at the top of her voice."[26]

By 1943, riding what she hoped would be the crest of prevailing opinion, Dorothy had worked out a set of "positive and constructive" peace proposals for Germany that included the restoration of the Weimar constitution, the retreat of the German armies to the borders of 1937, the complete disarmament of the country, and "the *compulsory* integration of Germany into any system of collective [European] security that emerges."[27] She hoped to see the end of "power politics" when the war was over. She wanted "a confederative system" for Europe, "with relegation to a federative organ of defense, currency, [and] communications."[28] She saw the need, very clearly, to counter Soviet strength. Although she had mainly admiring words for the people of the Soviet Union in their struggle against Hitler, she was wise enough — she was enough of "a student of history" — to know that Stalin would want to step in wherever Hitler left a gap.

"It ought to be clear to any statesmanlike mind," said Dorothy in a radio debate with Sir Robert Vansittart, "that our relations with Russia are of infinitely more importance than *anything* that happens to Germany after she has been defeated in this war":

> If we can continue in close agreement and in warm cooperation with Russia, we can, if we want to, deal out to Germany the fate of Carthage. We can wipe her physically off the map. I should be against this, because I have not a drop of Nazism in me. . . . On the other hand, we can, if we choose, behave like Christians, and give a new democratic Germany magnanimous treatment. I will go further: if we

are able to stick together with Russia, the Germans can go on goose-stepping in Berlin if they *really* like it. But I don't think they do. Their goose-stepping will be like the running of a squirrel on a wheel: they won't be able to go anywhere.[29]

"I do not think anyone doubts my feelings about Nazism," Dorothy said. "The rape and loot of nations and persons by the Nazis has no parallel in any modern history. If justice be an eye for an eye and a tooth for a tooth, and if statesmanship be this sort of justice; if silent and passive acceptance by large masses of the German people, themselves under Gestapo rule, constitutes collusion; then there is no fate for the German nation that is not deserved."[30] But retribution was not the function of statesmanship, so far as Dorothy was concerned:

> Victory of one nation over another does not establish the legitimate authority of the victorious over the defeated. It never has in human history, except where the defeated have been taken into the organized society of the victors as *equals,* subject to equal laws, and merged, with a large measure of popular consent. . . . Either a new Germany will be integrated into a new Europe, or a new Germany will be integrated into the Soviet Union. There is no such thing as a permanent no-man's land of eighty million people. . . . What is needed is not partisanship, but an almost disembodied disinterestedness, not passion, but intelligence, not physical heroism, but intellectual courage, not the vision of 1943, but the vision of 1963, at least.[31]

She was talking in a vacuum, unfortunately. As the war went on, it became more and more obvious that field strategy and military rationale, fueled by reports of Nazi atrocities, would win out over *Realpolitik* when it came to the future of Germany. Dorothy dated her own "profound alienation" from Allied policy from the day in January 1943 when Roosevelt and Churchill, after meeting in a tourist hotel in Casablanca, emerged with a demand for "unconditional surrender" by the Germans and the Japanese.[32] She regarded that demand as "a barbarity," "an absurdity," "an insanity," and she was convinced to the end of her life that the stubbornness of the Allies prolonged the war by at least a year, since it deprived "the forces in Germany that were anxious for peace" of any possible means of achieving it. Dorothy was not alone in thinking that "unconditional surrender" was an "astonishing" charge — no such thing had ever before been proposed, after all, in any war, by any nation[33] — but in the months to come she was forced to realize that she was seriously out of step with the mood of America. In 1944 Roosevelt's treasury secretary, Henry T. Morgenthau, Jr., came up with a plan to divide Germany when the war was over, with provisions for confiscating the Ruhr, stripping the Germans of their industrial capacity, and transforming the nation, somehow, into a "purely agricultural" state. Dorothy regarded Morgenthau as "an amorphous ass"[34] and wondered bitterly what he proposed to do "with thirty or forty million Germans who cannot possibly become peasants. Put them all on WPA?"[35]

"There is no question in my mind," said Dorothy, "that Germany now fights because her entire people are convinced that this time a lost war means a lost nation."[36] She refused to enter into "puerile, paratheological" discussions about "good" and "bad" Germans.[37] She would not be seduced by American chatter about "Prussian" militarism, nor "charge *particeps criminis* against everyone [in Germany] who did not choose martyrdom."[38] She was convinced that Nazi atrocities — such of them as had yet come to the attention of the outside world — were designed at least in part to keep the German people in line, and she advised Americans not to expect an overthrow of the Hitler regime through any ordinary avenue of "sedition" or revolt. The reason was simple: "The Nazi state has liquidated the power of every previous ruling class." The hand of despotism too tightly gripped every aspect of German life. It would make as much sense to ask why *Greece* did not rebel, or Holland, or Belgium, or France.[39]

"We face political problems of a decisive nature," Dorothy warned, "and they cannot be met by psychoanalyzing 70 to 80 million people and passing moral judgment on them. . . . It does not matter whether you assume Germany [to be] a race of angels, temporarily led by devils, or a race of devils led by their natural representatives. I do neither, not believing in the devil-angel theory of history."[40] Altogether Dorothy was disgusted with the "Hollywoodizing" of the war. It was forbidden in the United States, for example, to show newsreel films of American soldiers killed on the battlefield, and Dorothy remarked with a certain wisdom that "this country simply hates to face reality. . . . If I have to read another ad in which a wounded soldier tells me that he is fighting for fluorescent lighting, I will go on strike."[41] She loathed *Mrs. Miniver,* in which Greer Garson gave an Oscar-winning performance as a British housewife during the Blitz, declaring that it presented the war as "a conflict between the nice and the nasty" ("if it is, God help us!"); and when Samuel Goldwyn produced Lillian Hellman's *North Star* — "all about the Russian war," said Dorothy with a snort, "with, of course, a love interest" — she went into a rage over the romantic conceptions of "Miss Hellman's sentimental pink mind." Dorothy was fearful of the net effect of depicting the Germans as "stock villains" and the Japanese as "toothy apes." How did Americans imagine Hitler had sold his particular brand of anti-Semitism to the Germans? she asked. The answer: "Through cartoons, and the cartoon equivalent."[42]

"Wells," Dorothy wrote to her stepson, Wells Lewis, "I'm taking the war awfully hard. And often, often, a terrible fury possesses me, that maybe all the people who lead us won't be good enough to make it worthwhile. You know that I don't think so very highly of the human race, but even the Quintessence of Dust is worth more, I suspect, than 'they' think it is. I have such a deep, maybe crazy feeling that if anyone in a position of great power just appealed consistently and exclusively to the noblest and most creative instincts in 'mankind' — he could release a power that few believe exists. And even if he were crucified he couldn't be stopped."[43]

Thus it was that Dorothy, by the end of the war, developed a reputation for being not just "pro-German" but even (in the most superficial minds) "pro-Nazi." She was reduced to a state of perfect unbelief by the "infantilism" of her detractors. The writer Philip Wylie, in his own syndicated column, reflected the general opinion of the day when he called Dorothy "a turncoat, chin-deep in a crusade to appease the apostles of frightfulness."[44] British secret service operatives, meanwhile, were worried enough about her attitude toward Germany that they deemed it necessary to discuss the matter "frankly" with the Roosevelt administration.

"Dorothy Thompson has been a good friend of ours," said a Foreign Office report, "and on the side of the angels for a long time. . . . She has a powerful influence and would make a dangerous enemy. If [her] views [on Germany] become formally adopted as American policy, or widely held by public opinion, very serious complications may arise. . . . Miss Thompson would like a compromise peace a) in order to save bloodshed and b) more particularly because she is afraid of Bolshevism in Europe (Dr. Goebbels' line). We are all out for a complete military victory."[45] It is a moot question whether the gossip that now went around about Dorothy was inspired by British or even by American strategic concerns. It was rumored that her husband, Maxim Kopf, had been sent to the United States by "Pan-German interests" in order to marry her and "win her to the cause of a soft peace."[46] She was said to be angling for a position as ambassador to Berlin when the war was over. She was supposed to have remarked at a party that "the intellectual level in the United States is so low that I am moving to Germany for good." When this last canard turned up in Walter Winchell's column, Dorothy was "spitting mad."

"Don't you give a damn whether you lie or not?" she blasted Winchell. "I stand where I have always stood on the German question. I have never budged an inch."[47] Who was it, anyway, who had raised the loudest cry against the Germans? It was "those who held the Peace, because they held the Power, and let it drop through nerveless fingers in twenty years of do-nothingness."[48] Dorothy had not forgotten the days when she was called "a warmonger" because she knew — and dared to say — that appeasement of Hitler would lead to the conquest of Europe.

"The general thesis of those years was that the German people were no danger," she remarked bitterly, ". . . that whatever happened inside Germany did not concern us; it was a domestic affair." Now, with the end of the war in sight, there was a sudden clamor for "justice"; now there was "a race theory about the Germans," and a fashionable notion of collective guilt that made Dorothy "sick to my stomach."[49] When Philip Wylie called her "a turncoat," she wrote back to ask who, in fact, constituted "the collective guilty":

Do you want to indict the directors of General Motors? Did they not expand their plant in Germany for war purposes, under threat that otherwise their profits would be expropriated? Was their attitude any different from that of other industrialists? What reception did we receive in 1938, when a delegation of us addressed a Senate committee and begged for transitional admission of 300,000 European Jewish children under the age of 12 into the United States, arguing that otherwise they would all be killed? . . .

The atrocities did not surprise me. . . . They were going on in the years when statesmen of all nations, including our own, recognized the Hitler regime as "legal." They were going on when fashionable Americans visited the Nuremberg party rallies, and wrote glowingly of the Olympic games. They were going on when Mayor La Guardia granted the Bundists the right to hold meetings in New

York under police protection, and when I, who protested in a meeting, was attacked by the Civil Liberties Union for opposing free speech. . . . I saw plenty of atrocities inflicted by this regime in Germany, and upon Germans, before it exploded outward, and I knew that this regime would not be kinder to non-Germans than to its own people, and that the magnitude of the atrocities would increase. . . . A "turncoat" would now be following the trend of wartime opinion; I am against that trend. . . . My stand has been consistent almost to the point of painfulness. And you owe me, as a man of honor, a public apology.[50]

But the quarrel had only begun. In June of 1944, at Town Hall in New York, Dorothy took part in a debate on the future of Germany that became so acrimonious that the police had to be called in. The audience had been whipped into a fury, on the one hand by Dorothy's insistence that "flaws in the social and political structure of the Allied nations, as well as Germany, had brought on the war," and on the other by her opponent and arch-nemesis in the Good German/Bad German political fracas: the writer Rex Stout, whose Society for the Prevention of World War III had as its goal the complete destruction of Germany as a national entity. Before their quarrel was over, Stout would accuse Dorothy of "defending German murderers" and "mocking at the sufferings and torture of Hitler's victims."[51] Philip Wylie echoed this view when he answered Dorothy's letter about German atrocities and declared that he, along with "a multitude of other people," could not comprehend "the change in your spiritual orientation toward the savage affairs of this earth. . . .

"When you say that you knew that 'this regime' — i.e., the Nazis — 'would not be kinder to non-Germans than to its own people,'" wrote Wylie, "you have not only made a statement which does not, in my opinion, exactly correspond to many of your earlier statements, but also, in passing, takes away my breath, because it is surely one of the most prodigious understatements of the twentieth century."[52] Dorothy did not admit the argument:

Just what spiritual reorientation do you observe? That I call the atrocities "unkind"? I can hardly think of a stronger thing to say in a world where anything from a piece of china to a painting can be dubbed an atrocity. "Men loved unkindness then, but sightless in the quarry, I slept and knew not; tears fell down; I did not mourn. Sweat ran, and blood sprang out, and I was never sorry." . . .

Am I defending the criminals? Or Germans? No. I am not even defending the human race of which they are members. I simply cannot endure pharisaic hypocrisy. . . . I never scoffed at what you call . . . a "hard" peace. I have said over and over again that I cannot consider peace in terms of "soft" or "hard." I wanted to see an intelligent peace that would help restore civilization to this savage world. For savage it is, and savage it will progressively become, and into the abyss it is steering — oh generation of vipers![53]

She had never before taken a position so unpopular as this. Even her friend Max Ascoli, who normally found himself in sympathy with Dorothy on any "fundamental political problem," confessed that he had "reached the point where I believe in a Carthaginian Peace."[54] Maxim Kopf declared to anyone who asked that he could not "get sentimental about Germans,"[55] and Bill Shirer told Dorothy that in future they would have to avoid any discussion of the German question if they wanted to remain friends.[56] She was the only national commentator in 1945 who continued to insist that the Germans must be dealt with, first and foremost, as human beings. "Mere unpopularity," said Collier's magazine, "will never keep her from protesting that the Big Three and the Allied world are crazy if they think the German people must be punished for the sins of Hitler."[57]

"My own position is becoming dangerous," Dorothy confessed in her diary. "In the public prints I am entirely isolated." One day she ran into David Sarnoff, the head of RCA, who remarked that he saw "a great period of American prosperity" ahead, basing his prediction on the fact that "Germany and Japan, both great competitors of ours in the world market, will be finished." Dorothy appreciated Sarnoff's candor, if not the moral foundation for his satisfaction: "Apparently we have all accepted the Nazi theory, 'What's good for me is Right.' I think of Helmuth [von Moltke], Käthe Kollwitz, and Genia. I am glad that Genia is dead. Probably the others are, too. The world wears a terrible countenance of brass."[58] A much-publicized rift between Dorothy and the Writers' War Board, the result of her refusal to sign a statement that denounced "the German" (as opposed to the Nazi) "Will-to-Aggression," led to renewed accusations of "Nazi sympathizing."

"In every word I have published," Dorothy wrote in "On the Record," "I have tried to think of the effect in Germany itself. . . . I have asked myself whether what I wrote would encourage or discourage Germans from standing before Hitler."[59] It was a source of pride to Dorothy that the Nazi authorities had always endeavored to prevent the publication of her speeches in Germany. She was ready now to accuse the men and women who opposed her on the Writers' War Board — and specifically Rex Stout, who was calling her "a liar" — of "furnishing Goebbels with his most effective propaganda." Stout dismissed the charge as "fantastic" and resigned his position as a director of Freedom House, of which Dorothy was president. She countered shortly with her own resignation.[60] And in this burning, angry, caustic moment, Wells Lewis was killed. He was serving in France as an adjutant to Major General John E. Dahlquist, following his tour of duty in North Africa, and on October 29, 1944, during a lull in heavy fighting near Bruyères, he was shot in the head by a German sniper. He died instantly.[61]

It took two weeks for the news of Wells's death to reach America. On the day he died Dorothy was stumping for Roosevelt, delivering a thirty-minute radio speech in support of the President's bid for a fourth term in office. She had not intended to take any public stand in the election, and was moved to do so only by the negativism of the Republican campaign and "the snide personal whisperings about the President."

"They say he's tired," Dorothy declared. "And I say, you *bet* he's tired. Churchill is tired, Stalin is tired, Eisenhower is tired, MacArthur is tired, Nimitz is tired. Admiral King is tired."[62] And Dorothy herself was tired. Half a million copies of her speech were printed up and distributed around the country by the President's re-election committee. It "was, as the saying is, a sensation," said Dorothy, but she took no pleasure in the acclamation that came her way.[63]

"I often wish I could retire to a study instead of hurling words into the market place," she wrote.[64] For more than a year she had been working on a book, "The Moral Crisis of Our Times," but she could not write anything for it or even think about it without getting depressed. "It's all new," she advised Paul Brooks at Houghton Mifflin. "I am trying to think my way through some very big problems and I don't know yet just how I am going to come out. . . . Pray for me."[65] Word of Wells's death finally reached her on November 13, 1944, and when it did, for the first and only time in her life, she canceled a scheduled radio broadcast. It was a time of horror for the whole family. Michael Lewis heard the news from a friend at boarding school, who saw it in the papers and greeted him at breakfast with the words, "Too bad your brother was killed."[66] In Chicago, where he was staying at the Palmer House, Sinclair Lewis stubbornly ignored a telegram from Marcella Powers and only confessed that he knew about Wells's death when Howard Wilson, Dorothy's brother-in-law, tried to offer his condolences.

"Oh, *good* for you," said Red, *"you're* the one who got to tell it! All day everybody has been trying to tell me — the newsboy, the bootblack, the cigar counter man, the desk clerk, everybody's been trying to tell me. But great, great! *you're* the one who got to tell it." Then, as Mark Schorer reported, Red "settled down and spoke quietly and soberly about a German father, a Japanese father, fathers all over the world in many different countries to whom such news must be broken."[67] Red's broad-mindedness was limited strictly to unknown parents overseas, however: when Dorothy canceled her radio show in mourning for Wells, he accused her of concocting "a publicity stunt."

"Dorothy's just putting on an act," said Red. "She wasn't his mother. It's all self-dramatization."[68] But it was not. She was inconsolable.

"It is hard for me to explain what this boy meant to me," she wrote to Carl Zuckmayer. "He was in an intimate, complicated and infinitely comforting way something of my own." Six months after his death, during a tour she made of Europe at the end of the war, Dorothy was able to visit Wells's grave at Epinal. "I make myself recriminations that I did not do more," she confessed to Zuckmayer, "— do something active and positive to get him out of the hell in which he fought uninterruptedly for two years, but neither my own convictions nor his would allow me to do so. My grief is in every pore and I do not want it assuaged. It is part of me forever, and it is what remains to me of him."[69] There was a new dimension now to her arguments about Germany. When Oswald Garrison Villard, knowing the depth of her grief, wrote to her to express his sympathy and to say that Wells had "not died in vain," she answered only that she wished he was right.

"I don't feel that Wells' death is justified," Dorothy protested. "I feel it *must be* justified. Oswald, we must *fight fight* for a people's peace, and America must *lead.*"[70] The leaders of the Allied nations had already convened ten times, in various places around the world, to discuss the conduct of the war, the future of Europe, and the establishment of the United Nations. Borders were considered, as well as punishments, monetary policies, and future "spheres of influence." But Dorothy saw nothing on the horizon to give her any hope.

The conferences of Yalta, San Francisco, and Dumbarton Oaks left her muttering about "Vikingism" and predicting a "peace" that would be as horrible as the war.

"I did my best to draw comfort and faith from the statement of the Crimea conference," she wrote to a friend in February 1945, "nor would I write for the public what I really thought, or rather, perhaps, felt. . . . I see no end in sight of terror, no consequential moral position anywhere, and no definitions, either, of anything."[71] In other letters, and in a diary she kept that winter and later published in *The Commonweal* as "Apprehensions in 1945," Dorothy's vision was even bleaker: "I see ahead the disintegration of civilization, . . . monstrous crimes and crime waves — race wars — government by gangs. . . . Yet I hold my tongue — I abet with silence. Why? Because I am afraid — afraid of the campaign against me, and honestly torn with doubts [as to] whether expressing my indignation will help or injure the world I should like to see emerge."[72]

In March she took to her bed, stricken with flu and anxious to "awaken to another vision, fearing — knowing in my bones — that I shall not, glad, despite the health of my blood, for the time when I shall return to the quarry out of which I came, and to its peace. Sorry only, praying only, for my dearly beloved son."[73]

MANY times in later years Dorothy would remark that she had been tricked — "lied to" — when it came to the goals of America's leaders at the end of World War II.[74] The "disaster of the peace" might have been avoided, she thought, or at least mitigated, had Franklin Roosevelt lived; someone else, on the other hand, might have been elected President in 1944 had the White House been honest about the state of Roosevelt's health. Dorothy knew nothing about the secret wartime agreements among Roosevelt, Churchill, and Stalin — the promise to Russia of concessions in the Far East, for example, and the tacit acceptance of a permanent Soviet military presence in Europe. But she judged the Yalta conference, and all of the Allied conferences that followed, to be "a hundred percent Russian victory,"[75] the realization for Stalin of Hitler's global aspirations, "and by all of Hitler's methods short of war."[76] She could only conclude that Roosevelt meant to deal with the Russians when the fighting was over.

"What he apparently did not reckon with was his own death," Dorothy later reasoned, "and at the most critical moment, leaving the direction of affairs to the inexperienced and mediocre Mr. Truman." In July 1945, at Potsdam, the new President found himself ratifying the conquest of Eastern Europe as a fait accompli. While other commentators were waiting to see how Truman might shape up in the arena of foreign affairs, Dorothy gave him no quarter: "When the few historically minded survivors in some overlooked ivory tower ask themselves: from where shall we date this inversion of values, this rule of violence [in the Western world], they may name the First World War, or the Russian Revolution, or the 1936 Russian purges, or Mussolini's March on Rome, or the seizure of power by Hitler. But the seal of the dark ages for the Anglo-American world will be found to have been printed on the documents signed at Yalta and Potsdam."[77]

Dorothy was in London when Roosevelt died, in April 1945. She offered no eulogy, because her column was in suspension while she watched the Nazis "scram in wild confusion." She had simply been "compelled" to go, she said, and in her last communication with the President had asked for and received his help in obtaining for Maxim Kopf official accreditation as a war correspondent: the *Ladies' Home Journal* had agreed to publish Maxim's drawings of the Allied liberation if Dorothy could get him past the censors.[78] She waited out the fall of Hitler in Jerusalem, where she had gone from England to investigate the Palestine question and where she celebrated VE-Day at a concert hall with a thousand "Jewish patriots." Then, on May 8, one day after the German surrender, Dorothy and Maxim arrived in Rome. Before their tour was over they saw Vienna, Prague, Berchtesgaden, Dachau, and the bombed-out ruins of Berlin. Here, said Dorothy, "for the first time since the war, and for the first time since I said good-bye with the Gestapo's expulsion order in my pocket, I met the remnant of my old friends." Here she heard about the death of Helmuth von Moltke and hundreds of others who had opposed Hitler in the "officers' plot" of 1944. She learned about acts of heroism during the Battle of Berlin and about fights to the death over bits of sausage and half-empty jars of marmalade in the wake of the Russian advance.

"But we could not take up the thread, really," said Dorothy of her old companions; "for in no conversation before the fall would a gentlewoman have spoken of the rape of her daughter, quite casually, as a somewhat upsetting but rather minor incident, fortunate on the whole because the rapist had not been diseased, and there had been only one, not a dozen. . . . They were very glad to see me, as

I was glad to see them, for they had been among the resisters — not able to do much, really; pitiable when you think how much they risked for so little possible accomplishment."

> None of them knew of all that had gone on in the concentration camps, the gassing, for instance; but when it came out they were not surprised, nor shocked, either. For when you have lived through every kind of iniquity, through a total moral debacle, no new manifestation of that debacle is surprising. These were all highly civilized people; the unbridgeable chasm between myself and them was the chasm that would exist between people who had been to hell and those who had not, and who knew they were still in hell and probably you were, too, only you did not know it yet.[79]

She had suspended "On the Record" for most of her European trip, contenting herself with the steady gathering of news and a weekly broadcast to America over the Mutual Radio Network. "No words can describe the terrible spectacle of these crushed, burnt-out, abandoned crags and cliffs of broken mortar," she wrote after a tour of Frankfurt-am-Main. "Germany is knocked out for 100 years."[80] Dorothy wondered if the American people had any comprehension of what had really gone on in Germany. When she toured Dachau she was impressed most strongly not by the barracks or the gas chambers or the dreadful crematoria, but by the volumes of Goethe in the homes of the commandants, the evidence she saw that the Nazi exterminators had been "happy family men," devoted to their wives and children, appreciative of music, literature, and the arts.

"There is a medical term for this," Dorothy observed. "It is called schizophrenia."[81] The crimes of Dachau were not "primitive outbursts of fury, but highly rationalized and scientifically perpetrated." They had taken place not because "Germans" were bloodthirsty. They had taken place because the entire emphasis of modern life was "anti-human," "scientific," "efficient," and irreverent — "because the inhibitions which centuries of western culture imposed upon the individual" had been destroyed.[82]

> I have heard over and over again the words, "Such things never happened before anywhere else in the world" [wrote Dorothy]. But do people say, "Such things never happened before in *Germany?*" For that is also true. These monstrous crimes happened in our own civilization; in a white, European civilization, Christian for centuries, among a people in no way inferior to other western peoples in the

things of which our society is especially proud: science, technology, organization, production and a high standard of living. . . .

If only one could say, and dismiss it with that, "These people are savages." They are — but they are a new and terrifying kind of savage. . . . For modern man has set himself up in his own image; or rather, he has set up his own creations as the image of God. He is "functional." The S.S. administrators were but bureaucratic cogs in a smoothly oiled and functioning machine. . . . [The] concentration camps themselves were testing places of mass reactions. Does the world realize that some of the worst crimes in these camps were committed by the inmates? [83]

She was moving toward a position of "moral indignation and flaming rage" [84] that far exceeded anything that had compelled her during the rise of Hitler. She was setting herself in opposition not just to those who argued that Germany and the Germans should be punished "in kind," but to anyone who still believed — as she herself had once believed — that the answer to humanity's ills lay in scientific materialism, in "progress" and the march of technology. Her position, of course, had not really changed; it was no departure for Dorothy Thompson to call for a renascence of "spirituality" in response to the Nazi horrors.

"Our political life," she protested, "— all twentieth-century political life — approaches the same 'functional' concept. We are advised, even in our own country, to vote as 'workers,' or as 'employers,' to arrange ourselves in a 'system,' to fit ourselves into a 'plan' — as though man is a steam riveter, or a manufacturer, or a bureaucrat, or a salesman, and nothing else whatever. Is he a *conscience?* Can anyone *prove* conscience? Has anyone ever seen the soul? Can you measure it? Put it under a microscope? Cure its illnesses with sulfa and penicillin? Do you know that it exists? So argues the modern savage." She had asked a friend in Germany, a man who had "served twenty months in the dreadful death house of Mauthausen," which of the inmates in concentration camp had "behaved the best" under torture and confinement: "Businessmen? Intellectuals? What race? What political parties?"

Her friend thought about it "for a long time," and then answered, "Priests." [85] And even these had had to act spontaneously, individually, with no support from the Church at large. One of the first people Dorothy interviewed on her German tour, in May 1945, was the Protestant pastor Martin Niemöller, whose experiences in concentration camp had convinced him that there was "nothing left" in modern life that was not "corrupted and compromised." Only the *message* of Christianity, Niemöller told Dorothy, "had kept alive in people their recollection of morality and hope."[86] Only individual ministers, rabbis, priests, nuns, and lay worshipers had been strong enough to resist the Nazis:

> Various agencies of the United States Government and armed forces have made a study of the behavior of the prisoners at Dachau [wrote Dorothy]. Under the terrible pressures under which they were put, did their [political and nationalistic] beliefs determine their conduct? Did democrats or socialists or communists hold together to protect one another? Did Poles stick to Poles or Frenchmen to Frenchmen? Was political belief or patriotism a basis for morale or morality of behavior?
>
> No. That is the most tremendous lesson of Dachau. No. What was decisive for behavior was the individual human soul. What separated the saint from the sinner-under-pressure was a spark in the breast, an admonition in the heart . . . was *conscience*. . . . The lesson of Dachau is that no science, no technology, no political, social or economic systems, neither patriotism nor race, nor material standards of living, nor learning, nor civilization will save mankind. . . . Hitlerism is not a unique, isolated phenomenon, but a terrible example and warning. It is a symptom of universal moral crisis which even in cries for revenge and reprisal emits the animal-like cries of Nazism itself.[87]

Dorothy's articles on Dachau, which appeared, for the most part, in the *Ladies' Home Journal,* were written at a time when the atrocities of the war had barely ended and "the Holocaust" had not yet been defined as a historical concept, still less as a tragedy that related exclusively to the extermination of the Jews. In 1945 the Potsdam agreements, confirming the occupation of Germany and the division of Europe, led to the forced displacement of an estimated fifteen million persons of German extraction. These were not Nazis, or even native Germans, but *Volksdeutsche,* German-speaking peasants and merchants, and a smattering of aristocrats from noble families, whose ancestors had lived in the eastern reaches of Europe for hundreds of years. Two million of them, by the most conservative estimate, died of starvation, disease, beatings, or torture or in organized massacres before the end of 1947; five million more were "repatriated" into the Soviet Union, where, presumably, they too perished. In the western zones of Germany, after Potsdam, it was calculated that every fourth person was a refugee, and the famine that lasted there sporadically through 1949 claimed uncounted numbers of lives.[88] Dorothy was "horrified" by what she called "the Potsdam emanation" — she was "swallowed in the thundercloud of its greed, brutality, and unction."[89] Her postwar reputation as an anti-Soviet hard-liner was born partly of her insistence that the Allies had "sold out" to Russia in 1945, and that America had contributed, wittingly or not, to the deaths of millions of innocent people.

"If there were a scrap of imagination," wrote Dorothy, "an iota of intellect, a modicum of historical perspective, a shred of democratic principle, or even a whiff of morality operating at Potsdam, it was never indicated." Unlike many of her colleagues, she was not impressed by considerations of power politics or the general confusion of global war. She regarded the Potsdam agreements as "the lowest debasement of American history, . . . an appeal, not to reason but to revenge, and an invitation to loot, plunder, starve, dispossess millions, smash Europe, produce chaos, divide the Allies and, in fact, get us just to the point where we are this minute."[90] If Dorothy's thinking was turgid, if her opposition to Hitler had been supplanted, merely, by another obsession, she was not to be argued with on one score: the extermination of the German-speaking peoples of East Prussia, Silesia, Brandenburg, Bohemia, Transylvania, and the whole of modern Poland was no less horrible, "no less a crime against humanity," for being less systematic than the massacre of the Jews at Auschwitz.

"I imagine I am a great deal older than you," Dorothy wrote to Philip Wylie, who was moved, in the end, by her arguments about Germany and whom she counted now as a friend: "I've gone through a lot in my life watching the world go straight to hell."[91] She was deeply suspicious of the proposed trial of Nazi war criminals at Nuremberg — not because she thought they should not be punished, but because she feared "the rise of the People's Tribunal" and "the substitution of lynch law for habeas corpus." She was worried about form, as always, about precedent, about means and ends. She thought it would be better to shoot the Nazi leaders after military court martial[92] and not to confuse the issue with "international justice," which so far as she could tell was always shifting in the wind. She wanted to know if wartime agreements and "solemn covenants" meant anything, and if not, why not. If the United States was now a party to the prosecution of Nazis "for plotting a war of aggression," why should it not also demand the prosecution of the Soviet leaders, who in 1939 had signed a pact with Hitler? Why should there be no investigation of the Soviet massacre of Polish officers at Katyn? Why did the judges at Nuremberg not take some time off and travel into East Prussia, where they might see "more recent stacks of corpses. . . . Do they think that death by gassing is worse or better than death by beating, or death by imprisonment in filthy water up to the neck?" What would they make of the pillage in the East, the "rapine," the famine, the "suicide and despair?"[93]

"It is doubtful whether the sight and experience of monstrous suffering breed compassion," Dorothy wrote in "On the Record" at the end of 1945. "All the publicizing of the Dachau and Belsen horrors [has] not made mankind more tender of humanity." She had returned from Europe in the middle of July to find a nation flush with victory and preparing to relish its clout. In December, in a speech at Town Hall in New York, she warned her listeners that millions of people in the eastern zones of Europe were going to die if something was not done to prevent it.

"To drive the point home," she remembered, "I suggested that it would be more humane to re-open the gas chambers for German children," and to her horror — "just at Christmastime, perhaps in commemoration of the Babe of Bethlehem" — "the response was a scattered applause. The vicarious spectacle of the famished bodies and charred bones of Nazi victims had only turned the applauders into vicarious baby-killers themselves."[94] Dorothy's strongest attacks on the legitimacy of the Nuremberg trials, meanwhile, remained unpublished:

> Specifically mentioned as war crimes and/or crimes against humanity are: slave labor, forced deportations, political and racial persecutions, and cruel and unusual punishments. Yet everything of which the defendants stood accused and were convicted, is being done today by one or another of the accusers. It was the United States government and air force and no other that dropped bombs on Hiroshima and Nagasaki, both open cities, killing indiscriminately men, women and children, in a death whose horrors — to the honor of America — have been most eloquently revealed by an American and an American publication, John Hersey and The New Yorker. While we sit in judgment on war atrocities, we are also informed that the U.S. government has spent fifty million dollars . . . to perfect a poison, one cubic inch of which, properly diluted and sprayed from planes, could wipe out 180 million people! What a comment on a

judgment of crimes against humanity — what a waste of your money and mine.[95]

She had welcomed the atomic bomb ironically as "the greatest apostle of peace," seeing it as a "terrible instrument of destruction" that, "by opening before us the bottomless pit of hell," forced mankind to make a choice: "Repent or Die."[96] The reaction in the United States to the explosion at Hiroshima had been understandably jubilant; it had brought about the end of the war and convinced Americans that they were "supreme in the world," "that the exhilarating vision of an American Century," in Ronald Steel's words, "might now be turned into reality."[97] While journalists and editors and generals and statesmen all debated the *future* of atomic weapons — how they would be used, *if* they would be used, and to what extent the nation's power policy should be shaped around them — Dorothy took a different tack. She never once accepted the argument that the use of the bomb against Japan was justified because it served to shorten the war ("The only thing prolonging it," she said, "was the Allied demand for Unconditional Surrender").[98] But she did see a silver lining even in the awesome cloud of nuclear weapons: she believed that the atomic bomb clearly — "obviously" — made war obsolete. Not three days after the explosion at Hiroshima, she called for "total and universal disarmament" and declared that "a political deduction as logical as the instinct of self-preservation can immediately be drawn from this greatest of all human discoveries: There must be a world state. . . . War must be made illegal."[99] In November 1945 she proposed the establishment, at the minimum, of an international police force, "a kind of world sanitary corps" that would prohibit the manufacture and distribution of nuclear weapons.

"It should fly its own flag," said Dorothy, "— a flag of humanity. It should be publicized by an immense international bureau, as the protector of every man, woman and child on earth. . . . The proposals should be ratified, state by state, in enormous festivals."[100] To anyone who argued that her ideas were impractical, impossible, utopian, Dorothy answered that they were "child's play" in comparison with the "miracles of barbarism" that science had already put forth.

"At this moment," she wrote, "the greatest scientific minds in every country are concentrated on [designing] better and more powerful bombs and rockets. The amount of intelligence going into answering the question of how countries and peoples can be exterminated in a few minutes must be compared with the amount of intelligence and genius being expended on the narrow question of how to abolish war. On the widening or narrowing of that discrepancy depends the fate of this planet." [101] Dorothy was "profoundly disgusted" as time went on by the parade of international scientists who, when they were not attempting to justify their participation in the creation of the atomic bomb, were signing statements denouncing its use and placing responsibility for its future on the shoulders of "humanity." *Humanity* had not invented it, said Dorothy. *Humanity* was "fed up with the scoldings of the scientists." [102] She wanted laws against rearmament, laws against military conscription. She wanted a United Nations with *power*, not "a collection of foreign offices" engaged in "business as usual." She blamed the United States, the Soviet Union, Great Britain, and France for "emasculating" the United Nations at birth by insisting on the creation of the Security Council and on the reservation of the right of veto.

"The new League of Nations is not going to be one bit more effective than the old one was," she warned. "We are not going to organize the world for peace under law: we are not going to have a genuine international police force: and what it will amount to as far as American foreign policy is concerned is interventionism without positive responsibility. Between that foreign policy and one of splendid isolation, it is quite impossible for me to make a choice. I consider them both evil." [103] She foresaw an age of "endless minor wars" and "formless imperialism," "more and more atrocious Munichs," "lawlessness for the powerful and servitude for the weak." [104] She realized that her plea for world cooperation was visionary, and she braced herself for the inevitable accusation that she was thinking "like a woman." She knew she was — she was thinking for *all* women. She was about to enter a phase of her career that can only be called harshly anti-Communist, but she knew, on the most basic and truthful level, that "the people of the world are peace-loving, all, without exception," and that "no mother on earth wants her son slaughtered on a battlefield, or her children blown to bits in a cellar." She was proud to be "irrational" in the cause of survival:

It is, of course, entirely possible — quite coldly to be taken into calculation — that "the Big One" will be the last spot, people, and man, on a planet exploding itself out of the firmament. Then, if anywhere in the universe there is a graveyard for finished stars, the earth's obituary may be: It died because its inhabitants, being endowed with brains to penetrate the secret of all matter, preferred to perish rather than use them any further.[105]

In the light of Hiroshima, she invited Philip Wylie to join her in Vermont, "where every prospect pleases and even man is not — in the immediate neighborhood — particularly vile. I have rather a lot of room," said Dorothy, "the house is extremely comfortable, the cook (whom I have had for twelve years) excellent, and the landscape perfect. There are also martinis and Scotch — though you had better make it earlier than later. And butter and cream," she added. "And flowers."[106]

15

CHAPTER

AT the beginning of 1947, with the explanation that "space is tight" and that the column was "characterized by dullness and by a lack of any particularly significant new information or opinion,"[1] the editor of the *New York Post* dropped "On the Record" from its pages and deprived Dorothy Thompson of her outlet in New York City. "A full quarter" of Dorothy's annual income had come to her from the *Post,* but she was less concerned about the money than she was about the future of free thinking in America.

"It does not matter how 'courageous' a writer may be," she warned her friend Meyer Weisgal. "Courage becomes useless, for a courageous writer who is not published is not a writer at all. . . . I am under no illusions whatever about the probability of my finding another outlet in New York."[2] It was no secret that Ted Thackrey, the *Post*'s editor, had been scandalized by Dorothy's call for "understanding" in regard to peace with the Germans. In January 1945 Thackrey had taken the nearly unprecedented step of publishing a rebuttal to one of Dorothy's columns on his own editorial page;[3] and when, two years later, he made the decision to cancel "On the Record," he explained to an upset subscriber that "Miss Thompson's view has been orientated primarily by a consideration of the plight of the German people."[4] She was "vastly more disturbed [by] real or fancied 'persecution' of Germans," Thackrey charged, than she was by that of anyone who had suffered at the hands of the Nazis.[5] Dorothy was tired of defending herself, but she trotted out her arguments one more time.

"I cannot imagine," she wrote to Thackrey, "that anyone with a knowledge of my past could believe that I am vastly more disturbed by persecutions of Germans than of the Nazi victims. No one in America has written more about the Nazi persecutions, or more vigorously. I am concerned, however, that persecution should cease and *pro*secution take its place. . . . I disbelieve in racism, or in the racial-ethnic state, whether that theory be advanced by Germans, Slavs or Anglo-Saxons." Or, Dorothy might have added, by Jews: since 1945, starting just after her first trip to "the Holy Land," she had been giving considerable space in "On the Record" to the problem posed by Jewish emigration to Palestine and by the Zionist dream of a Jewish state. She had not, at this stage, worked out any clear editorial policy in regard to the disposition of the Palestinian Mandate. She was in something of a muddle, moving more or less reluctantly from the position she had always taken, one that was warmly supportive of Jewish hopes, toward a conviction that the proposed establishment of the State of Israel was a formula for disaster, "a recipe for perpetual war" in the Middle East. Dorothy had little doubt that her views on Palestine were the actual cause of her dismissal from the *Post*.

"I was in Palestine . . . ," she reminded Thackrey in November 1946, several months before she left the paper, "and I assure you, Ted, that the situation there is *not* the way it has been presented by many of the Zionists. It is one of the most complicated and difficult problems on the earth today."[6] Earlier in the year, Zionist terrorists under the leadership of the future Israeli Prime Minister Menachem Begin, among others, had detonated a bomb that blew up the entire west wing of the King David Hotel in Jerusalem, the headquarters of the British military authorities responsible for the administration of Palestine. Seventy-six people were killed in the blast, and Dorothy was far from alone in condemning the action as unconscionable. She believed herself to have been "very, very guarded" thus far in her criticism of Zionist tactics.[7] But her mail, which had once been filled with right-wing frothing about her "Jew-loving" tendencies, was now replete with accusations that she had turned traitor, that she was "anti-Semitic," that she had become, in the words of one hysterical reader, "the apostle of the Hitlerian technique," whose "filthy incitements to pogroms" would no longer be tolerated by New York's Jews.[8]

It was an organized campaign, and Dorothy knew it. "I am a very old hand, after all," she wrote to Meyer Weisgal, who was serving as the personal representative in America of Chaim Weizmann, the director of the Jewish Agency and the first president of the State of

Israel, "and when letter after letter is couched in almost identical phraseology I do not think the authors have been gifted with telepathy."[9] Weizmann himself had roundly condemned the terrorist actions of the Stern and Irgun gangs in Palestine, but Dorothy, as Weisgal explained, had "mistaken her cue." She was not Jewish; therefore "she was bound to be misunderstood."[10] Other editors at the *New York Post* (as well as his wife, Dorothy Schiff) would confirm that Ted Thackrey was "very close to the Irgunists and Menachem Begin"; that he regarded the creation of the Jewish state in Palestine as the only possible just response to the Holocaust in Europe; and that Begin, the Irgunists, the Stern gang, and other Zionist organizations had "an inordinate access" to the *Post*'s editorial board.[11] Dorothy's call for a halt to Jewish terrorism was perceived as indifference on her part to the fate of those Jews whom Hitler had failed to slaughter; her position on Palestine, in the minds of her Jewish readers, was connected directly to her defense of the Germans at the end of the war, and for the rest of her life, in spite of her record of friendship to the Jews and her undying opposition to organized bigotry, she was "officially anti-Semite."[12]

"I have had," she wrote to Helen Reid in April 1947, "I may say to you personally, a horrid time during the last two years at the *Post* — a horrid, undignified, embarrassing time."[13] In a letter to Sinclair Lewis she declared that she would like to give up "On the Record" altogether. "I am tired-tired-tired," she said. "And before I die I would like to write one or two good books, and I can't do it with this three-times-a-week business. And anyhow I don't know what to say. (Don't tell anyone.) But it seems to me that the world is stark insane. And the lying that goes on!"[14] Dorothy was especially upset about the fate of an article she had written for *Life* magazine, "The Germans Who Defied Hitler." It was the story of her friend Helmuth von Moltke and what she called "the German Underground," led by those officers and civilians — Claus Schenck von Stauffenberg, Otto Kiep, Ulrich von Hassell, Adam von Trott zu Solz — who were executed in 1944 after their failed attempt to seize power from the Nazi High Command.[15]

"The whole story of this plot has been completely distorted," Dorothy protested. "It was not a mere handful of military defeatists but a nation-wide plot, and I have positive reason to believe that early in 1944 they came in contact with our authorities and said they were prepared to strike, but that to be sure of the all but unanimous support of the [German] Army, they wanted to be able to offer the Ger-

man people an honorable peace under an anti-Nazi government.
. . . They got no answer, apparently, but Unconditional Surrender." [16] Henry Luce had accepted her story "on first reading," Dorothy reported, "and thought it the most sensationally interesting
article to come out of Europe to date. He also sent me a handsome
check." But in the end the article was never published: "Somewhere
along the line, and despite the publisher himself, the piece was
killed." To Dorothy, it was evidence that "the truth about Germany"
could never be told, and that anyone who hoped to tell it would be
putting his career on the line.[17]

"Ah, Grace," she wrote to Grace Lewis, "it is hard to live in these
days. . . . I am proud of my German friends! . . . They were the
moral and intellectual elite of the nation, and Helmuth and Wells
can shake hands in heaven." [18] The thought that Wells Lewis might
not have died had negotiations for peace been opened in 1944 would
haunt Dorothy to the end of her life: "I feel so full of grief and fury
that I am quite speechless. And, impersonally speaking, we shall pay
for years and years to come." [19]

She made her exit from the *Post* with perfect dignity, and while
she was grateful to the many friends who wrote to Ted Thackrey
asking where "On the Record" might now be found, she did not
expect or encourage a campaign for her reinstatement. Thanks to
her contract with the Bell Syndicate, she was still appearing in a
hundred and fifty newspapers around America, and when it came to
the editorial policy of any one of them, she was a strict proponent
of laissez-faire. At almost the very moment that Dorothy left the
Post, her colleague Bill Shirer was dismissed by CBS, on the ill-
concealed grounds that his commentary differed too markedly from
the corporate line; John Gunther requested that all of Shirer's friends
protest to William Paley, but Dorothy refused, explaining that as far
as she was concerned, business was business, the press was free, and
the news industry in America was changing to the point where soon
"all the old hands" would be unable to recognize it. She had not
been able to get a radio contract herself since 1945, and she did not
think it was because her views were unpopular per se.

"I think *all* serious commentators have suffered," she wrote to
Gunther, "with the public and sponsors, since the war; the interest
in public affairs and especially international affairs has certainly
lapsed." [20] Americans were looking for distraction after the years of
stress. War rationing had ended; long skirts were back; there was a
mania for Frigidaires, nylons, household appliances, and labor-saving

gadgets. There was also television to consider. "Indescribable inanity," Dorothy called it, as it tightened its grip on the American mind, "accompanied by violence. Every time I look at the television set somebody is shooting somebody. Boom boom."[21] She did not think "Uncle Miltie" was any sillier than "The Shadow" or "The Aldrich Family," but as a medium for numbing the perceptions, TV had far outstripped radio: it removed the last obstacle to uniformity in culture; it worked to obliterate distinctions of every kind. Long before she was dropped by the *New York Post,* Dorothy had to deal with editors at her syndicate who "kicked and squealed" and demanded to know why she *must* use "big words" in her copy — words like *autarchy* and *lacunae* and (as she once did) *unmitigated Buncombe.*

"I love to be precise," said Dorothy wistfully, "— perhaps it is my only literary virtue."[22] As early as 1943, two years after the advent of commercial television, she published a series of articles in the *Ladies' Home Journal* warning that America was becoming an illiterate nation. "I have, personally, a fight every day of the week with my syndicate," she wrote elsewhere, "because they say I don't write for the cultural level of my readers." But in "giving the public what it wants," Dorothy insisted, the moguls of popular entertainment were contributing directly to the decline of civilization.

"You ask yourselves," she wrote to MGM's Howard Dietz during the war, in response to Dietz's criticism of her views, "— I mean the industry does — Do we furnish what people want, and if the answer is yes, as evidenced in the box-office returns, the matter is settled. That is 'democracy.' . . . But suppose you look at it another way, and ask, 'What is the greatest potential cultural and educational medium for the masses in America?' Obviously the answer is, 'The movies.' And if you then ask, 'Are the movies raising the level to the extent that they could raise it?' the answer must certainly be: No."[23] And what movies had failed to do, television did not even attempt. Dorothy was in wholehearted sympathy with her friend Rebecca West, who lamented above all the absence of any real *meaning* in postwar American culture. In 1948, on a trip to New York, Rebecca saw Marlon Brando in *A Streetcar Named Desire* and remarked in a letter to Dorothy that it was "the most solemn dirt" she had ever witnessed: "Incoherent — the wrong story hitched on to characters it did not fit."

"It isn't *about* anything," Rebecca had complained to her companion that night.

"Well," said her friend, "what is?"

Rebecca was aghast: "Well, *Othello* is, and so is *King Lear*."[24] Rebecca and Dorothy both felt that the House Un-American Activities Committee was missing the point completely when it began to investigate suspected Communists in Hollywood.

"Those who believe that, on the whole, Hollywood exercises a bad influence, do not think so because they observe 'radical' tendencies," Dorothy wrote in "On the Record." "They deplore its fairly constant phoniness, its glamorizing of vulgar and tawdry standards, its creation of adolescent erotic ideals, the crudity and superficiality of its approaches to the real problems of life, its gooey sentimentality, and its apparent incapacity to create a work of art. . . . No art can be based primarily on the intention to make money. *No* art. . . . [Hollywood's] trouble is not that it is revolutionary, but that it is asinine."[25]

She was lucky to have found a friend in Rebecca, because in the 1940s and 1950s, as she went doggedly on in her criticism of American politics, culture, and morals, she was more and more isolated from the mainstream of public opinion. "It's time they started trusting you and me," Rebecca told Dorothy, "the President and Vice-President of the Pessimists' Club."[26] In 1947 Rebecca published her ground-breaking study *The Meaning of Treason;* before that she had covered the Nuremberg trials, and when it came to their views on "war guilt," she and Dorothy were on exactly the same wavelength: "Criminal acts are committed by individuals, not by those fictional bodies known as nations."[27] Dorothy and Rebecca might have been sisters in their devotion to the principles of enlightened individualism; in their abhorrence of communism as the "nazism" of the nuclear age; in their resolute closing of the gap that their personalities had set between them. Not since Rose Wilder Lane had Dorothy had a friend who understood her better.

"We were unlike in mind and temperament," Rebecca reflected, "but over what might have been an abyss [Dorothy's] warmth and affection and sense of fun built a bridge, and through the years she gave me not only friendship — but endless entertainment. I have never laughed so much with any other human being. I don't think the future will ever guess what she had to give of that."[28] They met for the first time in Berlin, in around 1924, when Rebecca, having ended her famous liaison with H. G. Wells, was struggling in an unsatisfying love affair with Lord Beaverbrook, the Canadian-born newspaper magnate. In a curious and completely English way, Rebecca was exactly like Dorothy. She had sprung from nowhere, so to speak; she was at once "the most conventional and unconventional person in the world,"[29] entirely self-created and conscious that she had wrested her own destiny from "whatever gods there be." She had a child by Wells, Anthony West, a troubled and lonely boy whom she raised, as Dorothy raised Michael Lewis, with only one theme in mind — that she knew best about everything under the sun. Rebecca was also a friend of Sinclair Lewis's, but in 1928 she had refused to attend his and Dorothy's wedding.

"I was abroad," she explained, "and even if I had been in London I doubt if I could have borne to go . . . , so sure was I that all would be for the worst."[30] Rebecca had a workman's admiration for Red, but she found him "impossible to love as one loved Dorothy,"[31] and when she came to the United States, as she did more and more often after World War II, it was frequently as Dorothy's guest. By that time they had both settled down in their final marriages, Dorothy to Maxim Kopf and Rebecca to Henry Andrews, a gentle, more than minutely boring City businessman whom Rebecca herself described as being "rather like a dull giraffe." On at least one occasion she contrived to have Dorothy invite her to New York "for some vague reason" just so she could get away from him.[32] It wasn't that her husband wasn't "sweet," said Rebecca: "Only as voluble as Ernestine Evans, and a promoter of chaos not to be believed. I wonder that I am sane."[33] As to the "chaos," it was Rebecca's experience that "the business of being a writer immediately involves one in a multitude of things which might have been specially designed to prevent one writing."[34] She had an ongoing problem with "squatters," for instance, and a host of distant cousins who appeared to have no homes of their own.

"Let her believe," said Dorothy about one of Rebecca's eternally undeparted guests, "— encourage her to believe — that you are an artist, and that all artists are ever on the brink of insanity."[35] Dorothy herself had become "*neurotic* about privacy" since marrying Maxim, and one of the reasons Rebecca was always welcome in her house was because she liked "Maxie" so much.[36] A high point of Dinah Sheean's acquaintance with both Dorothy and Rebecca was seeing them, after the Republican Convention of 1952, engaged in a hilarious imitation of Clare Boothe Luce, who had turned up in Chicago "in her peek-a-boo dress, with her Bo-Peep eyes" and her rather enormous ambition for a political appointment in the Eisenhower administration.[37] Normally Dorothy was careful to defend Clare "against her catty women 'friends,'"[38] but with Rebecca, sometimes, she might have been a teenager at an overnight slumber party. They exchanged recipes, dresses, effulgent praise. "When I think how calm and happy she was . . . ," said Rebecca of Dorothy in those years, "I could weep — but we all start as grazing land and end up as ploughed fields."[39]

In the future, Dorothy and Rebecca would be drawn together as much by sorrow and disappointment as in mutual admiration, but for now, while both were at the height of their powers, they regarded themselves as a united front in "The Age of Lunacy" (the phrase is Dorothy's).[40] Their political views were identical in the sense that they were based on a fundamental duality — "eternal duels," said Victoria Glendinning, Rebecca's biographer, "between light and darkness, good and evil, life and death, male and female."[41] In the thirties the enemy had been Hitler; in the forties and fifties it was Stalin and the leaders of the Soviet bloc. Dorothy moved away, eventually, from strict anticommunism, in the belief that the problems of mankind were essentially spiritual and that "the opposite of Communism is not any form of government, but in the spirit and faith that we live by."[42] But from 1946, roughly, through the middle of the Korean War, hers may be said to have been one of the strongest anti-Communist voices in America. There were many who believed that she was suffering from "the neurotic crisis that follows the loss of an *idée fixe*" (her obsession with Hitler, in other words);[43] and indeed, she observed in a letter to Frances Gunther that the United States, at the end of World War II, was still "inextricably tied to the enemy. We cannot imagine living without the enemy. We are in mortal fear of what would happen to all of us without an enemy. That terror — of life without the enemy — is what terrifies *me*."[44]

In 1946 Dorothy found out that Hermann Budzislawski, her prized research assistant and the man who had introduced her to Maxim Kopf, was a Communist.[45] Dorothy had been warned about "Budzi" when he first came to America, but she believed that talk was cheap and that stool pigeons were reprehensible, and when Budzi applied for his resident papers she appeared as a character witness in his behalf. Throughout the war Budzislawski lived with his wife and daughter in the Old House at Twin Farms — sleeping in Dorothy's beds, dining off her china, and briefing her daily from a leftist perspective that seemed to her to be entirely innocent in its sympathy toward the Soviet Union.

"His general line was that we must not disturb the war effort," Dorothy recalled; "that the alliance with Russia would work out for the benefit of all concerned; that the dissolution of the Comintern was a sincere gesture; that compromises would necessarily have to be made all around. . . . There was nothing unique about this — it was the [line] officially taken in Washington and London." Gradually Dorothy was able to discern that Budzislawski had been counseling her "from an extremely slanted position" and that rather a lot of "fellow-traveling" copy was going out under her name. But it was only in 1945, when she started cabling dispatches from Europe concerning Soviet "treachery" at the end of the war, that she began to wonder about Budzislawski's allegiance:

> I had talked with exiles from the Polish and Yugoslavian resistance movements [Dorothy remembered], who told tales of Communist terror, and in the British zone of Austria I saw with my own eyes thousands of men, women and children trying to escape into Austria from Yugoslavia and being pushed back weeping and screaming by British officers. . . . I read the articles of Jacques Duclos, the French Communist, . . . clearly foreshadowing the end of Soviet cooperation. I was in Europe when the twelve members of the Polish anti-Nazi underground were kidnapped to Russia at the opening of the San Francisco conference, and I was aware that almost the last thing F.D.R. did before his death was to send a protest to Stalin. From these and a thousand other clues I saw that while *we* had been fighting the war under a United Nations front, for the object of liberating the European nations from Hitler's yoke and making it possible for them to work out a new life "of their own choosing," the Communists had been exploiting the resistance movements with the object of making themselves and the Soviet Union dominant in all Europe. And much of this went into my cabled columns.

She had a showdown with Budzislawski almost immediately after her return from Europe in the summer of 1945. "He practically issued me an ultimatum to stop writing about these things," said Dorothy. "I reminded him that his services were those of a research worker and analyst and not of a monitor. Upon this, he almost burst into tears and assured me that he could not go on because, as he said, 'I don't want to be martyred.' His opinion was that the Soviets would sweep the world and that I would go down in that sweep, together with himself if he remained with me." What Dorothy did not realize was that Budzislawski, throughout the war, had been claiming to Communist party members that he himself was the author of "90 percent" of her material; when she began to turn severely anti-Soviet in her commentary, he was naturally put on the spot. Later, having left Dorothy's employ "without so much as a 'thank-you,' " he went back to Germany and was rewarded with a position as a professor of sociology at the University of Leipzig, in the Soviet Zone. By that time, too, he had revised his story somewhat: Dorothy Thompson was "a composite," he maintained, a whole collection of "anti-Socialist warmongers" who wrote under the name of a woman in order to gain sympathy for their cause.[46]

Dorothy was more disappointed, at first, than frightened or outraged by Budzislawski's treachery. "I long for a world, once again," she sighed, "like the world in which I grew up, where one could safely take for granted that one's fellow creatures were what they seemed to be." In 1949, at the height of the House Un-American Activities Committee's investigations of Communists in America, she went public with the story in a long article for the *Saturday Evening Post*, which she called "My Red Herring" but which the *Post*'s editors, in tune with the times, quickly renamed "How I Was Duped by a Communist."[47] Most of Dorothy's friends (and especially Jack Wheeler, her editor at the Bell Syndicate) had tried to discourage her from exposing herself in this way, but she regarded the exercise as "a public service" at a time "when many people [were] suffering from having had associations with Communists. . . . I think it useful," said Dorothy, "to show how this may occur, innocently, and even through one's better nature."[48]

Indeed, Dorothy's attitude toward the Un-American Activities Committee, the McCarthy "witch hunts," and the whole period of anticommunist agitation in the United States was neither so approving nor so confused as it appeared to her contemporaries. She had no objection in principle to congressional investigations of Communists and suspected Communists. She did not believe for an instant "that the fear of the West [was] hysterical or trumped-up."[49]

"I am absolutely convinced," she wrote to John Haynes Holmes, the chairman of the American Civil Liberties Union and minister of the Community Church in New York, "that the American Communist Party is a section of the International Communist Party, having no autonomous powers whatsoever, and [that it] is dedicated to the overthrow of this government and thereafter to the complete suppression of each and every form of civil liberty. . . . Had I been a German, I should have been in favor of the *suppression* of the Nazi Party as a murderous band of thugs, and that is equally my opinion of the Communists."[50] For all of that, Dorothy believed that McCarthyism, as a political force, was "childish, and positively useful to the cause it seeks to injure."[51] She foresaw "a lot of petty persecution and no solution whatsoever" so long as the Communist party remained legal in America.[52] By 1954 she was calling the Army-McCarthy hearings "the most ridiculous and scandalous performance of irresponsible sleuths in our history."[53] She wrote to Jimmy Sheean:

> You know I wouldn't lift a finger to defend anyone I suspected of being a Communist. . . . But this business of staging trials, as it were, outside the discomforts of law, . . . with the purpose, not of effecting legal penalties, but of punishing persons by bringing them into disrepute, is a travesty of justice. I said so when the New Dealers were similarly pillorying "Economic Royalists." Then my "liberal" friends branded me a "reactionary" and — recall — a "tool of Wall Street." But I just damned well knew that if this sort of thing could be done, by and by it would be the liberals' turn. It always is. Like packing the Supreme Court. If F.D.R. could do it, so could a successful political opponent sitting in his chair. . . . Let us, therefore, says I, abide by the law and by the spirit of the law, lest the two-edged sword be one day wielded against us.[54]

On the other hand, the threat was real — nobody who saw the collapse of Eastern Europe in the immediate postwar years could deny that the threat was real. "I submit that the nightmare world in which we live is the direct result of fighting a world war for no comprehensible objective," said Dorothy. "We fought only for victory and for Unconditional Surrender. One member of the coalition, however [Russia], fought for a clear objective: the extension of its global power, and the adding of the enemy potential to its own, as a step toward knocking out its wartime allies in the next round."[55] "The fact is," she went on, "Communism has become an instrument for a state which, throughout its history, has been Messianic and Imperialistic."[56] At heart, during the McCarthy years, Dorothy was grappling with the same issues that had preoccupied her during the heyday of the German-American Bund. She was dealing with questions of free speech; she was worrying about the breadth of foreign influence and the extension of constitutional protection to an organization that had as its goal the subversion of the Constitution.

"To my mind," she wrote, "any political activity is allowable in a constitutional order except fifth columns (which are traitorous) and organizations whose ultimate purpose is to abolish the civil liberties of the people. If Communists told their real aims they would be no menace at all. But prevarication concerning aims is a fundamental thesis of their strategy. There is a philosophical question involved here that cannot be answered so glibly as civil libertarians do."[57] The Constitution had never guaranteed the rights of any "socio-economic system," Dorothy conceded; it did, however, explicitly guarantee the rights of individuals, and she thought that one solution to the problem of communism in the United States might be to outlaw "*any* group that seeks to disrupt or remove or abrogate those [individual] rights."[58]

She reached the highest point of her anxiety in 1948, the "dreadful year" of the Berlin airlift[59] and the fall of Czechoslovakia to the Communist government of Klement Gottwald. In March Jan Masaryk, who had had a hand in bringing Maxim Kopf to America in 1941 and who had returned to Prague after the war as Czech foreign minister, was found dead in the courtyard outside his room in the center of the city. His friends would debate for many years about whether Masaryk had committed suicide (as Dorothy believed), in order to protest "the murder of his country" by the Communists,[60] or been assassinated by the very people whom, through his acceptance of their presence in the Czech government, he had helped to put into power.

"We *do* stand helpless before parties and movements whose essence is violence," Dorothy wrote after Masaryk's death, "because we are insufficiently prepared to oppose them by every peaceful, political, and legitimate means. You can invent any theory you like about the case of Jan Masaryk. But the plain fact is that the movement he helped support killed him. Today a set of unconscionable gangsters runs Czechoslovakia. . . . They are not even 'Communists' if Communism means anything at all. They are careerists. And they are trained instruments of Russian imperialism, as cynical as you will find."[61] Dorothy had seen Masaryk only days before he went back to Prague, at a party at John Gunther's; he had assured her then that the *independence* of Czechoslovakia was foremost on his mind, and that his government would surely reach some kind of understanding with Moscow.

"Socialist economics," Masaryk told Dorothy with a fine wave of the hand, "— okay. But if anyone tries to take away our freedom — freedom to think and say what you believe — the right to your own thoughts, your own soul. . . ."

"Could he have resisted?" Dorothy wondered later. "Who can resist a totalitarian state? Therein lies the absolute wickedness of the Potsdam jeer at the Germans for 'applauding' and 'blindly obeying' [the Nazis]. Shall we now calumniate the whole Czech people for also 'applauding' and 'obeying' with their lives at stake? Let those who are absolutely sure that they have the stuff of martyrs in them cast the first stone."[62] The death of Masaryk left Dorothy terrified. "I am afraid," she wrote to Marcia Davenport, Masaryk's lover, who was recovering from shock in London. "I am afraid all the time. I cry sometimes, and shiver, from an *unknown* fear. It was not my personal feeling for Jan but something else that made me have hysterics, right there in a hotel lobby, when I saw the headlines in the afternoon paper. I had to rush to my room with screams in my throat and tears falling like floods. . . . I am sorry, sorry, sorry, with part of the awful sorriness I feel over everything in this world."[63]

Her columns were filled with terrible warnings about what the future would hold if something were not done to revitalize American society. She never gave vent to her "anti-Soviet fever" without simultaneously lambasting the United States for its complacency and its refusal to stand by its democratic principles "in *all* matters, everywhere." Dorothy was worried especially about the decline of the religious spirit in America — referring not to "Churchianity," as she made the distinction (for she still despised the "pharisees and hypocrites" of organized religion), but to the "positive standards and values" that had built America from scratch. Many of her letters from this period closed with the dark advice that "Dostoevsky's prophecy" was about to be fulfilled, and that the earth, at the millennium, "would weep for its old gods."

"Woe to Those Who Destroy the Altars!" she cried in the *Ladies' Home Journal.* "For new altars will surely be built, to idols with terrible faces and bloody hands, carrying whips and swords. Such is the judgment of history, ancient and modern."[64] It was the banishment of "any notion of the absolute" that staggered Dorothy: the complete secularization of American life; the "doctrine of relativism" taught in the schools; the rejection of the idea that there even *might* be some power in the universe, some orderly force, that was "greater by far than man and his works."

"Do we think that only in this age men could have spread plagues," Dorothy wondered, "poisoned populations, taken slaves? That it was only lack of *know-how* that restrained our ancestors from such horrors even in war? They were restrained, as we are not, by imperatives which they (in their backwardness?) believed were fashioned of God."[65] The winter of 1947–1948 had seen the first of many attempts to ban the installation of Christmas trees, *crèches*, and other religious decorations in government buildings, and Dorothy was moved to swipe at atheists, "disgruntled rabbis," and that "cheap humanitarianism, or humanity worship," as she called it, which made no distinction between liberty and nihilism.[66] It was not the business of the state, said Dorothy, "to force, by its decisions, the clearance of the air for every cult or group" that might be offended by tradition. The "splintering" of America was a dangerous thing indeed.[67]

In the spring of 1948 she sent a letter to President Harry S Truman, begging him, as she had once begged Harold Nicolson when Hitler's armies were threatening Poland, to call "a day of national prayer" in response to the spread of communism in Europe. "I do not mean a day of sermons and speech-making," Dorothy explained, "but a day of intense concentration and silent prayer — everywhere — the mother in the home; the worker in the factory; the farmer in the spring plowing — all praying Our Lord's prayer, that His will should be done." The Communist presence was especially strong in Italy at that time, and Dorothy persisted in believing that through pure good will "and utter concentration" Americans might "contribute in some unfathomable way" to the triumph of freedom in the West.[68] In "On the Record" she related the tale of Jimmy Sheean's black cook, Eva, who, before accepting her post in the Sheean household, had announced that she would have to pray about it first.

"I find extraordinary sanity in her decision," said Dorothy. "Stated in secular terms, in concentrated meditation and a humble spirit, she wrestled with her conscience to find out what it was right for her to do. . . . In the present state of our civilization a worker (or employer) who asks himself such questions and regards the answers as a commandment of God may seem slightly touched, even to the beneficiaries. It is, however, a comment on the moral crisis of our times if so simple an ethical attitude seems crazy."[69] To drive her point home Dorothy devoted a number of columns to Mohandas K. Gandhi, who in January 1948 was killed in India, leaving behind a legacy of nonviolent resistance and immense spiritual power — "some sort of radiation," in Dorothy's ironic phrase, "that time and again caused weapons to drop from the hands of India's governors. Did [Gandhi] not really — one man alone — 'soften the hearts' of the violent?"[70]

But Truman was not Gandhi, and no day of prayer was on the White House agenda. The President was "unattended by the muses," Dorothy complained. He was an "intellectual nonentity." His "radio receiving stations [were] out of order."[71] The most that could be said for him was that he was preferable to Thomas E. Dewey, his opponent in the 1948 presidential election, whose ideas on battling communism, as they evolved, filled Dorothy with amazement. It was here that she most confused her readers, because while she was ready to attack communism at every turn as a vile and cowardly, irreligious thorn in the side of humanity, she did not believe that the United States was fitted to the role of world policeman. She was less afraid of a "Russian attack" than she was of a continual dissipation of American forces and morale. She was "petrified" about the consequences for America of making politics subservient indefinitely to military strategy.

"Every Communist victory in the world," she observed, "is, without exception, the result of two world wars fought as 'Crusades' for illimitable, millennial, and unattainable objectives. Only within the framework of such wars has it ever been possible for Communists to set up armies-within-armies and governments-within-governments with which they could turn a war initiated for other aims into a war victorious for their own. Communism is a virus activated by war, and thus far activated only by war."[72] The "conflict of ideologies," meanwhile, was "a lot of shadow-boxing — a search after scapegoats instead of after truth."[73]

"We are asked to contemplate . . . a hemorrhage of savings and income," Dorothy protested,

> along with inflation, declining purchasing power, hardly veiled military dictatorship over the economy, [the] inability of our youth to plan their lives or even envisage a stable future, as a means — of all things — of checking revolution. And we are expected to follow through until 800,000,000 people in other states overthrow their gov-

ernments (presumably with our aid and yet without war) or until these governments decide to come on their knees to the Canossa in Washington.

Gentlemen, would you kindly sit down for ten quiet minutes and think![74]

She appeared at all three national political conventions in 1948 in a mood of intense crabbedness — there were three conventions that year because former Vice President Henry A. Wallace was running for office as the candidate of the Progressive party. Dorothy was obsessed with Wallace, seeing in his populist campaign the classic shape of Communist exploitation, as well as another nail in the coffin of "reason and good will" in American life.[75] Wallace himself, as Dorothy knew, was not a member of the Communist party: "He is incapable of being anything that requires a mind built around coherent ideas," she said. But he was "surrounded" by Communists, and he was a tool of Moscow, in Dorothy's opinion, "if ever there was one." In column after column she attacked Wallace as the "American Fierlinger" — the reference was to Zdenek Fierlinger, the Czech prime minister who "looked the other way" when the Communists seized power in Prague — and at one convention press conference, while other reporters were wondering whether or not to take Wallace seriously, Dorothy rose to her feet and demanded that he answer the questions that were being put to him about his Communist connections. She won the silent admiration of every correspondent in the hall that day,[76] but more and more during this period, "out of temper" with the times, she was becoming a figure of fun among her colleagues. When she ran across a particularly unflattering photograph of herself in a New York paper, she marched off to Louis Nizer with the aim of filing suit.

"The malicious intention toward Dorothy could easily be discerned . . . ," wrote Nizer, who nevertheless talked her out of taking legal action. "[The photograph] caught her [with her] mouth wide open, eyes distended, hair standing straight up as if lifted by electric shock, copious breasts without a waistline so that they became part of a protruding stomach, and a clenched fist on top of a trunk-like arm to add a touch of belligerence to the pose."[77] Nor were press photographers the only cads on the political scene. H. L. Mencken was at the conventions that summer, presiding over the usual swilling of beer, and at the end of "the Wallace Show"

— "this grotesque combination of revolution and turkey-in-the-straw," Dorothy called it, "of snakelike venom and sentimental corn"[78] — he invited Dorothy to a farewell party at his hotel.

"She was drawn to the food like a castaway," said Alistair Cooke, who was covering the convention for the *Manchester Guardian* and counted himself a crony of Mencken:

> and [she] kept wolfing it helplessly and declaring between gulps that her doctor had warned her against letting her figure go to rack and ruin. Mencken twirled his cigar in his lips and relieved the general embarrassment by professing to be shocked at such an obviously inept diagnosis. "Never trust the medicos and butchers, Dorothy," he cried, and after a pause and a puff, "Why, Dorothy, you were never lovelier, you were never in better heft." He went on this way, and it was a relief to all of us to see Miss Thompson wriggle her great frame in simple delight. She was the only woman present, and after a while she too sensed our trade-union impatience with her and left. She was no sooner heard plodding down the corridor than Mencken looked at the froth on his stein and said sadly, "My God, she's an elephant, isn't she?"[79]

She actually voted for Norman Thomas, the socialist candidate, in 1948; it was her way of protesting the lack of any "serious ideas" in the major parties. "There are too many lawyers making our policy," she grumbled in a letter to Walter Lippmann. "The legal mind, which always thinks that you can win a case on points, is not at all equipped to guide any country in the present crisis."[80] Dorothy was waiting for "a statesman" to appear, someone who realized, as she did, that the really great problems were never " 'solved,' but slowly and imperceptibly *absorbed*, until one fine day it is seen that they simply no longer exist."[81] With this reasoning she reconciled her militant anticommunism with her steady faith in the balance of world power: "Peaceable relations between sovereign states can only be based on common interest, from the viewpoint of the security of each."[82] For the rest of her life she would function without a flagship paper, as an "independent" commentator, subject to cancellation without notice, censored regularly by local editors, and not knowing from one day to the next whether she would still be read by the thousands of people who wrote to praise or condemn her. "Politically," said one of her friends, "she was like a great ship left stranded on the beach after the tide had gone out."[83] There were many who thought she should have dropped "On the Record" in 1947, when the *New York Post* dropped her. Her old nemesis Clare Boothe Luce, in fact, even wrote to suggest it.

"There isn't another woman in America with as much brains and heart as you have," Clare remarked tactfully. "And courage. I wish you could cut free from that column altogether, for a half year, and let people miss you for a while. And *then* tell them." [84] But Dorothy was "stuck in the column position"; she was bound to its rhythms; she "needed the money." If she had one continuing function, she said, it was to be "a bubble in the mass," [85] "to forestall the prophecy (attributed to Churchill) that 'America will be the only great state to pass from infancy to senility without ever becoming adult.'

"Since this nation adores youth," Dorothy continued, "loves action, and despises thought (except the limited thought of the scientist, technician and 'expert'), and since most of our leaders (including the President of the United States) are abominably educated, such advocacy cannot be popular and is probably futile." [86] She sympathized with anyone who thought she had become boring, that she was "old and dull," that she was "pawing the air." But "in general," she maintained, "these are hard days in which to write," and she did not apologize for being being "wobbly." [87] It "nearly broke [her] heart," in the summer of 1950, when the United States sent troops to Korea, to find herself simultaneously defending the action and deploring its necessity — "wobbling" again. The Korean War was the direct result of "blind commitments," Dorothy charged, which had to be honored because they *were* commitments; it was too late now to ask if they were wise ones. [88] All she prayed for in the opening days of the struggle was that the United States would not regard the atomic bomb as a means of settling the matter.

"Many Americans," she observed, "including most atomic scientists, already have a deep sense of guilt about the use of the bomb against Hiroshima and Nagasaki, which all the rationalizations of this Administration have been unable to remove." Not for nothing were the 1950s the decade of Godzilla and the UFO. Dorothy was fascinated by the number of people who had suddenly begun to spot flying saucers in the sky and were convinced, on that account, that retribution was at hand. She was concerned as never before about "the atomization of morale." [89] At Twin Farms she detected "a weird sense of unreality" and watched as her husband painted a magnificent, eight-foot-high Resurrection. The body of Christ was "suspended," Dorothy reported, "and somehow rising, against a backdrop of rose-red, the color of sunrise." When she looked at Maxim's painting, she imagined that it was not of Christ but of Apollo, and "Christ or Apollo or both," she said, "I wish they would rise, or be born again."[90]

JIMMY SHEEAN was one of those people who had actually seen a flying saucer, in Springfield, Illinois, where he was visiting Governor Adlai E. Stevenson. "It harasses one's intellect, believe me," Jimmy remarked,[91] but by this time he was used to his own "unreasonable perceptions," to "dreams, visions, struggles and trances,"[92] and all of his friends were used to him. He was unmistakably the enfant terrible of the journalistic world, greatly beloved by a whole generation of foreign correspondents and their spouses; catered to by a series of exasperated and adoring women; put up with, tolerated, comforted, cajoled, and nursed through his "shemozzles" with limitless patience.[93] Dorothy was not the only witness present on the day in September 1947 when Jimmy came to her to say that he had to leave for India at once.

"I am at the end of my tether in the search for the meaning of life," he confessed. "I feel I shall find it through Gandhi. But the time is short, for Gandhi is going to be assassinated within six months, and by a Hindu. You know that, don't you?" And he looked at Dorothy "anxiously." For Jimmy, it was only the beginning of a long love affair with Eastern mysticism, a preoccupation that was almost as consuming as his passion for Italian opera. He was standing not forty feet away from Gandhi when the assassin's bullet hit, and later that year, when he came back to Twin Farms, he had a revelation of "a dreadful event" taking place in Jerusalem. He ran to Dorothy and cried, "Somebody is being murdered. I think it is the Mufti."[94]

The vision was correct in all particulars but one: the dead man was Count Folke Bernadotte, the Swedish prince appointed by the United Nations to mediate between the Arab and Jewish populations of Palestine. Bernadotte was shot by Zionist terrorists almost at the very moment Jimmy spoke about it; in future, Dorothy was inclined to heed her friend's premonitions.[95]

"As you know," she wrote to Jimmy, "I have stubbornly opposed for years modern rationalism, which is irrational, *au fond,* because it willfully excludes authentic experience."[96] She listened calmly when Jimmy told her that he was the only person alive who could bring peace to the Middle East — that he could "effect a pow-wow,"

August 1934: Dorothy arrives in Paris after her expulsion from Nazi Germany.

Helen Rogers Reid, publisher and editorial guiding spirit of the *New York Herald Tribune.* "We need a contract with Mrs. Sinclair Lewis," her memo read, "to do a column three times a week. . . ."

Sailing for Europe: Jimmy and Dinah Sheean.

Dorothy in 1937, following the debut of "On the Record." "Her gloom is gargantuan," said Ilka Chase, "but her fighting spirit is as unquenchable as Donald Duck's, and glows through the chaos like a steadfast flame."

Dorothy (*center*) at the rally of the German-American Bund in Madison Square Garden, February 1939. She is surrounded by a detachment of "Storm Troopers" and a body of New York City police, who are about to escort her from the building.

"Cassandra" in her heyday. She attended a rally for aid to Finland with former President Herbert Hoover and Fiorello La Guardia, mayor of New York (*opposite above*); sat at Columbia Pictures' "Roundtable of the Screen" with fellow journalists (*left to right*) Linton Wells, William L. Shirer, and Wythe Williams, who had given her her first break as a young journalist in Paris (*opposite*); and fought against polio with Mary Pickford (*at left*) and Eleanor Roosevelt (*above*).

May 1940: Dorothy inspects the French fortifications of the Maginot Line.

In London during the Blitz. She was a figure of benevolent inspiration very nearly the equal of Florence Nightingale.

With Clare Boothe Luce (*left*) in 1941. Their "feud," said Clare, was "somewhat overpublicized."

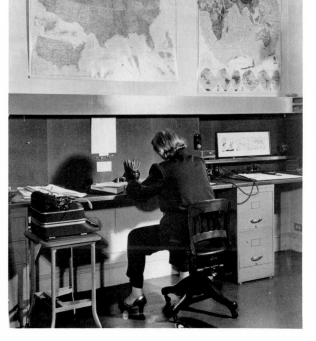

Dorothy at work in her office "command post."

Dorothy in her house at Turtle Bay, photographed for *Look* magazine. Her giant sofa had room for "five of the most distinguished bottoms in New York."

Michael Lewis, age twelve.

Dorothy being sculpted by Jo Davidson.

Maxim Kopf, Dorothy's third husband, with his portrait of Paul Robeson.

Dorothy at the end of World War II: "I see no end in sight of terror, no consequential moral position anywhere, and no definitions, either, of anything."

Dorothy and Maxim's wedding in Barnard, June 1943. He was "the man I should have married in the first place."

In Maxim's studio.

Rebecca West at Twin Farms.

Dorothy at her annual birthday celebration. Behind her is Dale Warren, her editor and "the best friend any woman ever had."

On the terrace of the Big House, *left to right:* Jane Gunther, Dinah Sheean, John Gunther, Dorothy, Jimmy Sheean.

Dorothy in Cairo, 1952.

Dorothy and Maxim in
Palestine, May 1945.

After Maxim's death.
Left to right: Michael,
Bernadette, Dorothy,
Gregory, and John Paul
Lewis.

Dorothy, Gregory, and
Bernadette in Sauk Cen-
ter, Minnesota, during
the Sinclair Lewis cele-
brations, July 1960.

Popperfoto

anyway, among the Zionist Chaim Weizmann, Azzam Pasha, the general secretary of the Arab League, and the Grand Mufti of Jerusalem, the spiritual head of Moslems in Palestine. Jimmy was friendly with all of the parties in the quarrel.

"There is nobody else in the world that I know of who stands in [the same] relation to these three men," he said to Dorothy just before the partition of Palestine and the birth of the State of Israel. "Therefore my duty as a human being is perfectly clear, inasmuch as there isn't anybody else to do it: I have to try to bring them together." [97] Jimmy felt the same way about the situations in India, where he regarded himself as the spiritual descendant of Mahatma Gandhi and a wise old man in the entourage of Jawaharlal Nehru, and in China, where he hoped to use his influence with the Soong sisters to effect peace, first on the mainland and later in Korea.

"It is all very well of you to tell me to mind my own business," Jimmy wrote to Dorothy during the Korean War, begging her for some "practical advice" about the situation in the Far East. "You always say that. . . . [But] remember I bear the *darshan* of the Mahatma.* It is mighty — mightier than the atomic bomb. . . . Since you have never been in India you do not realize the unbelievable *darshan* that I have. . . . I can absolutely guarantee that the government of India will do whatever I tell [it] to do. Now please, in the name of Christ Jesus Our Lord, *tell me something*." [98]

Dorothy had stepped in as a kind of guardian for Jimmy Sheean at a difficult time in his life. In 1945 Jimmy's wife, Dinah, had divorced him and fled home to her family in England. For ten years Dinah had tried to fit in with Jimmy's circle and to feel that she was something more than "a glorified object" alternately to be displayed or set aside as the mood struck. She had never felt a part of things at Twin Farms, but she was hardly alone in that respect among the wives of Dorothy's friends. Nobody forgot the night when Dorothy, during a lull in a fierce debate she was having with Jimmy and John Gunther about the future of Palestine, suddenly turned to Gunther's young wife, Jane, whom she ordinarily ignored.

"Why, Jane," said Dorothy, with no apparent intent to wound, "you have such pretty *feet!*" [99] She had "a curiously mixed attitude" toward other women. On the one hand she generally found them

---

* *Darshan* is a Hindu concept, not easily captured in a few lines but having to do with the blessing that accrues to a person through the viewing of another, more eminent human being.

dull and presumed them to be stupid; on the other hand, when the "high talk" ended, she cultivated "an air of protectiveness" toward them, "as if women were her special charge," as if she were obliged to guide them single-handedly through the maze of male concerns. Evelyn Baird, who was married to the arctic explorer Vilhjalmur Stefansson and lived not far away, in Bethel, remembered that the change in Dorothy's manner was sometimes lightning-quick: "It was like turning on a switch." She could be "cold" and even "rude" to the women in her house, and then suddenly she would be off in the kitchen, "rustling up some hot cakes" and advising her companions to stand their ground. "Say what you mean!" she commanded her women friends. "Say it out!!" As far as she was concerned, every woman she knew needed lessons in public speaking.[100]

"The trouble with you is you don't like these powerful women," Jimmy Sheean told Dinah as she packed her bags. "You don't like Dorothy, you don't like Clare Luce, you don't like Eve Curie."

"Nonsense, Jimmy," said Dorothy when she heard this story. "Dinah *adores* me."[101] But she was not surprised when Dinah went back to England. She realized that life with Jimmy would require more or less constant ingenuity, and that any woman in love with him was bound to have a rocky ride.[102] After Dinah left, Dorothy acted as a sponsoring angel not just for Jimmy but also for the Sheean children, Linda and Ellen, who lived with their father for months at a time in the Old House at Twin Farms. Jimmy had begun renting the place when Hermann Budzislawski vacated it; later on he bought it from Dorothy, and until he went bankrupt in 1953 he attempted to run it himself, "as a grown-up."[103]

"My sister and I were weeny Rosenkrantz and Guildensterns," Ellen Sheean recalled. "I think that possibly, with hindsight, Daddy was having a kind of breakdown at that time: Gandhi, Korea, complete writing block, McCarthy. . . . I jumble it all up as it seems to me so jumbled in the long, isolated summer times of those years." The Sheean girls were both tomboys, "unkempt, *farouche,* barefoot from June to September," and every now and then Dorothy would take them to Woodstock to have their hair cut and to buy them clothes that were not "raggedy." She enjoyed the opportunity to dote on "Jimmy's girls," and while she sometimes terrified the more introspective Linda (who always feared she was reading "the wrong books" when Dorothy asked her about it),[104] she was remembered by Ellen "with great fondness, love — but of a placid sort. She was sanity and safety." Both girls' most vivid memories were of Dorothy lying in bed writing her column:

> The BEST times [were] the ARTICLE MORNINGS [said Ellen]. I'd slop on the bottom of her bed surrounded with dictionaries and reference books. She'd be sitting up with the secretaries coming in and out, her rather sparse hair screwed up in a pink bandanna and [wearing] a frilly nightie and old sweater, at least two cigarettes going unnoticed and untouched (never knew anyone who smoked so much and so little, if you know what I mean) and the typewriter on the legs . . . writing at full speed and occasionally shouting, "Look up the spelling of . . ." or "What the hell's the capital city of . . . ?"and I'd shuffle through the books and feel wildly important.
>
> I realize now that she couldn't have needed me at all and it was just a kindness. But an imaginative and good one.[105]

She was still going out every morning in the summer and tending to her garden, which had become more colorful and rich and "immense" with each passing year. Ellen Sheean remembered Dorothy's "rather posh daisies" and the "*huge* roses" that were somehow "just like Dorothy" herself: "big and colorful and full-flower always." One summer, during a drought, Jimmy and his daughters led the whole neighborhood in a Hopi rain dance that actually — so everyone said — brought on "buckets of rain." It rained so hard and for so long that Jimmy felt obliged to apologize to the state authorities; he promised to do what he could to call off the torrents.[106] And nobody laughed when he said so. Vermont was a place where "character" was respected and where any kind of person might feel at home, be it Jimmy, who streaked through the woods during hunting season shouting at the deer, "Shoo! Scat, you fools! Hurry off to Canada!";[107] or Mrs. Lucille Miller, a famous local crackpot, who telephoned Twin Farms from time to time to "rant about Communism"; or a mysterious black woman, entirely conspicuous in those particular hills, who strolled down the drive one day singing "Jesus Walks This Lonesome Valley" and stayed long enough to engage Jimmy and Dorothy in a debate about the Second Coming.

They argued about any topic that might concern them, whether it was serious or unimportant or entirely incidental. They talked about the relative intelligence of cats and dogs; about houseflies, and whether they were more likely to find their way indoors in sunny or in cloudy weather; about the best way to grill steak ("But it *tastes* different" over charcoal, Jimmy insisted, "it *tastes* different. Won't you admit that it *tastes* different?").[108] Dorothy and Jimmy did not "fight" with each other in the ordinary sense. They "discussed" their business at the top of their lungs, and in the memory of Linda Sheean, "Dorothy never came to us; Daddy always went to her." He went to her "whenever she whistled," Dinah Sheean remarked sourly; year after year she "smothered him with the sledge-hammer repetition of her opinions on all subjects."[109] Jimmy told his friends that when he died, he wanted only women pallbearers at the funeral: Dorothy at the head of the procession, Dinah at the foot, Clare Boothe Luce on one side of the coffin, and Greta Garbo on the other.[110] After his experiences with Gandhi he changed his mind and declared that he wished to be cremated; Dorothy could flush the ashes down the toilet, if she liked.

"Ashes aren't like that, Jimmy," said Dorothy briskly. "They would ruin the plumbing."[111] Those of their friends who regretted that Jimmy had fallen so completely under Dorothy's spell (and there were many of these, especially among the tough-guy school of journalists) could not have known that her bossiness and her relentless pragmatism were about the only things that held him together in those years. When he found her one day tending a crabapple tree, he heaved a great sigh and lamented, "What sense is there in pruning trees and mowing lawns — it will all be destroyed."

"Well," said Dorothy, "when the end comes, Twin Farms is going to arrive in eternity washed and combed, with every hair in place."[112] She took all of Jimmy's feelings seriously, but she bade him to consider one thing well: why had he gone all the way to India "to find what is everywhere, and at home; to find, as it seems to me, Christ via Gandhi?" She did not think that Christ was "so small, or so confined" as the Christians made him. In the meantime, she advised Jimmy to remain *constant* to one belief or another; nine tenths of the spiritual life, she said, was a matter of practice.

"Might I say that Gandhi himself resisted the temptation of mysticism," Dorothy added. "So did Christ. Neither drowned himself in his revelation but sought to share it, in simple sweetness. . . . One does not have to 'understand' all this to *know* it."[113]

It was in the summer of 1947 that Jimmy Sheean first had the idea that Dorothy should run for President of the United States. His hope, as he expressed it in an article for *Look* magazine,[114] was "to convince the whole mass of the world's population that we want peace and mean peace. . . . I suggest," said Jimmy, "that only by symbols comprehensible to all peoples in all places can we overcome the wall that has been raised against us." And there could be no greater symbol of peaceful intention, surely, than the presence of a majestic woman at the helm of state. Jimmy was so "hipped on this idea" that he actually proposed it to Herbert Hoover, the Grand Old Man of the Republican party, who replied, of course, that it was "flatly impossible" — not because it was *Dorothy* who had been proposed, but because . . . well, it was flatly impossible.

"Sheean is an Irish soothsayer," Dorothy explained to Margaret Chase Smith, who later put herself forward as a Republican candidate for the presidency,

> with extremely remarkable super-sensory perceptions (as I believe they are called). . . . Although I don't in the least share [his] psychic visions, . . . I do believe that a woman in the White House could end the Cold War (a phrase no woman would ever have invented to start with). People have confidence in women to get them out of trouble. Otherwise the people (*not* the Church) would never have elevated the Virgin Mother to the role they did, quite clearly confident that they could count on Mary more hopefully than on the Holy Ghost. . . . A little more matriarchy is what the world needs, and I know it. Period. Paragraph. [115]

In 1946 Dorothy had published the first of many articles in the *Ladies' Home Journal* concerned directly with the role of women in the search for peace. "Security for all," she reminded her readers, "aggression for none — that is the fundamental thesis of the United Nations. [But] to make the thesis real, one sovereign right — the right to wage aggressive war — must be banned by all nations, and an international power must exist to see that the ban is observed. . . . It does not require a world government beyond one single world law: a law against aggression and *preparation for aggression*." [116] In "A Woman's Manifesto" and a dozen other columns — among them her moving "A Woman Says, 'You Must Come into the Room of Your Mother Unarmed'" and "If No One Else — We, the Mothers" [117] — Dorothy gave vent to her central thesis that "a corpse is neither a Communist nor a democrat" and "a heap of smoking rubble has no owners. . . . It is not Communism and Capitalism which cannot live in the same world. It is *armed* Communism and *armed* Capitalism, bending their theories to become instruments of combat." [118] As time went on Dorothy told her friends that she had "a lot to blame myself for" — that her own "youthful crusading" in the cause of "Freedom" had doubtless contributed to "the current complete lunacy" of the West.[119]

"There is, at present," said Dorothy, "literally nothing — nothing that *is* — which we can choose with the wholehearted conviction that it is good. We are all forced to be Hamlets, fearful that in attempting to deal with one evil, we shall invoke a worse: drive our most beloved mad, stab poor harmless friends through the curtain, and eventually bring down our house and kingdom on our heads." In "A Woman's Manifesto" Dorothy tried to express something that she knew it would be hard for most people to contemplate; she was aiming to hit "some new note," to "change the wavelengths," for better or worse.

"To my mind," she wrote, "it is simply futile to talk about peace and act according to the laws of power politics. *Is* there such a thing as an 'opinion of mankind' that could call the Great Powers to their senses? I think maybe the opinion of woman-kind could, and perhaps the opinion of the *small* nations, now being forced to choose with whom to line up, while their only real desire is to line up with neither. Can no one *express* this? . . . Must it remain only a private hope in private minds?"[120] Many of Dorothy's readers wrote to ask what she herself would do, how she would respond *personally* to the Soviet threat, and she answered that among other things she would "not expect the human mind to associate peace with growing armies" in what was the most obscene, crackbrained military buildup in the history of man.

"On the contrary," wrote Dorothy, "I would talk disarmament, day in and day out, upping every Russian proposal with a more radical one. . . . I would realize that whoever says that no agreement is possible or conceivable with a potential enemy, except at the point of a gun, is making himself co-responsible for war. . . . I would concentrate on thinking *what* is right, not who is right. In sum, I would seek to put the Russians on the spiritual defensive. But that assumes a genuine belief in spiritual forces."[121] Her editors at the *Ladies' Home Journal* were "uncomfortable" with the direction of Dorothy's thinking; a few of them, indeed, were "nauseated" by her "earth-motherish" tone.[122] But her calls for disarmament were among the most courageous writing she ever did:

> Gentlemen, beware! I come . . . not to beseech but to warn. I
> come humbly, but without fear. For I am pushed forward by the hosts

of the mothers, for whom you first groped in the dark, and without whom you wander now, in the dark. . . .

Gentlemen, we would relieve you of your fears. But first you must lay aside your guns. You cannot talk to the mothers with planes and atomic bombs. You must come into the room of your mother unarmed. Then we will show you that the healing power in the world is not where you search for it, is not in the earthquake and the fire, but in the still small voice; is not in the instruments of destruction, but in the universal will to creation; is not in the intellect, even, but in the emotion of the ideal — the unquenchable faith in life, the indestructible power of love.[123]

In 1948 "A Woman's Manifesto" was reprinted in the western zones of occupied Germany; through her agent in Hamburg, Dorothy continued to enjoy a wide German readership, and her appeals for disarmament were taken up as the central documents of a fledgling women's peace group, the World Organization of Mothers of All Nations (W.O.M.A.N.). This was the brainchild of Vilma Mönckeberg-Kollmar, who helped establish branches of W.O.M.A.N. around the world, including one in New York, of which Dorothy for a time served as chairman.[124] She never gave her support unequivocally to W.O.M.A.N.; in her own estimation she was too "apocalyptic" for committee work.[125] What she admired about W.O.M.A.N. was its singleness of purpose — its demand for the revision of the United Nations Charter (in order to "break the monopoly" of the Security Council) and its unflinching assertion that the Cold War would be ended only by "a change of thinking" on the global level. In July 1951 the President of the United States (not for the last time) declared that the goal of the arms race was "to put an end to war [by] building up such strength" that the Kremlin would have to capitulate. Dorothy, when she heard this, was moved to black humor:

I keep trying to imagine the moment when the President and the generals think we have sufficient military strength to put an end to war. There will be a three-, four- or five-million-man army; American air bases, all alerted, will ring the world from the British Isles to the South Seas; General Eisenhower will have licked the Europeans into a formidable force; Mr. [John J.] McCloy [the U.S. high commissioner in Germany] will have the West Germans goosestepping again; the assembly lines will be running out a plane a minute; the stockpile of atom bombs will be as high as the national debt; there'll be a tank in every garage and gunpowder in all the chicken. And there'll be so much armament as to make disarmament a really big, dramatic thing, big enough to throw every economy into a tailspin and millions of people out of work.

Then, at that point (determined by we know not what standards of measurement), the President will say, "Enough is enough. Now let's stop war." [126]

In 1951 W.O.M.A.N., under Dorothy's direction, asked that negotiations for an end to the Korean War be taken out of the jurisdiction of the United Nations and placed in the hands of the Quakers, the international Society of Friends. "The U.N. represents the contending forces," Dorothy explained, "who have devastated Korea in a Great Power struggle, and the representatives of each bloc will negotiate only with a view to the effect of the continuing Cold War." [127] In an open letter to other women's groups, Dorothy confirmed that W.O.M.A.N. had plans for "an international Pilgrimage" to the city of Berlin, where "the two conflicting Powers meet each other in the most dangerous tension. On that spot," she announced, in the city she had loved so much in the days of her apprenticeship, "the voice of Mothers should be raised above the present battle of ideologies in behalf of one eternal truth, recognized in every religion and every human soul: that peace lies in doing unto others exactly as you would have others do unto you. . . .

"I believe the voices that speak should be strong with indignation," Dorothy went on. "I believe [our] collective voice should be affirmative with pity and love. I imagine a great solemn festival, opened, perhaps, by Beethoven's Ninth Symphony, [and followed by] very short speeches in all languages." [128] These were to be delivered not in the form of "appeals," Dorothy advised, but as *judgment*. In a letter to Carl Zuckmayer she remarked that the pilgrimage to Berlin "must be *stupendous*, not by mere size, but by the drama of what occurs." There was to be no distinction made between one superpower and the other. There was to be "not one word about 'Democracy,' 'Freedom' — all verbal rubbish today." [129] There was to be, simply, "an unbending opposition to the force of arms, marshalled by any nation," for any reason whatsoever. Dorothy was willing to agree with anyone who told her that it might already be too late: her "Woman's Manifesto" was "frankly a *ballon d'essai*."

"But one does not have to believe that one will be successful," she

argued, "in order to advocate what one believes." And "if all popular peace demonstrations are to be confined to Communist or
Communist-inspired groups, we are handing them the greatest
weapon of psychological strategy that exists."[130] It was other
women, oddly enough, who attacked Dorothy most vociferously for
her "vague" and "unrealistic" proposals. It was Eleanor Roosevelt
who stated outright, in her capacity as leader of the American delegation to the United Nations' disarmament conference in Paris, that
W.O.M.A.N. was a tool of the Communists.

"At a time when Soviet-inspired and -directed 'peace movements'
are seeking to infiltrate and maneuver women's groups in various
parts of the world, and especially in Germany," Mrs. Roosevelt
warned, "it is essential for all women's organizations to be on guard,
and to be precise in the positions they take in order to avoid being
used in behalf of false peace propaganda." Mrs. Roosevelt was
alarmed enough by the prospect of the W.O.M.A.N.-sponsored "Pilgrimage to Berlin" that she sent out a form letter to women's groups
across America, in which she expressed her "shock" that Dorothy
Thompson, in her zeal for disarmament, could bracket the United
States "with the Soviet Union as equally guilty of bad faith" in
the Cold War.[131] And yet that was the central argument of
W.O.M.A.N.'s thesis: *all* of the great powers were guilty; the United
States, no less than Soviet Russia, was a menace to mankind so long
as it insisted on the maintenance and development of nuclear arms;
the leaders in Washington and Moscow, whether "pro-Jefferson or
pro-Marx," were in any case "definitely pre-Einstein."[132]

"We fail to find anything 'vague' in our proposals," Dorothy answered Mrs. Roosevelt. "Nor do we have faith that any scheme of
partial reduction of armies and armaments would work out in practice." The fifteen-year pause between the end of World War I and
the rearmament of Germany under Hitler, during which all of the
nations of Europe had struggled to find their way to "partial" disarmament, had ended with no positive result, and this "in a far more
favorable" atmosphere, said Dorothy, than currently existed: "This
whole period proves to us that if disarmament is necessary for peace,
it must be *total* disarmament, because no yardstick can be found for
a 'balanced reduction' of armed forces. That ground has already been
thoroughly explored."

"As far as the demonstration planned by W.O.M.A.N. in Berlin
is concerned," Dorothy went on, "we had hoped for, and anticipated

from the United States, nothing more than benevolent neutrality toward freedom of speech and opinion, which, if these rights mean anything, include the right to speak for oneself, at whatever risk, and against whatever prejudice. . . . I deeply regret that in your reply to the memorandum apropos the Woman's Manifesto . . . you found it proper to 'presume' that 'Miss Thompson has no intention of promoting Soviet objectives.' I think, Mrs. Roosevelt, that you need not 'presume' it, but that you absolutely know it." [133] In a letter to one of her editors at the Bell Syndicate, Dorothy remarked sulkily that she wished she "could write the sort of stuff that Mrs. Roosevelt writes in 'My Day,' but you have to be a President's wife, or widow, to get away that easy." [134] She would not be deterred, in any event, by the accusation that her position was "a boon" to the Communists; she did not care that the Soviet delegation to the Paris conference had recently come forward with arguments similar to her own.

"I have always chosen to follow the advice of St. Thomas à Kempis," she told Mrs. Roosevelt grandly, "not to enquire who advances an argument, but rather to enquire whether, in fact, it be true. . . . The 'plague on both your houses' which you deplore does not accurately describe the attitude of mind of W.O.M.A.N. . . . There *is* a plague on *all* our houses, which we earnestly desire to contribute to remove."

Dorothy "withdrew" from W.O.M.A.N. in 1952, exasperated by its failure of will and by its ultimate capitulation to the mainstream thinking of the day. Although plans for the march on Berlin eventually evaporated (which surprised Dorothy not at all), the effort had turned up support for her views in some widely divergent circles. For several years she carried on a mournful correspondence with Bernard Berenson, whose "utopian" views on ending war closely paralleled her own, and who agreed with her that "the age of darkness is not something distant. It is upon us; we are in it." [135] Pearl Buck wrote to say how "encouraged" she was that Dorothy had "so clear an understanding of the point at which our country stands." [136] And Walter Lippmann regretted no less than Dorothy that "the entire peace process is left to be a Communist monopoly." [137]

She went back to Twin Farms, as always, for restoration, and there she discovered that "the affection of friends, given and returned," meant more to her than ever. "All that remains for the time being," she had once written to Jan Masaryk, "as a source of comfort, recreation and faith, is private life, private friends, private beauties, private thought, and private memories."[138] In a letter to Jimmy Sheean she was cannier than that: "All I say is, don't let 'em get you. Keep your shirt on, your head on your shoulders, and remember we shall all die anyhow. . . . Don't join 'em brother, not either side of the maniac line-up. . . . Oh, as so many a poet has said: *Shit*."[139]

16

CHAPTER

MICHAEL LEWIS turned eighteen in the summer of 1948, and at the end of that year, "stunned with joy,"[1] he was accepted as a student at the Royal Academy of Dramatic Art in London. "*Nichts bleibt mir erspart,*" Dorothy sighed ("Nothing is spared me"). "I had hoped he would become a business magnate and support me in my old age, which looms on the horizon."[2] But acting was the only thing that interested Michael; it was quite plainly the passion of his life, and it did not require a great deal of argument before Dorothy was persuaded to "let him have at it." She was happy to think that her son might be on the right track at last; it had been a hellish few years in that regard.

"Mike is two inches short of six feet," Dorothy had written to Wells Lewis in 1942, when Michael was twelve, "and I think his growth has affected his wits. He gets terrible marks in school and lives entirely in a dream world, with himself as the star figure. One moment he is conducting a commando raid and the next exploring Alaska and the next committing some Chinese torture. I trust he will stop growing and grow out of it."[3] He did not: at the age of thirteen he "suddenly discovered sex" and began raiding Dorothy's liquor cabinet in more or less conscious imitation of his father.[4] Michael had built up an image of Sinclair Lewis as "a sort of renaissance prince, who lives in palaces, defies all conventions, is an internationally known drunk on two continents, immensely famous, and no matter what he does is saved by his wit and talent." Central to this picture, Dorothy feared, was Michael's view of himself as "a despised and bastard son."[5] Jimmy Sheean overheard a quarrel one day between Michael and the child of a neighbor in Vermont.

"My father is the best writer in America!" Michael said hotly.

"Oh, yeah?" his friend replied. "*My* father is the best dentist in Woodstock!"[6] And Woodstock was a lot closer to Barnard than Duluth, Minnesota, where Red holed up for a while during the 1940s; or Williamstown, Massachusetts, where he bought a farm that he only once invited Mike to visit; or Italy, where he would end his days in 1951, completely shattered by the abuse of alcohol, expiring (according to the death certificate) from "paralysis of the heart."[7] Dorothy doubted that in all the years of his parents' separation Michael saw his father more than ten times. Every now and then, entirely at Dorothy's urging, Red would conclude that some kind of reconciliation was in order, whereupon Michael would be summoned to appear at one of his father's houses. He looked forward eagerly to these trips, but invariably the meetings ended "in an aching disappointment."

"I can't really explain it," he told Dorothy later. "Every time I see Father I feel like a poor relation. . . . I am always embarrassed and he is embarrassed. I always hope we will find each other."[8] Over time, inevitably, Michael's confusion hardened into a fixed resentment. He begged Dorothy not to leave him alone with Red. He "failed, absolutely, to see any reason" why Red should be consulted about his upbringing.

"I really feel strongly about this," said Michael to Dorothy. "If you want to talk to a man, talk to *Maxim*. I certainly feel more like his son than my real father's, and why shouldn't I?"[9] At the same time, as he grew older, Michael did not hesitate to point to Red as an excuse for any failing of his own. If he was "self-destructive," it was "in the blood." If he was "intractable" and "childish" and "defiant," he was "like the old man."

"My father despised authority," said Mike conspiratorially. "Great men usually do."[10]

"He is so much like his father that it is to laugh and to weep," Dorothy exclaimed. "He has all Hal's charm, when he wants to turn it on, all Hal's consummate egotism, and also all Hal's puritan moral nature — when it comes to other people. I love him immeasurably, but never was I gladder to see anyone go off to school."[11] In 1943, when she found out that one of his teachers at Riverdale was homosexual and "a sadist,"[12] Dorothy yanked Michael out of term and sent him to the Putney School in southern Vermont. This was a famously progressive institution where students took a hand in the running of a farm while they contemplated literature, geography, and higher mathematics. The school had been warmly endorsed by all of Dorothy's friends, but Michael proved to be no happier with or better suited to country living than anything else.

"The child is all peaks and declivities," said Dorothy in exasperation. "His English teacher says that she has never known, in all the history of [her] teaching, a child who writes so easily, brilliantly, or with such a vocabulary, but that even in this course, where his gifts are greatest, he turns out Shakespearean prose and Kantian philosophy mixed with the cheapest pulp — a combination of noble literature and comic strips."[13] In this one respect, at least, Michael Lewis was the true child of both of his parents. The headmistress at Putney confirmed that he was a thoroughly bright young man, "full of imagination," but was "almost totally undisciplined," and possessed of an "overdramatic nature" that was a disturbance to everyone at the school; at the end of his first year he was not invited back.[14] "Apparently he has not comprehended a single lecture or theorem since the 4th grade," Dorothy remarked with a certain wonder. "If he doesn't reform he will be a movie star, at which point I shall disinherit him and blame it all on Red's complex."[15]

In 1944, in a complete change of approach, Dorothy sent Michael to the Valley Forge Academy, a military school, where, she insisted, he was "not unhappy" for the next two years: "He lost his slouchy, lurching way of walking, [and] admired himself in his uniform." Michael was strikingly handsome as he grew to maturity — six foot four inches tall and with a fleshy, sensual, even voluptuous body. But the discipline of Valley Forge did nothing to curb his reckless instincts. During summer vacations he was "hell to live with," and "once out of school he was wilder than ever, this always being expressed in girls and drink."[16] Michael Lewis was "abnormal" when he drank. He developed a passion for guns and cars, and by the time he was eighteen he was known throughout Windsor County as a rapscallion and a womanizer. Dorothy was so worried about him that in 1947 she considered having him "confined"; there was talk of "shock therapy,"[17] and at one point, desperate, she even appealed to Carl Jung for advice. She had never met Jung, but Freud was dead, and invariably Dorothy went straight to the top.

"I realize that the picture I am presenting of my son is that of a good-for-nothing young scamp," she wrote to the psychiatrist whom Jung recommended for Michael.[18] "I am sticking to objective details which I think you ought to know. They are by no means even the whole objective picture of my son's character. He is tender, humorous, witty, and *very* truthful. Oddly enough, although his conduct is often irresponsible, he has high esteem for responsibility. He *wants* to be good. He *wants* to achieve self-mastery. But, it seems to me, he does not know how, and is working under unconscious compulsions, and strong unconscious anxieties." Michael was suffering from "nameless fears."[19] His guilt was generalized; his capacity for drama was unequaled in the family. At Twin Farms one summer he buried himself up to the neck in a pile of manure, insisting that he was "worth no more than that" and that he would not come out for love or money.

"He doesn't need a psychiatrist," said Maxim Kopf. "He needs a kick in the pants."[20] Dorothy never denied that her son was "spoiled." But she regarded herself as "his greatest, indeed perhaps his only, emotional security," and she refused to let Maxim take a hand in disciplining him.[21] When, during a long weekend in New York around his sixteenth birthday, Michael and his friends "made a shambles" of the house in Turtle Bay, smashing furniture and objets d'art and entertaining "thoroughly disreputable young women overnight," Dorothy advised him in the most terrifying language she could muster that "responsible adults with normal cares [had] been seriously discommoded," and that his behavior would no longer be tolerated. She was prone to lecture Michael at the best of times:

> You may recall, my son [she wrote], the sermon that we listened to together in Valley Forge on Mother's Day. It was addressed not to sons, but to their mothers, and the pastor's advice to them was not to "humor" their sons, but to "honor" them. You have been humored, I am afraid, rather than honored. I wish to honor you. . . . Loving and honoring a person are not the same thing, you know. One can love someone more than one's own life, as I do you, and still see his faults with clear, and almost detached objectivity. Some mothers cannot; they are blinded by their love. But I am not such a mother.

She was "only trying to help," she said:

> We shall, of course, be very happy to see you [in Vermont], and no one will attempt to make you feel "ignominious." Feeling ignominious adds nothing to one's spiritual growth or development into happy and stable maturity, and it is therefore not with that object in mind that I, nevertheless, think you should, in returning, ponder a few things, and get them quite straight, . . . not with a view to remorse, but in anticipation of better and happier ways.[22]

"You ask me what I would do were I my own master," Michael wrote to his mother in 1946, after he was fired from a summer job she had found for him in the city, "and I will tell you. I believe that I would take a job, perhaps as a farm hand, and for a few years earn enough money to start me traveling. Then I would *travel,* really travel! as a stoker, a painter of decks, a night club waiter, anything just to see this wide world at first hand! I would do everything, see everything, and then, maybe, settle down later in life, I don't know."[23] A brief stint at the University of Chicago found Michael sleeping through most of his classes and "drinking from morning to night." It was a relief to Dorothy when he went to England. He sent her letters that she herself might have written in her younger days: lengthy travelogues, really, rapturous about "narrow streets" and British chimney pots, "loamy, sensuous green meadows" and the unending search for Beauty.[24] Michael seemed always to be conscious, when he wrote to his mother, that he was writing to Dorothy Thompson:

> I had a thought walking across the Deer Park at Oxford, which in a way now has become the banner and slogan of my existence. I said to myself, "Here Oxford was, when the world was mad, . . . a storehouse of beauty, an island, as it were, of art, and from this island and others like it came the light after the Dark Ages." Now, why may not an individual be such an island, in a world once more entering the night? . . .
>
> I want to live up to this, [but] backslide all the time, and sink low, and then I hate myself for it, and must cleanse myself afterwards by being among beautiful things, if it's [only] a meadow in the moonlight. . . . I know you understand, as you always understand, and you are so kind and generous and love me so much, and I give so little in return. Oh, please let me search and know that if I'm greedy, as I know I am, it is to taste everything. . . . I love you so much, and wish we could talk, and please dear Mummie take good care of yourself and stay well.[25]

She had sent him to England with a formal contract in his pocket: she would pay for his studies at the Royal Academy, for his lodgings in London, and for tutors (as she deemed them to be necessary) in history and foreign languages.[26] In return, Michael was to write to her every week and give her a strict accounting of his life and expenses. Dorothy took exactly the same approach in this matter that her own father had taken with her. She wanted details of Michael's studies; she wanted to know about his teachers and his friends. She expected him to call on *her* friends in London and, later on, in France, Germany, and Austria as well.

"If you are entertained," Dorothy advised, "always write the *moment* you leave, and send some small gift of chocolates or cigarettes, or flowers. . . . Don't be in a *rush*. I am willing to support you for four years to enable you to become as much a man of the theatre, in all its aspects, as schooling can make you."[27] It was Dorothy's not-so-private hope that Michael might turn away from acting eventually and become a director or a playwright. And indeed, during his two years at RADA, he left an impression that was not wholly promising. The faculty all agreed that he had talent, but he was "cocksure," frequently belligerent, and definitely too smart for his own good.

"They comment mostly on my 'originality,' " Michael wrote to his mother, "and say that I 'carefully think out' the things that I do. Some of the teachers like this, others do not. The Shakespearean producer said my Malvolio was too 'modern,' and when I asked her what she meant, that I thought Shakespeare was timeless, she thought me rude."[28] Throughout his career, Michael would rely more heavily on his splendid gift for mimicry than on any internal artistry as an actor. He was "devastatingly good at accents," and "brilliant" in character parts that gave him a chance to perform a solo turn.[29] But he had no use for "this 'people's theatre' crap," and it was his opinion that the American school of Method actors, the "Stanislavski crowd," was populated by "queers" and "dope fiends" and "racketeers like Jean-Paul Sartre."[30] Dorothy (who did not really disagree with him) urged him to take advantage, in that case, of everything that RADA had to offer. The "classical" approach, she maintained, was entirely to the good: "I do not share your cynical attitude toward the world. The world and art are not two different things. Art is only the world's highest expression of itself. Be true to it, and to yourself — to the self that you wish to be. And you will be it. . . . Never forget that what we become is the fruit of all our experiences — sensory, mental and spiritual. Keep away from the coarse and the ugly."[31]

She had enlisted the support of Dinah Sheean as a sort of chaperon for Michael at RADA. It was Dinah who found him inexpensive lodgings when he arrived in London, and Dinah who found him lodgings again when he was thrown out of the first ones for drunkenness. Mike was "such a confusing individual," Dinah remarked,

"— much more a child than his years, much more grown up than his years."[32] When he was drinking, however, he was just a drunk. He turned up one night in Piccadilly Circus, masked and brandishing a knife: "I'm Jack the Ripper!" he cried, badly frightening the prostitutes who worked the street.[33] Another time, at the beginning of 1950, he went home with an Austrian girl — an actress — and struck her before the night was over. The episode made the newspapers.

"My lawyer tells me the affair is 'slightly sordid,' " said Rebecca West, whose vast connections in British newspaper circles kept this particular scandal under control, "and [as] he has a fairly oldmaidish point of view, if there had been anything really rough he would have said so. Apparently the girl is trying to get some publicity out of it for her film career. My lawyer said that the way she had got right on to the *Daily Mail* did not suggest a modest violet."[34] Rebecca had known Michael in Vermont "as a tiresome and slightly alcoholic teenager";[35] she was hoping now to spare Dorothy any further distress. "Everybody here has been good about leaving Dorothy's name out," she reported. "Mike has appeared as the parthenogenic offspring of Red."[36] Mike himself, meanwhile, was frightened enough by his own behavior to agree that he needed professional help.[37]

"I never dreamed I could hit a woman," he told Dorothy later. "I must have been crazy. But I go haywire when Benny is not here."[38]

"Benny" was Bernadette Nansé, a French girl "of good family" who was studying English and working as an au pair in London. She and Michael had met in 1949 at the home of Baroness Moura Budberg, the Russian-born former mistress of Maxim Gorki and H. G. Wells. Moura herself was an astonishing creature, "the stuff that dreams are made of," massively constructed and in her early sixties, still weaving tales about her amorous past. No one knew whether or not to believe them. She was thought by many to have been a spy for Russia — or for Britain, or for both — and she did nothing to discourage the rumors that swirled around her all her life. When she was not working as a translator or script consultant for Alexander Korda, she was holding forth at her "wonderfully tatty and crowded" salon in the Cromwell Road, "gulping gin as if it were vodka" and looking like an overweight dowager empress in a room that dripped with icons.[39] Moura liked Dorothy's son — she *adored* Dorothy — and she was happy to see Michael and Bernadette come together under her roof. There was some speculation, in fact, that she had conspired in Bernadette's "seduction." Certainly she agreed with many other people that Bernadette was the nicest thing that had happened to Michael Lewis in a long, long time. She was "pretty," "charming," "feminine," "practical" — "in short," said Dorothy later, "very French."[40] Actually Bernadette was Alsatian, her widowed mother owning a modest business in the town of Altkirch, not far from the German border of Alsace-Lorraine. Michael wanted to elope with her almost from the moment they met, but Bernadette refused to marry without her family's consent, and in the meantime she tried to hold him to a strict sobriety.

"I think she has enough sense to realize," said Dinah Sheean, who was "bumbling along" in her role as chaperon, "that unless [Michael] can settle down in his own skin, she must try to control any serious feelings she may have about him."[41] This proved easier in the planning, naturally, than in the doing. When Dorothy arrived in London for a visit in 1949, she did not meet "Michael's girl," nor did she realize how far the affair had gone until later in the year, when Michael told her that he was determined to get married; that Bernadette had "saved his life"; that he would "be his own man" if it killed him. Dorothy immediately sent him to a psychiatrist and enlisted every one of her friends in England to help her break off the romance. She was encouraged by the fact that Bernadette's own mother, when she discovered the affair, called her daughter back to France, touching off a courtship-by-letter that lasted for more than a year.

"I think it perfectly preposterous," Dorothy scolded Michael in the summer of 1950, "that a young man who wants — of all things — to pursue a life in the theatre, and who is only twenty years old, and has never borne a single financial — or much of any other — responsibility, should contemplate marriage. I do not believe that *any* marriage that you would make at this time . . . has one chance in fifty of surviving."[42] For the rest of his time in England, thinking that it might distract him from Bernadette's charms, Dorothy urged Michael to "see other girls" (which he was doing in any case) and to broaden his education by any means possible. She hoped he would enroll in some European university when his course of study at RADA was over; the Korean War had broken out, and Dorothy was afraid that her son would be drafted.[43] In 1950 she ordered him to Spain, where Maxim Kopf had gone to paint the hills around Toledo. Mike was "well-behaved" during this trip, drinking little and showing certain signs of maturation that met with Dorothy's approval. She could not believe that this "teen-aged love affair" would continue to preoccupy Michael, but she was wrong: it did.

Over Christmas 1950 Michael went to Rome for what proved to be his final meeting with his father. Red was in a disastrous state by that time, his creative powers long ago evaporated, his private life reduced to the arbitrary companionship of maids and "secretaries." The last of these was Alec Manson, "a strange man of indeterminate nationality"[44] and the only witness to the degrading scenes of Michael's Christmas visit, when Red declared that he never wanted to see his son again and that if Michael had come to Italy only to get drunk and shack up with "floozies" — on Christmas Eve he spent the night with a prostitute on the Via Veneto — he could go back to England, "where he could do as he liked, and where he did not have to take into consideration other people's feelings."[45] There was something unbelievably hurtful about these words coming from Sinclair Lewis's mouth. Michael fled to Paris and then home to New York, where, five days after his arrival, he received the news of his father's death.

"I suppose I killed him," Michael groaned, in the same way he had blamed himself when Wells Lewis died. ("It should have been me," he had sobbed to Dorothy: "I am no good.")[46] Dorothy herself had just been hospitalized for exhaustion when she heard about Red, and she was not ashamed to admit that his death hit her "a much heavier blow in the solar plexus than I would have imagined."[47]

"I felt what I always felt with him," she wrote to Frances Perkins, "again that sense of having been a total failure, of having betrayed his hopes, and added to his sorrows. . . . Hal did not like pity, but the bleeding pity I always felt for him, at all times and under all circumstances, was a deep and ineradicable form of love, which my [present] husband, a man of the most delicate and sensitive perceptions, has always realized." It was Maxim, indeed, who had told Dorothy that if Red ever needed her, she would have to go to him: "It would be against your nature not to." No one wanted love more desperately, Dorothy agreed, "or more needed it, and no one more often doubted and rejected it" than Red: "His death brings me great pain. Above all the pain that he never knew my solitary tears."[48]

She sent Michael to the funeral in Sauk Center, Minnesota, Red's birthplace, where his brother Claude spoke a few words at the grave and accidentally tipped over the urn that held Red's ashes. It was twenty-two below zero and "blustery" that day, and a portion of

Red's remains blew out over the prairie before anyone could stop it. "But what does it matter," said Dorothy, "where a handful of ashes lies?"[49] Her tribute to Sinclair Lewis was published in "On the Record" on the sole condition, as she specified to her syndicate editors, that it not be cut by any newspaper, "nor sensationalized by reference to our past relationship." "Something has gone," Dorothy lamented in print, "— something prodigal, ribald, great, and high. The horizon is flatter. The landscape is duller."[50] She regretted the passing not just of Red but of other figures who inhabited a literary peak that seemed to her more and more remote: H. G. Wells and Edna Millay and Bernard Shaw, who had given her a tremendous laugh when she met him for the last time, in 1945.

"How do you see the future," Dorothy had asked Shaw, "— now answer honestly?" And "very *soberly*" Shaw had replied, "Three hundred years of the Dark Ages. After that, things will be fine."[51]

She gave her permission for Michael to marry Bernadette Nansé in the wake of his father's death. Michael was turning twenty-one that year and could do what he liked; he was scheduled also to receive a small inheritance from Red's estate. When Dorothy finally met Bernadette, just days before the wedding, she was forced to conclude that Michael, "for once in his life, probably knew what was good for him." The girl was "really charming," Dorothy reported. She was "not at all an intellectual type, . . . but anything but a simpleton," and because her devotion to Michael had "sustained such a long separation" Dorothy assumed it had "depth."[52] The wedding was performed on Michael's birthday, June 20, 1951, at the Church of Our Lady of the Snows in Woodstock; Bernadette's only condition had been that any children of the union would be raised as Catholics. The whole affair was "preposterous," but Dorothy was happy in spite of herself, because it was "perfectly beautiful at this moment on Twin Farms."[53] Very shortly afterward, Michael left for his first professional acting job, with the Barter Theatre in Abingdon, Virginia.

17
CHAPTER

DOROTHY was in New York the day after Michael's wedding, which was unusual for her at the beginning of summer: she had gone down on the overnight train to preside at a press conference in her living room at Forty-eighth Street, an inaugural seminar called to mark the founding of the American Friends of the Middle East (AFME). This was the "pro-Arab," "anti-Zionist," "anti-Israel" lecture bureau and cultural-exchange organization that was discovered, in 1967, to have been partially funded by the Central Intelligence Agency.[1] Dorothy knew nothing about the CIA's involvement (all of AFME's operating funds came from "private contributions" and foundation grants), but she served as AFME's president for more than five years, resigning only when her editors at the Bell Syndicate, under pressure from subscribers, asked her to make up her mind whether she was "a newspaper woman or a propagandist for the Arabs."[2]

"The Zionists would like us all to believe that there is no such thing as an Arab," Dorothy had written in the winter of 1950. "They also have adopted the attitude that the State of Israel, unlike every other state on earth, is sacrosanct, and outside any criticism whatsoever. This is the more irritating since the Jewish people as a whole have never been reticent in their criticisms of every other state and society on the globe."[3] As the decade progressed, Dorothy became so widely identified with the opposition to Israel in America that it was not unusual to hear her described as "a traitor" in the Jewish press. She was "a Goebbels-minded publicity agent," according to Rabbi Baruch Korff (who later achieved a certain fame as one of the last defenders of Richard Nixon during the Watergate crisis), "a mercenary, ill-motivated agent for the heirs of Nazism." [4] A correspondent for the *Jewish Advocate* in Boston went so far as to call Dorothy a "Jezebel," "a haggard witch," a "Lady Macbeth." [5] For her part, Dorothy believed that she had been made the victim of "a campaign of character assassination" unexampled in her thirty years of journalism. "Don't carry torches," her editors warned, when Dorothy, "fed up to the point of imprudence," undertook to criticize Israel as "the 49th state" of the Union, "the only nation in history to have been canonized at birth."

"When I asked whether that meant that one could criticize the British, the Dutch, the Russians or anyone else on the round globe," Dorothy remembered, "but not even *try* to counteract false Zionist propaganda," her editors responded that "the British, Dutch, etc., don't advertise," and that in the American press a hostility toward Israel was "almost a definition of professional suicide." [6] Dorothy would not be intimidated. "I refuse to become an anti-Semite by appointment," she declared. "I simply feel too old and too stubborn, if you like, to begin at my age to yield to this kind of blackmail." [7]

She had never recovered, in a professional sense, from her forced departure from the *New York Post* in 1947: she was not wrong in predicting that no newspaper in New York would dare to publish her column once her opposition to Zionism became known. The anger felt by many American Jews in the wake of Dorothy's defection was the more intense because she had been, up through the end of World War II, one of Zionism's most profoundly moving spokesmen. In May of 1942 she had appeared as a keynote speaker at the Biltmore Hotel in New York, where an international conference had been called to agitate for unrestricted Jewish immigration to Palestine. [8] There is no question that Dorothy, up to that point, was wholeheartedly sympathetic to the Zionist movement and convinced (as later she was not) that the Jews were "a separate people," "a sociological phenomenon" that needed to be dealt with as such after twenty centuries of persecution and oppression.

"The whole anti-Semitic movement is full of fetish and black magic," Dorothy had written in 1943. "It is a kind of modern witchcraft. Back of this black magic is the fact that the Jews *do* lead an abnormal life. They are a cohesive people without a place on earth of their own. That fact gives them, in the superstitious mind, an atmosphere of doom. An atmosphere of doom produces an atmosphere of fear." And a state of their own, "built by themselves and expressing their own peculiar culture and way of life," might liberate the

424 ■ AMERICAN CASSANDRA

Jews from their status as outsiders. It would end the "ghost story" of the Diaspora. It would allow any Jew, anywhere in the world, to make a choice: to become a member of the Jewish state, or to surrender his Jewishness (as distinct from his religious practice) once and for all to the country of his birth.

Indeed, it was with an eye to the *assimilation* of the Jews that Dorothy had first thrown her support behind political Zionism. She had been assured "time and again" (and for the first time in London, in 1920, during the Zionist conference that launched her career) that the Jewish state in Palestine would encompass "in equal partnership" the indigenous population of the region,[9] and that "actively dissident Arabs," if there were any, could be transferred "to other parts of the vast Pan-Arab Empire, which covers a territory as large as the United States."[10] Ignorant of Arab culture, badly informed about the history of the Middle East, Dorothy had not then imagined that a Palestinian shepherd would care very much whether he drew water from a well in Bethlehem or in Fez. Later she would deeply regret the cultural and racial prejudice that had allowed her to regard "the Arabs" as interchangeable bodies, indistinguishable one from another and superfluous in the face of Western plans, but even at the height of her devotion to Zionism she never suspected that whole populations (nearly a million people, by most estimates) would be uprooted from their homes in Palestine and driven into exile.

"I should be opposed to it if I were a Jew," Dorothy had warned, "with the undimmed memory of the dispersion of my own people in mind. I should not want any Arab to sit beside the waters of Babylon and weep because he remembered Zion."[11] Her first trip to Palestine in 1945 had convinced her that Zionism was *not* the "liberal crusade" she had thought it to be, "that the Zionist leaders envisaged," as she put it, "not a small state of Jews who chose to live in Israel, but a Zionist state destined to become the leading power in the Middle East, as the ward of world Jewry whatever their citizenship in other countries [might be]."[12] Dorothy was very much upset by Jewish terrorism in the quest for statehood. She was "shocked beyond measure" when Menachem Begin, one of the leaders of the Irgun group that was responsible for the massacre of more than two hundred and fifty Arabs at Deir Yassin, was accorded a hero's welcome by the Jews of New York, and when Ben Hecht, Peter Bergson, and other leading Zionists "put on a show in Madison Square Garden" and "slandered Great Britain" by displaying the Union Jack topped with the Nazi swastika.[13] The failure of Israel, after 1948, to agree to the fixing of its borders, to heed the call for the internationalization of Jerusalem, or to provide any relief or compensation for the Palestinian refugees led Dorothy to conclude that Zionism was "an aggressive, chauvinistic movement" and that the State of Israel was "an expansionist power" — "a creation of the United Nations, deriving its claim to legal existence from a United Nations decision made against the opposition of the whole Arab and Moslem world."[14]

Ultimately Dorothy was more worried about the effect of Israeli propaganda on American foreign policy than she was about the righteousness or iniquity of Israel itself. Israel was a fait accompli, and once it existed she did not recommend that it be disestablished or that its government be overthrown.[15] She was ahead of most of her colleagues in journalism in considering the problem of Israel at all (beyond merely hailing its creation as a humanitarian enterprise or, like Walter Lippmann, arguing that the Western allies ought to "impose peace" on the Middle East through the establishment of a joint Israeli-Palestinian confederation).[16] But just as Dorothy was one of the first — and only — American journalists to speak out in defense of the Arab nations, so was she the first and most prominent American journalist to be smeared with the label of "anti-Semite." In 1949 she spoke of her "ardent and absolutely sincere hope that Israel will flourish and give expression to the deepest moral instincts of the Jewish religion."[17] She hoped to see a negotiated resolution to the Arab-Israeli conflict that would recognize the just claims of *both* sides. She felt bound to repeat, nevertheless, that the Jewish state was "a secular, political" entity "with no prior claim on virtue," and that it must expect "to live in the same atmosphere of free criticism which every other state in the world must endure. . . .

"I often think that race relations were actually much better in this country," Dorothy went on, in a remark that was not designed to win her any popularity, "when we took good-natured flings at the characteristics of various national groups in our midst."[18] She resolutely denied any trace of anti-Semitism on her part: "I can say, with I think verity, that never in my life have I injured a Jew. I can say, with I think absolute truthfulness, that never in my life have I been prejudiced against a Jew, as Jew."[19] But her bias was strong enough, and the fight over Israel bitter enough, to allow her to comment privately "that the Jews, phenomenally brilliant individually, . . . are, collectively, the stupidest people on earth. I think it must come from cultural inbreeding — perhaps from physical inbreeding also — in a desire to retain a homogenous, in-group society in the midst of 'aliens.' "[20] There was a meanness to Dorothy's words, and a corresponding "stupidity," in the wake of the Nazi Holocaust — "the great European pogrom," she called it,[21] "the most ruthless persecutions ever visited in history upon so large a portion of humanity."[22] But here again, as Dorothy observed, justice could not be achieved through the balancing of "completely irrelevant equations." The "extermination of the European Jews could not be laid at the door" of the Arabs. The whole world had been riveted by a non sequitur.[23]

"Jews are Zionists," Dorothy explained with acid contempt, "— therefore non-Zionists are anti-Semites; anti-Semitism is illiberal — therefore anti-Zionists are reactionaries; Arabs are anti-Israel — American Jews are pro-Israel — therefore Arabs are the enemies of the United States, and criticism of Israel — or any of its policies — is anti-Semitic and anti-American."[24] When Dorothy went on lecture tours now, it was often to talk about the dangers posed to American Jewry by a division of its loyalties. She was seriously worried that there might be "a backlash."

"Really," she said, "I think continual emphasis should be put upon the extreme damage to the Jewish community of branding people like myself as anti-Semitic. It is a little beneath the dignity of anyone with my record to deny such charges in public, so they just tend to make anti-Semitism more respectable than it otherwise might be."[25] She was "highly distressed" to find out that children in Hebrew schools in New York City were being asked to pledge their loyalty "to God, to the Torah, and to the Jewish people and the Jewish State." She saw in this exercise "precisely what Hitlerism [had done] to Christianity in Germany. It is turning — or attempting to turn — a faith of universal and timeless wisdom and greatness into a nationalist and chauvinist credo."[26] In columns and speeches throughout the 1950s Dorothy railed against the rising tide of cultural pluralism, affirming that "America demands a single loyalty" and insisting that George Washington had known what he was talking about, in his Farewell Address, when he warned against fervent attachments and "permanent inveterate antipathies" toward other nations.[27] There was a real danger to the United States, Dorothy believed, in the "recrudescence of former loyalties" among ethnic and religious groups:

It may seem the utmost banality to re-affirm a proposition so obvious. But that it needs reaffirming is indicated by the way the concept of American "minorities" has crept into the American language. It must here be stated: *There are no minorities in the United States* [Dorothy's emphasis]. There are no national minorities, racial minorities, or religious minorities. The whole concept and basis of the United States precludes them. Every citizen of the United States and member of the American nation who was not born here came voluntarily as an individual, with one exception — the Negroes whose ancestors were imported as chattel slaves. Each member of this nation possesses his nationhood and his citizenship with equality of right and equality of obligation with every other citizen. Where, or if, his status . . . is prejudiced, he has the right . . . to fight for [its] *equalization.* . . . But he cannot fight for the recognition of a different national status, or a status as a "minority," for no such status is recognized or recognizable.[28]

She went back to the Middle East in 1950 — to Jordan, Lebanon, Syria, and Iraq — at the request of the United States government, which had asked her, "unofficially," to investigate political developments in the region. It was one of the peculiarities of American foreign policy at that time that the State Department, anxious about oil reserves and the spread of communism in the Gulf, was widely sympathetic to the Arab cause,[29] while Congress and all of the presidential candidates were unequivocally pro-Israel — "in the pockets of the Zionists," Dorothy said sulkily. She assured her editors at the Bell Syndicate that she was being sent to the Middle East "without other payment than expenses" and that she was expected only to file reports.

"I have made it clear that I will not go as a propagandist for any point of view," she remarked, "but as an objective observer and analyst. . . . I feel as though I were walking straight into the lion's mouth, but one might as well be hanged for a sheep as a lamb."[30] It was the first of four trips that Dorothy would make to the Arab world over the next six years, and it was the impetus for the founding of the American Friends of the Middle East. She sat on AFME's board of directors along with Garland Evans Hopkins, Cornelius Van H. Engert, Dorothy Kenyon, Virginia Gildersleeve, Harry Emerson Fosdick, and a number of other liberal educators and Protestant clergymen who realized, as she did, that the United States could shut its eyes to the realities of the Middle East only at its peril. In its daily operations AFME was concerned mainly with the promotion of Arab speakers in America and with cultural- and student-exchange programs on college campuses. It maintained an extensive clipping service and employed fifteen representatives overseas, but though it was clearly "pro-Arab" in outlook, it took no Arab subsidy and had no Arab members on its board.

"What I have tried to do," Dorothy asserted, "— leaving AFME aside — has been to explain *why* the Arabs think and feel as they do, and what would be the certain result of offending them on all and every occasion. . . . The American Zionists have misrepresented this civilization in a shocking way, as everybody who really knows anything about it would testify."[31] Later Dorothy would acknowledge that she had held on to her position at AFME longer than she otherwise might have because she was infuriated and made "stubborn" by Zionist opposition.[32] She was also fascinated, on a personal level, by the whole spectacle of the Middle East. She had not had so much fun since she was a young reporter in Europe. She dined with Ibn Saud, the founder and king of Saudi Arabia, at his harem in Riyadh, in "a palace that is straight out of the Arabian Nights, with a touch of Coney Island."[33] She got to know Cairo, Jidda, Damascus, Teheran, Baghdad, Beirut, Karachi, and Khartoum. In 1956, in the realization of a childhood dream, she "sailed into the Golden Horn at dawn,"[34] but she was under no illusions, all things considered, about the "magic" of the Middle East. She never went home without a bronchial infection and a bad case of enteritis. She described the Arab people privately as a "supersensitive" and generally troublesome bunch — "the victims of a psychological trauma involving 'status' and inferiority," as she told Rebecca West, "made more murderous by the fact that they damned well *are* inferior."[35] Dorothy was very funny sometimes in her correspondence from the desert:

> My own trip was fabulous [she wrote to Grace Lewis in 1952] — really fabulous — but extremely exhausting, for I kept a killing schedule, and the Middle Eastern climate is very hard on a Nordic like myself. When I finally got to Jidda, my last stop in Saudi Arabia and the end of the journey, . . . I was told that Eve (the first lady of humanity) had died in Jidda and was buried there, though just how she got from Mesopotamia to Jidda cannot be calculated by me. However, if she got there, I am sure that is where she died, and I

thought that I was going to follow her example. If the Russians want the Red Sea, they can have it so far as I am concerned.[36]

She got back to New York after her first Middle Eastern journey to find that new rumors had been circulating in the city about her personal and professional life. "She had lost her position in the metropolis," said Meyer Weisgal, Chaim Weizmann's representative in America; "her one-time friends [in the Jewish community] had turned on her in a gathering tempest of resentment."[37] It was said that she was alcoholic. She had "cancelled engagements without notice." She had accepted "a bribe" from Ibn Saud and a diamond brooch from King Farouk. Worst of all was the claim that Dorothy had been diverted from the cause of Zionism through the influence of her husband, Maxim Kopf, who was rumored to have been "a Nazi sympathizer" and even "a former member of the Nazi general staff."[38] Dorothy's secretaries and friends, most of whom did not share her hostility toward Israel,[39] were unanimous in their belief that these inventions were the work of Zionist propaganda. Virginia Shaw, who stepped in as Dorothy's chief secretary following the marriage and retirement of her elder sister, Madeline, remembered that Dorothy was always "scrupulously reliable" about her public commitments: in all the time Ginny worked for her (eleven years), she missed a scheduled appearance only once, because of flu.[40] And as to the other charges, "I never received a diamond brooch from anyone in my life," Dorothy mused somewhat ruefully.[41] Many times she said that if any other group or individual had libeled her in this way, she would have taken legal action without thinking twice about it.

"The reason I have not done so," she contended, "is simply because I fear the reaction that would follow from airing in public, as a libel suit would have to do, some of the methods these people use. It might reflect on the whole of American Jewry, which would be most unjust. I suspect, furthermore, that the people who are slandering me know this, and are therefore taking gross advantage of what might be called Christian patience."[42] Internal memoranda of the American Zionist Council, addressed "to the local committees," warned that there was "wide Roman Catholic interest" in Dorothy's pronouncements on the Middle East, and advised that "in view of the weight Miss Thompson's name carries, her misstatements and hostile propaganda must be challenged wherever she appears." The Zionist counterattack was meant to be conducted in "a dignified and effective manner,"[43] but inevitably "a few fanatics" slipped through the cracks — "and not one Zionist publication . . . ever defended me," Dorothy later pointed out, "not even for the right to express [my] views."[44] In the end, she avoided talking about the Middle East at lectures and public engagements unless the organization that was sponsoring her specifically asked her to. Once one did, she would hold it to its side of the bargain.[45] She had never organized "claques" to defend her, and would not start now, but she was fighting for more than her own interests. She was fighting "for all those people who want to keep alive the right to disagree with the totality of the trends of the times. . . . I have written and said what I believe to be the limpid truth, and with malice toward none. The test of the truth, in this question as in all others, will be made by the developments of history."[46]

She was more and more to be found, during the 1950s, as a guest speaker in out-of-the way towns and on college campuses; the days were over when Dorothy Thompson could command two or even three thousand dollars for a speech in New York. Quite calmly she pointed to 1949 as the year she "began [her] decline," and when the *Washington Star,* which regularly censored her columns on Zionism by refusing to publish them, threatened to drop "On the Record" altogether, she wondered if it might not be a good thing.

"I am sorry about the *Washington Star,*" Rebecca West wrote to Dorothy from London, "because I don't believe even you have the fortitude not to mind being ganged up on, glorious as your stand for principle may have been."[47] Rebecca was no less troubled than Dorothy by the postwar "Herrenvolk theory" regarding the Jews,[48] and when her own turn came (following some articles she published in the *Evening Standard* in London about "the Mosleyite Fascist revival"), she was no less infuriated than Dorothy to be castigated as an anti-Semite: "But the human race is so damn silly that it doesn't matter what happens to it, anyway, so let's cheer up."[49] A great deal of Dorothy's correspondence during this period was concerned with her mounting alienation from the profession she loved. She told Bernard Berenson that it was becoming more and more difficult for her to maintain any kind of respect for American journalism.

"For it seems to me," she said, "that the more powerful we become in terms of economics and military power, the more mealy-mouthed and intellectually timid we are. The idols of the marketplace rule everything. They rule so firmly that it is quite unnecessary for government to impose any censorship."[50] The political process itself, Dorothy thought, had less and less to do with the "informed reasoning" of the individual voter and more and more to do with the manipulations of the mass media and "the great organized pressure groups, with their power directly to command votes. . . . They, today, are the real Parties, the [only] issue between them being who gets the most noses in the troughs."[51] Grimly Dorothy looked back on a conversation she had had with Huey Long before his murder in 1935. She had asked Senator Long what he would do with the press if he ever came to power in a fascist America, and he had answered, "Nothing. They'd do it for me."[52] The presidential election of 1952, which gave Americans a choice between a barely retired general of the army (Dwight D. Eisenhower) and "Hamlet, Prince of Denmark"[53] (Adlai E. Stevenson), found Dorothy casting her vote only against "Truman and Trumanism." She had offered her services to Stevenson, initially, as an unofficial adviser in the campaign.

"I wonder whether I could be of any use to you?" she inquired of the Democratic candidate. "I do not mean, in the obvious way, as a campaigner, nor even giving you what boosts I can in the public prints. I mean, rather, occasionally calling your attention to information, ideas, and formulations that come from better or more knowledgeable minds than my own. I am a lonely worker, and get most of my information from reading, for which I have a great deal more time than you; probably more than most assistants around you." It was one of the pure horrors of modern times, so far as Dorothy was concerned, that a man might be elected President of the United States who, like General Eisenhower, never read anything more exacting than a mystery novel or a western. "I am aghast," she said, "when I think of the superficiality of most of the advisers [Eisenhower] is bound to attract."[54] No doubt she was pleased when Stevenson wrote back to say that he considered her "the best informed American on Europe" and that he would "eagerly welcome" anything she cared to send — "bits and pieces which you might care to write, which I might use in speeches, to at least make Americans aware of how little they know."[55] She sent him all manner of advice for a while, but she feared from the beginning that Stevenson was "miscast as a politician," and she voted for Eisenhower when the time came. It was difficult for anyone to make sense of her reasoning, then or later.[56]

"I am disappointed with both sides for avoiding the paramount issue before us today," she declared in "On the Record." "As I conceive it, that issue is the American commitment under the United

Nations Charter, which, as interpreted by President Truman, is — in my belief — a formula for permanent war, in the places, and on the terms, chosen by our enemies. . . . I would prefer, all things being equal, not to have any General for President. . . . But I believe a very real change is necessary in Washington."[57] Somewhat clumsily, perhaps embarrassed by her own tergiversation, she directed her attention to "popular delusions and the madness of crowds,"[58] but her sister, Peggy, for one, had more to say about Stevenson. Peggy was an ardent, lifelong Democrat.

"How you vote doesn't concern me or anyone else," she scolded Dorothy in a rare break with tradition, "but your column with its wide influence really distresses me, because . . . the one thing that has always stood out as a firm basis for your political ideas was your faith in the superior over the mediocre." Dorothy insisted under fire that she had "*not* come out for Eisenhower — I want a change of *party*."[59] She believed that there were "no real issues" between Republicans and Democrats, "no basic divergence" in their fidelity to the Cold War, and that making "a change" was all that mattered.[60] She did not let up for an instant in her appeal for "a revolution in thinking." When, two years later, General Douglas MacArthur joined in the call for "the total abolition of war," Dorothy hailed him as a visionary and a hero. MacArthur, she remarked, "whom no one will call a timid pacifist," had gone "to the heart and core of the matter, with a simplicity that — as he well knows — the 'peace' seekers . . . will call 'childish.'

"Well," continued Dorothy, "it was a child who observed that the Emperor was naked, and it was Christ who said that unless one becomes as a child one cannot enter the Kingdom of Heaven."[61] She was becoming more and more explicitly "Christian" in all of her commentary, a fact that was not lost on her Zionist opponents.[62] Her political philosophy was summed up "in the Evangelium," she claimed — in "those precepts of respect for truth, mercy, forgiveness, humility and charity, taught and admonished by Him whom I do not hesitate to call the Lord and Savior of my soul."[63]

"I believe in the teachings of Christ with my *mind*," Dorothy explained on Edward R. Murrow's CBS radio program, "This I Believe." "I believe in them with my whole experience. I believe them, intellectually, to be *true* above any knowledge of truth that has come to me from any other source."[64] Christianity was "a science of conduct," said Dorothy — a way of living, a point of view.[65] She counted as the greatest truth of all "that we reap what we sow, and that all that we do returns. . . . There is always a 'massive retaliation.' "[66] In 1954 she wrote two fine columns about the troubles of J. Robert Oppenheimer, the American atomic scientist whose security clearance was withdrawn by the Atomic Energy Commission on the orders of President Eisenhower. Oppenheimer, in his youth, had been "associated with Communists"; he was now opposed to the development of the hydrogen bomb, and he was presumed on that account to have "defects in his character." It was Dorothy's contention that "any person of position or influence who actually stands for something" in the modern world was a security risk by definition.

"Once every free mind and spirit knew that there is no freedom, national or personal, without risk," she wrote; "that to hold an opinion has often been incompatible with holding a job; that the survival of civilization depends not on technological achievements nor economic power, but on the wisdom of judgment, and on the strength of moral and intellectual character. The Greeks were right, and history has supported them, when they declared that 'Character is Destiny.'

"What, then, becomes of security if character fails?"[67] What was "security" anyhow, Dorothy wondered, but "a vast lie," "a fundamental untruth — the truth being that life is a very dangerous business, extremely dangerous, and that if you live it to its fullest you will suffer agonies, as well as experiencing great joy. . . . The truth of it is that you are going to die, absolutely, positively, beyond any question of a doubt, and it's not, therefore, it's not in the least secure."[68] She looked around America in the 1950s and saw a nation "exactly *adrift*," obsessed with "know-how" and devoid of reverence — a society composed, in her memorable phrase, of "literates illiterate in every higher sense," deprived of any authentic education or moral training, floundering "in an uncharted ethical miasma of 'being happy' " and staring at a horizon that technology had created beyond the line of human vision.[69] She told her friends that she did not enjoy being "a common scold" and said that it was not even in her nature.[70] But the times ensured it. "The twentieth century will be the earthquake and the fire," she had written once, "to its very end."[71]

IN 1953 Dorothy and Maxim had been married for ten years — "the happiest years of my life," said Dorothy, a decade of "closeness and a continual *gladness*" that was "very, very rare" and that rushed by more quickly than any she could remember.[72] Where her professional correspondence was filled with warning, protest, ire, and gloom ("Sometimes I think [I really do] that there is some cosmic disturbance in the universe which is making everybody slightly crazy. Sunspots"),[73] her private life flourished, having burst into happiness and then settled into "sheer contentment" and "the greatest peace" she had ever known.

"I now have an idea wandering loose in my head," she wrote to Bruce and Beatrice Gould at the *Ladies' Home Journal,* "something to the effect, in theme, that it is a challenge but not a horror [to live in modern times], and that 'in the mud and scum of things, always always something sings,' as a better writer than I remarked."[74] She had taken to quoting John Masefield in her letters and columns: "The days that make us happy make us wise."[75] She needed no proof that love was "a universal cosmic and creative force." She "wished to *testify* to that."[76]

She was out on the road, still, for weeks at a time, lecturing to women's clubs and to student unions and, more and more often, to teachers' organizations.[77] She had emerged in the postwar years as one of the most prominent critics of American public education, which she recognized as being in "deep, deep trouble" and which she insisted was "more important than the whole 'Cold War.' "[78] It was not only the enormous extension of educational services after 1945 that had guaranteed "the downward adjustment of standards" in the schools. It was the triumph of relativism, Dorothy charged. It was the emphasis on "self-expression." It was the thesis that "anything goes."

" 'Anti-discrimination' is a shibboleth of our times," she wrote, "like 'tolerance' (or anti-intolerance). . . . For the first time, as far as I know in any society, mediocrity has been clothed in the raiment of *morality*. It is 'anti-American' to be discriminating on any level — socially, racially, religiously, culturally. Everything and everyone is as good as anything and anyone, and whoever does not think so is an enemy of democracy. But if everything and everyone is as good as anything and anyone, then the measure of value *has* to be set at the lowest social and intellectual level. . . . And this simply means the disappearance of culture."[79] Dorothy did not expect American educators, burdened with certificates and theories of child development, to make a sudden volte-face into the classics. She *did* propose "that children should know how to read, to make a précis of *what* they read, to write correct and intelligent prose, to spell, and to command a vocabulary at the newspaper level."[80] She was not happy about the "unthinking" removal of the Bible from the schools, insisting that "we owe the fundamental tenets of our democracy — the idea, for instance, of 'brotherly love' — to this Book of Books" and that the "terse simplicity" and noble cadence of the English language would be lost forever without the context of Biblical diction.[81]

"I would not have the Talmud read in public schools," Dorothy added dryly, "nor the various Protestant or Catholic exegeses of the Christian dogma. . . . I am not a Jew, but I accept the greatest Jewish teachings. The Ten Commandments, for instance. And I cannot see why any Jew would object to having his children read the 13th Chapter of First Corinthians."[82] In the meantime, if Dorothy had the choice, she would forget entirely about IQ levels, a concept that she wished had never been invented.

"I am sure the I.Q. is not a static thing," she wrote, "— I know it is not. The mind can be improved by training and use, and the I.Q. will rise. I am sure that the average child is capable of more than its teachers — or rather the teachers' colleges — think it is. I also believe that the psychiatric approach [to life] is creating, not curing, neurotics. . . . I don't think Anita Loos was so far off the point . . . when she had her Lorelei [Lee, in *Gentlemen Prefer Blondes*] go to consult Professor 'Froyd,' who told her that all she needed 'was to cultivate a few inhibitions and get more sleep.' "[83] Dorothy was popular with her lecture audiences, for the most part, when she took on the icons of modern culture. She was amazed at the uproar that attended the publication of the Kinsey reports on American sexuality, saying that all anyone had to do to know what Dr. Kinsey knew was to spend a couple of summers in a small Vermont town.[84] Later on, when Simone de Beauvoir came out with *The Second Sex,* Dorothy remarked that she "found nothing new in it" and remained "unconvinced by [her] sister's large conclusions." Madame de Beauvoir had in common with Dr. Kinsey "a total lack of humor," said Dorothy, "thus proving that certain qualities are not a matter of sex. . . . I prefer men. But better keep off this subject. Nowadays every time one opens one's mouth a psychoanalyst peers into it."[85] In a letter to Rebecca West she took her point a step further. "Hasn't everyone a right to his own neurosis?" she cried. "Goddamn it!"[86]

She almost always went on her lecture trips alone; she took no secretary and handled her business herself on the road, hiring occasional help locally if and when she needed it. Frequently she would stay overnight in college dormitories, where she was accustomed to sit up till all hours talking to students and housemothers who were eager to hear her pronouncements. Dorothy told her lecture agents that she needed "eight hours sleep a night" and time to work on her column; other than that, she was free to go wherever and however the agency sent her. She had reason to believe that she was "the only person in the history of the state of Iowa" who had ever gone "from Sioux City to Ames by way of Fort Dodge." She got "mad enough to spit cats" when her directives were not followed, however, and was forced "to pep [herself] up with Benzedrine" many times in order to get through engagements that had been scheduled too close together.[87] Her husband hated the idea of Dorothy's taking drugs, and of her not eating anything before evening, as was also her habit.

"Please Dorothy take care of yourself," wrote Maxim, "eat a little at noon, don't go with an empty stomach into cocktails — It's poison! — Promise sweetheart to be careful. You are too precious!"[88] All of Maxim's letters to Dorothy were love letters. "Time went by so fast," he wrote near their tenth anniversary, "it was until now so short, and meanwhile I am growing old and older every day. . . . But one thing is sure, I love you so much, more than ever, and send you my heart."[89]

They rarely traveled together. When Dorothy was lecturing or "reconnoitering" in Europe, Maxim would either stay home in New York or go off on trips of his own to paint: to Paris, to Spain, twice to Tahiti. Normally Dorothy took no lecture dates "for any cause or at any price between June and October,"[90] but if, for some reason, she found herself away in the summer, Maxim would send her news from the farm: about the houses, the grounds, his studio, her flowers, the cows, the cars, the help, "crazy Jimmy Sheean," and "crazy Dinah," too.[91] The Sheeans had remarried in 1949; Dinah had "surrendered to destiny"[92] and rejoined her husband in Barnard, where life was "memorable for work and pleasure, for many guests and much good talk, as well as the beauty of the seasons and the sheer joy of the Vermont hills."[93]

In New York, meanwhile, for Dorothy and Maxim, it was still very much a question of dinners and concerts and nights at the theater; Dorothy's engagement books bear witness to a more or less constant coming and going, while her friends kept memories of a certain clockwork glamor at the house in Turtle Bay. "How to Give a Party and Like It" was the title of one of Dorothy's more lengthy unpublished manuscripts, in which she offered the advice to any novice hostess that she must be *natural,* above all things, in her approach to entertaining.

"A good party is one which the hosts not only give but go to," Dorothy observed. "If you know how to make a chicken pie which would be the pride of any grange supper, or a bang-up dish of scalloped potatoes, don't think they aren't good enough for your guests. They are good enough for a King."[94] Dorothy had actually served pie to kings, as well as to an assortment of Arab potentates and at least once to a Living Buddha, whom John Gunther, a well-known collector of the famous and original, brought to her house. Rudolf Serkin might be playing there, "casually in the evening," or Yehudi Menuhin, whose father was a great admirer of Dorothy's columns and sent them, clipped, in bunches to his prodigious son.[95] Elsa Maxwell was "a regular chum," as were Miriam Hopkins, Mady Christians, and Marian Anderson, whom Dorothy believed to be "an instrument of God," her singing "worth all the sermons I have ever heard."[96] Dorothy was even known to sing for her guests herself, but normally this happened only in the country, where she might sit up late with Carl Zuckmayer over a bottle of whiskey and trill out the songs of her childhood — "good old American songs and ballads" — while Zuckmayer played the guitar.[97] In New York she appeared in styles that were the height of fashion, in the wrapped-and-patted mode of the 1950s, her hair congealed into silver curls and her increasingly large frame tucked into suits and designer gowns. But an emissary of the State Department who came to see her at Twin Farms found her in the barn with Maxim, dressed in overalls and a faded neckerchief, her hands drenched in the blood of a sheep she was carving up for the freezer.[98] By the end of the decade she had grown comfortably into her elderly appearance: she had thinned down again somewhat, and her face had taken on a sleeker tone. She was still beautiful. She had "great bones."

On her sixtieth birthday, "still hale, hearty and not bereft of ideas,"[99] Dorothy swam the length of Silver Lake in Barnard while Maxim followed in a canoe. She described the exercise later as being "preposterously childish," and indeed she was not athletic in the usual sense. Since her graduation from Syracuse in 1914 she had "never willingly batted a ball over a net, around a course, into a basket or even through a wicket." The very idea of organized sports bored her to distraction — "strapping young men going into a huddle to tell each other secrets," she complained, "while one shivers in one's furs!"[100] In the early 1950s she joined the Sheeans, the painter

Sanford Ross, and Ely Culbertson, the bridge expert and notorious right-wing conspiracy theorist, and became a charter member of the Stebbins Pond Club in Barnard. This was a formal association of swimmers and boat owners who were anxious to preserve the privacy of Silver Lake; gradually, by grace of a number of ego-driven "improvements" on the clubhouse, Dorothy wound up as sole owner of what was meant to be communal property.[101] She bought the old inn on Barnard Green and razed it, erecting in its place a number of prefabricated houses that she proceeded to sell to her friends — in one case "over the third martini," to Dr. and Mrs. Stanley Sarnoff.[102]

"She was like that," said Lolo Sarnoff, a onetime refugee from Hitler whose family had escaped through Switzerland and whom Dorothy particularly liked for her beauty and her *savoir vivre.* "[Dorothy] was the kind of woman who went to Brentano's and bought a book on 'How To Build a House.' Then built it."[103] Mrs. Sarnoff was just one among a younger crowd in Barnard who, while they were scarcely uncritical of "Dorothy's empire," nevertheless took on many of the characteristics of a junior coterie. There was Rebecca Ross, Sanford's wife, who admired Dorothy mainly from a respectful distance. There were the Nicholses, Bill and Marithé (he was the editor of *This Week* in New York, she was a Czech beauty who was particularly fond of Maxim). There were the Wesbrooks, the Culbertsons, the Fullers, and the Joys. There was Lisa Sergio, "the Golden Voice of Europe," a former radio broadcaster in fascist Italy who came to the United States in 1937 and was taken more or less permanently under Dorothy's wing;[104] in Woodstock, Lisa lived with Ann Batchelder, her adoptive mother and the food editor at the *Ladies' Home Journal.* Dinah Sheean (for whom it was always a pleasure to see some "Mediterraneans" in Dorothy's "Teutonic" circle)[105] especially enjoyed the company of the writer Niccolò Tucci, who spent several summers in Barnard and described himself, not inaccurately, as "a Florentine, a Russian, a Parisian, an Interplanetarian, . . . the first conscientious objector to all future wars on scientific rather than religious grounds."

"Yes," said Tucci, who, like Lisa Sergio, had worked as a ghostwriter and interpreter for Mussolini before the war, "I *did* waste the best years of my life serving and praising one of the greatest imbeciles and criminals of the century, knowing that he was both, but 'hoping for the best.' " Tucci and Dorothy had an awful lot to talk about, as might have been expected.[106]

"You were timid last night," Tucci wrote to her after a long evening of whiskey and cigarettes at Twin Farms; "timid, baffled and not yourself. I have seen you that way before, just for brief moments, and I was pleased that you could have such moments, because that proved to me that your beautiful outbursts of ideas were not there all the time; in other words, they belonged to you as poetry belongs to a poet and painting to a painter: *quando tira il Dio* (when the God blows)." Now, when Dorothy was praised, it was as virtually a force of nature — "a lion and a child," Tucci called her, "an incendiary of certainties and a victim of doubts, . . . great and absurd as only noble people can afford to be."[107] Through Maxim, Dorothy met the Czech writer Johannes Urzidil, who wove her into *Das grosse Hallelujah* as "*die berühmte Frau*," Barnaby Nichols, the majestic, near-mythic "Famous Lady" of the fictional "Elm Tree Farm."[108] Stephen R. Graubard, who went on to become the editor of *Daedalus,* worked summers in Dorothy's garden. Henry Kissinger came for the weekend and left with the memory of an "inward generosity," an environment that transcended "the petty self-righteousness" of the age.

"It is not your hospitality primarily that we remember," Kissinger wrote to Dorothy, "but the atmosphere, and not your conversation as such but its style. At this moment, when mediocrity has almost succeeded in imposing its standards by calling them 'objective,' . . . it is much less important that our values be talked about than that they be lived. . . . All of us who are conscious of the emptiness of our period . . . gain strength from the knowledge that there exist a few islands where the great gesture is still possible without being sneered away."[109] And there was always a mingling of types in Vermont. One was as likely to find oneself in conversation with Alice Edmunds, the head housekeeper, as with Kissinger; or with Alice's handyman son, "Junior"; or with Walter Miller, who owned the general store; or with Naoma Hull, who brought the mail. Vermonters were "a strange, inbred" people, Dorothy kept on saying, "among whom one cannot take the obvious for granted."[110] She roared with laughter when she told the tale of a "city-slicker" who had come to stay in Barnard one particularly wet summer.

"Will it *ever* stop raining?" the fellow asked, and one of the locals, passing by, answered with assurance: "It always has."[111] Once a year, in summer, "the party of parties" was held at the hilltop farmhouse of Baron Louis Rothschild in nearby East Barnard. This was an open-air barn dance at which everyone in the neighborhood was welcome by blanket invitation — that meant "the local squirearchy," in Dorothy's report, "the native yokels," and "a remnant of the Austro-Hungarian Empire,"[112] among whom Louis and his wife, Hilda, were unquestionably the first. Hilda had been born in Vienna as a Princess von Auersperg; for a short time, before her marriage to Louis Rothschild, she worked as a secretary for Dorothy. Now she walked around Vermont "like everyone else, in a wraparound denim skirt," trailed by a herd of goats and "talking about her parquet floors."[113]

"There are by common consent numerous anomalies and inconsistencies and eccentricities in this countryside," Jimmy Sheean remarked in a letter to Dorothy, "attributed largely to you although you remain a monument to sanity throughout. Of all these things I do believe the weirdest is Hilda's new room in the barn. There I beheld an Ispahan carpet of 1790 or thereabouts, value anywhere from $35,000 to $50,000, used as a pretext for a room such as King Ludwig of Bavaria might have imagined. The only other article in this room is a Chippendale desk which itself is worth about $25,000. We are all crazy, it is true. But I do believe that our lovely, sainted Hilda, in all her grace and purity, has out-crazed the craziest of us."[114] Hilda was a woman of indestructible elegance, "like a lady greyhound," and her husband was the senior member of the Austrian branch of the Rothschild banking dynasty — placid, wise, courtly, funny, and, furthermore, stone deaf. Baron Louis had lately developed the habit of turning down his hearing aid in company; it was not unusual for him to put an end to conversation with the polite but autocratic words, "How very interesting. Now go home."[115]

In this case Dorothy took her cue from the Austrian nobility: she was going deaf herself, though years would pass before she would admit it. It remained "a convenient alibi."[116] Over time she experimented with a variety of electronic hearing devices, but abandoned them all when she realized what sort of "sounds and noises" she had thus far been spared.

"I could hear every tap dripping," she claimed, "every movement in the kitchen, and still had no better understanding of what people were saying."[117] Rebecca West suggested that Dorothy's undying loquacity — her gift for "tirades," "ranting," and "carrying on" — must have had its origins in deafness. "I do not recall her being anything like so talkative when she was young," said Rebecca.[118] Others allowed that there might be a connection between Dorothy's physical handicap and her mounting lapses of tact. She became more and more "controlling" as time went by. When her sister's husband,

Howard Wilson, lost his job and fell on hard times, Dorothy all but ordered him to move to Vermont and take charge of her chicken farm. "Howard didn't know the first thing about chickens," however (he was a graduate engineer),[119] and after she had set him up with Peggy in a small apartment on Twin Farms, Dorothy did little else but complain that he was failing to turn a profit.

"I am afraid I made an impulsive and unwise move in suggesting that Howard Wilson take it over," she confided to Dale Warren, who was still one of her dearest pals and her favorite "birthday child." "The work is too hard and the problems too unfamiliar for him or Peggy, and seeing Peggy heroically put her back into it (spending three hours a day on the chickens!) gave me a horrid feeling."[120] In 1951 the Wilsons escaped to St. Johnsbury, and three years later, finally, Dorothy gave up farming herself. Her "sincere ambition" had always been to make the venture pay. But it hadn't, she admitted, "and it won't. For when receipts are balanced against grain bills, extra labor in the haying season, expenditures for gas, seed and fertilizer, maintenance and repair of machinery and buildings, veterinarian fees, fencing, utilities and insurance, . . . it turns out that Mamma is supporting those lovely, big-eyed Jerseys with her typewriter." She would "drop a tear," she promised, "when the darlings are loaded onto trucks." But she would not "go on expending my life for cows."[121] She was sixty. She was tired. She was a grandmother.

In July 1954 Michael Lewis's wife, Bernadette, gave birth to their first child, a boy, while Michael appeared in a production of *My Three Angels* in Hyde Park, New York. Dorothy had refused even to consider the possibility that the baby might be born without her; she tried and failed not to interfere in her son's marriage. She made plans to suspend "On the Record" and pace the floors in Poughkeepsie during Bernadette's confinement, but Bernadette "jumped the gun on all of us" and delivered John Paul Sinclair Lewis two weeks prematurely.

"Of course I dashed into the car the next morning," Dorothy confessed, "and drove more or less like mad [to New York] through the most terrific storms of the summer."[122] She told her friends that John Paul, "the first Catholic child in the Lewis-Thompson family since the Reformation,"[123] was also "the most beautiful, virtuous and intelligent creature yet born on this planet." Within a year he was "talking continually, if not intelligibly, thereby demonstrating his legitimacy."[124] But his parents had been moving from theater to theater and from troupe to troupe, living in a series of "slummy bed-sitting room[s]," and Dorothy wondered if the baby would be brought up "in a bureau drawer." She wondered, too, whether Michael would prove to be any more "philoprogenitive" than Red.[125] Maxim advised her many times to "butt out,"[126] and she was aware enough of her shortcomings as a mother-in-law to devote a whole column to them in the *Ladies' Home Journal*. She understood that there were "savage tribes who push the old over cliffs when they are no longer able to hunt and fight." She hoped that she would not be one of these, a burden to the young.[127]

But she was worried about Michael, she was worried about Bernadette, and most of all she was worried about "the darling little boy."

18

CHAPTER

IT was Maxim Kopf's opinion that Bernadette Nansé was "too bourgeois" for Michael Lewis. This was no negative judgment of her; it was just that Bernadette "might have invented personally the middle-classed values of Alsace-Lorraine," while Michael had "not a shred of solid character" in him. One fine day, Maxim predicted, Michael would fall in love with somebody in the theater and ride off into a drunken sunset, leaving wife and child and Dorothy, too, to sweep up the dust of his whim. Maxim liked Bernadette. So did Dorothy, and the people who knew them all agree that she bent over backwards to help Bernadette feel welcome and a part of the family. It would have shocked her to know that Bernadette's own memories (so it was reported later) were mainly of being ordered around, condescended to, and interfered with by her mother-in-law.[1]

"If you, or rather Benny, shops carefully," said Dorothy in a letter to her son, ". . . you ought to be able to live . . . on an expenditure of not more than $1.50 per day ($3 for the two of you) or $21 per week." In a single paragraph Dorothy advised Bernadette how to economize on hardware, cleaning fluids, meat, cheese, gas, and electricity ("In buying meat," said Dorothy, "tell Benny I allow 1/2 pound per person for a meal, unless it is chopped meat [hamburger] where 3/4 lb. is plenty for two"),[2] and when John Paul Lewis was born, in 1954, word came down from the happy grandmother that it would *not* be necessary to shop for baby clothes at any modish establishment in New York: Sears would do nicely.[3] If Dorothy was meddlesome and a know-it-all, it is still a fact that Michael and Bernadette could not have lived in any kind of style without her assistance. Apart from the purely financial support she gave them (and gave them plentifully), she did not hesitate to pull any string at her disposal to help Michael in his career. Helen Hayes, Guthrie McClintic and Katharine Cornell, George Abbott, and Stella Adler all received letters at one time or another asking that they consider Dorothy's talented son for parts.[4] In the autumn of 1954 Michael went to work with the Lunts in *Quadrille;* "Baby brought him luck, say I," said Dorothy.[5] She was sure, however, that Michael would never earn enough money as an actor to support his family properly, and she took it on as her solemn duty to provide for John Paul and his brother, Gregory Claude, who was born in April 1957.

That same year, in a move that astounded her family and all of her friends, Dorothy sold the Big House and most of the land at Twin Farms. She went about it brusquely, even gruffly, and offered no better explanation than that she was "too old for all this business of lawns to be cut, etc."[6] Twin Farms itself had ceased to be a home, she complained: it was "a village," and it was costing her "a bundle."[7] Several years before, in a well-intentioned moment, Jimmy Sheean had persuaded her to sell him the Old House, across the valley, and then promptly gone bankrupt. His wife, Dinah, who had money of her own and might have been expected to rescue Jimmy from his financial difficulties, had by that time left again — fled Vermont permanently and "disappeared for the moment into the third dimension" as a consultant for Cinerama Productions.[8]

"It is, in fact, the end," said Jimmy. "I now retire for good and all into my so-called private life."[9] His plans were upset by the Internal Revenue Service, which in 1953 socked him for thousands of dollars in back taxes and put a lien on his income. For a while Jimmy worked as a ghostwriter on Marian Anderson's autobiography, which he proudly reported to Dorothy would be "the Goddamndest book that ever was, and no resemblance whatsoever to the old 'diva's memoirs' catshit. This is the real thing."[10] But "creative differences" with Miss Anderson left Jimmy once again in straits, and Dorothy was forced to buy up his mortgage and repossess the Old House. She assumed the liability gracefully enough, "for the sake of an ancient friendship that continues,"[11] but she lost a lot of money in the transaction. In 1956 Jimmy went to Italy, to Arolo, the village on Lago Maggiore where, as a young man, he had written the better part of *Personal History.* Here, at length, he would enjoy a contented life with Dinah, aware of his debt to Dorothy and not unmindful of his gratitude. "Bless you, dear Dorothy, forever and ever," he would write. "We have endured, and for this alone we shall see God."[12]

She made her own last tours of Europe and the Middle East in 1955 and 1956. In the first of these years she went to Russia, where she found "the smugness of the population" to be "absolutely unbearable" [13] and where she delivered herself of some pungent comments about her colleagues in journalism, whose ponderous style and almighty self-importance had risen, she believed, in direct ratio to their superficiality.

"All this attempting to peer beyond the Kremlin walls," Dorothy wrote with disdain, "— who will succeed whom — making a mountain out of a remark dropped by Bulganin at an embassy reception, etc., and never *looking*. They thought it remarkable of me to have spent two days in a public school!" [14] She looked everywhere in Russia for the human reality behind the socialist facade and by the end of her trip had an "overwhelming impression . . . of the liquidation of the revolution. All that is left is the dogma." [15] She was plainly thrilled when, a few months later, Nina Ponomareva, a world-class Soviet discus thrower, was arrested in London for shoplifting hats.

"Although usually on the side of law and order," Dorothy remarked, "my sympathy for Nina is such that I would gladly pay for the hats and her fine, too. For it is a pleasure to know that Nina is really a woman, with something more in her heart and head than the desire to heave a 2 pound 3 ounce disc. . . . Men seldom make passes at gals who weigh 210 pounds and are muscled like a heavyweight prizefighter. Yet a shy and loving heart probably beats beneath that tremendous diaphragm." [16]

She arrived back home after her Russian trip with "a terrible grippe" and a hacking cough that lasted for weeks, and she swore that she would curtail her traveling in the future. But a year later she was off again, this time in the company of Maxim Kopf and Virginia Shaw, her secretary — "Ginny," as a neighbor in Vermont recalled her: "Wonderful Ginny! A rock in a shaking world. Proud and strong and steady." [17] The junior Miss Shaw, in contrast to all of her predecessors, was not intimidated by Dorothy Thompson at any point in their association. She addressed Dorothy respectfully as "Mrs. Kopf," but otherwise she "took no guff." She argued with Dorothy; she actually talked back. She was presented, in a tender moment, with Christa Winsloe's watch, and more than once received a sincere apology from her employer for a stubborn or hastily considered remark: "You know," Dorothy would say, "I'm sorry, I was wrong."

"And that became a very important part of *me*," Ginny remembered, "to say you're wrong when you *are* wrong. . . . I miss Twin

Farms at night. I would just sit and listen, and listen, and listen." [18] During the Middle Eastern swing of 1956 Ginny was engaged as, among other things, a companion for Maxim; they went to Mykonos together while Dorothy dined in Athens with the King and Queen of Greece. ("My waistline is *not* contracting," Dorothy reported to a friend in New York. "We all have been eating like pigs.") [19] The tour began in Paris and moved on through Turkey to Lebanon, Egypt, India, Pakistan, Iran, Iraq, and the State of Israel, where Dorothy confronted a hostile press and tripped and fell as she walked through the Mandelbaum Gate into West Jerusalem. Her visit to Israel coincided almost exactly with the Suez crisis and the 1956 war; it was at this moment, while she was still abroad and with the Arabs at the front of the news, that Dorothy's editors demanded her resignation as president of the American Friends of the Middle East. She was "writing propaganda," they claimed. She was "carrying water on both shoulders." She had better "make up her mind" as to what was important to her.

She was furious, naturally. "What in the dickens is propaganda!" she cried. In Cairo she obtained a three-hour interview with Gamal Abdel Nasser and reported it verbatim in five extended columns: "I suppose they will call *that* scoop propaganda. They wouldn't if I had bagged an interview with Khrushchev." But she decided to resign from AFME rather than struggle any more. [20] She was getting ready to give up a lot that had mattered to her. She was drinking, too, much more than was sensible — although according to her staff and companions, Dorothy always had "all of her wits," even at the end of the longest nights by the fire. [21] If she was "ranting" more than usual, it was only in keeping with her state of general exhaustion and her mounting crankiness in off moments. A late column in "On the Record" ("Now Mama's Really Disgusted") called for a revolution of "nose-thumbers" in America, with a chorus of "loud derisive noises" and "gales of scornful laughter" for accompaniment.

"What this country needs are some old-fashioned American radicals," Dorothy proposed, "and some old-fashioned American constitutional conservatives, and a few thousand articulate citizens who still have some guts in their bellies and brains in their heads." [22] She was mindful of the folly of space exploration, wondering in column after column if there were not "an element of what normally would be called criminal insanity in some of modern scientific genius." Was it really necessary, Dorothy asked, "to do everything that a few men conceive it *possible* to do, regardless of the consequences?" She would have felt better about the race to the moon if she had had any reason to believe that scientific discovery was the actual purpose of the trip. But it was not, and she well knew it was not: "The object [was] the final perfection of war."[23] In the autumn of 1957, when the Russians launched *Sputnik* and sent American scientists and strategists into a jingoistic frenzy, Dorothy gave over her column in the *Ladies' Home Journal* to a meditation on the moon. "The Lady Can Be Vengeful," her title warned, and Dorothy rather hoped she would be: "A claim on the moon should be staked out, it seems to me, by the women of the whole world — including, of course, Russian women — to protect the chaste huntress, wielding love's bow, from the rape of the warriors."[24]

This was the tone of the final columns, the tone of the *Ladies' Home Journal* pieces and the thirty essays that Dorothy selected with the help of her sister, Peggy, and published in 1957 as *The Courage to Be Happy*.[25] "The Woman Poet,"[26] "The Little Towns," "The Baby in the Kitchen," "Only the Rose" — she chose the most serene and "womanly" columns from her twenty years with the *Journal* and offered them up as the pure expression of her life and character. Virgilia Peterson, writing in the *New York Times,* remarked that Dorothy managed to strike a note of "authenticity" no matter what she wrote: "For Miss Thompson has no pretensions. She is what she is."[27] The critic for the *New York Herald Tribune* called her "an American institution."[28] A portion of her royalties went directly to her sister (who earlier in the year had been diagnosed with Parkinson's disease), but it was not only on Peggy's account that Dorothy pestered and badgered and harassed her publishers into promoting her book.

"I was disappointed in the review in the N.Y. *Times* book section," she wrote to Dale Warren at Houghton Mifflin on the publication of *Courage*. "It's a magnificent testimony to my character — of the 'whether you agree with her or not' variety — but it seems to be my fate always to be judged as a conscience and a character rather than as a mind and a writer."[29] Dorothy was more than ever concerned about her larger reputation and about the mark, if any, that she would leave on the world. Her husband had been urging her for years to start working on her memoirs, and if she had not been so busy "terryhootin' around the world" (in Peggy Wilson's phrase)[30] she might have done so before shock, and sorrow, and the force of regret left her with no other solace. She did not cease to declare that she was tired of column writing and that she wanted "to do

something more permanent than contribute to the wastepaper basket."[31] She was anxious to establish a lasting place for herself in the
history of American letters.

She sold the house on East Forty-eighth Street at the same time
that she carved up Twin Farms, purchasing a seven-room cooperative
apartment on the East River so she and Maxim could live on a single
floor when they needed to be in the city. Maxim had suffered for
years from lumbago and high blood pressure; both he and Dorothy
still chain-smoked, too, "like all the chimneys of [their] childhood."[32] They were absurdly resistant to advice about their health.
They were perfectly obnoxious when it came to basic nutrition.
Many times Dorothy proclaimed that as a child she had eaten "a
single orange once a year" and that obviously she had not died of
scurvy: "What you don't know won't hurt you." At the end of 1957
she underwent an operation for the removal of "an enormous number of adhesions, and scar tissue" in her bowel. She wrote about it
gaily in her column, linking her abdominal troubles only to the stress
and strain of moving.[33] And when Maxim had his first heart attack
in May 1958, she joked that he had picked "a good time" for it:
they were just getting ready to take possession of the Old House at
Twin Farms — "the Sheean House," as Dorothy supposed it would
always be called.[34]

She had kept seventy acres of the Twin Farms property, most of
it wilderness, with a tiny strip of garden at the far side of the lawn.
She was "working like mad" to renovate the place, transplanting
perennials, ripping out baths, remodeling her kitchen, ransacking
files. ("In nightmares I have dreamed of the extinction of humanity,"
Dorothy confirmed, "not by H-bombs, but under a smothering of
paper.")[35] As she cleared out her houses she sent carloads of books
to libraries, charities, and soldiers overseas: "Scores of books on
'current' issues, already uncurrent; all the what-to-do-about-it volumes, how to deal with our defeated enemies, achieve eternal peace,
banish anxiety, become a success. . . . The annotations indicate
that I've read them all. [But] what's not in my head now never will
be."[36] She did not have "twenty minutes to sit down" during all that
spring at the farm. Walter Lippmann wrote to say that her commentary had "never been so original, so penetrating, and so full of
ripe wisdom";[37] she did not realize until months later, when Maxim
was dead, that she had been propelled, "consumed, eaten up by
fear."

"I did not know it then," she confessed, "— I did not let myself know it."[38] She battled the thought of Maxim's mortality right up to the last minute. He recovered from his first heart attack only to be stricken by a second within days of coming home from the hospital. It was the Fourth of July 1958 when he returned to Mary Hitchcock Hospital in Hanover, and it was the morning of the seventh when he died — around three o'clock, while Dorothy sat in a room at the Hanover Inn and flipped through a Gideon Bible. Later she swore that her hand opened the book spontaneously to that section of Psalm 119 entitled KOPH: "I cried with my whole heart, hear me, O Lord . . . I cried unto Thee."

For several weeks she went about her business "like an automaton." It had long been said of Dorothy that when a crisis hit, "the pieces flew together"; she was "obeying the pull of invisible strings."[39] "MAXIM DIED THIS MORNING AFTER CORONARY," she telegraphed a hundred friends. ". . . FUNERAL HERE THURSDAY AFTERNOON PRAY FOR ME — DTK."[40] Not long before, she had bought a spacious shaded plot in a corner of the Barnard cemetery, and it was here that she buried Maxim, under "a great boulder of blue limestone from the fields," with no religious ceremony apart from "the beautiful, beautiful prayer for the dead." She had not known before this how deeply her husband was loved in the community: a delegation of townspeople from Barnard came to her and asked if they might be pallbearers at the funeral.

"I saw our friends against a backdrop of trees," Dorothy remembered, "and masses and masses of flowers around the evergreen blanket that covered his body. I had not the slightest sense of his being in the ground, but a powerful sense of his presence. . . . This I felt with extreme intensity as, after the service, I turned, with my son, and walked away. I literally saw [Maxim] walking slightly ahead of me, with the air of one who would say that it had been a sweet party and gone off well."[41] Afterward Dorothy remarked that she felt as if she had been shot — "and I know when people are shot they don't feel anything. It is only when they begin to recover that the pain begins."[42] Ernest Cuneo, the chairman of the North American Newspaper Alliance, came to lunch at Twin Farms at the end of July and found Dorothy gulping Scotch by the cupful, while "the leaves rolled in the trees" and she "poured out her heart about Maxim." Her grief was terrible to witness, Cuneo reported: "Terrible. It put me in mind of Xanadu."[43]

"Only those who knew us very intimately, and they were not many, can possibly comprehend what has happened to me," Dorothy wrote to Bruce and Beatrice Gould, her editors at the *Ladies' Home Journal.*

> I always had the conviction that we would die simultaneously, in the same second, and now that I walk around, performing the normal duties of life, I have no feeling at all. I have, in fact, no comprehension that he is dead. I see him and hear him, and feel him patting my shoulder and saying rather roughly, "Now, don't carry on; it doesn't become you." . . . All this sounds horribly pathetic, but it mustn't be pathetic. He *hated* pathos, or any kind of sentimentality — imagined feelings. But he could make "You are the damndest sucker I ever knew" into a declaration of love to melt one's heart. . . . My dears — I have been *protected* — protected in every way, above all against myself. And now what shall I do?

At the end of August she gave up her newspaper column. "I have wanted to do so for at least two years," she said, "not only because the pressure of tri-weekly datelines makes any other large concentrated work impossible, but also because I feel the futility of writing, at this time, in that sort of medium."[44] Dorothy used the last edition of "On the Record" — she titled it *"Ave, Salve, Vale!"* ("Hail and Farewell") — to announce her retirement and to thank her fans. "One feels courtesy and gratitude toward one's readers and editors," she affirmed. "One does not abruptly sever relations of long standing."[45] The directors of the Bell Syndicate, having accepted her decision to retire, urged her to remember that if she ever changed her mind she would still have a place with them, at Bell. But she doubted very much that that would happen. She had "shot [her] mark."[46] She intended to continue in her duties as a contributor to the *Ladies' Home Journal,* but otherwise she was through writing columns. She would get to work on her memoirs. She would write "a history of my times."

"I want to digest the experiences of my life," she told Dale Warren, "and write a personal biography not just of myself but of this extraordinary century. . . . It will take me probably the rest of my working life to finish — I am sure a minimum of two years. And it will either be very important or I shall not publish it at all."[47] The demise of "On the Record" was reported in *Time* and *Newsweek* as an American event: Dorothy Thompson was "the first and finest of national newshens," said *Time.*[48] Within days she heard from eight different publishers who were eager to put her memoirs under contract (among them Doubleday, Simon and Schuster, Houghton Mifflin, and McGraw-Hill). But she had no plans that included editorial supervision.

"Delicious not to care whether I can do it or not," she wrote to Cass Canfield at Harper and Row. "Delicious no date lines, no fan mail (for or against). But forget it for the time being. Inside the Twentieth Century — and inside me, a person of no importance." She would let Canfield know when she had completed her manuscript — she would let them all know.[49] In the meantime she was going "to *work*, and work better than I have ever done. Maxim tells me that — that I must testify to what I know of life, and love, and wisdom."[50]

She stayed on at Twin Farms for the rest of the summer and well into the fall of 1958. "Here it is still absolutely beautiful," she wrote at the end of October, "even on sullen days, and even although the trees are beyond their violent but lovely prime. At this time of year we have a Mediterranean sky, completely different from the summer sky when everything on earth is green — Maxim said, 'Summer is spinach.' "[51] She had no intention of returning to New York without her husband. The "great anonymity of that city, its lonely crowds, . . . its daily, hourly crimes" would be intolerable without Maxim.[52] Michael came to visit "between plays"; Bernadette and the two young boys were constantly in the house, "and it seems to me," said Dorothy, "that people are eating, washing dishes, washing clothes and talking (about nothing of importance) *all* the time."[53] A reporter from the *Boston Globe* turned up to do a story on "the First Lady of American Journalism" and found her "horribly tired," "hunched forward," lighting and crushing out cigarette after cigarette and shaking her head in bewilderment over the gladiolus that had failed to come up that year.

"It's been the strangest summer," said Dorothy. She was reading *The Time of the Juggernaut* and reflecting on the organization of her memoirs. She had no idea of where to start. "Life is not something chronological," she explained, "in the sense of years. The movement of time is illusory." Her father, for example, had died almost forty years earlier, but "he has never been gone from me."

"What is the best thing you can say about yourself?" the *Globe*'s reporter asked.

"I never wrote to be popular," Dorothy answered. "It cost me a lot." She had plans to mount a traveling exhibition of Maxim's paintings and to publish a book of his work, but she was "finding it extremely hard to concentrate, hard to get at anything."[54] The children forced her to assume an outward cheerfulness, and the older boy, John Paul, gave her "a shy love" that touched her greatly.[55] But at night she was overwhelmed with loneliness. Probably she told no one when she began, propped up in bed, to write "letters" to her husband:

> Beloved: Why should I not write to you, even though I do not yet have your correct address, nor ever will until we meet, as I am reasonably sure we shall. (Though how — in what form — by what recognition — I cannot, indeed, even guess.) Still, I am here, in *this* life, and I am talking with you all the time, so I will write, as if you were in the South Seas, and I in Damascus! Then I was frantic at the separation and difficulty of communication. I cabled you, do you remember? I don't remember what, but I remember your reply: "Tahiti has changed, and I have changed, and I long for Vermont and you."[56]

And she went on to tell him about the changing of the seasons; about her plan to spend the winter in Hanover, where she would have access to the library at Dartmouth and could begin the research for her autobiography;[57] about John Paul, who was sick with something and running a fever: "He is in bed in the office where I worked yesterday, and afterward, at four, we had tea together, on a tray, with the best china. . . . I called him Mr. Lewis and crooked a refined finger." She was seeing old friends, to the extent that she could stand it: the Wesbrooks, Hilda Rothschild, and Lisa Sergio, who had stood by her from the beginning of Maxim's illness and was "a godsend," most assuredly. One night, driving to Barnard from Hartland-Four-Corners, Dorothy "mistook a curve" and found herself up on the edge of a bank. She had nearly flipped over in the car. "Afterward," she wrote, "I thought why I should have cared. But I have never thought of suicide, honestly, not *once*. How you would despise me! . . . No, I never thought of suicide. 'I will round out the circle of my life' — like you. But I think the circle will soon close. The test will be the book. If I can do it, I will, I think, live to complete it. If not — all the better."

She rented an apartment for the winter at 26 East Wheelock Street in Hanover. She had great plans at the start, not just to write her book (which she called "my *summa*") but to live at Dartmouth as a kind of literary hostess. She was looking forward to mingling with the students. "Perhaps I could do something to aid them in 'the art of contrary thinking,' " she wrote to Walter Lippmann, "by a little application of the Socratic method, after some suppers for hungry young men."[58] It was a shock for Dorothy to find out that the latest crop of Ivy League scholars had not a clue as to who she was. Stories made the rounds after her death of Dorothy in confrontation with some vaguely enthusiastic fans who wanted to congratulate her on her biting wit and clever poetry.

"I am afraid that you have me confused with that Parker woman," she was quoted as having said[59] (though these meanspirited words do not sound like her, and Dorothy Parker herself enjoyed no special vogue in the Eisenhower era). The staff at the Baker Library at Dartmouth remembered Dorothy's "huffiness" when she visited the stacks,[60] but Evelyn Stefansson, who had moved to Hanover with her explorer husband, Vilhjalmur, was more impressed by her "confusion" and her almost visible need for "intimacy." Hitherto Mrs. Stefansson (who would later become a psychotherapist) had judged Dorothy to be somewhat "unempathic." She was drawn to her now unexpectedly, one woman to another: "We touched each other finally."[61] Dorothy was not ready to admit that the peace and quiet of a college town was horribly unsettling to her nerves. She was sending out letters to acquaintances old and new, asking for memories of Hamburg, New York; of the woman suffrage campaign; of the National Social Unit. She stated her intention to reread "every one" of her articles and columns. But she was making no progress on her book. She lived in Hanover with her German maid, Waltraut Schmidt — "Traudl" — "organizing" her memoirs and drinking a great deal of Scotch. On November 13 she went to New York to "attend to some business affairs" and make arrangements for the upcoming exhibition of Maxim's paintings. She hoped to stay no more than ten days, but on the twenty-first she was rushed to University Hospital for an emergency operation on her bowel.

"I had known for a long time," she would admit later, "during and since Maxim's illness, that my 'insides' were not behaving normally. . . . However, in N.Y. my entire digestive system simply stopped operating altogether, and massive colonic irrigations and even castor oil sufficient to elicit an anti-fascist confession were useless. . . . I now know that I have been very ill, . . . and this relieves me of many self-recriminations which have depressed me, often to the point of tears." She lost a yard of her colon under the surgeon's knife and found herself recuperating, not without relief, at the Hotel Alden on Central Park West, one block from Michael Lewis's apartment and many miles from the disquieting calm of Hanover. The operation had actually served to clear her head. "For the first time," she remarked, "I really want to write."[62]

But New York proved to be no more agreeable than New Hampshire had been when it came to writing books. A diary that Dorothy began in January 1959 opened with the flat declaration that "conditions here are impossible. The telephone rings all day — no privacy — impossible." Ginny Shaw had been "let go" with the close of "On the Record" (she took a job at Harvard, and later one at Barnard College), and Dorothy had to make do with temporary and sporadic secretarial help. Faith Waterman, an old and valued friend who had first worked for Dorothy in 1947, now assumed the management of her still-voluminous mail, assuring her that she was not mistaken in thinking that it took half the day, every day, just to deal with her correspondence.

"There's a story in this," said Dorothy, who was finding nothing so concrete in her reminiscences of childhood. An extended essay about life at the turn of the century emerged as "The Age of Innocence," but it was "too slow," in Dorothy's estimation, and "too detailed": it collapsed beneath the weight of its pinafores and guimpes, its pickles and preserves. On January 18 Dorothy piled "papers — papers — papers" into seven cartons and trunks and set off for Southern Pines, North Carolina, the balmy retirement village where she had been asked to spend the remainder of the winter with Tish and Wallace Irwin. The Irwins had been friends of Dorothy's since 1928, when she had first come back to America with Sinclair Lewis. Wallace Irwin was now dying, and Dorothy was glad to be able to "help out" somewhere. "If I can't work here," she remarked of Southern Pines, "I can't work anywhere." Her diary of that winter confirms that, in fact, she could not work at all:

> *January 8:* How long is this business going to last — of being exhausted by *everything* (except sleeping!)?
>
> I don't think it's the operation (or only or chiefly). I have lived like an overwound watch spring for years. One can go on for a long time being propelled by tension. (Maxim thought it essential to anything creative.) Once the spring breaks the watch can't be rewound. It stops.
>
> *January 22:* I wrote about Tonawanda, suddenly remembering "The Scottish Woman" and her taking me to see the strange corpse.
>
> I don't know what all this has to do with my "life and times," but certainly my life had its essential pattern fixed before I was 12. Odd that I really never knew what I wanted to "do" with my life except live it, and not work from 9 to 5 in an office, at a "job." Journalism

was only a means to an end — to see, to learn, if possible to *be*. The means swallowed the end and the search for freedom became a (voluntary) slavery. I find today that the "success" I had means nothing to me whatever. I wonder *exactly* what went wrong.

January 23: Wrote all morning, struggling still with childhood memories. It is very difficult not to mix up what I really remember with what I have built up around a recollection or early impression. Also, 22 years of writing comment leads me to editorialize instead of letting incident or impression speak for itself. From being four or five I leap into being sixty, talking *about* something instead of reproducing it. This is an artistic failure.

January 31: My "obsession" with the book evaporates whenever I am not actually writing. In these last days I am again conscious that the whole project is probably an excuse to go on living, and again "Something comes to me in the night" telling me that I shall not do so for long — and the thought is not unwelcome. I look *forward* to nothing. It is an odd thought that my life at present probably means more to Tish than to anyone else. . . .

My insides aren't functioning well, and I think — "With Maxim's death, I lost my guts."

February 3: I woke up this morning and suddenly burst into sobs. I do not feel well — in fact I feel very unwell indeed. There are days when I do not want to go on anymore, and this has been one of them.[63]

She rose to her normal height of majestic self-confidence when Wallace Irwin died that spring; she was "a tower of strength" to Tish, and when the Irwin family gathered in mourning at Southern Pines, she delivered an impromptu sermon on the meaning of Wallace's life — "as if she had had religious training herself," said Polly Irwin, Wallace's daughter-in-law. Later, however, Polly was unable to recall a thing that Dorothy had actually said: she remembered only her presence, "her power," the *effect* of her words.[64] But the experience wore Dorothy to the bone — "Sickness and death seem to dog my footsteps," she wrote; "I feel like Typhoid Mary"[65] — and besides, Southern Pines was a crashing bore.

"One thing I *know* is that I *never* want to live in a resort," Dorothy proclaimed. "Climate is glorious but everyone here is old and preserving his health (or hers) and the only young people one sees are the colored. Awfully ingrown community and much easily hurt feelings. Awful!"[66] Dale Warren "invited himself" to visit and stayed eight days: no work got done.[67] Dorothy was happy to head north again in April. She had "waived a faithful oath" to herself and agreed to speak to the faculty at Syracuse University, where she saw her old roommates from college and had her picture taken with local dignitaries. Then she went back to Vermont, determined to prettify "the burying ground where Maxim's body lies" and to get down to work at last.[68] She was more grateful than ever now for the attention of her friends; after stopping to visit Marcel Fodor in Washington on her way north, she wrote to him from Vermont:

> My trouble, and a very real one, is that I am absolutely without any creative ideas or urges, and any kind of intellectual effort tires me horribly. I am no good for more than four or five hours, and have to drive myself to a pad or typewriter. . . . It is some comfort that I still get letters begging me to resume my column and saying that I was the only commentator who made any sense at all. But were this true it is still irrelevant, because nothing anyone thinks or writes affects the situation at all — everything is in the hands of the power elite. . . . I have practically abandoned reading newspapers for they merely repeat each other *ad nauseam;* fresh ideas do not emerge anywhere, or even good old-fashioned ones. No ideas.[69]

She made plans to spend three days a week that summer at Twin Farms and four at her Hanover apartment. She did her best to honor this commitment, but there were "constant distractions": renovations on the house, visits from grandchildren, runny noses, broken stairs. "Meanwhile I am trying to write an autobiography," she observed dryly, "— me and the twentieth century — but I am afraid, what I have long suspected, that the twentieth century is a bit too much to chew on. I have reached the age of ten, and think I will stay there. Mighty pretty country, and centuries removed from today."[70] In the middle of the summer Dorothy had a visit from Marguerite Jarvis, her best friend from Hamburg, New York, whose married name — Mrs. Thomas Bourne — she had never been able to remember in the intervening years. A miraculous normality attended the reunion of these two disparate friends. There was no condescension from Dorothy toward this woman who had never left Hamburg, and no exaggerated awe from Marguerite, whose existence as the wife of a small-town doctor had been rich and accomplished. Something "completely American" was going on here, something about Hamburg and that world and that generation that Dorothy hoped very much to be able to capture in her memoirs. But no work got done: on July 17, while lunching in Woodstock, she suffered a heart attack and wound up as a patient at Gifford Memorial Hospital in Randolph.[71]

She stayed in bed for about four weeks, amusing herself by reading and sending postcards to her friends. "I'm feeling fine," she wrote to Agatha Young, "only bored. . . . I don't wish you or anyone else were here."[72] At some level Dorothy must have realized that this latest reversal in her health would mean the end of her plans for her book. She turned her attention almost impishly to her malfunctioning organs, playing in the *Ladies' Home Journal* with "the everyday phrases that translate into *physical* terms the emotional states of the heart: My heart stood still . . . was in my boots . . . was in my throat . . . turned over . . . jumped . . . sank . . . leaped for joy . . . broke . . . melted . . . was full. Heartsick . . . wring the heart . . . 'the heart bowed down by weight of woe' . . . Richard the Lion-Hearted . . . heavyhearted, hardhearted, softhearted. A heart of stone . . . of lead . . . of ice."[73]

She had begun to dwindle, literally. She was turning into an old lady, and was "being treated," she complained, "as if I were a very old, valuable, and cracked piece of Chinese porcelain. One trouble with heart attacks is that although they are rather terrifying when they occur, one feels perfectly well when they are over, and it is hard to have to restrict one's physical and mental life for weeks, or even months, in order to assume that it won't happen again, after which of course it might happen anyway."[74] For the time being Dorothy was forbidden to climb stairs, which ruled out the apartment in Hanover, or drive a car, which kept her "pretty well grounded" at Twin Farms. She was "still taking a great deal of sedation of one kind or another," and she noted sorrowfully that "everything you take to slow up your heart action and keep down your blood pressure also slows up your mental processes."[75] Carl Zuckmayer, who had gone through the same thing a few years before, referred to it as "the *Vertrottlungskur*" (with apologies to Heine), and Dorothy agreed with him completely: "I am 'being cured to idiocy,' " she said.[76] She was in no condition, in that autumn of 1959, to deal with her wayward son, whose life suddenly went "straight overboard."

At the beginning of the year Michael Lewis had had the good fortune to be hired again by Alfred Lunt and Lynn Fontanne as a member of the touring company of the Lunts' revival of *The Visit*, Friedrich Dürrenmatt's wicked comedy about "the richest woman in the world," who bribes a small village, "somewhere in Europe," into murdering the man who once seduced her. Michael played the village policeman and by all accounts delivered one of the finest performances of his career. His success was accompanied by a rapid acceleration of his drinking, however, and by what Dorothy called "a sort of longing for the gutter."[77] Jimmy Sheean caught up with the *Visit* tour in San Francisco and reported to a friend that Lynn Fontanne was nearing the end of her patience:

> I got it quite clear in my head that Lynn really couldn't endure the boy and would be glad to have him fired, although she also says he is the best they have yet had for the part he is playing. . . . Alfred says he gets fired every single week by the managers, and he (Alfred) saves him every time because, he says, "this boy has genuine talent for acting." It was the most encouraging thing I'd heard about Mike for years! Lynn agrees about the talent but says he is quite awful to have in the company, especially on tour when they are so much together, because he gets really foully drunk and has fights with all the other actors, real fights. . . . Alfred has stood by him so far quite steadfastly but I have the distinct impression that Lynn would not repine if some day Alfred decided that the limit of endurance had been reached.[78]

Michael's predicament as a foil for the Lunts was no doubt exacerbated by the deterioration of his private life. In 1959, during an engagement in summer stock, he met and fell in love with Valerie Cardew, an English actress who was following him now on tour. Stories that reached Dorothy described Valerie as a "sex pot" and "death in the afternoon," but the information was exaggerated, and Dorothy was smart enough to realize that "the girl" herself was not at fault.[79] She knew, and had always known, that Michael had affairs. Everyone knew it, including Michael's wife, Bernadette, who was "French and practical" and not prone to hysterics. Until the marriage was actually over, however, Bernadette Lewis never told Dorothy how difficult her life with Michael had been: how often Michael came home drunk or did not come home at all; how he woke up regularly in "tenth-rate hotels," "rolled of his wallet" and unsure of anything but his need for another drink. It was a familiar enough story to Dorothy. She succumbed to a massive attack of self-recrimination on that score, but not before sending a resounding protest to Rebecca West:

It is his heartlessness about other people that drives me crazy. He seems to have no compassion whatever. When I had that heart attack last July [he] was awfully upset, but what he said was, "If Mother should die, *I* would be sunk." He is the only protagonist in all his dramas. . . . If I had my life to live over I would be damned careful by whom I had a child. And I would not choose a genius or a near-genius, and certainly not a drunkard. Love and kisses, nevertheless — Dorothy.[80]

Indeed, she took Michael's domestic troubles so completely to heart that she wound up in a psychiatrist's office herself, worried that she was having a nervous breakdown and that her inability to resolve the situation would destroy her once and for all. "The trouble with me is that I was given too much responsibility very early in life," she concluded, "and I take anything connected with my family very hard. In fact I take most things too hard. . . . *Meine Ruhe ist hin, mein Herz ist schwer.*"[81] Dorothy had no way of knowing whether Michael's passion for Valerie Cardew was "just a violent love affair, or whether it [was] much more profound."[82] She did not especially care. She was concerned about her grandchildren, five-year-old John Paul and rosy, two-year-old "Gwegowy," who had become (and would remain) the apple of his family's eye.[83] John Paul, in particular, was "a perfect seismograph of tension"; he did not need to be told about his father and Valerie to know that there was trouble in the house.[84] While sorting through papers for her autobiography, Dorothy may have reread her own letters from the 1930s, when the interests of her career and the demands of an impossible marriage had overridden any and every consideration of Michael Lewis's feelings.

"It's probably my early Puritan training," she reasoned, "but whenever Michael goes haywire I am overcome with the most suicidal feelings of guilt." She was now sending Michael letters that were as long and logic-ridden as any she had penned to his father. She wanted him to see a psychiatrist; she wanted him to see a clergyman; she had arranged a meeting with Marty Mann, who at that time had been sober longer than any other woman in Alcoholics Anonymous. Dorothy was desperate for Michael to go to AA, to "face reality" and live up to his responsibilities, but she had no better success with him than she had ever had with Red.[85] Michael returned from his tour in *The Visit* to announce that he was going to divorce

Bernadette and marry Valerie. Dorothy promptly slipped on a rug and cracked her ribs.

"According to the Psychopathology of Everyday Life," she moaned to Rebecca West, "I am certainly punishing myself for something."[86] It was Rebecca who urged her not to bother. In 1956 Rebecca's own son, Anthony West, had turned against her in a widely publicized roman à clef called *Heritage*. Although fictionalized, and tame by any later standard, it was the first in the school of "Mommie Dearest" memoirs,[87] and it left Rebecca with some very clear ideas about famous women and their children:

> I believe hostility to other people's work is an active factor in the lives of neurotics and psychotics — they don't approve of work, it's part of life, it sets their death wish into action. . . . I wonder if your Mike isn't unconsciously gunning for your autobiography. Don't let him get away with it. . . . It is a feminist work we have to perform. In the past women subscribed to the legend that the mother was always wrong, and gave themselves up to the sense of guilt. We have got to refuse to go under.[88]

But Dorothy was "under" already. "I realize there is nothing I can do," she wrote to Rebecca's husband, Henry Andrews, "and therefore do nothing — than which there is nothing harder." In the spring of 1960 Rebecca left for South Africa to report on apartheid for the *Sunday Times* of London. "How I wish the English rather than the Boers had the upper hand among the whites in South Africa!" Dorothy exclaimed when she heard this news. Not that it mattered: "Who won the Boer War anyway — or any other war?"[89] The depression she had battled since the death of Maxim Kopf had no chance of lifting under the added weight of Michael's divorce. "Things that I could do for years 'with my left hand' now exhaust me," said Dorothy. Her brain was operating "like a stuck phonograph record."[90] She was "drowning in drugs."[91]

In March she went back to Washington, to stay with Tish Irwin, whose apartment at 2101 Connecticut Avenue was the scene of Dorothy's last attempts at working. She spent hours and days with "good old Fodor," reminiscing about Vienna and Berlin and the golden age of foreign correspondence. Fodor, too, had been recently widowed, and his company "was the only thing all winter" that Dorothy really enjoyed — "apart from Tish and the kindness she showed me."[92] A concerted effort was made to revive her spirits. "JUST HAVE AN IM-PULSE TO SAY WE LOVE YOU DEARLY," Rebecca and Henry cabled from England. ("COULDN'T HAVE BEEN SENT TO A MORE GRATE-FUL ADDRESS," Dorothy answered. "RECIPROCAL.")[93] Later in 1960 Ginny Shaw spent some time with Dorothy in Vermont and departed with the thought that she should never have left her alone.

"I should have stuck with her," said Ginny regretfully. "I should have *made* her write the book."[94] There were awful scenes with Michael all that year: crying jags, shouting matches, drunken telephone calls. "Mother," said Michael, in his cups, "I will never be a happy man. I am doomed to unhappiness. I will go the way of my father." But he was "*not* like his father," said Dorothy in indignation, "for he lacks his father's extraordinary phosphorescence of mind and appalling energy and discipline in regard to his work."[95] Even the harshest of Dorothy's critics could see that she was devastated. At the end of 1960 she renewed her correspondence with Rose Wilder Lane, who had heard about her plans for an autobiography and rather showily returned to her batches of her letters from the 1920s. Dorothy's words of thanks and surprise — "I wrote you some time ago," she reminded Rose, "but never received a reply"[96] — were met with unconcealed bitterness.

"Oh come, Dorothy, really," said Rose. "You know that you cram-jammed your days with people and ideas that have nothing to do with me, and you've had no time nor need for our exchanging letters. . . . I believe that you had a letter in mind, but the cablegram came, the telephone rang, the car was waiting, and you'd be late. You've done what you wanted to do and got what you wanted to have; I wanted none of it for myself, but ever since we went walking in the valley of the Loire I've wanted for you whatever you wanted. So that's all right."[97]

"Yes, I *did* write you," Dorothy protested, "largely to ascertain whether you were still alive."[98] There was no point in arguing about it now, though. Rose began to melt, too, when she heard about Dorothy's troubles with her son. "I am so sorry," she wrote. "How futile, but what can I say? All my own griefs, tragedies, suddenly new again with news of yours. O Dorothy, *you* were to have none, they never should have happened to you."[99]

Dorothy had gone in the summer of 1960 to Sauk Center, Minnesota, the birthplace of Sinclair Lewis, where the citizens of "Main Street" had decided to honor Red as a favorite son. "Governor Orville Freeman proclaimed 1960 as Sinclair Lewis Year," Dorothy reported in an article for the *Atlantic Monthly*.[100] "The first weekends of July, August, and September were given over to a Lewis festival.

Nineteen sixty would have been the year of his seventy-fifth birthday, and is the fortieth anniversary of the publication of *Main Street,* the thirtieth of his winning the Nobel Prize." For three "gruelling" days Dorothy stayed in Sauk Center with Bernadette, her patient daughter-in-law, and young Gregory Lewis (whose brother, John Paul, had been stricken with measles and left behind in Minneapolis with a nurse). She wanted only to be present for the celebrations, she announced, and not to be "fussed over" by the locals. She herself did not know what had drawn her to Red's hometown:

> Some desire to pay tribute to him as an artist? Some appeal to a humorous sense of curiosity about how the satirizer of all boosters might now be celebrated by the same? . . . Or was there not another reason. . . ? Was it not a desire to learn, if I could, more about the man who for a few years had been the center of my existence, had fathered my only child, had caused me more grief than joy, but whom, after more than twenty years of total separation, I could never put out of my mind?

Dorothy's profile of Sinclair Lewis, "The Boy and Man from Sauk Center," was published in the *Atlantic* in November 1960 and was widely judged to be one of the finest works she ever produced. "It seems to me that you do as much in your handful of pages as I do in my whole monstrous book," said Mark Schorer,[101] whose eight-hundred-page *Sinclair Lewis: An American Life* would appear within months of Dorothy's death. Schorer had waited almost until the last minute before approaching Dorothy for an interview, only to discover, when he finally did, that her testimony changed the whole thrust of his book. "I think that I have known no other woman who was so completely without vanity," he remarked in his introduction. "I have known no other woman who could speak of her past as though it were the past of someone else."[102] He told Dale Warren that if *Sinclair Lewis* was to have any heroine, "that heroine will be Dorothy Thompson." But when Dale repeated these words to Dorothy, she murmured under her breath, "I seriously doubt if I will be the heroine of that book — or the heroine of any other book."[103] She was still in agony over the postponement of her memoirs.

"I am quite well again," she advised Schorer, "except that I tire very quickly and become discouraged about my book, perhaps because when I have the doldrums I see no earthly reason why I should write it at all. I know that such times are common to all writers and may indicate that I am less of a hack than I have thought . . . , but

I wish I were ten years younger. In years and in heart." [104] She had almost had a row with Dale when he pressed her to finish the book quickly and to limit it to three hundred and fifty pages. William L. Shirer had just had an enormous success with *The Rise and Fall of the Third Reich*, "which is pure journalism," Dorothy pointed out, "plus subsequent research," and which ran to eleven hundred pages on publication.

"I don't want a contract," Dorothy reminded Dale; "I don't want advice; when I have finished [the book] I am sure it will require rigorous cutting and editing. But I want a publisher — if there is such a one — who will be enthusiastic about it and think it unique, valuable, with fresh insights — and beautiful. And if there is no such publisher, well then there will be no such book — and then it goes into the wastepaper basket, or perhaps I will have a grandchild who will love to read it." [105] It took all the energy Dorothy had just to carry on; she was keeping Mark Schorer's words in mind. "You're just one of the great people," he had written to her in June 1960, "with one of the great, beautiful lives. . . . We can use some exempla of beauty and courage and intelligence and daring and — yes! — undemanding grandeur." [106] But the story was really over now: the autumn was blessedly quick.

She said good-bye to Vermont on October 25, 1960, boarding the train in White River Junction to go and spend another winter in Washington with Tish Irwin. In September Bernadette Lewis had taken both of her sons and left the country for Lisbon, where her sister was living and where she hoped she might put her own life back on track. Valerie Cardew was pregnant, meanwhile; if Michael's divorce came through in time, there would be another "legitimate" grandchild. Passing through New York on her way to Washington, Dorothy took time to meet Valerie and afterward pronounced her "sweet." She was not otherwise interested in pursuing the acquaintance. She arrived in Washington "looking like the wrath of God" — worn out, "disembodied and raddled from head to foot." [107] She took to her bed at once, and for the next six weeks she hardly left it.

She had decided that she needed a secretary on a part-time basis and was happy to find herself working, through one circumstance and another, with Alice Marie Tarnowski, the wife of Anton Tarnowski, a Polish count who had been friends with Maxim and with Rudi Rathaus, the best man at Dorothy's wedding in 1943. Alice was "competent and a darling," Dorothy wrote to John Gunther, [108] but her duties consisted mainly of standing by and taking down the odd dictation while Dorothy hacked and coughed and spit up blood (Alice noticed) into her handkerchief. When she was not asleep, Dorothy spent most of her time "yakking" with Tish. "They did nothing but drink and get waited on," said Don Irwin, Tish's son, while Alice Tarnowski remembered "endless conversation about *Willard*," Tish's chauffeur, who appears to have had rather a hectic schedule squiring ladies around town. Chief among Dorothy's interests that fall was the election of John F. Kennedy to the presidency: she had never had the slightest use for Richard Nixon, but neither was she able to imagine "a Catholic" in the White House, particularly one with such obvious movie-star qualities.[109]

"There is something about him," Dorothy remarked of Kennedy, "spoiled, and slightly neurotic. I have seen too many of these charismatic personalities in public life not to feel queasy about them."[110] She agreed with Fodor that television was "the best way to kill the last shred of intellect in people," and seconded his opinion that American politics, in the future, would function only on the most superficial level.[111] She envisioned "an alliance of organized minorities" in the United States, "consisting of organized labor (which means the Labor bureaucracy), organized ethnic groups (completely subservient to their self-appointed leaders), organized Jews (led and terrorized by the Zionists), organized educators (the NEA), and organized Catholics, [with] politicians outbidding each other for the favor of each. . . . This pattern," she ventured to say, "will encompass the ruin of the Republic."[112]

She made up her mind to go to Portugal at Christmas to visit her grandsons. She was astonished to think that "not so long ago" she had kept "ten balls in the air at once" and that now she could barely get across town without help.[113] On December 16 Tish Irwin and Alice Tarnowski saw her for the last time, "a frail and sick old lady," as she stepped into the elevator in the apartment building on Connecticut Avenue. Later in the week, in New York, Dinah Sheean joined Dorothy for lunch at the Cosmopolitan Club "and was *overwhelmed* with tenderness for her" — she who had once been "so grand and so vibrant." She was shrunken now, wizened, stooped, "her bosom gone," her gums stretched back from her teeth in a way that could only signify mortal illness.[114] Bill Shirer asked her to a cocktail party he was having, and when she arrived at the door he did not recognize her at all. He stared at her blankly.

"Bill!" cried Dorothy. "Bill, for Christ's sake, come off it! It's me, it's Dorothy!" She stood alone in a corner of the room for most of that afternoon, left out of the conversation, plainly confused by the chatter around her.[115] It was Jimmy Sheean's belief that Dorothy did not know who any of them were when he went out to Idlewild with Dinah and Michael to see her off on the plane to Lisbon: "She looked harassed, distracted, and the signs of great illness were upon her. . . . There was an irresistible sense of farewell." Her flight was called, "and she dived nervously into the appropriate doorway"[116] and flew off to her death, from a final heart attack, on January 30, 1961.

"She once quoted to me a line written by her friend, Carl Zuckmayer," Dale Warren remembered: " 'Home is not where you live, but where you want to die.' Most assuredly she did not want to die in a hotel room in Lisbon, alone in the middle of winter in the middle of the night."[117] She had left behind a letter for her son in Washington, a letter that Alice Tarnowski remembered she had dictated with some urgency. She wanted Michael to know that she had loved her life and that when death came, it would not be unwelcome. She asked for a plain funeral, an inexpensive urn to hold her ashes, and no ceremony beyond the simple prayers that Maxim had had.

"And I rather hope that people *will* send flowers," she added. What was the point of a funeral without flowers?

> I leave to you, your loved ones, and my grandchildren the memory of my love for you all; the wonders and beauties of this earth and universe that have given me so much joy; the solace of faith in a superhuman purpose and design; and the delights of art and of great minds.

"As I write this little note," Dorothy concluded, "I feel very grateful."[118] It was said that Michael swallowed nine brandies in succession when he heard that she had died.[119]

Epilogue

DOROTHY THOMPSON was not afraid of death — not at all, by her own account: " 'I pass death with the dying, and birth with the new-washed babe, and am not contained between my hat and boots.' " The words were Whitman's, more pertinent than ever, Dorothy thought, "in a civilization where perhaps the most needed of all things . . . is reconciliation with the idea of death."

Indeed, "the neurotic denial is very widespread," she wrote to John Gunther in 1949, when Gunther was struggling to reconcile the success of *Death Be Not Proud* with the loss of his only son, Johnny. "When Wells was killed," said Dorothy, "Red wrote me, 'Never mention it again to Michael!' Poor Red! Poor Michael, if I had followed that advice." She had an idea that "the miracle of death [is] no less than the miracle of birth, and everything is in the process of *becoming*. . . . Life, John, through all its transmutations, must be eternal. That was my childhood's faith. It is now both my faith and the conviction of my mind. Whatever comes to Johnny will be a miracle. Whatever comes will be a great renewal of life."[1]

She had suffered her second heart attack the day after New Year's in 1961. She had been planning to stay in Portugal for only a fortnight, but there was no question of her going home before her condition improved. The people who saw her at the British Hospital in Lisbon remembered her as "sunny," "cheerful," "animated," and "gay." She was "somebody who seemed to be at peace with herself," said Morris L. Nelson, an attaché at the American embassy who found himself serving as Dorothy's gofer and escort during her final illness. Michael flew over from New York at Bernadette's request, but flew home again after four days because his mother's spirits seemed to have rallied so dramatically.

"We went on a little sightseeing tour," she told Bernadette on the last day of her life, speaking of herself and the friendly Mr. Nelson. "After all, I've been in Lisbon for a month and I've seen almost nothing of the city."[2] She had left the hospital, against the advice of her doctors, and checked into the Reno Hotel, where she saw her grandsons for the last time just hours before she died. "I guess I must be a tough old girl," she scribbled on a card to Dale Warren.[3] She was found doubled over in bed on the morning of January 31, her dinner from the night before untouched, the telephone receiver knocked from its cradle in her attempt to call out for help. She died, as *Time* magazine entitled its obituary, "Without Regrets."[4]

She could not be cremated, as she had wished, because Portugal was a Catholic country. Her body was shipped to a vault in Woodstock, where it lay until the ground thawed in May and she could be buried next to Maxim. There was no eulogy — she had forbidden it — but a large crowd gathered at the funeral, among them Peggy Wilson, Hilda Rothschild, and a drunk and weeping Jimmy Sheean.[5] Dorothy herself had chosen the words for her epitaph: "Dorothy Thompson Kopf — Writer." Fourteen years later, when her son died of cancer, his family saw to it that his own grave, next to hers, would match the stately tone: "Michael Lewis — Actor. 'The rest is silence.'"

There was a daughter from Michael's second marriage, Lesley Lewis, a bright and pretty girl whose resemblance to her grandmother, as she grew older, stopped people in their tracks. The Barnardites talked about "spooks," and some of them claimed to have seen the ghost of Maxim Kopf in the trees around Twin Farms. In 1987 the Old House burned; apart from the chimney, the only thing left standing was a statue that Maxim had sculpted for the garden: a female figure, kneeling, faceless, but clearly stalwart, clearly Dorothy. It would have pleased her to know that when she died she was recognized as the greatest woman journalist of her time. She was "a phenomenal figure in American letters," said the *New York Times,* "a tireless worker" and "a good reporter."[6] It was high praise. The *Evening News* in Buffalo, commenting on the death of Erie County's native child, wondered if America would ever see her like again: "[She] never cared whose toes she trod on, what pride she undercut. . . . She was at every moment vibrant with her own emotions, implicated in her whole society's vision or action, committed without inner reserve."[7] She would not have thought journalism to be her most enduring achievement, however, nor wished it to be her only legacy to the granddaughter whom she never met:

> Well [she wrote once], it is our fate to live in a time of crisis. To live in a time when all forms and all values are being challenged. In other and more easy times, it was not, perhaps, necessary for the individual to confront himself with a clear question: What is it that you really believe? What is it that you really cherish? What is it for which you might, actually, in a showdown, be willing to die? . . . I say, with all the reticence which such large, pathetic words evoke, that one cannot exist today as a person — one cannot exist in full consciousness — without having to have a showdown with one's self, without having to define what it is that one lives by, without being clear in one's own mind what matters and what does not matter.[8]

That was the story she wanted to tell, the mission she had received in the parsonage at Hamburg. "Leave the interpretations to the analysts," she warned; "they're sure to be wrong."[9] She was "an overwhelming, larger-than-life figure" to women journalists of the next generation;[10] she was "double-portion" in the memory of her friends — among them Carl Zuckmayer, who remarked in his tribute to Dorothy that "anyone who knew her will always be grateful that she existed,"[11] and even Dinah Sheean, who, years later, a widow in London, sometimes thought that she could hear in the distance "Dorothy's satisfied, fat laugh," and imagined that Dorothy was "still talking somewhere, loudly, through all eternity."[12]

"Only yesterday," Rebecca West once reflected, "Henry and I were talking of a visit to America we hope to make in the next three months — and Henry said, 'Alas, no Dorothy!' And that is what she did: she made herself essential."[13]

Notes and Sources

DOROTHY THOMPSON'S papers are kept at the George Arents Research Library at Syracuse University, where Dorothy earned her undergraduate degree and where she hoped to see established a center for the study of journalism in the twentieth century. The material was catalogued in 1966 by Stephanie Leon and Susan D'Angelo, and the published inventory, with an introduction by Lisa Sergio, is available for consultation at almost any comprehensive research library.

The material at Syracuse is divided into ten series, arranged as incoming correspondence, outgoing correspondence, family papers, "Subject File" (consisting of miscellaneous materials, photographs, engagement pads, and so on), *Ladies' Home Journal* material, clippings and transcripts from "On the Record," individual manuscripts (published and unpublished, including speeches and radio broadcasts), notes and research materials, manuscripts by others, and oversize materials (scrapbooks, diplomas, scrolls, etc.). The archive is enormous, filling 150 research boxes and taking up 70 linear feet.

In citing material from Syracuse, I have used only the general designation SU, along with dates and titles where applicable and, occasionally, the Series number. The archive is extremely well organized, and there are no restrictions on access to it. I have cited material from other libraries and archival sources as necessary in the text.

During her lifetime Dorothy published eight books, all of them reprints or adaptations of her articles, columns, and radio broadcasts. They are listed here with their publishing data and cited in the notes by title only:

The New Russia. New York: Henry Holt, 1928.
"I Saw Hitler!" New York: Farrar and Rhinehart, 1932.
Dorothy Thompson's Political Guide. New York: Stackpole Sons, 1938.
Once on Christmas. London and New York: Oxford University Press, 1938 [unpaginated].
Refugees: Anarchy or Organization? New York: Random House, 1938.
Let the Record Speak. Boston: Houghton Mifflin, 1939.
Listen, Hans. Boston: Houghton Mifflin, 1942.
The Courage to Be Happy. Boston: Houghton Mifflin, 1957.

Three books have appeared since Dorothy's death that deal either directly or extensively with her life and career. These are Mark Schorer's *Sinclair Lewis: An American Life* (New York: McGraw-Hill, 1961), hereafter cited as Schorer; Vincent Sheean's *Dorothy and Red* (Boston: Houghton Mifflin, 1963), hereafter cited as Sheean; and Marion K. Sanders's *Dorothy Thompson: A Legend in Her Time* (Boston: Houghton Mifflin, 1973), hereafter cited as Sanders. There are, in addition, a number of in-depth profiles of Dorothy, which I have cited by author and title in the notes:

Alexander, Jack. "The Girl from Syracuse." *The Saturday Evening Post,* May 18 and 25, 1940; reprinted (1942) in *Post Biographies of Famous Journalists,* edited by John E. Drewry (Athens, Ga.: A University of Georgia Press Book, distributed by Random House).
Bottome, Phyllis. "Dorothy Thompson." Unpublished ms. [1943] at Syracuse.
"Cartwheel Girl." *Time,* June 13, 1939.
Fisher, Charles. "Dorothy Thompson, Cosmic Force." In *The Columnists.* New York: Howell, Soskin, 1944.
Harriman, Margaret Case. "The 'It' Girl." *The New Yorker,* April 20 and 27, 1940.
Kennedy, John S. "Global Lady." In *Molders of Opinion,* edited by David Bulman. Milwaukee: Brace Publishing, 1945.
Longmire, Carey. "God's Angry Woman." *Collier's,* June 23, 1945.
Marshall, Margaret. "Columnists on Parade" (No. VIII: Dorothy Thompson). *The Nation,* June 25, 1938.
Warren, Dale. " 'Off the Record' with a Columnist." *Saturday Review,* June 10, 1944.
———. "I Remember Dorothy." *The Courier,* Syracuse University Library Associates, Syracuse University, vol. IV, no. 2 (Summer 1964).
Wharton, Don. "Dorothy Thompson." *Scribner's,* May 1937.

I have used the following abbreviations in the notes and index:

DT   Dorothy Thompson
JB   Joseph Bard
JVS   (James) Vincent Sheean
LHJ   Ladies' Home Journal
MK   Maxim Kopf
MKS   Marion K. Sanders
ML   Michael Lewis
OTR   "On the Record"
PK   Peter Kurth
RW   Rebecca West
RWL   Rose Wilder Lane
SL   Sinclair Lewis

PROLOGUE

1. The account of DT's childhood, here and in chapter 1, is taken mainly from her autobiographical writings at SU. These are kept in Series 7 and include the rough drafts of her memoirs, written between 1958 and 1960 and titled variously "The Age of Innocence" and "The Wide, Wide World." I have referred to them hereafter as the DT Memoirs but have cited them only when it seems important to distinguish them from other sources. I have also relied extensively on "Goodbye, Little Angel," Margaret Thompson Wilson's charming memoir of growing up in Hamburg and Gowanda: Peggy's account was written in 1939–1940 at the request of Jack Alexander, who at that time was working on his profile of DT. Much of the Wilson material also appears in Alexander's "Girl from Syracuse." Other references as cited.

2. Quoted in J. W. Drawbell, Dorothy Thompson's English Journey (London: Collins, 1942), 251.

3. DT diary, typed, "November 20," kept during national lecture tour 1935–1936, hereafter cited as the Railway Diary (SU).

4. DT ms., unpublished, "Emotional Security," SU.

5. For the cyclone, see DT Memoirs; also different ms. drafts, "I Try to Think" and "Emotional Security," SU.

6. DT, Railway Diary, November 20, 1935.

CHAPTER ONE

1. Quoted in Lisa Sergio, "Dorothy Thompson, The Blue-Eyed Tornado," unpublished ms. in my possession.

2. From a loose ms., holograph, untitled, SU (Series 8).

3. J. W. Drawbell, Dorothy Thompson's English Journey (London: Collins, 1942), 202.

4. See DT, Railway Diary, undated entry [November 1935], an account of DT's visit to Harry Hill, "my favorite relative . . . the only member of the family who could pass for an Earl any day."

5. Sometime during the 1920s, in the only truly mysterious gesture of her life,

DT began to give her year of birth as 1894 instead of 1893. Ellen Sheean has suggested that she might have made the change out of pride, somewhere along the line, "so as not to be older than some man she was seeing." When she went to Europe for the first time, in 1920, she was still dating her age correctly, from 1893; and in June 1930, just before the birth of her son, she also gave her age correctly, as thirty-six (see her letters to RWL, at SU.) Otherwise she seems to have convinced herself that she had actually been born in 1894, and when her brother, Willard, in 1955, produced a family bible to prove her wrong, she snapped: "I don't give a damn, but having stood on its being 1894 through a series of Who's Whos, I shall keep to 1894 despite my annoying brother." (DT to H. L. Mencken, March 2, 1955, in the Mencken papers, New York Public Library.) On her gravestone in Barnard, nevertheless, in accordance with her own instructions, the correct date is given: 1893.

6. DT, "The American Way of Life," *LHJ*, April 1952.

7. Quoted in DT autobiographical sketch, 1951, SU.

8. DT, "I'm the Child of a King," *LHJ*, November 1959.

9. For information on Hamburg see Elton R. Heath, *Around Hamburg Village at the Turn of the Century*, with illustrations by Dorothy Markert, published by the Hamburg Historical Society, 1982.

10. DT, "Portrait of a Christian," screen treatment at SU.

11. DT, "The Little Towns," *LHJ*, February 1955; reprinted in DT, *The Courage to Be Happy*.

12. DT, "The American Way of Life."

13. DT, "The Little Towns."

14. DT, *Once on Christmas*.

15. DT Memoirs.

16. Peter Thompson's words are handwritten on a bound collection of obituary notices for Margaret Thompson, SU.

17. DT Memoirs.

18. From a loose manuscript, untitled, SU (see note 2).

19. DT speech, "I Knew a Christian," delivered November 29, 1939, on the occasion of bestowal of the Churchman Award upon Mrs. Eleanor Roosevelt, transcript at SU.

20. Peter Thompson's sermon, "Strength and Beauty," was delivered at Spencerport, N.Y., on February 20, 1910, and "published by request" (SU).

21. DT, "I'm the Child of a King."

22. DT, Railway Diary, November 20 [1935].

23. DT Memoirs.

24. DT, "Emotional Security," unpublished ms. at SU.

25. Quoted in DT, "Emotional Security," and in loose notes for her autobiography, SU (Series 7).

26. DT, "Emotional Security."

27. Drawbell, *English Journey*, 200.

28. DT, *Once on Christmas*.

29. DT, "I'm the Child of a King."

30. DT, "The Moments That Educate," *LHJ*, April 1954; reprinted in DT, *The Courage to Be Happy*.

31. DT, Railway Diary, January 14 [1936].

32. See DT, Railway Diary, account of her visit to Harry Hill.

33. DT, " 'Now Thank We All Our God,' " *LHJ*, November 1960.

34. DT, "The American Way of Life."

35. See the DT Memoirs; also MKS interview with (Peter) Willard Thompson, October 23, 1970, quoted in Sanders, 378 n. 9.

36. The narrative of Margaret Thompson's death is taken entirely from the DT memoirs.

37. DT, "Auntie and the Dragon," unpublished ms. at SU.

38. Wilson, "Goodbye, Little Angel."

39. John Gunther, "A Blue-Eyed Tornado," *New York Herald Tribune*, January 13, 1935.

40. DT, "Auntie and the Dragon."

41. Wilson, "Goodbye, Little Angel."

42. PK interview with Marguerite Jarvis Bourne, Hamburg, N.Y., September 13, 1987; and Marguerite Jarvis Bourne to DT, May 25, 1959, SU.

43. Heath, *Around Hamburg Village*.

44. DT, loose notes for autobiography, SU.

45. Sanders, 7.

46. DT Memoirs.

47. PK interview with Marguerite Jarvis Bourne.

48. Margaret Thompson Wilson, notes (handwritten) of a conversation with Marguerite Jarvis Bourne, Summer 1959, SU.

49. DT Memoirs.

50. DT, *Once on Christmas*.

51. DT, "The Theater: A Comment on America," *Tomorrow*, May 1942.

52. DT Memoirs.

53. DT, "The Theater: A Comment on America."

54. DT Memoirs.

55. DT autobiographical sketch, 1951.

56. George Abbott to PK, October 24, 1986; also in George Abbott, "*Mr. Abbott*" (New York: Random House, 1963), 39.

57. Warren, "I Remember Dorothy."

58. DT, Railway Diary, November 20 [1935].

59. Quoted in Drawbell, *English Journey*, 201.

60. PK interview with Freya von Moltke, Norwich, Vermont, December 6, 1985; also in Eugenia Schwarzwald, "*Eine Journalistin*," undated clipping at SU.

61. Wilson, "Goodbye, Little Angel."

62. Abbott, "*Mr. Abbott*," 7, 40.

63. PK interview with Marguerite Jarvis Bourne.

64. Wilson, "Goodbye, Little Angel."

65. Abbott, "*Mr. Abbott*," 40.

66. Wilson, "Goodbye, Little Angel."

67. Abbott, "*Mr. Abbott*," 7.

68. MKS interview with Willard Thompson, Sanders, 378 n. 12.

69. DT, "Emotional Security."

70. Quoted in Wilson, "Goodbye, Little Angel."

71. DT, "Emotional Security."

72. Wilson, "Goodbye, Little Angel."

73. Sanders, 12; the poem, "Way Down in Old Steuben," is at SU.

74. MKS interview with Willard Thompson, in Sanders, 13.

75. Wilson, "Goodbye, Little Angel."

CHAPTER TWO

1. DT, Railway Diary, December 11 [1935], recording conversation with Frances Moore.

2. DT, "Auntie and the Dragon," unpublished ms. at SU.

3. DT to JVS, April 13, 1951, SU.

4. Fanny Butcher, *Many Lives, One Love* (New York: Harper and Row, 1972), 20–21.

5. Quoted in Wilson, "Goodbye, Little Angel."

6. Sanders, 14.

7. Edwin Herbert Lewis to DT, May 28, 1928 (on the occasion of her marriage to Sinclair Lewis), SU.

8. The account of DT's days at Syracuse is taken from her various autobiographical writings and rough drafts at SU (Series 7). The material is not otherwise catalogued or identified, though one of the essays bears the title "Notes on College Days" and another was apparently written for publication in the *Nineteenth Century*. All quotes below are from this series unless otherwise indicated.

9. DT autobiographical sketch, 1957, written for publication of *The Courage to Be Happy*, SU, and in Houghton Mifflin Company archives, Houghton Library, Harvard University.

10. In her autobiographical sketches at SU, DT lists their names: Ethel Mead, Florence Lamb, Grace Griffith, and so on.

11. DT, untitled autobiographical ms., SU (Series 7), probably prepared as a speech to the faculty at Syracuse University, May 1959.

12. DT, "Are We in Peril?," ms. commissioned ca. 1940 by *Look* magazine, SU.

13. DT, loose ms., handwritten, SU (Series 8).

14. DT speech, "The Developments of Our Times," delivered in 1948 at John B. Stetson University, DeLand, Florida, as part of the Merrill Lectures. Published in 1948 by the University Press, DeLand.

15. From Ruth Hoople's notes on her friendship with DT, written for Jack Alexander ca. 1940 (SU).

16. DT, Railway Diary, December 11 [1935].

17. Letter (correspondent unknown) to John S. Kennedy, December 8, 1945, SU, written in response to Kennedy's profile of DT, "Global Lady."

18. Sanders, 32.

19. Bottome, "Dorothy Thompson."

20. Marjorie Shuler, "Expedition to Olympus," *Christian Science Monitor*, December 24, 1935.

21. DT, "Notes on College Days," SU; and notes of J. Winifred Hughes, prepared ca. 1940 for Jack Alexander's profile of DT (SU).

22. DT, Railway Diary, January 14 [1936]. The girl was Fanchon Arthur, for further information on whom see the Railway Diary and also DT, "The Moments

That Educate," *LHJ*, April 1954, reprinted in DT, *The Courage to Be Happy*. At the age of seventeen Fanchon entered a convent.

23. Quoted in Alexander, "The Girl from Syracuse."
24. Sanders, 18.
25. DT, Railway Diary, January 14 [1936].
26. DT Diary, 1920–1921, SU (hereafter referred to as the Europe Diary).
27. DT to Christa Winsloe, December 21 [1934], SU.
28. PK interview with Freya von Moltke, Norwich, Vermont, December 6, 1985.
29. Quoted in DT, "My First Job," ms. at SU.
30. Fisher, "Dorothy Thompson, Cosmic Force."
31. DT, untitled autobiographical ms., SU (Series 7).
32. DT, "My First Job."
33. DT to "Mr. Wright," June 11, 1920, SU.
34. Harriet Burton Laidlaw, "The Woman's Hour," *Forum*, November 1916.
35. DT to the *Buffalo Evening News,* undated, SU.
36. DT, "My First Job."
37. DT, Railway Diary, November 20 [1935].
38. From advice to "Organizers," and annual report (1917) of the New York State Woman Suffrage Party, in the Foley and Laidlaw collections, Schlesinger Library, Radcliffe College.
39. This story is told in every account of DT's career, but see especially Alexander, "The Girl from Syracuse," and Harriman, "The 'It' Girl." Quotes are from these sources.
40. Quoted in Charles Fisher, "Dorothy Thompson, Cosmic Force."
41. DT to "Mr. Wright," June 11, 1920.
42. DT to RWL, August 13, 1921. In the letter DT misquotes the lines from Longfellow. The letters between DT and RWL have been edited by William Holtz and prepared for publication as "The Correspondence of Dorothy Thompson and Rose Wilder Lane" (ms. in my possession). Many of the originals are in DT's papers at SU. I have cited them henceforth only by date.
43. Charles L. Dana, M.D., "Suffrage a Cult of Self and Sex" and "Anti-Suffrage News and Views," flyers prepared by the Woman's Anti-Suffrage Association, in the New York State Archives, Albany. Dr. Dana's remarks are truly breathtaking: "I am not saying that woman's suffrage will make women crazy. I do say that woman's suffrage would throw into the electorate a mass of voters of delicate nervous stability . . . and add to our voting and administrative forces the biological element of an unstable preciosity."
44. PK interview with Rinna Samuel (daughter of Barbara De Porte Grossman), London, October 5, 1987.
45. Ishbel Ross, *Sons of Adam, Daughters of Eve* (New York: Harper and Row, 1969), 175.
46. From a press release in the New York State Woman Suffrage Party collection, Library of Congress.
47. Gertrude Tone to DT, May 20, 1927, SU.
48. Sanders, 23.
49. Loose clipping [1923], SU.
50. Combined from Gertrude Tone's letters to DT of August 6, 1923, and May

20, 1927, SU; and to Pauline Newman, December 2, 1918, in the Newman papers, Schlesinger Library, Radcliffe College.

51. Gertrude Tone to Pauline Newman, November 9, 1918, in the Newman papers, Radcliffe.

52. DT diary, kept in Vienna and at the Villa Sauerbrunn, Winter 1932–1933, hereafter referred to as the Semmering Diary, SU.

53. See Gertrude Tone to Pauline Newman, February 12, 1920: "Everything spick and span here! Dorothy had even provided new chintz curtains and covers for my room. Talk about sublimation!" (letter in the Newman papers, Radcliffe).

54. DT, "The Developments of Our Times" (Merrill Lectures, Stetson University).

55. DT address, delivered to the Volunteer Land Corps, Twin Farms, Barnard, Vermont, August 29, 1942, transcript at SU.

56. DT, Europe Diary.

57. DT to Pauline Newman, September 8, 1918, in the Newman papers, Radcliffe.

58. For the Social Unit and Wilbur Phillips see Patricia Mooney Melvin in *American Community Organization: A Historical Dictionary* (New York: Greenwood Press, 1986). Phillips's papers are in the Social Welfare History Archives at the University of Minnesota, Minneapolis.

59. Edward Thomas Devine, "The Social Unit in Cincinnati," *Survey*, November 15, 1919.

60. Mary Burnett to DT, November 18, 1960, SU.

61. DT, "A Community Experiment Which Has Succeeded," *New York Times Magazine*, March 16, 1919.

62. DT, "The Developments of Our Times" (Merrill Lectures, Stetson University).

63. Typed copies (undated) are at SU.

64. Alexander, "The Girl from Syracuse."

65. "Cartwheel Girl."

66. Mary Burnett to DT, October 4, 1960, SU.

67. Devine, "The Social Unit in Cincinnati."

68. Alexander, "The Girl from Syracuse."

69. DT, Europe Diary.

70. DT to RWL, July 15, 1921.

71. DT, Europe Diary, in reference to plans for a novel based on her experiences with Wilbur Phillips.

72. Sanders, 33.

73. DT to RWL, July 15, 1921.

74. DT to Beatrice Sorchan, undated [but possibly part of DT's letter of November 13, 1920], SU.

75. DT to Pauline Newman, September 8, 1918.

76. DT, "The Developments of Our Times" (Merrill Lectures, Stetson University).

77. The application and a copy of the cover letter are at SU.

78. Peter Thompson to DT, June 21, 1920, SU.

79. Quoted in Eugenia Schwarzwald, *"Eine Journalistin,"* undated clipping at SU.

80. DT to RWL, September 14, 1921.

CHAPTER THREE

1. DT autobiographical sketch, 1957, written for publication of *The Courage to Be Happy*, SU, and in Houghton Mifflin Company archives, Houghton Library, Harvard University; and DT, "Water under Bridges," *Saturday Evening Post*, April 9, 1932.

2. DT to Beatrice Sorchan, June 26, 1920, SU.

3. Quoted in Sanders, 38.

4. DT to Beatrice Sorchan, June 26, 1920.

5. John Gunther originated this most famous epithet for DT, in "A Blue-Eyed Tornado," *New York Herald Tribune*, January 13, 1935.

6. Quoted in Wharton, "Dorothy Thompson."

7. Quoted in Harriman, "The 'It' Girl."

8. Quoted in Alexander, "The Girl from Syracuse."

9. See DT, "The Hope of a New Palestine," *The Outlook*, September 8, 1920.

10. DT to Beatrice Sorchan, November 18, 1920, SU.

11. DT autobiographical sketch, 1957.

12. DT to Beatrice Sorchan, November 18, 1920.

13. PK interview with Rinna Samuel, London, October 5, 1987.

14. Quoted in RWL, "The Pied Piper of Budapest," *San Francisco Bulletin*, July 15, 1922.

15. Quoted in J. W. Drawbell, *Dorothy Thompson's English Journey* (London: Collins, 1942), 178.

16. DT, Europe Diary.

17. DT to RWL, September 14, 1921.

18. DT, Europe Diary.

19. DT short story, "The Top Floor at Madame Tusson's," ms. at SU.

20. DT to Beatrice Sorchan, December 9, 1920, SU.

21. DT, Europe Diary.

22. DT to Beatrice Sorchan, October 22, 1920, SU.

23. DT and Barbara De Porte, "The Last Day," ms. at SU.

24. DT, Europe Diary.

25. DT to Beatrice Sorchan, November 18, 1920.

26. DT to Beatrice Sorchan, September 26, 1920, SU.

27. DT, Europe Diary.

28. DT to Beatrice Sorchan, October 22, 1920, SU.

29. DT, Europe Diary.

30. Sanders, 58.

31. DT, Europe Diary.

32. For RWL see Rose Wilder Lane and Helen Boylston, *Travels with Zenobia: Paris to Albania by Model T Ford*, ed. William Holtz (Columbia and London: University of Missouri Press, 1983); and Rose Wilder Lane and Roger Lea MacBride, *Rose Wilder Lane: Her Story* (New York: Stein and Day, 1977).

33. DT, Europe Diary.

34. Quoted in Lane and Boylston, *Travels with Zenobia*.

35. RWL to DT, January 21, 1928.

36. DT to RWL, September 14, 1921; and (reminiscing) September 25, 1960.

37. Paul Scott Mowrer, *The House of Europe* (Boston: Houghton Mifflin, 1945), 392.

38. DT to Beatrice Sorchan, November 18, 1920.

39. Quoted in Alexander, "The Girl from Syracuse."

40. Harriman, "The 'It' Girl."

41. DT to Beatrice Sorchan, December 9, 1920.

42. DT, ms. fragment, handwritten, SU, probably part of "The Tulip Box," DT's unfinished novel about her marriage to Joseph Bard.

43. The section on Vienna and DT's early days as a correspondent is based on her articles in the *Philadelphia Public Ledger* (on microfilm at SU); on her various manuscript drafts (cited by title); and on the notes of her conversations with Marcel W. Fodor in Washington, D.C., in 1959–1960, transcribed in preparation for her autobiography and hereafter referred to as the Thompson-Fodor Notes.

44. DT, "Oh, Thou, My Austria!," unpublished ms. at SU.

45. The phrase is Frederic Morton's, in "The Anschluss Remembered in Three Dimensions," *New York Times,* March 11, 1988.

46. DT, "The New Vienna," ms. at SU.

47. Quoted in RWL, *San Francisco Bulletin,* undated clipping [September 1922].

48. DT, "A Wreath for Toni," *Harper's,* July 1934.

49. Thompson-Fodor Notes.

50. DT, "Oh, Thou, My Austria!," SU, and Thompson-Fodor Notes.

51. DT, "The Tie That Binds the World Around," *Philadelphia Public Ledger,* January 8, 1922.

52. DT, "Oh, Absalom, My Son!," ms. at SU.

53. For the Atlantis and the *Schieber* in Vienna see DT, "The Market of the Profiteers," SU; and DT, "Enter the Sheriff Where Genius Supped," *Philadelphia Public Ledger,* June 18, 1922.

54. DT, "Enter the Sheriff Where Genius Supped."

55. DT in *Philadelphia Public Ledger,* June 10, 1922.

56. DT, "A Bath Abroad," ms. at SU.

57. *Philadelphia Public Ledger,* January 8, 1922.

58. DT, "The Tie That Binds the World Around."

59. DT, "Make Your Own Baedecker," ms. at SU.

60. Carl Zuckmayer, *A Part of Myself* (New York: Harcourt Brace Jovanovich, 1970), 340–341. See also Marcel Fodor to DT, June 27, 1948 (in reference to ca. 1921), SU: "I never heard anyone speak German as fluently and badly as you do."

61. Quoted in Junius Wood to DT, November 20, 1929, SU.

62. PK interview with Lilian T. Mowrer, Wonalancet, New Hampshire, August 25, 1986.

63. Harriman, "The 'It' Girl."

64. OTR (*"Ave, Salve, Vale!"*), August 22, 1958, SU.

65. Gunther, "A Blue-Eyed Tornado."

66. Thompson-Fodor Notes.

67. DT, "Woman Envoy Barred in U.S. Talks on Love and Divorce," *Philadelphia Public Ledger,* November 5, 1926.

68. In July 1921; DT's articles on microfilm.

69. *Philadelphia Public Ledger,* December 23, 1923.

70. Sanders, 67; and DT, "Karl's Departure Forestalls Putsch," ms. at SU.

71. Alexander, "The Girl from Syracuse."

72. Sanders, 68.

73. Here and for Fodor generally, PK interview with Denis Fodor, Munich, October 1, 1987.

74. Sanders, 67.

75. DT radio broadcast ("People in the News"), March 8, 1938, transcript at SU.

76. William L. Shirer, *Twentieth-Century Journey* (New York: Simon and Schuster, 1976), 439. For Fodor see also Martha Foley, *The Story of STORY Magazine* (New York: Norton, 1980), 87–88, and Foley's papers at the Mugar Library, Boston University.

77. John Gunther short story, "Dorothy," ms. copy in my possession courtesy of Jane Gunther.

78. DT to RWL, September 14, 1921.

79. Sanders, 75.

80. PK interview with Denis Fodor.

81. DT, "A Bath Abroad."

82. DT, "Amazing Hungary," *Contemporary Review,* September 1921.

83. DT, "The Last Days of the Habsburgs," ms., SU.

84. DT, "Agitation for Karl Grows in Hungary," ms. at SU.

85. DT, "The Revival of Duelling in Hungary," ms. at SU.

86. Quoted in Sanders, 71.

87. DT articles in the *Philadelphia Public Ledger,* March 30 ("George Washington Found in Ancient Austrian Castle"), February 12 ("Captured Lincoln's Assassin"), and December 24, 1922 ("Europe's Youngest Queen — Mariora of Jugo-Slavia Just Loves Her New Tasks"), respectively.

88. I have relied on three sources primarily for the Habsburg adventure: DT's manuscript draft "The Last Days of the Habsburgs," at SU; DT, "Water under Bridges"; and Rose Wilder Lane's serial in the *San Francisco Bulletin,* September 1922, quoting DT on the episode at Tata. Other references as cited.

89. Alexander, "The Girl from Syracuse."

90. Sanders, 69–70.

91. DT to Gertrude Tone, undated [1922], in Eileen Agar's collection.

92. DT, Railway Diary, December 11 [1935]; and Europe Diary (concluding entry), SU.

93. DT to Gertrude Tone, undated [1922].

94. DT, Railway Diary, November 20 [1935].

CHAPTER FOUR

1. DT, "In the Streets of Vienna on Riot Day," *Philadelphia Public Ledger,* February 5, 1922.

2. Toni Stolper quoted in Sanders, 82.

3. This story is told repeatedly, but see especially DT, "In the Streets of Vienna," and the reminiscences of Elisabeth Marton, Columbia Oral History Project, Butler Library, Columbia University.

4. DT to RWL, August 13, 1921.

5. DT, "Oh, Absalom, My Son!" ms. at SU.

6. DT, "Vienna Fast Becoming European Arts Center," *Philadelphia Public Ledger*, December 26, 1923.

7. Here and generally, see Hilde Spiel, *Vienna's Golden Autumn* (New York: Weidenfeld and Nicolson, 1987); and Ilsa Barea, *Vienna* (New York: Knopf, 1966).

8. DT to JB, undated, SU; and quoted in Sheean, 18.

9. Harriman, "The 'It' Girl."

10. DT, Railway Diary, December 20 [1935], "Later."

11. Sheean, 17.

12. DT to JB, undated [May 1927], in Eileen Agar's collection.

13. JB to DT, undated [ca. 1926], SU.

14. PK interview with Eileen Agar, London, March 11, 1986.

15. Eileen Agar (in collaboration with Andrew Lambirth), *A Look at My Life* (London: Methuen, 1988), 56.

16. From "The Tulip Box," DT's fictionalized account of her marriage to Joseph Bard (called "Jenö" in the text), SU.

17. See Louis Untermeyer, *Bygones* (New York: Harcourt Brace and World, 1965), 82: "As I remember it, he [used] three different colored inks: black for German, blue for English, and red for French."

18. DT, "The Tulip Box."

19. Combined from DT to JB, April 3, 1927, in Eileen Agar's collection, and January 27, 1927, SU.

20. Untermeyer, *Bygones*, 82.

21. Bottome, "Dorothy Thompson."

22. DT to RWL, September 3, 1921.

23. RW to JVS, December 25, 1963, in Houghton Mifflin Company archives, Houghton Library, Harvard University.

24. DT to RWL, July 15, 1921.

25. JB to DT, September 1, 1922, SU.

26. Bottome, "Dorothy Thompson."

27. DT to RWL, September 24, 1921.

28. PK interview with Eileen Agar.

29. DT, Railway Diary, November 20 [1935], "Later."

30. Agar, *A Look at My Life*, 66; and Sanders, 75.

31. DT to RWL, July 15, 1921.

32. DT to RWL, September 3, 1921.

33. DT to RWL, July 15, 1921.

34. Harriman, "The 'It' Girl."

35. Peter S. Drucker, *Report from Atlantis* (New York: Harper and Row, 1979), 53.

36. DT to RWL, September 3, 1921.

37. Bottome, "Dorothy Thompson."

38. John Gunther short story, "Dorothy," ms. copy in my possession courtesy of Jane Gunther.

39. Carl Zuckmayer, *A Part of Myself* (New York: Harcourt Brace Jovanovich, 1970), 340–341.

40. DT to Gertrude Tone, undated [1922], in Eileen Agar's collection.

41. DT to RWL, July 15, 1921.

42. DT to Gertrude Tone, undated [1922], in Eileen Agar's collection.

43. JB to DT, letters of August 18, September 9, August 20, and undated, respectively, 1922, SU.

44. DT to JB, December 16, 1926, SU.

45. DT to JB, December 27, 1926, in Eileen Agar's collection.

46. DT to JB, July 26, 1927, in Eileen Agar's collection.

47. The wedding took place on April 26, 1923.

48. DT to RWL, September 3, 1921.

49. DT, Railway Diary, January 8 [1936].

50. DT to JB, undated, SU.

51. The section on DT and the foreign correspondents is taken from the Thompson-Fodor Notes; from "The Old Outcasts," DT's unpublished ms. about her early career, SU; and from her radio broadcasts ("People in the News") of March 1 and 8, 1938, in which she discusses "the boys," her colleagues, individually (transcripts at SU). All other sources as cited.

52. PK interview with Denis Fodor, Munich, October 1, 1987. "I depended for current news on string correspondents," said DT, "all attached to services in the States. . . . They had no concept of American news. They sent in stories by mail, except in cases of outstanding distinction, but only a fraction of the material could be used, but all of it had to be read.

"Two outstanding stories were sent . . . every fall or winter, usually in November. They ran like this: Wolves had gotten into such-and-such a village in Herzogovina and eaten up a 13-year-old girl. The other was usually from Yugoslav correspondents, who said that a shark had been sighted in Abbazia (then Italian), to frighten off the tourists." (Thompson-Fodor Notes.)

53. Here and generally see John Hohenberg, *Foreign Correspondence: The Great Reporters and Their Times* (Oxford: Oxford University Press, 1964), 266–282.

54. PK interview with George Seldes, Hartland, Vermont, December 4, 1985.

55. Oswald Garrison Villard, *The Disappearing Daily* (New York: Knopf, 1944), 219–220.

56. Quoted in Bottome, "Dorothy Thompson."

57. William L. Shirer, *Twentieth-Century Journey* (New York: Simon and Schuster, 1976), 438. *The New Yorker,* in its 1947 profile of John Gunther, called him "an Adonis" without flinching.

58. John Gunther, *A Fragment of Autobiography* (New York: Harper and Row, 1962), 5–6.

59. PK interview with Dinah Sheean, Paris, July 18, 1986.

60. Hohenberg, *Foreign Correspondence,* 271–272.

61. PK interview with Dinah Sheean.

62. See Martha Foley, *The Story of STORY Magazine* (New York: Norton, 1980). Also in manuscript in the Foley papers, Mugar Library, Boston University.

63. PK interview with Dinah Sheean.

64. JVS quoted on Edgar Mowrer in *Dictionary of Literary Biography,* vol. 29, ed. Perry J. Ashley (Detroit: Gale Publishing, 1984), 256.

65. See Dinah Sheean to PK, October 24, 1986, in reference to "the kind of man in Pana, Illinois . . . who sneered at Jimmy for not being great on the football field, for reading up a silver maple tree, where he was hidden from everyone except his mother."

66. John Gunther, "The Fabulous Jimmy," in *Book-of-the-Month Club News*, undated [but 1949, on publication of JVS's *Lead, Kindly Light*].

67. In general use; see Sheean, 73–74.

68. PK interview with Dinah Sheean, London, May 20, 1986; and quoted in Sanders, 105.

69. Sheean, 3.

70. H. R. Knickerbocker to DT and SL, May 27, 1928, SU.

71. Quoted in Alexander, "The Girl from Syracuse."

72. Sigrid Schultz was an exception, and was outraged when she heard about Seldes's remark. See her correspondence with Seldes, November 9, 1975, in my possession.

73. Harriman, "The 'It' Girl."

74. DT, "On Women Correspondents and Other New Ideas," *The Nation*, January 6, 1926.

75. DT, "Outline for a talk before the Ohio Newspaper Women's Assn.," dated "October 10," attached to diary, typed, August 24, 1931, SU.

76. Harriman, "The 'It' Girl."

77. This is rather confusing, but DT's marriage to SL in 1928 eliminated the problem. See notes in Sanders, 382.

78. Thompson-Fodor Notes, SU. Competition was fierce among newspapermen, and "bribery was very common to get expedition for a scoop." DT related the story of a fellow correspondent, Lincoln Eyre, who once tried to block his colleagues' dispatches from Eastern Europe by filing 5,000 words taken straight from the Bible, thereby tying up the telegraph wires.

79. Another story that appears in nearly every account of DT's life and career. See "The Old Outcasts," and also DT's letter to Ernest Jones, April 24, 1956, SU; her loose autobiographical materials, SU; and Sanders, 94. MKS takes the view that DT invented the better part of the Polish tale, but this would seem to be in error: DT's Warsaw dispatches, running in the *Public Ledger–New York Post* syndicate in May 1926, refer to her having "travelled throughout the night by motorbus, in peasant carts, and finally on foot. . . . Your correspondent has been in revolutionary Poland since early Friday morning; by train crossed Czechoslovakia, traversed that part of Poland which was formerly Upper Silesia, entered former Russian Poland and finally pulled up at Skiernevitz, at the gates of Warsaw. From there to Warsaw the rails had been destroyed." Generally I have found no substantiation for MKS's hostile contention that DT "produced only one successful work of fiction: her own legend."

Of Sigmund Freud, DT said only that "I had met him, though we were not friends." Notes of an interview with Freud can be found at SU, in which DT records that "he would not undertake to psychoanalyze the world," and quotes him: "I never take a patient unless I can offer some hope."

80. DT, "On Women Correspondents."

81. DT, "Outline for a talk before the Ohio Newspaper Women's Assn."

82. DT, "On Women Correspondents."

83. For Genia, see DT, "The Most Beautiful Form of Courage," *LHJ*, August 1955, reprinted in DT, *The Courage to Be Happy*; and Drucker, "Hemme and Genia," in *Report from Atlantis*. All quotes are from these sources unless otherwise cited.

84. Lilian Mowrer, *Journalist's Wife* (New York: Morrow, 1937), 217.

85. For von Moltke and DT see Michael Balfour and Julian Frisby, *Helmuth von Moltke: A Leader against Hitler* (London: Macmillan, 1972).

86. See Alice Herdan-Zuckmayer, *Genies sind im Lehrplan nicht vorgesehen* (Frankfurt-am-Main: S. Fischer Verlag, 1979), which is also an excellent account of Genia's activities as seen through the eyes of one of her students.

87. DT, "Wassermann Seeks Life in U.S. Veiled from Europe," *Philadelphia Public Ledger*, February 13, 1926.

88. Gunther, *A Fragment of Autobiography*, 5.

89. OTR ("A Generation of Journalists Passes"), May 25, 1958.

90. PK interview with Lilian T. Mowrer, Wonalancet, New Hampshire, August 25, 1986; and quoted in Mowrer, *Journalist's Wife*, 215.

91. DT to JB, loose pages, undated, SU.

92. DT speech, "The Developments of Our Times," delivered in 1948 at John B. Stetson University, DeLand, Florida, as part of the Merrill Lectures. Published in 1948 by the University Press, DeLand.

93. For Weimar Berlin, see DT's articles in the *Public Ledger* and the *New York Post*, 1925–1928, SU. The best general work in English is still Otto Friedrich's *Before the Deluge* (New York: Harper and Row, 1972).

94. DT, "The Developments of Our Times" (Merrill Lectures, Stetson University).

95. DT, "Even Wagner's Heroes Now Find Valhalla in the Movies," *Philadelphia Public Ledger*, October 8, 1922.

96. DT, "Police Exposition Thrills Public with Room of Horror," *Philadelphia Public Ledger*, November 6, 1926.

97. From DT's introduction to Carl Zuckmayer's *Second Wind* (New York: Doubleday, Doran and Co., 1940), viii–ix.

98. Mowrer, *Journalist's Wife*, 216–217.

99. PK interview with George Seldes. For the Adlon, see also Gerhard Masur, *Imperial Berlin* (New York: Basic Books, 1970).

100. DT radio broadcast ("People in the News"), March 8, 1938, transcript at SU.

101. Sigrid Schultz, oral reminiscences, William E. Wiener Oral History Library of the American Jewish Committee, New York City.

102. DT radio broadcast, March 8, 1938.

103. Claud Cockburn, *Discord of Trumpets* (London: R. Hart-Davis, 1956), 90.

104. In *Journalist's Wife*, Lilian Mowrer comments on the nature of the "journalistic existence, the essence of which is the unexpected, the improvised and the hurried," and quotes her admonition to her four-year-old daughter when she and Edgar Mowrer prepared to leave Berlin on their various assignments: "Now if you fit in and don't make a fuss, you can come along with us. If not, of course you must remain at home. It is entirely up to you." (Pages 215–216.)

105. DT to Phyllis Bottome, January 7, 1927, SU.

106. PK interview with Eileen Agar.

107. PK interview with Lilian Mowrer.

108. JVS to Dorothy de Santillana, December 11 [1963], in Houghton Mifflin Company archives, Harvard.

109. Gunther, "Dorothy."

110. Untermeyer, *Bygones*, 83.

111. DT to JB, December 16, 1926.

112. DT to JB, January 25, 1927, SU.

113. DT to Phyllis Bottome, January 27, 1927, SU.

114. DT to RWL, January 10, 1927.

115. DT to JB, January 25, 1927.

116. PK interview with Eileen Agar.

117. Quoted in Sanders, 106.

118. PK interview with George Seldes.

119. Quoted in Agar, *A Look at My Life,* 55.

120. DT to JB, December 26, 1926, SU.

121. DT to Eileen Agar, December 7, 1926, in Eileen Agar's collection.

122. Bottome, "Dorothy Thompson."

123. DT to JB, undated, SU.

124. Quoted in DT to JB, January 19, 1927, SU.

125. DT to JB, February 27, 1927, SU.

126. See in particular JB's undated letter to DT in which he speaks of Gertrude Tone as "a bad influence. Dorothy Dear — get away from the influence of that strange crowd of hysterical women among your American friends — they have a mad *'Lebensform'* and *'qui en mange en meurt!'* " (SU).

127. DT to JB, April 3, 1927, in Eileen Agar's collection.

128. "She was not a patient of [Freud's]," said Dale Warren, "but at the time of the break-up of her first marriage his few well-chosen words proved very much to the point: 'Buy a new wardrobe and change your lipstick.' " (Warren, "I Remember Dorothy.")

129. Combined from DT to JB, January 25, February 1, and undated, 1927, SU, and April 3, 1927, in Eileen Agar's collection.

130. Quoted in Sanders, 97.

131. Quoted in DT to JB, January 12, 1927, SU.

132. DT to Phyllis Bottome, January 7, 1927, SU.

133. Quoted in DT to JB, January 14, 1927, SU.

134. DT to Phyllis Bottome, January 7, 1927.

135. DT to JB, January 12, 1927.

136. Combined from DT to JB, January 12, 1927, and December 31, 1926, SU.

137. DT to JB, undated fragment, SU.

138. Combined from RWL to DT, January 25, and February 16, 1927.

139. Combined from RWL to DT, undated [January] and February 16, 1927.

140. DT to JB, April 3, 1927, in Eileen Agar's collection, and undated, SU.

141. DT to JB, undated [May 1927], "Sunday night," in Eileen Agar's collection.

142. DT to JB, June 4, 1927, in Eileen Agar's collection.

143. DT to JB, February 14, 1927, SU.

144. DT to JB, February 1, 1927, SU.

145. DT to Phyllis Bottome, undated, SU; and to JB, July 4, 1927, in Eileen Agar's collection. Also PK interview with Eileen Agar.

146. For JB's published writing, see his novel, *Shipwreck in Europe* (New York: Harper and Brothers, 1928); poem, "Aurora Mediocritas," *The Dial,* March 1928; "Why Europe Dislikes the Jew," *Harper's,* March 1927 (which DT insisted was more her work than JB's); and especially "The Tale of a Child," in *The World's Greatest Short Stories* (London: Odhams Press, n.d. [ca. 1934]).

147. PK interview with Eileen Agar.

148. PK interview with Dinah Sheean.

149. Combined from DT to JB, January 6, 1927, in Eileen Agar's collection, and January 19, 1927, SU.

150. DT's articles on Chamberlin and Levine ran through June 1927. She dismissed them both (privately) as "the lowest form of bird life." (Quoted in Ramon Guthrie to Harris Whitteman, Jr., undated [Summer 1927], in the Guthrie papers, Baker Library, Dartmouth College.)

151. PK interview with George Seldes.

152. DT to SL, April 29, 1937 [possibly unsent], carbon copy at SU.

153. Brendan Gill, *Here at the New Yorker* (New York: Random House, 1975), 63.

154. Peggy Bacon quoted in Schorer, 502.

155. Mary Welsh Hemingway, *How It Was* (New York: Knopf, 1976), 234.

156. DT, "The Boy and Man from Sauk Center," *Atlantic Monthly*, November 1960.

157. PK interview with Lilian Mowrer.

CHAPTER FIVE

1. PK interview with Lilian T. Mowrer, Wonalancet, New Hampshire, August 25, 1986.

2. DT diary, January 1942, SU.

3. For SL's courtship of DT, see Schorer, 484–501; Sheean, chapters 1 through 4; Sanders, 111–130; Alexander, "The Girl from Syracuse"; and other sources as cited.

4. Sheean, 23.

5. DT to JB, July 11, 1927, in Eileen Agar's collection.

6. Schorer, 488–489.

7. DT to JB, July 11, 1927: "Tell Eileen that the Gunthers are here — Frances more of a leprechaun than ever and John a big white bear."

8. Schorer, 489; and Sheean, 26.

9. SL, "Air Trip to Vienna Most Exciting Part of Riot, Sinclair Lewis Finds," *Philadelphia Public Ledger*, July 20, 1927; and SL to Alfred Harcourt, July 26, 1927, in *From Main Street to Stockholm: Letters of Sinclair Lewis, 1919–1930* (New York: Harcourt, Brace, 1952), 250.

10. DT to RWL, January 17, 1928.

11. Schorer, 13–15.

12. Ibid., 16.

13. John Hersey, "First Job," *Yale Review*, vol. 76, Winter 1987.

14. DT diary, loose, April 15, 1932, SU.

15. SL, quoted in *Dictionary of Literary Biography*, vol. 9, ed. James J. Martine (Detroit: Gale Publishing, 1981), 171.

16. Schorer, 182.

17. Mark Schorer, essay on SL in *Encyclopedia Americana*, vol. 17 (Danbury, Conn.: Grolier, Inc., 1989), 273.

18. Quoted in Schorer, 311.

19. Ibid., 513.

20. Quoted in *The Man from Main Street: A Sinclair Lewis Reader,* ed. Harry E. Maule and Melville H. Cane (New York: Random House, 1953), xiv.

21. Schorer, 468.

22. DT, loose essay about SL, handwritten ca. 1959 for Mark Schorer, SU.

23. Sheean, 11.

24. Hersey, "First Job."

25. Ramon Guthrie, "The Birth of a Myth, or How We Wrote *Dodsworth,*" ms. in the Guthrie papers, Baker Library, Dartmouth College.

26. Hersey, "First Job."

27. Sheean, 10.

28. Ibid., 8.

29. Brendan Gill, *Here at the New Yorker* (New York: Random House, 1975), 63.

30. Hersey, "First Job."

31. Schorer, 501.

32. Quoted in Alexander, "The Girl from Syracuse."

33. Sheean, 10.

34. Ellen Sheean to PK, undated [March 1986].

35. PK interview with Lilian Mowrer.

36. Schorer, 467.

37. This was the kind of word game SL played to excess. See SL to Grace Lewis, January 1, 1928, in the Grace Hegger Lewis papers, Humanities Research Center, University of Texas at Austin.

38. Grace Lewis Casanova, *Half a Loaf* (New York: Liveright, 1931), 218.

39. Quoted in Schorer, 473.

40. Quoted in Hersey, "First Job."

41. See Guthrie's letter to Hanna Josephson, November 12, 1951, at the American Academy and Institute of Arts and Letters, New York City.

42. DT to JB, July 11, 1927.

43. DT to RWL, January 17, 1928.

44. SL, "Air Trip to Vienna."

45. Quoted in Sheean, 26. SL's articles appeared in the *Ledger-Post* syndicate on July 19, 20, and 21, 1927.

46. DT to JB, July 31, 1927, in Eileen Agar's collection.

47. Sheean, 29.

48. DT to JB, August 22, 1927, in Eileen Agar's collection.

49. SL to Grace Lewis, November 26, 1927, in the Lewis papers, Austin.

50. SL to H. L. Mencken, April 8, 1928, in the Mencken papers, New York Public Library.

51. Schorer, 505.

52. In DT diary, June 8, 1928, SU (generally known, and hereafter referred to, as the Honeymoon Diary).

53. DT to JB, December 13, 1927, in Eileen Agar's collection.

54. DT diary, October 3 [1927], SU.

55. DT to JB, October 25, 1927, in Eileen Agar's collection.

56. See Alexander, "The Girl from Syracuse": "A belief that had survived throughout the history of the human race seemed to her to be worthy of a com-

petent, up-to-date investigation. Unfortunately for theological letters, the project never came off."

57. DT diary, September 9, 1927, SU.

58. DT to JB, November 17, 1927, in Eileen Agar's collection.

59. DT diary, February 12, 1928, SU.

60. DT diary, September 1927, at SU.

61. Schorer, 503.

62. According to Sigrid Schultz, DT came to her around this time to say that *two* men had asked her to marry them: Sinclair Lewis and — Sigrid thought, though DT did not mention his name — H. R. Knickerbocker, with whom DT did, probably, have an affair, and who was having difficulties with his wife, Laura. "Well," said Sigrid, "better go with the one who's already started his divorce," to which DT replied, in this account, "Yes, he'll probably be more useful to me than the other." It should be noted that Sigrid remained hostile toward DT to the end of her life. (Sigrid Schultz oral reminiscences, William E. Wiener Oral History Library of the American Jewish Committee, New York City.) Sigrid told MKS that Laura Knickerbocker was "unhappy" about her husband's attentions to DT and therefore eager to see DT united with SL: "We must all pull together," said Laura, "to make this thing work." (Sanders, 114.)

In an interesting variation on this story, George Seldes maintains that the entire colony of foreign correspondents in Berlin "joined forces" with Knickerbocker to divert Lewis's attention away from *Laura,* with whom he was "smitten," and toward DT. "We were all in on it," said Seldes. (PK interview with George Seldes, Hartland, Vermont, December 4, 1985.)

63. Steven Marcus, *Representations: Essays on Literature and Society* (New York: Random House, 1975), 53–55. Marcus's essay, which appeared originally in the *New York Review of Books,* is particularly nasty and unaccountably superior in its attitude toward DT.

64. DT to SL, November 12, 1927, SU.

65. DT to SL, undated [November 1927], SU.

66. DT to SL, undated [November 1927], SU.

67. DT to SL, November 11, 1927, SU.

68. DT to JB, November 17, 1927, in Eileen Agar's collection.

69. DT to SL, November 18, 1927, SU.

70. DT to SL, undated [November 1927], "Saturday," SU.

71. DT to SL, November 21, 1927, SU.

72. DT to SL, undated [November 1927], SU.

73. DT to JB, November 17, 1927.

74. DT to SL, November 16, 1927, SU.

75. SL to DT, November 7, 1927, SU.

76. SL to DT, November 8, 1927, SU. "Frau Valentin" was Antonina Vallentin Luchaire, who wrote from Berlin for the *Manchester Guardian* and whom DT later sponsored for entry into the United States.

77. DT diary, September 1927, SU.

78. SL to DT, November 27, 1927, SU.

79. SL to DT, November 25, 1927, SU.

80. SL to DT, November 28, 1927, SU. SL was in Russia from November 30 through December 10, 1927.

81. Schorer, 494. This exchange is repeated endlessly in the accounts of DT's marriage to SL. See Sanders, 122; Alexander, "The Girl from Syracuse"; and DT's own letter to Arthur Lyons, of April 17, 1939, SU.

82. DT to Mark Schorer, December 14, 1958, in the Schorer papers, Bancroft Library, University of California at Berkeley.

83. Sheean, 73. His account of the life and death of Rayna Prohme is told in more detail in *Personal History* (Garden City: Doubleday, Doran and Co, 1935).

84. DT to SL, November 21, 1927.

85. DT to SL, undated, "Thanksgiving," SU.

86. DT to SL, November 21, 1927.

87. SL to DT, November 16, 1927, SU.

88. DT to SL, undated [from Italy, 1928], SU.

89. DT to JB, November 17, 1927.

90. DT to SL, letter written as diary entry, March 12, 1928, SU.

91. DT to JB, March 10, 1928, in Eileen Agar's collection.

92. DT to JB, December 13, 1927, in Eileen Agar's collection.

93. DT to RWL, January 17, 1928.

94. DT to SL, November 25, 1927, SU.

95. DT to SL, undated [1928], SU.

96. DT to Margaret Thompson Wilson, March 21, 1928, SU.

97. DT to JB, March 10, 1928.

98. DT to SL, April 27, 1928, SU.

99. DT to Margaret Thompson Wilson, March 21, 1928.

100. Eileen Agar (in collaboration with Andrew Lambirth), *A Look at My Life* (London: Methuen, 1988), 80–81: "Both Dorothy and Hal were hard at [work], their mechanised muses demanding to be fed. But then one night at dinner all hell broke loose. Dorothy got up from the table saying that she must find some missing pages from the manuscript she was writing. . . . Lewis was very drunk, and obviously feeling that his work was of more moment than Dorothy's, he erupted bitterly. After all, he said, he had written a few books himself in his time that were somewhat more important than her bloody manuscript. He was completely plastered and ended up by stalking out of the room into the garden, where he tripped in the dark amongst the rose bushes and fell into an intoxicated sleep."

101. Schorer, 519.

102. Sheean, 88.

103. SL to Grace Lewis, May 6, 1928, in the Lewis papers, Austin.

104. SL to DT, April 28, 1928, SU.

105. DT to SL, May 2, 1928, SU.

106. DT to SL, April 30, 1928, SU.

107. DT to SL, undated [May 1928], SU.

108. Margaret Thompson Wilson to DT, April 17, 1928, SU.

109. Quoted in Random House publicity materials for *The Man from Main Street;* and in Schorer, 473.

110. *New York Times*, April 24, 1928. DT wrote to Mark Schorer on July 1, 1959: "I probably told you that I had something of a quarrel with Lewis about *Elmer Gantry*. I thought the book utterly failed of a foil. It lacked the indignation that a man with any deep religious instinct would have felt, and therefore it lacked

truth, or so I thought. Of course with my background and memory of my father I could not accept Elmer as representative" (letter in the Schorer papers, Berkeley).

111. Marguerite Jarvis Bourne to DT, May 1, 1928, SU.

112. *New York Times,* May 15, 1928.

113. Sheean, 97.

114. Quoted in Sanders, 135.

115. DT to Mark Schorer, December 14, 1958, in the Schorer papers, Berkeley; and quoted in Schorer, 502.

116. DT, Honeymoon Diary. The Honeymoon Diary is quoted extensively in Sheean, chapter 5.

117. Louis Untermeyer, *Bygones* (New York: Harcourt Brace and World, 1965), 84.

118. Combined from DT to RWL of June 25 and July 23, 1928.

119. RWL to DT, July 11, 1928 [unsent].

120. RWL to DT, July 13, 1928.

121. DT to RWL, July 23, 1928.

122. DT to RWL, January 17, 1928.

123. DT to RWL, June 25, 1928.

CHAPTER SIX

1. DT to H. R. Knickerbocker, December 24, 1928, in the Knickerbocker papers, Butler Library, Columbia University.

2. Twin Farms was also called Summerfield, and according to Vermont tradition took different names from different owners: it was "the Crowell Place," "the Connett Place," and later, of course, "the Lewis Place."

On March 12, 1934, SL wrote in response to a U.S. Department of Agriculture questionnaire regarding Twin Farms: "To keep your statistics accurate, you *must* distinguish between working-farms and country estates. I paid $10,000 (cash) for my place of 300 acres in Barnard, but that is no criterion of farm land values, because on the place were two houses, one completely furnished, with four bathrooms and electric light plant etc. . . . For actual farming purposes (but I farm none of it except for a vegetable patch) it would not have been worth over $3000. [Signed] Sinclair Lewis" (letter in the Wilbur Collection, Bailey-Howe Memorial Library, University of Vermont, Burlington).

3. *New York Times,* August 28, 1928.

4. Quoted in Wharton, "Dorothy Thompson."

5. Schorer, 508–509.

6. H. L. Mencken to Sara Haardt, August 29, 1928, in *Mencken and Sara: A Life in Letters,* ed. Marion Elizabeth Rodgers (New York: McGraw-Hill, 1987), 392.

7. Charles Angoff, "Dorothy Thompson: Kansan in Westchester," in *The Tone of the Twenties* (South Brunswick, N.J.: A. S. Barnes and Co., 1966), 115. Mencken's views were not uniformly negative; mainly he liked to be funny. On August 31 he wrote to Gretchen Hood: "I had dinner with Lewis and his wife in New York last Tuesday. She seems very nice. She is as far from No. 1 [Grace Lewis] as you could imagine. No. 1 was very affected; No. 2 is natural and charming. She has rosy cheeks, and is wide enough to look solid and substantial. I liked her very

much." (*"Ich Kuss die Hand"*: *The Letters of H. L. Mencken to Gretchen Hood*, ed. Peter W. Dowell, [Tuscaloosa, Ala.: University of Alabama Press, 1986], 121.) And at the time of SL and DT's marriage, Mencken sent his heartiest congratulations: "May the lady bear in mind that trials are put upon us on the earth that we may be properly prepared for the horrors of Heaven. I request and instruct you to kiss her hand for me" (Mencken to SL, 27 April, 1928, SU).

8. DT to H. L. Mencken, September 12, 1928, in the Mencken papers, New York Public Library; and at SU.

9. See Schorer, 509; and Sheean, 126–40.

10. Sheean, 128, 131.

11. DT, undated report on Twin Farms, addressed to "Margaret," SU.

12. Sheean, 136.

13. See SL to Alfred Harcourt, July 16, 1929, in *From Main Street to Stockholm, Letters of Sinclair Lewis, 1919–1930* (New York: Harcourt, Brace, 1952), 276–277.

14. DT to H. R. Knickerbocker, December 24, 1928.

15. SL, "A Letter to Critics," *The Nation*, September 16, 1931.

16. Quoted in DT, "Give Me Vermont," *House and Garden*, July 1947.

17. Sheean, 130–131.

18. Quoted in DT, "Give Me Vermont."

19. Sheean, 131, 132, 134–135.

20. DT to JB, October 10, 1928, in Eileen Agar's collection.

21. Ramon Guthrie to Harris Whitteman, Jr., October 10, 1930 [or 1931?], in the Guthrie papers, Baker Library, Dartmouth College.

22. DT to H. R. Knickerbocker, December 24, 1928.

23. See DT's two letters to SL of October 27, 1929, and her diary of September–October 1927, SU.

24. Schorer, 511.

25. DT to H. R Knickerbocker, December 24, 1928.

26. DT to SL, October 27, 1929, SU.

27. Schorer, 510.

28. Sheean, 146.

29. DT diary, February 13, 1929, SU.

30. DT to Richard Buhlig, July 4, 1930, SU. Buhlig was a concert pianist and a great friend of DT's from Vienna. "He is that extraordinary creature," she told Mencken, "a literate and articulate musician" (DT to H. L Mencken, March 24, 1930, SU).

31. The phrase is DT's, from DT to SL, April 29, 1937, written from Bronxville, carbon at SU.

32. Schorer, 511.

33. For the Dreiser flap, see W. A. Swanberg, *Dreiser* (New York: Scribner's, 1965), 342–346. Other references as cited.

34. Swanberg, *Dreiser*, 343.

35. DT to RWL, February 28, 1929.

36. Swanberg, *Dreiser*, 344.

37. DT to RWL, February 28, 1929. See also Swanberg, who agrees that Dreiser was "churlish" in this matter.

38. Quoted in Swanberg, *Dreiser*, 345, taken from the *New York Evening Post*,

November 14, 1928. DT herself had "given the scoop" to the *Post*. Several months later, on February 16, 1929, *Vogue* announced that she was contemplating a suit against Dreiser (she wasn't), but the incident was not widely reported in the press until two years later, when Dreiser and SL had their famous slapping match at the Metropolitan Club in New York (see my chapter 7).

39. DT to RWL, February 28, 1929.

40. Sheean, 148.

41. Quoted in the *Literary Digest*, April 11, 1931, on the occasion of the Lewis-Dreiser "fistfight" in New York.

42. Schorer, 529.

43. These words were spoken many times, and have been reported to me by many people.

44. Quoted in Sara Mayfield, *The Constant Circle* (New York: Delacorte, 1968), 139.

45. DT to RWL, February 28, 1929.

46. Quoted in Ramon Guthrie, "The Birth of a Myth, or How We Wrote *Dodsworth*," ms. in the Guthrie papers, Dartmouth.

47. Ramon Guthrie to Hanna Josephson, November 12, 1951, in the Guthrie papers, Dartmouth.

48. Quoted in Schorer, 519.

49. DT to "Bill" [probably Woodward], from Monterey, March 14, 1930, in the Ben Stolberg papers, Butler Library, Columbia University. For DT and SL in this period, see Louis Adamic, *My America* (New York: Harper, 1938), chapters 6 and 7.

50. Quoted in Schorer, 521.

51. See DT to JB, August 20, 1930, in Eileen Agar's collection: "I had an easy pregnancy and a quite phenomenally easy confinement"; and DT to Sidney Howard, July 12, 1933, hoping that Polly Howard's obstetrician "is one of those who gives his patients a rectal anaesthesia which mine gave me and which is one of God's (or scientists') gifts to womankind" (letter in the Sidney Coe Howard papers, Bancroft Library, University of California at Berkeley).

52. Quoted in Sheean, 171.

53. DT to RWL, March 1, 1930.

54. DT to SL, October 27, 1929, SU.

55. RWL to DT, March 8, 1930.

56. RWL to DT, December 29, 1929.

57. DT to SL, undated [April 1929, from Quebec City], SU.

58. SL to DT, undated [March 1929], SU.

59. SL to DT, undated, SU.

60. SL to DT, undated ["13th of July"], SU.

61. DT to SL, undated [April 1929, from Quebec City].

62. SL quoted in Schorer, 531.

63. Ibid., 532.

64. DT to H. L. Mencken, March 24, 1930, in the Mencken papers, New York Public Library; and at SU.

65. DT to Helen Woodward, February 21, 1930, SU.

66. DT to RWL, February 19, 1930.

67. DT to RWL, February 28, 1929.

68. Sheean, 172–173.

69. DT to Jay Allen, August 27, 1946, Special Collections, Baker Library, Dartmouth College.

70. Schorer, 533.

71. Ramon Guthrie to Mark Schorer, August 11, 1961, in the Guthrie papers, Dartmouth.

72. DT considered the names Stephen and Nancy before settling on Michael, which JVS insists was chosen because of SL's "youthful enthusiasms for English novels (in a period when every boy was called Michael in English novels)." See Sheean, 183; and also DT's correspondence with Lilian Mowrer, undated, SU.

73. Sheean, 179–181.

74. H. R. Knickerbocker to DT and SL, June 28, 1930, SU.

75. H. L. Mencken to DT, undated, SU.

76. Quoted in Schorer, 536–537.

77. DT to Helen Woodward, October 9, 1930, SU.

78. DT to Richard Buhlig, July 4, 1930.

79. DT to Tish Irwin, November 26, 1930, SU.

80. Schorer, 537. Martha Foley came to Twin Farms around this time and was given a tour of the "Big House." "Where's Michael's room?" she asked. "You didn't show it to me."

"He lives with the servants in our other house down the road," DT answered. "Hal can't stand having him around, poor baby." (Martha Foley, *The Story of STORY Magazine* [New York: Norton, 1980], 216.)

81. Sheean, 190.

82. DT to JB, August 20, 1930.

83. DT to Helen Woodward, October 9, 1930.

84. PK interview with Erna Heininger, Burlington, Vermont, January 1988.

85. See SL's letter to DT of August 15, 1934: "I came back from my trip to find the Old House simply lost, not to us alone but to Micky and Pammy [Wilson, DT's niece], who were become mere excrescences in a house the porch and every room of which simply swarmed with four hearty, cheerful, well-mannered, and most Godawfully inundating Wallers, Mrs. [Waller, DT's secretary] and her three healthy young. . . . Between you and me, I have had, for an undomestic gent, rather a full measure of kids heaped upon me, this summer when I meant to be tranquil."

86. DT to JB, August 20, 1930.

87. SL to H. L. Mencken, undated [summer 1930], in the Mencken papers, New York Public Library; and at SU.

88. DT to Helen Woodward, October 9, 1930.

89. PK interview with Dinah Sheean, Paris, July 18, 1986.

90. DT to Helen Woodward, October 9, 1930.

91. Sheean, 177.

92. Schorer, 539.

CHAPTER SEVEN

1. Quoted in Schorer, 546.

2. Ibid., 452.

3. Ibid., 543.

4. Sheean, 195.

5. RWL to Laura Ingalls Wilder, undated [December 1930], in "The Correspondence of Dorothy Thompson and Rose Wilder Lane," ed. William Holtz, ms. in my possession.

6. For this and DT's full account of the trip see "At the Court of King Gustav," *Pictorial Review,* April 1931.

7. Schorer, 551.

8. DT, "At the Court of King Gustav."

9. Schorer, 552.

10. For SL's speech see Schorer, 552–554; and Marquis Childs in the *New York Times Book Review,* January 11, 1976.

11. *Chicago Tribune,* December 14, 1930, clipping at SU.

12. Schorer, 551.

13. DT, "At the Court of King Gustav."

14. *Time,* December 22, 1930.

15. Quoted in Ramon Guthrie to Mark Schorer, August 21, 1961, in the Guthrie papers, Baker Library, Dartmouth College.

16. DT to Mark Schorer, July 1, 1959, in the Schorer papers, Bancroft Library, University of California at Berkeley.

17. RWL to DT, December 24, 1930.

18. Telegram at SU.

19. DT, "Poverty De Luxe," *Saturday Evening Post,* May 2 and 9, 1931.

20. DT, "Back to Blood and Iron," *Saturday Evening Post,* May 6, 1933.

21. DT, "Poverty De Luxe."

22. DT, "Something Must Happen," *Saturday Evening Post,* May 23, 1931.

23. DT, "Poverty De Luxe."

24. SL to DT, February 12, 1931, SU.

25. DT to SL, undated [February 1931], SU.

26. See DT's correspondence with Oswald Garrison Villard, in the Villard papers, Houghton Library, Harvard University, especially her letter of July 31, 1931.

27. DT, "Something Must Happen."

28. *Saturday Evening Post,* July 23, 1932; May 6, 1933; and August 6 and 20, 1932, respectively. See also "Will Gangs Rule the World?" (July 16, 1932); "The Militant Disarmed" (September 17, 1932); and "Room to Breathe In" (June 24, 1933).

29. Ishbel Ross, *Ladies of the Press* (New York: Harper and Brothers, 1936), 365.

30. John Gunther to DT, February 10, 1950 (in specific reference to her articles in the *Saturday Evening Post*), in the John Gunther papers, University of Chicago.

31. DT, "*I Saw Hitler!*," 5.

32. Ibid., 32.

33. Ibid., 4.

34. DT, "The Gray-Squirrel Complex," *Saturday Evening Post,* February 20, 1932.

35. DT to SL, "February 2" [marked 1931, but in fact 1932], SU.

36. DT to SL, November 10, 1931, SU.

37. DT, "The Gray-Squirrel Complex."

38. DT to SL, December 6, 1931, SU.

39. DT, "Poverty De Luxe."

40. The Hitler interview was first published in April 1932 as an article in *Cosmopolitan* magazine.

41. William L. Shirer, *Berlin Diary* (New York: Knopf, 1941), 17.

42. DT, "*I Saw Hitler!*," 11, 20.

43. Ibid., 5–6.

44. DT, Semmering Diary; and DT, "The Technique of Terror," *Saturday Review*, September 7, 1935: "This breeding of supermen by decree! This death-loving philosophy! One feels that the explanation of the Nazi revolution does not lie in history at all, but in Kraft-Ebbing [sic]." See also her review of Ernst Toller's *I Was a German*, in the *Saturday Review*, March 31, 1934.

45. DT, "*I Saw Hitler!*," 12–18.

46. John Gunther memo [to JVS?] on reading the draft of *Dorothy and Red*, September 12, 1963, in Houghton Mifflin Company archives, Houghton Library, Harvard University.

47. William L. Shirer, *Twentieth-Century Journey, Volume II: The Nightmare Years* (Boston: Little, Brown, 1984), 118.

48. DT to Raoul de Roussy de Sales, July 12, 1942, SU.

49. Shirer, *Berlin Diary*, 16.

50. DT, "Back to Blood and Iron."

51. From DT's introduction ("This Book") to her book *Let the Record Speak*, 2–3.

52. DT, "I Try to Think," unpublished ms. at SU.

53. DT, "Room to Breathe In."

54. DT to SL, March 13, 1933, SU.

55. DT speech, "The Developments of Our Times," delivered in 1948 at John B. Stetson University, DeLand, Florida, as part of the Merrill Lectures. Published in 1948 by the University Press, DeLand.

56. DT to SL, undated [February 1932], SU.

57. DT to SL, February 2, 1932, SU. A series of letters dating from this period of ML's illness is at SU.

58. The bulk of the quoted material below is from DT's holograph draft of her reminiscences of SL, prepared ca. 1959 for Mark Schorer, at SU (Series 7). Other references as cited.

59. DT diary, April 15, 1932, SU.

60. William L. Shirer, *Twentieth-Century Journey* (New York: Simon and Schuster, 1976), 451.

61. Joseph F. Donelan, Jr., letter to the editor, *New York Times Book Review*, July 19, 1987. Donelan was Lou Florey's son-in-law.

62. DT to SL, undated [1933], SU.

63. DT diary, February 13, 1929, SU; and quoted in Sheean, 123.

64. DT diary, April 15, 1932, SU.

65. PK interview with Pamela Wilson Reeves, Holden, Massachusetts, June 26, 1988.

66. Quoted in Sheean, 263.

67. Quoted in DT to SL, April 29, 1937, SU.

68. Schorer, 596.

69. DT to SL, April 29, 1937.

70. Quoted in Schorer, 568.

71. RW to JVS, December 25, 1963, in Houghton Mifflin Company archives, Harvard.

72. DT to SL, undated [July 1941], in the Lewis family collection.

73. DT, Railway Diary, November 18 [1935].

74. Quoted in Schorer, 624.

75. DT to SL, undated [March 1935], SU; and quoted in Schorer, 607.

76. Quoted in Schorer, 603–604.

77. DT to Mark Schorer, December 14, 1958, in the Schorer papers, Berkeley; and quoted in Schorer, 630.

78. DT to SL, April 29, 1937.

79. DT to SL, March 22 [1933, from Portofino], SU.

80. DT to SL, undated [March 1933], SU.

81. SL to DT, July 16 [1934]; undated [Spring 1933]; and November 18 [1931], SU.

82. SL to DT, undated [ca. 1933], SU.

83. SL to DT, undated [but with reference to Whitsuntide, thus May 13, 1932]; July 27, 1932 [signed "Von Papen"]; and undated ["June 28, Thursday," signed "Tiny"], SU.

84. Brendan Gill in "The Theatre," *The New Yorker,* March 19, 1979 (review of Sherman Yellen's play *Strangers,* about DT and SL).

85. For the Lewis-Dreiser fight see Schorer, 561–563; W. A. Swanberg, *Dreiser* (New York: Scribner's, 1965), 372–373; *New York Times,* March 21, 1931; and the *Literary Digest,* April 11, 1931.

86. Quoted in Schorer, 573.

87. SL to DT, November 21 [1931], SU.

88. Barbara De Porte Grossman told MKS that she and other friends of DT's from suffrage days (notably Mary Gawthorpe) were "outraged" by SL's representation of the feminist movement in *Ann Vickers* (Sanders, 172).

89. In correspondence with Philip Goodman, H. L. Mencken described himself as "pleasantly disappointed" by *Ann Vickers:* "I expected something truly appalling, but what I found was simply a bad novel, with a few bright spots. . . . I see little trace of Dorothy in it. She may have given Red some of his materials, but I believe she is too shrewd to have been responsible for the general tone of the book. It might have been written by Fannie Hurst" (H. L. Mencken to Philip Goodman, combined from letters of December 29, 1932, and January 15, 1933, reprinted in *The Letters of H. L. Mencken,* ed. Guy J. Forgue [New York: Knopf, 1961], 355).

90. DL to SL, November 24, 1931, SU. At this time the heroine of SL's novel was called "Ruth Vickery."

91. SL to DT, November 21 [1931].

92. DT to SL, November 24, 1931.

93. Published in the *Saturday Evening Post,* April 9, 1932.

94. DT to SL, November 10, 1931, SU.

95. DT to SL, December 3, 1931, SU.

96. DT to SL, November 24, 1931.

97. Thompson-Fodor Notes.

98. Quoted in Sanders, 174.

99. SL to DT, undated [May 13, 1932], SU.

100. SL to DT, May 4, 1932, SU.
101. DT to SL, undated [Spring 1932], SU.
102. DT to RWL, July 28, 1932.
103. DT to H. R. Knickerbocker, October 9, 1932, in the Knickerbocker papers, Butler Library, Columbia University.
104. DT to Tish Irwin, June 20, 1931, SU.
105. DT to SL, November 8 [marked 1933, but in fact 1932], SU.
106. "Jimmy says 'E' is probably not Edgar Mowrer," says a 1963 memo from Joyce Hartman to Paul Brooks at Houghton Mifflin, written during preparation for the publication of JVS's *Dorothy and Red*. But there was no one else at the Semmering party that winter with the first initial "E." (Memo in Houghton Mifflin Company archives, Harvard.)
107. DT, Semmering Diary.
108. DT, Railway Diary, November 7 [1935].
109. DT, Railway Diary, November 7 [1935], "Later."
110. At SU (Series 8).
111. DT to H. R. Knickerbocker, October 9, 1932.
112. Shirer, *Twentieth-Century Journey*, 449.
113. DT to H. R. Knickerbocker, October 9, 1932.
114. PK interview with Lilian T. Mowrer, Wonalancet, New Hampshire, August 25, 1986.
115. Thompson-Fodor Notes.
116. PK interview with Lilian Mowrer.
117. All quotes to the end of the chapter are from DT, Semmering Diary, unless otherwise indicated.
118. Christa Winsloe, *The Child Manuela* (New York: Farrar and Rhinehart, 1933; reprinted in German, with an introduction by Christa Reinig, as *Mädchen in Uniform*, Munich: Frauenoffensive, 1983).
119. DT to SL, March 26, 1933, SU.
120. Helen Wolff to PK, May 29, 1987; and PK interview with Helen Wolff, Hanover, New Hampshire, August 22, 1987.
121. Sheean, 239–240.
122. DT to SL, March 25, 1933, SU.

CHAPTER EIGHT

1. Quoted in Schorer, 579–580. Goodman's letter was dated February 3, 1933.
2. SL to DT, February 12, 1933, SU.
3. SL to DT, February 18, 1933, SU.
4. SL to DT, March 4, 1933 [on board the *Europa*], SU.
5. DT to SL, March 13, 1933, SU.
6. See her letter to SL, March 25, 1933, SU.
7. DT to Christa Winsloe, undated, SU (Series 8).
8. DT, "Back to Blood and Iron," *Saturday Evening Post*, May 6, 1933.
9. DT to SL, March 13, 1933.
10. DT to SL, undated, SU.
11. Harriet Cohen, *A Bundle of Time* (London: Faber and Faber, 1969), 174–178. DT's letter is dated March 18, 1933.

12. DT to SL, March 13, 1933.

13. Ronald Steel, *Walter Lippmann and the American Century* (Boston: Atlantic Monthly Press, 1980), 300.

14. SL to DT, March 4, 1933.

15. DT to SL, undated [March 1933], SU.

16. From DT to Harriet Cohen, March 18, 1933, quoted in Cohen, *A Bundle of Time*, 177.

17. Combined from DT to SL, March 26, March 30, and undated [March] 1933, SU.

18. Holograph at SU (Series 7).

19. The vast majority of Christa Winsloe's letters to DT from the period 1933–1935, kept in a single file at SU, are undated, written in stream-of-consciousness style, often illegible, and organizable only through guesswork. I have not cited them individually in the notes hereafter. The translations from the German are mine.

20. Sheean, 269.

21. JVS memorandum, undated [1963], in Houghton Mifflin Company archives, Houghton Library, Harvard University. He adds: "Hilda [Rothschild] tells me she got this [information] from Emily Carter — rather a dubious source, I believe."

22. Margaret Thompson Wilson to JVS, November 18, 1963, copy in my possession.

23. DT to SL, undated [Spring 1933], SU.

24. Quoted in Sanders, 190.

25. PK interview with Lilian T. Mowrer, Wonalancet, New Hampshire, August 25, 1986.

26. DT to Christa Winsloe [unsent?], undated, ["Sunday," ca. 1933–1934], SU.

27. Quoted in *New York Times*, May 12, 1933.

28. DT to Sidney Howard, undated [1933] in the Sidney Coe Howard papers, Bancroft Library, University of California at Berkeley.

29. Sheean, 234.

30. DT remembered "these sessions with Sidney and Red as among the happiest events in our married life." (DT to Dale Warren, September 10, 1953, SU.)

31. Quoted in Schorer, 588.

32. DT to Christa Winsloe, March 31, 1934, SU.

33. For DT's diabetes, see her letter to Christa Winsloe, March 31, 1934; and Sanders, 190. Mysteriously, there is no further mention of it in DT's correspondence.

34. Quoted in Charles Angoff, "Dorothy Thompson: Kansan in Westchester," in *The Tone of the Twenties* (South Brunswick, N.J.: A. S. Barnes and Co., 1966), 121.

35. DT to SL, undated, SU.

36. Angoff, "Kansan in Westchester," 120.

37. Quoted in Dale Warren, "Notes on a Genius: Sinclair Lewis at His Best," *Harper's*, January 1954.

38. Sheean, 235.

39. Brendan Gill, *Here at the New Yorker* (New York: Random House, 1975), 65.

40. DT report on SL, prepared for Mark Schorer, 1959, SU.

41. Quoted in Schorer, 579.

42. Ibid., 589.

43. Quoted in DT to Mark Schorer, December 14, 1958, in the Schorer papers, Bancroft Library, University of California at Berkeley.

44. Schorer, 595.

45. DT, Railway Diary, December 5–6 [1935].

46. DT to JB, January 7, 1935, in Eileen Agar's collection.

47. DT, undated memorandum, SU.

48. Quoted in Warren, "Notes on a Genius."

49. DT to SL, undated ["Bronxville — Monday," 1937], SU.

50. Quoted in Schorer, 619; and PK interview with George Seldes, Hartland, Vermont, December 4, 1985.

51. Margaret Thompson Wilson to JVS, November 18, 1963.

52. Schorer, 601. DT wrote to Schorer on July 1, 1959: "I was rather touched to learn that Red was constantly on the phone with the Rutland *Herald* (probably Vermont's leading newspaper) at the time I was thrown out of Germany, anxious to know every scrap of news as it came in. But he was obviously more interested than concerned, for Jerry [Ziegler] tells me that he chortled, 'That gal will know how to take care of herself' " (letter in the Schorer papers, Berkeley).

53. SL to Marie Mattingly Meloney, June 27, 1934, in the Meloney papers, Butler Library, Columbia University.

54. SL to DT, July 25, 1934, SU.

55. Sanders, 199 (from United Press dispatch of August 26, 1934).

56. DT to JB, January 7, 1935.

57. DT, "Good-by to Germany," *Harper's*, December 1934.

58. DT, "Room to Breathe In," *Saturday Evening Post*, June 24, 1933.

59. DT, "Good-by to Germany."

60. Quoted in the *New York Times*, August 27, 1934.

61. Quoted in the *New York Times*, August 26, 1934.

62. Sheean, 249.

63. Quoted in Bella Fromm, *Blood and Banquets: A Berlin Social Diary* (New York: Harper and Brothers, 1942), 169.

64. Quoted in the *New York Times*, August 26, 1934.

65. The letter was dated August 24, 1934, and addressed to "Mrs. Dorothea Lewis, Hotel Adlon, Berlin." For many years it hung, framed, in Dorothy's office. The full text is given in the *New York Times*, August 26, 1934.

66. *New York Times*, August 26, 1934.

67. Ibid., September 15, 1934.

68. *Time*, September 3, 1934.

69. Quoted in the *New York Times*, August 26, 1934.

70. Quoted in the *New York Times*, August 27, 1934.

71. *New York Times*, September 15, 1934.

72. She never came back from Europe during this period without being asked to confirm or deny that her marriage was on the rocks. In 1932, during a shipboard interview, a reporter suggested to DT and SL (who for once were traveling together) that *Ann Vickers* must have been based on their own happy marriage. "Lewis burst into loud guffaws," Don Wharton wrote in *Scribner's*, "but it is recorded that his

wife 'stamped her foot angrily and demanded of the reporters: "How do you know we are happily married?" ' And it is also recorded that she asked Lewis 'to deny the advance notice, but he was quite overcome by mirth and did not do so.' " (Wharton, "Dorothy Thompson.")

73. DT, "Back to Blood and Iron."

74. DT speech, delivered to the Foreign Policy Association, Philadelphia, October 25, 1934, transcript at SU.

75. DT to Marie Mattingly Meloney, November 10, 1934, in the Meloney papers, Columbia.

76. Schorer, 608.

77. DT, "Back to Blood and Iron."

78. DT, "Room to Breathe In."

79. DT to SL, undated [1935, from Washington], SU.

80. Combined from two undated letters from DT to SL, written from Washington ["Stoneleigh Court"], 1935, SU.

81. DT speech, "A Nation of Speculators," April 25, 1937, transcript at SU.

82. DT speech, "The Death of Democracies," delivered at the Harvard Club, March 14, 1937, transcript at SU.

83. DT, "Our Ghostly Commonwealth," *Saturday Evening Post,* July 27, 1935.

84. DT to SL, undated [1935–1936], SU.

85. From DT's statement before the Senate Committee on the Judiciary, 75th Congress, 1st Session on S 1392, March 31, 1937, reprinted in *Basic Issues of American Democracy,* ed. Hillman M. Bishop and Samuel Hendel (New York: Appleton-Century-Crofts, 1948), 194–201.

86. OTR, September 22, 1937.

87. OTR, November 2, 1936.

88. OTR, April 4, 1938.

89. OTR ("Ruffled Grouse"), February 17, 1937.

90. DT, Railway Diary, December 5–6 [1935].

91. See *New York Times,* September 28, 1934; and DT speech, "The Changing Status of Women," transcript at SU.

92. There was talk of a radio contract for DT as early as 1933, but, she reported, "I didn't get the idea that the National Broadcasting Company or Columbia were exactly champing at the bit to get me. I would rather do it than anything I can think of. Fifteen minutes a week on the outstanding news event of the week would be more fun than a picnic." (DT to Ben Stolberg, June 21, 1933, in the Stolberg papers, Butler Library, Columbia University.)

93. Sheean, 254.

94. Wharton, "Dorothy Thompson."

95. DT to JB, January 7, 1935.

96. DT to SL, undated [ca. 1935], SU.

97. Schorer, 613.

98. Granville Hicks to "Mr. Friedman," April 17, 1953, in the Granville Hicks papers, SU.

99. Quoted in Schorer, 611; and in Malcolm Cowley, *The Dream of the Golden Mountains* (New York: Viking, 1980), 297.

100. DT to Mark Schorer, May 26, 1959, in the Schorer papers, Berkeley.

101. Quoted in Schorer, 611; and in Cowley, *The Dream of the Golden Mountains*, 297.

102. Granville Hicks to "Mr. Friedman," April 17, 1953.

103. Quoted in Schorer, 601.

104. United Press interview with DT, December 1, 1935, quoted in Sanders, 204.

105. Quoted in Marjorie Shuler, "Expedition to Olympus," *Christian Science Monitor*, December 24, 1935.

106. DT debate with Sir Gerald Campbell, April 1935, transcript at SU (Series 7).

107. DT speech, "The Changing Status of Women."

108. DT, "Will the Next Epoch Be a Matriarchy?," unpublished ms. at SU.

109. DT debate with Sir Gerald Campbell, SU.

110. DT to Mark Schorer, February 3, 1960, in the Schorer papers, Berkeley.

111. DT, Railway Diary, November 28 [1935].

112. Combined from DT to Gustav Stolper, March 7, 1936, at the Leo Baeck Institute, New York City; and DT speech, "A Nation of Speculators."

113. DT to Gustav Stolper, November 7, 1935, at the Leo Baeck Institute, New York City.

114. DT, Railway Diary, December 8 [1935].

115. DT, Railway Diary, December 9 [1935].

116. DT, Railway Diary, January 10 [1936].

117. DT, Railway Diary, undated entry.

118. DT, Railway Diary, January 10 [1936].

119. Quoted in DT, Railway Diary, December 3 [1935].

120. Quoted in DT, Railway Diary, November 18 [1935].

121. DT, Railway Diary, undated entries [January 1936].

122. DT, Railway Diary, December 11 [1935].

123. DT, Railway Diary, November 20 [1935].

124. DT to Christa Winsloe, December 21 [1934], SU.

125. DT, Railway Diary, undated entry [autumn 1935].

126. DT to Christa Winsloe, December 21 [1934].

127. DT, Railway Diary, December 8 [1935].

CHAPTER NINE

1. Sheean, 258, 281–282.

2. For Mrs. Reid, DT, and the *Herald Tribune*, see Richard Kluger, *The Paper: The Life and Death of the New York Herald Tribune* (New York: Knopf, 1986), especially 286–288.

3. Ibid., 286.

4. SL to Irita Van Doren, November 24, 1939, Library of Congress.

5. DT to Walter Lippmann, April 5, 1936, in the Lippmann papers, Sterling Library, Yale University.

6. Harriman, "The 'It' Girl."

7. DT to Helen Rogers Reid, January 20, 1936, in the Reid papers, Library of Congress.

8. Walter Lippmann to DT, March 20, 1936, in the Lippmann papers, Yale.

9. H. L. Mencken, quoted in "Personal Journalists," *Saturday Review*, December 12, 1936.

10. Charles Fisher, *The Columnists* (New York: Howell, Soskin, 1944), 9.

11. Frederick Lewis Allen, *Since Yesterday* (New York: Harper and Brothers, 1940), 273.

12. *New York Times*, February 1, 1961.

13. Harriman, "The 'It' Girl."

14. Schorer, 622.

15. Quoted in Schorer, 617. The note dates from March 1936.

16. Clippings at SU.

17. Sheean, 266.

18. OTR ("The Corporations Tax Bill"), March 18, 1936. Copies of nearly all of the columns in "On the Record" were kept by DT's secretaries, either in transcript or (during the first ten years) in scrapbooks. I have cited the columns by date and have given the title where possible, though with DT's wide syndication these varied from place to place. This was especially true after 1947, when DT had no flagship paper in New York. For transcripts after 1947, I have given the date of release, not the date of publication.

With the debut of "On the Record," DT's secretarial staff was greatly enlarged, and her files, generally, are more extensive and better organized for the period 1940–1958 than for the earlier decades of her career. She developed the habit of penciling her replies to professional correspondence at the bottom of the letters she received, which she then gave to her secretaries for typing. Since her letters were invariably transcribed exactly as she wrote them, I have quoted, in a few cases, directly from this holograph material.

19. Quotes on OTR from Harriman, "The 'It' Girl"; "Cartwheel Girl" (*Time*); and Fisher, "Dorothy Thompson, Cosmic Force."

20. Fisher, "Dorothy Thompson, Cosmic Force."

21. OTR ("Political Dictionary"), March 20, 1936.

22. OTR ("Devil's Choice"), March 22, 1936.

23. OTR ("The Floods"), March 24, 1936.

24. OTR ("Invitation to Death"), April 4, 1936.

25. OTR ("Fishing in Politics"), April 9, 1936.

26. See Ronald Steel, *Walter Lippmann and the American Century* (Boston: Atlantic Monthly Press, 1980), 318.

27. DT to SL, undated [1936], SU.

28. DT to Oswald Garrison Villard, August 15, 1936, in the Villard papers, Houghton Library, Harvard University.

29. OTR ("The President's Speech"), November 2, 1936.

30. OTR ("A New Definition of Democracy"), October 1, 1937.

31. OTR ("Notes on the Roar Machine"), June 16, 1936.

32. DT, "Notes on the Common Man," ms. draft, SU.

33. OTR ("In Defense of Adults"), April 16, 1936.

34. OTR ("Mr. Galloway and Mr. Payne"), June 7, 1937.

35. DT, "An Open Letter to Anne Lindbergh," *Look*, March 25, 1941.

36. From DT, introduction to Marcel W. Fodor, *The Revolution Is On* (Boston: Houghton Mifflin, 1940).

37. OTR ("Time to Take Stock — I"), April 11, 1938.

38. OTR ("To My Valentines"), February 12, 1937.

39. OTR ("The Cornucopia Club Meets"), October 15, 1937.

40. OTR ("Governor Aiken of Vermont"), December 8, 1937.

41. OTR ("Green Mountain Holiday"), January 16, 1939.

42. OTR ("Governor Aiken of Vermont").

43. DT, "An Open Letter to Anne Lindbergh." See also OTR ("Concerning Vermont"), September 29, 1937: "Farming can be either an industry or a way of life. If it is an industry it needs to be run like an industry, with capital, with cost accounting, with science, with organized attempts to constantly broaden the market, and to profitably cheapen the product by rationalization. But the farmer, even when what he has is a soil factory and not a farm, wants to be treated as an agrarian. He asks to be considered the backbone of the nation. He holds himself out to be the figment of Jefferson's dream, when, as a matter of fact, he is a speculative businessman."

44. See OTR ("It Can Happen Here"), May 28, 1936; and ("The Lunatic Fringe — I and II"), July 21 and 23, 1936.

45. OTR ("Ourselves and Crime"), April 25, 1936.

46. DT radio broadcast, "Millinery Madness," excerpted in *Reader's Digest*, January 1939. "Since I did not grow up in Andalusia," DT went on, "and never learned to walk with a basket on my head, I find it difficult to adjust my balance to supporting a lark-kidney-and-beefsteak pie, with one of the dead larks rampant. And I believe the place for mixing bowls is in the kitchen and the place for crepes Suzette is in the dining room, not on my head."

47. DT to "Mr. Schreiber," undated ["Statement — Battle for Russia"], SU.

48. OTR ("Minority Report"), November 25, 1940.

49. See DT to Mark Schorer, October 19, 1958: "Nor is [George Jean] Nathan right that my reflections of S.L.'s observations were responsible for my success as a columnist. A conversation at breakfast in which he made some mordant observations on political matters led me to write 'Grouse for Breakfast,' and having invented the phrase I then continued, but only occasionally, to re-invent the Grouse. But actually the Grouse was usually myself" (in the Schorer papers, Bancroft Library, University of California at Berkeley).

50. OTR ("Grouse for Breakfast"), October 9, 1936.

51. OTR ("Ruffled Grouse"), February 17, 1937.

52. See Sheean, 301; Warren, " 'Off the Record' with a Columnist"; and DT, "I Try to Think" (unpublished ms. at SU), quoting her critics: " 'Don't get so wrought up,' they said. 'Don't be a Cassandra.' An unpleasant woman, draped in black and wailing on the walls of Troy! How come this role for someone by nature cheerful and of hearty appetite?"

53. Quoted in Warren, "I Remember Dorothy."

54. OTR ("On Further Thought"), February 10, 1937.

55. The series was recorded as part of New York's "Town Meeting of the Air," and the opening lecture, followed by an audience "question-and-answer" session, is on disk at the National Archives in Washington. "Essentials of Democracy" was also published in pamphlet form (SU).

56. She frequently gave over her column to passages from her favorite books, always with the proper credit, but sometimes without commentary. On June 14, 1937, she quoted verbatim nearly a thousand words from James Henry Breasted's

Conquest of Civilization and titled the column "Share Cropping — Taxation — Relief — Currency Depreciation — Fascism and Bolshevism in Ancient Rome."

57. OTR ("On Further Thought").

58. OTR ("Bases of the Lack of Confidence"), January 12, 1938.

59. From DT's statement before the Senate Committee on the Judiciary, 75th Congress, 1st Session on S 1392, March 31, 1937, reprinted in *Basic Issues of American Democracy*, ed. Hillman M. Bishop and Samuel Hendel (New York: Appleton-Century-Crofts, 1948), 194–201.

60. Quoted in Fisher, "Dorothy Thompson, Cosmic Force."

61. Quoted in Harriman, "The 'It' Girl."

62. For Station KWK, see the *New York Times*, September 2, 1939, and Harriman, "The 'It' Girl."

63. Quoted in Harriman, "The 'It' Girl."

64. DT's letter about her night on the town with Harry Hopkins is reproduced in Robert Sherwood, *Roosevelt and Hopkins* (New York: Harper and Brothers, 1948), 86–87.

65. The author of this ditty was John Mackey; it dates from October 1938. Clipping in the file on DT in the Sophia Smith collection, Smith College.

66. See DT to Helen Rogers Reid, January 21, 1937, in the Reid papers, Library of Congress.

67. "Cartwheel Girl."

68. Charles Angoff, "Dorothy Thompson: Kansan in Westchester," in *The Tone of the Twenties* (South Brunswick, N.J.: A. S. Barnes and Co., 1966), 116.

69. *Time*, December 27, 1937.

70. Alexander, "The Girl from Syracuse."

71. Quoted in Sheean, 262.

72. Quotes from General Hugh S. Johnson, in OTR ("The Front Spirit"), October 11, 1940; Fisher, "Dorothy Thompson, Cosmic Force"; Marshall, "Dorothy Thompson" ("Columnists on Parade"); and Longmire, "God's Angry Woman," respectively.

73. Harriman, "The 'It' Girl."

74. Fisher, "Dorothy Thompson, Cosmic Force," 17.

75. John Chamberlain, "Miss Thompson Goes to War," *New Republic*, August 24, 1938 (review of *Dorothy Thompson's Political Guide*).

76. Marshall, "Dorothy Thompson."

77. John Chamberlain, "Delilah of the Ink-Pot," *New Republic*, September 27, 1939 (review of *Let the Record Speak*).

78. Quoted in OTR ("The New Game"), June 18, 1937.

79. Heywood Broun, "The Right People," *New Republic*, September 29, 1937.

80. Fisher, "Dorothy Thompson, Cosmic Force."

81. Marshall, "Dorothy Thompson."

82. OTR ("The Right to Insecurity"), May 11, 1938.

83. OTR ("The Fine Arts Bill"), May 23, 1938.

84. Quoted in Sheean, 315.

85. George Seldes, "Servants of the Lords," in *Lords of the Press* (New York: Blue Ribbon Books, 1941 [but copyright 1938]), 352.

86. See DT's letter to George Seldes, December 13, 1938, SU.

87. DT remarked succinctly in a letter to Alfred Lilienthal: "I don't know whether

I'm a 'liberal' or a 'conservative.' The words seem to me to have lost their meaning. I don't believe that money is the main thing in life, and from that I deduce other things" (letter of May 6, 1942, SU).

88. OTR ("Concerning a Point of View"), August 13, 1937.

89. DT, "To Freedom!," *LHJ*, December 1937.

90. DT, "Dramatizing Democracy," *LHJ*, February 1939.

91. DT commencement address, delivered at Syracuse University, May 30, 1937, transcript at SU.

92. DT, "Liberalism and Morality," *LHJ*, January 1938.

93. DT, "An Open Letter to Anne Lindbergh."

94. DT remarked in an undated letter to "Mr. Dennis": "I am convinced that we will have socialism all over the world, and I am deeply concerned to see my way to the answer to the question: What kind of socialism?" (SU).

95. DT, "An Open Letter to Anne Lindbergh."

96. Jay Franklin, quoted in Seldes, *Lords of the Press*, 352.

97. DT commencement address, Syracuse University.

98. DT speech, "The Coming American Revolution," undated [but ca. 1940], transcript at SU.

99. DT commencement address, Syracuse University.

100. DT, "The Coming American Revolution."

101. DT to Paul Scheffer, December 30, 1938, SU.

102. OTR ("A New Definition of Democracy"), October 1, 1937.

103. For DT's association with the *Journal* see Bruce and Beatrice Gould, *American Story* (New York: Harper and Row, 1968).

104. DT, "How to Destroy Civilization," *LHJ*, January 1939.

105. DT speech, "The Changing Status of Women," transcript at SU.

106. DT, "It's a Woman's World," *LHJ*, July 1940. See also her article "If I Had a Daughter," *LHJ*, September 1939, which for sheer sophistry is unequaled among DT's pieces: "If I had a daughter, I would tell her that she has to choose [between a husband and a career]. I would tell her that if she feels in herself some talent for the development and expression of which everything else is worth the sacrifice, to go ahead and develop it, but to know that the development will cost her a great deal." She did not have, and never had had, any intention of following her own advice.

107. DT, "The World — and Women," *LHJ*, March 1938.

108. OTR ("To Thomas Mann"), April 14, 1937.

109. DT commencement address, Syracuse University.

110. Fisher, "Dorothy Thompson, Cosmic Force."

111. DT, introduction to Kurt Schuschnigg, *My Austria* (New York: Knopf, 1938), xxv: "This, then, is a memorial, with even the introduction written by one who would have died for Austria — not for Austria the state, but for Austria the idea; supra-national, integrating, all-inclusive, Christian and humane."

112. OTR ("Write It Down"), February 18, 1938.

113. OTR ("Rebirth at Easter"), April 10, 1939.

114. OTR ("Resistant Pacifism"), December 22, 1937.

115. DT, *Refugees: Anarchy or Organization?*, 11–12.

116. OTR ("Women and Children First"), April 30, 1937.

117. Schorer, 628–629.

118. DT to SL, undated [ca. 1938–1939], SU.

119. DT to SL, August 29, 1937 ["On our parting"], SU.

120. Quoted in Schorer, 613.

121. See Louis Untermeyer, *Bygones* (New York: Harcourt Brace and World, 1965), 85.

122. Quoted in Harriman, "The 'It' Girl."

123. Sheean, 255–256.

124. John Hersey, "First Job," *Yale Review*, vol. 76, winter 1987.

125. PK interview with Dinah Sheean, Paris, July 18, 1986.

126. Quoted in Harriman, "The 'It' Girl."

127. Quoted in Sanders, 227.

128. Quoted in Schorer, 632.

129. Sheean, 291.

130. Quoted in Schorer, 635.

131. SL, *Gideon Planish* (New York: World Publishing Co., 1944), 320–323. Two plays of SL's, *Queenie and the Jopes* and *Felicia Speaking,* were also based on a central character, a "Talking Woman," reminiscent of DT. The various drafts of *Queenie* (with annotations by Helen Hayes, who considered taking the role) are at SU.

132. See Sanders, 226; and Schorer, 628.

133. DT to SL, April 29, 1937, SU.

134. SL to DT, January 28, [1939], SU.

135. DT to SL, April 29, 1937.

136. DT to SL, undated [1937, from Bronxville], SU.

137. DT to SL, April 29, 1937.

138. DT to SL, undated [1937, "Bronxville — Monday"], SU.

139. DT to Wells Lewis, undated [1937], in the Grace Hegger Lewis papers, Humanities Research Center, University of Texas at Austin.

140. DT to Mark Schorer, February 3, 1960, in the Schorer papers, Berkeley.

141. DT to SL, April 29, 1937.

142. Schorer, 631.

143. PK interview with Lisa Sergio, Washington, D.C., November 23, 1985.

144. Ethel Moses quoted in Sanders, 226.

145. SL to DT, January 28 [1939].

146. See his different letters to DT, mostly undated, 1939–1941, SU.

147. Combined from DT to SL, undated, and April 29, 1937, SU.

CHAPTER TEN

1. DT to Helen Rogers Reid, January 28, 1937, in the Reid papers, Library of Congress.

2. DT to John Moses, June 24, 1938, SU.

3. Harriman, "The 'It' Girl."

4. Charles Fisher, *The Columnists* (New York: Howell, Soskin, 1944), 17n., 168.

5. Ronald Steel, *Walter Lippmann and the American Century* (Boston: Atlantic Monthly Press, 1980), 342.

6. DT to John Moses, June 24, 1938.

7. DT to Alexander Woollcott, "August 14" [probably 1939], in the Woollcott papers, Houghton Library, Harvard University.

8. PK interview with Dennis Fodor, Munich, October 1, 1987.

9. DT to Wells Lewis, undated [1937], in the Grace Hegger Lewis papers, Humanities Research Center, University of Texas at Austin.

10. Dinah Sheean to PK, February 12, 1987.

11. PK interview with Denis Fodor.

12. Alexander, "The Girl from Syracuse."

13. Dale Warren was actually the head of the publicity department at Houghton Mifflin, but in DT's case, for many years, he functioned as what would now be called an acquiring editor.

14. Warren, "I Remember Dorothy."

15. Quoted in Harriman, "The 'It' Girl."

16. Quoted in an untitled manuscript by Avery Strakosh (at SU), later adapted and published as "House of Maps and Worlds," *Look,* April 7, 1942.

17. Warren, " 'Off the Record' with a Columnist."

18. PK interview with Lisa Sergio, Washington, D.C., November 23, 1985.

19. "Cartwheel Girl."

20. Strakosh ms., SU.

21. Bottome, "Dorothy Thompson." DT was outraged by Phyllis's depiction of her character. "I wish you would read this from the pen of my 'friend' Phyllis," she wrote to Dale Warren in February 1943, after Phyllis had forwarded a copy of the manuscript. "I think it is very cruel. I think it is in terrible taste. And I think it is very untrue. But, of course, in the latter matter I may be woefully prejudiced. I am furious at her attempt to describe and psychoanalyze my life with Red, about which she knows literally nothing. I want to stop her from publishing this, but I suppose there is no way to do it." In fact, when Phyllis heard about DT's objections, she withdrew her piece from a proposed collection of published profiles. (DT to Dale Warren, "Filed, 2/25/43," in Houghton Mifflin Company archives, Houghton Library, Harvard University.)

22. PK interview with Virginia Shaw and Madeline Shaw Green, Ridgefield, Connecticut, August 25, 1988.

23. Harriman, "The 'It' Girl."

24. Alexander, "The Girl from Syracuse." See also Diana Cooper, *Trumpets from the Steep* (Boston: Houghton Mifflin, 1960), 16: "The conversation [at Dorothy's] was always above my head. The Tripartite Agreement, the Treaties of St. Germain and Sèvres were argued, and I do not remember once opening my mouth."

25. Much of the research material in Series 8 at SU deals directly with the production of OTR and includes reports of DT's conversations with the members of the "brain trust."

26. The words are her own. See DT to Franklin D. Roosevelt, undated [November–December 1940], SU; and at the Roosevelt Library, Hyde Park, New York.

27. Alexander, "The Girl from Syracuse."

28. PK interview with Polly Irwin, Chevy Chase, Maryland, October 23, 1986.

29. *New York Times,* May 23, 1976.

30. PK interview with William I. Nichols, Paris, January 17, 1986.

31. Quoted in Harriman, "The 'It' Girl."

32. Alexander, "The Girl from Syracuse."

33. Quoted in Sanders, 229.

34. See Max Ascoli to DT, August 22 and 28, 1939, SU: "I miss you. . . . Yes, I miss you: but I must say that I miss you in the right way. I miss the good companion, the sister mind . . . and I miss your dear warm heart. All the rest is something that is neither in nor out of my mind. It is simply something which does not exist — and should never have existed."

35. Ilka Chase, *Past Imperfect* (New York: Doubleday, Doran and Co., 1942), 244–248.

36. Quoted in Sanders, 225.

37. PK interview with Rinna Samuel, London, October 5, 1987.

38. Quoted in Strakosh ms., SU.

39. Fisher, "Dorothy Thompson, Cosmic Force."

40. Alexander, "The Girl from Syracuse."

41. DT to Alexander Woollcott, August 14 [1939?], in the Woollcott papers, Houghton Library, Harvard University.

42. Quoted in Sanders, 247.

43. Charles Fisher, "Dorothy Thompson, Cosmic Force."

44. Warren, " 'Off the Record' with a Columnist."

45. Sari Juhasz quoted in Sanders, 259.

46. PK interview with Dinah Sheean, London, February 10, 1986.

47. Klaus Mann, *The Turning Point* (New York: Marcus Weiner, 1984), 296, 340. A German adaptation of Mann's original English text exists as *Der Wendepunkt: Ein Lebensbericht* (Munich: Spangenberg, im Ellermann Verlag, 1981).

48. Alexander, "The Girl from Syracuse."

49. Chase, *Past Imperfect,* 245.

50. OTR ("On Party Material"), March 29, 1939.

51. See *The Letters of Aldous Huxley,* ed. Grover Smith (New York: Harper and Row, 1969), 593.

52. Waverley Root, *The Paris Edition,* edited and with an introduction by Samuel Abt (San Francisco: North Point, 1987), 45–46.

53. Warren, "I Remember Dorothy."

54. Quoted in Mann, *Der Wendepunkt,* 476.

55. PK interview with Denis Fodor, Munich, October 1, 1987.

56. PK interview with Madeline Shaw Green.

57. Alexander, "The Girl from Syracuse."

58. Quoted in Harriman, "The 'It' Girl."

59. Fisher, "Dorothy Thompson, Cosmic Force."

60. Alexander, "The Girl from Syracuse."

61. Strakosh ms., SU.

62. In 1938 she also published a small memoir for children, *Once on Christmas,* with illustrations by Lois Lensky. The book was a reprint of a 1937 Christmas Eve radio broadcast. It recounted the Thompson family Christmas in Hamburg, New York, in 1900 and was dedicated to Michael Lewis.

63. *New York Times,* September 2, 1939.

64. Lewis Gannett, "Books and Things," *New York Herald Tribune,* August 25, 1939.

65. *Christian Science Monitor,* February 14, 1940.

66. DT to Alexander Woollcott, November 8, 1937, in the Woollcott papers, Harvard.

67. Kennedy, "Global Lady."

68. DT radio broadcast ("Blue Network"), September 6, 1939, transcript at SU.

69. Harriman, "The 'It' Girl."

70. Harriman, "The 'It' Girl;" and PK interview with Dinah Sheean, Paris, July 18, 1986.

71. Warren, "I Remember Dorothy."

72. PK interview with Madeline Shaw Green and Virginia Shaw.

73. DT to Pearl S. Buck, May 10, 1938, Records of the Central Committee on Friendship Dinners, Schlesinger Library, Radcliffe College.

74. DT to Marie Mattingly Meloney, April 3, 1939, in the Meloney papers, Butler Library, Columbia University.

75. PK interview with Ellen Sheean, Paris, July 18, 1986.

76. See her undated letter to Stan Rhoades, SU.

77. Sheean, 139–140.

78. Quoted in Warren, " 'Off the Record' with a Columnist."

79. Warren, "I Remember Dorothy."

80. DT to George Powell, undated, SU.

81. DT radio broadcast ("People in the News"), February 15, 1938, transcript at SU.

82. DT, "100% Uninhabitable," LHJ, October 1939.

83. DT, "Give Me Vermont," House and Garden, July 1947.

84. PK interview with Lisa Sergio.

85. PK interview with Denis Fodor. Concerning one of her very first fender-benders, she wrote to her friend Tish Irwin: "The chief fault seems to have been mine — I wasn't on my side of the road, but in the middle. Wheel tracks showed it. Never before having driven six thousand pounds of steel, the shape and size of a motor bus, I thought I was on the right, when I wasn't" (DT to Tish Irwin, June 20, 1931, SU).

86. Recounted in letter of Laura Z. Hobson to DT (asking DT to confirm the story), January 27, 1954, SU.

87. Sheean, 137.

88. PK interview with Elisabeth Marton, New York City, April 8, 1987.

89. Paul Brooks to DT, November 3, 1943, in Houghton Mifflin Company archives, Harvard.

90. It was the tale of "Harriet," called Harry by her family.

91. DT to American Academy and Institute of Arts and Letters (in response to an Academy questionnaire), February 14, 1939, in the Academy archives, New York City.

92. Dale Warren to DT, March 20, 1940, in Houghton Mifflin Company archives, Harvard.

93. DT, Railway Diary, January 9 [1936]; and DT to Dale Warren, undated, SU.

94. PK interview with Denis Fodor.

95. DT enlisted the aid of all her friends and colleagues to help secure a position for Fodor in America. See her letter to John Gunther of August 26, 1940: "You and I have got to do something about Fodor. He is going to have a much harder time

in this country than he himself dreams of unless we do. The best solution for him will be if he can get a place in a University where he can teach the diplomatic and political history of Central Europe on which his information is second to none, as you know." (Letter in the Gunther papers, University of Chicago.)

96. DT, "Notes on College Days," ms. ca. 1947, SU.

97. PK interview with Denis Fodor.

98. Dinah Sheean to PK, June 4, 1986.

99. Warren, " 'Off the Record' with a Columnist."

100. DT, "It's a Woman's World," *LHJ*, July 1940.

101. Quoted in Warren, " 'Off the Record' with a Columnist."

102. PK interview with Charlotte Cramer Sachs, New York City, December 21, 1987.

103. Quoted in Warren, "I Remember Dorothy."

104. DT to George Powell, undated [but wartime, ca. 1942], SU.

105. Quoted in Peter S. Jennison, *The History of Woodstock, Vermont, 1890–1983* (Woodstock, Vt.: The Countryman Press, 1983), 190; and PK interview with William I. Nichols.

106. JVS to John Gunther (quoting SL), May 24, 1963, in Houghton Mifflin Company archives, Harvard.

107. Dinah Sheean to PK, August 21, 1986: "What I remember best about the [Zuckmayers] is their physical appearance. . . . Carl dressed in full 'tract,' with Lederhosen, beflowered braces, and a feather in his hat, of course. . . . Licce all in browns and grays and with sensible shoes . . . like the bird kingdom, with the male having all the plumage." See also Alice Herdan-Zuckmayer, *Die Farm in den grünen Bergen* (Frankfurt am Main: Fischer Bucherei, 1956).

108. For Rosenstock-Huessy see Michael Balfour and Julian Frisby, *Helmuth von Moltke: A Leader against Hitler* (London: Macmillan, 1972).

109. Meyer Weisgal, *Meyer Weisgal . . . So Far* (New York: Random House, 1971), 194.

110. Quoted in Sanders, 239.

111. For the section following, see two works by David S. Wyman, *Paper Walls: America and the Refugee Crisis, 1938–1941* (Amherst, Mass.: University of Massachusetts Press, 1968) and *The Abandonment of the Jews: America and the Holocaust, 1941–1945* (New York: Pantheon, 1984). In the latter he speaks of DT (page 320) as an "exception" among her colleagues: "[M]ost American intellectuals were indifferent to the struggle for rescue." I have also referred to Sheldon Spear, "The United States and the Persecution of the Jews in Germany, 1933–1939," *Jewish Social Studies*, October 1968.

112. According to Spear, in "The United States and the Persecution of the Jews," "The American Jewish Committee and B'nai B'rith were the most persistent among Jewish organizations in urging the U.S. to intercede diplomatically."

113. OTR ("An Appeal to Jews and Christians"), January 21, 1938.

114. Quotes from DT, "Escape in a Frozen World," *Survey Graphic*, February 1939, and DT, *Refugees: Anarchy or Organization?*, 5–6, 39.

115. DT, "Escape In a Frozen World."

116. The article, "Refugees," which ran in *Foreign Affairs* in April 1938, was later expanded to become *Refugees: Anarchy or Organization?* "Personally," said

DT, "I wish it were being published in paper at 25 cents!" (DT to Robert Haas, undated [June 1938], in Random House archives, Butler Library, Columbia University.)

117. DT, *Refugees*, 103–104.
118. "Refugees, Inc.," *Time*, August 8, 1938.
119. DT, "Refugees."
120. DT, "Escape in a Frozen World."
121. DT, "A Not Fantastic Dream," *LHJ*, March 1939.
122. Hamilton Fish Armstrong, introduction to DT, *Refugees*, xi.
123. Quoted in Spear, "The United States and the Persecution of the Jews."
124. Harriman, "The 'It' Girl."
125. Alexander Woollcott to Rebecca West, February 21, 1938, reprinted in *The Letters of Alexander Woollcott* (New York: Viking, 1944).
126. OTR ("Shadow Boxing"), September 8, 1937.
127. OTR (" 'Peace' — And the Crisis Begins"), October 1, 1938.
128. DT radio broadcast, November 14, 1938, transcript at SU.
129. OTR, November 14, 1938.
130. DT to "Geoffrey" [probably Parsons], letter draft, undated, SU.
131. DT radio speech, November 14, 1938.
132. Open letter from DT, as Chairman of the Journalists' Defense Fund, sent to contributors and subscribers, November 1938, SU.
133. DT's hate-mail is still in her file at the Federal Bureau of Investigation, No. 9-7990, released to me in January 1988 (FOIA request No. 276,798).
134. DT speech, untitled, Detroit, March 17, 1939, transcript at SU.
135. Harriman, "The 'It' Girl."
136. DT speech, untitled, Detroit, March 17, 1939.
137. Wyman, *Paper Walls*, 18. The book provides a concise and entertaining rundown of Father Coughlin's career.
138. OTR ("Towards a Showdown"), September 1, 1936.
139. DT speech, "Freedom's Back Is against the Wall," delivered as a commencement address at Russell Sage College, June 8, 1937, transcript at SU.
140. For the German-American Bund, see Leland V. Bell, "The Failure of Nazism in America: The German-American Bund, 1936–1941," *Political Science Quarterly*, December 1970, 585–599, and Joachim Remak, " 'Friends of the New Germany': The Bund and German-American Relations," *Journal of Modern History*, March 1967, 38–41. A useful guide for the section below was *The German in America: 1607–1970: A Chronology and Fact Book*, comp. and ed. Howard B. Furer (Dobbs Ferry, N.Y.: Oceana Publications, 1973).
141. DT radio broadcast ("People in the News"), September 1937, transcript at SU.
142. DT to Helen Rogers Reid, March 3, 1939, in the Reid papers, Library of Congress.
143. *New York Times*, December 23, 1938.
144. "America's 'Isms,' " *Newsweek*, March 6, 1939.
145. "The Nazis Are Here," *The Nation*, March 4, 1939. For the Bund rally see also A. J. Smith, "I Went to a Nazi Rally," *Christian Century*, March 8, 1939, and Stanley High, "Star-Spangled Fascists," *Saturday Evening Post*, May 27, 1939.
146. "There are ways of dealing with dealers in poison words that do not con-

stitute infringement of free speech," DT wrote. "The publication of anonymous pamphlets ought to be forbidden by law. Anyone who has anything to say to the public ought to be compelled to accept responsibility for saying it. Letterhead organizations ought to be investigated. The financial sources and the interlocking directorates of organizations indulging in political propaganda ought to be made public. The disposition of funds collected from the public for propaganda purposes ought to be revealed. What became of the money raised for the defense of the Scottsboro boys? What became of all the moneys raised for various forms of relief for Spain?" (DT, "Propaganda Bogey," *LHJ*, December 1939.)

147. For DT at the Bund rally see Sanders, 235, and Associated Press and United Press International dispatches, February 20, 1939.

148. *Newsweek*, March 6, 1939.

149. "Notes and Comment," *The New Yorker*, March 4, 1939. This unsigned piece was written by Wolcott Gibbs.

150. OTR ("Who Loves Liberty?"), January 10, 1938.

151. "The Nazis Are Here."

152. "Notes and Comment," *The New Yorker*, March 4, 1939.

153. OTR, March 17, 1939.

154. DT to "Geoffrey," letter draft, undated.

CHAPTER ELEVEN

1. OTR ("Ten Minutes — And a Check"), January 25, 1939: "Pneumonia! Pneumonia! Did you ever think that a great wave of relief would sweep over you, that almost a song would sing in your heart because a doctor told you your boy had pneumonia!"

2. DT to SL, undated [1939], SU.

3. PK interview with Lilian T. Mowrer, Wonalancet, New Hampshire, August 25, 1986.

4. Betty Gram Swing to DT, undated ["Thursday," April 1938], SU.

5. Quoted in Sanders, 244–245. The Frances Gunther papers are at the Schlesinger Library at Radcliffe College, and as of this writing are unprocessed.

6. PK interviews with John Paul Lewis, Washington, D.C., November 24, 1985, and Winnetou (Zuckmayer) Guttenbrunner, Saas-Fee, August 11, 1986.

7. PK interview with Dinah Sheean, London, February 10, 1986.

8. Marianne Kortner Brün to PK, September 15, 1988.

9. PK interview with Denis Fodor, Munich, October 1, 1987.

10. DT to Betty Gram Swing, April 21, 1938, SU.

11. PK interview with Pamela Wilson Reeves, Holden, Massachusetts, June 26, 1988.

12. PK interview with Lisa Sergio, Washington, D.C., November 23, 1985.

13. DT, loose essay about SL, handwritten ca. 1959 for Mark Schorer, SU (Series 7).

14. SL to ML, "Five days before Christmas, 1939," SU.

15. See especially DT's letters to Wells Lewis of 1942–1943, in the Grace Hegger Lewis papers, Humanities Research Center, University of Texas at Austin.

16. DT to SL, undated, SU. She has penciled at the top of the letter, "This was never sent. To a few that were I received replies chiding me for my 'self pity.' "

17. PK interviews with John Paul Lewis and Lisa Sergio.

18. DT to Dr. Bernard Pacella (recounting ML's childhood medical history), June 18, 1960, SU.

19. PK interview with Denis Fodor. For more on Dr. Traeger (and a far more favorable opinion of his practice) see John Gunther's *Death Be Not Proud* (New York: Harper and Brothers, 1949).

20. DT to SL, undated [1939], SU.

21. ML's letters to DT are at SU (Series 3).

22. DT to Henri Bernstein, undated [but November 1944, in response to Bernstein's note of condolence on Wells's death], SU.

23. The manuscript and reviews of Wells Lewis's *They Still Say No* (New York: Farrar and Rhinehart, 1939), are at SU.

24. Max Ascoli to DT, November 13, 1944, SU.

25. DT to Grace Lewis, November 1, 1945, in the Lewis papers, Austin.

26. PK interview with Lisa Sergio.

27. OTR ("A Reaction to the Republican Convention"), June 26, 1940.

28. DT to Grace Lewis, November 1, 1945.

29. PK interview with Dinah Sheean.

30. Schorer, 645.

31. DT to SL, undated [1939], SU; and quoted in Sheean, 306–309.

32. Kitty Carlisle, *Kitty: An Autobiography* (New York: Doubleday, 1988), 88–89.

33. For Marcella Powers, see Schorer, 651–652 and *passim*.

34. Schorer, 659.

35. See DT's telegram, undated [1939], to Louis B. Mayer, and her letter to Bruce Gould, March 5, 1951, SU. Around this time DT also proposed a screen treatment of her romance with SL, partly in order to counter a film in development at Paramount called *Arise My Love*, which was based loosely on the same story. Neither film was ever made.

36. For Kortner's reminiscences of DT, see Fritz Kortner, *Aller Tage Abend* (Munich: Kindler-Verlag, 1959), chapter 28.

37. PK interview with Denis Fodor.

38. PK interview with Madeline Shaw Green, Ridgefield, Connecticut, August 25, 1987.

39. The best account of the German cultural emigration is Anthony Heilbut's *Exiled in Paradise: German Refugee Artists and Intellectuals in America* (New York: Viking, 1983).

40. For DT and Brecht see Kortner, *Aller Tage Abend*, 349, and James K. Lyon, *Bertholt Brecht in America* (Princeton: Princeton University Press, 1980), 141.

41. DT, "Beware of Geniuses," *LHJ*, December 1956, reprinted in DT, *The Courage to Be Happy*.

42. DT to John Anderson, February 28, 1940, SU.

43. The account of the production of *Another Sun* is taken from PK telephone interview with Celeste Holm, August 22, 1987; from Cheryl Crawford, *One Naked Individual: My Fifty Years in the Theatre* (New York: Bobbs-Merrill, 1977), 108–110; and from DT to Fritz Kortner, February 23, 1940, SU. Other sources as cited.

44. DT earnestly solicited funds for the production from any source she could think of. See her telegram (undated) to Bernard Baruch: "The play will be produced

in any case because if necessary I will finance it myself but some stubborn streak in me tells me that other people ought to be willing to back it on my own faith in it and in the cause for which it was written. . . . All you have to lose is $5,000 — I have to endure the critics. . . . I am going to give my royalties to the Jews, Poles, Czechs and Finns anyhow" (SU).

45. Quotes from Fisher, "Dorothy Thompson, Cosmic Force"; and "Cartwheel Girl."

46. Cheryl Crawford, *One Naked Individual*, 110.

47. Warren, " 'Off the Record' with a Columnist."

48. *New York Times*, February 24, 1940.

49. Quoted in Harriman, "The 'It' Girl."

50. Apart from Kortner, Miss Holm, and Miss Hofer, the cast of *Another Sun* included Hans Jaray, Kate Warriner, Adrienne Gessner, and Leo Bulgakov.

51. DT to John Anderson, February 28, 1940.

52. In March 1940 DT wrote to Meyer Weisgal: "[My] experience in the Broadway theatre, whatever it may have revealed to me as a playwright, revealed a great deal to me as a journalist. The Broadway theatre is a combination of crap-game . . . and trade-union dictatorship. . . . Financially, Broadway is on the level with horse-racing or lotteries, only the chances in these are somewhat better than in the theatre." (Quoted in Meyer Weisgal, *Meyer Weisgal . . . So Far* [New York: Doubleday, 1971], 195.) See also "Swords Crossed with Dorothy Thompson," *Equity*, December 1939: "I could tell you things about the Musicians' Union that would make your hair stand on end."

53. See Cornelius Traeger to DT, August 27, 1940: "I was terribly upset to read the last paragraph in your letter regarding the Wells-Kortner episode. . . . All that Wells knows about Kortner from me is his relationship with you respecting the production of the play. However, Dotty, he is not stupid and you are not a good dissembler and I am sure Wells arrived at his own conclusions" (SU).

54. Fritz Kortner to DT, September 4, 1941, SU.

55. SL to DT, January 28 [1939], SU.

56. DT to Madeleine Clark, undated [1940], SU. Also in this vein, in the autumn of 1939 Rinna Grossman (later Samuel), the daughter of DT's friend Barbara De Porte, arrived in New York as a student at Russell Sage College. During a visit to Central Park West, she was treated "very summarily" by DT. DT was "ill at ease," Mrs. Samuel recalled, "and so was I, but *I* was eighteen, after all." Mrs. Samuel asked if DT could help her secure a job as a copygirl with the *Herald Tribune*, and DT answered, "No, I'm afraid not, I can't even do that for Michael, whom I love very much."

"Of course it was a lie," said Mrs. Samuel later, "and not a nice lie," because it was "obviously unnecessary and not thought about." She remembered leaving DT's apartment, "probably in tears," thinking, "How can it be? How *can* it be?" (PK interview with Rinna Samuel, London, October 5, 1987.)

57. SL to DT, March 19 [1939?], SU.

58. For Rosie Waldeck see her memoirs, *Prelude to the Past: The Autobiography of a Woman* (New York: William Morrow, 1934), and Malcolm Cowley, "Valuta Girl," *New Republic*, December 5, 1934.

59. Sanders, 210n.

60. A lengthy but rather useless file on Rosie Waldeck, released at my request,

is available for reading at FBI headquarters in Washington (FOIA request No. 276, 804). The Berlin journalist Bella Fromm adopted Rosie's own line in regard to her falling-out with DT: "Countess Waldegg [sic] had been secretary to Dorothy Thompson for years. Dorothy fired her when she discovered that Waldegg mixed in Dorothy's love affair with the German actor Fritz Kortner, in New York." (Loose memo in Bella Fromm papers, Box 52, Folder 1, Mugar Library, Boston University.)

61. Quoted in Ronald Steel, *Walter Lippmann and the American Century* (Boston: Atlantic Monthly Press, 1980), 360.

62. For DT's trouble with the servants, see her FBI file (No. 9-7990), in which, in spite of extensive Bureau excisions, Kortner's influence is still apparent; also see Cornelius Traeger to DT, August 27, 1940: "I was completely bowled over when I heard the story of your German servants. I am sure that if we knew the extent of Fifth Column activities in this country we would be appalled. In any event, I am glad you are rid of them, and I am sure that Michael will enjoy the companionship of a stable young man over the over-fervent Mimi."

63. Quoted in Charles Angoff, "Dorothy Thompson: Kansan in Westchester," in *The Tone of the Twenties* (South Brunswick, N.J.: A. S. Barnes and Co., 1966), 117.

64. DT to SL, undated [1938–1939], SU. While preparing for her autobiography, DT read through her letters and dated them from memory, sometimes erroneously. Here she has written "1938," but since she makes reference to Hamilton Fish Armstrong's "last book on the Munich conference," the letter would date from the end of that year at the earliest.

65. For Rose Lane's later years, see her obituary in the *New York Times*, November 1, 1967.

66. "The Correspondence of Dorothy Thompson and Rose Wilder Lane," ed. William Holtz, ms. in my possession.

67. RWL to DT, June 1, 1939.

68. DT to RWL, June 6, 1939.

69. DT to Meyer Weisgal, August 10, 1940, SU.

70. DT to SL, undated [1939], SU.

71. Cornelius Traeger to DT, August 5, 1940, SU.

72. DT to SL, undated [1939], SU.

73. Sanders, 226.

74. Quoted in Alexander, "The Girl from Syracuse."

75. DT to SL, undated [1938–1939], SU.

76. For Toller's death see the *New York Times*, May 23, 1939.

77. DT speech, "America," delivered at the Forum in Los Angeles, April 13, 1939, and reprinted in DT, *Let the Record Speak*, 371–387.

78. DT speech, May 8, 1939, delivered at the international PEN conference, transcript at SU.

79. OTR ("Death of a Poet"), May 24, 1939.

80. Enit Kaufman (illustrator) and Dorothy Canfield Fisher, *American Portraits* (New York: Henry Holt, 1946), 276.

81. OTR ("Now or Never!"), March 18, 1938.

82. DT speech, untitled, delivered in Detroit, Michigan, March 17, 1939, transcript at SU.

83. OTR ("The Balance Sheet of History"), June 3, 1940.

84. DT speech, untitled, delivered in Detroit, March 17, 1939.

85. See DT, "You Don't Know the Half of It," unpublished ms. dated March 15, 1939, SU.

86. OTR ("Diary Between Peace and War"), September 3, 1939. The text of this column was adapted from letters DT had received from Max Ascoli, who was sailing for Europe when war broke out. (Original letters at SU.)

87. DT radio broadcast, September 6, 1939, transcript at SU.

88. Diary of Raoul de Roussy de Sales, October 7, 1939, typed copy at SU.

89. Quoted in de Sales diary, May 4, 1939, SU.

90. The definitive biography of Charles Lindbergh has yet to be written. For his activities as an American isolationist, see Wayne S. Cole, *Charles Augustus Lindbergh and the Battle Against Intervention in World War II* (New York: Harcourt, Brace, Jovanovich, 1974).

91. See the diary of Harold Ickes, September 23, 1939, Library of Congress. On March 29, 1940, Ickes observed that DT was "writing magnificently on the international situation" and that she would be "perfect" as a candidate for "Minister of Propaganda."

92. OTR ("Col. Lindbergh and Propaganda"), September 20, 1939.

93. DT, "What Lindbergh Really Wants," ms. prepared for publication in *Look* magazine, SU.

94. De Sales diary, September 21, 1939, SU.

95. Letters in DT's FBI file (No. 9-7990), where she is described as "Miss Dorothy Thompson — Victim."

96. Quoted in Longmire, "God's Angry Woman." In 1942 DT actually *was* bitten in public, though not by a Nazi per se. According to an account in the *New York Post* (February 12, 1942, clipping at SU), she had gone to the Café Royal, a famous hangout of the Yiddish theater in New York, where "a blonde dripping diamonds, pretty hefty . . . and as drunk as a skunk," sat making loud remarks about "dirty Jews" and shouting "Heil Hitler!" at the clientele. Escorted outside by the café's management, she "raged" for a while on the sidewalk and then "attacked" DT when she tried to leave.

"It all happened so fast," DT recalled. "I can't describe it adequately. She kicked me, I think, and she tried to punch me. Then she bit me on the finger. And then she went away.

"It was nothing, really," DT concluded. "Just an irresponsible drunk. Make a joke of it." But the headlines were priceless: "Dorothy Thompson Bitten by Blonde," "Bitten — On the Record," "Dorothy Thompson Encounters a Drunk," etc.

97. Quoted in Warren, "I Remember Dorothy."

98. *New York Times*, February 24, 1941.

99. *New York Journal and American*, October 19, 1939.

100. DT's undated draft reply is at SU.

101. De Sales diary, May 9, 1939, SU: "I understand the words but I don't know what it means. Christianity? Fundamentally I don't know what it is. For that matter neither does Dorothy. It is a kind of atmosphere of tolerance in which democratic capitalist commercialism flourishes."

102. The copy at SU is undated, but see Nicolson's reply, note 103 below.

103. Harold Nicolson to DT, August 29, 1939, SU.

104. *Time*, March 20, 1939.

105. Ferris Greenslet to DT, May 3, 1940, SU.

106. DT diary, March 23 [1940], SU.

107. DT to Franklin D. Roosevelt, March 5, 1945 (but in reference to 1940), at the Roosevelt Library, Hyde Park.

108. DT to the Honorable James A. Farley, November 11, 1939, SU: "The Pope's Encyclical has been the one ray of light among all the international speeches and documents of the last months." See also OTR, February 13, March 6, and November 1, 1939 ("The Papal Elections," "Pius XII — the Former Diplomat," and "The Philosophy of Pius XII").

109. DT, "Meaning for Us All," *LHJ*, February 1959.

110. Quoted in DT, "The Most Beautiful Form of Courage," *LHJ*, August 1955, reprinted in DT, *The Courage to Be Happy*.

111. OTR, May 13, 1940.

112. DT radio broadcast, untitled, condensed and reprinted in *Current History*, June 1940.

113. OTR ("The Front Spirit"), October 11, 1940.

114. PK telephone interview with Julian Bach, May 9, 1987. See also Sanders, 261.

115. PK interview with Jane Gunther, Greensboro, Vermont, July 30, 1987.

116. Quoted in Sanders, 276–277.

117. Quoted in the *Springfield Union*, August 28, 1940, clipping at SU.

118. DT speech, "There Are No Neutral Hearts," broadcast July 21, 1940, over the Canadian Broadcasting Corporation; reprinted in *Life*, January 27, 1941, as " 'There Was a Man.' "

119. DT, "Democracy and Britain," *LHJ*, November 1941.

120. See the *New York Times*, January 23, 1941, and OTR ("The Union of the English-Speaking World"), January 10, 1941.

121. OTR ("The 1940 Elections"), May 15, 1940.

122. Helen Rogers Reid to DT, telegram, April 15, 1940, in the Reid papers, Library of Congress.

123. DT to Paul Block, June 7, 1940, SU.

124. OTR ("The Presidency"), October 9, 1940.

125. OTR ("The Next President"), April 5, 1940.

126. For Willkie see Steve Neal, *Dark Horse: A Biography of Wendell Willkie* (New York: Doubleday, 1984), and Richard Kluger, *The Paper: The Life and Death of the New York Herald Tribune* (New York: Knopf, 1986), 322–329.

127. Kluger, *The Paper*, 323.

128. Quoted in James T. Patterson, *Mr. Republican: A Biography of Robert A. Taft* (Boston: Houghton Mifflin, 1972), 221.

129. DT to Paul Block, June 7, 1940.

130. The words are Roosevelt's, in a letter to Morris Ernst concerning DT (May 18, 1940, Roosevelt Library, Hyde Park). See also Ernst to Edwin M. Watson, September 22, 1940, Hyde Park.

131. DT to Paul Block, June 7, 1940.

132. DT radio broadcast, October 29, 1944 (but in reference to the 1940 election), published by the National Independent Committee for Roosevelt and Truman, SU.

133. OTR ("The Presidency").

134. PK interviews with William I. Nichols, Paris, January 17, 1986, and Lisa Sergio.

135. OTR ("To Mark Sullivan"), October 28, 1940.

136. DT to Edgar Mowrer, October 24, 1940, SU.

137. "A Letter from Dorothy Thompson: Seven Reasons Why She Is Voting for President Franklin D. Roosevelt," October 25, 1940, published by the New York State Independent Voters Committee for Roosevelt and Wallace, SU.

138. For commentary, see the clipping from *PM* magazine, "*Herald Tribune* Gags Dorothy Thompson," in the Reid papers, Library of Congress; and the *New York Times,* October 17, 1940.

On October 14 Interior Secretary Harold Ickes heard DT speak in Buffalo before "a paid audience" of 6,000 people. "She is a handsome woman," he recorded in his diary, "and she avoids the mistake, that so many women make, of being as unfeminine as possible.

"After the address I went up to introduce myself. She told me that the *Herald Tribune* had refused to print her column that morning. She had written on the theme that cognizance ought to be taken in this campaign of the attitude of the dictators toward the candidates and their reputed desire that Willkie be elected. This does not necessarily mean that Willkie would be more sympathetic or more disposed to deal with them than Roosevelt, but it does mean that they know they can do nothing with Roosevelt and for that reason they prefer to go along with Willkie, even if, later, they find him as stern as the President now is. If the dictators are not supporting Willkie, it is difficult to explain why all the Bunds and the fifth columnists, and the Nazi-minded people in this country are working for him, reportedly on orders through the diplomatic offices in this country of Germany and Italy." (Ickes diary, Library of Congress.)

139. Correspondence in the Reid papers, Library of Congress.

140. Quoted from the *New York Sun* in *Current Biography 1940* (entry for Dorothy Thompson), 798.

141. DT diary (loose), October 10, 1940, SU.

142. DT to Ogden and Helen Rogers Reid, January 8, 1941, in the Reid papers, Library of Congress.

143. For Clare and DT see Stephen Shadegg, *Clare Boothe Luce* (New York: Simon and Schuster, 1970), 119–122; and Alden Hatch, *Ambassador Extraordinary* (New York: Henry Holt, 1956). Also Clare Boothe Luce to PK, January 24, 1987.

144. Clare Boothe Luce to John S. Mayfield, reprinted in *The Courier,* published by the Syracuse Library Associates, Syracuse University, September 1963.

145. DT to Mrs. Henry R. Luce, Sr., undated [October 1940], SU.

146. Neal, *Dark Horse,* 186.

147. DT to Wendell Willkie, April 8, 1940, in the Willkie papers, Lilly Library, University of Indiana, Bloomington; and to Irita Van Doren, undated (condolences on Willkie's death), Library of Congress.

148. DT to Franklin D. Roosevelt, undated [November–December 1940], SU.

149. DT to Ogden and Helen Rogers Reid, January 8, 1941.

150. DT to Helen Rogers Reid, November 10, 1940, in the Reid papers, Library of Congress.

151. OTR (" 'The President of the United States' "), January 20, 1941.
152. DT to Ogden and Helen Rogers Reid, January 8, 1941.

CHAPTER TWELVE

1. Quoted in Fisher, "Dorothy Thompson, Cosmic Force."
2. Joseph M. Proskauer, address, January 24, 1939, printed privately, copy at SU. An account of the dinner is given in the *New York Times,* January 25, 1939.
3. A copy of Churchill's telegram, sent through the U.S. ambassador to London, is in the Wendell Willkie papers, Lilly Library, University of Indiana, Bloomington, and reproduced in the *New York Times,* May 7, 1941, and the *Herald Tribune* of the same date. Both articles contain extensive coverage of the tribute dinner proceedings. The *Herald Tribune*'s account also reproduces the text of DT's speech concerning the inauguration of the Ring of Freedom.
4. Diary of Raoul de Roussy de Sales, May 7, 1941, typed copy at SU.
5. James W. Gerard to Franklin D. Roosevelt, May 8, 1941, at the Roosevelt Library, Hyde Park.
6. For the Ten Articles of Faith, see the pamphlet prepared in May 1941 to announce the formation of the Ring of Freedom. The following quotations, unless otherwise cited, are from this booklet and from DT's cover letter, sent to potential Ring subscribers and dated May 16, 1941 (SU). In private correspondence DT described her Ten Articles as "Christian principles, although I haven't said anything about Christianity in them" (DT to William M. Forsythe, July 1, 1941, SU).
7. De Sales diary, May 7, 1941.
8. DT to Tommy Dix, June 13, 1941, SU.
9. From DT address to the United Jewish Appeal, delivered at the Plaza Hotel in New York City, May 27, 1941, transcript at SU.
10. DT to Eleanor Roosevelt, January 29, 1941, SU.
11. A famous story. See John Gunther, *Roosevelt in Retrospect* (New York: Harper and Brothers, 1950), 36.
12. For DT and Roosevelt, see also Raymond Gram Swing, *"Good Evening!" A Professional Memoir* (New York: Harcourt, Brace and World, 1964), 283. Later DT declared that she had "thrown out all the manuscripts" she had prepared for the Roosevelt administration and was "queasy" about taking credit for any of the President's speeches: "The speeches were President Roosevelt's, and I was not expected to take any credit for them then, nor do I care to do so posthumously, especially since I haven't got the documents. At the time in question I was doing so much broadcasting and writing that I had files and files full of stuff which I simply threw into the ashcan. . . . I do recall that in the Cleveland and Boston speeches in the 1940 campaign [Roosevelt] used long passages of the material I had submitted, and that practically everything he said about the German question in the foreign policy speech in New York in September 1944 was verbatim from a text I had submitted" (DT to Professor H. F. Harding, November 24, 1954, SU).
13. See Barnaby Conrad, "Portrait of Sinclair Lewis," *Horizon,* March 1979.
14. DT's letters to FDR are at the Roosevelt Library at Hyde Park and in copy at SU.
15. In 1942 a penciled note from DT concerning wartime propaganda was thus

submitted, "without Protocol," through the agency of Arthur Bliss Lane (Roosevelt Library, Hyde Park).

16. DT to Franklin D. Roosevelt, May 6, 1942, Hyde Park.

17. Gunther, *Roosevelt in Retrospect*, 28.

18. PK interview with Dinah Sheean, London, February 10, 1986.

19. DT to Morris L. Ernst, May 6, 1941, in the Ernst papers, University of Texas at Austin.

20. Ferris Greenslet to DT, May 24 and June 5, 1940, in Houghton Mifflin Company archives, Houghton Library, Harvard University; and DT to Dale Warren, undated, SU. See also DT's reply to Greenslet of June 30, 1940: "At present I am so tired and exhausted and in such a depressed frame of mind that I think the best thing to do is nothing, for a while, anyway. I just can't have the burden of doing a book. I don't know clearly enough what I think" (letter in Houghton Mifflin Company archives, Harvard).

21. DT to Matthew Woll, undated, SU.

22. Harriman, "The 'It' Girl"; and quoted in Bottome, "Dorothy Thompson."

23. Clifton Fadiman to PK, April 3, 1987.

24. DT to Elmer Rice, June 2, 1941, Library of Congress.

25. DT, "This War and the Common Sense of Women," *LHJ*, April 1942 [but written with a three-month lead, thus January 1942].

26. DT to Elmer Rice, June 2, 1941.

27. Phyllis Bottome to DT, April 5, 1941, SU.

28. OTR ("The Abbey — The Museum — The Commons"), May 14, 1941.

29. The full account appears in J. W. Drawbell, *Dorothy Thompson's English Journey* (London: Collins, 1942). Further material is in the James Wedgwood Drawbell papers at Mugar Library, Boston University. Quotes below, unless otherwise indicated, are from Drawbell's commentary, in the Boston archives.

30. Quoted in Bottome, "Dorothy Thompson."

31. Quoted in Drawbell, *English Journey*, 207.

32. Quoted (years later) in OTR ("We Must Push for a Cease-Fire in the Straits"), April 6, 1955.

33. Correspondence, reviews, and commentary on *Dorothy Thompson's English Journey* are in the Drawbell papers, Boston University.

34. Correspondence in DT's FBI file (No. 9-7990).

35. SL to DT, July 3, 1941, in the possession of the Lewis family.

36. Combined from DT to SL, July 6, 1941, and undated, both in the possession of the Lewis family.

37. SL to DT, July 11, 1941, in the possession of the Lewis family.

38. DT to Wells Lewis, undated [ca. January 1942], in the Grace Hegger Lewis papers, Humanities Research Center, University of Texas at Austin.

39. DT to Bruce and Beatrice Gould, April 25, 1955, SU.

40. Sanders, 32. Beatrice Sorchan quoted DT ca. 1920: "Someday I'm going to own one of these houses."

41. DT to Wells Lewis, undated [ca. January 1942].

42. Avery Strakosh, "House of Maps and Worlds," *Look*, April 7, 1942.

43. PK interview with Dinah Sheean.

44. Quoted in Sanders, 299.

45. Script by Edward Chodorov and H. S. Kraft (clippings at SU). In his memoirs,

Louis Nizer confuses the Chodorov-Kraft *Cue for Passion* with Elmer Rice's play of the same name. There *was* some dispute at the beginning of 1941 about the probable basis for the character of Louise Frayne in Rice's *Flight to the West,* but in a letter to the *New York Times,* Rice denied that she was based on DT (*New York Times,* January 19, 1941).

46. For Nizer and DT see, Louis Nizer, *Reflections Without Mirrors* (New York: Doubleday, 1978), 147–152.

47. De Sales diary, November 1, 1941, SU.

48. DT to Wendell Willkie, October 14, 1941, in the Willkie papers, Bloomington.

49. DT to Wells Lewis, undated [ca. January 1942].

50. DT speech, "The Security of the Nation," delivered in Washington, D.C., before the United States Chamber of Commerce, February 27, 1949, transcript at SU.

51. PK interview with Denis Fodor, Munich, October 1, 1987.

52. DT, "This War and the Common Sense of Women," *LHJ,* April 1942 [but written with a three-month lead, thus just after Pearl Harbor].

53. DT to "Johnny" [probably Gunther, but possibly Farrar], undated, SU.

54. DT diary, January 2, 1942, SU.

55. Schorer, 684.

56. DT diary, January 30, 1942, SU. The diary was not kept for the remainder of that year.

57. DT to Lawrence H. Grieg, May 22, 1946, SU. For several years DT had been sending money to Christa in France, initially out of the Journalists' Defense Fund and later out of her own pocket. There are four letters from Christa at SU recounting her life at Cagnes-sur-Mer. Simone Gentet was described after her death as "a hysterical, dissolute morphine addict and alcoholic," but there is no independent confirmation of this testimony.

Concerning Christa's death, see the letters to DT of Hertha von Gebhardt (January 6, 1946); Helene Meier-Graefe (July 28, 1946); and especially Henri Bonnet, who was the French ambassador to the United States after the war (all at SU). Bonnet wrote to DT on December 7, 1946: "Miss Christa Winsloe is dead. She was not captured by the *maquis* but murdered by a man named Lambert, who killed her, falsely pretending that he was fulfilling orders from an underground movement." Christa died on June 10, 1944. In reply to my own enquiries, police authorities in the department of Saône-et-Loire confirmed that four defendants — Claude Lambert, Antoine Desbois, Pierre Desbois, and Gabriel Ravat — had been charged with the murder of Christa Winsloe and Simone Gentet and, in 1948, acquitted. No further light has been shed on this matter. (Letter to PK of June 19, 1987.)

58. PK interview with Lili-Charlotte Sarnoff, Bethesda, Maryland, November 23, 1985.

CHAPTER THIRTEEN

1. DT to SL, May 3, 1942, SU.

2. DT to Wells Lewis, June 10 [1943], in the Grace Hegger Lewis papers, Humanities Research Center, University of Texas at Austin.

3. Virtually all of Dorothy's letters to Maxim Kopf, many of which date from

the time of their courtship and marriage, are in the possession of the Lewis family and were made available to me only for the purposes of this book. Most of them are undated, headlined only "Tuesday," "Thursday night," "Saturday," and so on. The same is true of Maxim's correspondence (though a greater number of his letters to DT are on file at Syracuse). For these reasons, in the notes for this chapter, with two exceptions, I have not cited the individual letters from which quotations have been drawn, though in general they were written in the period 1942–1943.

4. DT to Wells Lewis, undated [November 1943], in the Lewis papers, Austin; and quoted in Sheean, 323.

5. For the Volunteer Land Corps see OTR ("Spring Is Coming"), March 11, 1942; and further (for the Land Corps's antecedents in Vermont and DT's role in its development), Jack J. Preiss, *Camp William James* (Norwich, Vt.: Argo Press, 1978).

6. DT to Robert Littell, October 26, 1942, SU.

7. Quoted in Lawrance Thompson and R. H. Winnick, *Robert Frost: The Later Years* (New York: Holt, Rinehart and Winston, 1975), 98.

8. DT to Lester Bernstein, August 6, 1942, SU.

9. DT address to the Volunteer Land Corps, Twin Farms, August 29, 1942, transcript at SU. The Land Corps operation ultimately was "taken over by the federal government," said DT, "in the Victory Farm Volunteers, organized after we went into the war. . . . During its life, which covered two summers, it absorbed an amount of my time which I could not conceivably continue to give." (DT to Ellen J. Pattison, March 13, 1952, SU.)

10. DT to Wells Lewis, December 27, 1942, in the Lewis papers, Austin.

11. PK interview with Madeline Shaw Green, Ridgefield, Connecticut, August 25, 1987.

12. Biographical and autobiographical materials concerning MK are in Series 3 at SU. These include press releases and news clippings as well as transcripts of his own dictations, which DT took down by hand and hoped one day to see published. All quotes below, from and concerning MK, are taken from this series unless otherwise indicated.

13. DT to "Fritz" [probably Shey], July 15, 1959 (in reminiscence of MK).

14. *New York Times*, January 11, 1942. After MK's death, in 1958, DT arranged for the publication of a commemorative volume of his work, entitled *Maxim Kopf* (New York: Praeger, 1960), which includes not only reproductions of his paintings but essays about his life and art, including "Maxim Kopf's Prague Years," by his friend Johannes Urzidil, and DT's own, "My Husband, Maxim Kopf," which appeared originally in October 1958 in the *Ladies' Home Journal*.

15. Sheean, 323.

16. PK interview with William I. Nichols, Paris, January 17, 1986.

17. PK interview with Ellen Sheean, Paris, July 18, 1986.

18. DT to Gustav Stolper, undated [in reply to Stolper's of April 23, 1943], in the Stolper collection, Leo Baeck Institute, New York City.

19. The quote is from "Wild Swans," which Millay published in 1921 in *Second April* (New York: Mitchell Kennerley): "Wild swans, come over the town, come over/The town again, trailing your legs and crying!"

20. See Louis Nizer, *Reflections Without Mirrors* (New York: Doubleday, 1978), 148–150.

21. Dinah Sheean to PK, July 3, 1986.

22. PK interviews with Dinah Sheean, Paris, July 18, 1986, and Ellen Sheean; and Richard Edes Harrison to PK, undated [May 1987].

23. Sanders, 304–305.

24. DT to Helen Rogers Reid, May 24, 1943, in the Reid papers, Library of Congress.

25. DT to Wells Lewis, undated [November 1943].

26. She appears to have said this rather often, for Jane Gunther also remembers it. See Cass Canfield, *Up, Down and Around: A Publisher Recollects the Time of His Life* (New York: Harper and Row, 1973), 156.

Leland Stowe had dinner with DT shortly after her marriage and recalled that "she was blooming like a 20-year-old bride. So strikingly aglow that I told her so, provoking this response: 'Lee, Max is wonderful — and especially in bed!' To which I replied: 'And that's just how you look.' " (Leland Stowe to PK, August 12, 1987).

27. PK interview with William I. Nichols.

28. Rebecca West to JVS, December 25, 1963, in Houghton Mifflin Company archives, Houghton Library, Harvard University.

29. PK interview with Lisa Sergio, Washington, D.C., November 23, 1985.

30. Rebecca West to MKS ("I am also sorry that you think so poorly of Max Kopf"), March 20, 1973, in Houghton Mifflin Company archives, Harvard.

31. PK interview with Dinah Sheean.

32. MK to DT, May 6, 1953, SU.

33. MK to DT, combined from letters of October 24, 1954, and undated, SU.

34. DT to Gustav Stolper, undated [April 1943].

35. PK interview with William I. Nichols.

CHAPTER FOURTEEN

1. These remarks are among the loose autobiographical material in Series 7 at SU, typed on DT's personal stationery and headlined "Notes for comment in book."

2. DT's comments are combined from a transcription of a recording in the National Archives of her radio debate with Lord Vansittart, September 30, 1943, as part of "America's Town Meeting of the Air," and from a letter to Joachim Jaenicke, January 10, 1944, SU.

3. DT to Franklin D. Roosevelt, October 13, 1942, in the Roosevelt Library, Hyde Park.

4. DT to Franklin D. Roosevelt, undated [addressed "To the President of the United States (without Protocol)"], Hyde Park.

5. DT, "Children and Working Mothers," *LHJ*, July 1942.

6. DT, "Keeping Up the Place in Wartime," *LHJ*, August 1943.

7. DT, "That They Do Not Die in Vain," *LHJ*, January 1943.

8. DT, "A Suggestion for the Peace," *LHJ*, February 1943.

9. Dale Warren [?] to Paul Brooks, undated ["5/42"] from Ipswich, Massachusetts, in Houghton Mifflin Company archives, Houghton Library, Harvard University.

10. DT to John Moses, July 2, 1942, SU.

11. After the war, in an undated letter to Jenö von Moltke, Helmuth's brother,

DT confirmed that Hans "was in fact Helmuth, whose anti-Nazi feelings I never doubted for a moment, any more than I doubted that he would attempt with whatever means he had to fight the regime." Count von Moltke's widow told DT later that she "only heard about 'Listen, Hans' after the war. Helmuth did not know about it either."(Freya von Moltke to DT, December 4, 1946, SU; and PK interview with Freya von Moltke, Norwich, Vermont, December 6, 1985.)

12. DT to Philip Wylie, August 3, 1945. The DT-Wylie correspondence, quoted extensively in this chapter, is in the Wylie papers at Princeton University.

13. DT radio broadcast, April 24, 1942, reprinted in DT, *Listen, Hans*, 160.

14. Dale Warren [?] to Paul Brooks, undated ["5/42"].

15. Reported to DT by a German correspondent, K. Rommel, in a letter of March 12, 1947, SU.

16. Entry of April 5, 1942, in *The Goebbels Diaries* (New York: Doubleday, 1948), 160–161.

17. Combined from DT radio broadcasts of April 3 and 10, 1942, reprinted in DT, *Listen, Hans*, 140–151.

18. Dale Warren to DT, April 24, 1942, SU: "Ernestine is here with one of her good ideas."

19. Dale Warren memo to editorial staff at Houghton Mifflin Company, June 11, 1942, in Houghton Mifflin Company archives, Harvard.

20. Malcolm Cowley, "But Listen, Dorothy," *New Republic*, December 28, 1942.

21. Carl Zuckmayer to DT, December 7, 1942, SU.

22. DT to Wells Lewis, December 27, 1942, in the Grace Hegger Lewis papers, Humanities Research Center, University of Texas at Austin.

23. *New York Times*, November 29, 1942.

24. *Atlantic Monthly*, January 1943.

25. *Christian Science Monitor*, December 23, 1942.

26. *New York Times*, November 28, 1942.

27. DT's proposals for Germany are contained, among other places, in a loose memorandum from 1944 headed "Unconditional Surrender," SU. See also "The Thompson Case," *Newsweek*, October 9, 1944 (alternating with Rex Stout's call for the annihilation of Germany), and DT to "Mr. Barton," undated [1944], SU.

28. Quoted in Longmire, "God's Angry Woman."

29. Transcribed from DT radio debate with Lord Vansittart, September 30, 1943, National Archives.

30. DT, "Germany Must Be Salvaged," *The American Mercury*, June 1943.

31. DT, "Germany — Enigma of the Peace," *Life*, December 6, 1943. In formulating her proposals for the future of Germany, DT did not rely solely on her own expertise. In 1943 she developed a multipage "questionnaire" concerning the German nation and people and sent it to a variety of exiled politicians and thinkers in the United States, including Paul Tillich, Bertholt Brecht, Jacques Maritain, Heinrich Brüning, and Alexander Kerensky. Their responses were incorporated into the various dissenting statements she made the following year, 1944, when the Writers' War Board issued a manifesto denouncing, in perpetuity, the "German Will-to-Aggression." DT was one of only four members of the board who refused to sign the release, "because it is," she said, "on the whole, an insult to my intellectual

integrity" (DT letter of June 21, 1944, to the Writers' War Board). The records of the Writers' War Board are at the Library of Congress; DT's questionnaire and various responses are at SU.

32. See DT's letter to "Mr. Sudermann," April 6, 1948, SU: "I have been really *suffering* over the international situation since approximately the beginning of 1943, when it became clear that the war had taken on a life of its own — as these modern mass wars are likely to do — and that America was beginning to think of herself as the future 'policeman of the world,' without the foggiest notion that even for so great and powerful a nation as ours, politics would always remain the 'art of possibilities.' "

33. See, for instance, the memo of JVS to Joyce Hartman at Houghton Mifflin, November 6, 1963, in Houghton Mifflin Company archives, Harvard: "So much of this Americanism is allusive. Roosevelt's impetuous expression, 'unconditional surrender,' for example, which stunned all of our allies, just came out of his American unconscious, a Civil War memory, which, since they did not share it, meant nothing at all (or rather meant something utterly impossible) to our astonished friends."

34. DT to Robert Sherwood, August 22, 1947, SU.

35. DT to Hugh Gibson, February 25, 1943, SU.

36. DT to "Mr. Barton," undated [1944].

37. OTR ("In Self-Defense"), February 2, 1945.

38. DT to Philip Wylie, July 20, 1945, in the Wylie papers, Princeton.

39. See "The Thompson Case," *Newsweek,* October 9, 1944. In April 1944, at the bottom of a letter Clifton Fadiman had written to her about the Germans, DT penciled a reply to him: "The resistance of people *qua* people and without leadership is hooey in general and everywhere. In Germany it is actively impossible. Those who *did* resist or who might have resisted were arrested at the beginning and many are dead" (Clifton Fadiman to DT, April 3, 1944, SU).

40. OTR ("On Being a Sentimentalist"), October 22, 1943.

41. DT to the editor of the *Waupun Leader-News* (Wisconsin), May 2, 1944, SU.

42. DT to Quincy Howe, May 7, 1943, SU; and to Wells Lewis, undated [November 1943], in the Lewis papers, Austin.

43. DT to Wells Lewis, November 10, 1943, in the Lewis papers, Austin.

44. The phrase is quoted in DT's letter to Wylie of March 16, 1945. Actually he had called her a "turn*skirt,*" which he described in his reply (undated) as "a word of my own invention. . . . Since turnskirt is my own property and only mine, I think you will admit that I, alone, can define it. It is a word which might occasion thought on the part of the person to whom it is applied — but it is hardly a slanderous word — inasmuch as it clearly connotes a woman's privilege to change her mind and heart at any time." (Both letters in the Wylie papers, Princeton.)

45. Combined from British Foreign Office memoranda of January 18 and 25, 1943, reference No. FO 371/34456 114745 ("Dorothy Thompson"), London. Much of the material about DT in the Foreign Office archives concerns her role in regard to the prevailing American attitude toward British war propaganda in the 1939–1941 period. Internal memoranda in London (dated 1940) speak of her as "America's most popular serious columnist."

46. See the letter of Bill Ormerod, the director of the British Information Service in New York (and a good friend of DT's), to the British Embassy in Washington, May 5, 1944 (labeled "Secret"), in the Foreign Office archives, London.

47. The draft of DT's undated letter to Winchell is at SU.

48. DT speech, delivered to the Forum on the Future of the World Order at the Plaza Hotel, New York City, May 11, 1942, transcript at SU.

49. DT to Philip Wylie, March 16, 1945.

50. DT to Philip Wylie, combined from letters of March 16 and July 20, 1945, in the Wylie papers, Princeton.

51. For DT and Stout, see John McAleer, *Rex Stout: A Biography* (Boston: Little, Brown, 1977), 330–332, 352.

52. Philip Wylie to DT, undated [March 1945].

53. DT to Philip Wylie, July 20, 1945, in the Wylie papers, Princeton. Wylie's novel, *Generation of Vipers,* was published in 1942 by Farrar and Rhinehart.

54. Max Ascoli to DT, August 21, 1944, SU.

55. Quoted in Longmire, "God's Angry Woman."

56. PK interview with William L. Shirer, Lenox, Massachusetts, January 28, 1988; and William L. Shirer, *Twentieth-Century Journey* (New York: Simon and Schuster, 1976), 450.

57. Longmire, "God's Angry Woman."

58. DT diary, loose [January 1945], SU.

59. OTR ("Hard Hearts — But Hard Heads!"), October 4, 1944.

60. For the Freedom House upheavals see McAleer, *Rex Stout* (which, following Stout's recollections, is biased against DT); and the *New York Times* for October 21, 23, and 25, 1944.

61. For Wells's death, see the report sent to DT by Major General Dahlquist (Headquarters, 36th Infantry Division, Office of the Commanding General), May 28, 1945; and DT to Grace Lewis, August 15, 1945, in the Lewis papers, Austin.

62. DT radio broadcast, October 29, 1944, transcript published by the National Independent Committee for Roosevelt and Truman, SU.

63. DT, "The Return to the Grand Manner — An Heroic Age Calls for Heroic Expression," *Saturday Review,* December 2, 1944. An interesting letter from DT to Robert Sherwood dates from the fourth Roosevelt campaign: "If you can give the President a message for me, tell him this: As I see it, a large part of the Republican tactic is to make such a snide campaign that it will really work on the President's temper, anger him, bring him down to their level and wear him down. They know he is tired and that he has times of great discouragement, and they want to make him more discouraged. Beg him to ignore them and to put himself on a level so sovereign, so far above, that they seem like ants and bedbugs in comparison. Always remember the good old American adage, 'Never have a pissing contest with a skunk.' Now, if ever, the President must be Olympian" (DT to Robert Sherwood, October 17, 1944, in the Sherwood papers, Houghton Library, Harvard University).

64. DT to C. F. Kuehale, July 8, 1944, SU.

65. DT to Paul Brooks, August 13, 1943, in Houghton Mifflin Company archives, Harvard.

66. Quoted in DT to Dr. Bernard Pacella, June 18, 1960, SU.

67. Schorer, 722.

68. DT to Carl Zuckmayer, November 16, 1944, quoted in Sanders, 310.

69. Quoted in DT, "The Boy and Man from Sauk Center," *Atlantic Monthly*, November 1960.

70. DT to Oswald Garrison Villard, November 14, 1944, SU.

71. DT to "Lawrence" [probably Westbrook], February 22, 1945, SU.

72. DT to Oswald Garrison Villard, November 12, 1945, in the Villard papers, Houghton Library, Harvard University. "Apprehensions in 1945" appeared three years later, unedited, in *The Commonweal*, on January 30 and February 6, 1948.

73. DT, "Apprehensions in 1945."

74. See, for instance, her letter to "Mr. Sudermann," April 6, 1948.

75. DT diary, loose [January 1945].

76. OTR ("The 'Mystery' of Soviet Policy — I"), March 6, 1946.

77. DT, "Violence Is the Enemy," *Maclean's*, July 1, 1946.

78. DT to Franklin D. Roosevelt, March 5, 1945, Hyde Park.

79. DT, "The Last Time I Saw Berlin," *Saturday Review*, March 15, 1947. She was proud of this essay and called it variously "Reunion in Berlin" and "When God Is Dead."

80. OTR ("Good-bye to Germany"), June 29, 1945.

81. DT speech, November 21, 1957 (in reference to the Nazi death camps), delivered to the Washington Institute on Muslim-Christian Cooperation, transcript at SU.

82. DT, "From the Holy Land," *LHJ*, July 1945.

83. DT, "The Lesson of Dachau," *LHJ*, September 1945.

84. DT to Philip Wylie, August 3, 1945, in the Wylie papers, Princeton.

85. DT, "The Lesson of Dachau." See also DT to "Miss Stang," April 9, 1946, SU: "Do you not believe you have a 'soul'? Does it have to be proved to you, any more than it must be proved to you that you love? Do you not feel an affinity to the beautiful, the just, the noble, the creative, the great? Do you need a logical argument to prove what you already *know*? . . . I would warn you against believing only what can be proved by your mind. For we all *know* much more than we *think*. . . . We know when the soul is insulted, as Whitman said."

86. OTR ("Martin Niemöller"), May 15, 1945. Niemöller, a future president of the World Council of Churches, was an author in 1945 of the "Stuttgart Declaration of Guilt," an indictment of the Protestant clergy under the Nazi dictatorship.

87. DT, "The Lesson of Dachau."

88. For the chaos and murder in the East, see above all Douglas Botting, *From the Ruins of the Reich* (New York: Crown, 1985).

89. DT to Philip Wylie, August 3, 1945.

90. OTR ("It Had to Turn Out This Way"), July 17, 1946.

91. DT to Philip Wylie, August 3, 1945.

92. See "The Thompson Case," *Newsweek*, October 9, 1944.

93. DT, loose ms., "War Guilt = World Guilt," SU.

94. OTR ("The Atomization of Civilization"), December 12, 1945.

95. DT diary, loose, October 2, 1946, SU (Series 4).

96. OTR ("The Atomic Bomb and God's Peace"), November 28, 1945.

97. Ronald Steel, *Walter Lippmann and the American Century* (Boston: Atlantic Monthly Press, 1980), 425.

98. DT speech to the Washington Institute on Muslim-Christian Cooperation, November 21, 1957.

99. OTR ("Disintegration — Or Integration"), August 10, 1945.

100. OTR ("The Atomic Bomb and God's Peace").

101. DT, "Atomic Warfare," loose ms. [labeled "unused"] at SU.

102. OTR ("Are the Scientists Members of Humanity?"), August 26, 1949.

103. DT to George Field, July 7, 1944, SU.

104. DT, "Apprehensions in 1945."

105. DT, "Toward the Big One," *LHJ*, January 1946.

106. DT to Philip Wylie, August 3, 1945. Wylie responded on August 8: "You have certainly shown, rather overwhelmingly, that you have the dimensions attributed to you by your many friends. Somebody comes along and persecutes you and reviles you, falsely — so you do not merely invite them to reason with you, you ask them for a week-end. Strangers, to boot. It is a sure thing that the Scriptures contain no example of equal variety and merit" (letter in the Wylie papers, Princeton).

CHAPTER FIFTEEN

1. *New York Times,* March 8, 1947; and Ted O. Thackrey to H. McAllister Griffiths, March 18, 1947, SU.

2. DT to Meyer Weisgal, March 5, 1947, SU.

3. *New York Post,* January 30, 1945. See also DT's reply in OTR ("In Self-Defense"), February 2, 1945.

4. Ted O. Thackrey to H. McAllister Griffiths, March 18, 1947. "If it were not for the continuing severity of newsprint shortages," Thackrey went on, "Miss Thompson's column would have had a better chance of continuing presentation."

5. Ted O. Thackrey to DT, October 28, 1946, SU.

6. DT to Ted O. Thackrey, November 3, 1946, SU.

7. DT to Meyer Weisgal, March 5, 1947.

8. Telegram from Herbert Hollander to DT, undated [but in response to her column of July 24, 1946 ("Russia — Poland — Germany"), in which she condemned Jewish terrorism in Palestine], SU.

9. DT to Meyer Weisgal, March 5, 1947.

10. Meyer Weisgal, *Meyer Weisgal . . . So Far* (New York: Doubleday, 1971), 197–198. Weisgal's account of DT's troubles with the American Zionists, while inaccurate in certain details, is fair and worth reading. "The issue was an uncomfortable one," he acknowledged; "as a Jew, I was allowed to share Weizmann's views on the terrorists; but Dorothy was not in the same position." And further: "The editor of the *Post* at that time, Ted Thackeray [*sic*], was a good friend of the Etzel, the major terrorist organization in Palestine."

11. Jeffrey Potter, *Men, Money and Magic: The Story of Dorothy Schiff* (New York: Coward, McCann and Geohegan, 1976), 201.

12. DT to JVS, January 27, 1949, SU: "The Zionist propaganda here has gone on being boundlessly related to no standards whatever of truth."

13. DT to Helen Rogers Reid, April 4, 1947, SU, in the Reid papers, Library of Congress.

14. DT to SL, April 21, 1947, SU.

15. DT's manuscript is at SU. "Nothing united these men," she wrote, "except patriotism, moral disgust, [and] revolt against arbitrary rule, terror, legalized crime, and aggressive war. The binding emotion was a European and world humanistic outlook." A fascinating inside view of the plotters can be found in Princess Marie Vassilchikov's *Berlin Diaries: 1940–1945* (New York: Knopf, 1987).

16. DT to Grace Lewis, August 15, 1945, in the Grace Hegger Lewis papers, Humanities Research Center, University of Texas at Austin.

17. DT to "Dr. Barnes" [Harry Elmer?], May 12, 1950, SU.

18. DT to Grace Lewis, August 15, 1945.

19. DT to SL, April 21, 1947.

20. DT to John Gunther, undated [1947], SU.

21. DT diary, January 5, 1952, SU. On March 27 of that year she wrote to David Sarnoff: "T.V. at first had a devastating effect on our household! Somewhat like a crystal ball — hypnotizing. We looked at everything — good, bad, and indifferent, cursing ourselves. . . . Some of the commercials are sick-making."

22. See DT's letter to Jack Wheeler, undated [1946], SU.

23. DT to Howard Dietz, April 28, 1943, SU.

24. RW to DT, July 28, 1948, SU.

25. OTR ("Hollywood and the Communists"), December 1, 1947.

26. RW to DT, February 26, 1948, SU. For RW see Victoria Glendinning, *Rebecca West* (New York: Knopf, 1987). There are two Rebecca West archives in the United States, one at Yale University's Beinecke Library, and the other (where most of DT's letters to RW are kept) at the McFarlin Library of the University of Tulsa, in Tulsa, Oklahoma.

In spite of their close association and the fact that RW's markets were generally more prestigious (or at least more highbrow), there was little or no professional jealousy between DT and RW. "I might have done it myself if I had been clever enough," said DT of RW's work (quoted in Sheean, 265), while RW remarked to DT that her column in the *Ladies' Home Journal* was "the best feature in all American journalism. I never miss reading you there, and I am never disappointed." (RW to DT, December 15, 1957, SU.)

27. Quoted in Glendinning, *Rebecca West,* 184.

28. RW to Dale Warren, January 18, 1965, in the West papers, Beinecke Library, Yale.

29. DT to Harold Ross, February 17, 1950, SU.

30. RW to Anne Ford, September 10, 1963, in Houghton Mifflin Company archives, Houghton Library, Harvard University.

31. RW to Dale Warren, February 24, 1965, in the West papers, Yale.

32. RW to DT, August 31, 1946, SU.

33. RW to DT, February 26, 1948, SU.

34. RW to DT, September 30, 1958, SU.

35. DT to RW, undated, SU.

36. DT to RW, January 6, 1954, in the West papers, McFarlin Library, University of Tulsa. "I send love to all the household," RW closed her letter to DT of July 28, 1948, "and please pinch Max's behind for me" (SU).

37. PK interview with Dinah Sheean, London, May 21, 1986.

38. DT to Mrs. Henry R. Luce, Sr., undated [October 1940], SU.

39. RW to John Gunther, July 12, 1961, quoted in Glendinning, *Rebecca West,* 245.

40. She used it as the title of OTR, October 29, 1947.

41. Glendinning, *Rebecca West,* 211.

42. DT to Harry S Truman, March 19, 1948, SU.

43. OTR ("The First Days of Peace"), August 20, 1945. "[The] anti-Soviet fever is high on this farm," JVS reported from Vermont. "Dorothy Thompson thinks the Russians are at the bottom of everything, including the diseases that inflict her chickens." (JVS to Leigh White, September 12, 1946, in the Sheean papers, SU. [A small collection of Sheean letters and manuscripts, donated to Syracuse by JVS, is catalogued separately from DT's papers.])

44. DT to Frances Gunther, undated, quoted in Sanders, 313.

45. For the Budzislawski affair, see DT's unedited manuscript, "My Red Herring," and her letter of February 1, 1949, to the editors of the *Neue Zeitung* (Berlin), SU. Quotes below are from these sources unless otherwise indicated.

46. See the *Tägliche Rundschau* (Berlin), December 1, 1948, quoting Budzislawski's "revelations" about DT.

47. Published in the *Saturday Evening Post,* April 16, 1949.

48. DT to Ben Hibbs, January 27, 1949, SU.

49. DT to John M. Whitcomb, March 30, 1948, in the Clift collection, Sterling Library, Yale.

50. DT to John Haynes Holmes, October 21, 1949, SU.

51. OTR ("The Age of Lunacy"), October 29, 1947.

52. See OTR ("The Labor Situation"), April 2, 1941.

53. OTR ("Cohn Called McCarthy Victim"), July 23, 1954.

54. DT to JVS, October 27, 1947, SU. "If I knew of any communist who was in an important public position I would not wait for the Un-American Activities Committee to get busy," DT remarked elsewhere, "but [would] expose him immediately. But when it came to committing myself to tattling on people whom I had not seen for years, about whose activities past and present I was not absolutely informed, I don't think I could bring myself to do it. It's against all my upbringing." (DT autobiographical sketch, ca. 1957, written for the publication of *The Courage to Be Happy,* SU; and in Houghton Mifflin Company archives, Harvard.)

55. OTR ("When Is War Not War?"), July 12, 1950.

56. DT to John M. Whitcomb, March 30, 1948.

57. DT to "Mr. Muste," April 6, 1948, SU.

58. OTR ("Mr. Truman's Loyalty Test Order — I"), April 2, 1947.

59. She wrote to Walter Lippmann at the end of August 1948, in regard to the Berlin blockade: "If we leave Berlin, as many hints indicate we contemplate doing, the results will be catastrophic. . . . For the first time, we shall deliberately have delivered 2.5 million people to the Soviets, in full knowledge of what awaits them, and after repeatedly saying we would not. People in and out of Germany will no longer trust us. It might have been better to have left Berlin to the Russians, but it is too late now, as, in my opinion, it is too late to reverse the idea of a West German state, although, like you, I felt at the time that it was another of those impulsive mistakes we so often make. On the other hand, I do not see how the present Berlin situation can be indefinitely prolonged. If we are compelled to make a radical sacrifice of our position there, we should, I think, hold a plebiscite and allow the

population to vote whether they will stay with the Russians or leave with us. . . . Presumably we could airlift people out as well as airlift supplies in. Anyhow, we must not turn over a single unwilling person to the Russians. If we have to give them Berlin, give them its rubble, not its people. For we have put these people on a spot" (DT to Walter Lippmann, August 31, 1948, in the Lippmann papers, Sterling Library, Yale).

60. See OTR ("Masaryk Kept His Word of Honor to Dead Father"), March 10, 1948.

61. DT to "Mr. Muste," April 6, 1948.

62. DT, "Good Night, Sweet Prince," ms. at SU; published in condensed form in *Life,* March 22, 1948.

63. DT to Marcia Davenport, March 25, 1948, SU. For Davenport's account of Jan Masaryk's death (and much besides), see Marcia Davenport, *Too Strong for Fantasy* (New York: Scribner's, 1967).

64. DT, "Woe to Those Who Destroy the Altars!" *LHJ,* November 1946.

65. OTR ("Magnet Pull in Gandhi Fast"), January 23, 1948.

66. DT, "What Juvenile Crime Reflects," *LHJ,* October 1946.

67. DT, "Woe to Those Who Destroy the Altars!" She wrote in OTR concerning the constitutional separation of church and state: "The specific meaning was, and is, that no church and its clergy shall be maintained by the taxpayer nor have transferred to it functions of the civil power. This prohibits such state support as is granted the Roman Catholic Church in Spain, for instance, or the Anglican Church in England.

"But there is not the slightest implication in this that would withdraw the nation and all its public institutions from Christian culture. . . . Christianity is threaded into the whole fabric of our civilization, into our history, law, customs and very language. If everything of Christian religious significance were barred from our schools, we would have to bowdlerize our culture out of existence" (OTR [" 'God Rest Ye Merrie, Gentlemen' "], December 17, 1947).

68. DT to Harry S Truman, March 19, 1948. On March 24 she wrote to Ernest Bevin, the British foreign secretary, on the same theme: "Also, use imagination! The world is perishing for lack of it! Launch it with churchbells, fill the air with the great religious music, call on everyone to pray for the freedom of Europe and for peace!" (DT to Ernest Bevin, March 24, 1948, SU).

69. OTR [untitled], May 31, 1946.

70. DT to Harry S Truman, March 19, 1948.

71. DT to Walter Lippmann, January 19, 1951, in the Lippmann papers, Yale; and to Adlai E. Stevenson, September 25, 1952, SU.

72. OTR ("Cohn Called McCarthy Victim").

73. DT to Frank G. Gill, April 12, 1950, SU. "This present theological struggle," she went on, "called the 'Cold War,' between a 'Private' and 'Free' Enterprise that doesn't work, and a collectivist system that also doesn't work (in terms of human security, stability and serenity) only escapes being hideously *boring* by being so extremely dangerous."

74. OTR ("U.S. Cannot Afford to Dictate"), July 9, 1951.

75. In January 1948 alone DT devoted ten columns in OTR to Wallace and the specter of American communism.

76. See Eric Sevareid to PK, April 21, 1987: "In a mass press conference in the Bellevue-Stratford, Wallace was dodging around on the questions about his 'guru.' ([Westbrook] Pegler had been writing scathing columns about this.) Dorothy stood up and demanded Wallace answer the questions. We all silently applauded her, including, I thought, Henry Mencken, who was there and, I think, said something himself. Pegler was there and had to stand up because Wallace, not seeing him, had talked about 'Pegler stooges.' To my amazement the tough-writing Pegler was so nervous he could hardly talk."

77. Louis Nizer, *Reflections Without Mirrors* (New York: Doubleday,1978), 151.

78. OTR ("The Wallace Show"), July 28, 1948.

79. Alistair Cooke, *Six Men* (New York: Knopf, 1977), 111–112.

80. DT to Walter Lippmann, January 1, 1951, SU.

81. DT to Edward Donohoe, February 1, 1948, SU.

82. DT to Adlai E. Stevenson, September 25, 1952.

83. Stephen R. Graubard quoted in Sanders, 341.

84. Clare Boothe Luce to DT, April 14, 1947, SU.

85. DT to Professor William Yale (quoting Robinson Jeffers's "Shine, Perishing Republic"), July 29, 1952, SU.

86. DT to Grove Patterson, September 21, 1954, SU.

87. See DT's correspondence with Paul Bellamy, editor of the *Cleveland Plain Dealer* (who in 1949 made the decision to drop "On the Record"), November–December 1949, SU. "This is the first time I *ever* intervened for myself to ask an editor whether he wouldn't reconsider," said DT. "And I hope you do not take offense at what is really an expression of admiration." Elsewhere she declared that "today's editors are, for the most part, the most poltroonly in my experience." (DT to "Dr. Barnes," May 12, 1950.)

88. See OTR ("Americans Will Pay — Because We Have To"), July 17, 1950.

89. OTR ("Don't Use Atomic Weapons!"), July 19, 1950.

90. DT to Carl Zuckmayer, July 21, 1950, SU.

91. JVS to DT, December 1, 1952, SU: "Nobody else in Springfield seems to have seen or noticed the thing! People never do look up."

92. JVS to DT, February 15, 1948, SU.

93. This was the word DT ordinarily used to describe JVS's brainstorms. See, for instance, her diary for New Year's Day, 1952, SU: "At midnight we called the Sheeans in Vermont and Jimmie was obviously in a shemozzle (about Einstein)." She obstinately persisted in her own spelling of "Jimmy."

94. Quoted in OTR ("Vincent Sheean Relates Own Spiritual Growth"), July 25, 1949.

95. She sent him a telegram after Gandhi's death: "THE BURDEN UPON YOU WAS YOU KNEW IT HAD TO HAPPEN OUT OF THAT TRANSCENDENTAL LOGIC WHICH THIS TERRIBLE AGE DENIES. . . . BURDEN ON YOU NOW IS DIGEST IT IN GANDHI'S OWN SANITY. MY THOUGHTS AND PRAYERS ARE WITH YOU" (DT to JVS, undated, SU).

In January 1951, in a night that Jane Gunther remembers vividly, JVS "foresaw" the death of Sinclair Lewis and was so upset to find the next morning that Red had died that he sent a note to DT: "I am appalled to realize (and I may as well tell you because I know the Gunthers will) that I spent a good deal of time last night . . . declaring that [Red's] time was up and that he should now die. This is the sort of frightful coincidence that makes life so hard to understand. . . . The horrible thing is that [Red] was probably dying just at that moment, or a little earlier or later" (JVS to DT, January 10, 1951).

96. DT to JVS, February 6 [1948], SU.

97. JVS to DT, February 15, 1948.

98. JVS to DT, October 31 [1952?], SU. DT did not share his fascination with the East. "We have all overrated the Orient anyhow," she wrote in a loose memorandum at SU. "As far as I know history, there has never been anything in the Orient except one or the other form of despotism. . . . China has always been corrupt and maybe always will be."

99. PK interviews with Dinah Sheean and with Jane Gunther, Greensboro, Vermont, July 30, 1987.

100. From PK interviews with Dinah Sheean, Evelyn Stefansson Nef, Washington, D.C., October 25, 1986, and Lili-Charlotte Sarnoff, Bethesda, Maryland, November 23, 1985.

101. PK interview with Dinah Sheean.

102. "I go obstinately on and on treating Jimmy as if he were a normal husband to whom I could say things about situations and people," Dinah Sheean wrote to DT in 1951, following her remarriage to JVS. For a while Dinah had toyed with the idea of finding "a really intelligent priest" to bring Jimmy back to Catholicism, the religion of his youth, "but Monsignor Vance said that he thought it would be extremely dangerous — he feels Jimmy's mania would *use* any religious belief, that he would be more likely to *become* the Sacred Heart of Jesus than submit to it, and that any moment he might translate me into the personification of evil which it was his duty to expunge." (Dinah Sheean to DT, May 17, 1951, SU.)

103. PK interview with Dinah Sheean.

104. PK interview with Linda Sheean, New York City, January 8, 1987.

105. Ellen Sheean to PK, undated [March 1986].

106. PK interviews with Linda Sheean and with Ellen Sheean, Paris, July 18, 1986.

107. JVS to Virginia Shaw, undated ["Nov. 24, Saturday" — 1952?], SU.

108. Sheean, 291.

109. Dinah Sheean to Max and Marion Ascoli, December 12, 1947, in the Ascoli papers, Mugar Library, Boston University.

110. From a loose memorandum on JVS in the Irita Van Doren papers, Library of Congress.

111. PK interview with Dinah Sheean. See also JVS to DT (concerning the death of Edna St. Vincent Millay), October 22, 1951, SU.

112. Quoted in DT to Walter Lippman, June 21, 1951, SU.

113. DT to JVS, February 6 [1948], SU.

114. JVS, "A Woman For President," *Look,* July 13, 1949, ms. at SU.

115. DT to Margaret Chase Smith, June 5, 1950, SU. She reported further on JVS's plan: "The trouble was he couldn't find a candidate. Mrs. Roosevelt is too old and too silly in many of her judgments and associations. Claire [*sic*] Luce has retired from politics and is too much of the glamour-type. Sheean was finally reduced to picking on me, which would certainly require several kinds of miracles, apart from the fact that I am so ungifted politically that I couldn't be elected dogcatcher in my own village — if we had a dog-catcher."

116. DT, "The Progress of a *Journal* Editorial," *LHJ*, February 1950.

117. In *LHJ*, November 1947, February 1946, and July 1947, respectively.

118. DT, "A Woman's Manifesto," *LHJ*, November 1947.

119. DT to Professor William Yale, July 29, 1952.

120. DT to Jan Masaryk, November 9, 1947, SU.

121. OTR ("A New Approach"), October 10, 1951.

122. On September 11, 1947, Bruce Gould wrote to DT with a sampling of editorial comment concerning the Woman's Manifesto: "Let this oracle be dumb or at least less pontifical." "Just so much ranting rhetoric to me." "The great mother-force speaking through D.T. makes me quietly want to retch." "This is fantastic! It reads like a burlesque of William Jennings Bryan and Amy [*sic*] Semple McPherson." (Letter at SU.)

123. DT, "A Woman Says, 'You Must Come into the Room of Your Mother Unarmed,' " *LHJ*, February 1947.

124. Incoming correspondence concerning W.O.M.A.N. fills nearly two boxes at SU; DT's letters are arranged chronologically in her outgoing correspondence. There is also a file on W.O.M.A.N. at the Schlesinger Library at Radcliffe College, in the archives of Women United for the United Nations.

In 1947, in OTR, DT spelled out W.O.M.A.N.'s position quite clearly: "The view that we have advanced is that as long as sovereign states possess war-making powers, armament races are inevitable, fear makes real co-operation impossible, and fear will eventually result in war. We wish to see the abolition of one single sovereign right: the right to wage international war; and consequently, and logically, the right of any nation to maintain an army, navy or air force, or manufacture any weapons beyond those used in the normal internal policing of states. We wish to see this prohibition written into the constitutions of all nations and made the first law of the United Nations. We wish to see aggressors defined, in conformity with the Nuremberg trials, as those who order and participate in breaches of this law. . . . Beyond this, we would respect the right of every state to have any social system it desires. I have said this over and over, in the press and on the platform" (OTR, ["Russia and Palestine — Machiavelli Wins"], May 19, 1947.

125. When someone from *The Survey* wrote to her in around 1952 asking her to become a "*Survey* Associate" she penciled her reply: "Every time I associate myself with some group I rapidly find myself disassociating from it. I'm just not group-minded — and I keep changing my mind, as I grow more mature (or more senile). (The difference is hard to discern.) . . . I would not be any good to you at all. More likely a pain in your neck" (penciled note at SU).

126. OTR ("The Big Moment"), August 6, 1951.

127. OTR ("Proposes Quakers Write Peace"), July 11, 1951.

128. DT letter of July 9, 1951, SU (sent to women's groups around the United States).

129. DT to Carl Zuckmayer, January 22, 1951, SU.

130. DT to Eleanor Roosevelt, January 7, 1952, SU.

131. Eleanor Roosevelt, letter addressed to "Dear Friend," December 21, 1951, SU (sent to women's groups around the United States).

132. "The theory held by most of our people that America would never strike first is dubious," DT observed. "There is nothing in the American mind that would cringe from socking another fellow first, if convinced that he intended to, and could,

kill us otherwise. This is true of all peoples." (DT, "Atomic Warfare," loose ms. [labeled "unused"] at SU.)

133. DT to Eleanor Roosevelt, January 7, 1952.

134. DT to Joe Agnelli, February 15, 1952, SU.

135. OTR [untitled], January 4, 1952. "I fear our U.S.A. destiny is to parallel Rome, who acted as undertaker to the Ancient World." (Bernard Berenson to DT, January 8, 1953, SU.)

136. Pearl S. Buck to DT, October 1, 1951, SU.

137. DT to Walter Lippmann, March 1, 1952, SU.

138. DT to Jan Masaryk, November 9, 1947.

139. DT to JVS, undated [1946–1950], SU.

CHAPTER SIXTEEN

1. ML telegram to Dinah Sheean, December 10, 1948, SU.

2. Combined from DT to Carl Zuckmayer (in reference to ML's career), July 21, 1950, SU; and to Arthur Vandenberg, December 22, 1948, SU.

3. DT to Wells Lewis, December 27, 1942, in the Grace Hegger Lewis papers, Humanities Research Center, University of Texas at Austin.

4. DT to Wells Lewis, June 10 [1943], in the Lewis papers, Austin.

5. DT to Alec Manson, undated [January 1951], SU.

6. PK interview with Ellen Sheean, Paris, July 18, 1986.

7. *Paralisi cardiaca*. See Schorer, 814.

8. Quoted in DT to Alec Manson, undated [January 1951].

9. ML to DT, undated [1946], SU. "Why should I send my father a Christmas card?" ML asked his mother. "He divorced *us*, didn't he?" (Quoted in Dale Warren to DT, undated ["Fri.," 1960], SU.)

10. Quoted in DT to Dr. Bernard Pacella, June 18, 1960, SU.

11. DT to Wells Lewis, undated [November 1943], in the Lewis papers, Austin.

12. See DT's letter to Dr. Bernard Pacella, June 18, 1960.

13. DT to Wells Lewis, undated [November 1943].

14. The letters and reports of the faculty at Putney are in the files labeled "Michael Lewis" at SU (Series 3).

15. DT to Jay Allen, August 27, 1946, special collections, Baker Library, Dartmouth.

16. DT to Dr. Bernard Pacella, June 18, 1960.

17. See Dr. Hans Huessy to DT, August 15, 1947, SU.

18. A telegram from Carl Jung (undated) is at SU: "ADVISE COUNSELLING DOCTOR BENNETT 99 HARLEY STREET LONDON LETTER FOLLOWS JUNG." But no letter remains on file.

19. DT to Dr. E. A. Bennett, September 21, 1949, SU.

20. PK interview with Virginia Shaw, Ridgefield, Connecticut, August 25, 1988.

21. DT to Louis Nizer, November 12, 1946, SU; and to Dr. E. A. Bennett, September 21, 1949, SU: "I have not the slightest doubt that I was too indulgent [with Michael]. . . . It is perhaps a fault of my generation, who in families like my own were brought up terribly strictly, that we try to spare our children the same disciplines. I do not mean that I have let him have everything he wanted; I do mean that

his punishments were light, and that I unquestionably took too many responsibilities off his shoulders."

22. DT to ML, August 8, 1946, SU.

23. ML to DT, May 27, 1946, SU.

24. ML to DT, December 29, 1948, SU.

25. ML to DT, July 31, 1950, SU.

26. Copies of this extraordinary document are at SU, with the heading: "CONTRACT BETWEEN MRS. DOROTHY THOMPSON KOPF, HEREINAFTER REFERRED TO AS 'THE PARTY OF THE FIRST PART,' AND MR. MICHAEL LEWIS, HEREINAFTER REFERRED TO AS 'THE PARTY OF THE SECOND PART,' RESPECTING MUTUAL RIGHTS AND OBLIGATIONS DURING THE YEAR 1949."

27. Combined from DT to ML, January 30, 1949, and July 1, 1950, SU.

28. ML to DT, February 12, 1949, SU.

29. PK interview with Ellen Sheean (who as a girl idolized Michael and who later became an actress herself).

30. ML to DT, undated [February 1949], SU.

31. Combined from DT to ML, June 18 and July 1, 1950, SU.

32. Dinah Sheean to DT, July 19, 1949, SU.

33. DT to Dr. Bernard Pacella, June 18, 1960.

34. RW to Dinah Sheean, December 5, 1950, in my possession.

35. RW to MKS, March 20, 1973, in Houghton Mifflin Company archives, Houghton Library, Harvard University.

36. RW to Dinah Sheean, December 5, 1950.

37. See Dr. E. A. Bennett to DT, March 31, 1950, SU: "[Michael] went on to say that it worried him tremendously that you regarded him as abnormal and felt that he needed to have continuous psychiatric treatment. He agrees that he does need a certain amount of treatment, particularly for what he describes as his laziness. But he is inclined to separate this off from everything else."

38. Quoted in DT to Dr. Bernard Pacella, June 18, 1960.

39. PK interview with Dinah Sheean, London, May 21, 1986. For Moura Budberg see the memoir of her daughter, Tania Alexander, A Little of All These (London: Jonathan Cape, 1986).

40. DT to Helen Rogers Reid, August 13, 1951, in the Reid papers, Library of Congress.

41. Dinah Sheean to DT, July 30, 1949, SU.

42. DT to ML, July 12 [1950], SU.

43. She was thinking about the death of Wells Lewis. See DT to ML, October 3, 1950, SU: "This is urgent. Do not postpone it. There is . . . always a chance that if you have to serve your time, you will serve it in the entertainment field of the army, and I assure you I shall do everything possible to secure such a berth for you. I am absolutely hard-boiled this time, and shall pull every string I can."

44. DT, "The Boy and Man from Sauk Center," Atlantic Monthly, November 1960.

45. Alec Manson to DT, December 20, 1950, SU.

46. Quoted in DT to Dr. E. A. Bennett, September 21, 1949.

47. DT to Dale Warren, January 15, 1951, SU. "At such moments," she said, "all the old pains, hurts, joys, regrets, feelings of failure, etc., come back in a wave. . . . I can hardly today think of Red without getting knots in my bowels. I was

afraid of him, Dale, always afraid of him. Admiration and pity I felt, but fear more than either."

48. DT to Frances Perkins, February 9, 1951, in the Sinclair Lewis collection, Macalester College Library, St. Paul, Minnesota.

49. DT, "The Boy and Man from Sauk Center." In an essay about SL ("Portrait of Sinclair Lewis") Barnaby Conrad wrote: "Sinclair Lewis died in Rome of alcoholism. I heard of a final macabre irony: a friend of mine went into the United States Embassy in Rome and saw a consular official down on her knees with a broom and pan. 'What are you doing?' he asked her. 'Sweeping up Sinclair Lewis,' was the answer. Red's ashes had been put in a safe pending final disposal and the urn had fallen out, its contents spilled" (*Horizon*, March 1979).

50. DT, "Novelist's Death Ends Tradition," undated clipping at SU. This was a special edition of "On the Record," twice as long as other columns in the series and not published by all of DT's subscribers.

51. DT to William R. Mathews, December 4, 1952, SU.

52. DT to Bruce and Beatrice Gould, July 2, 1951, SU; and to Helen Rogers Reid, August 13, 1951, in the Reid papers, Library of Congress.

53. DT to Jean Marie Richards, June 27, 1951, SU. She had stayed in close touch with Miss Richards, her former mentor at Syracuse, and helped raise a fund for her care when Miss Richards was dying of cancer.

CHAPTER SEVENTEEN

1. For DT and AFME, see DT's open letter to the *New York Times* of July 29, 1951; and the chapter on "Exploiting Anti-Semitism" in Alfred M. Lilienthal, *The Zionist Connection* (New York: Dodd, Mead, 1978), especially 418–420. A thoroughly hostile account of AFME's activities can be found in Hertzel Fishman, *American Protestantism and a Jewish State* (Detroit: Wayne State Press, 1973), 102–107. Fishman calls AFME "the most important pro-Arab group organized since the founding of the state of Israel." Even a number of DT's anti-Zionist friends were disturbed about its intentions. See, for instance, the reminiscences of Bruno Lasker in the Columbia University Oral History Project, page 518: "I found that the proposed organization was not, as I had thought, simply a committee to familiarize Americans more with the culture and economies of the people of the Middle East, but that Miss Dorothy Thompson and the clerical and other people who worked with her were definitely interested in supporting the Arab claims as against those of Israel. In other words, it was wholly political. Though I might have had a great deal of sympathy with it, I did not like to participate in something that I knew so little about. I only like to be connected with organizations in which I can be active myself. More especially, Miss Thompson refused to say where the funds came from, and that decided me to retreat at once, which I did."

It is worth pointing out that no one who knew her ever doubted that DT was honest in her espousal of the Arab cause. "It has not," she remarked, "in any way, been profitable for me. . . . It has lost me thousands of previous admirers and scores of personal friends. It has closed platforms to me which once eagerly sought me as a speaker. It has mobilized against me one of the most powerfully organized and zealous groups in American public life. It has contributed to diminish my income. And it has often filled my heart with tears." (DT, undated statement [ca. 1957], SU.)

For the CIA's involvement with AFME, see the *New York Times,* February 17, 1967; and the *Washington Post,* May 1, 1969. My FOIA request yielded nothing from the CIA but a stack of newspaper clippings and an outrageous bill for xeroxing. DT's papers contain no reference to the matter, nor was she ever concerned with the collection or distribution of funds within AFME.

2. Jack Wheeler to DT, December 8, 1956, SU.

3. DT to Ben Hibbs, December 29, 1950, SU.

4. Quoted in DT to Baruch Korff, January 13, 1954, SU. Rabbi Korff's remarks appeared in a letter to the *Manchester Union Leader* (New Hampshire), November 17, 1953.

5. See Joseph S. Shubow's "Reply to Dorothy Thompson" in the *Jewish Advocate* (Boston), March 3, 1949. Rabbi Shubow's attack was prompted by DT's comments on the film version of *Oliver Twist,* which Jewish groups in the United States had boycotted as anti-Semitic. "Rightly or wrongly," said DT, "I do not think *Oliver Twist* has contributed anything to creating anti-Semitism. It has been an English classic for a hundred years, during which Jews have enjoyed in England full civil rights and risen to posts of highest eminence. Regarding the film itself I cannot say, since Jewish pressures in this country have prevented it from being shown." (DT to the *Jewish Advocate,* March 9, 1949, SU.) She was severe in her condemnation of the Anti-Defamation League of B'nai B'rith: "The Anti-Defamation League exists to defame as anti-Semites everyone who treats the State of Israel as every other state of the world is treated, and blasts as 'anti-Semitic' every book in which a Jew appears in an unfavorable light." (DT to Paul Hoffman, April 27, 1953, SU.)

6. Combined from DT to JVS, January 27 and February 10, 1949, SU.

7. DT to Ben Hibbs, December 29, 1950, SU.

8. Throughout the war DT was ardent in her championship of Jewish emigration to Palestine. On June 26, 1941, she cabled Winston Churchill: "CONGRATULATIONS ON YOUR GREAT SPEECH. IN BROADCAST I MADE TO ENGLAND TODAY I WANTED TO SAY A WORD FOR PALESTINE COLONISTS AND PLEAD IN THE NAME OF HUMANITY THAT THEY BE FULLY ARMED FOR THEIR DEFENSE. I REFRAINED FOR OBVIOUS REASONS OF TACT YET WE IN AMERICA HOPE AND PRAY THAT THE PEOPLE WHO HAVE TRIED WITH THE WORK OF THEIR HANDS TO BUILD UP A REAL HOMELAND FOR THE RACE FIRST AND LAST TO BE PERSECUTED BY HITLER WILL NOT BE ALLOWED TO PERISH LIKE RATS UNABLE TO PROTECT THEMSELVES. YOUR WITTHHOLDING WEAPONS FOR THEM FOR SELF DEFENSE IS HURTING YOUR CAUSE WITH MANY MILLIONS OF CHRISTIAN AMERICANS. I PLEAD WITH YOU IN HEAVEN'S NAME DO SOMETHING QUICKLY. FAITHFULLY YOURS," etc. (telegram in the British Foreign Office archives, reference No. FO 371/34456 114745 ["Dorothy Thompson"], London).

9. See her article in *The Outlook,* "The Hope of a New Palestine," September 8, 1920; and her speech at the "Balfour Meeting" in Carnegie Hall, November 1, 1943, transcript at SU: "No one has ever challenged the right of the Arabs to live in Palestine on terms of personal equality with the Jews and everyone else. . . . The right of Arabs to live in Palestine belongs to them not as Pan-Arabians, but as human beings. If western civilization is going to establish the theory that sections of the earth are to be set off for the exclusive use and development of persons descended from persons that have been indigenous there for centuries, then all civilization will stagnate and ours in particular will. Least of all can the British support such a concept. Least of all can we of the United States."

10. The words are John and Frances Gunther's, in an open letter to President Roosevelt, signed by DT and other prominent journalists to protest "the application of the proposed British government plan for Palestine" (May 1939, SU).

11. DT, "Chaim Weizmann" (published in *Jewish Frontier*, July 1942, as a tribute to Dr. Weizmann on his seventieth birthday), ms. at SU. Weizmann and DT were excellent friends. In her essay she spoke of his "always courteous obstinacy" and his "unremitting tenacity" and called him "a complete Jew. He is as Jewish as Churchill is English, or Wendell Willkie American, or as Bismarck was Prussian. . . . He is the epitome and apotheosis of his race."

12. DT statement, undated [1957], SU.

13. DT to the *Jewish Advocate* (Boston), March 9, 1949; and to "Mr. Travis," undated, SU.

14. OTR ("Palestine's Fate up to the U.N."), September 22, 1948.

15. See DT's letter to Herman Lissauer, September 7, 1941 [in error for 1951], SU: "I have said, in print, that relations between Israel and the Arab States can never be radically improved (a consummation devoutly to be wished) until the whole Palestine issue is settled, as it presently is not. . . . I have never suggested that the frontiers should be pushed back to where they were at partition. I have said they should be fixed. For the Arab world suffers from what amounts to a neurosis that Israel has boundless ambitions in the Middle East, and that any steps she may take to realize them . . . will never be opposed by the United States. . . . On these matters I have been a reporter, rather than a commentator, and it is a reporter I prefer to remain."

16. See Ronald Steel, *Walter Lippmann and the American Century* (Boston: Atlantic Monthly Press, 1980), 453–454.

17. DT speech, "Israel, Judaism and the American Jew," delivered at the Warwick Hotel in Philadelphia, November 1,1949, transcript at SU.

18. DT to William Zukerman (editor of the *Jewish Newsletter*), April 6, 1951, SU; reprinted in the *Jewish Newsletter*, February 20, 1961.

19. DT to "Mr. Travis," undated.

20. DT to "Mr. Churchill," January 22, 1953, SU.

21. See DT's letter to "Mrs. Marvin," undated, SU.

22. DT speech, November 1, 1943, Carnegie Hall, transcript at SU.

23. DT was anxious to refute the suggestion that she was indifferent to the sufferings of the Jews during World War II. In April 1953 she complained about an article published about her in *The Reconstructionist:* "[The author] gives the impression that the extermination of six million Jews didn't affect me, and in fact bored me. My reaction [to his questions] was — it must have been, because I know too well how I feel about this — that the extermination of the European Jews could not be laid at the door of the Arab world. . . . And I went on further to elaborate something which I deeply feel, namely that it is wrong, and tends to separate the suffering of the Jews from world suffering, to put the Jews in an altogether peculiar position. At least six million Germans perished [in the war] and they were certainly not all Nazis. During the bombing of Dresden, during the last days of the war, a minimum of 100,000 people were estimated to have perished, among them women and children. Hundreds of thousands of people perished in concentration camps who were not Jews. The French claim that over a million Frenchmen perished in those camps, and they were certainly not all Jews. Thousands of Germans, among

them some of my old friends, were executed by Hitler for anti-Nazi activities. I tried to extend Mr. Remba's sympathy somewhat beyond the sufferings of the Jewish people to encompass the terrible agonies through which a very large part of mankind went between 1939 and 1945 — which agonies have by no means ended since then" (DT to Eugene Kohn [editor of *The Reconstructionist*], April 21, 1953, SU).

24. DT to Paul Hoffman, April 27, 1953.

25. DT to William Zukerman, April 6, 1951.

26. Quoted in Elmer Berger's speech before the Fifth National Conference of the American Council for Judaism (of which Rabbi Berger was the founder), April 22, 1949, copy at SU.

27. See DT speech, "Israel, Judaism and the American Jew"; and DT, "America Demands a Single Loyalty," *Commentary*, March 1950. There is a balancing reply from Oscar Handlin in the same issue.

28. DT speech, "Israel, Judaism and the American Jew."

29. See JVS to DT, February 13 [1948], in reference to Philip Ireland, first secretary at the American embassy in Cairo: "He is thought to be pro-Arab anyhow (so is everybody else who has been more than six months in the Middle East). . . . As a matter of fact, he'll probably be moved out of Cairo sometime soon — a man knowing anything about Arab affairs is bound to be sent to Sweden" (letter at SU).

30. DT to Alfred M. Lilienthal, October 16, 1950, SU.

31. DT to Professor Max Lerner, February 24, 1956, in the Lerner papers, Sterling Library, Yale.

32. See her letter to Jack Wheeler at the Bell Syndicate, January 9, 1957, SU.

33. DT to Grace Lewis, July 1, 1952, in the Grace Hegger Lewis papers, Humanities Research Center, University of Texas at Austin.

34. DT to Agatha Young, November 26, 1956, in the Agatha Young papers, Berg Collection, New York Public Library.

35. DT to RW, September 8, 1956, in the West papers, McFarlin Library, University of Tulsa.

36. DT to Grace Lewis, July 1, 1952.

37. Meyer Weisgal, *Meyer Weisgal . . . So Far* (New York: Random House, 1971), 198.

38. PK interviews with Dr. Alfred M. Lilienthal, Washington, D.C., November 19, 1987; Hans Bethmann, Washington, D.C., November 18, 1987; Virginia Shaw (Ridgefield, Connecticut, August 25, 1988); Lisa Sergio (Washington, D.C., November 23, 1985); and John Paul Lewis (Washington, D.C., November 24, 1985). In February 1953 the following item appeared in the *California Jewish Voice:* "Dotty DID marry a guy of whom it is said that he was either a 'white roosian' or a former nazi sympathizer. It's difficult to believe that a brilliant newspaperwoman, or man, could completely lose his sense of perspective because of a compatible bed-fellow" (clipping at SU). MK was innocent, by all reliable accounts, of putting any "pressure" on DT's thinking. See Weisgal, *Meyer Weisgal . . . So Far,* 199.

39. See Stephen R. Graubard to DT, June 30, 1956, in which he recounts his visit to Bernard Berenson in Italy: "I should add that his opinion of you is not just high, but really (for B. B.) ecstatic. I think that you should know that he has heard that you are pro-Arab, and that information has pained him. I tried to explain your position as best I could but he did not seem prepared to move on that point. 'Dorothy is wrong, and you must tell her so,' were the final instructions" (letter at SU).

40. PK interview with Virginia Shaw.

41. DT to William Zukerman, April 9, 1951, SU.

42. DT to Mrs. E. H. Bingham, May 22, 1951, SU.

43. Letter of Jerome Unger, executive director of the American Zionist Council, March 20, 1951, Library of the American Jewish Committee, New York City.

44. DT to Max Lerner, February 24, 1956.

45. See Grace Sims Peat to Mrs. E. H. Bingham, May 23, 1951, SU.

46. DT to "Mr. Travis," undated; and DT loose statement, undated [1957], SU.

47. RW to DT, January 24, 1949, SU.

48. RW to DT, June 7, 1950, SU: "I couldn't sympathize with you more in your troubles with your Jewish friends. Unless one subscribes to the Herrenvolk theory regarding them they turn and rend one, no matter what one's services may have been. But this is an unjust world."

49. RW to DT, July 19, 1954; and see Victoria Glendinning, *Rebecca West* (New York: Knopf, 1987), 201–203.

50. DT to Bernard Berenson, January 22, 1952, SU.

51. OTR ("What Are the Basic Issues?"), March 12, 1956.

52. See, for instance, DT to Franklin D. Roosevelt, undated [ca. 1940], Roosevelt Library, Hyde Park.

53. DT to Professor William Yale, July 29, 1952, SU.

54. DT to Adlai E. Stevenson, August 1, 1952, SU. See also her letter to Marc de Conti, March 22, 1951, SU: "The older I get the more I stay in my study instead of running around interviewing 'leaders.' This is not supposed to be the way a journalist should act, but I am convinced that one trouble with our 'leaders' is that they never have time for contemplation or meditation."

55. Adlai E. Stevenson to DT, August 5, 1952, SU.

56. DT to JVS, November 16, 1952, SU: "I wish [Stevenson] would get out of politics and become President of Columbia University. . . . We have, as far as I can remember, had only two introverts for President. One was Lincoln. If Booth hadn't killed him he probably would have ended as an acute case of melancholic insanity."

57. OTR ("A Vote Against Trumanism"), October 24, 1952.

58. OTR ("Both Men of Talent, Character"), November 3, 1952. "The result of the election was not quite as much of a surprise to me as to you," DT observed in a letter to JVS, "though I had guessed that Adlai might win. I did not see the tidal wave [for Eisenhower] that evidently was there, and figured that only a tidal wave . . . would put out the incumbents. In short, I thought that if the election were going to be close, Adlai would win, and I thought it would be close." (DT to JVS, November 16, 1952, SU.) MKS remarks that DT's prediction of a Stevenson presidency "must have been based on a reading of tea leaves" (Sanders, 345), but at the time of the 1952 election, following the upset victory of Harry S Truman four years before, only a fortune-teller would have put any faith in public-opinion polls.

59. Margaret Thompson Wilson to DT, October 26, 1952, SU. DT's reply is penciled at the bottom of the letter.

60. See OTR ("The Issues Were Obliterated"), July 29, 1952.

61. OTR ("The Way to Abolish War Is to Abolish It"), January 31, 1955.

62. "Over the years," wrote MKS, "she offered a variety of explanations for her change of heart [about Zionism]. According to Vincent Sheean, she claimed that while she was hospitalized in Jerusalem, Jesus of Nazareth appeared to her in a

vision, holding out his arms to the dispossessed Palestinian Arabs." The source for this statement was Dinah Sheean, who wrote to MKS on April 10, 1972, that it had "the ring of truth . . . as Dorothy was so deeply Christian." (Sanders, 322–323 and 404n.) But to me Mrs. Sheean remarked, after confirming the story, "Mind you, Jimmy had done some pounding on Dorothy before Jesus came on the scene."

63. DT speech before the Institute on Muslim-Christian Cooperation, Washington, D.C., November 21, 1957, transcript at SU.

64. DT, "This I Believe," ms. at SU.

65. DT, "A Reason to Live and a Reason to Die," *LHJ*, October 1952.

66. DT, "Religion in American Life," *LHJ*, December 1951.

67. OTR, April 21 ("Was Oppenheimer Wrong in Opposing H-Bomb?") and June 21, 1954 ("Definition of 'Security Risk' Has Changed with Events").

68. DT, "Education for Democracy," unpublished ms. at SU.

69. See DT, "Why and What Should Johnny Read?" *LHJ*, October 1956; and DT speech, "Which Way, America? The Progressive Decay of Standards," delivered before the 38th Annual Meeting of the United States Chamber of Commerce, Washington, D.C., May 2, 1950, transcript at SU.

70. DT to Jay Franklin, September 16, 1954, SU.

71. DT to Ted O. Thackrey, November 3, 1946, SU.

72. DT to Bruce and Beatrice Gould, July 16, 1958, SU.

73. DT to Henry Andrews, September 7, 1951, SU.

74. DT to Bruce and Beatrice Gould, July 30, 1955, SU.

75. See, for instance, her letter to the nefarious William Loeb (whom she greatly admired), February 8 [1950?], SU. DT was quoting from John Masefield's "Biography" (in *Poems* [New York: Macmillan, 1929], 105): "But trust the happy moments. What they gave/ Makes man less fearful of the certain grave,/ And gives him wide compassion and new eyes./ The days that make us happy make us wise."

76. DT to J. H. Shrader, December 30, 1953, SU. "If I were asked to state the essence of Christianity," she wrote later, "I could only fall back on the one and saving word, love. Love is the meaning, the intention. . . . We are to know God, if we ever do, through love" ("Meaning for Us All," *LHJ*, February 1959).

77. Generally she offered her sponsors a wide range of topics. In 1954 she listed as her prepared lectures for that season: "On Education," "Religion and Our Civilization," "Western Law and the Modern People's Tribunal," "Germany, Europe and America," "The Crisis in the Middle East," and "The Crisis of the West."

78. DT to Howard L. Fernau, April 10, 1953, SU. See also her different articles on public education in *LHJ;* and "The Literate Illiterates," *Time*, October 8, 1956.

79. DT to "Mrs. Bolsky," February 7, 1952, SU.

80. DT to Mrs. W. H. Newton, February 6, 1953, SU. And further to Howard L. Fernau, April 10, 1953: "The member of your state board who thinks there is 'no need to teach spelling' is representative of many. Would he agree that the *aim* of education is illiteracy? . . . Or shall spelling become an 'expert technique,' limited to proof readers decoding the manuscripts of writers? Profession: Speller."

81. DT, "Do Our Schools Need an S.O.S.?" *LHJ*, February 1953. See also DT, "The Old Bible and the New," *LHJ*, March 1953, reprinted in DT, *The Courage to Be Happy,* and DT, "The Limits of Public School Education," *LHJ*, April 1953.

82. DT to "Miss Sommerville," February 20, 1953, SU.

83. DT to Mrs. W. H. Newton, February 6, 1953. Dale Warren remembered a

night at Twin Farms when DT unburdened herself about modern psychology: "Whereas I have the profoundest admiration for the genius of Sigmund Freud, I have the profoundest distrust of the therapy known as psychoanalysis." She mentioned the death of George Gershwin: " 'He began to complain of excruciating headaches [she exclaimed], and what do those Hollywood intellectuals do? They send him to a psychoanalyst, who puts him on a couch to talk about his love-life while (thumping her own brow vigorously) all the time he is dying of a brain tumor!' " (Warren, "I Remember Dorothy.")

84. See DT, "Some Observations on a Sensational Book," *LHJ*, May 1948; and DT to Dr. Gordon Bates, May 17, 1950, SU: "Whatever value these studies may have — which is extremely dubious from any scientific viewpoint — they amount in popular publication to the distribution of pornography and should be confined, in my opinion, if published at all, to scientific journals."

85. OTR [untitled], May 18, 1953.

86. DT to RW, January 6, 1954, in the West papers, Tulsa.

87. DT to Virginia Shaw, undated [November 1948], SU.

88. MK to DT, March 13, 1950, SU.

89. MK to DT, February 27 [1953], SU. The letter was signed "Your nervous type" — this appears to have been a joke between them.

90. DT to Mrs. C. R. Sellers, April 21, 1954, SU.

91. MK to DT, March 30, 1950, SU.

92. PK interview with Dinah Sheean, London, May 21, 1986.

93. Sheean, 323.

94. DT, "How to Give a Party and Like It," unpublished ms. at SU.

95. For Menuhin, see DT to Anne O'Hare McCormick, February 7, 1944, SU; and Yehudi Menuhin to PK, September 7, 1987: ". . . my father's reverence and esteem for her [were] passed to me."

96. In 1958 DT sponsored Marian Anderson, who was black, for membership in the Cosmopolitan Club in New York. "I consider Miss Anderson not only one of the greatest artists in this country today," she wrote in her proposal, "but one of the greatest spiritual forces in the world." (Letter of January 30, 1958, SU). Mainly, however, and throughout her career, DT shied away from commentary on the status of black people in America. "It is my belief," she wrote on February 1, 1948, "that the social, intellectual, and legal advance in the status of American negroes, during the less than three generations which have elapsed since the abolition of chattel slavery, is nothing short of remarkable, despite the fact that it falls far short of liberal aspirations or avowed ideals. . . . I fully expect continuous advance. I do not await retrogression." (DT to Edward Donahoe, SU.) In later correspondence she ventured that there was considerably less "caste spirit" in America than elsewhere — "except, alas, for the negroes. Of them one can only say that they're better off than any other *negroes* in the world." (DT to D. Wilkinson-Fox, March 8, 1955, SU.) But in 1957, during the Little Rock crisis, she condemned President Eisenhower's use of federal troops to ensure racial desegregation in the schools on the grounds that "it invades what has hitherto been recognized as the functions of the states, and intervenes in two especially delicate fields, racial relations and the education of children and youth. It violates taboos, as powerful a social force as exists. It is a boon to the worst type of agitator and to every subversive element. It has not mollified race relations but inflamed them, at a time when their

improvement was notable. It has engineered hysteria even in children, and created a climate in which education is impossible. It has led to a serious clash between state and Federal authorities. And all this was foreseeable by anyone with imagination." (OTR ["Respect for Force Is Not Respect For Law"], September 30, 1957.) "The perennial question asked by whites," DT also remarked, " 'Would you *marry* a negro?' is, of course, a silly question, because there are very few people anyone would, or could, marry." (DT to Edward Donahoe, cited above.)

97. PK interview with Winnetou (Zuckmayer) Guttenbrunner, Saas-Fee, August 11, 1986.

98. Roger W. Tubby to PK, August 18, 1987.

99. DT to Bruce and Beatrice Gould, August 24, 1954, SU. Note that DT was still calculating her date of birth one year late, thus in 1894.

100. DT, untitled ms. at SU; edited as "Look Again" and published in *Holiday*, June 1946.

101. PK interview with Rebecca Brock Richardson (formerly Rebecca Ross), Charlottesville, Virginia, October 22, 1986.

102. PK interview with Bob Sarnoff, Woodstock, Vermont, December 4, 1985.

103. PK interview with Lili-Charlotte Sarnoff, Bethesda, Maryland, November 23, 1985

104. See Dale Warren's memo to the Houghton Mifflin Company, September 17, 1964, in Houghton Mifflin Company archives, Houghton Library, Harvard University; and Lisa Sergio's memoir of DT, "Dorothy Thompson: The Blue-Eyed Tornado," unpublished ms. in my possession.

105. See Dinah Sheean to Max Ascoli, June 3, 1975, in the Ascoli papers, Mugar Library, Boston University: "How well I remember the joy of *you*, an Italian, appearing in Dorothy's Teutonic world in Vermont — *what a relief!*"

106. See the entry on Tucci in *Contemporary Authors* vols. 81–84, ed. Frances Carol Locher (Detroit: Gale Publishing, 1979), 571–572; and DT's correspondence at SU concerning his efforts to be naturalized as an American citizen: "Mr. Tucci . . . has become fanatical about human freedom, about the liberty of the person, about the unlisted 'freedom to move,' about the oppression of bureaucracies, and the irrational stupidity of war. Thomas Jefferson would, I think, sympathize with most of his views. I am not sure, however, how many people today would sympathize with Jefferson's" (DT to Judge John C. Knox, December 8, 1947, SU).

107. Niccolo Tucci to DT, undated [ca. 1954], SU.

108. Johannes Urzidil, *Das grosse Halleluja* (Munich: Albert Langen–Georg Müller Verlag, 1959).

109. Henry Kissinger to DT, September 22, 1954, SU.

110. DT to Princess Anna Schwarzenberg, December 2, 1953, SU.

111. Quoted in DT to Dale Warren, January 15, 1951, SU.

112. DT to Esther Adams, July 21, 1954, SU.

113. PK interview with Ellen Sheean, Paris, July 18, 1986.

114. JVS to DT, undated ["Monday, June 22" — 1952?], SU.

115. PK interview with Dinah Sheean.

116. Warren, "I Remember Dorothy."

117. DT to Marcel W. Fodor, October 20, 1958, SU.

118. RW to Dale Warren, January 18, 1965, in the West papers, Beinecke Library, Yale University.

119. PK interview with Dinah Sheean.

120. DT to Dale Warren, January 15, 1951, SU.

121. DT, "The Farm Problem and Me," *LHJ*, July 1954. "My advice to anyone is not to go into the dairy business," she wrote, "— stick to something useless, such as flowers." (DT to Celeste F. Wessell, December 29, 1953, SU.)

122. DT to Agatha Young, August 5, 1954, in the Young papers, Berg Collection, New York Public Library.

123. DT to Clare Boothe Luce, April 22, 1955, SU. See also her letter to Norman and Katherine Littell, August 25, 1954, SU: "The christening ceremony astonished my Protestant mind. As far as I can recall Protestant ceremonies concentrate on dedicating the child to God, but the devil is very present in the Catholic [service], being exorcised in many points of the ritual. I think it all very pre-Christian and pagan. . . . At the moment when Satan was being driven from his bosom, and sent flying horns and tail, the baby gave one enormous yawn."

124. DT to H. L. Mencken, March 2 and September 13, 1955, in the Mencken papers, New York Public Library.

125. DT to Dale Warren, December 29, 1953, SU.

126. PK interviews with Madeline Shaw Green, Ridgefield, Connecticut, August 25, 1988, and Virginia Shaw.

127. DT, "The White Sofa," *LHJ*, February 1957, reprinted in DT, *The Courage to Be Happy*.

CHAPTER EIGHTEEN

1. PK interviews with Dinah Sheean (London, May 21, 1986); Madeline Shaw Green and Virginia Shaw (Ridgefield, Connecticut, August 25, 1988); Lisa Sergio (Washington, D.C., November 23, 1985); and John Paul Lewis (Washington, D.C., November 24, 1985).

2. DT to ML, January 16, 1952, SU.

3. Sanders, 351.

4. DT's letters to these people are at SU.

5. DT to Barbara Morgan, September 30, 1954, SU.

6. DT to Dale Warren, September 27, 1957, in Houghton Mifflin Company archives, Houghton Library, Harvard University.

7. DT to H. V. Kaltenborn, June 28, 1958, SU. She sold the place "to an Englishman named, believe it or not, Mr. Albertini. He seems to be well-heeled, and will pay cash." (DT to Dale Warren, September 11, 1957, SU.) The Big House at Twin Farms has gone through several owners since, and at this writing (December 1989) is on the market for nearly three million dollars.

8. Dinah Sheean to DT, March 8, 1953, SU.

9. JVS to DT, December 29, 1953, SU.

10. JVS to DT, undated, SU.

11. DT to JVS, August 13, 1955, SU.

12. JVS to DT, undated ["April 30"], SU.

13. DT to "Dr. Blesch" [Josephine? or in error for Rudolf Flesch, the author of *Why Johnny Can't Read*, who corresponded with DT about the Soviet system of education?], January 4, 1956, SU.

14. DT to Paul Scheffer, January 6, 1956, SU.

15. DT to Beth and Don Wesbrook, January 9, 1956, SU.

16. OTR ("The Revolt of the Hatless"), September 3, 1956.

17. Peta Fuller to DT, July 14, 1958, SU.

18. PK interview with Virginia Shaw.

19. DT to Agatha Young, November 26, 1956, in the Young papers, Berg Collection, New York Public Library.

20. DT, December 24, 1956, SU (letter mimeographed and sent to friends and family at Christmas). Publicly DT gave as her reason for quitting AFME her belief "that the presidency should be filled by someone with more time than I can give to it, pressed as I am by my own work, and absent as I so often am by travel. . . . [But] I do not propose to sever my association with the people with whom I have been working so long, and to whose knowledge, intelligence, character and encouragement I owe so much as a citizen and a writer." (DT press release, April 12, 1957, SU.)

After her death AFME established the Dorothy Thompson Memorial Fund, to award grants to journalists for travel and study in the Middle East: "Her unusual vision still guides AFME's activities. Her own words, always so eloquent and often so prophetic, will serve as a continuous source of inspiration." (Undated pamphlet in the Urzidil-Thiesiger collection, Leo Baeck Institute, New York City.)

21. PK interview with Virginia Shaw.

22. OTR ("Now Mama's Really Disgusted"), May 28, 1958: "Some years ago Philip Wylie wrote a book castigating American mores with the title *Generation of Vipers*. He was wrong. This is a generation of mush-mouths — not a sting in a carload — governed by political illiterates, two-penny patrioteers ready to save the nation at any moment by being elected; hucksters in the form of 'Public Relations Counsellors'; intellectual charlatans; and plain idiots."

23. DT, "We Can Conquer Minds and Hearts," *LHJ*, July 1952, reprinted in DT, *The Courage to Be Happy*.

24. DT, "The Lady Can Be Vengeful," *LHJ*, November 1958.

25. DT described her sister as "the world's most representative female reader of the Middle Brow," and as "a very gifted and somewhat frustrated woman [whose] works are largely confined to personal letters." (DT to Dale Warren, April 14, 1957, and to Paul Brooks, August 20, 1957, both in Houghton Mifflin Company archives, Harvard.)

26. This was DT's tribute to Edna Millay, cut "drastically" for publication in *LHJ* but printed in toto in *The Courage to Be Happy*.

27. *New York Times Book Review*, November 17, 1957.

28. *New York Herald Tribune Book Review*, November 24, 1957.

29. DT to Dale Warren, undated ["Sunday"], in Houghton Mifflin Company archives, Harvard.

30. Margaret Thompson Wilson to DT, December 20, 1956, SU.

31. *Newsweek*, September 1, 1958.

32. Warren, "I Remember Dorothy."

33. DT, "Speaking of Operations," *LHJ*, January 1958.

34. DT to H. V. Kaltenborn, June 28, 1958; and to Dale Warren, September 27, 1957.

35. DT, "Speaking of Operations."

36. OTR ("A Moving Story"), October 7, 1957.

37. Walter Lippmann to DT, July 10, 1958, SU.

38. These words are taken from "letters" that DT wrote to her husband after his death in 1958; they are still in the possession of the Lewis family and are quoted more extensively below.

39. For this and more on MK's death see Sergio, "Dorothy Thompson: The Blue-Eyed Tornado."

40. Copies of the telegram are at SU and in the Urzidil-Thiesiger collection, Leo Baeck Institute.

41. DT, August 25, 1958, SU (signed "Dorothy T. K." and sent out, mimeographed to "Dear Friends" and family).

42. DT to Dale Warren, August 1, 1958, SU.

43. PK interview with Ernest Cuneo, Crystal City, Virginia, November 17, 1987.

44. DT to Bruce and Beatrice Gould, July 16, 1958, SU.

45. OTR ("*Ave, Salve, Vale!* — II"), August 18, 1958.

46. Jack Wheeler to DT (bearing DT's penciled reply), August 20, 1958, SU.

47. Letter quoted in memo of Dale Warren to the Houghton Mifflin Company, August 4, 1958, in Houghton Mifflin Company archives, Harvard.

48. "Off the Record," *Time*, September 1, 1958. She was described in the article as "an erratic, headstrong conservative"; glancing reference was made to her interview with Hitler ("in 1932 she produced a book on Adolf Hitler [and] decided he would never reach power") and to "her last, most persistent bug: the failure of U.S. policy in the Mideast." An undated text at SU, which DT drafted as a form letter, was careful to assure her readers that in closing "On the Record" she had "*not* been 'shut off,' " and that when her memoirs appeared they would contain "an *extensive* study of the Middle East."

49. DT to Cass Canfield, undated [August 1958], SU.

50. DT to Bruce and Beatrice Gould, July 16, 1958.

51. DT to Mark Schorer, October 19, 1958, in the Schorer papers, Bancroft Library, University of California at Berkeley.

52. DT to Bruce and Beatrice Gould, July 16, 1958.

53. DT to Peta Fuller, September 24, 1958, SU.

54. Mary Cremmen's interviews with DT appeared in the *Boston Globe* on September 7, 8, and 9, 1958 (clippings at SU).

55. DT to RW, August 28, 1958, in the West papers, McFarlin Library, University of Tulsa.

56. This and the following excerpts are from manuscripts that were made available to me by the Lewis family.

57. DT was especially happy about working in the Dartmouth library because it had open stacks and she was therefore not obliged to fill out a form every time she wanted a book. She explained — and I heartily agree — that in research work one often has no idea of *what* one wants to see until one sees it: a chance to roam in the stacks is the equivalent of heaven.

58. DT to Walter and Helen Lippmann, July 15, 1958, in the Lippmann papers, Sterling Library, Yale.

59. In Sanders, 342.

60. PK interview with Philip N. Cronenwett, Hanover, New Hampshire, May 5, 1987.

61. PK interview with Evelyn Stefansson Nef, Washington, D.C., October 25, 1986.

62. DT to Mark Schorer, December 14, 1958, in the Schorer papers, Berkeley; and to Dale Warren, December 17, 1958, SU. "I was haunted by the fear that they might discover a malignancy," she wrote to Schorer, "and I be condemned, not to immediate death (which is an idea I could easily bear) but . . . to a long-drawn-out and horrible fatality." She told Ginny Shaw that she *would* commit suicide if she found out she had incurable cancer, and she tolerated no one's criticism of such an obviously personal decision.

63. DT's last diary (for 1959) is at SU.

64. PK interview with Polly Irwin, Chevy Chase, Maryland, October 23, 1986.

65. DT diary, January 28, 1959, SU.

66. DT to Mark Schorer, March 17, 1959, in the Schorer papers, Berkeley.

67. DT to Bruce Gould, March 31, 1959, SU.

68. DT to Mark Schorer, April 1, 1959, in the Schorer papers, Berkeley.

69. DT to M. W. Fodor, June 26, 1959, SU.

70. DT to Malcolm R. Lovell, July 1, 1959, SU.

71. She had been visiting that day with Paul Scheffer, a former correspondent for the *Lokal Anzeiger* in Berlin, whom she had known for decades, first in Germany and later in America. During the spring of 1942 Scheffer was arrested in New York and interned as a suspected enemy agent. His FBI file (which is enormous, if nothing else) contains a great deal about DT's efforts to have him released and recognized as an "asset" to the United States in wartime. He was "an old, old friend," she declared, "with whom I have maintained some sort of relationship. He is a German national but not a pro-Nazi." After the war, when Scheffer's career was in ruins, DT took the lead in establishing a fund for his support. He lived in Woodstock until his death in 1963.

72. DT to Agatha Young (postcard), August 15, 1959, in the Young papers, Berg collection, New York Public Library.

73. DT, "May I Tell You about My Heart Attack?" *LHJ*, April 1960.

74. DT to Max Ascoli, September 2, 1959, in the Ascoli papers, Mugar Library, Boston University.

75. DT to Mark Schorer, October 3, 1959, SU.

76. DT to Walter Lippmann, October 5, 1959, SU.

77. DT to RW, December 1, 1959, SU.

78. JVS to Hilda Rothschild, November 28, 1959, SU.

79. She wrote to Johannes Urzidil on February 16, 1960: "Those who have seen the girl on tour (she has been with him most of the time) report an entirely different impression than I got more or less from hearsay. (A much more favorable one)" (letter in the Urzidil-Thiesiger collection, Leo Baeck Institute).

80. DT to RW, December 1, 1959.

81. DT to Mark Schorer, January 12, 1960, SU. DT is quoting Gretchen's words at the spinning wheel in Goethe's *Faust* ("My peace is gone. My heart is heavy").

82. DT to Dr. Pincus Berner, February 11, 1960, SU.

83. A typical remark: "The little birds are very beautiful and promise to be less evanescent than their predecessors unless Gwegowy gets his hands on them, though so far he has displayed a quite remarkable instinct for keeping his hands off Gwannie's treasures." (DT to Dale Warren, July 2, 1959, SU.)

84. DT to Gertrude and Johannes Urzidil, undated, in the Urzidil-Thiesiger collection, Leo Baeck Institute.

85. "I should never have written you, as I did initially, about Valerie's reputation," DT wrote to ML on February 22, 1960. "Nevertheless the facts are that she has had a very rackety life, and what most frightened me was that *you* said that she was a reflection of yourself. The last thing you need, Michael, as a life companion, is that. For what *is* yourself? I do not think — I know — that you do not know." (Letter at SU.)

86. DT to RW, December 1, 1959.

87. There was nearly a breach in DT's friendship with RW over the publication of *Heritage,* which DT read at RW's request and dismissed as "definitely a *novel,* and, I think, a very good one. . . . Dear Rebecca, stop having fits, and stop being wounded in your respectability. You are not, you never have been, and you never will be 'respectable.' . . . [You] are great enough and famous enough and *sovereign* enough to rise above this situation." (DT to RW, January 27 and 28, 1956, in the West papers, Tulsa.) RW judged these remarks to be "so very rude and so very silly that if you [DT] were not my dearly loved friend of many years I would never speak to you again." (RW to DT, February 1, 1956, SU.) And at the top of DT's pages RW noted, years later: "How different were her letters to me when her [own] son went off the rails."

88. RW to DT, December 6, 1959, SU. Whatever RW's crimes against Anthony may have been, her letter is a joy to read in this era of unforgiving "adult" children: "I'm not responsible, and I won't serve any good purpose by pretending that I am. And as for you — there is Red's blood in Mike, and also there is the same awful need in both Mike and Anthony for a gimmick that will make them as much noticed by the world as their parents are. Anthony has as his gimmick his hatred of me, and his incessant moralizing. Mike has gone in for the beatnik gimmick. This is an odd pitfall that we couldn't have foreseen. Let us not beat our breasts, we will only spoil our elegant contours and do no good. . . . AND DO NOT WORRY ABOUT MIKE'S FINANCIAL WELL-BEING. . . . YOU ARE NOW IN YOUR MIDDLE SIXTIES AND A YOUNG MAN WHO TOOK ANY OF YOUR EARNINGS WOULD NOT PROFIT BY IT BUT WOULD BE SPIRITUALLY DAMNED FOR IT FOREVER. IF ANY MONEY PASSES IT SHOULD — BY EVERY CANON OF CIVILIZED SOCIETY — PASS FROM HIM TO YOU. THE OTHER WAY ROUND IT WOULD NOT WORK. REMEMBER THAT, YOU BAD, SILLY GIRL."

89. DT to Henry Andrews, April 5, 1960, SU.

90. DT to Bernadette Lewis, March 8, 1960, SU.

91. ML to DT, February 9, 1960, SU.

92. DT to M. W. Fodor, June 10, 1960, SU.

93. The cables, undated, are at SU.

94. PK interview with Virginia Shaw.

95. DT to Mark Schorer, August 18, 1960, SU.

96. DT to RWL, September 21, 1960.

97. RWL to DT, September 25, 1960.

98. DT to RWL, September 25, 1960.

99. RWL to DT, November 18, 1960.

100. DT, "The Boy and Man from Sauk Center," *Atlantic Monthly,* November 1960.

101. Mark Schorer to DT, December 12, 1960, SU.

102. Schorer, xviii. He wrote to Ramon Guthrie on August 17, 1961: "Dorothy, by the way, did read the entire book last October, when I came to Barnard with the final sections for this expressed purpose. She cried when she finished and gave me her generous blessing. . . . She also made such corrections of fact as occurred to her" (letter in the Guthrie papers, Baker Library, Dartmouth College). Schorer had written to thank DT just weeks before her death: "I have said to you before that no opinion was more important to me than yours on this matter, and if I have not already said, I want to say now, that the great reward of having written the book for me is having you as my friend" (Mark Schorer to DT, December 12, 1960).

103. Quoted in Warren, "I Remember Dorothy."

104. DT to Mark Schorer, May 3, 1960, in the Schorer papers, Berkeley.

105. DT to Dale Warren, August 27, 1960, SU. She wrote to her friend Ernestine Evans on September 22: "The last I heard from Houghton Mifflin was the advice to write my book before next May and confine it to 350 pages. I wrote them back to go jump in the Atlantic Ocean — which they have not done" (letter at SU). At the end of 1960 Margot Johnson, who was acting as DT's literary agent, secured a contract for DT's memoirs with Harcourt, Brace and Company, but DT refused to sign it on the grounds, again, that she could not be held to "artificial" restrictions and deadlines. (Margot Johnson's papers are in the Sophia Smith Collection at Smith College in Northampton, Massachusetts.)

106. Mark Schorer to DT, June 2, 1960, SU.

107. DT to Mark Schorer, November 9, 1960, in the Schorer papers, Berkeley.

108. DT to John Gunther, November 9, 1960, SU.

109. PK interview with Alice Marie Tarnowski, Washington, D.C., October 24, 1986; and with Don and Polly Irwin.

110. DT to Bruce Gould, November 9, 1960, SU.

111. M. W. Fodor to DT, October 11, 1960, SU. "I don't call that journalism what the younger generation is doing," Fodor wrote to DT on September 16 [1959?], ". . . aber man muss leben ["but you've got to live"]" (letter at SU).

112. DT to "Mrs. Schuyler," September 2, 1958, SU.

113. DT to Mark Schorer, November 9, 1960, in the Schorer papers, Berkeley.

114. PK interview with Dinah Sheean.

115. PK interviews with William L. Shirer, Lenox, Massachusetts, January 28, 1988, and Jane Gunther, Greensboro, Vermont, July 30, 1987.

116. Sheean, 326–327.

117. Warren, "I Remember Dorothy."

118. DT to ML, December 9, 1960, SU.

119. PK interview with Lisa Sergio.

EPILOGUE

1. Combined from DT to John Gunther, February 14, 1949, and undated, in the Gunther papers, University of Chicago.

2. Quoted in Sanders, 370–371.

3. Quoted in Warren, "I Remember Dorothy."

4. *Time*, February 10, 1961.

5. PK interview with Evelyn Stefansson Nef, Washington, D.C., October 25, 1986.

550 NOTES AND SOURCES

6. *New York Times,* February 1, 1961 (editorial).

7. *Buffalo Evening News,* February 1, 1961.

8. DT speech, untitled, January 24, 1939, delivered at the tribute dinner given in her honor by the Committee for the Relief of German-Christian Refugees, New York City, transcript at SU.

9. Quoted in Warren, "I Remember Dorothy."

10. Mary McGrory to PK, January 24, 1986.

11. Carl Zuckmayer, *"Die Geschichte von Dorothy Thompson,"* in *Aufruf zum Leben* (Frankfurt-am-Main: S. Fischer-Verlag, 1977), 30.

12. PK interview with Dinah Sheean, Menton, France, June 4, 1987.

13. RW to Dale Warren, February 24, 1965, in the Rebecca West papers, Beinecke Library, Yale University.

Index

Cummings, Homer, 206
Cuneo, Ernest, 449
Curie, Eve, 260, 261, 329, 402
Curie, Marie, 260
Currie, Mrs. (cook), 197
Curtis, Cyrus H. K., 84
Czechoslovakia, 60, 61, 68, 329; Communist government in, DT's views on, 393–394, 397; DT and, 71, 87, 174, 482n.79; Fodors in, 174, 272; Germans/Nazis vs., 267, 272, 280–281, 310, 317; MK in, 350, 353; refugees from, 512–513n.44. *See also* Prague

Dachau, 374, 376, 378; DT at, 373, 374
Daedalus, 439
Dahlquist, John E., 370
Daily Mail, 418
Damaged Goods (Brieux), 35
Damascus, 428
Dana, Charles, 475n.43
Danbury, CT, 305
Daniel, Anita, 354
Darrow, Clarence, 145
Dartmouth College, 139, 232, 347, 452–453, 546n.57
Darwin, Charles, 32
Davenport, Marcia, 166, 176, 394
Davenport, Russell, 176
Davidson, Jo, 329
Death Be Not Proud (Gunther), 177, 466
Debs, Eugene, 54
Decker, A. R., 85
Deir Yassin, 424
Delta Democrat-Times, 296
Democracy, 327, 408, 434; in Britain, 318; Christianity and, 237, 515n.101; DT as advocate of, 32, 44, 188, 229–230, 236, 237, 241–242, 269, 279, 285, 309, 315, 317, 328–331, 435; DT's criticism of, 195, 209, 237, 386, 408; in Europe, 54, 317; in Germany, 47, 363; journalism and, 220, 321; liberal, 241–242; nazism and, 163, 186; refugee resettlement and, 279; Social Unit and, 44; in U.S., 18, 188, 209, 220, 226, 330, 394; woman suffrage and, 42. *See also* Freedom; Free speech
Democratic party, 228; DT and, 234, 322, 431 (*see also* Roosevelt, Franklin Delano: DT's opposition to/criticism of); DT's friends/colleagues in, 41, 257, 432; Re-

publican party vs., DT on, 207, 240, 432
Denmark, 263, 315, 329
Dennis, Mr., 504n.94
De Porte, Barbara ("Varya"), 43, 495n.88; daughter of, 513n.56; DT's European trip with (1920), 47–48, 49–54, 55, 56, 471–472n.5; DT's planned Russian trip with, 47–48, 52, 53, 57; marriage/Grossman and, 50, 54, 57, 68; Zionism and, 49, 50
Depression, 156, 205, 206, 207, 208, 277, 305, 320; Germany and, 156, 157–158
de Sales, Raoul de Roussy, 258, 274, 311, 313, 329, 330, 340, 515n.101
Desbois, Antoine, 520n.57
Desbois, Pierre, 520n.57
De Valera, Eamon, 266
De Voto, Bernard, 136
Dewey, Thomas E., 320, 396
Diaspora, 49, 424
Dictatorships: DT's views on, 202, 207–208, 208–209, 264, 396; European, and view of Roosevelt-Willkie campaigns, 517n.138; Hitler and, 159; Lindbergh and, 312; Munich Agreements and, 281; Roosevelt and, 188, 208, 223, 230
Dietz, Howard, 386
Dionne quintuplets, 225
Disarmament: DT and, 379, 406–410; in Europe/France, between the wars, 158, 160; of Germany, 363; "peace women" and, 65; UN Paris conference on, 409, 410
Dodd, William E., 203
Dodsworth (SL), 122, 124, 126, 127, 138, 144, 174, 194, 215
Dollfuss, Engelbert, 199, 282
Donovan, William J., 359
Dorfman, Ania, 260, 355
Dorothy and Red (JVS), 496n.106
Dorothy Thompson Emergency Squad, 202
Dorothy Thompson's English Journey (Drawbell), 337
Dorothy Thompson's Memorial Fund, 545n.20
Dorothy Thompson's Political Guide (DT), 264
Dostoevsky, Fyodor, quoted by DT, 394
Drake, Sir Francis, 318
Drawbell, J. W., 335, 336, 337
Dreiser, Theodore, 122, 153; plagiarism of DT's work, 142–144, 171–172, 490–